On their own behalf

# On the Boundary of Two Worlds: Identity, Freedom, and Moral Imagination in the Baltics

## 37

# On their own behalf

Ewald Ammende, Europe's national
minorities and the campaign for
cultural autonomy
1920-1936

Martyn Housden

Amsterdam - New York, NY 2014

Cover image: Ewald Ammende (centre, front) and a group of unknown diplomats aboard a Hanseatic charabanc. Image from the Russian State Military Archive, Moscow.

The paper on which this book is printed meets the requirements of "ISO 9706:1994, Information and documentation - Paper for documents - Requirements for permanence".

ISBN: 978-90-420-3876-9
E-Book ISBN: 978-94-012-1147-5
© Editions Rodopi B.V., Amsterdam - New York, NY 2014
Printed in the Netherlands

'Since our specific character derives from being born almost without instinct, it is only by training and experience that our lives as men take shape; they determine both the perfectability and corruptibility of our race. Thus the history of mankind is necessarily a whole, i.e. a chain formed from the first link to the last by the moulding process of socialization and tradition.'
Johann Gottfried Herder, 'Book IX' in F.M. Barnard (ed.), *J.G. Herder on Social and Political Culture*. CUP, 1969, p. 312.


'Man—freed from the traditional bonds of the medieval community, afraid of the new freedom which transformed him into an isolated atom—escaped into a new idolatry of blood and soil, of which nationalism and racism are the two most evident expressions.'
Erich Fromm, *The Sane Society*. London: Routledge and Kegan Paul, 1963, p. 58.


'Since national identities still matter to people in Central Europe, it is important to conceptualize the possibility of a nationalism that is liberal.'
Stefan Auer, *Liberal Nationalism in Central Europe*. New York: RoutledgeCurzon, 2004, p. 10.

# Table of Contents

| | | |
|---|---|---|
| Preface | | ix |
| Images | | xiii |
| Introduction | Why Baltic history is more difficult to write than German history | 1 |
| ONE | Brave new world: enterprise and aid | 13 |
| TWO | Liberal nationalist | 39 |
| THREE | Becoming a minority | 61 |
| FOUR | Achieving cultural autonomy | 83 |
| FIVE | Minority interests—European interests— global interests | 113 |
| SIX | Establishing the European Congress of Nationalities | 139 |
| SEVEN | The General Secretary: early optimism and its frustrations | 169 |
| EIGHT | 1929: year of the minorities | 199 |
| NINE | International national community thinking and a different kind of Pan-Europe | 213 |
| TEN | Critical challenges | 237 |
| ELEVEN | The new nationalist wave | 263 |
| TWELVE | When friends won't help | 285 |
| THIRTEEN | Aftermath | 311 |
| FOURTEEN | Fateful context | 329 |
| FIFTEEN | At Stalin's throat | 353 |

SIXTEEN          Admitting defeat                                    375

Conclusion       The need for more histories of national              391
                 minorities

Bibliography                                                          397

Index                                                                 407

# Preface

This book has taken a very long time to produce. My first article about Ewald Ammende and national minorities was published in 2000 and, symptomatically, very soon had to be corrected.[1] Even now, after researching his life and times for over 15 years, the study does not 'feel' complete. This might be a surprise given that Ammende was hardly a top echelon statesman in inter-war Europe—how much can there be to say about him?—but his course followed many paths less frequently explored in English-language histories and his career was forged in close association with a number of people and organisations which require closer scrutiny than they have received so far. For example, as yet there is no book about the Association of German Minorities in Europe;[2] likewise, the more you read the proceedings of the European Congress of Nationalities, the more it becomes obvious that every one of its participants deserves study in his or her own right—they all came with agendas attached. Equally, it would be possible to write lengthy studies about the politics of the Baltic German Party and the practice of cultural autonomy.[3] So, this book has been completed in the spirit of contributing to a historiographical area where there will be many developments in the future and where perspectives are likely to shift as a result.

It is notoriously easy to make mistakes in Central and Eastern European History, not least because some of its problems have no ideal answer. Take a simple issue: which place names should be used? The ethnic Germans who populate this text always spoke of Reval, Pernau and Dorpat (for instance), never Tallinn, Pärnu and Tartu. Hence two of their main newspapers in Estonia were *Revaler Bote* / *Revalsche Zeitung* and *Dorpater Nachrichten*. That names mattered to the historical actors was shown when the former newspaper had to change its title for a brief time during 1934–35 because the use of the word 'Reval' became unacceptable to the government of the day. Hence for a while the paper was published as *Estländische Zeitung*. To be true to the historical actors, really this study should use the original Germanic place names. Doing so, however, would alienate contemporary audiences in the Baltic, hence the study uses current place names with historic counterparts bracketed afterwards the first time the name is used in a chapter. Likewise, the names of some of the actors themselves are problematic. For example, should a Russian family name be spelled 'Kurtschinsky' (as in the original German-language documents) or

---

[1] 'Ewald Ammende and the Organisation of National Minorities in Inter-war Europe', German History 18 (2000) 439–60 followed by 'Ambiguous Activists. Estonia's Model of Cultural Autonomy as Interpreted by Two of its Founders: Werner Hasselblatt and Ewald Ammende', *Journal of Baltic Studies* 35 (2004) 231–53.

[2] This point was made numerous time by John Hiden.

[3] For at least a chapter studying the practice of cultural autonomy, see D.J. Smith and J. Hiden, *Ethnic Diversity and the Nation State*. London: Routledge, 2012, chapter 4.

'Kurchinskii' (as in at least one recent English text)? Really I should write the individual's name as he wrote it himself when using the Latin alphabet, but I haven't come across documents showing this. In the end, I have opted for the simplest course and have left personal names as they stand in the original German documents.

It goes without saying that many people have helped this project along. Above all, John Hiden was squarely to blame for getting me interested in Ammende in the first place. Without his intellectual spark, knowledge, connections and generosity of spirit, this study would have been inconceivable.[4] David Smith can hardly be ignored. It's only due to his selflessness and capability as a linguist that I gained access to Ammende's papers in Moscow; he also facilitated research visits to Estonia. David's tireless and deep engagement with Baltic Studies has enabled me to give several papers at conferences about national minorities, also to write occasional essays about Ammende and his concerns. The latter have been valuable vehicles for trying out different approaches to the most salient topics. David, Gábor Batonyi, Tom Lane and Roger Fellows have all contributed to this project through discussion and comments on the text, but also—and let's not under-estimate this—their sustained companionship. The latter has provided a necessary source of motivation. Without it, such a long-term project would have been impossible.

It is also a pleasure to recognise the support offered by all of the staff at the archives and institutions visited during the research process, in particular: Jürgen Warmbrunn and Peter Wörster of the Herder Institute, Marburg; Joachim Tauber of the Nordost Institut, Lüneburg; Bernhardine Pejovic and Jacques Oberson of the League of Nations Archive at the United Nations Library, Geneva; Viesturs Zanders of the Baltic Central Library, Riga (not to mention Valters Ščerbinskis whose help also has been very much appreciated); staff of the Russian State Military Archive, Moscow; staff of the Political Archive of the German Foreign Ministry, Berlin; staff of the Federal Archive, Koblenz; staff of the Institute for Contemporary History, Munich; staff of the Estonian National Library, Tallinn; staff of the Estonian State Archive (Madara branch), Tallinn; staff of the Latvian State Library, Riga; staff of the Central Zionist Archive, Jerusalem; staff of the Hebrew Union College, Cincinnati and staff of the British Library, Boston Spa. I must also thank Frank Nesemann very much indeed for passing on some important information from his work at the Central Zionist Archive, Jerusalem. Lene Auestad and Johnathan Davidoff are to be recognised too for allowing me to give papers to their conference series 'Psychoanalysis and Politics'. The

---

[4] For a discussion of John's contribution to Baltic Studies and the study of national minorities, see M. Housden and D. Smith (eds), *Forgotten Pages in Baltic History. Diversity and Inclusion.* Amsterdam: Rodopi, 2011, introduction.

proceedings of these events have provided a thought-provoking analysis of national belonging.[5]

Naturally the research effort standing behind this book had to be financed. Between 1995 and 1998 the British Council funded John Hiden and myself to research security in the Baltic region. During these years it became clear that national minorities were of critical significance. Thereafter I received two small personal research grants from the British Academy, the first for archive visits and the second to enable the microfilming of Ammende's papers in Moscow. The University of Bradford contributed to a visit to Germany, a conference paper delivered to the American Association of Baltic Studies, New York and a visit to Moscow. David Smith and the Centre for Russian and East European Studies at the University of Glasgow enabled me to give papers are conferences in Glasgow and Belfast.

A debt of gratitude is also due to both Eric van Broekhuizen and Leonidas Donskis. Rodopi and the series *On the Boundary of Two Worlds. Identity, Freedom, and Moral Imagination in the Baltics* always have stood full-square behind this book. Confidence in their support has been invaluable throughout the writing process.

Last but not least, as with everything, I had better mention the unrelenting, unwavering support of Gillian, Patrick and Alexander. All three, in their rather different ways, are invaluable.

*Martyn Housden*
*Penistone, 30 May 2014*

---

[5] Published volumes are L. Auestad (ed.), *Psychoanalysis and Politics. Exclusion and the Politics of Representation*. London: Karnac, 2012 and L. Auestad (ed.), *Psychoanalysis and the Nation*. London: Karnac, 2014.

# Images

## 1. Villa Ammende

## 2. and 3. The villa inside and from the side

**4. The front door**

**5. A young Ewald Ammende with his father**

## 6. Ewald Ammende, 1892–1936

## 7. Werner Hasselblatt, 1890–1958

Martyn Housden

**8. Paul Schiemann, 1876–1944**

Images 1 to 4 are photographs taken by M. Housden. Image 5 is from the Russian State Military Archive. Images 6 and 7 are from *Kölnische Volkszeitung*, Special Supplement, August 1929.

The author has made every effort to trace the copyright holders of the photographs used in this book. Unfortunately it has proved impossible in the cases of 5, 6 and 7. Information would be welcomed about the copyright holders of these images in order to acknowledge them full in future editions of this book.

*Introduction*

# Why Baltic History is more difficult to write than German History

## 1. *On their own behalf.*

The title of the book reflects the determination of members of the European nationality movement to represent their own agenda on national and international stages during the inter-war years. As members of Europe's national minorities, they wanted to participate in policy-formation rather than be passive objects of decisions made by governments that too often had too little to do with them. Cultural autonomy, the Association for German National Minorities in Europe and the European Congress of Nationalities all were pressed forwards by members of minority populations and were fashioned according to the priorities they set for themselves. Ewald Ammende, a Baltic German from Pärnu (Pernau), Estonia is central to the narrative. He was a member of a Central and Eastern European national minority who dedicated much of his life to 'wheeling and dealing' with statesmen and the officials serving them as he attempted to write minority interests into state initiatives. His concerns ran alongside those of fellow 'Estonian Germans' Werner Hasselblatt (co-author of Estonia's cultural autonomy law), Axel de Vries (editor of *Revaler Bote*) and Ferdinand von Üxküll-Guldenbrand (sometime editor of the ethnic German journal *Nation und Staat*). For much of his life—until the early 1930s anyway—Ammende also was heavily involved with the famous 'Latvian German' politician and editor of *Rigasche Rundschau*, Paul Schiemann.[1]

In a way, therefore, this is a story about those rather lacking in power (i.e. national minorities) attempting to influence those better positioned to exercise it (i.e. state governments—which tended to represent majority nationality groups—and the League of Nations). The minority figures chose diverse strategies to make their case, from purely ethical to essentially tactical arguments. They were equally flexible about the methods of communication they employed, including personal appeals, rationally composed memoranda and targeted press campaigns. As the members of minorities made their case, they showed the wide range of possibilities open to human beings. At times they put Europe's statesmen to shame—making them appear self-interested, narrow-minded, lacking in imagination and morally blind. On other occasions, the interventions of at least Ammende, Hasselblatt, Üxküll and de Vries, displayed exactly the same unappealing

---

[1] 'Estonian Germans' and 'Latvian German' are in inverted commas simply to recognise that when all of these men were born in the nineteenth century, there were no independent Estonian or Latvian state.

qualities. Hence as the characters populating these pages attempted to supplement the state-dominated system of international affairs that emerged after the First World War, and as they built up their own experimental non-governmental institutions, they produced a body of work that—when taken as a whole—was undoubtedly innovative, but which nonetheless has to be interpreted with care.

## 2. Not a conventional biography: the main protagonist and his context

This book has been difficult to piece together and the intrinsic difficulties made it an interesting exercise in writing history. Originally it was supposed to be a conventional biography of Ewald Ammende, but ultimately this became impossible. Writing a biography of a member of, say, the Third *Reich* is relatively straight forward because so much of the context surrounding the life has been narrated *ad nauseam* such that a great deal of knowledge can be taken for granted. In the case of an individual such as Ammende however, far less can be taken as read. Compared to the history of Germany, for example, the histories of national minorities, Estonia and the League of Nations are all far less well established and less widely appreciated. It followed that, time and again when trying to explain the trajectory of Ammende's life, it proved necessary to appear to leave the man to one side and explain the context in which he was working. Hence, although Ammende's life is a main strand running through this book, the text has to deal extensively with the national and international environments in which he operated. In fact, at times it will appear to become as much an examination of historical context as of the figure who originally was supposed to be central.

It is worth spelling out, however, that a couple of times here I have used the word 'appear' because it is not always straightforward to identify exactly where Ammende's personal activity ended and 'pure' context began. For example, although Ammende did not participate in the *Riigikogu* debates about cultural autonomy (because he was not a parliamentary deputy in Estonia), nonetheless he did participate in a key newspaper (*Revaler Bote*) which reported and discussed the proceedings at length; likewise he belonged to the intellectual community which championed cultural autonomy (e.g. he was friends with Werner Hasselblatt, a key parliamentary activist engaged in the autonomy project). Equally, although Ammende personally was not a key League of Nations statesman engaged in reforming that organisation's method of protecting national minorities, nonetheless he lobbied people who were (including Adatci), he was engaged with the League of Nations Union organisation (helping feed ideas into the League via that channel) and, again, he was involved in publicising debates as they happened in Geneva. Hence, even when this study appears to drift away from Ammende and discusses context, often it is actually outlining an environment into which Ammende and his activism were stitched one way or another. That is to say, 'context' can amount to aspects of the wider world which interested Ammende extensively and which he had been attempting to influence by whatever means were available.

It is only fair to warn the reader that Ammende personally will appear to retreat into the background for periods when the study discusses the nature of Baltic German society after the First World War (chapter 3), the process of achieving cultural autonomy (chapter 4), the international system for protecting national minorities (chapter 5), élite political efforts to reform the international protection of national minorities (chapter 8) and the decline of European politics in the 1930s (chapter 10). In fact, biographical purists might even observe that much of the discussion of the European Congress of Nationalities (chapters 7 and 9) concerns not just Ammende but other participants in the organisation too. On this score, it has to be said that Ammende played the part of an organiser whose vision involved the empowerment of not just himself, but of other Europeans with whom he shared minority status. Hence he provided a platform not only for himself and members of his Baltic German community, but for others too. In this respect, to understand Ammende's work it is necessary to pay attention not just to the words of the man himself, but to those who surrounded him as well.

## 3. Methodology: sources

Archive sources for this project proved more of a challenge than expected. With German history, for example, you might be lucky enough to find the necessary sources neatly collected in the Federal Archive system, albeit supplemented by a manageable number of supplementary papers located in one or two additional places. Ammende's work, however, left a trail that was much trickier to follow. Important documents are in the National Archive and Estonian National Library, Tallinn; Paul Schiemann's papers are in Riga; the political holdings of the German Foreign Ministry are in Berlin; microfilms of Josip Wilfan's papers are in Koblenz; NSDAP documents are in Munich; League of Nations documents are in Geneva; Motzkin's papers are in Jerusalem; and Ammende's private papers are in Moscow. Obviously research has to take into account all of these sources, but there are more. The published proceedings of the European Congress of Nationalities can be accessed in the Herder Instiute, Marburg, but they don't provide the full picture. In an ideal world you would chase up the correspondence of each of the key participants, whether in Romania, Czechoslovakia, Poland, the Baltic States, Spain or Israel—perhaps Wales as well. But how long would this take and how much would it cost?

Nor is geographical distribution the only problem. Ammende's papers number tens of thousands of pages. To make matters worse, his handwriting often was messy, so his notebooks dealing with South Tyrol, for example, are difficult to read. Moreover, the documents in Moscow are incomplete. Sometimes sections where you'd expect correspondence with fellow Estonian German Werner Hasselblatt are completely empty. Also there is the fact that the Moscow documents end in about 1928; so where are Ammende's papers dealing with the critical years 1929–34?

Moreover, there is the matter of language. I am a British historian with a background in writing about Germany. For years I have gone through Baltic German documentation and countless editions of *Revaler Bote / Revalsche Zeitung*, but at the end of the day there is a feeling that it has not really been enough. Certainly, Baltic Germans reported and translated what Estonian colleagues were saying during, for example, parliamentary debates about cultural autonomy, but this is a poor substitute for reading those Estonians in their own language, whether in archives or in newspapers such as *Päevaleht*. To make matters worse, there is always the question of what exactly Estonia's Russian community was discussing during the cultural autonomy debates. By the time you start dealing with the European Congress of Nationalities, of course, the language problem becomes worse still. True, Spanish Catalans expressed themselves in German when they were in the congress itself, but what about correspondence among themselves? What about representatives at the congress who were Poles, Ukrainians, Zionist Jews or Hungarians? In other words, writing this book largely through the medium of German-language sources means that it has a one-sided quality. Research using any of the other languages that are part of the story surely will give different perspectives.

It follows that although this book is just about twice the length originally anticipated, it is a very long way indeed from being any kind of definitive study. If writing history is compared to a race, this is only just getting off the starting blocks.

### 4. Ammende the sphinx

Nor is it easy to provide a clear conventional story-telling framework for Ammende. Write about a Nazi and you are dealing with a 'villain'; write about a member of the League of Nations and maybe you are describing a would-be hero or heroine; in either case it is relatively easy to adopt a consistent approach to the character throughout the study. Ammende, on the other hand, displayed a morally ambiguous character. His work, from the 1920s at least, has been counted a positive contribution to European affairs, yet in the 1930s—most notably with respect to the Jewish Question—he was shown wanting.[2] But if he could make the sort of mistakes he did in the 1930s, should we then re-evaluate even his 'positive' work from the previous decade? In the light of his later mistakes, should we be less generous in the interpretation of earlier work and emphasise more fully the possibility of

---

[2] W. Schlau et al, *Die Deutschbalten*. Munich: Langen Müller, 1995, p. 87.

cynicism and self-interest in behaviour that equally could be taken as idealistic? Are we dealing with a character who changed from good to something else or the continuity of a cynicism that at times was only masked?

Interpretation is not helped by the fact that Ammende could not always be his own person. As a private individual and a member of a national minority, there was a limit to how much he could achieve personally. To make things happen, he always had to be prepared to strike a bargain with a budget-holder. In attempting to gain purchase with policy-makers, he had to be prepared to deploy tactical arguments as well as attempt to take the moral high ground. There is a sense, therefore, that at key points it was a struggle for Ammende to get to the point he really wanted to make. Consistently he was buffeted by superior political forces; if time and again he had to be prepared to play politics from a position of weakness in order to make things happen, how should we judge his behaviour?

Ammende's motivations certainly encompassed the following: humanitarian urges, emotional outrage, a quest for money, national pride, anti-Communism, desire for importance and desire for adventure. How exactly all of the characteristics stood in terms of a hierarchy of significance is not always clear even when you are dealing with some fundamentally important periods of his life.

## 5. National identity and peace

Unavoidable in this study is an evaluation of Ammende's position as an activist for the rights of national minorities. As he campaigned on their behalf, emphasising the importance national identity could hold for people, was he wrong-headed and divisive (a potential nationalist) or simply expressing a reality of how society has long been organised?

It is obvious that national, cultural and linguistic differences exist between people. It is also true that in modern multi-ethnic societies, decisions have to be taken about the expenditure of resources that must take into account the needs of different national and linguistic groups. Such decisions might concern, for instance, access to education or the provision of state-sponsored media. Under such circumstances, a debate about the just apportionment of social resources according to the needs of different national groups becomes unavoidable. Equally, in such societies there have to be debates about how to ensure social integration, in particular the best way to structure the education system to bring it about. Should there be only common schools or should they be divided by language? In cases where schools teach in more than one language, what should be the balance of language tuition and at what point should non-mother-tongue language be introduced? In circumstances where different national cultures represent the past differently, should History be taught uniformly in all state schools, or should there be variations depending on the students' backgrounds? Indeed, how should educational institutions be managed and balanced: locally or centrally?

In other words, for so long as national differences exist—and whether we like it or not—, there is no denying that public systems have to take them into account. Consequently debates about appropriate and inappropriate, just and unjust responses to actual national social divisions have to be attended to. Most basically, it is a matter of attempting to accommodate national diversity effectively and fairly.

Yet with all this said, national identity remains problematic. We'd all be horrified if we were not treated fairly because of our national background; but how should we be treated if our particular national group has been associated with the oppression of others in the past? And what if this nationally-based historic behaviour has become institutionalised in a way that affects the present and which might affect the future? Should, for instance, property be confiscated today on account of nationally-based injustices perpetrated in the past? In short: how should we respond to present nationally-based inequality if it is a continuation of past injustice? Should people today lose resources because of the behaviour of their forefathers?

More dramatically, even if we accept we have to manage multiple national identities in society, is doing so anything more than a necessary evil? Should we expect that sooner or later national identity is always likely to stop being benign? Is it inevitable that such a powerful source of social division eventually will produce sectarianism, 'othering' and persecution? As Kevin Myers puts it in the context of Northern Ireland:

> I saw murder face to face, and heard the keen of bereaved
> and broken hearts. I witnessed the bloody chaos that results
> when the tribe is exalted over the individual and when
> personal morality is abandoned to the autonomous ethos of
> some imagined community, independent of God and law.[3]

In this light, what should be the relationship between national identity and social harmony? Can a society ever really be stable and secure if it is home to significant national divisions, or is such a structure more of a kind of waiting room for future conflagration?

But is something apart from national difference *per se* the key here? Although typically Erich Fromm favoured internationalism over national difference in the modern world, he also recognised that security of identity and faith in what one is are critical for individuals and for long-term social stability.[4] In this respect a sense of security experienced when expressing

---

[3] K. Myers, *Watching the Door*. Brooklyn: Soft Skull Press, 2009, introduction.
[4] For Fromm on the nation, see M. Housden, 'Psychoanalysis and Peace: Erich Fromm on History, Politics and the Nation' in L. Auestad (ed.), *Nationalism and the Body Politic*. London:

one's national identity might be more important to the maintenance of social harmony—more important than whether or not a territory is shared by a number of different national groups.

In this light it's not impossible that a sense of national belonging might offer something helpful to many humans. Citing Eric Fromm again, the importance of national belonging is as follows:

> To the degree to which the individual, figuratively speaking, has not yet completely severed the umbilical cord which fastens him to the outside world, he lacks freedom; but these ties give him security and a feeling of belonging and of being rooted somewhere. I wish to call these ties that exist before the process of individuation has resulted in the complete emergence of an individual 'primary ties'. They are organic in the sense that they are a part of normal human development; they imply a lack of individuality, but they also give security and orientation to the individual. They are the ties that connect the child with its mother, the member of a primitive community with his clan and nature, or the medieval man with the Church and his social caste. Once the stage of complete individuation is reached and the individual is free from these primary ties, he is confronted with a new task: to orient and root himself in the world and to find security in other ways than those which were characteristic of his pre-individualistic existence. Freedom then has a different meaning from the one it had before this stage of evolution is reached.[5]

Following Fromm's reasoning, in a practical sense, a society of national groups that offer individuals a sense of belonging might actually be more stable than one of more completely 'free' people acting for themselves and potentially making bad mistakes in the process. Perhaps we might say national belonging can offer a kind of emotional security. Fromm recognises the power that national belonging can exert, although he chooses cases where the satisfaction of an emotional need was abused by criminal politics:

> Fascism, Nazism and Stalinism have in common that they offered the atomized individual a new refuge and security. These systems are the culmination of alienation. The

---

Karnac, 2014. For Fromm on security and identity, see E. Fromm, *To Have or to Be?* London: Continuum, 2009, p.139. For a recent extended treatment of Fromm's life and work, see L. Friedman, *The Lives of Erich Fromm: Love's Prophet.* New York: Columbia University Press, 2013.
[5] E. Fromm, *Fear of Freedom.* London: Routledge and Kegan Paul, 1960 edition, p. 20.

individual is made to feel powerless and insignificant, but
taught to project all his human powers into the figure of the
leader, the state, the 'fatherland,' to whom he has to submit
and whom he has to worship. He escapes from freedom into
a new idolatry. All the achievements of individuality and
reason, from the late Middle Ages to the nineteenth century
are sacrificed on the altars of the new idols.[6]

But what if that emotional need could be satisfied by a kind a national
identity that was constructive, open and rejoicing in difference rather than
destructive, aggressive and exclusionary? Under such circumstances, could
national belonging become a force for good?

Furthermore, what do you do when, for whatever reason, people
perceive their national identity as offering them something fundamental—
when they feel pride and fulfilment through belonging and contributing to a
given body of national culture? Do you try to break down national divisions,
risking being perceived as assaulting something essential to individuals and
stimulating a hostile response, or do you recognise the perception of
difference and try to work with what you have got?

For today's educated audiences it is easy and tempting automatically
to prioritise universal human values over all other features of life; but is it
always right to do so? If all that really matters is what we *share* by virtue of
being human, then what is wrong with policies promoting cultural
assimilation? Likewise, what is wrong with a political system that
emphasises common human qualities such as the capacity for labour over
everything else? To complicate things further, if Hannah Arendt is right that
national identity becomes important the moment it comes under attack, it
might not be a long way to a position that would be ironic indeed. That's to
say, if we prioritise what we share to the point that we begin attacking
national differences, then we might simply end up retrenching people within
those differences, possibly enhancing potential inter-group resentments and
antagonisms into the bargain.[7] It is also ironic that while Erich Fromm is
suspicious of the appeal of 'the nation' in the modern world, he is equally
critical of people being assigned the role of small cogs in massive
administrations, corporations or political systems. He calls for society to be
given much more manageable, local dimensions, just in areas other than
nationality.[8] But if we are prepared to agree it is more human to divide a
multi-national corporation into smaller units, to localise giant bureaucracies

[6] E. Fromm, *The Sane Society*. London: Routledge, Kegan Paul, 1963 edition, p. 237.
[7] H. Arendt, 'We Refugees', available online at
www.stanford.edu/dept/DLCL/files/pdf/hannah_arendt_we_
refugees.pdf (accessed 5 December 2013). For a perceptive essay on this, see G. Agamben, 'We
Refugees', available at http://jft-newspaper.aub.edu.lb/reserve/data/soan201-sk-mod7-
agamben/Module7-G_Agamben-WeRefugees.pdf (accessed 5 December 2013).
[8] Fromm, *To Have or to Be?*, chapters 8 and 9.

and political systems, should we not also accept it might actually be better (in some ways at least) to sub-divide Mankind into smaller units which might include nations?

In the end, we might just be making an obvious point: when you are dealing with extremes, the choice between retrenched nationality or total universality risks problems. Overly and aggressive national differentiation can lead to provocations between groups, while over-homogenisation and loss of individuality in a massive, uniform crowd threatens to produce rebellion just as surely. In a sense, therefore, to the question of whether we want universal humanity or a diversity of national identities, maybe the answer is pretty simple: we want the best of both options and the worst of neither.

Perhaps the potential problems with universal humanity and national multiplicity do not so much lie with the ideas themselves. As a colleague pointed out, you can criticise policies based on either possibility. For instance, if different national groups are educated apart, people can complain about barriers being thrown up; if they are educated together there are complaints about attempts at assimilation.[9] The point becomes, therefore, what exactly people do with the principles before them. An emphasis on universality can be wrapped up with respect for all, the appreciation of universal rights and the generalisation of compassion, but also has led to the repression of difference. An appreciation of national diversity can lead to cultural vibrancy and richness of options, but equally has led to 'othering', unhealthy pride, repression, suspicion and conflict. Under the circumstances, it's the spirit of enactment that becomes decisive.

This discussion is fundamental to helping us start interpreting Ammende's life, but to make things more awkward still, he would gladly have styled himself a peace-activist. Given this, we are faced with the following question (which still looks odd at first sight, notwithstanding the prior discussion): can you be a peace activist if your world view accepts national difference as fundamental? Even if armed with the best spirit in the world, are you really likely to start talking peace when using the vocabulary of national difference? Even in the light of what we've said so far, the very idea still seems odd to modern ears. But we have to recognise we live in the post-Holocaust world—a place where nationalism is taboo because we've seen its worst case scenario. It is also a place where at least some populations in Central and Eastern Europe were significantly 'un-mixed' as a consequence of the Second World War. Likewise, we live in the post-Soviet world, a place still coming to terms with the heritage of Communist nationality policies and population movements. So our intellectual 'baggage' is likely to be different to that of the people populating this study. They had ideological and cultural values *not* born of Nazism and Stalinism, but of the massive, multi-ethnic, complicated Habsburg and Russian Empires. True,

---

[9] Anna Verschik in conversation.

these heritages fed into National Socialism, but nonetheless, should we allow that they permitted more flexibility than this? Should we allow the possibility that in the 1920s at least, before National Socialism arrived full-force in Europe, it was plausible that activism on behalf of nationality could be counted as peace activism? Could a structuring of societies around ethnic belonging have been viewed as a justifiable route to social cohesion, harmony and stability? Was it appropriate to give Herder a chance to prove his reading of Mankind to be productive?

Despite everything, giving priority to the nation still does sound like a justification for division, while talk of universality sounds more like peace, so all the more reason to attend carefully to the detail of any given historical situation—the context, contents and spirit of the policies about national belonging. The empirical point leaves the door open for activists on behalf of national minorities to be promoters of peace, but it recognises that they might also be something else. It is the actual lives in question that are all important to the assessment.

### 6. Ammende's life and Central and Eastern Europe in the 1920s

The existence of national minorities goes to the very heart of the history of Central and Eastern Europe. It was a defining point of what the region used to be. Jewish minorities are no longer there in such great numbers following the Holocaust; Ukrainian minorities are not there in such numbers after the alteration of Poland's frontiers; many ethnic German groups fled their homes at the end of the Second World War, while the Baltic Germans left their homeland in the Nazi-orchestrated resettlement (*Umsiedlung*) of 1939. So in Central and Eastern Europe after the First World War you encountered something fascinating: a sophisticated multi-ethnic population adjusting to a post-colonial environment.[10] At the same time, people were existing under the terms of a peace settlement made by a set of Great Powers which didn't necessarily understand the subtleties of their region.

The 1920s especially was a decade of possibility and uncertainty for Central and Eastern Europe. Based on the Wilsonian principle of self-determination, new democracies were set up for rule by formerly subject peoples, but other options were close at hand. Communism lurked in Russian lands to which, until recently, some Central and Eastern European states had been attached. Revolutionary possibilities were still abroad in large parts of Europe. At the same time, in Italy a different kind of anti-democracy was underway. Meanwhile, at the international level, the tremendous experiment of the League of Nations had been inaugurated—an ambitious undertaking which aspired to organise the peace of the world. It would attempt to do this not only by arranging élite politics in such a way that statesmen would be

---

[10] 'Post-colonial' because of the supersession of the Austro-Hungarian, Russian and German Empires.

persuaded to exclude war as a problem-solving device, but also by introducing social arrangements to ensure mass societies would be insulated against war-like appeals. Several of the League's experimental strategies were played out especially in Central and Eastern Europe—for example, conflict regulation over the Åland Islands, epidemic prevention over typhus in Poland, repatriation of prisoners of war across the Baltic Sea, the management of Russian refugees, the application of territorial autonomy (for instance over Gdańsk / Danzig), but also the protection of national minorities in newly established and extended states.[11] Through it all (and accepting the presence of Communism and Fascism), the 1920s experienced a substantial sense of idealism and optimism. It was a time to try to put many bad things behind oneself and progress towards better options. With so much happening all at once, it seemed that if even private individuals were prepared to engage with policy-making, perhaps they would indeed be able to influence national or even international affairs. Nationally, then, a great deal was in the melting pot and internationally it was as if the 1920s provided the foundations for a 'New Enlightenment'. But could Mankind take full advantage of the situation?

Ewald Ammende and the Baltic German community were determined to try to do so. Dissatisfied with the way de-colonisation was being played out in the Baltic region, and critical of the concept of self-determination as it was being applied there, he and members of his community began promoting an alternative vision for Europe, one in which society would not be structured along the lines of nation states where minorities received specific—and possibly rather limited—rights, but a world based on a more complete idea of national coexistence, where states were more completely shared by the nationalities living in them. His conception of Central and Eastern Europe certainly was more fully one of the region as a multi-cultural space than was the case in the minds of either the Allied peace-makers of 1920s or the statesmen populating the League; so the challenge was how to realise it—especially given that Ammende and his colleagues in general had only modest levels of influence in government circles.

This was also a time when physical movement was in people's minds. As a student, Ammende split his time between Riga, Moscow, Kiel and Tübingen. As a businessman, he had travelled to Ukraine, but knew well that his home town of Pärnu was connected internationally by trade. He had a brother in Mukden (Manchuria), another relative in Liverpool (perhaps involved in a rubber factory) and, apparently, a family connection in the Caucasus. As a student he became interested in German ethnic groups and travelled among them. As a nationality activist, he travelled the length and

---

[11] See M. Housden, *The League of Nations and the Organisation of Peace*. Harlow: Pearson, 2012. Also M. Housden, 'Securing the Lives of Ordinary People. Baltic Perspectives on the Work of the League of Nations' in M. Housden and D. Smith (eds.), *Forgotten Pages in Baltic History. Diversity and Inclusion*. Amsterdam: Rodopi, 2011.

breadth of Europe exploring minority affairs. He had an office in Vienna and set up the European Congress of Nationalities which met in Switzerland and Austria. He was forever lobbying in Berlin. Later in life, agitating against Soviet Commuism, he travelled beyond the confines of Europe. Ammende's life, therefore, spoke of a cosmopolitanism redolent of a former élite member of a world empire. It also reflected the possibilities open to a mentality unrestricted by the political division of Europe that occurred as a result of the Cold War. For Ammende, Europe stretched from the Atlantic to the Urals and was a place full of opportunities, while the wider world was there to be explored too.

## 7. Structure

Many intricate strands run through this study. Taking Ammende's life as a prime thread, its approach is more or less chronological but, given the tendency in life for several things to happen at once, this could not always be the case. The text examines Ammende's origins as a businessman in Pärnu (where he was born in 1892) before moving on to look at his involvement in the achievement of cultural autonomy in Estonia in 1925. Already, however, he had been involved in international organisational work, establishing the Association of German Minorities in Europe in 1922, and as his project in Estonia was finished, Ammende moved on more fully to work internationally, playing a leading role in setting up the European Congress of Nationalities in October 1925. From this platform, he and a wide variety of Europe's nationality spokesmen attempted to engage with the League of Nations as a means to promoting the place of national minorities in Europe. At this point, Ammende's life and work became just one part of a bigger continental story involving the rights of national minorities as a whole as championed by European statesmen as important as Gustav Stresemann.

Catastrophe struck, however, certainly in 1933 as Hitler came to power in Germany, although already there were signs of the 'hollowing out' of at least the movement of German minorities well before this. In autumn 1933 Jewish groups left the congress, destroying its moral validity once and for all. By this point Europe's political climate was deteriorating rapidly and increasingly Ammende had begun to look for fresh challenges, not least publicising famine in Ukraine, as he had done already in the 1920s. Ammende's commitment to anti-Communism left traces throughout his life and was wrapped up with his death too, since in 1936 he was undertaking a world cruise for the sake of his health, while also exploring the consequences of the Comintern around the globe. He died in Beijing of a stroke suffered on a train while apparently on his way to Manchuria. This study attempts to describe and assess Ammende's work and concerns, as well as to locate them in the framework of the times.

*Chapter One*

## Brave new world: enterprise and aid

### 1. Made in the Baltic

Pärnu's (Pernau's) old town appeals to the historical imagination. It has narrow streets and plaster shop fronts painted either white or a pastel colour. There is a town hall which would look quite at home in Helsinki and delicately impressive churches. Pärnu is home to the remains of medieval fortifications and the only seventeenth century city gate preserved in the Baltic States. There are tree-lined residential streets of wooden homes and a string of spa gardens (including a skateboard park) which lead from the commercial centre to the beach front. The beach is quite short, but receives character from a notable sea-front hotel built between 1935 and 1937, also a wooden *Kursaal*. A neo-classical mud baths (completed in 1927) is close by. Admittedly there is also a new hotel owned by a Scandinavian chain, but it's situated at the far end of the promenade.

Mid-way between the town centre and the beach, there's a large red and orange brick villa which has been designated an Estonian national monument. Designed by the St. Petersburg architects F. Mieritz and Y. Gerassimov, it was completed in 1905 and is an early example of *art nouveau*. Standing in its own sedate gardens, it gives a sense of time suspended. Inside, there are chandeliers, net curtains and everything that speaks of comfortable bourgeois life as experienced in the early twentieth century.

Villa Ammende was commissioned by Hermann Ammende, a successful businessman who inherited his trade empire from grandfather Christian Ludwig and father Iakov Dietrich. The villa served as a family home until it was taken over by the municipality after the family business hit hard times in the late 1920s. Between 1927 and 1935 it functioned as a casino.[1] Today, the building underlines that this was a local business family which, for a time at least, experienced substantial material success; and the house served as either home to or as an emotional base for one of Hermann's three sons who is the subject of this study—Ewald Ammende.[2]

In the 1920s, Pärnu had a community of about 1,200 ethnic Germans. They included a number of established families, not least the Ammendes, who were deeply involved in local affairs. In general, these Germans regarded themselves as responsible, disciplined and conscious of their traditions. They were said to be practically-minded, and perhaps it was

---

[1] For pictures of Villa Ammende, inside and out, see www.ammende.ee/ (consulted 9 September 2013).
[2] The other two brothers were Erich and Edgar.

not unexpected that Pärnu's ethnic Germans formed the only comparable community in Estonia outside Tallinn which was doing well in material terms. It was able to fund mother-tongue schools more generously than was normal and enjoyed the advantages offered by living on the coast. The town had a thriving port with a trading hinterland that, before 1914 at least, had stretched far into Russia. Then there was the beach.[3] Even during a cool summer, Pärnu had its attractions. Admittedly the daily concerts given by a military choir were not well attended when the sun failed to shine, but still plenty of people could take bicycle trips around the town. Even if, in 1924, there was a shortage of good quality hotels and restaurants, even if the bathing facilities needed improvement, even if the plaster was crumbling in some parts of the old town, Pärnu was still reckoned a good resort for youngsters.[4]

In the early years of Estonia's independence, concern about his home town held an important place in Ewald Ammende's mind and journalism. This was so much the case that, at times, it could almost seem as though local and family issues framed his wider political concerns.[5] In 1926, in the context of discussing a council plan to develop the town, he put his name to a lengthy discussion of Pärnu's possible future as a spa and seaside resort likely to attract crowds from Estonia and the surrounding countries.[6] It's quite possible, of course, that given its engagement in local affairs, the Ammende family had a hand in generating the council's initiative in the first place. Perceptively, the article argued that following the collapse of the Russian Empire, there were enhanced possibilities around the Baltic region, and so the town should do its best to capitalise on them.

Ammende highlighted that the town had a good sized, clean beach fit for further development. At the time, it did not have a promenade, but it could be turned into a proper, sophisticated '*Plage*' (his word) complete with beach businesses and windbreaks. Quite correctly he said the spa area and commercial centre flowed together well, but there was still plenty of land available for future development. He recommended improved hotel provision and the use of mud from nearby fens for medicinal baths. He said the town should create a central spa organisation to manage events for visitors across the summer months and build a '*Kurhaus*' to cater for their needs. Ever the pragmatist, Ammende added that Finland had particularly stringent anti-alcohol regulations and Latvia did not serve alcohol at weekends, so his home town could make money by offering a nice place for Finns and

[3] H.v. Berg, 'Rund um die kleineren Städte der Heimat', *Revaler Bote* 20 September 1924.

[4] 'Rund um die kleineren Städte der Heimat', *Revaler Bote* 28 June 1924.

[5] Ewald Ammende's personal papers contain extensive correspondence about a wide array of family business projects, for instance trading with agents in Ukraine. 1502–1–47, Moscow. See also 1502–1–87 and 1502–1–21 (among others), Moscow.

[6] E. Ammende, 'Pernaus Zukunft als Kur- und Badeort. Kann Pernau zu einem Konzentrationspunkt des Reise- und Kurverkehrs Estlands und seiner Nachbarländer werden?' *Revaler Bote* 17 November 1926.

Latvians to drink as much as they wanted. By contrast, he thought German tourists would be interested to visit a 'foreign' place with an historic German community.

Ammende was commentating on a major project to modenise Pärnu. Given the number of important buildings still existing today which date to the 1920s and 1930s, clearly the initiative was carried forward in some ways at least. All that Pärnu needed in addition was an improved rail connection, better roads to Tallinn and Riga (plus a good coach service), as well as steamers going to the Latvian capital, Helsinki and German ports on Rügen and at Stettin. He even looked forward to an air link between Estonia and Finland. Ammende supported all these possibilities and it is easy to imagine that his enthusiasm for all and any measures to increase the financial viability of the town reflected at least in part the fact that, by this point, the family business was experiencing difficulties.

A further article in the main ethnic German newspaper based in Tallinn (*Revaler Bote*) presented even more ambitious plans for the opening up of Estonia to Europe-wide tourism. Although the piece was anonymous, probably it owed something to Ammende since in part at least it fitted with the concerns of his journalism mentioned already.[7] It contended that Europeans were tired of visiting Italy (as Ammende himself had done in the early 1920s) and proposed that increasingly Scandinavia was an attractive destination, particularly given its historical position of mediating between East and West. Pärnu would benefit from the trend, it was said, with an improved rail connection to Tallinn. Then visitors could see Estonia's old Hanseatic capital before passing on to the beach at Pärnu, the ruins at Viljandi (Fellin) and the university city of Tartu (Dorpat). Pleasure cruises could run along the country's rivers and around Lake Peipsi until tourists came to the gateway to Russia—Narva. As they circulated around the country, visitors could take trips to the islands (most notably Saaremaa, formely Oesel) and to religious sites in the south east of Estonia. Echoing a point made elsewhere under Ammende's name directly, the article added that Estonia had plenty of places where alcohol could be drunk in comfort, but even Tallinn needed a restaurant with an international reputation.

Ammende was deeply interested in all manner of Estonian affairs, not least transport—and particularly railways. He became involved in attempts to provide a broad gauge link between Pärnu and the main line running from Riga towards the Russian heartland. Ammende collected papers about his local council's investigation into just such a possibility in 1924.[8] When a national debate took place about how best to integrate Estonia into the emerging European transport network, consistently Ammende

[7] 'Estland als Touristenland', *Revaler Bote* 17 November 1926.
[8] See various of Ammende's papers from 1925, 1502–7–19, Moscow. Also E. Ammende, 'Pernau', *Revaler Bote* 24 May 1924.

championed a rail link running through Pärnu over the development of a line from Tallinn through Tartu.[9]

Transport was important not just for tourism. Pärnu's port served the local flax and wood industries. During the time of the Russian Empire, its growth had been restricted artificially by transport policies prioritizing Riga. Certainly a new railway line serving western Estonia and its rich agricultural land would bring Pärnu closer to its rural hinterland. This alone would generate an economic upswing, but possibly it would also facilitate the recovery of lost markets and the future acquisition of raw materials in Russia. Unfortunately there was a feeling that Pärnu was being sacrificed to the needs of south eastern Estonia and that Tallinn did not need the competition of another Estonian port, certainly not one less susceptible to the winter freeze.[10] The issue was held so important that one of Ammende's close associates, a member of the *Riigikogu*, Werner Hasslblatt, raised the matter of Pärnu's place in the national rail system in a parliamentary budget speech given during 1925.[11]

During his life, Ewald Ammende was active in places markedly different from Pärnu's flat and coastal character. He travelled extensively around Europe, then on to the USA, Canada, South America, Japan and India, before dying in Beijing. Yet he never broke his connection with his family's home in Estonia. He remained the product of a distinctive community that responded with creativity and determination to radical change after the Russian empire's collapse.

## 2. Baltic Germandom

It was significant that Ewald Ammende was German but not from Germany. He was an *Auslandsdeutsche*, not a *Reichsdeutsche*. For a variety of historical reasons, including both self-motivated migration and deliberate imperial settlement projects, in the 1920s a large number of German communities existed beyond the geographical area most readily associated with Germany today, including Romania, Ukraine, the Volga, northern Italy and Yugoslavia.[12] Notwithstanding the suggestion that one of Ewald's paternal forebears hailed from somewhere in the Caucasus, life in Pärnu and his mother's lineage defined him as a member of a distinctive, small and élite

---

[9] E. Ammende, 'Die estnische Presse zum Bau der südestländischen Aunschlußbahn', *Revaler Bote* 28 March 1924. Additional detail is provided in H.v.B., 'Rund um die kleineren Städte der Heimat'.

[10] H. v. B., 'Rund um die kleineren Städte der Heimat'.

[11] 'Die Budgetrede des Abg. W.Hasselblatt', *Revaler Bote* 22 January 1925.

[12] For a brief overview of the history of ethnic Germans, see U. March, *Die deutsche Ostsiedlung*. Bonn: Bund der Vertriebenen. 1998. A whole series of studies is available from the publisher Langen Müller as part of the following series: *Studienbuchreihe der Stiftung Ostdeutscher Kulturrat*.

group, one that might have lived in 'the East', but which kept alive ties with 'the West'. He was a Baltic German.

By the community's standards, the Ammendes were *nouveaux riches*. They were 'tradesmen' who had made their fortune in the late nineteenth century rather than 'landed aristocracy' with wealth based on estates owned over centuries. And Estonia had been a good place to become wealthy through trade. Descriptions of Tallinn from before 1914 portray a medieval, walled city transforming into a modern metropolis thanks to the export of corn originating from the Volga and the import of goods as varied as oranges, coal and cotton.[13] Sometimes ships were four deep at the docks and grain elevators worked day and night. All this trade lay in the hands of German-owned firms, some of which were centuries' old. Hence Thomas Clayhills and Sons may have been founded in Dundee in 1633, but by the start of the twentieth century it was run by ethnic Germans. The concern controlled a third of the grain passing through Tallinn before the First World War.[14] Even if facilities in Estonia were smaller than counterparts in Riga and St. Petersburg (and Pärnu port was smaller than Tallinn), still enough wealth to go around flowed through them. An economic boom trickled down across the land, as credit institutions sprang up which farmers could use. Transport systems began modernising, as did local paper and copper industries. Trading contacts were cultivated across the Russian Empire, involving anything from Black Sea cement to asbestos from the Urals. The Ammendes rode the crest of this economic wave. That their villa was built in the revolutionary year of 1905 suggests, perhaps, that the economic success of the period enabled too many to overlook, or at least live with, society's latest problems.

But being a Baltic German involved more than participation in a frequently wealthy community, it involved character and leadership. Within the Russian Empire, the Baltic provinces of Estonia (northern Estonia as defined today), Livonia (central Latvia plus southern Estonia) and Courland (southern Latvia) were run autonomously on behalf of the Tsar by Baltic German interests which held sway over other local population groups which, often, far outnumbered them numerically. In this respect, the history of the Baltic Germans is that of an élite colonial population.[15]

In 1180, the Bishop of Bremen instigated a mission by the German Orders to bring Christianity to the Baltic, in the process thwarting Danish ambitions there.[16] As a result, Riga was founded in 1201 by Bishop Albert

---

[13] C.G. Ströhm, 'Reval vor dem Weltkrieg', *Revalsche Zeitung* 12 October 1935 (75th anniversary edition).

[14] For an outline of the career of influential merchant Etienne Baron Girard de Soucanton, including his role in Thomas Clayhills and Son, see 'Estländische Charakterköpfe', *Revalsche Zeitung* 12 October 1935.

[15] W. Schlau, 'Die Deutschen im Baltikum von 1180–1939/41' in W.Schlau (ed.), *Die Deutschbalten*. Munich: Langen Müller, 1995, p. 33.

[16] For an overview of the ensuing events, see A. Plakans, *A Concise History of the Baltic States*. CUP, 2011. Also Schlau (ed.), *Die Deutschbalten*. Recent brief pamphlets outlining the

von Buxhöveden. Although Tallinn had been established by Waldemar II of
Denmark in 1219, it was consolidated in 1230 by the Brothers of the Sword.
The mission led to the settlement in the region of German noblemen who
brought no German peasants with them. Consequently they built a largely
agrarian feudal state stretching from Klaipėda (Memel) to Narva in which
Germanic estate owners controlled 90% of land tilled by Baltic serfs. This
was a complicated state in which landowning élites formed noble
corporations (*Ritterschaften*) governing rural areas, while a number of towns
practiced autonomous administration too. So, for example, Lübeck's legal
code was applied in Tallin, Narva and Rakvere (Wesenberg), while
Hamburg's was used in Riga. Moreover, as German business interests
penetrated the region, so German businessmen began forming urban élites in
towns such as Riga, Tallinn and Tartu. All three belonged to Hanseatic
networks stretching at least as far as Novgorod. So, from early times German
involvement in the Baltic had a three-fold basis: Christianity, colonisation
and profit.

The dissolution of the German orders in the mid-sixteenth century
paved the way for subsequent Polish and Swedish control, later Russian
supremacy. In 1721 Estonia and Livonia became part of Peter the Great's
Russia, elements of the 'window to the West', while in 1795 (as a result of
the third partition of Poland) Courland was added to Russia's possessions.
These changes did not have consequences as dramatic as might have been
expected, since generally the Baltic region was permitted a considerable
amount of autonomy. The *Ritterschaften* emerged as *de facto* regional
governors, preserving their interests and being responsible for the area's
inhabitants. For long periods, the established feudal bodies administered their
territories according to established German practices, worshipped according
to Protestant religion and maintained a German legal system.

In 1632, even though the Baltic was under Swedish domination, a
German-language university was founded at Tartu. In 1802 it was re-founded
under Tsar Alexander I. It trained doctors, lawyers and administrators who
served the Russian Empire loyally and was a fundamental part of intellectual
life in the Baltic. Paralleling developments elsewhere in Europe, the late
eighteenth century saw an 'Enlightenment' in the Baltic, a period during
which J.G. Herder taught in Riga (1764–69) and Immanuel Kant published
the first edition of *The Critique of Practical Reason* in Jelgava (Mitau).
Germans travelled from the Baltic provinces to Germany to extend their
education (particularly in Kaliningrad [Königsberg] and Jena), while a
migration of *Literaten* made the reverse journey. The result was the enhanced

---

essentials of the historical sweep are March, *Die deutsche Ostsiedlung* and H. von zur Mühlen,
*Die baltischen Lande. Von der Aufsegelung bis zum Umsiedlung*. Bonn: Bund der Vertriebenen,
1997. Also of interest is A. de Vries, *Das Deutschtum in Estland*. Brandenburg: Sidow and Co.
Undated (but circa 1930). See also M. North, *Geschichte der Ostsee. Handel und Kulturen*.
Munich: Beck, 2011, especially chapter 2.

ability of the already high-powered community to produce distinguished artists, scientists and administrators for the Russian Empire, but also to maintain close links between the region and Germany's cultural and intellectual life. In 1881, for instance, as well as 24 Baltic German scholars, Tartu University had 19 professors from Germany itself. In the same year, 36 professors and lecturers in the German *Reich* were of Baltic origin. The group prided itself on its ability, and on applying this quality for what it perceived as the general good. As Hamilkar von Fökersahm put it, 'A person's worth does not come from the rights which he exercises, but rather from the duties which fall to him.'[17]

As the nineteenth century progressed, pressures on the Baltic German community began to mount. The survival of picturesque medieval towns and corporatist methods of social organisation gave truth the comments of one Baltic German commentator: 'The Middle Ages were the present-day.'[18] A Russian state, struggling to modernise, had to target such an anomaly, particularly one right by the imperial capital. Desire to resist early threats to this autonomous way of life led Carl Schirren famously to draft his 'Livonian Answer' to St. Petersburg. He advocated that the community do all it could to 'hold out' or 'persevere'.[19] Russian concerns about the region increased after the foundation of the German Empire in 1871 and there followed more determined moves to impose Russian ways of life on the provinces. Under Alexander III, Russian became the language of instruction in all schools (1887). Similar reforms followed in Tartu University, with its name being Russified in 1889.[20] The police and court systems were also changed (1888/9) and pastors persecuted.[21] A number of German intellectuals left the Baltic for Germany where some became anti-Russian publicists. Carl Schirren did so, becoming a professor at Kiel, but also Julius Eckart, Theodor Schiemann and Paul Rohrbach.

From the mid-nineteenth century on, the Baltic peoples were also experiencing growing national awareness. Freed from serfdom in 1820, they had benefitted from increasing numbers of schools across the region, often supported by local churches. Latvian and Estonian newspapers were appearing by 1864 and song festivals became popular.[22] Creeping industrialisation drew Baltic peoples into urban areas where most swelled the

---

[17] Quoted in Schlau (ed.), *Die Deutschbalten*, p. 72.
[18] For a description of the systems of government, see M. Garleff, 'Relations between the Political Representation of the Baltic Provinces and the Russian Government, 1850–1917' in G. Alderman (ed.), Governments, *Ethnic Groups and Political Representation*. Aldershot: Dartmouth Publishing, 1993. For Wittram's comment, see p. 205.
[19] Schlau (ed.), *Die Deutschbalten*, p. 75. Schirren himself lost his post in History at Tartu University in 1869 and went to Germany.
[20] The change was from Dorpat to Yurev.
[21] Schlau (ed.), *Die Deutschbalten*, pp. 78–82; Garleff, 'Relations between the Political Representation of the Baltic Provinces and the Russian Government', pp. 220–4; de Vries, *Das Deutschtum in Estland*, p. 6.
[22] Mühlen, *Die Baltischen Lande*, p. 11.

proletariat, although some joined the ranks of the bourgeoisie. Between 1867 and 1897, the proportion of Latvians in Riga grew from 23.5% to 41.64% and of Estonians in Tallinn from 51.8% to 88.7%. Just as dramatically, between 1897 and 1902 Tallinn's working class population grew from 2,500 to 30,000. In 1904 this was the first large urban area which voted for an Estonian-Russian (rather than German) municipal council.[23]

By the start of the twentieth century, Russification of the administration and the education system was depriving young Baltic Germans of avenues for jobs while the slowly developing Estonian middle classes were beginning to compete with Baltic German businesses. At the same time, a few notable liberal voices began to emerge in the predominantly conservative Baltic German community, including Christoph Mickwitz, (editor of *Revalsche Zeitung*) and Paul Schiemann (his junior). The latter envisaged a future in which the still-remaining feudal privileges of the *Ritterschaften* would be liquidated and the franchise for elected administrative bodies would be extended. Some German communities began slowly to move with the times more successfully than others; this happened in Riga, Jelgava, Viljandi and Pärnu.[24]

Yet even during the pre-First World War period, Baltic German social life remained dominated by corporatist organisations. In Tallinn, although other organisations existed, élite social circles were divided between the *Aktienklub* for the nobility, the *Revaler Klub* for the *Literaten*, the House of the Black Heads for business interests and the Canute Guild for artists.[25] Even liberally-inclined Germans from this milieu later admitted they had too little to do with Estonians and nothing to do with Russians.[26] When communication happened, it was in German language. Occasionally, relations between groups became particularly sour. On one occasion, for instance, in Tartu an ethnic German leader organized a boycott of shops run by Estonians displaying too much national sentiment.[27]

The troubles of this old colonial society boiled over in 1905. In the countryside, outrage flared against Baltic German estate owners and German pastors who were interpreted as agents of imperialism. About 200 German estate houses and pastors' dwellings were burned and 82 Baltic Germans were killed.[28] In the towns, unrest reflected social democratic class-discontent and demands for national autonomy. Eventually the unrest was 'managed'.

---

[23] Schlau (ed.), *Die Deutschbalten*, p. 80; S. Page, *The Formation of the Baltic States. A Study of the Effects of Great Power Politics upon the Emergence of Lithuania, Latvia and Estonia*. Cambridge: Harvard University Press, 1959, p. 15.

[24] P. Schiemann, *Zwischen zwei Zeitaltern. Erinnerungen 1903–1919*. Lüneburg: Verlag Nordland-Druck, 1979, p. 65.

[25] Schiemann, *Zwischen zwei Zeitaltern*, p. 26.

[26] Ibid, pp. 46–7.

[27] Ibid, p. 62.

[28] Schlau (ed.), *Die Deutschbalten*, p. 81; G. von Rauch, *The Baltic States. The Years of Independence. Estonia, Latvia, Lithuania 1917–1940*. London: Hurst, 1974, p. 15.

On the one hand, the Tsar issued a manifesto promising freedom of confession and nationality; on the other, Baltic Germans collaborated in reprisals against revolutionary ring-leaders and helped impose summary punishments.

Notwithstanding the economic success of the Baltic provinces, 1905 displayed the fragility of Baltic German society. A contemporary commented that in the wake of 1905, an order based on medieval corporatism (*Stände*) began to give way to something less hide-bound.[29] The more inclusive German Associations (*Deutsche Vereine*) were established to draw Germans together and help organize their schools. The German community began acquiring the property which would comprise the backbone of its educational system. At the same time, Estonians and Latvians began organising themselves politically more extensively than before.

This society could hardly survive the outbreak of war against the German Empire. Although generally Baltic Germans served loyally in the Russian armed forces, St. Petersburg regarded them as potentially subversive. Consequently, many were either incarcerated or deported from the forward military areas. Dramatic change came with the revolution of March 1917 when, in Estonia, the old feudal administrative organisations were overturned in favour of the democratic *Maapäev* (constituent assembly). The October revolution ushered in more dramatic possibilities, as Socialist Balts declared independence within a Bolshevik framework. Already, however, some Estonian leaders, such as Jan Tõnisson, had begun proposing that Estonia withdraw from any Russian-dominated state structure to claim autonomy.[30]

Baltic German noblemen regarded the changes as disastrous and attempted to cultivate contacts with the German High Command. When local Communist authorities uncovered the contacts, on 9 February 1918 Tallinn's Soviet declared all Baltic Germans outlaws. Thereafter, 500 members of the nobility were imprisoned by the Red Guard and deported to Siberia.[31] On 24 February, however, German troops took Tallinn, an event Baltic Germans viewed as a kind of salvation.[32] Although the *Maapäev* declared Estonia's independence, Estonian, Latvian and Lithuanian territory all now experienced a period of German occupation. The Baltic's place in a German sphere of influence was consolidated by Brest-Litovsk and by the calling of a regional representative assembly in which Baltic Germans outnumbered Latvians and Estonians 35 to 23. To complicate the situation further, on 3 May 1918, effectively Britain, France and Italy recognised the *Maapäev*.[33]

1918–19 saw the creation of one of the most powerful stories in the history of Estonian Germandom. The Baltic Regiment was formed, in which

[29] H. Koch, 'Die Zeit des deutschen Vereins in Estland', *Revalsche Zeitung* 12 October 1935.
[30] Rauch, *The Baltic States,* pp. 29-31
[31] Schlau (ed.), *Die Deutschbalten*, p. 84.
[32] 'Der 25 Februar 1918', *Revalsche Zeitung* 12 October 1935.
[33] Von Rauch, *The Baltic States* pp. 47–48.

Baltic Germans fought alongside Estonians to fend off Bolshevik forces and then to push towards St. Petersburg. Subsequently lists of Baltic German casualties appeared on the front of the community's newspapers on anniversaries. Surviving leaders, such as Viktor von zur Mühlen, were fêted as heroes.[34] The Baltic Regiment had stood firm against the Bolshevik assault of November 1918.[35] As the Baltic German press later remembered, Estonian War Minister Konstantin Päts had been joined by ethnic Germans Baron Stackelberg, Harry Koch and Max Bock (all of whom were members of the constituent assembly of 1919) in making an appeal on behalf of the provisional government both to mobilise volunteer forces and to call for *Reich* German troops to deploy to the region.[36]

There was undoubted heroism in a military unit that often lacked basic equipment, but probably the arrival of Finnish volunteers during December was the most important reason why Estonia remained free of Bolshevism at this point.[37] Despite the sacrifices of Baltic Germans, the arrival of peace certainly did not guarantee their traditional position in society. Baltic Germans only comprised about 1.7% of Estonia's population. Even though there were also Swedes (0.7% of the population), Jews (0.4%) and Russians (8.2%), the democratic system introduced in June 1920 created a parliament (*Riigikogu*) in which parties representing national minorities only ever contributed 3 to 8% of deputies.[38]

Given these new circumstances, some Baltic Germans decided the community's historic place in the region had ended and emigrated to Germany.[39] Many of those who stayed experienced deep dismay and resentment at the decision of the Estonian constituent assembly in 1919 to expropriate the massive landed estates which, until that point, remained disproportionately in German hands. Now, Baltic Germans lost 90% of their lands. This was a tremendous hammer blow, since land ownership not only represented centuries' old wealth but was a component of community identity.[40] Between 1914 and 1920, therefore, the Baltic Germans were transformed from a privileged, powerful élite staffing a relatively successful corner of a world empire, into a tiny, struggling segment of a small independent state bordering Bolshevik Russia. Those who remained in Estonia had to re-evaluate their relationship to their homeland.

---

[34] See, for instance, *Revaler Bote* 18 May 1920, *Der Aufstieg* 3 December 1933 and *Revalsche Zeitung* 4 December 1933.

[35] A. Tönisson, 'Ehre den Gefallenen!', *Revalsche Zeitung* 12 October 1935.

[36] See *Revalsche Zeitung*, 2 December 1933.

[37] Von Rauch, *The Baltic States* p. 53.

[38] M. Garleff, *Deutschbaltische Politik zwischen den Weltkriegen*. Bonn-Bad Godesburg: Verlag Wiisenschaftliches Archiv, 1976, pp. 76–7.

[39] Schlau (ed.), *Die Deutschbalten*, p. 66.

[40] 'Wie erhalten wir unser Deutschtum?', *Revaler Bote* 3 October 1922.

## 3. Re-thinking the Baltic German mission

To contemporary commentators, Baltic German personality was distinctive. The oldest German colony living in a foreign environment, the community described itself as sensitive to foreign cultures and always ready to overcome new hardships.[41] The need to survive under often difficult situations traditionally had led to an emphasis on vitality and strength—characteristics which had allowed the community to flourish in the Russian empire. But once banished to the peripheries of the Estonian state experiment, commentators questioned what the purpose of their lives had become. For one journalist, the community had to 'stay at its post' and fulfil morally valuable service to the new state.[42] A further interpretation maintained that the fate of Baltic Germans was wrapped up with that of Estonians and that they should hold firm; from the position of a national minority they should pursue constructive work in the Baltic.[43] Such messages were resolute, but not without a certain pathos. The latter article raised the possibility of future martyrdom.

Community leaders discussed ways in which the First World War had precipitated a crisis in Baltic German identity. In 1891, Max Hildebert Boehm was born near Cēsis in Livonia. In time, he became a radical conservative thinker on nationality issues, but from an early point, he recognised difficulties facing the Baltic German community. In the early 1920s he discussed the psychological challenges owing to the Baltic Germans' loss of their traditional sense of mission associated with their long-standing supremacy in the region.[44] Boehm argued that, in fact, a great deal of the Baltic German world had been placed under threat by 1905, particularly since the German Empire had not really cultivated connections with German communities abroad. He accepted their world lay in ruins in the wake of the First World War, thanks to German defeat and the upwelling of anti-German feeling in the lands of the former Russian Empire; but he also wondered if it was not now time for a new historical phase to start. He proposed that the German communities in the states bordering Bolshevik Russia recover their self-reliance and oppose anarchy, disorder, corruption and mass cowardice in the region. In other words, Baltic Germans could help defend Europe against the 'Russian-Asiatic threat'.[45] Furthermore, he

---

[41] De Vries, *Das Deutschtum in Estland.*

[42] 'Unser heisiges Erbe', *Revaler Bote* 31 January 1920.

[43] 'Glaube und Heimat', *Revaler Bote* 6 February 1920.

[44] M.H. Boehm, 'Baltische Sendungskrise I' and 'Baltische Sendungskrise II', (1924) pp. 164–5 and 179–81. This idea of crisis was not a new theme for Boehm. In 1915 he had already discussed the way Russification was threatening Baltic identity. With Europe at war, he looked to Germany to take the Baltic into its sphere of influence in order to shore up Germanic influence in the region. M.H. Boehm, *Die Krise des deutschbaltischen Menschen. Eine Studie zum Kulturproblem der Ostseeprovinzen Russlands.* Berlin: Verlag der Grenzboten, 1915. Nachlass Boehm 1077 / 17, Koblenz.

[45] Boehm, 'Baltische Sendungskrise II' p. 181.

recommended that Germans' traditional strengths would enable them to capitalize on the East's new economic possibilities much more effectively than, say, Jews or Russians could.[46]

Boehm wanted to recover suitable elements of tradition and apply them to the 1920s. Admittedly many Baltic Germans could not be so flexible; they could not reconcile themselves to the Estonian state, were suspicious of democracy, did not view Estonians as equals and mourned all that they had lost as a result of the post-war settlement. Yet for at least some educated figures, ties to community and region endured. By 1923, the editor of *Revaler Bote* (and parliamentary deputy for the Baltic German Party), Axel de Vries, was encouraging his readers to participate in forthcoming elections, even though their impact would be small.[47] He applauded the emergence of the independent Estonian state for marking the end of foreign rule in the area and as a vehicle which could be drawn towards western culture. Whilst maintaining that Estonians were poor at political-administrative work and unlikely to achieve heroics on the battlefield, he admitted that relations between them and ethnic Germans had improved over the last three years. Moreover, the German minority, he proposed, had important qualities, including invulnerability to corruption, which it should teach the new polity. On this basis, de Vries recommended whole-hearted German engagement with the state, a strategy quite in line with the historic civilizing mission of monks, knights and merchants in the region. So changes that provoked crisis for some were interpreted in terms of continuity based on adaptation by others.

The key Estonian German newspaper *Revalsche Zeitung* (re-named *Revaler Bote* after the First World War until the early 1930s) had been founded in 1860 as a response to Russification. Determined to shore up Baltic German identity and community, it was always more than just a local broadsheet. In its fashion, it provided thoughtful discussions of prevailing issues and commentated extensively on global events. Estonian German *prominenti* published in it and had their activities reported.

In line with de Vries's call for positive community responses to a changing world, it carried an article applying Carl Schirren's historic message to the 1920s: '*Ausdauer ist die Summe unserer Politik*' ('Perseverance is the sum of our politics').[48] Another author observed both that Estonia's Germans were no longer split into different traditional classes and that in a number of ways they were better off than before 1914. For instance, there was no imperial secret police force and everyone enjoyed

---

[46] Boehm, 'Baltische Sendungskrise II' p. 180.
[47] A. de Vries, 'Der estländische Freistaat und die Deutsch-Balten', *Revaler Bote* 29 September 1923.
[48] Auch ein Deutscher, 'Was nun weiter?!', *Revaler Bote* 27 November 1924.

freedom of speech and belief. He recommended that ethnic Germans promote their identities according to the new, progressive conditions.[49]

Rootedness in an formerly élite national minority and awareness of proud traditions both framed how Baltic Germans conceived the future. Ewald Ammende was part of this heritage.

### 4. Ewald Ammende: roots and early pre-occupations

Ewald Ammende was born on 22 December 1892. His grandfather had been a *Ratsherr* and his father both *Stadtrat* and deputy mayor. The family participated in local welfare and educational initiatives.

Ewald was the middle brother of three who graduated from Pärnu's grammar school in 1909 and then opted not to study in the rarefied atmosphere of Tartu University, but at the technical college in the regional centre, Riga. He began with Economics, writing an early dissertation about the Netherlands' trading power. Perhaps he felt the Baltic had something to learn from Dutch experiences.[50] A certain restlessness was soon making itself known in Ammende's character. In 1913 and 1914 he made research visits to England, France and the Balkans, also to the Volga (Kama and Düna) and northern Russia. In 1914, he spent time at Moscow's Institute of Economics.[51]

Following the war, Ammende began developing an interest in journalism. His father was an admirer of Paul Schiemann's liberalism. Before the First World War, Schiemann had worked in Tallinn as a journalist, but after the war he was soon playing a formative role in one of the most important German-language journals in Eastern Europe, *Rigasche Rundschau*. Ewald acquired some shares in the paper and between 1919 and 1922 collaborated in its management. At the same time, he returned to his studies. He attended Cologne University (1919–20) before gaining a doctorate from Kiel University (1922). His thesis reflected Ammende's roots:

---

[49] H. v. Berg, 'Nationale Selbstbesinnung', *Revaler Bote* 8 January 1924.

[50] The biographical details are compiled from F. von Üxküll-Güldenbrand, 'Dr. Ewald Ammende', *Nation und Staat* (1936) pp. 531–7; M.H. Boehm, 'Ewald Ammende als Mittler der Europäischen Volksgruppen', *Jahrbuch des Baltischen Deutschtums* 10 (1963) pp. 55–60. W. Lenz (ed.), *Deutschbaltische Biographisches Lexikon. 1710–1960.* Cologne: Böhlau Verlag, 1970; W. Killy (ed.), *Deutsche Biographische Enzyklopädie.* Munich: K.G.Sauer, 1995; B. Schot, *Nation oder Staat? Deutschland und der Minderheitenschutz. Zur Völkerbundspolitik der Stresemann Ära.* Marburg-Lahn: Herder Institute, 1988, pp. 102–5; M. Garleff, 'Deutschbaltische Publizisten: Ewald Ammende—Werner Hasselblatt—Paul Schiemann', *Berichte und Forschungen* 2 (1994) pp. 189–229. See also Ewald Ammende's CV located at 1502–1–30, Moscow and his article 'Die Hungerkatastrophe und der Wiederaufbau Russlands (undated), 1502–1–78, Moscow. His dissertation is located among Ammende's papers in the Moscow archive.

[51] Ammende was exempt from military service from 1910 to 1914 on account of family circumstances. 1502–1–1, Moscow.

*German Minorities in Europe. Their Development, Organisation and Attempts at Association.*

Ewald Ammende was memorable. M.H. Boehm recalled him as well-liked—a dynamo able to drive projects along.[52] Equally, he could be erratic and tactless.[53] For example, he was arrested in Cologne during his student days. Returning home one evening with a friend, Ammende was confronted by a policeman for singing too loudly. The Baltic German objected to being called 'a Russian peasant' and a scuffle ensued in which the policeman wielded a walking stick and Ammende lashed out with dangerously pointed shoes. He suffered a fine of RM 3 or a day in prison.[54] He had a 'devil may care' quality. Later in life, Ammende gave a speech hostile to the League of Nations while one of the organisation's functionaries stood by and observed.[55]

Ammende did not see combat during the First World War. In 1910 he was exempt from military service on the grounds of family commitments. In 1915 he began operating as a commissioner procuring supplies for the Livonian population.[56] Even this sort of work was not without its dangers and in March 1917 Hermann Ammende was arrested temporarily by Bolshevik authorities.[57] At about this time, Ewald was cultivating trading contacts in Ukraine. He visited Kiev, obtaining a shipment of sugar for the Baltic provinces. Visiting eastern Moscow, he negotiated safe passage for a cargo of rice. That December he travelled to St. Petersburg in an effort to acquire petrol.[58]

Ammende maintained the provisioning of Livonia and Estonia under German occupation. He was Representative of the Chairman of the Supply Office for Estonia (a post which enabled him to travel widely) and outlined his responsibilities and concerns in two memoranda.[59] Even before the First World War, he said, Estonia was not self-sufficient in food. The expansion of war industries around Tallinn strained the supply situation further. Consequently Baltic authorities deployed agents around Ukraine, the Volga valley and the Black Sea to source sugar, grain, other foodstuffs and animal fodder. The advent of German occupation and civil war in Ukraine, however, had made the sourcing of supplies harder than ever. Consequently the

---

[52] Boehm, 'Dr. Ewald Ammende' p. 55. Documents about Ammende's student days are available at 1502–1–1, Moscow.

[53] Quoted in J. Hiden, *Defender of Minorities. Paul Schiemann, 1876–1944.* London: Hurst, 2004, p.114.

[54] 1502–1–1, Moscow.

[55] 'Le Congrès des Nationalites Européennes a Vienne 29 Juin - 1 Juillett 1932', 4/6638/6638. Box S 338. League of Nations Archive, United Nations Library, Geneva.

[56] According to Ammende's CV located at 1502–1–30, Moscow.

[57] The event is recorded in 1502–1–15, Moscow.

[58] See 1502–1–11 and 1502–1–47, Moscow.

[59] 'Zur Verpflegungsfrage in Livland und Estland' and an untitled memorandum. Neither is dated, but references to the German occupation of Estonia suggest they were written in 1918. 1502–1–46, Moscow.

territory had to rely increasingly on foodstuffs coming from Poland and Lithuania. Since their delivery was uncertain, Estonia's food situation became precarious. Things could well have been worse still for Riga, which seemed to be surviving thanks largely to the black market. Ammende concluded that, when it came to provisioning the Baltic, it was just about impossible to replace Ukraine as a critical supply source.

Ammende watched as conflict followed conflict; revolution wreaked havoc; old empires gave way to new states; workforces were disrupted and populations uprooted; property and resources were damaged; and established economic relationships were challenged. His journalism during the immediate post-war period showed a fascination for both newness and the possibility that established economic requirements would still need to be respected somehow. Change was clear when he visited Trieste in 1921.[60] Historically this had been a major port serving the Austro-Hungarian Empire. The peace settlement, however, allocated it to Italy. Deprived of an imperial hinterland which had embraced territory in Hungary, Yugoslavia, Czechoslovakia and southern Austria, Ammende observed that the city had become marked by a mood of depression reflecting a drop in trade of at least 30%. Political isolation, high tariffs and assertive trades unions securing massive pay rises for dock workers were all damaging the port's competitiveness. As a result, trade was shifting towards Hamburg. Bearing Trieste's economic weakness in mind and the fact that goods from the Balkans and Central Europe would still need an outlet to the sea, Ammende recommended that northern sea ports should take the initiative and offer alternatives.

Of course local interest was implicit in Ammende's analysis. If there was trade from Central Europe requiring an outlet to the sea, then clearly there was a possible benefit for Pärnu and hence for the Ammende family. Already in 1918 Ammende had written about the need for better transport links between his home town and key inland economic areas. In line with later concerns, he wrote a piece, apparently for a local newspaper, called 'The North Livonian Trade Route' which advocated connecting his home town to the main broad gauge railway system linking Riga to the Russian heartland.[61] He made his case with historical arguments, maintaining (for instance) that Hanseatic trade routes had run through Pärnu to Tartu (a gateway to the Russian heartland) before proceeding to Pskov and Novgorod. It was only the construction of imperial railway lines to Riga and Tallinn that consigned Pärnu to the status of rather a second class port with a small hinterland compared to those other cities. He suggested that linking Pärnu to the modern rail network would permit the re-acquisition of historic trade and the re-invigoration of Estonia's economy. In due course, Estonia's railway system was overhauled at least in part, with the introduction of state-management for

---

[60] E. Ammende, 'Italien und das tote Triest', *Revaler Bote* 22 October 1921.
[61] 'Der nordlivländische Handelsweg'. 1502–1–35. Moscow.

the Tallinn-Pärnu narrow gauge railway and various improvements for the national railway system.[62]

So changes, such as the collapse of Trieste, were creating opportunities for the Baltic ports. Exploiting these, plus the attachment to Europe's main transport system, could bring personal and regional benefits alike, as well as preparing Estonia for increased advantage once access to the Russian heartland became possible once more. Of course, Ammende's post-war arguments were located in the context of serious difficulties. Not only had access to Ukrainain and Russian resources become impossible for the time-being, but for him the Baltic region had lost its unity. All Ammende could do was highlight opportunities and pitfalls in the prevailing order of things, in the process recommending ways to capitalize on the former while minimizing the latter.

### 5. Economic concerns for the region and continent

Congruent with his interest in business and economics, Ammende also watched closely negotiations that occurred about a possible customs union between the Baltic States, although especially between Latvia and Estonia since in imperial times Pärnu had been part of Livonia and had looked to Riga as its provincial centre. In an early article, Ammende discussed whether the removal of trade tariffs between Estonia and Latvia would result in southern Estonia becoming an economic colony of the Latvian capital.[63] Such fears led to the maintenance of a tariff fence between the two countries and the destruction of railway tracks at the border crossing points Valga and Misaküla.[64]

Ammende thought tariff barriers were harming both Estonia and Latvia. To his mind, southern Estonia was being drawn towards Riga economically despite artificial efforts to prevent the trend. The Latvian capital was an important source of at least sugar, flour and salt. The Latvian transport system was well-organised and cheap. Even travel restrictions on Latvian business people could not off-set the fact that Tallinn was not competing effectively with Riga.[65] For Ammende, the situation could only be improved once trade restrictions were abolished. Only then would southern

---

[62] 'Übernahme der Pernau-Revaler Schmalspurbahn', *Revaler Bote* 2 November 1923; 'Das Projekt des Umbaues des Revaler Eisenbahnnotenpunktes', *Revaler Bote* 22 August 1924.

[63] Undated article, 'Soll Südestland eine Handelskolonie Rigas werden?' 1502–1–60, Moscow. Also 'Zur Frage der Zollunion mit Lettland', 1502–7–19, Moscow.

[64] E. Ammende, 'Nochmals zum litauisch-lettländisch-estnischen Wirtschaftsbund', *Revaler Bote* 10 June 1921.

[65] In his article, Ammende also commented that businesses in Tallinn feared competition from Jewish firms in Riga. 'Was solide und lebensfähig ist, muss und wird sich gleich wie vor dem Kriege gegen die Rigaer Juden halten, während was unfähig arbeitet auch unter dengegenwärtigen Verhältnissen nicht geschützt werden kann. Jedenfalls wäre es falsch, die Zollunion der Furcht einiger Revaler Firmen vor dem Rigaer Judentum zu opfern.' 'Zur Frage der Zollunion mit Lettland', 1502–7–19, Moscow.

Estonia be able to export its own goods to Latvia and ship its flax through Riga. Repeating his argument that southern Estonia needed a better railway system, he concluded that artificial barriers could not overpower economic realities forever and it was harmful to attempt to do so.

It was typical of Ammende that his thoughts about the nearby Latvian-Estonian border were part of a 'bigger' concern. When he attended the Genoa conference as a journalist for *Revaler Bote*, Ammende interviewed Professor Cassell who believed that national borders were damaging Europe's post-war economic recovery.[66] New borders were hindering trade and artificial, politically-motivated efforts were being made to separate states from areas to which they belonged 'naturally' by virtue of geography and economics. In Cassell's view, the restrictions imposed between Estonia and Latvia had to be lifted to improve the area's long term prospects. The Balkanisation of the Baltic, he felt, had gone far enough. He recommended the economic union of Latvia, Lithuania and Estonia, a measure which could serve as a model for the rest of Eastern Europe.

Ammende wanted to emphasise that the Baltic was open for business. He believed that Western Europe was only interested in his home region in so far as it could function as a single economic unit stretching from Klaipėda to Narva.[67] He felt the creation of such a unit was more realistic than the forging of a united economic bloc comprising all the states bordering Bolshevik Russia—a *Randsstaatenpolitik* favoured by some European statesmen. While he accepted there might be a case for the states having a political or military association, he maintained economic union was only feasible for states with geographical, historical-cultural and, of course, pre-existing economic ties. He rejected, therefore, the possibility of economic unity between states as different as Finland and Poland. The former was too Scandinavian, the latter was so large it had to have its own imperatives.

Ammende regarded as unsuccessful past attempts to weld together economically dissimilar states bordering Russia such as that which happened at Bilderlingshof in 1920. Since then, economic barriers to economic union in Eastern Europe had only intensified. Even in the Baltic region, Ammende felt Lithuania was now diverging economically from Latvia and Estonia. Consequently unless statesmen acted quickly, even a Baltic customs union might prove unattainable. He argued that the Baltic States should act unilaterally and swiftly to create a customs union embracing all three. As a first step, he proposed establishing a joint Latvian and Estonian chamber of commerce. Once the Baltic States were united economically, it would be all the harder for Moscow to divide them to its advantage and they would be

---

[66] E. Ammende, 'Professor Cassell über die Konferenz von Genoa und das europäische Sanierungsproblem', *Revaler Bote* 3 June 1922.
[67] E. Ammende, 'Der Lettisch-Estnisch-Littauische Bund', *Revaler Bote* 11 May 1921. E. Ammende, 'Nochmals zum litauisch-lettländisch-estnischen Wirtschaftsbund', *Revaler Bote* 10 June 1921.

better placed eventually to provide a transit land to Russia operating on their own terms rather than those of the eastern neighbour.

Customs union is not a classically exciting topic, but Ammende compiled ringing arguments for it. Woodrow Wilson's 14 points might have promoted the autonomy of nations, but this had to have limits. Separate states were responsible for the promotion of general welfare through participation in the international economy, their individual success depending on the quality of their contribution to the whole. In this context, the Baltic States had to provide solid foundations for free trade. Being too small and weak to stand alone, they had to strengthen themselves through association in order to fulfil important tasks such as providing a 'window' to Russia. As Europe was currently experiencing a trade slump in the wake of the First World War, it was a perfect time to prepare for the future. In a world where it would be impossible to insulate themselves, they had to look for a role that would be appreciated by the international community. They should become a mediator between East and West rather than a barrier between the two.[68]

Ammende saw economic union as the foundation for Baltic economic success, something which would, in turn, provide the states with political weight internationally. In the event, although some steps were taken to set up a Baltic customs union (for example, measures to facilitate travel between Latvia and Estonia), they were too limited;[69] and so the creation of a Baltic Association of all three states remained an aspiration.[70] Lack of progress reflected the existence of vested interests in both countries which saw no advantage in union. These interests pointed out that to be effective, customs union would require extensive economic harmonisation between states (for instance, regarding taxation).[71] Hence, in 1925 and 1926 Ammende was still lobbying government ministers on the topic and arguing for customs union over national egoism.[72]

All of these concerns existed against a backdrop of terrific change. Empires had been broken up and established economic relationships had been disrupted. At the same time, even a quick glance at newspapers like Tallinn's *Revaler Bote* showed that economies were globalizing. The paper advertised not just domestic products (such as Le Coq beer), but Sunlight soap and Ford cars. It began advertising not just steamers travelling from Estonia to German and Finnish ports, but to Dundee, Hull and Liverpool. Soon it was promoting flights between Tallinn and Helsinki. Ammende showed himself adept at keeping abreast of the new possibilities. He foresaw the day when a good

---

[68] E. Ammende, 'Nochmals zum litanisch-lettländisch-estnisch Wirtschaftsbund', *Revaler Bote* 7 June 1921. See also 'Der Baltische Staatenbund', *Revaler Bote* 21 May 1921.

[69] 'Abschluß des estländisch-lettländischen Vertrages', *Revaler Bote* 2 November 1923

[70] For continuing negotiations, see for instance 'Die estländisch-lettländische Zollunion', *Revaler Bote* 11 August 1924.

[71] A.M. Luther Ltd to Ammende, 22.5.1922. 1502–1–24, Moscow.

[72] See the letter of Ammende to an unnamed minister, May 1925, 1502–7–19, Moscow. Also E. Ammende, 'Scheitern der Zollunion?', *Baltische Blätter* (1926).

road would link Tallinn and Riga, enabling people to travel between the two with an overnight stop at Pärnu. More unexpectedly, in 1922 he floated the idea of making a documentary feature film shot from a plane as it flew from the Baltic to Italy. He liked the title 'From the Mountains to the Sea'.[73]

And when the Estonian economy hit the rocks, Ammende tried to engage with that situation constructively.[74] In 1924, he discussed how best to stabilise the Estonian Mark and encourage foreign investment. Rather than change the currency or link it to the value of Sterling or the US Dollar, he recommended stabilizing the currency as it was. Exports and imports should be balanced by reducing non-essential imports. He wanted the state budget to be balanced too, a measure requiring stringent austerity initiatives such as cutting foreign diplomatic missions, defence expenditure and the number of interior ministry officials. Estonia needed a more realistic understanding of what it could afford. Government spending had to be done in such a way that it would boost national productivity, as improving the rail system would do. Such steps would increase national wealth and foreign investment and, as a result, lead to increased government spending in the longer term. As Ammende put it: 'Reduce unproductive expenditures and ... raise productive expenditures—in the future this must be the principle of our state's economic policy.' When Estonian Finance Minister Strandmann identified 12 principles for economic stabilization, he did indeed recognise the need to cut government spending.[75]

### 6. Business, Russia and peace

After the war, Ewald Ammende provided a constructive commentary on the possibilities facing the Estonian state, yet he was particularly fascinated by how relations with Russia would unfold. As early as 1920, newspapers in Tallinn were discussing what would happen when Bolshevism collapsed. Some expected this to happen sooner rather than later given Communism's denial of property ownership and the increasing signs of moral degeneration (including corruption and anti-Semitism) observed in the lands ruled from Moscow.[76] There was some anticipation of the Soviet lands breaking up into smaller units, with 'foreign' border lands (such as Ukraine) going their own way. Ammende had some sympathy with the view, and wrote an unpublished article advocating the creation of a union between the Baltic States, Ukraine and White Russia if the Soviet state did indeed fall apart.[77]

---

[73] Letter from Ernst to Ammende, 1 August 1922. 1502–1–21, Moscow.

[74] E. Ammende, 'Der Kampf um die Estmark. I', *Revaler Bote* 12 April 1924 and 'Der Kampf um die Estmark. II', *Revaler Bote* 16 April 1924. Also E. Ammende, 'Zum Abbau', *Revaler Bote* 15 May 1924 and 'Wie führen wir den Abbau durch?', *Revaler Bote* 4 June 1924.

[75] 'Die Leitsätze für die Stabilisierung der Estmark', *Revaler Bote* 12 June 1924.

[76] 'Das Russlandproblem', *Revaler Bote* 24 April 1920.

[77] Unpublished article dated 30.12.25, 1502–7–19, Moscow.

But Ammende thought of Russia in other ways too. He was aware of ideas originating in France which looked to the stimulation of Russia's economy from abroad, zone by zone and working from the periphery towards the heartland. By contrast, Latvian Finance Minister Kalinin believed that Russian reconstruction should start at the core, beginning with the re-development of an express rail link to the Russian interior.[78] Once modern transport was in place, other things would follow. Kalinin's position was, actually, one with which Ammende sympathized. He wanted Russia accessible to business—not least for the benefit of the family firm, but for the global economy too. Without its markets and raw materials, he felt post-war reconstruction could never be driven ahead properly.[79]

These ideas shed fresh light on Ammende's insistence on Baltic economic unity and the need for a rail link between Pärnu and Pskov. Ultimately they were necessary elements of post-war world economic recovery and long-term regional, even global economic well-being and hence peace. This awareness of how themes hung together must have encouraged *Revaler Bote* to send him to Genoa as a correspondent and naturally he produced a whole string of articles about the event, including a series of interviews with figures such as Czech President Beneš, German Foreign Minister Rathenau and Polish Foreign Minister Skirmunt.

As Ammende put it, the time had come to stop wasting resources on arms and to channel them into more worthwhile areas, such as cultural life. He looked to the Genoa conference to provoke reduced defence spending especially in Eastern Europe, and advocated that Estonia remain aloof from bloc-based politics which might draw the state into military commitments. He wanted Tallinn to seek common cause not with the victors or vanquished of the First World War, but with neutral states such as Sweden, Denmark, Norway, Holland, Switzerland and Spain. Such a strategy, he felt, was necessary to help transform the international mood from one dominated by military preparedness to one characterised by peaceful economic exchange. Only after such a development would it be possible to focus more clearly on reconstruction within Russia—a topic vital to the future of the Baltic States and in which they had to play a fundamental part.[80]

Naturally, Ammende's reporting from Genoa explored the geo-political games in play there. France was singled out as using the conference for national interests, while Britain attracted praise for promoting reconciliation and common economic gain. Quickly he saw that in many

---

[78] E. Ammende, 'Auf dem Wege nach Genua', *Revaler Bote* 12 April 1922.
[79] E. Ammende, 'Die Hungerkatastrophe und der Wiederaufbau Russlands'. 1502–1–78, Moscow.
[80] E. Ammende, 'Die baltischen Staaten und die Genua Konferenz. Abrustung und Neutralität', *Revaler Bote* 31 March 1922; 'Die baltischen Staaten und die Genua Konferenz. Der Wiederaufbau Rußlands und das Prinzip der "offenen Tur"', *Revaler Bote* 1 April 1922 and 'Die baltischen Staaten und die Genua Konferenz. Unsere Taktik in Genua', *Revaler Bote* 8 April 1922.

areas genuine progress would be impossible. Poland, for instance, would never be persuaded to disarm. Ammende even regarded the German-Russian agreement at Rapallo as a distraction from a full consideration of how the Russian economy might be assisted towards reconstruction. Yet, notwithstanding the event's deficiencies, Ammende conveyed the considerable drama of Genoa and what was at stake there.[81] He enthused that scientists and business people were present to impress upon politicians that real work had to be achieved. He was delighted that Estonia contributed a representative to the sub-commission on transport. He applauded the realization that successful relations had to be created in Central Europe if the whole continent was to be a long-term success. He also conjured up the uncertainty surrounding the conference, stressing that by the third week its likely conclusions still were unclear; but Ammende's most evocative prose was saved for one topic in particular.

The Genoa conference started at 3 pm on 10 April 1922, in the Hall of the Georgian Brotherhood, where Christopher Columbus had once met the city's businessmen. With Lloyd George, Lord Curzon, Josef Wirth, Walther Rathenau and Eduard Beneš among those present, and just five minutes before the event was due to start, the Soviet delegation, led by Chicherin, paraded in. It was the first time that Moscow's Foreign Commissar had represented his country at a fully international conference, and Russia's representatives had been protected exhaustively by the Italian police ever since they crossed the Brenner Pass. Security was so formidable it put Ammende in mind of how the Tsar had been protected in the years just before the war. He described the entrance:

> The delegates have taken their places. The room is packed
> tight. Then the men from another world—the men who,
> after all the years of battle, hatred and wildest annihilation,
> take their place for the first time among the representatives
> of the European states—, the representatives of the Soviet
> Union permit Europe—the European statesmen who have
> all gathered here—to wait for them.

This was the atmosphere in which Lloyd George delivered his ringing opening address calling for decisive constructive work; but Ammende was

[81] See for example, E. Ammende, 'Die Eröffnung der Genuakonferenz', *Revaler Bote* 20 April 1922; 'Zur Chronik der Genuakonferenz. Die Presse in Genua', *Revaler Bote* 21 April 1922; 'Die Baltischen Staaten in Genua', *Revaler Bote* 27 April 1922; 'Zur Chronik der Konferenz von Genua', *Revaler Bote* 28 April 1922; 'Zur Chronik von Genua. Erregte Stunden', *Revaler Bote* 4 May 1922; 'Polen und der deutsch-russische Block', *Revaler Bote* 13 May 1922; 'Die bisherigen Ergebnisse der Genuerer Konferenz', *Revaler Bote* 13 May 1922; 'Die wirtschaftlichen Entscheidungen der Konferenz von Genua', *Revaler Bote* 27 May 1922; 'Rußland, Deutschland und die baltischen Staaten. Ein Gespräch mit Walter Rathenau', *Revaler Bote* 31 May 1922 and 'Skirmut über Genua und die baltische Frage. Ein Interview', *Revaler Bote* 2 June 1922.

fascinated by the Soviet delegation, and Chicherin in particular. One evening
the Soviets arrived at the municipal palace for a reception, the politicians
dressed in tails, behind them elegant women and men in cavalry uniform.
Ammende felt their splendour recalled the glittering world of Empire. He
went on:

> ... Chicherin, the red-haired weakling in a tailcoat and white
> bow tie, is now the greatest sensation. What he used to be,
> what he did, no longer concerns anyone. And while the
> upper crust bow down in the most objectionable way before
> their new hero—the man they have fought, insulted,
> despised and ridiculed over the last four years—there stand
> outside, behind a chain of military and security men, those
> who cannot enter this place where affluence and power are
> collected in white tie and tails.[82]

Ammende proposed that Chicherin and the capitalist élites around
him both were guilty of hypocrisy. The former was playing a part which
formerly had repulsed him; the latter were dealing with a man representing a
system they rejected out of hand. But at Genoa, Russia's economic potential
was as important to the international community as it had been to the
Ammende family firm. While everyone agreed on that point, there was scant
accord on anything else. Wherever you turned, there were problems
associated with the development of Russia. Hence Ammende recognised
there were many Polish businesses (particularly Jewish ones) that, given their
expertise, could help get Russia moving again. In the wake of the Russo-
Polish war, however, there was little interaction between the two states.
Hence Ammende called on Russia and Poland to put aside their past
differences. He called on the latter to stop acting as a barrier to flows between
East and West, and to participate in a mediation initiative between the two
states.[83]

Genoa gave Ammende the opportunity to interview Walther
Rathenau.[84] It was a rich encounter in which the German Foreign Minister
interpreted the conference as a major step towards the normalisation of
international relations. Accepting that the rail system in Europe and Russia
needed extensive development and that the Soviet agricultural economy had
to be modernized, Rathenau also spoke directly about the Baltic Sea region.
Understanding that close cultural and historic ties bound Germany,
Scandinavia and the Baltic States, Rathenau stressed that the Baltic coast

---

[82] E. Ammende, 'Zur Chronik der Genua-Konferenz. Die Stadt empfängt', *Revaler Bote* 13 May
1922.
[83] E. Ammende, 'Polen und der deutsch-russische Block', *Revaler Bote* 13 May 1922.
[84] E. Ammende, 'Rußland, Deutschland und die baltischen Staaten. Ein Gespräch mit Walter
Rathenau', *Revaler Bote* 31 May 1922.

should not be taken away from Russia completely. Rather, he wanted access to it mediated by the Baltic States, with them providing the most important route for German-Russian trade. The theme, no doubt, was at the front of his mind in the light of the Treaty of Rapallo, an agreement he termed 'a pure and genuine peace treaty'. Perhaps to Ammende's surprise, Rathenau said that Russia was in the process of discovering an order more appropriate to its people than that inherited from Peter the Great.

The economic themes concerning Ammende personally were little different to those occupying Europe's foremost statesmen. The creation of a durable, affluent European economy lay at the heart of the continent's prospects for stability. This economic goal required the re-gaining of access to Russian economic space, an objective calling for both the development of an effective transport system and the unification of the Baltic States as a launch pad for accessing the lands to the East. So projects advocated to help Pärnu were part of a package Ammende thought necessary to assist not just Estonia but Europe as a whole. His thinking really was marrying local and continental experiences. He was also implying, whether intentionally or not, that the regeneration of Europe drequire sound economic development at key local levels.

### 7. Soviet hardship

If, at this time, Russia was central to many concerns for European regeneration, then there was no escaping the dire conditions afflicting the territory. In this connection Ammende showed that, even at a relatively early age, his interest in practicalities could not be divorced from political and humanitarian engagement.

For commentators situated in the states neighbouring Bolshevik Russia, it was axiomatic that, despite the territory being rich in natural resources, Communism had caused such massive economic collapse that the lands could not look after their own people, never mind generate the sort of surpluses which previously had funnelled through Tallinn and Riga.[85] Ammende had witnessed the situation first hand. In 1921 he published *Europe and Soviet Russia*, a collection of four essays based on what he had seen in Moscow and St. Petersburg (by that point Petrograd) while staying there at the behest of the Estonian Red Cross.[86] In the first instance, he was investigating the situation of Estonian nationals in Soviet prisons. This, actually, was a very personal mission since his brother, Edgar was imprisoned in early 1921, apparently on suspicion of financial improprieties while trying to conduct business in Russia. Soon he was suffering from typhus.[87] Ammende was all the more horrified that prisoners were not even

---

[85] See, for instance, 'Die Barbarisierung Rußlands', *Revaler Bote* 20 October 1920.

[86] Evald Amende [sic], *Europe and Soviet Russia*. Riga: R.Ruetz and Co, 1921.

[87] Letters of January to April 1921. 1502–1–84, Moscow. Edgar seems to have been imprisoned

receiving their basic nutritional requirements. That Soviet authorities found it
so hard to supply fundamental human needs had substantial international
importance because hundreds of thousands of prisoners of war from Central
Europe were still in Russian camps, and they were little better off than
Ammende's brother.[88]

There was almost too much to criticize. The Soviet transport system
was utterly disorganized, but the Soviet secret police (*Cheka*) was a particular
problem. It was preventing liberalization of the economy, in the process
forcing people to sell their property on the black market and to become
criminals. *Cheka* officers behaved as a law unto themselves, implementing
body searches of diplomats, imprisoning Estonian citizens without reason and
removing selected refugees from trains arbitrarily.[89] The organisation was
even subverting attempts (favoured by Lenin and Moscow's Foreign
Ministry) to develop trade agreements with the West. Meanwhile, Westerners
(including Red Cross representatives) were not necessarily that much
better—travelling to the suffering country to exploit it. Capitalising on
popular misery, they were acquiring once expensive artefacts—art treasures,
family heirlooms and so on—at bargain basement prices. Moscow tolerated
the activity because the 'entrepreneurs' carried Bolshevik propaganda as they
left.[90] The situation was outrageous.

Ammende found this 'money-grubbing' and 'speculation' to be
deeply unsavoury. He called for western governments (including the Baltic
States) to send only resolutely moral characters to Russia, otherwise the
corrupt practices picked up there would infiltrate their own lands. He
proposed that relations with Russia should be well-regulated in order to
promote the reform of Bolshevist policies, or else, like the USA, western
states should consider having nothing to do with the place.[91]

Given his background, of course Ammende absolutely rejected
Communist economics. Looking at Bolshevik Russia, he saw a system on the
verge of breakdown. Agricultural production had slumped and cities were
starving. St. Petersburg had a mortality rate of about 95/1,000, with children
and the infirm suffering grievously. Taking everything into account,
Ammende felt things had gone too far for Russia to save herself.[92] Already he
was anticipating the possibility of unrest spilling over Soviet borders as
hardship and uproar threatened to generate refugee movements. The only

---

in January and released in April.

[88] 'Die verzweifelte Lage der Gefangenen in Sibirien', *Revaler Bote* 4 February 1920. For a
study of the repatriation of these prisoners of war, see M. Housden, 'When the Baltic Sea was a
"bridge" for humanitarian action: the League of Nations, the Red Cross and the repatriation of
prisoners of war between Russia and Central Europe 1920–22', *Journal of Baltic Studies* 38
(2007) pp. 61–83.

[89] Ammende, *Europe and Soviet Russia* pp. 17–22.

[90] Ibid, pp. 23–7. See also E. Ammende, 'Ssowjetrußland und wir', *Revaler Bote*, 1 June 1921.

[91] Ammende, *Europe and Soviet Russia*, p. 27.

[92] Ammende, *Europe and Soviet Russia*, p. 14. See also his article 'Eindrücke aus
Ssowjetrußland', *Revaler Bote* 9 May 1921.

hope rested with some kind of foreign intervention, most likely involving the supply of aid.

## 8. Famine

But there was one hardship with which Ammende engaged with special determination. He became a prime publicist of the famine afflicting Russia between late 1920 and 1922. At an early point, he corresponded with the League of Nations on the matter.[93] He compiled a lengthy report about the stricken areas which he used as a source for articles distributed to Europe's press.[94] While Soviet authorities said about 13 million people were affected by starvation focused on Ukraine, Ammende proposed the true figure was nearer 30 million. He believed fully a third of the population of European Russia was suffering some kind of hunger in the early 1920s.[95]

This was far more than a domestic Russian affair. Before the war, the Volga, Kama, Ukraine and Crimea had all been major producers of grain (supplying the Russian Empire and export markets alike), yet now they were suffering famine. Ammende believed, therefore, that crisis in this region was likely to be exported across Russia and beyond. To make matters worse, he feared the catastrophe would be prolonged because of prevailing chaos in the Soviet transport system. On this account it was unlikely that seed crops would be supplied to the troubled regions in time for the next harvest. Therefore Ammende called for the supply of large quantities of aid to Russia. Solving the sapping effects of such a massive famine had to be a pre-requisite for doing worthwhile business with the territory. Movements across the border during the famine might only spread typhus and cholera. As he put it in bullet points concluding his report: there could be no Russian economic recovery until the epidemics in Russia and the hunger causing them were solved; this required co-ordinated action by international interests involved in relief; it required the Russian transport system to be restored; and until all of this was achieved there could be no serious progress for the world economy.

In this light, Ammende looked to the statesmen gathering at Genoa to save Russia's people from collapse. He was certain that famine in southern Russia was the single biggest problem facing the world in the early 1920s, and those statesmen could not avoid addressing it.[96] As he said, 'It becomes

---

[93] Ammende to the League, 20 June 1921. 12/14312/14182. League of Nations Archive, UN Library, Geneva. Also his letter to the League of 20 August 1921.

[94] 'Die Hungerkatastrophe und der Wiederaufbau Russlands'. Signed 'Ewald Ammende, Member of the Estonian Red Cross'. 1502-1-78. Moscow. Examples of his journalism about the famine include E.Ammende, 'Die deutschen Wolgakolonisten vor dem Untergang', *Revaler Bote* 2 August 1921, 'Die Russlandhilfe und der Völkerbund', *Revaler Bote* 8 October 1921 and 'Den an der Wolga untergehenden Menschen muß geholfen werden', *Revaler Bote* 29 October 1921. See also Ammende, *Europe and Soviet Russia*, chapter 6, 'Relief for Starving Russia'.

[95] For an objective recent word on these themes, see O. Figes, *A People's Tragedy*. London: Jonathan Cape, 1996, pp. 775–85.

[96] Ammende, *Europe and Soviet Russia*, p. 7.

more and more evident that the European states cannot prosper for the long run if Russia—one third of our continent—is perishing economically and morally.'[97]

Ammende's discussion of famine in Ukraine had a number of different strands. It sought a sympathetic response to human suffering while, more pragmatically, maintained that strict economic necessity dictated intervention. Moreover, Ammende argued that a mission to save Russia would help European states overcome the tensions they still experienced as a residue of war. Humanitarianism would become a project behind which Europe could begin to unify. In other words, Ammende made the point strongly that saving Russia was in the political interest of Europe itself.

## 9. Conclusion

In the early 1920s, Ewald Ammende had his fingers in many pies. He was, however, more than a dilettante because his interest in the family business and role as a journalist dictated his concerns would never be fleeting. From the outset, he knew well that business patterns had changed. The collapse of old empires and the emergence of new, smaller states had transformed the condition of markets, the supply of raw materials and the requirements of an effective transport system. At many different levels (from local to global), he was promoting engagement with these new conditions of life in post-war Central and Eastern Europe. Ultimately he was optimistic he could find ways to create durable peace in Europe based on an effective economy stretching from the Atlantic to the heart of Russia. This was the mentality of a humanitarian with a business edge. He believed that the best way to secure Europe was to create viable, self-sustaining liberal capitalist economies which would make peace profitable for all (his own family included), and which might eventually help bring about change within the suffering Bolshevik empire. In terms of his view of the world, he shared much with the peacemakers of the period for whom free trade was a power for good.[98]

---

[97] Ibid, p. 6.
[98] J. Robinson, O. Karbach, M.M. Laserson, N. Robinson and M. Vichniak, *Were the Minorities Treaties a Failure?* New York: Antin Press, 1943, p. 32.

## Chapter Two

## Liberal nationalist

### 1. Introducton: the German diaspora

Although Ammende was always interested in the economics of a profitable, peaceful Europe, he was even more deeply absorbed by a different topic. As a member of a distinctive national group in a multi-national empire, he was fascinated by national identity.

Ammende's doctoral research analysed the distribution, status and aspirations of German national minorities in Eastern Europe. In a text apparently developed from his thesis and intended for publication, he examined the German nation not as defined by state borders, but as a shared community of blood, language and culture.[1] These qualities bound people together more fundamentally than a formality like 'state citizenship'. In a further essay, Ammende underlined how seriously he took the history of the German diaspora in the Russian Empire. German minorities, he said (perhaps rather wishfully) had grown into a self-conscious, organised cultural community (*Kulturgemeinschaft*). Clearly Ammende had spent no small amount of time on historical research. He discussed everything from the invasion of the Baltic region by the Teutonic Orders to the creation of a small German community in Moscow during the reign of Ivan the Terrible. He proposed there had been three main phases of German migration to Russia. The first, during the Middle Ages, followed Hanseatic trade routes and led to the settlement of Germans in communities which became outposts of western culture and trade. The second occurred during the eighteenth and early nineteenth centuries, when, unable to make a living in Germany, small trades people moved to the Volga, the Caucasus and the Vistula. Last, in the late nineteenth century, Germans moved around the Russian Empire according to the dictates of industrialization. In the process, for instance, they helped Łodz become 'the continent's Manchester'. At this time, settlers from the Volga moved on to Siberia.[2]

Ammende was deeply sensitive to the experiences of German communities living in the midst of other national cultures. They had valuable pasts, characteristic identities as well as the capacity to civilise and enrich all around them. Ammende's championing of these groups determined that he would be at odds with the totalitarian politics that gained ground in the wake of the First World War. These movements threatened both minority national identities and the centuries of productive, co-operative cultural work minorities had achieved.

---

[1] Untitled, 1502–1–57, Moscow.
[2] Untitled, 1502-1-53, Moscow.

## 2. The collapse of Russia

Ammende was fascinated by Russian society, but believed it was precarious in the extreme. In 1921 he visited Russia for the first time in three years on behalf of the Estonian Red Cross. His train inched over the badly damaged bridge at Lugo and he felt the track to be as delicate as the basis of life in the country he was entering.[3] Either could fall apart at any moment. What he witnessed confirmed the initial impression. With little to eat and unable to return home years after war had ended, Hungarian prisoners of war at Andronnikoff camp by Moscow were threatening hunger strike.[4] The prisoners were administered by Hungarian Communists and Ammende felt they were particularly unlikely to find freedom quickly; not that Estonian refugees were faring much better. Strewn across Russian lands for many reasons, they were attempting to travel to their new nation state, but risked getting stuck and starving at any point *en route*.[5] This was a hard place in which to survive.

Ammenede, like other Baltic Germans, believed enmity towards 'foreigners' was well-established in Russian society. Correspondingly, in 1924, *Revaler Bote* ran a story describing an anti-German pogrom which happened in Moscow in 1915 with the tacit approval of the city's mayor.[6] But if contempt for foreigners was nothing new in Russia, the characteristic became exaggerated under Bolshevism. Not only had Baltic German aristocrats been deported to Siberia when the Red Army occupied the Baltic provinces in 1918, but local groups were permitted to loot and commit outrages against their perceived 'enemies'. At this time, revolutionary tribunals meted out dreadful 'justice' to anyone, but especially to ethnic Germans.[7]

Even after the Bolsheviks left the Baltic territories, Baltic Germans kept a weather eye on revolutionary excesses. In November 1919 *Revaler Bote* reported mass executions organised by Felix Dzerzhinsky's extraordinary committee in Moscow. Certainly these were happening at the Lubjanka and in Petrowski Park, but after an assassination attempt against Lenin, roughly 1,000 people were shot near Chodinka field.[8] With Russian

---

[3] 'Worin die Stärke des Bolshewismusses liegt.' 1502–1–78, Moscow.
[4] For the story of the return home of the POWs, see M. Housden, 'When the Baltic Sea was a "Bridge" for Humanitarian Action: the League of Nations, the Red Cross and the Repatriation of Prisoners of War between Russia and Central Europe, 1920–1922,' *Journal of Baltic Studies*, 38 (2007), pp. 61–84.
[5] These details can be found in Evald Amende [sic], *Europe and Soviet Russia*. Riga: R. Ruetz and Co, 1921, chapter 4. The Tallinn newspaper for which Ammende wrote, also carried stories about the POWs. See for example *Revaler Bote*, 7 June 1920.
[6] 'Der grosse Moskauer Pogrom 1915', *Revaler Bote* 25 January 1924.
[7] Report about Communist takeover of Riga at end of WW I. Possibly written by Schickedanz. Z2368. Institute for Contemporary History, Munich.
[8] 'Wie die Bolschewisten hinrichten', *Revaler Bote* 12 November 1919.

society suffering perpetual power cuts, factory closures and the interminable need to queue, members of the middle classes were being compelled to undertake forced labour. The experience was killing many older people, while survivors faced the additional risk of being taken to Kronstadt where they might be used as hostages.[9] The newspaper stories resounded with subtext: the Baltic was extremely fortunate to have fought off Bolshevism and further east the successes of the traditional German 'civilising mission' were being destroyed. Russia was being barbarised; everything was in a state of regress. In rural areas, threshing machines had vanished and there had been a return of oxen and the flail.[10] Society had fallen to such a point that, even in Russia's most westernised city, it was necessary to fight the spread of cholera.[11]

Russia's education system was barely functioning. Educational buildings were dilapidated; teachers were supervised by a staff-student Soviet; private lecturers could no longer teach in universities; and student recruitment had become politicized such that barely half those attending courses in St. Petersburg were qualified to do so because they had been selected according to their family's proletarian credentials, not academic attainment.[12] Axel de Vries (who became editor of *Revaler Bote* and was Ammende's friend) found this loss of advanced culture more shocking even than economic collapse. He believed Russia's educated circles (fragile at the best of times) faced extinction, with catastrophic consequences. Applying anti-Semitic arguments (as he did on other occasions too), de Vries complained that Jews were now likely to find advantage and dominate Russia's 'intelligentsia'. He also bemoaned the fact that general educational levels would remain appallingly low. In a country which had 18 million illiterate peasants, he cited the example of leader of a local village Communist party who tried to make a student fall in love with him by applying witchcraft as taught by his grandmother. De Vries argued that Orthodox religion was in the process of being replaced by a strange mixture of Marxism and heathenism. He foresaw the 'absolute moral and spiritual barbarisation' of Russia.[13]

Ammende was also vocal in denouncing the treatment of Russia's intellectuals. In St. Petersburg, the death rate of this group was thought to be 12%.[14] More practical-minded than de Vries, he advocated an extensive relief operation to assist them. The Quakers, he said, were proving aid would not be pilfered by the Red Army automatically.[15] Promoting the need for action,

---

[9] 'Selbsterlebtes aus der Bolschewisten-Zeit in Petersburg und Zarskoje Sselo 1918–1919 (Teil 1)', *Revaler Bote* 11 November 1919.
[10] 'Die Barbarisierung Rußlands', *Revaler Bote* 20 October 1920.
[11] 'Die Cholera in Petersburg', *Revaler Bote* 16 June 1920.
[12] 'Die Schulen in Ssowjetrussland,' *Revaler Bote* 19 November 1920.
[13] A. de Vries, 'Die Sowjetunion nach dem Tode Lenins', *Baltische Blätter* (1924), pp. 79–81.
[14] Ammende, *Europe and Soviet Russia*, pp. 32–3.
[15] Ibid, p.34.

Ammende made contact with Maxim Gorky, who lived in Russia's former capital.[16] In spring 1921, Ammende smuggled a letter by him out of Russia highlighting the 'tragic' position of 'scientists and scholars, inexperienced in the struggle for their livelihood'.[17]

For Ammende, inside Russia a collapse was occurring on a scale impossible to ignore. He said:

> It is the duty of the Baltic States, and in common moral questions (the care for prisoners, arrest of hostages)—the duty of all European States represented in Moscow, to protest by a common, coordinated and conscious action through their Representatives in Moscow against the wilfulness in this country, and hence to insist on immediate redress.[18]

For Ammende, the moral and intellectual turmoil of Russia could not be separated from economic disaster. Town and country no longer understood each other and urban Communists would not let the peasants do their job. A cycle of persecution of the peasantry leading to rural unrest and further persecution was offering little promise of economic improvement, even in the longer term. Imperial trading systems had broken down to the point that largely a barter economy was left. Ammende wondered if the failure of Russia would become so serious that, one day, the state of Europe would be compelled to intervene in its affairs simply for the sake of self-preservation.[19]

### 3. Starvation

Bolshevism was a man-made catastrophe, but Russia was suffering a natural one as well. At the start of July 1921, *Revaler Bote* reported a meeting of Russian agronomists in Moscow.[20] The tone of the piece raised suspicions that it was propaganda, but in fact it seemed reasonably accurate. While alleging that in some locations the Russian harvest had been mis-managed (for example being carried out too early and mis-recorded), the piece also noted that in some places the harvest had failed so badly that refugee movements were under way. It maintained that Russia needed to import grain

---

[16] Ibid, chapter 5.
[17] The letter is reproduced as follows: 'Gorky—The Humanitarian', *Russian Review*, 27 (1968), pp. 351–3. See also Ammende to the League of Nations, 30 August 1921. 12/14312/14182. League of Nations Archive, UN Library, Geneva.
[18] Ammende, *Europe and Soviet Russia* pp. 18–21. See also E. Ammende, 'Eindrücke aus Ssowjetrußland', *Revaler Bote* 9 May 1921.
[19] Ammende, *Europe and Soviet Russia* chapters 1 and 2.
[20] 'Die große russische Hungersnot. Lehrreiche Folgen der Agrarreform', *Revaler Bote* 8 July 1921.

on a massive scale. A week later, the paper reported famine in the Volga where whole villages were deserted as their inhabitants had left for Turkestan, Kirgizia and Central Russia in search of food. 6,000 cases of cholera had been reported already spreading north from the Black Sea, most likely transported by refugees.[21] Within a week, the Supreme Central Executive Committee of the Russian Soviet Republic was issuing emergency orders and there were fears that 10 million people would need foreign assistance to avoid starvation.[22] Before long, there were stories of anarchy breaking out in the affected areas and of food shipments being robbed before they arrived at their destinations. It seemed that only coastal and peripheral famine areas could be helped, that nothing could be done for interior areas.[23]

*Revaler Bote* had no time for Bolshevism, often linking the rise of extremist politics with war, epidemics and famine,[24] but there was a more balanced narrative too that recognized the confluence of man-made and natural disaster. The journal understood that before 1914 harvest yields in south and south east Russia had been highly variable and that there had been droughts on a number of occasions, most notably in 1891. Since the black soil area stretching from Ukraine to the North Caucasus retained little moisture naturally, it was particularly vulnerable to dry periods. The author contended that, in 1921, natural susceptibility had been turned into a full-scale disaster by Communism's agricultural policies. The elimination of large estates, leading to the eradication of stockpiles of agricultural supplies and the destruction of understanding about how best to work the land contributed to the emergency. Bolsheviks had no idea how to manage rural communities. Attempts to turn peasants into forced labourers were leading to resentment and passive resistance. Meanwhile, élite government officials, including perhaps Lenin himself, failed to recognise the signs of drought which had been evident that spring. With time wasted, starvation was now abroad across Saratov, Samara, the German Volga colonies, Zarizyn, Astrakan, Don, Kuban and Terek. People were eating grass, acorns or anything they could get their hands on.[25]

But there was no denying the politics of the famine. A group called 'the Pan-Russian Committee to Aid the Starving' (a non-Bolshevik organisation of Russians) formed quickly.[26] *Revaler Bote* maintained that through support of this organisation, the wider 'civilized' world could engage with Bolshevik Russia. Aid for starving people was deemed the best anti-

[21] 'Der Hunger kommt' and 'Die Cholera in Ssowjetrussland' both in *Revaler Bote* 15 July 1921.
[22] 'Russland. Aufruf der Ssowjetregierung in Veranlassung der Hungersnot', *Revaler Bote* 20 July 1921.
[23] 'Anarchistische Verpflegungszustände in Folge der Hungersnot', *Revaler Bote* 3 August 1921; 'Der Volkskommissar für Gesundheitsschutz über die Hungersnot der Kinder', *Revaler Bote* 3 August 1921.
[24] 'Die russische Tragödie', *Revaler Bote* 21 July 1921.
[25] 'Die katastrophale Hungersnot in Südosten Russlands', *Revaler Bote* 21 July 1921.
[26] 'Das Allrussische Komitee zur Hilfsleistung für die Hungernden', *Revaler Bote* 27 July 1921.

Bolshevik propaganda possible and Russian patriots were called on to participate. In this light, humanitarian assistance became action designed to pave the way for a post-Soviet future.

Ammende was at home within this intellectual framework. He believed the famine was so significant it could bring down the Bolshevik state;[27] but he also emphasised the experiences of the historic ethnic German communities living at the heart of the Volga. Their forebears had settled during the time of Catherine the Great; Bolshevism had established them as an independent administrative unit, the Volga-German community;[28] but now they were experiencing crisis. In late July, the administrative leader of the Volga Germans, *Herr* Schneider, said that production had failed on 70% of their arable land and the rest had been damaged severely. Consequently 300,000 'Volga-colonists' would die without outside assistance.[29] Ammende painted a grim picture of communities on the edge of extinction. As someone who had shared a life in the Russian Empire with the Volga Germans, Ammende was moved by their suffering and wrote that a community related in blood and culture to the Baltic Germans, with a 200 year history, was staring at its own destruction. He proposed it was the particular duty of every German to aid them.

In a later article (and contrasting other articles in *Revaler Bote*— although in line with his earlier comments over the hardships of intellectuals), Ammende stressed that aid would reach the people who needed it. Again he cited the Quakers who were working successfully with Russian children in Samara. They had transported 18 wagon loads of supplies at least as far as Moscow. With a rhetorical flourish aimed at White Russians in exile, Ammende observed you could not expect starving people to rise up against a state. They were too weak for that.[30]

Although famine had taken hold of an area prone to it, Ammende and his colleagues at *Revaler Bote* still maintained that the Bolshevik government was responsible for the severity of the event. So, if Soviet newspapers blamed the crisis on war, capitalists and bandits, Baltic Germans blamed lack of culture and organisation.[31] With some level of sympathy for Russia's plight, *Revaler Bote* could agree with reports in *Pravda* suggesting

---

[27] Ammende, *Europe and Soviet Russia*, pp. 3– 4.

[28] For a study of the Volga Germans, see F.C. Koch, *The Volga Germans. In Russia and the Americas, from 1763 to the Present*. Pennsylvania State University Press, 1977, pp. 12–17. For interesting *Revaler Bote* reporting on the Volga Germans, see J. Schleuning, 'Die Autonome Sozialistische Ssowjetrepublik der Wolgadeutschen', *Revaler Bote* 25 March 1924 and J. Schleuning, 'Die Autonome Sozialistische Ssowjetrepublik der Wolgadeutschen', *Revaler Bote*, 28 March 1924. These reports concern especially the setting up of the Autonomous Soviet Socialist Republic of the Volga Germans.

[29] E. Ammende, 'Die deutschen Wolgakolonisten vor dem Untergang', *Revaler Bote* 2 August 1921

[30] E. Ammende, 'Den an der Wolga untergehenden Menschen muß geholfen werden', *Revaler Bote* 29 October 1921.

[31] 'Die Hungersnot in Russland', *Revaler Bote* 3 August 1921.

Russia's railways were wrecked after prolonged periods of conflict (with only 2,000 of 11,000 locomotives functioning), adding that Communist party members—after years of upheaval and conflict were unable to work in famine relief on account of a 'sense of demobilisation'.[32] At the same time, however, more critical voices were evident, alleging for example that in the face of the greatest famine known to Mankind, 10 million souls were being sentenced to death by the incompetence and criminality of a dictatorship.[33]

Ammende accepted that, even if Bolshevism did not cause the famine, it took decisions certain to promote the suffering of victims. An unpublished essay made his position clear.[34] Noting that 2 million people had died of starvation, that ethnic German villages were being devastated, that 13 million people were starving and 30 million going hungry, Ammende related a conversation with Soviet Foreign Commissar Chicherin at Genoa. The Soviet wrote off the famine as a concomitant of necessary agrarian restructuring. With this, the famine victims became acceptable losses to the Soviet project.

Ammende contrasted Soviet complacency with international concern. The American Aid Administration organised by Herbert Hoover was supplying food to the Volga, Odessa and Cherson, with only a very small percentage pilfered during transportation. *Save the Children* was sending aid and reporting more lost between London and Riga than Riga and Saratov. Quaker organisations had been working since 1919 to help Russia and now were taking food to stricken areas. Meanwhile, the League of Nations' High Commissioner for Russian Refugees, Fridtjof Nansen, was supplying 375,000 people around Saratov and Samara. Red Cross organisations were assisting specific regions too.[35] The human cost of this engagement was high. A number of aid workers had died in service: Dr. Ferrar (of the League of Nations' Epidemic Commission), Dr. Pardo (of the Italian Red Cross), Dr. Gürtner (a member of the German medical expedition) and Sister Lindskog from Sweden. 60% of Quakers working in Bulusk had contracted typhus. But there were the psychological pressures too. On a daily basis, daily the workers were faced with two or three times the number of people they could help and so had to deal with utter desperation. One English aid worker near Balashow had committed suicide.

---

[32] 'Von Zustand der russischen Bahnen' and 'Das Versagen der Kommunisten im Kampf gegen den Hunger', *Revaler Bote* 31 August 1921

[33] 'Die Frage der Garantien in der Hungerhülfe für Rußland', *Revaler Bote* 31 August 1921.

[34] 'Die Hungerkatastrophe und der Wiederaufbau Russlands', undated but written at about the time of the Genoa Conference.1502–1–78, Moscow.

[35] International aid to Russia was reported regularly in the Tallinn press, see for instance 'Bekanntmachung des Estnischen Roten Kreuzes in Sachen der Hilfeleistung an Rußland', *Revaler Bote* 11 August 1921; 'Die Russische Hilfsaktion', *Revaler Bote* 15 August 1921; 'Zur Hilfsaktion für Rußland', *Revaler Bote* 17 August 1921; 'Das russische Hilfswerk und wir', *Revaler Bote* 26 August 1921; also *Revaler Bote* 31 August 1921.

From the Urals to the Baltic, Ammende heard 'a groaning...passing through the pained Russian country'.[36] He declared:

> The world must recognize that Bolshevism and the Russian nation are two different things which are not to be mixed up.... [I]t is an unavoidable humane duty to help the suffering people in Russia as the Russian nation cannot perish because of the Bolshevists.[37]

Proximity of the Baltic States to Russia, plus understanding on the part of the Baltic peoples for life in that country, dictated their governments should lead the publicity of the famine. Furthermore, if too little was done to alleviate starvation, Ammende felt anarchy would spill across Russia's borders into neighbouring territories. Assistance to Russia, therefore, was a matter of self-interest for the Baltic States.[38]

The scale of the crisis dictated that Ammende have a special interest in the League of Nations' response to it.[39] He noted extensive discussions about the best way to structure the relationship between the League and the Red Cross, and observed that Russian émigré groups were lobbying aggressively against the provision of any aid on the grounds that it would only help the Bolshevik regime.[40] In fact, in June 1921 Ammende had contacted the League's Information Section to report about food shortages and to pass on Gorky's letter, but he also advised that food should be sent to the country before Russia's ports started icing up in October.[41] A couple of months later, he wrote to the secretary of the Information Section providing details about the Russian Relief Committee in Moscow (it had been formed recently, was recognised by the Bolshevik government and comprised political figures active before 1914).[42] On another occasion, he provided information about the Relief Committee for Russia which was based in Riga and attached to the Latvian Red Cross.[43]

---

[36] Ammende, *Europe and Soviet Russia*, p. 42.

[37] Ibid, p. 45.

[38] Ibid, p. 7.

[39] The League of Nations Archive, Geneva has an extensive documentary record relating to the Russian famine of the 1920s. It includes boxes R 656, R 657 and R 1754.

[40] E. Ammende, 'Die Russlandhilfe und der Völkerbund', *Revaler Bote* 8 October 1921.

[41] Letter from Ammende, 20 June 1921. R 656. Famine in Russia. 12 / 14312 / 14182. League of Nations Archive, UN Library, Geneva

[42] Letter from Ammende, 20 August 1921. R 656. Famine in Russia. 12 / 14312 / 14182. League of Nations Archive, UN Library, Geneva. In this letter, Ammende also records that he met Fridtjof Nansen and they discussed the famine.

[43] Letter from Ammende, 29 July 1921. R 656. Famine in Russia. 12 / 14501 / 14182. League of Nations Archive, UN Library, Geneva.

## 4. Analysing Bolshevism

In the light of Russia's hardship, presenting a critical analysis of Bolshevism became an obsession for Ammende. Certainly this reflected damage done to his family (in terms of imprisonment and destruction of the family business), but it also spoke of humane instincts horrified at the suffering of helpless people trapped behind political borders. Ammende was so much of a determined opponent of Bolshevism that, although the term 'Cold War' really only applies after the Second World War, there was something of the prototype 'Cold Warrior' about him. The characteristic was shared by many Baltic Germans. Theirs was a conservative community which interpreted Soviet Russia not just as a personal threat, but as a challenge to the whole idea of western civilisation. For Eduard von Stackelberg, Bolshevism's thirst for central control negated every spontaneous and creative human instinct. Apocalyptically, he feared Lenin's successor would attempt to set the world alight through revolution.[44] Axel de Vries took it as axiomatic that Moscow would do all it could to destabilise the liberal world, including fomenting unrest between majority and minority national groups wherever they existed, especially in the ethnically diverse lands of Central and Eastern Europe.[45] He believed the Communist movement had understood the strength of nationalist sentiment and consequently had granted national self-determination to many peoples inside the Soviet Union. Hence different nationalities within the Soviet system could use their own languages for, say, administration and education. But Communists wanted to de-stabilise Central and Eastern Europe by exploiting national tensions there. Everywhere they were trying to appear saviours of oppressed nationalities. De Vries considered Bolshevism's combining of social and national dissatisfaction to be particularly dangerous.[46]

The anti-Communism of, say, de Vries was wrapped up with a number of prejudices. Communism was believed 'Asiatic' and at times his rejection of it became anti-Semitic, as the following reflection of an audience watching a ballet in Moscow shows:

> ... this is the reality—the victory of the East, above all the victory of Jewish people. From the box on the left there shine on us the white faces of fanatical young Jewesses, wide burning eyes, full of the will to power and domination: it is the box for the offspring of the Communist Party. From the most pure Sepharid type to the negro-

---

[44] E. v. Stackelberg, 'Rußland am Scheidewege', *Baltische Blätter* (1925), pp. 357–9.

[45] See, for example, A. de Vries, 'Europa und Moskau', *Baltische Blätter* (1925), p. 5.

[46] A. de Vries, 'Ssowjetrußland und das Nationalitätenproblem', *Revaler Bote* 28 August 1924 and A.de Vries, 'Die Gefahren der ssowjetrussischen Nationalitaetenpolitik', *Revaler Bote* 20 September 1924.

oriental half-breed—it is like a kaleidoscope of Jewish types is passing us by.[47]

*Revaler Bote* reported extensively on Bolshevism's plans to promote revolution abroad. It carried Lenin's speech to the Third International of July 1921 which advocated careful planning for revolution in capitalist lands.[48] Already it had reported that Moscow's press was advocating heightened revolutionary action in the West (although especially in the Baltic States), with professional malcontents slated to take over the leadership of workers' organisations. Stories followed of Bolshevik agitators becoming active in Estonia's border areas, not least in the vicinity of Narva.[49]

In early 1924, the Estonian police arrested a number of individuals suspected of acting in Moscow's interests.[50] Interior Minister Einbund said 150 people had been apprehended for criminal activities traceable to the Third International's agenda.[51] On 1 December 1924, Tallinn experienced a Communist putsch which was small, but nonetheless shocking for local residents.[52] *Revaler Bote* ran stories about Bolshevik activity abroad. In October 1924 there were reports of the Red Army repressing unrest in Georgia and in December about Bolshevism manipulating discontent among national minorities in Romania.[53] In this heady atmosphere, Ammende not only rejected Soviet Communist economics and politics, but became a publicist denouncing what he saw as Moscow's attempted expansion. Most notably he wrote an essay 'Moscow's new offensive'.

## 5. Moscow's new offensive

The article, attempting to reveal a truth about events across Europe, displayed raw anti-Bolshevism.[54] In common with Interior Minister Einbund, Ammende believed the Third International had planned how best to spread Communism beyond Soviet borders. He thought Bolshevism was applying a new kind of warfare to subvert the states on its borders, the '*Randstaaten*', or what Ammende also referred to humorously as 'the bourgeois chain' stretching from the Baltic to the Black Sea. Bolshevik strategy was to promote the belief that these states were oppressing their national minorities and then to present Moscow as their minorities' liberator. In this light,

[47] A. de Vries, 'Asiatische Mission', *Baltische Blätter* (1925), pp. 98–9.
[48] 'Schluss des Kongresses der III. Internationale', *Revaler Bote* 21 July 1921.
[49] 'Bolschewistische Absichten gegen die baltischen Staaten', *Revaler Bote* 15 June 1921 and 'Bolschewistische Agenten an der estnische Grenze', *Revaler Bote* 20 July 1921.
[50] 'Zu den Massenverhaftungen der Kommunisten', *Revaler Bote* 24 January 1924.
[51] 'Der Minister des Inneren zu den Kommunisten-Verhaftungen', *Revaler Bote* 31 January 1924.
[52] For reports of this event, see *Revaler Bote* 1, 2, 3, 4 and 6 December 1924.
[53] C. v. Kügelen, 'Der Aufstand in Georgien und sein Echo', *Revaler Bote* 20 October 1924 and 'Die bessarabische Gefahr', *Revaler Bote* 9 December 1924
[54] E. Ammende, 'Moskaus neue Offensive', *Baltische Blätter* (1925) 15 and 22 January 1925.

establishing the Soviet Republic of Moldova on the borders of Bessarabia was presented as a strategy to stimulate unrest in Romania and Poland. Ammende believed Moscow's plans had three phases. First came subversion (*'Die Unterhöhlung'*), then an uprising (*'Der Aufstand'*) and lastly union with the Soviet state. It followed that initially a network of Communist organisations and placemen would be built up across a given territory, with part of the armed forces being won over. Then a coup would be staged before a piece of theatre in which, on the basis of supposed national 'self-determination', the new government would request Moscow's protection.

Ammende argued that Moscow was tackling the perceived weakest links in the bourgeois chain first. His home state was experiencing an economic crisis, was closest to the influential St. Petersburg (Petrograd) military district and had seen extensive efforts to build up networks of Soviet sympathisers. Moscow also believed it would be relatively easy to whip up discontent among Lithuanians, Ukrainians and White Russians living in Poland. Destabilisation strategies could then be exported from Polish territory to other states, perhaps Finland and eventually Bulgaria, Romania and Yugoslavia.

So how should the capitalist world protect itself? Ammende rejected the build up large military forces alone; you never knew whose orders they might obey. He praised on-going efforts to create defensive agreements between Latvia, Lithuania and Estonia, but feared that even these could be subverted at some point. Ultimately, he felt there was only one way to fend off the Soviet threat: states had to consolidate themselves domestically such that conditions were removed which could turn millions of inhabitants into internal enemies. Certainly this meant that, say, Estonia and Poland required external assistance to solve their economic problems, but it also meant that the national chauvinism intrinsic to a number of *Randstaaten* had to be superseded. In particular, the oppression of national minorities had to be tackled by the League of Nations putting into effect post-war agreements on minority protection. Finally, Ammende argued that western states had to avoid falling prey to Moscow's strategy of 'divide and rule'. To this end, he applauded steps by the Baltic States to pull together, but remained concerned that the Treaty of Rapallo might force a wedge between Germany and the rest of Europe.

In 'Moscow's new offensive' Ammende addressed themes which, by 1924, had concerned him for a number of years. As he had put it in an unpublished essay, Bolshevism had nothing to offer Europe because it killed enterprise. Proper reconstruction required the continent to be united as a capitalist economic community striving for improved productivity and possibly regulated by a pan-European economic council. The states had to strive towards equality, understanding and the supersession of past injustices. On-going hostilities between victors and vanquished in the First World War had to be shelved, as did imperialist ambitions.[55] So Ammende was envisioning the creation of a unified, organic, economically-balanced, capitalist Europe, but this should not over-shadow the importance he attached to at least some non-economic aspects of the continent, particularly the management of his long-standing interest—national minorities.

### 6. National minorities and the Association of German Minorities in Europe

After the First World War, the treatment of national minorities was an international question. In the name of 'self-determination' the peace settlement had broken up the old empires of Central and Eastern Europe and recognised independent states including Finland, the Baltic States, Poland, Czechoslovakia, Hungary, Romania and Yugoslavia. But 'self-determination' was only possible up to a point, because these lands were home to multiple and interspersed national groups. Hence, for example, Estonia was inhabited not just by a majority Estonian population, but also by Russians, Germans, Swedes and Jews. The importance of how national minorities would fare in the re-structured Europe was reflected in the reporting of ethnic German newspapers across Central and Eastern Europe, including *Revaler Bote*.

*Revaler Bote*'s editorial team was always deeply interested in the experiences of national minorities in the lands between Berlin and the Soviet frontier. In 1923, Ammende applauded electoral success by German minorities in Yugoslavia and observed that ethnic Germans had parliamentary representation in Estonia, Latvia, Poland, Yugoslavia, Romania and Italy, while Germans in Lithuania were just starting to organise. In the same edition, by chance a number of Hungarians discussed an earlier article by Ammende which shed an unfavourable light on the quality of life available to ethnic Germans in Hungary.[56] In Romania, *Revaler Bote* was always interested in the fate of the *Siebenbürger Sachsen* community. Their schools were said to be facing 'Romanianisation'.[57] Regarding Czechoslovakia, when Ammende interviewed Eduard Beneš in 1922, they

---

[55] E. Ammende, 'Worin die Stärke des Bolshewismusses liegt.' Unpublished manuscript, 1502–1–78, Moscow.
[56] E. Ammende, 'Der Deutsche Wahlsieg in Jugoslawien', *Revaler Bote* 24 April 1923. A year later the paper also reported on the closure of German cultural organisations in Yugoslavia, see 'Verbot des deutschen Kulturbundes in Südslawien', *Revaler Bote* 23 April 1924 and 'Die Schließung des deutschen Kulturbundes in Jugoslawien', *Revaler Bote* 26 April 1924. E. Ammende, 'Ungarn und seie deutsche Minderheit', *Revaler Bote* 25 June 1923 and E. Ammende, 'Was die deutschen und ungarischen Minderheiten voneinander trennt', *Revaler Bote* 30 June 1923. See also Elmer Viranyi, 'Ungarn und das Minoritätenproblem', *Revaler Bote* 19 May 1923.
[57] 'Zur Schulfrage in Rumänien', *Revaler Bote* 29 April 1924 and E. Neugeboren, 'Der Kampf um die deutsche Schule in Rumänien', *Revaler Bote* 22 August 1924.

discussed poor relations between ethnic Germans and Czechs.[58] As for Poland, articles reported ethnic Germans in the *Sejm* complaining about co-nationals being ejected from the country.[59]

The reporting of *Revaler Bote*, as written by members of a German national minority, displayed a clear awareness that they were party to important developments during a significant phase of European history; but there was also a clear and persistent fear of persecution. A number of reasons stood behind this. Before the First World War, ethnic Germans in Austria-Hungary and parts of the Russian Empire (such as in the Baltic States) often had been a social élite. The collapse of empire, however, led to their position being levelled out in new states where they were a numerical minority and where parliamentary politics was dominated by peoples who previously had felt second-class citizens in their own lands. Hence ethnic Germans faced expropriation for the good of the new state and suspicion if they found themselves living in strategically sensitive zones. Worse, memories of war-time occupation by German troops complicated post-war inter-ethnic relations further.

The Great Powers and the organization they created—most notably the League of Nations—understood that problems over the treatment of national minorities could fast become a source of international friction. Unfortunately, once established the League was wary of being accused of interfering in the domestic affairs of sovereign states. Consequently its mechanism for addressing minority protection compromised between international and state interests. The balancing act soon drew criticism from even quite disinterested observers.[60] But even if the League's system was imperfect, still it underlined the importance of the principle of tolerating national minorities. Hence, Ewald Ammende once quoted with approval a speech by Swiss statesman Giuseppe Motta to the League's Third Assembly which stated clearly the need to promote good relations between different national groups. Actually, Ammende cited Switzerland as an ideal type of state in which different national groups co-existed with respect and fellow-feeling.[61]

Speaking generally, when the new or significantly enlarged states of Central and Eastern Europe negotiated to join the League of Nations, each was required to undertake guarantees concerning their treatment of national

[58] E. Ammende, 'Die Kleine Entente. Ein Interview mit Bensch, dem tschecho-slowakischen Premier', *Revaler Bote* 29 May 1922

[59] 'Über die Lage der völkischen Minderheiten in Polen', *Revaler Bote* 11 August 1923.

[60] For a discussion of the League's minority' system as a compromise, see R.N. Kershaw, 'The League and the Protection of Linguistic, Racial and Religious Minorities' in *Problems of Peace. Third Series*. OUP, 1929. For a contemporary academic critique of the question, see H.R.G. Greaves, *The League Committees and World Order. A Study of the Permanent Expert Committees of the League of Nations as an Instrument of International Government*. OUP, 1931, pp. 15–16.

[61] E. Ammende, 'Beschlüsse über den Minoritätenschutz der dritten Völkerbundversammlung', *Revaler Bote* 7 October 1922.

minorities. Based on a communication between Clemenceau and Polish Foreign Minister Paderewski dated 24 June 1919, such protection was taken as a principle of international law.[62] In due course, the peace settlement made extensive provision for how minorities should be treated.[63] Poland agreed a minority treaty with the Great Powers on 28 June 1919 and this served as a model for subsequent agreements with Czechoslovakia, Yugoslavia, Romania, Greece, Albania, Lithuania, Latvia and Estonia.[64] The fact that there was a gap of four years between Poland's signing of the model treaty and the agreement of some other states to similar provisions indicates that, soon after gaining independence, some Central and Eastern European statesmen were reluctant to relinquish any of their newly found sovereign autonomy. Negotiations between Estonia and the League were particularly protracted and showed a rather unflattering determination on the part of elements of the Estonian establishment not to offer international guarantees to minorities.[65] Nonetheless, eventually all the agreements were made.

The internationalisation of the national minority issue across bourgeois, capitalist Europe attracted Ewald Ammende immensely. As early as 1917 he had participated in the Congress of Germans held in Moscow but now his interests developed in tune with the new times. He would work with Rudolf Brandsch (a leading representative the *Siebenbürger Sachsen* whom he had met during his doctoral research) in founding the Association of German Minorities in Europe (*Verband der deutschen Minderheiten in Europa*).

Born in 1880, Rudolf Brandsch had more political experience than Ammende. Drawn from a family of Protestant churchmen, before the First World War he had been a deputy in the Hungarian parliament, while after the war he was elected to the Romanian parliament. He provided the initial impetus for convening representatives from the various major ethnic German groups around Europe. It was, however, Ammende who drafted the document which defined the group's formative framework, tasks and practical programme. This memorandum later was published in the journal of German minority groups, *Nation und Staat*.[66]

The Association of German Minorities in Europe aimed to unite and strengthen ethnic German groups outside the German state. In so doing, it was filling a long-standing gap, as Paul Schiemann observed. In his opinion,

---

[62] *Ten Years of World Co-operation*. Geneva: Secretariat of the League of Nations, 1930, p. 355
[63] For instance, Article 85 of the Treaty of Versailles made provision for the treatment of Germans who now found themselves resident in Czechoslovakia, while Article 91 dealt with Germans who were now living in Poland.
[64] K. Aun, *Der völkerrechtliche Schutz nationaler Minderheiten in Estland von 1917 bis 1940*. Hamburg: Joachim Heitmann, 1951, p. 25. For a fuller discussion of the League's minority provisions, see *Ten Years of World Co-operation*, chapter 9.
[65] These negotiations are recorded in the minutes of the Council of the League of Nations and published in the *League of Nations. Official Journal* for the period in question.
[66] E. Ammende, 'Gründe, Aufgaben und Programm für eine Zusammenkunft der Vertreter aller deutschen Minoritäten in Europa', *Nation und Staat*, October 1932, v.6, pp. 63–6.

Bismarck and the German Empire had done too little to promote a sense of solidarity among the German communities abroad.[67] But the Association had very current concerns, not least providing material and ideological support to its members.[68] It aimed to strengthen ties between German communities within the same state, to promote contacts between ethnic Germans in different states and to build up a strong mentality for business and enterprise. It was supposed to promote the return of ethnic Germans to areas from which they had begun emigrating after the First World War, including the Baltic States. To Ammende's mind, the Association had to strengthen ideas of national consciousness rootedness in the homeland, self-sacrifice and duty.[69] From the outset it was understood that the project required the underpinning of German-language schools serving the various ethnic German communities of Central and Eastern Europe.

The Association believed the promotion of minority rights was critical for Europe:

> Minority protection legislation and the cultural autonomy of minorities ... really are the only means to defeat the cancer in the body of our continent, namely national hatred— which causes ninety nine percent of the cases of oppression and violence towards national minorities.[70]

But there was a lot of work to do, since in the post-war world no German minority had attained full equality with whichever majority people inhabited any new state. Since the cultural life of a minority was always curtailed by the demands of the majority, Ammende's memorandum proposed that no German group was yet in control of its own cultural life: they all lacked 'cultural autonomy'. With this said, Ammende recognised there were benefits to life in post-war Europe. So, whereas before the war national minorities had been unable to contest their rights, now it was perfectly possible. Hence, he thought, representatives from all these groups should draw together to share their experiences and plot a way forward. By planning a common strategy towards international organisations such as the League of Nations, they could have a greater impact than if they acted individually and in disorganised fashion.

But the attainment of minority rights for German national groups was made more challenging by the German state's place in the international order. With that state accorded pariah status (e.g. denied membership of the League), Ammende suggested that the millions of Germans living outside the 'home' state should become promoters and disseminators of German culture

---

[67] P. Schiemann, 'Eine Auseinandersetzung', *Baltische Blätter* 1925.
[68] 'Arbeitsprogramm des Vorstandes des Verbandes'. Undated typescript, 1502–1–61, Moscow.
[69] Ibid.
[70] Ibid, p. 63.

and champions of post-war reconciliation. Success here would re-define minorities as something other than a source of tension between the different European states (since no 'home' state could be indifferent to the treatment of related minorities 'abroad'); they would become bonds bringing together different areas of the continent.

At this early point, Ammende recognised there was a positive purpose to *all* minorities drawing together, but even so he felt specifically ethnic Germans had a particular duty to fulfil. Taking their groups as a whole, they were the most numerous single national minority and could be found more or less across the length and breadth of Europe. More contentiously, Ammende also believed that culturally they were the most highly developed national minority.[71] If they could organise and pursue their rights, then it would be an important step on the way to solving the national minority question in general. In his words:

> The co-operation of all German minorities and their consolidation as a community of common interest would be an extraordinary step on the way to the organisation of Europe's minorities and to the solution of one of the most important problems in the world. So the community of German minorities would not just be fighting for their own interests, but for those of minorities in general.[72]

Ethnic Germans were to be the 'pioneers' of minority protection.

Ammende wanted a prospective meeting of German minority representatives to achieve a number of tasks in quite specific ways. He was clear that minorities should pursue their goal of establishing autonomous cultural lives in loyalty towards the state in which they lived. To this end, they should *not* engage in any *political* initiative benefitting the German state, since that would subvert their position in their home state. It followed that Ammende recommended setting up a liaison office for ethnic German groups not in Berlin, but in Vienna. He was adamant that the project should not take on the character of an 'irredenta group'. This was the best way to ensure credibility for concerted action in respect of national governments, the League of Nations and, indeed, similar organisations which might be formed by other national minorities. It would be the most effective way to pursue rights for German minorities, to ensure respect for German culture and address matters of interest to all Germans (including the treatment of Volga Germans).

An initial meeting of German minority representatives occurred in Vienna in October 1922, followed by the first full meeting of the Association

---

[71] 'Among all European minorities, the Germans constitute the mostly widely distributed and in many cases culturally the most highly developed element.' Ibid, p. 64.
[72] Ibid.

of German Minorities in Europe in the same city in July 1923.[73] The latter was attended by representatives drawn from 11 separate states. Those attending from the Baltic pushed hard for a rejection of irredenta politics. Minorities needed to fight for their rights within the framework of the laws of the states in which they lived. In this context, it was agreed that the quest for the 'cultural autonomy' of German national minorities within their home states was fundamental.[74]

When Ammende contacted a journalist from the *Basler Nachrichten* to publicise the work of the Association, he exhibited pride at what had been achieved. By bringing together German spokesmen from different minorities located across Europe, something of genuinely historic importance had been realized. He was happy to highlight that specifically *German* minorities were the first to pursue a progressive approach to the European national minority question and added that all present rejected attacking the states in which they lived. The most important thing was to prove that chauvinism *per se* was destructive.[75]

At subsequent meetings, the Association addressed all manner of issues. In line with Ammende's deep anti-Bolshevism, the meeting in Vienna in July 1924 registered concern about the Soviet Union using its 'national republics' as propaganda tools to generate unrest among oppressed national minorities in Europe.[76] This gathering included representatives interested in the Volga, Black Sea and Caucasus regions of the Soviet Union.[77] Yet Ammende's biting critique of minority protection in the early 1920s was not reserved for the Communist state alone. From about the time of the Genoa conference, Ammende took an interest in the ethnic German community of South Tyrol. Increasingly the group was living under Fascist hegemony, as Mussolini formed a governing cabinet in late 1922 and established dictatorship in mid-1924.

## 7. South Tyrol

In some respects at least, South Tyrol's Germans were more vulnerable than many ethnic German communities living in Central and Eastern Europe. The latter groups, so long as they were located in new or expanded states, could look to the League of Nations for a kind of protection. By contrast, although Italy annexed South Tyrol from Austria-Hungary under the terms of the

---

[73] B. Schot, *Deutschland und der Minderheitenschutz. Zur Völkerbundspolitik der Stresemann-Ära.* Marburg/Lahn: J.G.Herder-Institut, 1988, p. 103.
[74] 'Eine deutsche Minderheitentagung', *Revaler Bote* 11 July 1923. The press report is confirmed and extended in 1502-1-56, Moscow.
[75] Letter of Ammende to Oerl of 6 November (1923), 1502-1-23, Moscow. Ammende's correspondence with Oerl shows clearly that he understood the importance of good publicity for minorities' issues with the international press.
[76] 'Der deutsche Minderheitenkongreß in Wien', *Revaler Bote* 11 August 1924.
[77] Schleunig to Ammende, 11 June 1923. 1502-1-23, Moscow.

Treaty of Saint-Germain, she was on the victorious side in the war and had increased her size only to a limited extent. Hence, no special provision was instituted to ensure the protection of Italy's minorities—neither the Germans of South Tyrol nor the Slovenes and Croats who lived in the north east of the country (not least in the region around Rijeka—formerly Fiume—which was seized in the wake of the war). Hence the question of Italy's national minorities was not subject to international supervision and there was no outside authority competent to intervene formally if the country's government turned against these people.[78]

The vulnerability of Italy's minorities, plus the inclusion of ethnic Germans among them, led Ammende to begin collecting information about the Italianisation of the South Tyrol.[79] He obtained copies of an Alpine newspaper called *Der Tiroler* which reported that on 7 August 1923 the word 'Tyrol' had been banned.[80] For ethnic Germans, the expression was central to their identity. Simply put, they defined themselves as 'Tyrolians' (*Tyroler*). The measure was in addition to steps taken to close primary schools mainly attended by ethnic Germans and to sideline the use of German language in communications with state authorities. The newspaper's tone was of rage not so thinly concealed. The South Tyrol was a centuries' old homeland of this particular German community—an historic mountain people, who experienced an organic connection to the Alps.[81]

Ammende collected evidence of Tyrolian readiness to mobilise in the face of persecution. He acquired a mimeographed sheet entitled 'Letter from South Tyrol' dated 11 October 1923.[82] A year after Fascism had come to power the leaflet denounced the policy of Italianisation as pursued especially by Senator Tolomei. People had less freedom than in the old Austrian state. Laws were no longer published in German, German institutions in effect had been wound up, state officials could no longer use German language and German names had been changed. In the face of this pressure, the leaflet urged people to stand firm in the name of their heritage. A further newspaper article proposed that about a quarter of a million people were under threat.[83]

Armed with his information, Ammende began to write. An apparently unpublished article was called 'Fascist dictatorship in the South

---

[78] For the League to have taken up the cause of Italy's national minorities, someone would have to have argued that their treatment was causing the threat of war, affectively applying Articles 12 or 15 of the Covenant.

[79] Ammende's papers in Moscow include a number of handwritten note books about the South Tyrol.

[80] 'Wir wollen sein ein einig Volk von Brüdern', *Der Tiroler* 11 August 1923. 1502–1–60, Moscow.

[81] 'Die unwandelbaren Berge', ibid.

[82] 'Südtiroler Brief', 1502–1–60, Moscow.

[83] 'Das namenlose Land. Der Leidensweg Südtirols. Italien will 250,000 Deutsche Entnationalisieren', *Südtirol* 24 September 1924. Ibid.

Tyrol'.[84] Using rather pejorative terms, he proposed Italian Fascism was determined to Italianise everything south of the Brenner Pass; it aimed to create a nation of 'Sicilians'. To this end, there was no place for ethnic German mayors and German schools had been closed in Bolzano (Bozen) and Salum (among other places). A further memorandum discussed what had been going on.[85] On 27 September 1919, Italian statesman Tittoni had told the League of Nations that Italy would treat the national minorities of Istria and Trentino much better than minorities had been treated by the imperial Austrian regime. Nonetheless, a law passed on 1 October 1923 compelled German schools to teach Italian language from the very first year of tuition, a step generally believed to herald the eventual end of 400 ethnic German educational facilities. Ammende proposed that no measures quite so damaging had been undertaken anywhere in Eastern Europe, not even in Russia, and added that the principle Italy was setting might have serious consequences there. In short, if Italy could treat her minorities badly, why should not other states follow suit? The version of the article published in *Revaler Bote* made clear the emotion Ammende felt about what was happening to ethnic Germans in Italy and beyond:

> This action will awaken outrage and indignation
> everywhere that Germans live. It seems that wherever the
> German nation lies defeated on the floor, every German is
> an outlaw, a defenceless victim—of foreign violations.[86]

Italian pressure on the South Tyrol turned out to be inconsistent. By January 1924 Ammende was noting that ethnic German schools were permitted to teach religious education in the pupils' mother tongue and that first year primary school pupils could use the same language.[87] Nonetheless he had publicized a vitally important issue and raised questions about the long-term sustainability of ethnic German communities in Europe.

## 8. Conclusion

As will become apparent, Ammende's concerns about the treatment of German minorities in Italy and, for that matter, across Europe, were intimately related to his understanding of how ethnic Germans in Estonia

---

[84] 'Die Diktatur des Faschismus in Südtirol', unpublished typescript. 1502–1–65, Moscow.

[85] Undated typescript memorandum. 1502–1–61, Moscow. A revised version of the manuscript subsequently was published as E. Ammende, 'Der Untergang der deutschen Schulen in Süd-Tirol', *Revaler Bote* 14 November 1923.

[86] E. Ammende, 'Der Untergang der deutschen Schulen in Süd-Tirol', *Revaler Bote*, 14 November 1923. For a further report on the Italianisation of German schools in South Tyrol, see 'Um die deutschen Schulen in Süd-Tirol', *Revaler Bote*, 29 November 1923.

[87] E. Ammende, 'Eine Milderung der italienischen Schulpolitik in Süd-Tirol', *Revaler Bote* 7 February 1924.

should respond to the challenges of the post-war world. He was convinced that they should seek the autonomous management of their cultural lives while combining for common purpose in order to promote their concerns internationally. In the process, they were to remain loyal to their host states. His interest, of course, extended to ethnic Germans in Moscow's new empire, where he perceived a threat not just from national prejudice but also from Communist ideology (which, he believed, debased past cultural achievement while turning national difference into a vehicle for revolutionary struggle) and economic collapse (epitomised by the famine of southern Russia ravaging, amongst others, the Volga Germans).

To Ammende's mind, threats to the construction of successful multi-national states were posed especially by chauvinism—not least in the form of Italian Fascism—and Communism. More than a few subsequent commentators agreed his priorities. In the 1950s, Karl Aun recognised that the question of national minorities ran to the heart of the inner security of the state. He observed that democracies had obligations to guarantee their citizens equality, protection and the pre-requisites to enable them to realise their full selves (including the development of national culture), but also that minorities had a duty to respond with loyalty to the state which delivered all this.[88] At a time when Moscow was trying to exploit national divisions for cynical purposes abroad and overlooking the demise of long-established communities at home, and while nationally-inclined politicians at the helm of various European states in the early 1920s started putting the needs of majority national groups ahead of those of minorities, Ammende was looking for an alternative approach. Already he was beginning to wonder why all of Europe could not be more like Switzerland—a place where different national communities appeared to mix without conflict but with personal fulfilment.

At this point, Ammende's framework of thinking was largely that of a liberal nationalist. He regarded national identity as something fundamental to a human being—as something requiring expression if life was to be lived in 'full colour'. At the same time, in the early 1920s at least, he rejected totalitarian politics—both left and right. Discussing nineteenth century Britain, E.F. Biagini has noted how ideas of democracy, community and liberalism cohered.[89] This was the case for Ammende too. It was plain that he believed the best possibility for diverse national communities to co-exist was in a democratic state operating according to liberal values, construed both in terms of the economy and wider civic standards.[90] He would have had sympathy with liberalism as defined by a recent political commentator:

---

[88] K. Aun, *Der völkerrechtliche Schutz nationaler Minderheiten in Estland von 1917 bis 1940.* Hamburg: Joachim Heitmann, 1951, pp. 9–12.
[89] 'Introduction: Citizenship, Liberty and Community' in E.F. Biagini (ed.), *Citizenship and Community. Liberals, Radicals and Collective Identities in the British Isles 1865–1931.* CUP, 1996, pp. 1–2.
[90] For Ammende's ideas on economics, see chapter 1.

Liberalism embraces individuality, religious and social diversity, and commercial energy, enshrining toleration and personal liberty as core political values. It protects personal liberties by imposing procedural and substantive limits on the ways that persons or governments can interfere in the lives of others... [It involves] ... [i]ndividuality and social pluralism, liberty, legality, rights, limited government, and public reasonableness... [It stands for] ...peace through toleration, law-bound liberty, and a rights-oriented conception of justice. Less often noted, perhaps, is that liberal constitutionalism attempts to combine liberal freedom with reasoned self-government.[91]

When the same commentator maintained that 'community' gives content to liberalism, Ammende also would have agreed because, for him, the traditions and achievements of given national communities had a formative importance for their members.[92] That is to say, the potential of individuals was conditioned in large measure by the inherited qualities of national background as passed on through upbringing, language and education. So, democracy, community and liberalism were inescapable values for Ammende. They provided a route map for much of his work as it developed until at least the end of the 1920s.

---

[91] S. Macedo, *Liberal Virtues. Citizenship, Virtue, and Community in Liberal Constitutionalism.* Oxford: Clarendon Press, 1990. pp. 9, 12 and 40.
[92] Ibid, p. 17.

*Chapter Three*

# Becoming a minority

## 1. Experimenting with liberal nationalism: an alternative to the nation state?

Ammende was certain that in Central and Eastern Europe, the emerging Soviet Union too, there existed a massive, potentially coherent German 'community of blood, language and culture', membership of which was determined by the personal convictions of any given individual.[1] So how did this certainty translate into the pursuit of democratic politics in the framework of the post-war settlement?

Baltic German commentators felt a transition from the idea of liberal nationalism to political practice should not have been difficult. Werner Hasselblatt observed that for centuries Baltic Germans had maintained their élite position under diverse political leaderships precisely because they recognised the existence of fundamentally different relationships between the individual and the state, and the individual and the national group. He also thought it was perfectly possible to experience separately loyalty to both homeland and nation.[2] In other words, people like Hasselblatt argued that, historically, ethnic German communities in Central and Eastern Europe always had been able to balance the dual roles of preserving their distinct national identities with full participation in multi-national civic society. In this light, what could be more natural than adapting to the new times and fresh challenges?

By necessity, the position of members of national minorities had to be more subtle than the one outlined by John Stuart Mill:

> Where the sentiment of nationality exists in any force, there
> is a prima facie case for uniting all the members of the
> nationality under the same government, and a government
> to themselves apart.[3]

Such a view took little account of the complex demography of a region like Central and Eastern Europe. It was unfortunate, therefore, that after the First World War, the victorious powers, with their Wilsonian ideas of self-determination, were a bit too hasty in the application of a comparable political approach there. It threatened to consign a national minority such as

---

[1] See 1502–1–57 and 1502–1–53, Moscow.
[2] W. Hasselblatt, 'Die Baltische Deutschen in der Nationalitätenfrage', *Europäische Revue* (1927) pp. 420–21.
[3] J.S. Mill quoted in P. Gilbert, *The Philosophy of Nationalism*. Boulder, Colorado: Westview Press, 1998, p. 64.

the Baltic Germans to submergence beneath the agenda of majority populations. Logically, commentators like Ammende and Hasselblatt rejected the application of a blunt nation state model to their homeland. For them, nation state thinking was a Western European model not readily applicable to the lands further east. As Hasselblatt put it, in the 1920s, too often the nation state marginalised alternative ideas of a state built on the rule of law, geography, economics or tradition. It marginalised the idea of a historic homeland too.[4] For someone like this, there had to be an alternative to the nation state:

> The possible solution to the problem lies in proclaiming an anational state, in the separation of culture and state, in the complete removal of culture from the affairs of the state.[5]

For people such as Ammende and Hasselblatt—in Latvia, Paul Schiemann—, the idea of a given territory being home to a single nation state, being run by a sole majority national group and embodying a single national culture, was fundamentally flawed.[6] Moving towards an anational state was an important strategy in the effort to supersede it.

For the lands of former large multi-nationality empires, the necessity of linking nation and state was not self-evident; in some respects, it was even an obviously incorrect thing to do. Nonetheless the idea of linkage came to the fore in wake of the First World War. On the one hand, the victorious Allies had included promises of self-determination for subject peoples in their war aims—most famously in Wilson's 14 Points. On the other hand, and pragmatically, they were faced with the collapse of old empires. In political terms, how was the region to be organised now? At the time, how many reliable state models existed apart from the nation state? Even if, say, Ammende had pointed to Switzerland, this state was organised geographically to take account of national diversity: different cantons were identified as home to different nationality groups. A system like that would have been no use to the Baltic Germans because they (like various other groups in Central and Eastern Europe), were not always settled in geographically discrete communities. Different national groups could inter-

---

[4] W. Hasselblatt, 'Neuzeitliche nationalpolitische Problem', *Baltische Monatsschrift* (1927) p.469.

[5] Ibid, p. 475. Paul Schiemann's work is also relevant here, see X-M. Núñez Seixas, *Entre Ginebra y Berlin. La Cuestion de las Minorias Nacionales y la Politica Internacional en Europa 1914-1939*. Madrid: Akal, 2001, pp. 476–80 and J. Hiden, *Defender of Minorities. Paul Schiemann, 1876–1944*. London: Hurst, 2004, especially chapter 7. For a study of the relevance of particularly Schiemann's work today, see I. Ijabs, 'Strange Baltic Liberalism: Paul Schiemann's Political Thought Re-visited', *Journal of Baltic Studies* 40 (2009) 496–515.

[6] E. Ammende, 'Gründe, Aufgaben und Programm für eine Zusammenkunft der Vertreter aller deutschen Minoritäten in Europa', *Nation und Staat* Oct 1932, v. 6 p. 63. Also W. Hasselblatt, 'Die nationale Autonomie als Ziel der europäischen Nationalitätenpolitik' in *Zehn Jahre Deutschpolitisches Arbeitsamt*. Reichenberg: Sudetendeutschen Verlag, 1929, p. 10.

penetrate extensively.[7] Within the Estonian state, the national minority question could not be solved by recourse to territorial federalist thinking. If Baltic Germans were just a small fraction of the Baltic population, if they could be dispersed and isolated, what convincing state model was available to take account of their needs?

Organising Estonia's society was all the more difficult because, in the early 1920s, international law was in its infancy. Then, even more than today, states were considered sovereigns of their territories.[8] Hence the League of Nations was not understood to be a supra-national government, more an association of national governments. Under the circumstances, how far could the League expect to go to protect national minorities? Furthermore, it was not entirely clear what constituted a national minority. Were Jews, for instance, a religious or national minority? Unsurprisingly then, Werner Hasselblatt described the legal regulation of minorities as 'a new legal territory which is still in the process of being created'[9]

The attempt to create a state that took account of dispersed and numerically small national minorities, such as the Baltic Germans, led to an experiment of international importance—a fact well understood by its pioneers.[10] Baltic German commentators also knew their concerns went straight to the heart of the issues facing Central and Eastern Europe more generally.[11] Hasselblatt stated their intellectual framework as follows:

> Everyone should be able to determine his nationality and that of his children without losing equality with the other citizens of the state. Every child must be able to enjoy education in his mother-tongue without his parents having to pay more than other state citizens. Citizens of the same nationality should be allowed to administer their mother-tongue schools. After all, they are the only ones who understand these schools properly. Of course, what is true for schools is also true for many other cultural issues.[12]

---

[7] A. de Vries, 'Unsere Kultur-Autonomie. Ihre Bedeutung', *Sonderausgabe. Revaler Bote* 23 February 1925.

[8] The obligations statesmen from Central and Eastern Europe had to undertake to the League of Nations, guaranteeing the protection of their national minorities, were the exceptions that proved the wider rule.

[9] Hasselblatt, 'Die nationale Autonomie als Ziel der europäischen Nationalitätenpolitik', p. 14.

[10] A. de Vries, 'Zur Annahme des Autonomiegesetzes in Estland', *Baltische Blätter* (1925) 15 February 1925. Also A. de Vries, 'Vor dem Beginn der Autonomie-Verhandlungen in der Staatsversammlung', *Revaler Bote* 26 September 1924

[11] W. Hasselblatt, 'Die Baltische Deutschen in der Nationalitätenfrage', *Europäische Revue* (1927) p. 425.

[12] W. Hasselblatt, 'Die nationale Autonomie als Ziel der europäischen Nationalitätenpolitik' in *Zehn Jahre Deutschpolitisches Arbeitsamt*. Reichenberg: Sudetendeutschen Verlag, 1929, p. 18.

In the quest to achieve their ends, Baltic Germans contributed significantly to Estonia's cultural autonomy law which received its third and final reading in the Estonian parliament (*Riigikogu*) on 5 February 1925. It permitted significant national minorities to constitute themselves as public-legal corporations (i.e. as legally-recognised components of the state) and to be led by a central cultural body elected by the minority itself which had the primary function of organising the minority's education system.[13]

Admittedly, Estonia's law was building on a number of recent precedents. The Polish Minority Treaty of 1919 and the Upper Silesia Convention of 1922 both contained provisions permitting national minorities to control important institutions, including schools.[14] The Polish treaty, in fact, allowed Polish minorities particularly extensive rights in this regard.[15] Also, in 1919 (after local Jewish Bundists had promoted the idea of national personal autonomy), Latvia passed a law allowing autonomous schooling for national minorities.[16] Nonetheless, in the post-war world, Estonia's cultural autonomy law was the most extensive attempt by an independent state to address constructively the realities of life in a multi-national territory. It was a path-breaking measure which opened up possibilities beyond those conceptualised by the Great Powers or the League of Nations. With it, according to Axel de Vries, the Gordian knot of national minority rights finally had been cut.[17] The law was celebrated as the foundation upon which all subsequent attempts to legislate about the rights of minorities would have to be constructed.

Nor were Baltic Germans the only ones to fête the new law. Widely-travelled and influential English academic C.A. Macartney said it put relations between Estonia's minority and majority peoples on a 'very satisfactory footing' and that according 'to the repeated statements of minorities and majorities alike it has proved a brilliant success.' He added that unfortunately 'few states have been so wise or so liberal as Estonia.'[18] Pablo de Azácarte, one time director of the Minorities Section of the League of Nations, maintained that Latvia and Estonia 'were wise enough to

---

[13] For an outline and discussion of how the system was supposed to work, see *Revaler Bote, Sonderausgabe* 23 February 1925.
[14] See S. Barbieri, *National Minorities in Post-Revolutionary and Soviet Russia (1917–1932). Theoretical Framework and Institutional Arrangements.* Doctoral thesis: University of San Marino, 2007/2010, particularly chapter 3.
[15] Ibid, p. 24.
[16] P. Schiemann, 'Die Überwindung des nationalen Hasses', *Rigasche Rundschau* 26 July 1919 in H. Donath (ed.), *Paul Schiemann. Leitartikel, Reden und Aufsaetze. Band II 1919-19.33. Heft 1: Juli 1919 bis April 1920.* Frankfurt a.M., 1986. For discussion of the role of Bundists in developing ideas of cultural autonomy, see R. Gechtman, 'Conceptualizing National Cultural Autonomy—From the Austro-Marxists to the Jewish Labor Bund' in *The Simon Dubnow Institute Yearbook* (2005).
[17] A. de Vries, 'Zur Annahme des Autonomiegesetzes in Estland', *Baltische Blätter* (1925) 15 February.
[18] C.A. Macartney, *National States and National Minorities.* OUP, 1934, p. 395–6 and pp.406–08.

establish on their own account a regime of wide cultural autonomy for the German minorities, which, if it did not entirely put an end to the aggressiveness of the latter, at least considerably lessened it.'[19] Central European minority activists agreed Estonia's law was 'more generous' than anything implemented by other states and went 'far beyond' the country's 'international requirements'.[20] They knew that since the ethnically perfect nation state was unattainable in Central and Eastern Europe, and assimilation promised resistance leading to unrest and instability, the only option was to incorporate minorities into prevailing political structures. Writing towards the end of the Second World War, Jankowsky believed that the 'decentralization of national-cultural affairs' as occurred in Estonia had been a valid response to the challenges at issue, and that the cultural autonomy law 'should serve as a guide in the reconstruction of east-central Europe'—at least for situations where numerically small and dispersed minorities existed.[21]

More recent commentators have not disputed positive evaluations of the legislation. According to Uibopuu, the sovereignty of the people 'rarely found such comprehensive expression' as in Estonia's inter-war constitution, which of course provided the context for cultural autonomy.[22] Michael Garleff described cultural autonomy as 'a domestic-legal regulation of minority protection which was unique for this time'.[23] Wilfred Schlau *et al* counted it a constructive contribution to the solution of Europe's national minority problem.[24] For Kari Alenius, the law was 'exceptional in the atmosphere of that time', while for Smith and Hiden cultural autonomy went 'to the very heart of questions about the future of what was then optimistically termed the New Europe'.[25] So what was the fuller context for the creation of Estonia's cultural autonomy law?

## 2. No longer an élite

There was no small degree of irony about the origins of cultural autonomy. A piece of legislation widely regarded as a triumph of liberalism was generated in significant part by a conservative, old imperial élite—the Baltic Germans.

---

[19] P. de Azcárate, *League of Nations and National Minorities. An Experiment.* Washington: Carnegie Endowment, 1945, p. 28.

[20] J. Robinson, O. Karbach, M.M. Laserson, N. Robinson and M. Vichniak, *Were the Minorities Treaties a Failure?* New York: Antin Press, 1943, p. 226.

[21] O.I. Jankowsky, *Nationalities and National Minorities.* New York: Macmillan, 1945, pp. 147–66.

[22] H-J. Uibopuu, 'The Estonian Republic in its Constitutional Development 1918–40', *Internationales Recht und Diplomatie* (1972) p. 234.

[23] M. Garleff, *Deutschbaltische Politik zwischen den Weltkriegen.* Bonn: Verlag Wissenschaftliches Archiv, 1976, p. 106.

[24] W. Schlau *et al*, *Die Deutsch-Balten.* Munich: Langen Müller, 1995, p. 88.

[25] K. Alenius, 'The Birth of Cultural Autonomy in Estonia: How, Why and for Whom?' *Journal of Baltic Studies* 38 (2007) 446. D.J. Smith and J. Hiden, *Ethnic Diversity and the Nation State.* London: Routledge, 2012, p. xiv.

Their key concern was to define a new position for themselves. No longer a thinly-spread leadership cadre, they had to adjust to being a small numerical minority amongst the peoples over whom formerly they had wielded imperial authority. The transformation was difficult:

> Peoples who had long suffered as minorities now found large numbers of their former oppressors handed over to them, and the temptation to act vengefully was strong.... The new political entities of Eastern and Central Europe looked upon themselves as national states, and were eager to inaugurate policies of consolidation. It was not unreasonable to expect that newly emancipated and inexperienced ruling peoples might make drastic demands for uniformity.[26]

As French statesman Georges Clémenceau put it to Polish Prime Minister Jan Paderewski, although admittedly referring to lands and populations being transferred to Polish administration, the different peoples often had been 'estranged by long years of bitter hostility', the period 1914–18 being only the most recent and dramatic phase of a much longer period of unease.[27] Hence in the wake of the First World War, Baltic Germans struggled to make the transition from ruling caste to bit-part players in states now largely belonging to someone else. They had to fight the feeling of being barely tolerated.[28]

In 1922 Estonia's inhabitants comprised 969,976 Estonians, 91,101 Russians, 18,319 Germans, 7,850 Swedes, 4,566 Jews and 15,239 people with different nationalities.[29] All the minorities together barely made up 15% of the Estonian population. With the Estonian state established as a popular democracy, it was always likely to be difficult for minorities to make their voices heard in the *Riigikogu*. Today commentators recognise that liberal democracies can marginalise non-mainstream groups, but the prospects were particularly bleak for a former imperial élite.[30]

Between 1921 and 1929, the German national group was represented by four, three and finally just two delegates in the *Riigikogu*. During the same period Russians were represented by one, four and two delegates and the Swedish minority by no one at all.[31] Worse, the German

---

[26] I.L. Claude, *National Minorities. An International Problem*. New York: Greenwood, 1955, p. 13.

[27] Robinson, Karbach, Laserson, Robinson and Vichniak, *Were the Minorities Treaties a Failure?* p. 23.

[28] Schlau *et al*, *Die Deutsch-Balten*, p. 87.

[29] Garleff, *Deutsch Baltische Politik zwischen den Weltkriegen*, p. 163.

[30] S. Auer, *Liberal Nationalism in Central Europe*. New York: RoutledgeCurzon, 2004, p. 36.

[31] G. von Rauch, *The Baltic States. The Years of Independence. Estonia, Latvia, Lithuania 1917–1940*. London: Hurst, 1974, pp. 137–8.

population was falling. According to official figures, the number of ethnic Germans in Estonia declined from 18,319 in 1925 to 16,346 in 1930.[32] People were both emigrating to Germany and leaving the national group while remaining in Estonia. That is to say, before 1914, if an Estonian married a Baltic German, then the former was pulled into the community of the latter; but in the 1920s, inter-marriage led to the family becoming Estonian.[33]

The consolidation of the Estonian state was pursued at the expense of the Baltic Germans. Agrarian reform led to the expropriation of large landed estates by the state for social re-distribution. Since historically the German minority had held disproportionate amounts of land, it was hit particularly hard by the measure. Baltic Germans often thought land reform was directed specifically against them and was motivated by national prejudice. It was described, for instance, as 'rape of the national minority by the majority' and 'an instrument of annihilation against the Baltic Germans'.[34] The minority felt its assets were being stolen in institutionalised fashion to benefit the ethnic majority;[35] but the Baltic Germans were concerned about more than just the economics of land loss.

For many in the community, land ownership was integral to their national identity and, in this light, agrarian reform was perceived as a fundamental assault on their nationality. Baltic German commentators of the time believed that community identities were being maintained more successfully in agricultural than urban environments and that there was something special about belonging to a farming community bound intimately to the homeland's soil.[36] The sense of vulnerability felt by Baltic Germans was heightened by the outlawing of some of their traditional social organisations (e.g. the guilds) and because they were left, in the post-war world, without an over-arching organisation binding them together for mutual support and common purpose.[37]

So how were the Baltic Germans to respond? *Revaler Bote* asked directly whether they should leave Estonia or assimilate, but rejected both options.[38] Assimilation was denounced as particularly damaging, since it would deprive an individual of everything valuable in him or her. The essay called on Baltic Germans to remember their moral qualities and maintain their traditional readiness to work for the general community. If Germans lost sight of this characteristic, there would be no purpose remaining in the Baltic; it was the heritage they had to bequeath to their children. A further article

---

[32] Ibid, p. 166.
[33] Ibid.
[34] Baron W. Wrangell, 'Minoritätenfragen und Agrarreform', *Revaler Bote* 18 February 1922; also Axel de Vries, 'Ist die Agrarfrage eine Minoritätenfrage?', *Revaler Bote* 20 February 1922.
[35] 'Das Eigentumsrecht und die Deklaration der Minderheitsrechte', *Revaler Bote* 11 June 1923.
[36] 'Wie erhalten wir unser Deutschtum? Teil I', *Revaler Bote* 3 October 1922.
[37] 'Wie erhalten wir unser Deutschtum? Teil II', *Revaler Bote* 4 October 1922.
[38] 'Unser heisiges Erbe', *Revaler Bote* 31 January 1920.

stated the case even more clearly.[39] It explained the purpose of the Baltic Germans remained to pioneer Western European culture in their region—that is to say, to promote Lutheran religion, the *Rechtsstaat*, together with German ideas of honour and duty. At a time when their homeland still needed them, the anonymous article recommended Germans 'stay at their posts' to fulfil this mission in co-operation with the Estonian people.

Naturally there were different ways to interpret the 'mission' now falling to the Baltic Germans. With a rhetorical flourish, Werner Hasselblatt asked whether, with the creation of an independent Estonian state, the mission of the Baltic Germans had come to an end.[40] He maintained, however, that there was plenty of work still to do. He wanted Baltic Germans to help prevent Soviet penetration from the East while promoting a western orientation for the Estonian state. Commitment to this purpose would give the Baltic German community a reason for existence and prevent its disintegration.[41] Axel de Vries suggested Estonian independence created the conditions for many positive possibilities in the Baltic region. It permitted a much fuller incorporation of the area into the West European cultural circle. The author assumed that the greater the participation of Baltic Germans in the Estonian state, the greater the degree of incorporation likely. So notwithstanding that Baltic Germans had already made significant sacrifices benefitting the Estonian state, de Vries argued they had to hold firm to the mission championed by Germanic settlers over the centuries and keep pulling Estonia towards the West's cultural orbit. This work should continue even if the Baltic Germans had no hope of a political majority. Whether working in national or local offices, he said Germans still should contribute to the common good.[42] This view seems to have won the day, being incorporated in the programme of the Baltic German Party in Estonia drawn up in April 1924. It said the community should act as a bridge for German culture to their new state with a view to anchoring it in the western cultural sphere.[43]

## 3. National community and cultural autonomy

There were, however, a whole series of issues that had to be addressed. For instance, deprived of its élite social status and traditional mechanisms of social organisation, how should the Baltic German community structure itself now? This question was clear even in 1919, when (for instance) delegates from the Lutheran parishes across Estonia met in Tartu (Dorpat) to discuss the organisation of church communities. Harry Koch and August Spindler

---

[39] 'Glaube und Heimat', *Revaler Bote* 6 February 1920.
[40] Speech by Hasselblatt to Baltic German Party given in period 1923–4. Fond 1000, File 173. Madara archive, Tallinn.
[41] W. Hasserlblatt, 'Leitsätze zum Referat über innere Organisationsprobleme des Deutschtums'. 1502–1–111. Moscow.
[42] A. de Vries, 'Eine national-politische Pflicht', *Revaler Bote* 1 December 1923
[43] 'Programm der deutsch-blatischen Partei in Estland'. Fond 1000, File 173. Madara.

were present, individuals who would play significant roles in the cultural autonomy project.[44] Organisations also sprang up seeking to promote German-language schools in Estonia, for example German School Aid (*Deutsche Schulhilfe*).[45] Other associations promoted welfare and culture, with Ewald Ammende's home town of Pärnu (Pernau) being richly endowed with German community-based, charitable organisations.[46]

The changes of the time were accompanied by a stock-taking of traditional notions of community. Heinrich Pantenius, a senior education figure among Estonia's Baltic Germans, proposed that old ideas based on a stratified society (i.e. in terms of class and profession—effectively a *Standesstaat*) were defunct; they had to give way to an inclusive community of equals (*Volksgenossenschaft*).[47] With the power of the Baltic German nobility broken thanks to land reform and mass democracy, the sole issue was to survive and persevere (*ausharren*). Absolutely all Baltic Germans who were doing so (i.e. not just members of the most élite groups) deserved support. Pantenius also argued that survival required a re-think about the functions Baltic Germans should undertake in Estonia. They needed an education system that recognised Germans would no longer be working so intensively in the state administration, also that well-trained doctors and lawyers would simply choose to emigrate. The community's best prospects would come with involvement in business (like earlier members of the Hanseatic movement), and the education system should equip new generations to become self-sufficient in their traditional homeland. Pantenius concluded:

> If we want to protect our national group, then three things are important above all others. First there should be a firm, tight union of absolutely all of the members of our national community (*Volksgenossen*) in the legal framework of a cultural self-administration. Second [there should be] the attempt to secure our economic situation through greater activity in trade and industry; and finally, thirdly, [there should be] a well-planned network of schools, not designed according to unclear ideals, but rather addressing the real demands of the present time.

---

[44] 'Delegierten Versammlung der deutschsprachigen Gemeinden', *Revaler Bote* 13 November 1919.

[45] 'Aufruf an alle Deutschen Estlands', *Revaler Bote* 22 April 1922.

[46] 'Die ordentliche Generalversammlung des Verbandes deutscher Wohltätigkeits- und Kulturvereine', *Revaler Bote* 6 May 1922.

[47] H. Pantenius, 'Wie bewahren wir unser Volkstum?', *Revaler Bote* 7 April 1923. See also 'Politische Wochenschau. 14 April 1923', *Dorpater Nachrichten*. Edition not dated, but rough period identified in title. Fond 1000, File 173. Madara.

A month later, the same author wrote that a classless national community (or *Volksgemeinschaft*) was beginning to develop. (Later, the phrase 'national community' [*Volksgemeinschaft*] would become linked with especially Hitler's Nazi party, but in the early 1920s in the Baltic region, this connection did not exist.) In deep existential crisis, Baltic Germans finally were ignoring each individual's social origins.[48] The old fixation on social background had only led to a splintering of the community, but Pantenius wondered if the needs of the new times might stimulate the growth of an organic national whole (*Volksorganismus*). Likewise, Werner Hasselblatt hoped that one day the group would hold common feelings and sentiments.[49] The Baltic German political party took up the cause of creating a national community. It tried to define itself as more than a narrow political organisation aiming at parliamentary representation, rather it wanted to unite the whole community.[50] Addressing a party meeting in early 1924, Harry Koch said Baltic Germans had a moral mission to create a national community (*Volksgemeinschaft*) that would be 'a living organism embracing every possible member of the national group'. It would be structured through cultural organisations and cemented by the duty of all Baltic Germans to participate. If the community did not band together to achieve this, Koch felt it would be ruined.[51] In Latvia, Baltic Germans agreed all their members should form a national community, and that creating such a body would pave the way for cultural autonomy.[52]

In mid-March 1924, Ammende explained the need to construct a national community to a meeting of the German Cultural and Welfare Associations in Estonia. Anything else would lead to a division of the community's material and intellectual strengths.[53] Understandably, then, when the Society of German Associations in Estonia met at the end of that month, there was general agreement to create such an organisation and that so doing would create the conditions for cultural autonomy.[54] The meeting reasoned that, since the old guilds and traditional methods of social organisation were impossible, something new had to be established to re-vitalise the community. Representatives from School Aid (*Schulhilfe*), the Baltic German Party and Baltic German parliamentary deputies would plan

---

[48] H. Pantenius, 'Die Idee der deutschen Volksgemeinschaft', *Revaler Bote* 7 May 1923. Other relevant essays by Pantenius include 'Volksgemeinschaft und kulturelle Selbstverwaltung I', *Revaler Bote* 4 May 1925 and 'Volksgemeinschaft und kulturelle Selbstverwaltung II', *Revaler Bote* 5 May 1925. See also H. Pantenius, 'Berufswahl und Schule', *Revaler Bote* 29 September 1925.

[49] W. Hasselblatt, 'Leitsätze zum Referat über innere Organisationsprobleme des Deutschtums'. 1502–1–111. Moscow.

[50] 'Ein außerordentlicher Delegiertentag der D-B Partei', *Revaler Bote* 18 December 1923.

[51] 'Alle Mann ans Werk', *Revaler Bote* 20 February 1924

[52] P. Meyer, 'Um die deutsche Autonomie', *Revaler Bote* 13 March 1924.

[53] 'Auf dem Wege zur deutschen Volksgemeinschaft', *Revaler Bote* 2 April 1924.

[54] See Ammende's comments in Proceedings of DB Party 6 December 1923. Fond 1000, File 173. Madara.

such a body. Ammende gave another speech arguing that a private initiative to create a national community would prepare the way for a much grander, civic counter-part.[55]

Ammende's thinking about the national community remained under-developed theoretically. Although obviously he knew 'national community' identified a group linked by blood, inheritance, culture and language, he left it to others to dissect exactly what this implied;[56] and while Ammende thought about national cultures in terms of hierarchy (with German culture being superior), he did not take this sentiment as far as some. His speeches and essays did not have a counter-part to the following written by Pantenius:

> Only now, at a time of crisis, slowly there arises from the deepest recess of the German soul, like a new revelation, the idea of the national community (*Volksgemeinschaft*). A yearning after a living community (*Lebensgemeinschaft*) comes into being, one in which there would be no gruff contradictions of interest as there were before. One in which it says: one for all, and all for everyone—who is German.... It is nothing other than that call: back to whatever is natural...[57]

Also Pantenius said that a national community was:

> ... a natural (*naturgeborene*) living community (*Lebensgemeinschaft*) of a nation whose members are clearly aware that without exception they all are bound together tightly by blood, by the same language and by an intrinsic (*Wesensverwandte*) way of thinking and feeling, and who want absolutely to remain bound together tightly. And in such a social form, the whole is just as much completely necessary for the existence of the individual as the individual is indispensible for the total whole.[58]

Many Baltic German commentators said a true national community had to be organic, hence Baron von Wrangell spoke about creating a 'living organism';

---

[55] 'Jahrestagung des Verbandes deutscher Vereine in Estland am 30 März 1924', *Revaler Bote* 24 May 1924

[56] For Ammende discussing the nature of German communities in Central and Eastern Europe, see his long memorandum located at 1502–1–53, Moscow. He uses the word '*Kulturgemeinschaft*'.

[57] H. Pantenius, 'Volksgemeinschaft und kulturelle Selbstverwaltung I', *Revaler Bote* 4 May 1925.

[58] H. Pantenius, 'Volksgemeinschaft und kulturelle Selbstverwaltung II', Revaler Bote 5 May 1925.

but ideas like this were absent from Ammende's more practical attitude.[59] He did not understand a 'nation' in ways that were *excessively* mystical or biological.

Ammende's pragmatism found an echo in the writings of others. In late 1923 'S.K.' said that the Baltic German Party should unite the German community not as 'a thing in itself', *but as a loyal part of the Estonian state*. He stated that the key phrase was not just 'national community', but there had to be 'service to the nation', 'service to the homeland' (i.e. Estonia) and 'bridge-building' (*Brückendienst*).[60]

## 4. National minorities and security

The issues facing Estonia's Germans were out of all proportion to their numbers and stretched far beyond the borders of their new state. Solving the national minority question was central to the preservation of peace in Europe. It had consequences for the domestic security of states (since dissatisfied minorities could promote unrest) and for international relations (because no government could ignore the fate of co-nationals abroad).[61] National minorities understood much of this. As Ammende put it, 'the best security for the prosperous development of our land lies in the structure of sincere and friendly relations between majority people and minorities.'[62] Likewise, a series of articles in *Revaler Bote* outlined how the rise of the national idea in the nineteenth century had generated violent pressures within multi-national states. The series recommended that the solution to such pressures was to offer autonomy to national minorities within existing political structures under international guarantee.[63]

Many international politicians agreed; they understood the importance of dissatisfied national minorities. In 1916 German agencies had helped organise a Congress of Nationalities at Lausanne with a view to mobilising nationality groups inside the Russian Empire. The conference was part of a general initiative to disrupt the Russian war effort.[64] Naturally, by the 1920s government policies were emphasising prevention rather than promotion of state-breaking activities associated with minorities. Clemenceau said:

---

[59] Baron v. Wrangell, 'Zu den Wahlen in den deutschen Kulturrat', *Revaler Bote* 20 August 1925.

[60] S.K., 'Das neue Programm der deutsch-baltischen Partei', *Dorpater Nachrichten* 20.11.23. Fond 1000, File 173. Madara.

[61] K. Aun, *Der völkerrechtliche Schutz nationaler Minderheiten in Estland von 1917 bis 1940.* Hamburg: Joachim Heitmann, 1951. p. 9.

[62] E. Ammende, 'Unsere Autonomie', *Estländisch-Deutscher Kalendar* (1925) pp. 66–70

[63] 'Auf dem Wege zur nationalen Autonomie', *Revaler Bote* 18 November 1921, 22 November 1921 and 25 November 1921.

[64] T.D. Musgrave, *Self-Determination and National Minorities.* Oxford: Clarendon, 1997, p. 15. In more detail, see S. Zetterberg, *Der Liga der Fremdvölker Russlands 1916–1918.* Helsinki: Finnish Historical Studies, 1978.

> Nothing, I venture to say, is more likely to disturb the peace of the world than the treatment which might, in certain circumstances, be meted out to the minorities.... If this Conference (i.e. Versailles) is going to recognize these various powers as new sovereignties within definite territories, the chief guarantors are entitled to be satisfied that their territorial settlements are of a character to be permanent, and that the guarantees given are to insure the peace of the world. It is not therefore, the interventions of those who would interfere, but the actions of those who would help.[65]

He recognised that the position of minorities had to be guaranteed by international supervision to forestall eventual calamity.

Commentators later agreed with Clemenceau. In the 1960s, Alfred Cobban noted that 'zones of small, internally divided states constitute the belts of greatest weakness in the thin crust of international peace'.[66] This was especially so when small states existed close to much more powerful counterparts. It was, then, in the interests of peace that Cobban said the 'multinational state must re-enter the political canon, from which, as Acton many years ago declared, it should never have been expelled'.[67] Acton had believed that 'civilised life' required people of different nationality groups to integrate peacefully in the same state; anything else spelled 'moral ruin'.[68] As Jankowsky had already put it, 'No state can enjoy domestic tranquillity when some of its minorities entertain hopes of its destruction.'[69] He looked to states to adopt structures that would not promote the welfare of a single nationality group but of multiple nationality groups—facilitating the loyalty of all who lived within them. With minorities integrated into political institutions, states would become partnerships rather than agencies of oppression.

Such issues found a hearing in the 1920s. Despite the short-coming of Wilsonian ideas of self-determination, the President's drafts of the Covenant of the League of Nations recognised national minorities should receive the same treatment within a state as everyone else.[70] But, as far as politicians and commentators were concerned, it was unclear how the welfare of minorities would be achieved.

---

[65] Quoted in Robinson, Karbach, Laserson, Robinson and Vichniak, *Were the Minorities Treaties a Failure?*, p. 21.
[66] A. Cobban, *The Nation State and national Self-Determination*. London: Collins, 1969, p. 17.
[67] Ibid, p.128.
[68] Acton quoted in E.H.Carr, *Nationalism and After*. London: Macmillan, 1945, p. vi and p. 66.
[69] Jankowsky, *Nationalities and National Minorities*, p. 145.
[70] Robinson, Karbach, Laserson, Robinson and Vichniak, *Were the Minorities Treaties a Failure?*, p. 8. Aun, *Der völkerrechtliche Schutz nationaler Minderheiten in Estland von 1917 bis 1940*, pp. 10–11.

## 5. The origins of cultural autonomy and the importance of education

Ewald Ammende believed Estonia was well placed to address its national minority issues. There were not that many members of national minorities in the country, on the whole they were culturally well-developed and most Estonians were tolerant. Under these circumstances, for Ammende, cultural autonomy was the obvious way forward.[71] Estonian officials pointed out it had always been implicit in the framework of the Estonian state. The Manifesto to the Peoples of Estonia of 24 February 1918 promised 'national-cultural autonomy' to Russians, Germans, Swedes and Jews on Estonian territory. Following German occupation, on 16 November 1918 the Constituent Assembly issued a declaration promising the rights of minorities would be guaranteed. A law on primary schooling of May 1920 allowed different languages to be used in education. Furthermore, the constitution of June 1920 guaranteed minorities the rights which would feed into cultural autonomy.[72] Commitment to the rights of minorities was also reflected in Estonia's international obligations. Guarantees for national minorities were included in the Peace Treaty of Tartu (concluded between Estonia and Russia on 2 February 1920) and in the accord signed by Estonia, Latvia and Poland on 17 March 1922.[73] Eventually, on 17 September 1923, Estonia made a declaration to the League of Nations placing the rights of minorities under international guarantee.

The cultural autonomy model of social organisation did not arise out of the blue; it had deceptively extensive roots in the pre-1914 world.[74] It has been described as 'Herderian', since it expressed the conviction that Europe's national groups were defined by common language, custom, collective life and culture—also that national diversity is beneficial so long as it promotes harmonious society.[75] In pre-war Austria-Hungary, Otto Bauer and Karl Renner explored ideas of cultural autonomy, while Viennese lawyer Karl Laun discussed it in international perspective. The latter recommended there should be free choice of nationality, national autonomy, the right of minorities to raise their own taxes and education in the mother-tongue. In the Russian Empire, Jewish activists including Simon Dubnow and Vladimir Medem pursued ideas of cultural autonomy, while Baron Alexander von Meyrendorff did so in the *Duma*.[76]

---

[71] E. Ammende, 'Unsere Autonomie', *Estländisch-Deutscher Kalendar* (1925) pp. 68.
[72] E. Maddison, *Die nationalen Minderheiten Estlands und ihre Rechte,*. Tallinn: 1926, pp.1–5. See also D.J. Smith and J. Hiden, *Ethnic Diversity and the Nation State.* Abingdon: Routledge, 2012, chapter 3.
[73] Aun, *Der völkerrechtliche Schutz nationaler Minderheiten in Estland von 1917 bis 1940*, pp. 24–44.
[74] See, for example, Smith and Hiden, *Ethnic Diversity and the Nation State*, chapter 1.
[75] Núñez Seixas, *Entre Ginebra y Berlin*, pp. 459–60.
[76] For more detailed discussions, see Garleff, *Deutschbaltische Politik zwischen den*

This was an eclectic mixture of sources for an idea—a Romantic philosopher, Austro-Marxists, a professional lawyer, East European Jews and imperial nobility—yet they shared a desire to promote a society in which national minorities were accommodated not through mechanisms of territorial organisation, but through rights attached to individuals. Furthermore, since most of the rights at issue (such as the use of language) could hardly be practised by one person alone, cultural autonomy required recognition of collectivities. In this connection, Hasselblatt once criticised pre-war Austria-Hungary for failing to recognise legally the existence of separate national groups. While the state legislated for the equality of different languages, it created no institutions to promote the interests of its different national groups. Hasselblatt felt this deficiency contributed to the collapse of the empire and quoted Karl Renner's view that separate national groups should be allowed to take over given state functions.[77]

Control of the education system was understood to be vital to the long-term survival of a national group. From January 1920 at the latest, Estonia's Germans were arguing that, since the Estonian state was not yet fully formed, there was an opportunity for them to build their particular educational requirements into its emerging structures.[78] Education was central for several reasons. It was a vehicle for the transmission of language and culture from one generation to the next. It provided the community's young people with the skills necessary for them to build successful lives. Also schools provided focal points around which communities could unite. For Axel de Vries, therefore, a system of local organisations coming together to support German-language schools across Estonia could provide a foundation for the construction of a national community as a whole.[79]

De Vries believed Pärnu's German community was particularly well organised when it came to supporting German-language education. This became clear in a couple of articles written by Hermann von Berg.[80] Pärnu was described as a self-confident town in which the local German-language school was a social hub. It had been used as military offices during the war and had been damaged as a result. In January 1919, a co-educational German school was re-opened (presumably in the same buildings); it was a grammar

*Wektkriegen*, pp. 104–8; Y. Plasseraud, *Les États Baltiques des Sociétés Gigognes*. Brest: Armeline, 2006, 2nd Edition, pp. 90–101; also E. Nimni, 'National-Cultural Autonomy as an Alternative to Minority Territorial Nationalism' in D.J. Smith and K. Cordell (eds.), *Cultural autonomy in Contemporary Europe*. London: Routledge, 2008. Nunez Seixas, *Entre Ginebra y Berlin*, pp. 464–5.

[77] W. Hasselblatt, *Über die Kulturautonomie. Buchmanuskript und Anlagen*. Riigiarhiiv, Tallinn, pp. 60–61.

[78] 'Zur Bildung einer Dorpater Ortsgruppe der deutschbaltische Partei', *Revaler Bote* 31 January 1920.

[79] A. de Vries, 'Selbsthilfe. Deutschtumsarbeit in Estland'. *Rigasche Rundschau* 28 November 1924.

[80] H. v. B., 'Rund um die kleineren Städte der Heimat', *Revaler Bote* 20 September 1924 and H. v. B., 'Rund um die kleineren Städte der Heimat', *Revaler Bote* 4 October 1924.

school unable to offer Greek language. By 1924, it was attended by 305
children (155 boys and 150 girls), the ratio of German to non-German being
5:1. The annual education of each child cost Estonian Marks (EM) 8,000 and
the school had 8 trained and 10 untrained staff, plus 6 part-time teachers.
Although the library was short of books, the gym hall was well equipped. It
lent its facilities to the Russian school in the afternoon.

Pärnu's German community supported the school well. Mr.
Ammende was president of the German School Association (presumably this
was Ewald's father rather than Ewald himself). It had 296 members and
worked closely with the School Aid organisation in Tallinn (Reval). The
Pärnu organisation received EM 500 per year from each family with a child
at the school and organised an annual collection which brought in EM
523,000 in 1922, EM 85,000 in 1923 and EM 46,000 in 1924. Hermann von
Berg's journalism emphasised the strength of collective spirit that this small
community enjoyed. He made plain there were also women's organisations
(in which Mrs. Ammende—presumably Ewald's mother—participated), plus
various charitable and welfare organisations aiming to help the poor, sick and
elderly. Pärnu's German community was only about 1,200 strong, but clearly
it was awash with civic engagement.

So how was schooling organised in Estonia and what were the
practical problems facing the German community over it? 88.9% of school
children went to Estonian schools, 8% to German schools, 0.4% to Swedish
and Latvian schools and 0.1% to Jewish schools.[81] The disproportionate
importance of education to the German community as a whole was reflected
in it spending EM 5,085 to educate each child annually, as against the
national average of EM 3,229. Average German spending was only exceeded
by average Jewish spending, which was EM 5,984.[82] In Estonia, education
was not the sole preserve of the state. Before the First World War, it had been
organised extensively by private societies, a trend which continued after
1918, for instance with School Aid and the Association of German
Societies.[83] These organisations managed ethnic German schools, whether
organising their funds and budgets or supervising the teaching staff.[84] Of
course, towns such as Pärnu and Tartu had their particular local educational
associations too. So in the early 1920s, the German education infrastructure
in Estonia was a many-headed beast.

In the early 1920s there were said to be 18 private and 6 public
schools catering for Estonia's Germans.[85] Of the public schools, 2 were in
Tartu, 3 in Tallinn and one in Mustjala (Mustel). Elementary schooling was

---

[81] 'Von der Tätigkeit der Gesellschaft "Deutsche Schulhilfe" in Estland', *Revaler Bote* 23 April
1924
[82] Ibid. The figure of EM 8,000 is given earlier in the text.
[83] Rauch, *The Baltic States*, p. 140.
[84] 'Von der Tätigkeit der Gesellschaft "Deutsche Schulhilfe" in Estland', *Revaler Bote* 23 April
1924
[85] H. v. Berg, 'Unser Schulwesen', *Baltische Blätter* (1924).

not yet free for all ethnic Germans—an important issue for the community's poorer members—even though article 12 of the Estonian constitution promised this would be the case. As a rule, private schools were elementary and middle schools rolled into one. Roughly 4,000 children attended German schools, with 2,700 in private institutions and 1,300 in public ones. There was over-provision. Before the period of Russification (which started in the early 1880s), August Spindler said there had been just 8 German schools preparing children for university, but in the early 1920s there were 14.[86]

There was, however, a feeling that these schools were not fulfilling their potential in the post-war world. Herman von Berg was critical that *per capita* spending on German education was so high. In total, every German was said to be paying about EM 1,000 Estonian annually towards the community's education, and that was too much. With education in small towns costing on average twice as much as education in large towns, he suggested the former should only provide elementary schools, while middle schools should be located in regional centres. Greater efficiency here would open the way to teachers getting paid properly and to the employment of more specialist staff. The management of provincial schools was also said to be deficient. The regions were trying to improve their schools without paying attention to national trends and they were also offering syllabuses that were overly academic (i.e. they were ignoring applied training relevant to the prevailing necessities of life).

Repeating a view already associated with Pantenius, he wondered if there was a danger of too many professionals being created by the community. Spindler proposed that many children would be better served by shorter periods of education to equip them for more mundane careers. Pentenius reiterated that intellectual education alone was no good for Baltic Germans in the post-war world. He said trade, industry and skilled manual labour should be the order of the day from then on.[87]

Could the community maintain so many schools for the long-term?[88] On the one hand, Spindler wondered if teachers would accept starvation wages indefinitely; on the other hand, he noted that there was a problem with the community's demography. Certainly Germans were dispersed, comprising low percentages of the population across the whole of Estonia (which made locating schools in rural areas problematic), but—worse—only 25% of the community was aged under 20 (six years previously, the statistic had been 30%). By contrast, 40% of Estonians were under 20. The lack of young people clearly had implications for any German education system.

---

[86] A. Spindler, 'Einzelfragen betr. die deutsche Kulturselbstverwaltung', *Revaler Bote* 5 August 1925.

[87] H. Pantenius, 'Berufswahl und Schule', *Revaler Bote* 29 September 1925.

[88] Spindler, 'Einzelfragen betr. die deutsche Kulturselbstverwaltung'.

It was generally recognised that German education needed to re-organise.[89] There was no single umbrella organisation; 18 different German schools (presumably the private ones) existed under 13 different local administrations, with at least some school catchment areas cutting across administrative boundaries, so complicating funding arrangements. The scarce number of Germans in many rural areas raised questions about how they could be catered for properly.[90] Yet the schooling question was vital. Appropriate education and the survival of national culture were felt to go hand in hand and the administration of educational institutions by other ethnic groups was regarded as inhibiting proper cultural development.[91] Securing educational and cultural freedom was understood to be a necessary step if Germans were to feel comfortable in, even patriotic about, their new state.

The importance of schooling for the Baltic German community was reflected in its press and a number of contributors, such as Pantenius, worked in German-language schools. The press discussed educational issues of the day, for instance teaching Estonian language from the third grade, maintaining class sizes of at least 20 and lack of co-ordination between different German charities.[92] There were reports of School Aid meetings and initiatives, such as plans to rationalise the network of schools.[93] Educational philosophy was aired. Pärnu's mayor, Johannes Beermann, once discussed how education was vital to passing on not just rote learning, but community values.[94]

This was an exciting time for educationalists in the Baltic States. Given the emergence of independent states, the region's system of schooling had to be re-structured. The changes were reflected in the press and in parliament, where themes were debated such as the existence of too many teachers left over from Tsarist times and the need for new teacher training facilities.[95] Although ethnic Germans recognised they had to take account of developments within the national educational system, nonetheless they felt the issues facing them were more urgent than those facing the Estonian population. A passionate article in *Revaler Bote* suggested that across Europe education was becoming a means to de-nation national minorities.[96] Hence,

---

[89] A.V., 'Selbsthilfe. Deutschtumsarbeit in Estland', *Rigasche Rundschau* 28 November 1924.

[90] H.P. [Pantenius] 'Schulzwang', *Revaler Bote* 3 March 1920.

[91] 'Wie bewahren wir unser Deutschtum?', *Revaler Bote* 6 October 1922. Other parts of this article were published on 3 October 1922, 4 October 1922 and 5 October 1922. This set of articles underlines the important connection that existed between education, culture and the lasting general organisation of the German community in the new Estonian state.

[92] H.P., 'Zur Lage unserer deutschen Schulen', *Revaler Bote* 16 August 1921.

[93] 'Die Deutsche Schulehilfe in Estland im Jahre 1924', *Baltische Blätter* (1925).

[94] J. Beermann, 'Beginn des Unterrichts in unseren deutschen Schulen', *Revaler Bote* 15 September 1921.

[95] '2. Staatsversammlung', *Revaler Bote* 1 August 1923. See 'Das Gesetzprojekt betr. die Lehrerseminare'.

[96] 'Zur Frage des Schulwesens der völkischen Minderheiten', *Revaler Bote* 1 September 1923.

in Czechoslovakia, Czechs were being appointed to teach in German schools—the implication being that German children were suffering. The Tallinn paper argued that Estonia's Germans needed to organise schools for themselves. Their educational system had to be administered and staffed by ethnic Germans from top to bottom, and they had to organise their school network according their particular needs. The article, apparently written by Dr. Spindler, suggested that only private German schools would meet their needs, adding that constructing such a system would be tremendously expensive and require considerable sacrifices.

The comments led to an exchange of views with Pantenius who maintained that private provision alone would never be adequate.[97] They agreed, however, that a German school system had to be as independent as possible from Estonian control—a proposition that raised the question of how the demands of German identity would be balanced against duties to the Estonian homeland and wider society. For some, it also raised the issue of how to balance the community's position inside Estonia with a desired close relationship to Germany. A few years later, Werner Hasselblatt said this:

> We do not want to tend our culture as if it were something in a greenhouse located in a foreign national environment—which enjoys all too little warmth here anyway—artificially and in virtual isolation; rather, we need and lay claim to fertilization and stimulation by the cultural development of the great mother nation.[98]

How, then, to develop your own identity, be loyal to Estonia and cultivate appropriate relations with Germany? Time would show how difficult this balancing act would be.

### 6. Interpreting cultural autonomy: the problems of nationality and appropriate education

The Baltic German communities of the period experienced significant divisions and disagreements. So when Estonia passed the cultural autonomy law in February 1925, many felt it left a lot unsaid and was only acceptable as a temporary measure.[99] As time went by, increasingly important differences of opinion became apparent between leadership figures such as Paul Schiemann (based in Riga) and Werner Hasselblatt (from a family based in Tartu). Despite being a generation older, the former was more of a progressive democrat than the latter—and more than most other Baltic

---

[97] H. Pantenius, 'Zur Schulfrage', *Revaler Bote* 12 September 1923.
[98] Hasselblatt, 'Die nationale Autonomie als Ziel der europäischen Nationalitätenpolitik', p.21.
[99] See, for instance, A. Spindler, 'Einzelfragen betr. der Kulturselbstverwaltung', *Baltische Blätter* (1925), 1. August 1925.

Germans, come to that.[100] For instance, in 1925 Baron Stackelberg wrote to
Hasselblatt as follows concerning cultural autonomy:

> I can only express the hope time and again that it will
> actually be possible to reach the goals identified by you of
> an organic Baltic German society, even though the path lies
> through the sterile plains of democratic mechanistic
> administrative methods.[101]

In a later article, Hasselblatt outlined a positive attitude towards the pre-1914
corporatist system of social organisation practised in the Baltic region. Also
he bemoaned the fact that Estonians were trying to drive Germans out of the
region, proposing that his community develop a renewed kind of corporatist
organisation as a means of resistance to change.[102] Elements within the Baltic
German community were interested in restoring as much of their 'glorious'
past as possible, rather than simply moving with the newer times.

Disagreements over adopting a progressive or restorative attitude to
post-war life in the Baltic region were also expressed in debates about who
should be defined as German. This was evident in *Revaler Bote* in early
1921. How should Estonia's Germans define themselves? Pantenius argued
that language criteria alone would not do—citing the example of Jews who
shared the same national groups but spoke German in Berlin, French in Paris
and English in London.[103] In response, an anonymous reader argued that
nationality could never be just a matter of free choice: if someone was born
of German parents and could only speak German, then he or she was
German; but if none of these points applied, he or she was not German. The
author also felt that if the parents were not members of an 'indo-Germanic
race', a child could never be German even if he or she received a German
education. By contrast, if a Swedish family moved to Berlin and their child
went to school there, that child should be treated as German. With all this
said, the author accepted that if a child was a national mixture (for instance
with different parents and able to speak different languages), then it was up to
the individual to decide how to construct his or her identity.[104] A further
anonymous contribution to the discussion attempted to distinguish 'race' (a

---

[100] For comparisons between Schiemann and Hasselblatt, see Seixas, *Entre Ginebra y Berlin* pp.
480–1 and M. Garleff, 'Nationalitätenpolitik zwischen liberalem und völkischem Anspruch.
Gleichklang und Spannung bei Paul Schiemann und Werner Hasselblatt' in J. von Hehn and C.J.
Kenez (eds.), *Reval und die Baltischen Länder*. Marburg: Herder Institute. 1980.

[101] Stackelberg to Hasselblatt, 27.12.25. Fond 1000, File 172. Riigiarhiiv, Madara branch.
Tallinn.

[102] W. Hasselblatt, 'Die Baltische Deutschen in der Nationalitätenfrage, *Europaische Revue*
(1927) pp. 424–25. The article interprets cultural autonomy as a vehicle for the re-introduction of
corporatist social models. The view was also pedalled in Hasselblatt's unfinished manuscript,
*Über die Kulturautonomie. Buchmanuskript und Anlagen*, p. 47.

[103] H. Pantenius, 'Volkszugehörigkeit und Autonomiegesetz', *Revaler Bote* 10 January 1921.

[104] 'Zur Frage der Bestimmung der Nationalität', *Revaler Bote* 16 January 1922.

scientific concept to do with biology), '*Volk*' ('all the inhabitants of a geographical area'), 'nation' (a *Volk* organised into a given state) and 'nationality' (a category concerning not so much inheritance, blood and political mobilisation as culture and language).[105] With that, the discussion was pretty much back to its starting point.

August Spindler contributed to the discussion of nationality with an essay that provided insights into life in a multi-nationality part of Central and Eastern Europe.[106] Half-jokingly he criticised Estonians for being too defensive about their own culture, saying that sometimes, among themselves and in an attempt to appear intellectual, they preferred to speak bad Germans rather than good Estonian. More seriously he looked to the creation of a society where there would be peaceful competition between Estonian and German school systems—the rivalry keeping both parties on their toes. But he said this about national belonging:

> Take the case of an Estonian who has lived among Germans since his youth and who feels attracted to German culture: why shouldn't he regard himself ultimately as German and be recognised generally as the same? Likewise, no one should throw stones at a German who becomes Estonian or Russian for similar reasons.

Nationality was like a religious confession; Spindler said people could cross from one to another if they honestly felt it was the right thing to do. Observers only became cynical about changes of religion if they were made opportunistically, perhaps for career advantage. Hence Spindler complained that in 1918 several thousand people registered as German who in the 1922 census gave themselves a different nationality. There was, he felt, too much opportunism in Estonia at the time.

The debate about nationality was highlighting a genuine area of confusion (i.e. how to decide who belongs to which nationality in an area that had been ethnically mixed for centuries) and the situation was only made worse by an article by Eugen Maddison (an official of the Estonian state with a particular interest in cultural autonomy). Having stated a rather relaxed attitude to defining nationality (since he believed it depended on either 'blood' or special circumstances, involving perhaps language), he continued:

> That which nature gives cannot be taken away by any law. A Jew is a Jew; a Russian is a Russian; a Swede is a Swede, etc etc. And no 'denial of nationality' or 'Christening' makes a difference here.

---

[105] 'Zur Frage der Bestimmung der Nationalität', *Revaler Bote* 4 February 1922.
[106] A. Spindler, 'Nationalitäten-Chaos', *Revaler Bote* 11 June 1925.

There was, then, a tension between the capacity of individuals to choose nationality for themselves and the possibility that some of the decisions could be disputed.

The possibility that personal confessions of nationality could change over time, could be made for reasons of opportunism or could be questioned were far from trivial for a German community concerned to define itself clearly. After all, the debate was close to implying either there was no such thing as a national group (it was an arbitrary construct) or it could never be defined clearly (which amounted to the same thing). From the point of view of a legislative project, a position amounting to 'you know a German when you see one' was not adequate.

On top of this, there was debate over the nature of the education system the German community should create. German schools were split between public and private systems and subordinated to too many local administrations. Moreover, the community itself was overly fragmented, lacking co-ordination and devoid of an appropriate sense of mission.[107] There was a great deal of work to do.

## 7. Conclusion

The intricate discussion about German schooling did not always reach definitive conclusions, but it did show that the community was dedicated to dealing with its problems independently. Naturally, in this context, Ammende was one of a number of spokespersons pushing hard for some kind of system of cultural autonomy. Repeatedly he emphasised that the minority question was the single most important issue of the day, not least because however the borders of Central and Eastern Europe were drawn, there would always be national minorities. Given recent developments in technology and chemistry, any fresh outbreak of war threatened the destruction of western culture once and for all, so Ammende argued it was imperative to abolish tensions surrounding the nationality question. This required some kind of autonomy (whether territorial or personal) being guaranteed to minorities. He looked to Estonia to show Europe the way forward.[108] Notwithstanding all the possible disagreements and difficulties about the concepts and practices implicit in addressing minority affairs, all the *Riigikogu* had to do was agree a suitable law about cultural autonomy. Especially in the light of the progressive views on display in the Manifesto to the Peoples of Estonia and the Estonian constitution, how hard could that be?

---

[107] S. K., 'Wie erhalten wir unsere Volkskultur?', *Revaler Bote* 14 October 1924.
[108] E. Ammende, 'Unsere Autonomie', *Estlaendischdeutscher Kalender* 1925. Dorpat: H. Laakmann. 1925. Baltic Central Library, Riga.

## Chapter Four

## Achieving cultural autonomy

### 1. Beginnings: 1919–22

Many of the values associated with cultural autonomy were reflected in Estonia's constitution of 15 June 1920. It guaranteed equality of nationalities (article 6), education in one's mother tongue (article 12), the right of all Estonian citizens to choose their nationality (article 20), the possibility for national minorities to set up autonomous organisations (article 21), the use of a minority language as an official means of communication in areas where minorities were in the majority (article 22), and the right of Germans, Russians and Swedes to petition central government in their own languages (article 23).[1]

The constitution, of course, had its own history and followed the Manifesto of the Peoples of Estonia (23 February 1918)[2] and the declaration of the Constituent Assembly (23 April 1919).[3] Equally, in 1919, Estonia's German community already had begun discussing the possible forms cultural autonomy could take, for instance based on public or private foundations. Nonetheless, according to one of the co-authors of the eventual cultural autonomy law, Werner Hasselblatt, the year of the constitution—1920—marked the real starting point of the autonomy project.[4] That February, *Revaler Bote* reported that the Central Rada in Ukraine had adopted a law guaranteeing its minorities national autonomy.[5] In the first instance, it was envisaged as affecting Russians, Poles and Jews, although it could be extended to smaller minorities such as Germans and Czechs if 10,000 of their members requested the right. Each minority was empowered to elect a central assembly and the activities of this body ultimately would be authorised by Ukraine's central representative body. Nationality registers were to be compiled and published; the central government would provide funding to

---

[1] W. Hasselblatt, *Von der Kulturautonomie zum Nationalitätenkongress*, Herder Institute, MSS 53. See chapter 4, 'Das Gesetz über die Kultur Autonomie mit dem Motivenbericht'. C. Hasselblatt, 'Minderheitenpolitik in der Republik Estland in Geschichte und Gegenwart' in *Zeitschrift für Ostforschung* 43 (1994) pp. 557–8.
[2] For a compy in the original Estonian, see http://www.estonica.org/en/Manifesto_to_All_Peoples_ of_Estonia/?large (consulted 5 March 2014).
[3] For some details about the Constituent Assembly, see http://www.estonica.org/en/The_state _order_of_Estonia_in_its_historical_development/Manifest_of_Independence_and_election_of_ the_Constituent_Assembly/ (consulted 5 March 2014). For an accessible and succinct discussion of some of the background to cultural autonomy, see D.J. Smith and J. Hiden, *Ethnic Diversity and the Nation State*. London: Routledge, 2012, chapter 3.
[4] W. Hasselblatt, 'Die Organisationsform unseres kulturellen Eigenlebens', *Estländischdeutscher Kalender* 1925. Dorpat: H. Laakmann, 1925. Baltic Central Library, Riga. p. 71.
[5] 'Völkische Autonomie in der Ukraine', *Revaler Bote* 28 February 1920.

support minority activities, and the minorities were given the right to tax their own members. *Revaler Bote* concluded:

> This Ukrainian law is an organic construction which derives logically from the principle of the right to self-determination for nationalities.... And it can serve as a template for all the other countries in which several national groups live side by side, and want to maintain their special character and indeed form a unit.

Subsequent articles about Ukraine noted, for instance, that General Wrangell had promised equality of belief and nationality to all groups living there, also that he would allow full autonomy to the Cossack areas of Don, Kuban and Terek.[6]

The existence of an independent Ukraine was short-lived, with Wrangell's resistance to Bolshevism dissipating by the end of 1920, but the Ukrainian agenda of national autonomy spurred on events in the Baltic. In early June 1920 (just before the constitution was agreed), a delegation of representatives drawn from the minorities—Professor Popow (a Russian), H. Westerbloem (a Swede), J. Klatschko (a Jew) and Dr. A. Spindler (for the Germans)—handed a memorandum on cultural autonomy to the Prime Minister.[7] In a rather pedantic text, they complained that while an early draft version of Estonia's constitution had included a section 'national minorities', this had been dropped. They complained that provision for the minorities to impose taxes on their own community for cultural purposes had been withdrawn. As a result, they doubted that cultural autonomy would work properly, since without the capacity to raise taxes independently, a national group would not be able to support the full extent of its cultural life. In fact, the petitioners did not want state funding alone to support cultural autonomy, since this could come with an agenda set by the government and, ultimately, voters drawn from the majority national group. They wanted a balance of state and independent financial support for the project.

The memorandum emphasised that the minorities would not use autonomy to pursue activities against the interests of the state before proposing a number of improvements to the, then, still draft constitution. It recommended the constitution talk specifically of autonomous institutions, that the Jewish group be identified by name, that every citizen be able to determine his or her nationality freely, that minorities be permitted to establish their own educational and welfare institutions, that autonomous

---

[6] 'General Wrangells politisches Programm', *Revaler Bote* 21 August 1920. Also 'Von der südrussischen Front', *Revaler Bote* 9 September 1920. Wrangell (or Wrangel) was born in Zarasai (today in Lithuania).

[7] 'Denkschrift über die kulturelle Autonomie der völkischen Minderheiten I', *Revaler Bote* 8 June 1920, See also 'Denkschrift über die kulturelle Autonomie der völkischen Minderheiten II', *Revaler Bote* 9 June 1920.

institutions be subject to government supervision, and that national cultural organisations be empowered to tax members of their national group. The memorandum made plain that cultural autonomy was an idea whose time had come in Estonia and, by November, it was part of the electoral platform of the Baltic German Party.[8]

When, during the run up to municipal elections, members of the Baltic German Party met at the House of Blackheads in Tallinn (Reval) in February 1921, national cultural life was high on the agenda. Senior teacher Behrsing, cited Renner (specifically *The Self-Determination of Nations*) and highlighted that an independent cultural life ought to be based on a national group establishing itself as a public-legal corporation. Only this status would guarantee it the necessary rights.[9] Subsequent discussion emphasised that the Baltic German community had roles to fill in respect of both nationality and state. In particular it was argued that a nationally autonomous education system should be sponsored, at least to some extent, by the state in which it was rooted. As a report of the meeting put it:

> If the state maintains a national school, then it knows what is going on. It needs loyal citizens of the state, and a state citizen becomes loyal when he knows that his rights to his national culture will not be curtailed.

Discussion also heard that state money alone would never be enough to maintain the sort of schools Germans wanted; that the system would not be led by bureaucracy, but by men and women of character; that new textbooks would have to be written; and that older children especially would need a good technical education, perhaps including some elements of agricultural training. Although the meeting was, apparently, poorly attended, it was clear that some members of the community at least were thinking carefully about what cultural autonomy would entail.

Unsurprisingly, when the first Estonian parliament met in April 1921, supported by a Swede and a Russian, four Baltic German deputies presented a memorandum outlining how minority communities might establish themselves autonomously.[10] The draft owed much to E. von Bodisco, an ethnic German.[11] It took time, however, before the *Riigikogu* would begin to focus on the sort of legislation that Estonia's minorities were demanding.

---

[8] 'Wahlplattform der Deutsch-Baltische Partei in Estland', *Revaler Bote* 18 November 1920.

[9] 'Eine Parteiversammlung der Deutsch-Baltischen Partei', *Revaler Bote* 19 February 1921.

[10] Hasselblatt, 'Die Organisationsform unseres kulturellen Eigenlebens', pp. 70–1.

[11] E. Hausen, 'Unser Kampf um die Autonomie. Ein Rückblick', *Revaler Bote. Sonderausgabe* 23 February 1925.

## 2. March 1923: failure in the *Riigikogu*

A parliamentary commission finally was established to investigate cultural
autonomy in summer 1922, but its work only became intensive in early 1923,
at which point the press began discussing policy possibilities at length.[12]
Ammende prepared a piece for *Revaler Bote* in which, interestingly, he
assumed membership of the German community would depend on more than
just an individual's choice.[13] Quoting Paul Schiemann, he said that
supporting ethnic German schools was an obligation determined by birth. He
said:

> We really want an organisation which possesses the
> authority and legal competences to enlist *all the members*
> [emphasis added] of our minority as a group to co-operate
> in our nationality's cultural development according to their
> capacities for material sacrifices.

He proposed that the provision of autonomy to 30,000 Germans in Estonia
(his figure) would put that country in a good position to argue for the better
treatment of 100,000 Estonians living in Russia; it would impress the
international community and ensure that Estonia was taken seriously by the
League of Nations. He added that it would promote the security of the
Estonian state by allowing it to consolidate itself internally, in effect that the
move would forestall any possibility of subversion by Bolshevik Russia. He
went on to say that Estonia was well positioned to be generous over
autonomy because there were only 30,000 Baltic Germans in the country
(again, his figure) and they were not interested in irredenta. They were deeply
attached to their Baltic *Heimat*.

In time, *Revaler Bote* published a draft version of the parliamentary
commission's work: 'The legislative project for the temporary self-
administration of national minorities'.[14] At this point, self-administration was
held to include the management of schools, cultural organisations and welfare
organisations too. An elected cultural parliament (here called a *Volkstag* or
national council) would be empowered to create binding regulations in all
these areas. The newspaper emphasised that the establishment of an

---

[12] For a discussion of the early work by the commission, see 'Motivenbericht zum Gesetzprojekt
über die zeitweilige Ordnung der Selbstverwaltungen der nationalen Minderheiten', *Revaler Bote*
2 March 1923. Apparently its work was summarised in a pamphlet written by A. Spindler, *Die
kulturelle Autonomie der völkischen Minderheiten* (publication details unknown). For further
information about Spindler's involvement with cultural autonomy, see Smith and Hiden, *Ethnic
Diversity and the State*. London: Routledge, 2012, chapter 3.
[13] E. Ammende, 'Ist das estnische Volk an einem Zustandbekommen der Minderheiten-
Autonomie interessiert?', *Revaler Bote* 27 February 1923.
[14] 'Gesetz-Projekt über die zeitweilige Ordnung der Selbstverwaltung der nationalen
Minderheiten, *Revaler Bote* 2 March 1923.

autonomous institution would not release citizens from their duties towards the wider polity and would not conflict with the interests of the Estonian state.

In fact, the autonomy commission had supervised the drafting of several legislative proposals before the most recent version was presented to parliament in March 1923, at which point the bill received its first reading. Although the first reading was passed, the law was deemed too important for it to proceed to a second reading at once. Hence the first Estonian parliament broke up for the summer before the autonomy bill had become law.[15] Nonetheless, the debates of the time were instructive. Parliament heard Foreign Minister Hellat argue that an autonomy law would bolster Estonia's place in the European community of states and forestall the possibility of Baltic Germans complaining to the international community about their treatment.[16] From a relatively early point, however, there was also pessimism that the legislation would not be agreed before the parliament had to be dissolved and fresh elections held. As might have been expected of a new state, there was a glut of parliamentary work which deflected attention from the affairs of minorities. Also a new law on the self-administration of local governments was in preparation, and it was deemed impossible to pass a law on cultural autonomy ahead of this.[17] There was a suggestion that perhaps a temporary autonomy law might bridge the gap until a definitive piece of legislation could be agreed, but even this begged too many questions. It was inevitable, unfortunately, that the failure to agree autonomy in the first half of 1923 led to animosity. On behalf of the minority groups in the *Riigikogu*, Hermann Koch made a speech which denounced the Estonian politicians Martna (Social Democrat) and Tõnisson (People's Party) for filibustering, not to say stirring up national hatred. Koch observed that the terms of the Estonian constitution had not been fulfilled.[18]

Commentators analysed the failure to agree the autonomy law at length. Axel de Vries wrote an essay 'The victory of the nationalist spectre' arguing that the multi-party members of the parliamentary commission all agreed the draft proposal, but specifically the nationalist fervour of Jaan Tõnisson—albeit supported by the Social Democrats—had wrecked the legislation.[19] Likening Tõnisson to traditional Russian nationalists, de Vries said Estonia had missed an opportunity to define itself as a truly liberal state and to write its name in any book about the peaceful progress of humanity. In a further article which argued the international community was watching how Estonia was dealing with its minorities, de Vries likened Tõnisson to a

---

[15] Hasselblatt, 'Die Organisationsform unseres kulturellen Eigenlebens', p. 72.
[16] 'Das Autonomie-Gesetzprojekt im estländischen Parlament', *Baltische Blätter* (1923), p. 63.
[17] 'Der Stand der Autonomie-Frage', *Revaler Bote* 2 Feburary 1923
[18] 'Zur Vorgeschichte des Autonomie-Gesetzprojektes', *Baltische Blätter* (1923). See also 'Deklaration der Abgeordneten der schwedischen, russischen und d-b. Minderheiten im Parlament betreffend das Autonomiegesetz-Projekt', *Revaler Bote* 9 March 1923.
[19] A. de Vries, 'Der Sieg des nationalistischen Phanotoms', *Revaler Bote* 9 March 1923.

Tsarist Russifier. Since Tõnisson himself had been forced to use Russian in primary school, really he should have been more generous towards his country's Germans.[20]

The whole issue of autonomy was so important that *Revaler Bote* reproduced the speeches of the parliamentary deputies who had supported the law.[21] Max Bock (of the Baltic German Party) questioned why the Social Democrats had turned against the law when the Social Democrat member of the commission (called Palwadre) had agreed the draft, also when Jüri Jaakson (of the People's Party) had chaired the general group investigating autonomy.[22] German deputy von Wetter-Rosenthals emphasised that cultural autonomy was unexceptional; it was only a logical consequence of democratic ideals.

That parliamentary discussion had not been conducted in lofty terms alone but included emotional historical baggage was emphasised by Deputy Lattik (Christian National Party) when he proposed that Tõnisson was motivated by historical hatred—and perhaps he was not alone, since Martna had shouted out that Baltic German culture amounted to the application of increasing numbers of police and Cossacks to keep society under control.[23] When Foreign Minister Hellat complained that Tõnisson was making things more difficult for Estonian diplomats, the reply came that he was only acting in accordance with the state of Estonia's internal relations and that there was no point in Estonians 'putting a noose around our neck!'[24] More reasonably, Tõnisson maintained that the non-territorial autonomy demanded by the Baltic Germans would only disappoint them. He recommended that autonomy should be organised not across the whole state (as the Baltic Germans wanted), but in line with local systems of self-government. He added that, in any case, individual school councils could always be led by members of minorities in so far as local conditions dictated.

Autonomy based on local administration was not acceptable to Baltic Germans for obvious reasons. As Werner Hasselblatt pointed out in a private letter, since Germans did not live in clearly defined settlements, they could never gain control of any local administrations and so the acquisition of autonomy based on persons rather than territory had to be a matter of life and death for them.[25] And despite Tõnisson's irritation with the cultural

[20] A. de Vries, 'Der Schutz der nationalen Minderheiten im Lichte der letzten Staatsversammlungsdebatten', *Revaler Bote* 9 March 1923.
[21] 'Die Reden der deutsch-baltischen Abgeordneten zum Autonomie-Gesetzprojekt', *Revaler Bote* 9 March 1923.
[22] There was a general parliamentary committee investigating cultural autonomy, but often it delegated detailed work to a sub-committee.
[23] 'Staatsversammlung', *Revaler Bote* 9 March 1923.
[24] 'Staatsversammlung', *Revaler Bote* 10 March 1923.
[25] Fond 1000, File 172. Deutsch-Baltische Partei. Korrespondenz des Abgeordneten W.Hasselblatt. 1921–25 Hasselblatt to Prof. Erich Kaufmann, 23.7.23.

autonomy project as was shown in March 1923, a number of Estonian politicians were much more sympathetic.

According to recent work by Kari Alenius, parliamentary records show that from 1918 on, a small but significant number of Estonian politicians 'continuously, systematically and strongly' supported the proposals for cultural autonomy being made by the minorities, even though doing so 'incurred the wrath' of other members of the majority population.[26] As Alenius adds, the 'goodwill of the majority was an absolutely necessary prerequisite to passing the law on autonomy.'[27] A handful of German deputies in the *Riigikogu* could never have hoped to bring about legislation without the assistance of influential Estonian figures. Among them, Konstantin Päts (Agrarian Party) agreed that autonomy based only on local administrative arrangements would be nonsensical.[28] He stated that Russians, Germans, Swedes and Jews all lived differently and this reality had to be given practical form. When Tõnisson complained the proposal would cause the Estonian state to hand over elements of its sovereignty to the minorities, Päts stated they would not set up bodies akin to Swiss cantons or North American federal states, but self-administering organisations which would be part of the state and which could not, therefore, come into conflict with it. He accused Tõnisson's ideas of being out of date, adding that Estonia's external relations were vitally important and that they alone might provide weighty reasons to pass a cultural autonomy law.

### 3. Dealing with disappointment

Despite the parliamentary disappointment of March 1923, German publicists kept pushing the autonomy agenda. Spindler urged German voters not to become apathetic, but to vote in forthcoming elections specifically to help achieve cultural autonomy.[29] Max Bock emphasised that autonomy would promote the rootedness of the Baltic Germans in their *Heimat* and assist understanding between different nationality groups in the region.[30] Despite these words, meetings of the Baltic German Party held after the Estonian parliament was dissolved showed the situation to be serious. Parliamentary debate about cultural autonomy had become mired and it was not clear how exactly progress could be achieved. It was not always clear that the German community would be able to decide what to do next.

A meeting of the Baltic German Party held on 10 June 1923 discussed whether to co-operate with other minorities to achieve autonomy,

---

[26] K. Alenius, 'The Birth of Cultural Autonomy in Estonia: How, Why and for Whom?' *Journal of Baltic Studies* 38 (2007) p. 448.

[27] Ibid.

[28] 'Staatsversammlung', *Revaler Bote* 13 March 1923. A study of the differences of opinion between Estonian politicians at this time would be interesting.

[29] Sp. 'Die kommende Parlamentssession', *Revaler Bote* 7 April 1923.

[30] M. Bock, 'Unsere wichtigste Aufgabe im neuen Parlament', *Revaler Bote* 14 April 1923.

whether a national register should be voluntary or somehow compulsory, the extent of state control over any autonomous cultural organisation, how to persuade Estonians to support the initiative and whether their agenda should be linked to planned reforms of the local administration.[31] The list of issues and potential stumbling blocks was so lengthy it must have been tempting for the community to give up the project, but positive voices kept coming to the fore. Ammende did not attend the meeting, but de Vries spoke up, saying that autonomy would proof the Baltic Germans against irredenta. Spindler added his voice, saying that experiments in autonomous education were underway in Latvia and Romania, so these should provide information for them to draw on.

In mid-July 1923, German and Russian deputies submitted a petition to parliament demanding that, following its first reading, work continue on the autonomy bill. Now, however, the situation was complicated by senior Estonian politicians Jaakson [32] and Tõnisson (both of the People's Party) submitting alternative legislative ideas based on cultural autonomy rooted in local administrations (as opposed to being organised on a whole-state basis).

Between August 1923 and May 1924 the work of the parliamentary commission proceeded, with a fresh proposal being agreed eventually by all its multi-party members and receiving another first reading in parliament in June 1924.[33] In the earlier year (1923), Werner Hasselblatt had been elected a deputy for the Baltic German fraction. Ewald Ammende had encouraged him to engage in politics with a view to promoting especially cultural autonomy.[34] Once elected, Hasselblatt joined the parliamentary commission. Later he recalled long and hard arguments with deputies such as Ado Anderkopp (Labour Party) who remained suspicious of non-territorial autonomy since there had never been such a thing before. He feared it could create a 'state within a state'. By contrast, Päts remained more sympathetic.[35]

During this period, cultural autonomy still raised hot passions. When parliament re-convened in August 1923, a debate about the reform of Estonia's teacher training facilities saw Communist deputies arguing strenuously that there should not be a two tier educational system in which provision reflected a family's ability to pay.[36] The argument had implications for any proposal about minorities establishing autonomously funded schools. Undeterred, deputies drawn from the minorities presented a draft proposal to

---

[31] Minutes of the meeting of the delegates of the DB Party on 10 June 1923. Madara. Fond 1000, File 173.
[32] There was a general parliamentary committee investigating cultural autonomy, but often it delegated detailed work to a sub-committee.
[33] Hasselblatt, 'Die Organisationsform unseres kulturellen Eigenlebens', p. 72.
[34] W. Hasselblatt, *Von der Kulturautonomie zum Nationalitätenkongress*, Herder Institute, MSS 53. pp. 14-5.
[35] W. Hasselblatt, *Über die Kulturautonomie. Buchmanuskript und Anlagen*. Riigiarhiiv, Tallinn. p. 98.
[36] '2. Staatsversammlung', *Revaler Bote* 1 August 1923.

the government suggesting they be allowed to administer many of their own affairs until a definitive law finally was agreed. It proposed that autonomous bodies with a status analogous to local administrations be set up to manage minority schools, to run minority welfare provision and to supervise minority religious affairs.[37] Minorities would also be permitted to tax themselves and would organise their schools in consultation with local administrations. Resistance remained in some Estonian quarters, however, with *Revaler Bote* publishing a translation of an essay from the Estonian press suggesting that the law might lead minorities to fund their churches better than Estonian parishes.[38] This discussion made plain that the issues of autonomous religion, welfare and education were closely intertwined.

Now the Baltic German community began to show increasing interest in the concerns of Estonians. Axel de Vries took up a number of points raised in an article probably written by former Foreign Minister Piip and published in *Vaba Maa*. Unfortunately the discussion was ill-tempered. Piip's article was said to characterise Baltic Germans as ungrateful and to accuse them of making excessive demands when minority protection was framed as an international rather than a domestic affair. The article was also criticised for implying that Germans would only be given autonomy once they dropped their complaints over land reform.[39] In reply, de Vries maintained that minorities only wanted what was in the constitution, that autonomy was the best way to prevent irredenta and that discussions of culture were serving as a mask for economic and political attacks on members of the German nobility and middle classes. The same article from *Vaba Maa* was discussed by a separate author who described it as self-congratulatory. Estonians seemed to believe they were pioneering minority rights while very little was actually happening. Like de Vries, this author (S.K.) rejected the idea there could be any trade off between cultural autonomy and land reform; rather, economic loss had helped make cultural autonomy necessary in the first place, as a means for the minority to sustain itself.[40]

By October 1923 the Jaakson-Tõnisson proposals had become so important that deputies representing the national minorities took time during parliamentary debate to condemn them.[41] Hasselblatt explained they approached autonomy in terms of organisation through local administrations, hence neglecting any over-arching structure uniting a whole national community ('*Kuppelbau*'). The result would be the fragmentation of the minorities. Whilst doubting that the proposal fulfilled the terms of the

---

[37] 'Gesetzprojekt über die zeitweilige Ordnung der Selbstverwaltung der nationalen Minderheiten', *Revaler Bote* 10 August 1923.
[38] 'Bemerkungen zum Gesetzprojekt über die Autonomie der Minderheiten', *Revaler Bote* 11 August 1923.
[39] A. de Vries, 'Die Rechte der völkischen Minderheiten', *Revaler Bote* 15 August 1923.
[40] S.K., 'Offenes Spiel', *Revaler Bote* 20 August 1923.
[41] '2. Staatsversammlung', *Revaler Bote* 10 October 1923.

constitution, in deference to Jaakson and Tõnisson Hasselblatt agreed that it should be subjected to further parliamentary scrutiny. Sjeljugin, speaking on behalf of ethnic Russian deputies, agreed on the grounds the outcome probably would be to show how unacceptable the proposals were.

Discussion of the latest events once again spilled into the press. August Spindler complained there were now three draft autonomy projects on the table: one worked out by the minorities (aiming at nationally-organised autonomy), the Tõnisson-Jaakson draft (proposing locally-organised autonomy), plus a compromise penned by Päts and Anderkopp (which the minorities had accepted).[42] Spindler was dismissive of the Jaakson-Tõnisson proposal since autonomy run through local administrations would be so expensive that only the larger groups of minorities found in major urban centres would be able to afford mother-tongue schools. Certainly it would be impossible to co-ordinate a network of German schools across the country and so they would be unable to design the best way to cater for ethnic Germans in sparsely populated areas. Spindler also criticised the financial strictures included in the Jaakson-Tõnisson plan, not least the stipulation that no more money *per capita* should be spent on the education of a German child than an Estonian one. This, he felt, would lead to reduced quality of German teaching staff and educational materials. Spindler believed the Jaakson-Tõnisson proposal would annihilate the German schooling system. For the community to survive, it had to be recognised in its entirety as a legal entity. All of these points were repeated in the parliamentary commission when it met mid-way through October.[43]

Admittedly there were some signs that a dialogue was developing between majority and minority peoples and *Revaler Bote* published an interview with Interior Minister Karl Einbund (Agrarian Party—later known as Kaarel Eenpalu) which originally was published in *Päevaleht*.[44] The minister emphasised that the government had an obligation to provide autonomy to the minorities as promised in the constitution. He explained also that it had to cultivate trust between the minorities and the Estonian state, between the minorities and Estonians. Showing balance, Einbund maintained that, having lost their earlier élite status, some Germans were unhappy with the new state and, reciprocally, Estonians suspected the group of potential disloyalty; but he called for all this to change. In his own words, 'It should be clear there are no "foreigners" (*Fremdstämmigen*) in the Estonian Republic.' The government had to accept that everyone had equal rights and obligations; anything else would only promote difficulties in the future. *Revaler Bote*'s editorial comment at least praised Einbund for his commitment to equality.

---

[42] A. Spindler, 'Das neue Gesetzprojekt btr. die kulturelle Selbstverwaltung der völkischen Minoritäten', *Revaler Bote* 13 October 1923.

[43] 'Das Autonomieprojekt in der Parlamentskommission', *Revaler Bote* 20 October 1923.

[44] 'Der Minister des Inneren K. Einbund über die Minoritäten in Estland', *Revaler Bote* 20 October 1923.

Sure enough, when—in late November 1923—the commission discussed again whether cultural autonomy should be organised locally or nationally, Einbund supported the minorities' view in the face of Jaakson. But still the situation remained deadlocked.

## 4. From spring to October 1924: hopes still unfulfilled

By the start of 1924, the Baltic German community would have been excused at least a degree of disillusionment, yet some of their number tackled the stalemate head on. The indefatigable August Spindler argued the minorities' case powerfully. Democracy, he said, involved the negation of foreign domination, so no nationality should seek to control another. In fact, each group should govern itself, at least over matters concerning it intimately. Naturally he meant Estonians should not decide matters affecting German culture, since protests were bound to result—as was happening in Poland, where ethnic Germans were complaining about the Polish state.[45]

Ammende and Hasselblatt did what they could to move things forwards. The former held critically important private conversations with Tõnisson which, on 18 March, were expanded to include Hasselblatt and Pantenius.[46] They met in Pärnu and agreed that autonomy should involve the complete separation of politics and culture, also that local cultural bodies should be established to look after regional cultural life. Little by little, some kind of meaningful compromise was emerging. It was agreed that local electoral districts would elect members of local cultural councils (*Kulturkuratorien*) which in turn would send representatives to a central cultural council (at this point called a national council or *Volksrat*). The proposals provided the foundation for a basic agreement with the People's Party, although disagreements still remained. Most obviously (and perhaps at odds with the constitution), Tõnisson felt welfare should not be administered autonomously, and so the German participants decided to leave the topic for another day. There needed to be discussions about the exact character of a national register too.[47]

At the request of the Democratic Bloc, the outcome of the meetings was written down and handed to the parliament's chair. It had been agreed that a national minority's cultural life should be put in its own hands through the creation of a public legal institution. This would both guarantee the project being democratic and facilitate state supervision of a minority's activities (i.e. lots of separate local organisations would be much harder to supervise). It would recognise the complete separation of cultural and

---

[45] A. Spindler, 'An die Gegner der Kulturautonomie der völkischen Minderheiten' in *Estland*. Reval: Nord- und Ostdeutsche Forschungsgemeinschaft, 1924. pp. 4–8.

[46] Alenius highlights the importance of the discussions of 18 March in bringing about cultural autonomy. Alenius, 'The Birth of Cultural Autonomy in Estonia', p. 448.

[47] 'Auf dem Wege zur Kultur-Autonomie', *Revaler Bote* 22 March 1924.

political affairs and would neither create a privileged position for minorities nor damage them. Voting would take place according to local electoral districts created as *Kulturkuratorien*, which in turn would elect representatives to a central cultural council (now called a cultural council or *Kulturrat*). This central body would create an executive to manage the group's educational system, organise its cultural and welfare projects and establish levels of self-taxation.[48]

Within a fortnight, the government issued a declaration stating cultural autonomy would be realised in the near future.[49] Unexpectedly, a stormy debate followed because some deputies (including Päts and Einbund of the Agrarian Party) felt the declaration had not gone far enough. Einbund said clearer thinking was necessary to do justice to a multi-faceted issue. Minorities should be encouraged to feel fully-fledged citizens and more thought should be given to how best they should organise so as to avoid conflict with the interests of the state.[50] This was the point at which Ammende addressed the Association of German Welfare and Cultural Associations in Estonia on the subject 'Do we need a national community (*Volksgemeinschaft*)?'[51] The meeting decided, unsurprisingly, that they did need a national community constructed as a public legal organisation.

Things began to move again at the start of May 1924 when the key sub-committee of the parliamentary commission adopted a revised version of a temporary autonomy law.[52] It addressed the national self-administration of mother-tongue educational institutions, both cultural and welfare organisations, and incorporated the principle that minorities settled in territorially well-defined patterns would be able to administer themselves autonomously through established systems of local government.[53] Progress came to a halt, however, when Hasselblatt proposed that, at the outset, *all* Germans should have their names inscribed on a national register which would define the German community and electorate.[54]

These developments pulled Ammende back into the fray with an article entitled 'Before the decisive step'.[55] He proposed that no significant differences now existed between the majority and minority populations over autonomy and five years of work by his minority was almost coming to

[48] Letter to the President, 18.3.24. Fond 1000, File 173. See also Garleff, *Deutschbaltische Politik zwischen den Weltkriegen*, p. 110.
[49] 'Die Regierungsdeklaration', *Revaler Bote* 2 April 1924.
[50] '2. Staatsversammlung. 3 Session, 24 Sitzung. Am 4 April 1924', *Revaler Bote* 5 April 1924.
[51] 'Auf dem Wege zur deutschen Volksgemeinschaft', Revaler Bote 2 April 1924.
[52] 'Gesetz über die zeitweilige Ordnung der Selbstverwaltung der völkischen Minderheiten', *Revaler Bote* 5 May 1924.
[53] The recognition of both cultural and territorial autonomy was important because whilst the former was preferable for Germans and Jews, the latter was applicable to Russians, who were settled in more coherent patterns.
[54] 'Der Gesetzantrag über die Autonomie der völkischen Minoritäten', *Revaler Bote* 10 May 1924.
[55] E. Ammende, 'Vor dem entscheidenden Schritt', *Revaler Bote* 10 May 1924.

fruition. The length of time he accepted as inevitable, since Estonia was pursuing path-breaking work but, since there was substantial international interest in what was being done, he proposed a speedy conclusion would impress the League of Nations. Ammende added that Einbund's recent interview had been published in about 40 different newspapers around Europe.

Meanwhile, the parliamentary investigative body's work continued. Mid-way through the month, the most recent draft law passed its third reading in that body without difficulty. There was just one problem for ethnic German commentators: provision was being made for members of the national minorities to leave the national group freely and at any time. This, *Revaler Bote* noted, could generate problems of internal discipline for the group. No doubt they were thinking that individuals would leave if self-taxation became too expensive or even after their own children had been through the German-language school system.

The cultural autonomy bill received another first reading in parliament at the start of June 1924, when it was opposed by just 4 Social Democrats.[56] Social Democrat Jans complained that existing social divisions in Estonian society posed a barrier to autonomy. For centuries, he said, Russians and Germans had lived next to each other without becoming close.[57] If an autonomy law was passed, the position would become entrenched, national minorities would exist as separate entities, and tensions would build up within the state. The speaker wondered what exactly the Germans were up to. He said Spindler's recent book about autonomy was so democratic you'd have thought a Social Democrat had written it, but he then cited other undemocratic comments by Spindler. Jans argued that someone like Spindler was only using democratic arguments to get what he wanted. Once the aim was reached, nothing would be given back to wider society. Jans got carried away by the occasion, proposing that Baltic Germans were not really a national group because they had no workers or farmers; they were just déclassé noblemen and landowners used to renting out their estates. He said they were trying to create 'a reactionary shock organisation' (*reaktionäre Stoßorganisation*) and suggested their system would be so expensive it could only be supported by external funding (i.e. from Germany). At that point, Axel de Vries shouted out, 'That is a provocation!' Eventually Hasselblatt entered the debate. He pointed out that Germans had helped fight Bolshevism only to have their land removed from them; he noted that elsewhere in Europe (even in Georgia), Social Democrats favoured autonomy, but not in Estonia; and he even defended Spindler's prior anti-democratic comments. More importantly, he added that Baltic Germans were tied to their homeland

---

[56] A.V., 'Die erste Lesung des Autonomie-Gesetzes', *Revaler Bote* 7 June 1924.
[57] '2 Staatsversammlung. 4. Session. 17 Sitzung am 6 Juni 1924', *Revaler Bote* 7 June 1924.

and wanted to fulfil their cultural mission there to the benefit of the Estonian state. This was the purpose of cultural autonomy.[58]

Russian deputy Sjeljugin was doubtless correct that current political problems were being complicated by historical experiences and the desire to settle old scores.[59] He admitted that Estonians certainly had suffered in the Russian Empire, but proposed that Russians in Estonia wanted to keep their national-cultural identity in order, for instance, to enjoy Pushkin, Tolstoy and Dostoyevsky in the original language. If they could not do this, they might become motivated to act against the welfare of their home state. Jans responded by criticising Russian groups in Tartu and Tallinn for seeking out contacts with German groups (termed 'the most reactionary of people'). These German reactionaries, he said, wanted to prevent the growth of democracy and it was imperative to fend off their conspiracies. He added that in Russian culture, democracy was more a matter of lovely words than of substance.

At that point, Einbund took the floor. He said they had to view autonomy through the prism of Estonian aspirations in imperial times. Estonians had wanted self-determination then, and so they should comprehend the position of Estonia's minorities today. He emphasised there were no grounds to believe the minorities would use autonomy for subversive ends, adding that it would be easier to supervise autonomy if it were organised on a public-legal basis rather than privately. He said the real issue was the extent to which their policies turned Estonia's minorities into loyal citizens. Anderkopp (Labour) added that they should think about the tens of thousands of Estonians living in Russia. They could not demand prerogatives for them which the Estonian state itself did not grant.

Jaakson's (People's Party) contribution was less constructive. Although he admitted autonomy was promised in the constitution, he questioned whether welfare systems (including hospitals and asylums) should really be part of it. So although the bill was passed by a large majority on 6 June 1924, its troubles were not over. Axel de Vries was right to note at once that individual articles in the law could yet cause difficulties.[60]

In mid-June 1924, an interview with Eugen Maddison (director of the Department of Administrative Affairs, Interior Ministry) appeared in German- and Estonian-language newspapers.[61] It was subtitled 'Must the welfare system be subordinated to the new system of autonomy or not?' Although Hasselblatt did his best to keep cultural autonomy on the parliamentary agenda, with the issue about welfare in the background and

---

[58] Ibid.
[59] Ibid.
[60] A. de Vries, 'Die erste Lesung des Autonomie-Gesetz', *Revaler Bote*, 7 June 1924.
[61] 'Wie muß die Autonomie der Minderheiten beschaffen sein?', *Revaler Bote* 13 June 1924

parliament scheduled to close, the project was set to be sidelined once more.[62]

Again, Ammende produced a piece of journalism. After five years without autonomy, he said, the German community was struggling. Without a central organisation, it was impossible to manage educational and other matters rationally and so its culture was being damaged.[63] He complained that the government wanted to use parliamentary time to deal with economic crisis, and expected the minorities' assistance here, but would not help them in return. Ammende proposed, therefore, that parliament should adopt cultural autonomy, create conditions for co-operation between majority and minority nationality groups, then tackle the economic crisis based on a united front. He also emphasised that the more quickly Estonia moved, the more likely it was to be the first country in Europe to regulate its minority issues comprehensively. Nonetheless, discussion of cultural autonomy foundered because when it was next due for discussion, parliament lacked a quorum.[64] Days later it was struck off the list of work to be achieved before parliament's summer break.[65] The Baltic German press complained that although Einbund had spoken in favour of autonomy, the Agrarian Party had agreed to drop it.[66] The action was interpreted as petty revenge because the minorities had not supported that party over legislation about new agricultural settlers. In amongst the inevitable complaints, some began suggesting the Germans should constitute themselves as a national community on a private legal basis, with a view to moving to a public legal foundation once the legislation finally was passed.[67]

Parliament began sitting again in September and, optimistically, *Revaler Bote* suggested the legislation could received a second reading soon. The paper was wrong.[68] On 17 October 1924 the legislation was returned to the parliamentary commission's sub-committee for revisions—something Baltic Germans considered an act of bad faith by the government.[69] That day saw another stormy debate in parliament. Hasselblatt's view that the law should cover both culture *and* welfare provision was rejected and, later, claims for autonomous welfare provision would be dropped by the minorities (notwithstanding the constitution's provisions). Kornel (People's Party) argued autonomy in both areas went too far. Rei (Social Democrats) said it would be too expensive for Russians and Germans to set up their own hospitals. Wirma (Social Democrat) said the law left too much unsaid; for

---

[62] '2. Staatsversammlung. 5. Session am 13 Juni 1924', *Revaler Bote* 14 June 1924

[63] E. Ammende, 'Ein Appell', *Revaler Bote* 16 June 1924.

[64] '2. Staatsversammlung. 5. Session, 3. Sitzung am 14 June 1924', *Revaler Bote* 16 June 1924.

[65] A. de Vries, 'Eine verpaßte Gelegenheit', *Revaler Bote* 19 June 1921.

[66] '2. Staatsversammlung. 5 Session, 5 Sitzung am 18 Juni 1924', *Revaler Bote* 19 June 1921.

[67] H.F., 'Gedanken zur Autonomiefrage', *Revaler Bote* 7 July 1924.

[68] A. de Vries, 'Vor dem Beginn der Autonomie-Verhandlungen in der Staatsversammlung', *Revaler Bote* 26 September 1924.

[69] Hasselblatt, 'Die Organisationsform unseres kulturellen Eigenlebens', p. 72.

instance, what would happen if an autonomous administration came into conflict with a local administration?[70] When de Vries complained that Germans had been waiting five years for autonomy, an Estonian snapped back 'We have been waiting 800 years!' In the end, a vote of 29 (comprising the Agrarian Party, People's Party, National Liberals, Settlers Party and most Social Democrats) to 14 (the minorities, the Christian Party, the Labour Party, plus two members of the Agrarian Party—including Einbund—and two Social Democrats) rejected the law as it stood. In response, Baron Schilling (Baltic German Party) read a statement questioning the government's commitment to consolidating peace inside Estonia.

Mournfully, ethnic German journalists began forecasting that autonomy was unlikely to be implemented before the start of 1927.[71] They bemoaned the lack of courage displayed by the majority population and questioned whether there was any real political will to solve the nationality question.[72] When, however, the parliamentary commission debated the autonomy law again, the outcome was unexpected. By 7 votes to 3 it decided that parliament's decision to return the law to it was unconstitutional and so it had to go back to that body![73]

German commentators took up the cudgels again. An article signed 'A German too' echoed Carl Schirren's famous sentiment, saying the main thing was for Baltic Germans to 'persevere' (*Ausdauer*).[74] Axel de Vries echoed the view in a series of articles.[75] Stating that autonomy was coming slowly, he maintained they had to keep fighting or else betray their forefathers' inheritance. More pragmatically, he proposed that indecision over autonomy was weakening the state, specifically it was preventing minorities participating in the construction of Estonia as a bulwark against external threats. As he put it:

> ... how can it be forgotten for a minute that someone is waiting beyond Estonia's borders until unemployment, economic crisis and political indecision have prepared the ground adequately for the overthrow of the state?

---

[70] 'Vertagung des Autonomiegesetzes in Estland', *Baltische Blätter* (1924). Also see '2. Staatsversammlung. 6. Session, 20. Sitzung. Am 17. Oktober 1924', *Revaler Bote* 18 October 1920.

[71] 'Vertagung des Autonomiegesetzes in Estland', *Baltische Blätter* (1924). Also 'Deklaration der deutsch-baltischen Fraktion anläßlich der Vertagung des Autonomiegesetzes', *Revaler Bote* 22 October 1924.

[72] A. de Vries, 'Ein schwarzer Tag', *Revaler Bote* 18 October 1924.

[73] 'Der Beschluß der Staatsversammlung zum Autonomiegesetz', *Revaler Bote* 28 October 1924.

[74] Ein Deutscher, 'Was nun weiter?', *Revaler Bote* 22 November 1924 followed by Auch ein Deutscher, 'Was nun weiter?!', *Revaler Bote* 27 November 1924.

[75] A. de Vries, 'Der Weg in die Zukunft. I', *Revaler Bote* 25 November 1925; 'Der Weg in die Zukunft II', *Revaler Bote* 26 November 1924; and 'Der Weg in die Zukunft III', *Revaler Bote* 27 November 1924.

In this light, de Vries argued that inaction over cultural autonomy was not just a betrayal of the minorities, but of the majority population too.

## 5. The extra element: Communism

De Vries was alluding to the threat of Communism, both in the form of the Soviet state and of individual sympathisers. As he wrote his most recent articles, a major trial of Communists was taking place in Tallinn. 88 people were accused of subversion and eventually some would be executed.[76] Commenting on events, de Vries maintained that Communist Russia, through the Third International, was fomenting revolution in neighbouring states. He cited demonstrations against the Tallinn trial staged in St. Petersburg as evidence of a concerted Bolshevik policy to undermine self-defensive steps taken by countries such as Estonia.[77]

The trial of the Communists had a substantial background. In 1921, reporting maintained that the proceedings of the Third International proved Moscow was anxious to destabilise the Baltic States. Lenin closed the assembly with a call for the preparation of revolution in capitalist lands and stories followed of Bolshevik agitators on Estonia's borders, also of Soviet troop deployments to the same region.[78] In January 1922 alleged Communist spies had been arrested across Estonia (although especially around Tartu) collecting military intelligence.[79] Reports followed that the Estonian Communist Party was receiving orders from the Third International and distributing calls for working class revolt. That spring, 115 Communists were arrested and tried by a military court.[80] They included *Riigikogu* deputies Sergei Andrejew, Eduard Kegu, Paula Järw and Johannes Wanja—plus former deputy Soans.

The Communist spectre did not go away. In April 1923 there were reports of Communists in St. Petersburg planning outrages against Estonian statesmen.[81] Several months later, there followed fresh reports of mass arrests of Soviet agents in Estonia.[82] Allegedly treasonous material was being

---

[76] 'Der große Kommunistenprozeß', *Revaler Bote* 17 November 1924. Also 'Politische Wochenschau', *Revaler Bote* 22 November 1924; and 'Der große Kommunistenprozeß', *Revaler Bote* 25 November 1925.

[77] A. de Vries, 'Das Echo des großen Kommunistenprozesses', *Revaler Bote* 21 November 1924.

[78] 'Bolschewistische Absichten gegen die baltischen Staaten', *Revaler Bote* 15 June 1921; 'Der Kongress der III. Internationale', *Revaler Bote* 15 July 1921; 'Bolschewistische Agenten an der estnische Grenze', *Revaler Bote* 20 July 1921; 'Schluss des Kongresses der III. Internationale', *Revaler Bote* 21 July 1921; 'Bolschewistische Truppenansammlungen an der estnische und finnischen Grenze', *Revaler Bote* 24 August 1921.

[79] 'Aufdeckung einer großen Spionageorganisation in Eesti', *Revaler Bote* 26 January 1922.

[80] 'Die kommunistische Geheimorganisation in Estland', *Revaler Bote* 22 March 1922.

[81] 'Terroristische Pläne der Kommunisten in Estland?', *Revaler Bote* 17 April 1923.

[82] 'Massenverhaftungen von Kommunisten', *Revaler Bote* 23 January 1924 and 'Zu den Massenverhaftungen der Kommunisten', *Revaler Bote* 24 January 1924.

circulated and 50 arrests followed a meeting of 200 Communists in Tallinn on the night of 22–23 January 1924. Those detained included *Riigikogu* deputies Janson, Keerdo, Tomp and Allik. 80 buildings were searched around the capital and former parliamentary deputy Hansen was arrested. Parliamentary deputy Reesen was arrested in Viljandi (Fellin), although he escaped while being transferred to the capital, and deputy Kangur was arrested in Narva. In total, 100 people were arrested across the country. Given the number of *Riigikogu* deputies involved, these were dramatic events. At the end of the month, Interior Minister Einbund stated 150 Communists had been detained and that an investigation was underway concerning an attempt to introduce a workers' dictatorship in Estonia. He alleged that Soviet Russia was funding Communist activity in the country and that the Third International was promoting subversion.[83] By November 1924, the trials of the accused were well underway.[84]

In this context, a modest Communist coup broke out. It started at 5.30 am on 1 December 1924 and involved attacks on several military and civic institutions around Tallinn. Groups of 5 to 10 armed men attacked police offices, railways stations, government buildings (including the War Ministry) and communications offices. An attempt to break into Einbund's flat failed, but the events led to the death of several police officers and Transport Minister Kark. 40 more people were hospitalised. The events only lasted a few hours. Both the police and military remained loyal to the state and the actions seem to have involved a few hundred participants who were out of harmony with Estonia's workers. De Vries characterised them as in the pay of a foreign power, and subsequent newspaper reporting maintained that between 80 and 100 of the putschists had crossed into Estonia from the Soviet Union on 28 and 29 November.[85]

In the days and weeks that followed, soul searching began about how best to respond to the events.[86] De Vries recommended, on the one hand, that Estonia develop its defence system along Finnish lines, and added, on the other hand, that parliamentary squabbling had to end for the common good.[87] There was a tense atmosphere when the new parliament met on 18 December. Jaakson was Prime Minister and discussions had already begun about how to respond to 1 December. He announced steps to strengthen the army, to bolster the state security laws and to introduce a civil defence system (i.e. in

---

[83] 'Der Minister des Inneren zu den Kommunisten-Verhaftungen', *Revaler Bote* 31 January 1924.
[84] 'Der große Kommunistenprozeß', *Revaler Bote* 17 November 1924.
[85] A. de Vries, 'Nach dem Putsch', *Revaler Bote* 2 December 1924. Also 'Der kommunistische Putschversuch und seine Lehren', *Revaler Bote* 3 January 1925 and 8 January 1925.
[86] For further reports of the putsch, see for instance 'Zum gestrigen Kommunistenputsch', *Revaler Bote* 2 December 1924; 'Weitere Einzelheiten vom Kommunistenputsch', *Revaler Bote* 3 December 1924; 'Weitere Einzelheiten von Kommunistenputsch', *Revaler Bote* 4 December 1924; 'Weitere Einzelheiten vom Kommunistenputsch', *Revaler Bote* 6 December 1924.
[87] De Vries, 'Nach dem Putsch'. For more about the relevance of the Finnish defence model, see A. de Vries, 'Der innere Schutz', *Revaler Bote* 10 January 1925.

line with de Vries's suggestion). More generally he stated a commitment to address the country's economic problems and to pursue autonomy legislation.[88] The security dimension of cultural autonomy was to the fore when Schilling spoke. In the wake of the failed coup, he said everyone living in Estonia was a member of the same community of fate, adding that they all needed civic peace in terms of economics and nationality affairs.

That Bolshevism could promote unrest in western neighbours had long been feared by Baltic Germans. In 1919, Paul Schiemann told Latvia's parliament that defence against the danger in the East involved 'social war'. Governments had to promote social peace, not least by addressing economic and nationality questions.[89]

During autumn 1924 (with feelings about the lack of cultural autonomy still raw), Tallinn's ethnic Germans had begun arguing that Moscow was attempting to exploit the nationality question to undermine her neighbours. De Vries explained that inside Russia minorities were being permitted self-administration not just for reasons of domestic expediency, but so the Soviet state could establish itself at the head of the nationality movement in Eastern Europe.[90] The aim ultimately was to bind together the twin forces of nationalism and social-economic unrest in order to create a revolutionary force capable of challenging bourgeois governments in the border states. De Vries said this insight gave the concerns of German minorities a new salience. Their desire to establish a state incorporating the effective management of cultural rights amounted to defence against subversion by Moscow.

The line was promoted in *Revaler Bote* in the weeks after the Tallinn putsch,[91] but no one was more active or impassioned about Moscow's strategy to subvert her western neighbours than Ewald Ammende. This was the environment in which he published the essays 'Moscow's new offensive' (see chapter 2). They were reproduced across Europe and argued there was a definite model of Soviet subversion.[92] With comments sure to cause a stir in Estonia, Ammende pointed out how easy it would have been in December for Russian troops to have crossed the border at Narva or for the navy to have landed at Tallinn. He said no one, not even the League of Nations, could have stopped that happening. Discussing how to forestall Moscow's subversion, Ammende said this:

---

[88] Apart from Jaakson's speech, see 'General Laidoner über die innere und äußere Sicherheit des estländischen Staates', *Baltische Blätter* (1925).
[89] 'Eine programmatische Rede des lettländischen Abgeordneten Schiemann', *Revaler Bote* 16 December 1919. Schiemann was concerned that land reform was promoting social unrest.
[90] A. de Vries, 'Die Gefahren der ssowjetrussischen Nationalitätenpolitik', *Revaler Bote* 20 September 1924.
[91] See 'Die bessarabische Gefahr', *Revaler Bote* 9 December 1924.
[92] E. Ammende, 'Moskaus neue Offensive', *Baltische Blätter* (1925), 15 January 1925 and E. Ammende, 'Moskaus neue Offensive', *Baltische Blätter* (1925) 22 January 1925.

Even the implementation of economic restructuring cannot
help if it is not accompanied by the supersession of the real
and greatest cancer afflicting almost all of the border states
today (although Estonia perhaps least of all), namely the
oppression of all national minorities—national chauvinism.

Europe had to abandon policies which assimilated children (as happened in
Romania) and forego national triumphalism (as occurred in Poland); instead
the League of Nations' provisions for the protection of minorities had to be
applied thoroughly.[93]

### 6. The consequences of 1 December 1924

Anti-Communism energised Ammende, but had consequences for Estonia's
political processes too. On 16 January, Ammende met with senior member of
the People's Party Jaan Tõnisson. Their discussions probably involved some
horse-trading, since Tõnisson suggested autonomy could be dealt with in
association with the budget (perhaps indicating that German backing for the
budget would be balanced by his party's support for autonomy). He also said
that the law should not address welfare organisations. Although the Baltic
Germans were not going to get everything they wanted out of autonomy,
nonetheless purposeful movement was now under way. The next day, on 17
January 1925, de Vries, Hasselblatt and Ammende met with State President
Jaakson and Interior Minister Einbund.[94] They agreed that autonomy
legislation should be passed quickly, cementing relations between majority
and minority peoples and protecting the homeland from internal and external
threats. So, about six weeks after the failed Tallinn coup, participants in the
autonomy debate finally were reaching an accommodation, and concern for
the social bases of national security certainly seems to have been important in
helping the process along.

The Estonian politicians were as good as their word. On 28 January
1925 the autonomy law received its second reading in the *Riigikogu* and was
passed in 20 minutes without debate and with Tõnisson's assistance.[95] At 9
pm, after the house had been in session for two hours, parliament was
inquorate. Still, Tõnisson, acting as speaker, allowed proceedings to progress,
reasoning that it would be wrong to delay autonomy any longer. At this point,
just two changes were made to the law: the cultural parliament was to be
elected every three years (previous drafts had not given a definite time limit)
and, as Tõnisson requested, welfare autonomy was dropped. Subsequent

---

[93] E. Ammende, 'Die Abwehr der neuen Moskauer Offensive', *Rigasche Rundschau* 14 January
1925.
[94] 'Zur Frage der Annahme des Autonomie-Gesetzes', *Revaler Bote* 17 January 1925.
[95] 'Das Autonomiegesetz in 2. Lesung angenommen. 2. Staatsversammlung. 7. Session, 9.
Sitzung', *Revaler Bote* 29 January 1924.

discussions in the press suggested Tõnisson wanted welfare autonomy to be dealt with by parliament separately because it was a complicated area.[96] It was also noted that Tõnisson did not like the word *Volksrat* ('national council' or 'people's council'), but *Kulturrat* ('cultural council').

In January 1925, Tõnisson and the Baltic Germans—with Ammende as mediator—were working in a kind of harmony. All of the Estonian's concerns were accommodated in the final law which received its third reading on 5 February 1925. This was opposed by just one vote. De Vries termed the legislation the first serious effort to address the rights of national minorities, adding that it would allow bourgeois Europe to draw the teeth of Moscow's nationality-based propaganda.[97]

## 7. The cultural autonomy law

The Law on the Cultural Self-Administration of National Minorities allowed national groups with over 3,000 members to run their own educational and cultural affairs. It permitted them to set up registers of members based on free choice. Elections of representatives would lead to the creation of a central cultural council (*Kulturrat*) with between 20 and 60 members based in Tallinn, a central cultural executive administration linked to this body, plus a series of regional cultural bodies (*Kulturkuratorien*) to supervise cultural affairs in the provinces. The cultural council and its executive would run their own educational facilities and (in association with local councils) design a network of schools to cover the whole country. The cultural council also received powers to raise taxation from the members of the national register to help fund these schools.[98]

The new law was momentous and *Revaler Bote* celebrated with a special edition.[99] The paper set out a wealth of articles all making the case in favour of Estonia's new experiment in the management of relations between national groups. One of the authors of the cultural autonomy law and a prime participant in the parliamentary planning process during 1923–25, Werner Hasselblatt, applauded the statute as an important step on the way to the creation of nationality law. He added his belief that the state could only benefit from the proper organisation of the minorities living on its territory.[100] In line with his earlier writings, de Vries said that at a time when Moscow was pushing revolution, Estonia had responded by mobilising the strongest state-building principle of all: the self-determination of national minorities.[101]

---

[96] "'Kultur- und Wohlfahrtsrat" oder "Kulturrat"?', *Revaler Bote* 31 January 1924.
[97] A de Vries, 'Zur Annahme des Autonomiegesetzes', *Revaler Bote* 6 February 1925.
[98] For a study of the law by one of the Estonian civil servants who created it, see E. Maddison, *Die nationalen Minderheiten Estlands und ihre Rechte*. Tallinn, 1926.
[99] *Sonderausgabe. Revaler Bote* 23 February 1925.
[100] W. Hasselblatt, 'Grundsätzliches und Allgemeingültiges im Autonomiegesetz', *Sonderausgabe. Revaler Bote* 23 February 1925.
[101] A. de Vries, 'Unsere Kultur-Autonomie. Ihre Bedeutung', *Sonderausgabe. Revaler Bote* 23

Noting that the rise of new states built on the nationality principle had only led to a Europe more divided and unstable than ever before, he applauded the idea of transferring self-determination from the political to cultural sphere. He added that previously only one country had taken seriously the possibility of organising multiple nationalities in an enlightened way, namely Switzerland; but while the Swiss did this on a territorial basis, Estonia had minorities which inter-penetrated geographically and so had opted for a personal system.

Pantenius applauded the fact that mother-tongue education had become something no longer reliant on the whim of the majority national group.[102] He felt that only such an educational experience would enable an individual to discover 'the best and most noble properties of his soul and spirit'. Now the job of the German community was to establish a properly functioning and unified school system. August Spindler maintained that finally a 'turning point' had come, and he took the time to recognise that Estonians such as Anderkopp (Labour Party), Päts (Agrarian Party) and Laidoner (Defence Minister) had been instrumental in helping bring it about.[103] Now the onus was on Estonia's Germans to prove they were not just a small group of noblemen and bourgeoisie, but a proper national group. Erich Hausen contributed an historical article explaining the genesis of the undoubtedly pioneering legislation.

Not to be outdone, Ewald Ammende contributed three articles.[104] He argued that the law would not lead to the encapsulation of the group within the state—perhaps to the creation of a state within a state—but would be an important pre-requisite for better co-operation with the majority. The possibility of self-taxation for educational and cultural purposes would permit the members of the German community to fashion their lives exactly as they wanted, that is to say expensively or cheaply. In this respect, their futures would be put firmly in their own hands. Ammende also went out of his way to put Estonia's developments into international perspective. He maintained that the loss of the First World War had led to a kind of spiritual awakening among ethnic Germans across Central and Eastern Europe. Now these people were organising in ways that had absolutely nothing to do with irredenta, but which were essentially loyal to the state in which they lived and likely to promote good relations between majority and minority peoples. As such, they were involved in projects concerned with the accommodation of national minorities into majority states in manners which were novel and of continental significance. As he put it:

---

February 1925.

[102] H. Pantenius, 'Schule und kulturelle Selbstverwaltung', *Sonderausgabe. Revaler Bote* 23 February 1925.

[103] A. Spindler, 'Ein Wendepunkt', *Sonderausgabe. Revaler Bote* 23 February 1925.

[104] E. Ammende, 'An die Gegner der Autonomie!', 'Die deutschen Minderheiten in Europa. Ihre Organisation—Ihre Ziele—Ihre Bedeutung' and 'Die Struktur unserer Selbstverwaltung', *Sonderausgabe. Revaler Bote* 23 February 1925.

German minorities with their pioneering work are not just
of the very greatest importance for their states and for the
entire German nation. No, they are of the very greatest
importance for the cultural development of Europe as a
whole.

As a journalist had once put it, in East and South East Europe, Germans were
the cement binding societies together and the elements likely to promote the
consolidation and improvement of relations around Europe. Laws such as
that passed in Estonia would permit such groups to bind themselves together
better than ever, so facilitating their economic activities, assisting their long-
term survival and underpinning their ability to act as a bridge between
Germany and their homelands.

## 8. The *Kulturrat*

With barely a pause for breath, as soon as the cultural autonomy law had
been passed, the Baltic German Party set up a committee, chaired by
Hasselblatt (with other members including Spindler, Pantenius, Bodisco,
Koch and von Lilienfeld) to work out how to pursue cultural autonomy in
practice.[105] Quickly the committee foresaw an autonomy institution that
would have separate departments dealing with the national register,
schooling, finance, relations between the central council and regional
*Kuratorien* and for organising elections. They prepared the route to
autonomy quickly and at noon on 11 April 1925 Hasselblatt, Baron Schilling
and Johannes Beermann (chairman of the Association of German Societies)
handed to the state president their formal declaration of intent to establish
cultural autonomy.[106] Subsequently President Jaakson and Interior Minister
Einbund issued the necessary regulations for the compilation of lists of
electoral candidates and voters.[107] By early May, the autonomy committee,
headed by Hasselblatt had drafted a provisional timetable for the compilation
of voter and candidate lists, an election period and the convening of the
cultural council (*Kulturrat*) itself.[108] There followed all manner of articles in
the press commentating on the cultural autonomy process at every step of the
way.[109] There were, for instance, frequent exhortations for all members of the

---

[105] 'Vorarbeiten für die Autonomie', *Revaler Bote* 3 March 1925.

[106] 'Zur Verwirklichung der Autonomie', *Revaler Bote* 11 April 1925.

[107] 'Regierungsverordnung über Zusammenstellung der Wählerlisten für die Wahlen zum ersten
estländischen deutschen Kulturrat', *Revaler Bote* 27 April 1925.

[108] 'Zur kulturellen Selbstverwaltung', *Revaler Bote* 6 May 1925.

[109] For example, see 'Verordnung über die Organisation der Kulturselbstverwaltung der
Minderheiten', *Revaler Bote* 20 June 1925, 'Verordnung über die Wahlen in den estländischen
deutschen Kulturrat', *Revaler Bote* 20 June 1925 and 'Verordnung zur Führung der
Nationalregister', *Revaler Bote* 20 June 1925. Also 'Die erste Aufgabe ist erfüllt', *Revaler Bote*

community to participate enthusiastically in the project. Hence Pantenius argued that even though cultural autonomy might not be perfect, people should become involved or else be consigned to life on the sidelines of society.[110] Sounding a more conservative note, Baron von Wrangell called on all Germans to participate in the creation of 'a living organism'.[111] Then, on 1 November 1925, the cultural council finally met in the House of the Ancient Brotherhood of the Black Heads in Tallinn.

Essentially the country had been divided into ten voting districts in order to elect a cultural council with 41 members.[112] The body was empowered to issue binding legislation in the field of culture, manage its budget, prescribe taxes for cultural purposes, appoint administrative staff and run the cultural administration which now had six offices (i.e. the original five plus one for sport and youth). It seems that 11,682 ethnic Germans had inscribed their names on the electoral lists, with 5,171 being located in Tallinn, so it was no small achievement for such a numerically limited group finally to have attained their goal.[113] It was understandable that the first meeting of the cultural council was a celebratory affair. On 1 November there was a service in the Nicolai Church before the inaugural meeting in the White Room in the House of the Blackheads. Present were 38 members of the cultural council.[114] They included Spindler, Schilling, Thomson, Maydell, Koch, Wrangell, Bodisco, Stackelberg and Pantenius, but apparently not Ewald Ammende who was required in Pärnu to participate in a 135 year old celebration. Also present were Estonian political figures such as Einbund, Foreign Minister Birk, Education Minister Ney and parliamentary deputies Päts, Jöeäär, Grigorjew and Sjeljugin; for the German Foreign Ministry, Ambassador Frank and Dr. Weyrauch were present. All heard Hasselblatt give a lengthy speech discussing 'the herald of public conscience, of national freedom and national peace'. On a number of occasions he specified that the new administration would have to grow 'organically', as opposed to mechanically.

Perhaps rather surprisingly there was a debate about whether or not the German group wanted to activate cultural autonomy.[115] More surprising still, a number of voices were raised expressing concerns about the project, at least in the form in which it was to be taken forward. Bodisco worried they were only being regulated by a framework law, so it was hard to judge where

---

29 September 1925.

[110] H. Pantenius, 'Berufswahl und Schule', *Revaler Bote* 29 September 1925.

[111] Baron v. Wrangell, 'Zu den Wahlen in den deutschen Kulturrat', *Revaler Bote* 20 August 1925.

[112] Hasselblatt, 'Die nationale Autonomie als Ziel der europäischen Nationalitätenpolitik', p. 19.

[113] 'Die erste Aufgabe ist erfüllt', *Revaler Bote* 29 September 1925.

[114] 'Die kulturelle Selbstverwaltung wird verwirklicht. Auf seiner gestrigen Eröffnungssitzung beschloß der erste Estländische Deutsche Kulturrat die Durchführung der kulturellen Selnstverwaltung', *Revaler Bote* 2 November 1925.

[115] 'Die Debatten im Kulturrat über die Frage der Verwirklichung der kulturellen Selbstverwaltung', *Revaler Bote* 5 November 1925.

exactly the project would go. In more outspoken fashion Baron Stackelberg was reported as follows:

> The construction of the law is democratic and it must be feared that it contains a concession to the mechanistic spirit of the age. Baltic Germandom has always rejected every kind of mechanistic form of organisation, since it has always created for itself an organic form of life. We should not allow ourselves to be forced to retreat to the standpoint of being a national minority in the sense that we renounce our historical worth in the region. We can and should never be evaluated according to our number. We should not forget that the decisive thing about a community is not its number, but its spirit.

A member of the cultural council called Greinert chipped in saying that, after this law, he felt there was a real danger of Germandom losing its Baltic character. During the interchange, Hasselblatt intervened to say that they had to be careful about accepting the law if they really believed it would preclude an organic growth of the community. (Elsewhere he had already said that the law would permit the German community to become a corporation [*Körperschaft*].)[116] Of course, having got this far there was no real chance of the law faltering and points such as that made by Pantenius (namely that autonomy would finally permit the unification of an administration of German schools) carried the day. Harry Koch was elected president of the cultural council and was received by the state president on 2 November.[117]

This was the signal for work to start in earnest, and the German experiment began—followed by Jewish autonomy being established in autumn the next year.[118] The German cultural council spent time discussing how to organise the taxation system, how to provide a mobile library, how to organise cultural lectures, how to provide appropriate history textbooks to schools, how the cultural administration could take over German schools and how to define an appropriate mission for them. In the early days of the council, Ewald Ammende wrote reports about its proceedings and initiatives. Perhaps he soon began to feel a little alienated by some of the conservative rhetoric because Ammende found himself emphasising that cultural autonomy should serve the interests of all classes of German society, not just an educated élite. With this said, it was also characteristic of his restless personality that, once the basic end had been achieved, he was ready for a

---

[116] 'Geleitworte', *Revaler Bote* 29 September 1925.
[117] 'Das vorläufige Präsidium des Deutschen Kulturrats beim Staatsältesten', *Revaler Bote* 3 November 1925.
[118] 'In der Frage der Unterrichtssprache in den jüdischen Schulen Einigung erzielt', *Revaler Bote* 20 October 1926.

new, even more ambitious agenda.[119] So having been a founder member of the cultural council elected in Pärnu, by November 1926 (at which point discussion of cultural autonomy had become extremely detailed) Ammende had stood down.[120]

## 9. Conclusion

Recently Yael Tamir declared that the 'era of homogeneous and viable nation-states is over (or rather, the era of the illusion that homogeneous and viable nation-states are possible is over, since such states never existed)'.[121] Tamir welcomed the possibility of 'liberal nationalism', that is to say the idea that all nations deserve to be allocated equal rights, regardless of whether they happen to control a given popular state.[122] To this way of thinking, individuals should be free to decide their own nationality and all nations should be guaranteed some kind of public space for their expression.[123] With a particular eye on Central and Eastern Europe, Stefan Auer has gone on to argue that, since many individuals do not want to live without a sense of their particular nationhood, a certain kind of national awareness (or nationalism) can play a valuable role in sustaining liberal democracy.[124] That is to say, consciousness of belonging to a given national group can promote a sense of community solidarity, reinforce the idea that society is based on partnerships and obligations which continue across time, and, by fostering ideas of community-based pride, encourages people to transcend their limitations for the sake of common benefit.[125]

To these ways of thinking, there is nothing intrinsically malign in 'nationalism'. Pride in a particular heritage can just as much find expression through friendliness towards other nationalities, through tolerance, openness, inclusivity and work for common good as it can through more negative orientations and behaviours. By the same token, political stability does not have to be based on 'cultural, linguistic, or religious uniformity'; it can be founded on national pluralism too.[126]

In all fairness, recognition that some degree of pride in national background is not automatically a bad thing and that the alignment of a single nation with a single state can be damaging is not exactly new. To quote Lord Acton again (see also chapter 3), 'the combination of different nations in one

---

[119] For instance, E. Ammende, 'Die Arbeit unserer Kulturverwaltung schreitet fort', *Revaler Bote* 12 March 1926, and E. Ammende, 'Die zweite Tagung unseres Kulturrats', *Revaler Bote* 13 March 1926. For a report on the first year of Kulturrat's work see 'Die Arbeit der Deutschen Kulturverwaltung im Jahre 1925–26', *Revaler Bote* 20 November 1926.
[120] 'Zu den Wahlen in den deutschen Kulturrat', *Revaler Bote* 5 September 1925.
[121] Y. Tamir, *Liberal Nationalism*. New Jersey: Princeton University Press. 1993, p. 3.
[122] Ibid, p. 9.
[123] Ibid, p. 150.
[124] S. Auer, *Liberal Nationalism in Central Europe*. New York: RoutledgeCurzon, 2004, p. 8.
[125] Ibid, p. 10.
[126] Tamir, pp. 165–66.

state is as necessary a condition of civilized life as the combination of men in society.'[127] After all, tolerance can hardly be nurtured when difference is too rarely encountered.

Positive attitudes such as these towards national identity may well rely on its expression being depoliticised or at least taking only particular forms. Certainly it should not undermine a sense of 'us' which can be shared by *all* the peoples living in a given region.[128] Hence, if people are separated by national culture, they must be bound together by a commitment to other features of life and the over-arching state, perhaps through respect for shared values enshrined in the state (such as in its legal system), its promotion of economic well-being and so on. If such a framework can be constructed, then perhaps it is indeed correct to maintain, as David Miller does, that nationality might be able to play a liberalising and progressive role in society—as something enriching and providing of choice rather than confrontational and alienating.[129]

Thoughts such as these found counterparts in the cultural autonomy project championed by the inter-war Baltic German community in Estonia. That is to say, *as Ammende interpreted it (although clearly the views of, say Stackelberg were rather different)*, cultural autonomy was an attempt to find space for all national groups in a modern state, to revise the nation state into something more flexible, to remove national cultures from the political sphere, to permit the German community to be at peace with itself and to achieve its potential, and in the process to strengthen the foundations of liberal democracy. As it was construed by Ammende in the early to mid-1920s, cultural autonomy had much about it that was progressive in a way we can still recognise today. After all, for Ammende, it was plain that after the First World War the Baltic German community had to change and adapt to radically new conditions; cultural autonomy was his chosen vehicle facilitating the necessary transformation.

And so an idea promoted by Austro-Marxists and Russian Jews was enacted by a former imperial élite at least partly in the face of Estonia's social democratic party and aided eventually by the Estonian People's Party. At the time, certainly it found notable supporters. Speaking at the German House in Stuttgart on 21 May 1925 Gustav Stresemann applauded the project. Moreover, today interest is still being shown in cultural autonomy as a tool for managing multi-nationality societies in Hungary, Romania and Russia. Non-territorial cultural autonomy also has supporters among Romani spokespeople.[130]

---

[127] Quoted in E.H. Carr, *Nationalism and After*. London: Macmillan, 1945, p. 66.

[128] This point was made by Werner Hasselblatt long ago, 'Staatskrise und auslandsdeutsche Nationalitätenpolitik', *Baltische Monatsschrift* (1929).

[129] D. Miller, *On Nationality*. Oxford: Clarendon Press, 1995, chapter 6.

[130] For discussions of these points, see D. Smith and K. Cordell (eds.), *Cultural Autonomy in Contemporary Europe*. London: Routledge, 2008.

None of this means cultural autonomy was without its flaws. For people such as Stackelberg and perhaps Hasselblatt, it was rather a Trojan horse for something more reactionary and divisive—a perspective which makes autonomy look like a vessel which could be filled with whatever content an activist chose. Of course there have to be question marks over a system that was quite so appealing to those at odds with the liberal democracy of the day. We should also pause to consider whether we should support a system promising separate schooling by nationality. David Miller, for instance, has argued schools should be places where those from different backgrounds are thrown together in order to build common experiences. They should not reinforce separateness and perhaps aspirations for superiority.[131] Cultural autonomy has also been criticised on the basis of providing a foundation for co-nationals to penetrate other states, as serving the interests of strong over weak minorities and as requiring the broadcasting of every person's nationality.[132] In fact, there might well be reservations about the expectation that, in a region with complex demographic and nationality structures and in which individuals can have complex personal heritages, national affiliation appears to be reduced to a single, static choice.

No doubt Ammende and his colleagues would have had something to say about all these points. For instance, Ammende maintained it was quite impossible to come up with a single school system that could actually do full justice to the requirements of children from diverse national backgrounds.[133] Also at various times he observed that competition between different nationality groups would always happen to some extent. But such a view was mild in comparison to others that could be found in Europe in the 1920s. In the form that Ammende pushed it, and in the context of the day in Estonia, cultural autonomy was a tool for use against both nationalism and Communism. On balance and in so far as it was a mechanism likely to provide the opportunity for reconciliation between minorities and the new state in which they lived, it was something supportive of the young Estonian democracy, not subversive of it.

This chapter is not meaning to imply that cultural autonomy was or is a universal panacea for addressing the concerns of national minorities. Rather, it was a system for dealing with minority issues that was adopted by a specific group under given historical circumstances. It was not without its problems, but we should still recognise one or two things. In a situation where good will between nationality groups could not be taken for granted, cultural autonomy was better than forced assimilation or revanche. At least it

---

[131] Miller, *On Nationality*, p. 142.
[132] X-M. Núñez Seixas, *Entre Ginebra y Berlin. La Cuestion de las Minorias Nacionales y la Politica Internacional en Europa 1914-1939*. Madrid: Akal, 2001, pp. 473–4.
[133] See his discussion of Polish schooling in Germany in his memorandum of 'Denkschrift zur Frage der Behandlung der Nationalitäten in Deutschland mit besonderer Rücksicht der Rückwirkung auf das bodenständige europäische Auslandsdeutschum', 28 October 1924, 1502-1-110, Moscow.

created a pause for the discovery of fellow feeling between mutually suspicious nationality groups and, in this light, offered a step on the way towards acceptance and integration. With something of a confidence-building measure about it, cultural autonomy was a move towards the discovery of a peaceful, nationality-based *modus vivendi*.

*Chapter Five*

# Minority interests—European interests—global interests

## 1. Introduction

The world, and especially Europe, was not the same after the First World War. More than ever, vital international connections were understood to exist. After all, it had proved impossible to confine an outrage committed in the Balkans. It was also agreed generally that no such cataclysm should happen again. Against this backdrop, in October 1925 the European Congress of Nationalities (*Europäische Nationalitäten Kongresses*—full formal name Congress of the Organised National Groups in the States of Europe, *Kongress der organisierten nationalen Gruppen in den Staaten Europas*) began to meet. Its participants believed it heralded a new direction in European nationality affairs. Paul Schiemann likened the magnitude of the changes under way to the consequences of the Thirty Years War for religious identity. After that, it became unacceptable for European states to define their citizens' religion for them; Schiemann proposed that the legacy of the First World War, coupled with the calling of the congress, marked the end of a state's power to determine a citizen's nationality.[1] Of course, his view proved too simple. To many minds state citizenship and nationality had to stay closely aligned.

Nonetheless, for a cosmopolitan like Ammende, achieving cultural autonomy within Estonia was more a start to a life's mission than an end. As befitted a member of an international trading family, his perspectives on life always transcended a single state boundary. At a time when international politics was coming ever more to the fore, with the creation of the Paris Peace Treaty and the League of Nations, it was inevitable that someone of Ammende's mindset would be drawn increasingly towards the international stage. In time, he emerged as an indefatigable lobbyist of the League and national governments alike, in the process becoming a rarity: a member of a Central and Eastern European national minority who fashioned an international political role for himself during the inter-war years.

Working though the European Congress of Nationalities, Ammende's ambition became to integrate the interests of German ethnic groups in Europe with those of the continent's other main national minorities. The strategy was supposed to prevent German minority objectives being interpreted as part of a German nationalist agenda, since benefit for ethnic Germans would have to bring more general benefit too. It also meant that, when he spoke, Ammende could claim to be representing not just several

---

[1] 'Rede des Abgeordneten Herrn Dr. Schiemann zur Eröffenung der Ersten Nationalitäten-Tagung der Europäischen Staaten.' R60463, Political Archive of the Foreign Ministry, Berlin.

million ethnic Germans, but tens of millions of other national minority people into the bargain. He also maintained the project would benefit states and majority populations, since the decent treatment of minorities would remove a source of friction from international affairs and reduce the prospect of neighbours trying to interfere in each other's domestic affairs.

## 2. The League of Nations and its security mission

Robert Cecil said the League of Nations was 'a great experiment'.[2] It was rooted in the Covenant of the League of Nations with a preamble specifying that 'organised peoples' would act justly and maintain their treaty obligations.[3] Time and again, League officials and supporters emphasised that peace needed to be organised. Early South African proponent of the League, J.C. Smuts, interpreted the organisation as taking up the mantle of organiser of the continent's affairs from the recently defunct European empires.[4] Later, William Rappard worked in the League's Mandates Section and in a book analysed the 'Organization of Peace'.[5] Amongst other things, this involved the creation of disinterested points of view, channels of co-operation, international law and morality, international solidarity and steps for the avoidance of war.[6]

In the first instance, the League was supposed to be a security organisation. It stood for 'collective security' as outlined in the first 18 articles of the Covenant and its law-abiding members would combine to face down (though diplomatic, economic and military action) any state threatening aggression.[7] This was a minimal aim, however, because for supporters of the League it was never enough to 'forbid war'.[8] It was not even enough to mediate disputes as they arose. As the 'Organization of Peace' implied, the very causes of conflict had to be tackled.[9] Nor was the League ever intended to be a 'super-state' working through diktat alone. To be effective in its mission to underpin peace in the world, it had to 'become part and parcel of the common international life of States, ...an ever visible living, working organ of the polity of civilization.'[10]

---

[2] R. Cecil, *A Great Experiment*. London: Jonathan Cape, 1941.

[3] http://avalon.law.yale.edu/20th_century/leagcov.asp (consulted 11 October 2013).

[4] J. Smuts, *The League of Nations: a Practical Suggestion*. London: Hodder and Stoughton, p. 11 and p. 28.

[5] W.E. Rappard, *The Geneva Experiment*. OUP, 1931, chapter 3 is entitled 'The League and the Organization of Peace'.

[6] Rappard, *The Geneva Experiment*, p. 88.

[7] Robert Cecil quoted in A. Sharp, *The Versailles Settlement: Peacemaking in Paris, 1919*. Basingstoke: Palgrave, 1991, p. 62.

[8] Cecil in J. Robinson, O. Karbach, M.M. Laseron, and M. Vichniak., *Were the Minorities Treaties a Failure?* New York: Antin Press, 1943, p. 32. See also Smuts, *League of Nations*, pp. 12–17.

[9] Smuts, *League of Nations*, p. 70.

[10] Ibid, p. 8.

In this context, the management of national minorities in the new and enlarged states of Central and Eastern Europe was critical. One commentator assessed there were twenty million members of minorities in post-war Europe, with ten million in Poland alone comprising 31% of its population.[11] Following the growth of national awareness during the nineteenth century, and as a result of heightened national differences resulting from the First World War, it was imperative that the 'legitimate claims of nationalities and minorities' be addressed.[12]

The position of national minorities was all the more sensitive given the rhetoric of national self-determination which accompanied the final stages of the war. The Treaty of Brest-Litovsk, removing Russian troops from, among other places, the Baltic region, Finland and Ukraine, helped prepare the way for a new ascendancy of nation-state-thinking in the region. Then, among the Allied Powers, on 5 January 1918, Lloyd George explained that, to create peace, 'a territorial settlement must be secured on the right of self-determination or the consent of the governed'.[13] Three days later, in his Fourteen Points, Woodrow Wilson also emphasised the need for self-determination for subject peoples of European empires. On 11 February 1918 he spoke to congress:

> National aspirations must be respected; peoples may now be dominated and governed by their own consent. Self-determination is not a mere phrase, it is an imperative principle of action which statesmen will henceforth ignore at their peril.[14]

Self-determination was regarded as a self-evident democratic right, because it was assumed that those sharing the same language and national culture would best run their lives for themselves.

Alfred Cobban judged national self-determination 'a very important part' of peace.[15] Unfortunately most influential statesman were unclear about the complexity of providing self-determination for the kaleidoscope of national groups inhabiting Central and Easter Europe. There, it was impossible to avoid creating national minorities; but how could self-determination be applied to them? They could not claim it in the same way as majority populations, but neither could they be denied it completely. To complicate things further, as soon as minorities claimed the right to express their separate nationality, they could be accused of somehow limiting the

---

[11] O.I. Jankowsky, *Nationalities and National Minorities*. New York: Macmillan, 1945, p. 111.
[12] Ibid, p. 13.
[13] F.P. Walters (formerly deputy sec gen of the League of Nations), *A History of the League of Nations*. OUP, 1952, reprinted 1960, p. 20.
[14] T.D. Musgrave, *Self-Determination and National Minorities*. Oxford: Clarendon, 1997, p. 24.
[15] A. Cobban, *The Nation State and National Self-Determination*. London: Collins, 1969, p. 18 and p. 104.

possibilities open to the majority national group among whom they lived, a situation likely to provoke resentment and its consequences. This was why the Great Powers began designing measures for the protection of minorities, something which implied restrictions on the exercise of a nation state's sovereignty. Naturally, such measures were not always welcome to politicians taking power after a life-time of second class status in an old empire.[16]

In due course, at least some figures looked beyond the limitations of self-determination, hence Winston Churchill's characterisation, made in 1930 of the Treaty of Versailles as the 'apotheosis of nationalism'. He regretted that Europe was 'organised as it never was before, upon a purely nationalistic basis.'[17] This principle was particularly damaging given the psychological mood of Central and Eastern Europe after the First World War, at least as some Western political commentators understood it. J.W. Headlam-Morley, an influential East Europeanist in the London Foreign Office, described the area as 'dead lands':

> Across the continent of Europe, from the Baltic to the
> Adriatic, there runs a … band of death—not physical but
> national, states, nations, and peoples broken up, wrecked,
> and destroyed—for more than 1,000 miles.[18]

Only a little later, founder of *Journal des Affaires Étrangers*, Albert Mousset, identified Eastern Europe as the seat of Europe's destructive passions owing to the 'open wounds' left by prior conflict.[19] Exaggeration apart, the region retained a difficult heritage that had to impact on its new political systems and polities—likewise the national minorities entwined in them.

Co-existence between majority and minority required tolerance—including acceptance of the prevailing democratic politics. Minorities had to be loyal to the states in which they lived and majorities had to treat them with equality and understanding. Indeed, majorities had to accept, as Austria's Chancellor Seipel said, that maintaining a separate national identity did not amount to disloyalty; it too was a feature of self-determination.[20] Unfortunately, even though states could be quick to call for the protection of co-nationals left abroad as a result of the post-war settlement, they were not always so ready to reciprocate in respect of minorities living on their own

---

[16] Walters, *A History of the League of Nations*, p. 91.

[17] E. Reves, *The Anatomy of Peace*. London: Penguin, 1947, pp. 173–4.

[18] W.B. Newsome, '"Dead Lands" or "New Europe"? Reconstructing Europe, Reconfiguring Eastern Europe: "Westerners" and the Aftermath of the World War', *East European Quarterly*, 36 (2002).

[19] Ibid.

[20] Robinson, Karbach, Laseron, Robinson and Vichniak., *Were the Minorities Treaties a Failure?* p. 99 and p.102.

lands. The situation was less than ideal, particularly given the international political architecture of Central and Eastern Europe. To quote Alfred Cobban:

> ...other zones of small and internally divided nation-states lie in the penumbra where the shadows of two great powers [i.e. Russia and Germany] intersect. Such zones are faults in the political structure of the world, and like geographical faults they are the areas in which disturbance is most likely to arise.[21]

In such a structure, persecution of a national minority which was co-national with a powerful neighbour threatened at least a serious international row. Worse, it might lead one state to attempt to interfere in the domestic affairs of another—a situation always likely to endanger peace. If the borders could not be re-drawn, and if small states could not be abolished, how was peace to be secured?

In the wake of the First World War and the creation of new democratic nation states in the lands between Germany and Russia, power lay with national majorities by virtue of voting strength.[22] Under such circumstances, if minorities could not carve out a space for personal control, how could their national cultures avoid eventual submergence beneath the majority? So, as happened in the case of Estonia's cultural autonomy, they began trying to limit the role of the state to that of provider of services to be enjoyed by all inhabitants of a given area (for example, law and order, defence, and economic development), while allowing space for independent national cultural development.[23] From an early point, some particularly far-sighted individuals even advocated that the League of Nations should reflect this national cultural complexity. As Ernst Wittermann told the *Deutschen Auslandsinstitut*, Stuttgart, in 1922:

> We should refer especially to the demand raised from different sides that the League of Nations not be an association of states, but rather an association of peoples; this highlights that the League must grow out of the free will of peoples; consequently the League would be regarded as a superior community of peoples, in which the peoples band together for the common protection of peace.[24]

---

[21] Cobban, *The Nation State and National Self-Determination*, p.18.
[22] B. Schot, *Deutschland und der Minderheitenschutz. Zur Völkerbundspolitik der Stresemann-Ära.* Marburg/Lahn: J.G.Herder-Institut, 1988, p. 24.
[23] Ibid, p. 120.
[24] Ibid, pp. 121–22.

There were, therefore, two linked problems: how to create nationally-inclusive democracies in Central and Eastern Europe, and how to ensure all national groups could find a voice on the international stage.

### 3. The context for pursuing the rights of national minorities

Spanish diplomat and official of the League of Nations' Minorities Section, Pablo de Azcárate, said this:

> Homogeneity never has been, nor ever can be, an ideal for the organization of human societies. On the contrary, diversity of mentalities, temperaments, aptitudes, ideas, beliefs, has always been rightly considered as a source of material and moral prosperity and strength in nations and states—provided, of course, that in these social groups the rational principles of solidarity prevail over the primitive instincts of struggle and destruction.[25]

Likewise, other voices disputed that the assimilation of minority national cultures was necessary to prevent the fragmentation of a state.[26] Certainly the problem of what do with national minorities had pre-dated the First World War. In the nineteenth century, for the most part it was assumed that national minorities were the domestic affair of the state where they lived, e.g. the regulation of Poles living in the German Empire was assumed the business of Berlin alone. After the Treaty of Versailles, however, things became more complicated. Theoretically-speaking, it was hard to deny that democratic states were supposed to protect *all* their citizens, including national minorities. As Karl Aun said, once the inhabitants of a state were more than 'just subjects', the state was supposed to assist all of them in 'realizing their full selves'.[27] On this basis, 'the international protection of national minorities' became a matter 'of the rights of the individual and those of democracy'.[28]

After the First World War, both the domestic treatment and international regulation of national minorities came to the fore. Not least, the wartime experience of managing populations, both one's own and those under occupation, had heightened awareness of the issue. Correspondingly, one of the key bodies charged with defining borders for the Paris Peace Conference was called the Committee on New States and the Protection of

---

[25] P. de Azcárate, *League of Nations and National Minorities. An Experiment.* Washington: Carnegie Endowment., 1945, p. 17.
[26] Cobban, *The Nation State and National Self-Determination*, p. 126–8.
[27] K. Aun, *Der völkerrechtliche Schutz nationaler Minderheiten in Estland von 1917 bis 1940.* Hamburg: Joachim Heitmann, 1951, p. 10.
[28] Ibid, p. 13.

Minorities.[29] The committee interpreted minority rights as including language rights and cultural protection, supplemented by political, civil and religious liberties.

The development took place in a complicated historical context. Rights had been granted to religious minorities in the Westphalia settlement of the 1640s. The Congress of Vienna (1815) granted Poles the right to maintain their own national institutions even though they lacked a state at the time; also the Treaty of San Stefano (concerning the treatment of Armenians inside the Ottoman Empire) and later the Congress of Berlin (1878) provided international recognition that new states in particular should treat minorities decently.[30] Statesmen had also been quick to link minority issues to the pursuit of the First World War. For instance, the Allies had deployed nationality as a justification for going to war, Prime Minister Asquith telling the House of Commons the following on 5 August 1914:

> If I am asked what we are fighting for, I reply.... We are fighting to vindicate the principle which, in these days when force, material force, sometimes seems to be the dominant influence and factor in the development of mankind, ...that small nationalities are not to be crushed, in defiance of international good faith by the arbitrary will of a strong and overmastering power.[31]

Arguably more cynically, in June 1916, German interests organised a Congress of Nationalities in Lausanne to play to the interests of minorities in the Russian Empire.[32]

After the First World War, not all minority initiatives were enlightened. The Treaty of Neuilly (1919) led to Western Thrace being split from Bulgaria and, eventually, to the exchange of Greek and Bulgarian populations. More dramatically, at the Lausanne Conference on 30 January 1923, a convention was agreed between Turkey and Greece authorising the exchange of about 2 million people. The measure was particularly notable because it gained the support of the League of Nations' High Commissioner for Refugees, Fridtjof Nansen. If comparable political actions were not to become commonplace across Central and Eastern Europe, there was only one possibility: adequate institutions placed under international guarantee had to regulate relations between majority and minority populations.[33] As a later commentator put it:

---

[29] J. Jackson Preece, *National Minorities and the European Nation-States System*. Oxford: Clarendon, 1998, p. 69.

[30] Ibid, chapter 4.

[31] Robinson, Karbach, Laseron, Robinson and Vichniak., *Were the Minorities Treaties a Failure?* p. 3.

[32] Musgrave, *Self-Determination and National Minorities*, p. 15.

[33] P. de Azcárate, *League of Nations and National Minorities. An Experiment*. Washington:

An international public law guarantee for minorities was indispensable to the international and internal peace of Europe after the First World War, both for the sake of the minorities and for the majorities with whom they had to live within common frontiers. Such a guarantee served the interests of Europe and the whole world in which these states of many races, faiths and languages formed an integral part.[34]

The Allied Powers began underpinning the rights of national minorities in Central and Eastern Europe even before the League of Nations was created. Their work took the form of a minority treaty with Poland signed on 28 June 1919 which provided a model which other minority treaties would follow.[35] It guaranteed all Polish citizens equality and liberty regardless of their race, nationality, religion or linguistic background, and added extensive provision for the autonomous management of institutions for Jewish communities.[36] Six months later, on 13 February 1920, the Council of the League began supervising the protection of national minorities, one of the 'most difficult and delicate tasks' it ever faced.[37] This responsibility only hinted at the full array of difficulties the League would encounter over the next few years. Minority issues coloured disputes over the Åland islands, Vilnius and Klaipėda (Memel), not to say tensions over Upper Silesia and Gdańsk (Danzig).[38] Regulating minority questions was never going to be an easy task.

### 4. Protecting the rights of minorities

The minority protection agreements involving the states of Central and Eastern Europe were 'one of the cornerstones' of the new 'peace structure'.[39] Their importance was underlined by the amount of time the League of

---

Carnegie Endowment, 1945, p. vii and p. 24.

[34] Robinson, Karbach, Laseron, Robinson and Vichniak., *Were the Minorities Treaties a Failure?* p. 26.

[35] Aun, *Der völkerrechtliche Schutz nationaler Minderheiten in Estland von 1917 bis 1940.* footnote 52, pp. 25–6. Horace G. Alexander, *The Revival of Europe. Can the League of Nations Help?* London: Allen and Unwin, 1924, p. 168.

[36] For the text of the treaty, see
http://www.macalester.edu/courses/intl245/docs/treaty_poland.pdf (consulted 13 October 2013). Articles 8 to 11 discuss the rights of the Jewish community in particular.

[37] *Ten Years of World Co-operation. Secretariat of the League of Nations.* 1930, p. 357.

[38] For a brief summary of these issues, see M. Housden, *The League of Nations and the Organisation of Peace.* London: Longman, 2012, chapter 3. Also F. Kellor, *Security against War. Volume 1.* New York: Macmillan, 1924.

[39] Robinson, Karbach, Laseron, Robinson and Vichniak., *Were the Minorities Treaties a Failure?* p. v.

Nations spent on minority issues. Before 1923, they accounted for about 15% of the time of the Council of the League.[40] Unfortunately the system it was administering has also been described as 'very confused and cautious', and indeed was soon being assessed a failure.[41] Leading members of minority organisations soon began criticising the League's work, for example describing minority rights as a kind of charitable donation made to impoverished second-class citizens or to people who were not really part of the state.[42]

Certainly the League's minority protection system was always imperfect. Generally, the Great Powers—but many other states too—were reluctant to encourage national minorities either to claim autonomy or to engage directly with the League of Nations.[43] In a memorandum from 1919 discussing how minorities might raise concerns with the League, Foreign Office analyst Headlam-Morley said it would be dangerous for them to do this direct, i.e. without their communications being mediated by their representative government.[44] Since the League of Nations was a composite of states, it became rare for national minorities to enter its élite setting in person. Probably the only members of national minorities who enjoyed face to face discussions with the Council were two ethnic Swedes from the Åland islands, at the time when the territory was disputed by Finland and Sweden.[45] The framers of the League had been determined to tread carefully over the relationship between minorities and that organisation. They knew an appeal to an authority 'superior' to the state in which minorities lived could be taken as subversion, so making delicate political relationships more difficult than ever. Alternatively, an international legal confrontation could be sparked between a minority and a government, maybe involving the Permanent Court at The Hague.  Such a possibility would reduce the readiness of states to commit themselves to wider League activities and values.[46]

So the interest of the Great Powers to implement the rights of national minorities had limits. As League of Nations official R.N. Kershaw put it, the minorities were not being offered 'the moon'.[47] Most importantly, the Great Powers never inaugurated a global system of minority rights, in fact, not even an all-European one. The aim was not to create a general international law of the rights of national minorities, only to address the

---

[40] X-M. Núñez Seixas, *Entre Ginebra y Berlin. La Cuestion de las Minorias Nacionales y la Politica Internacional en Europa 1914-1939*. Madrid: Akal, 2001, p. 521.

[41] Ibid. p. 520.

[42] W. Hasselblatt, 'Neuzeitliche nationalpolitische Problem', *Baltische Monatsschrift* (1927), pp. 472–6.

[43] Schot, *Nation oder Staat?* p. 6.

[44] Núñez Seixas, *Entre Ginebra y Berlin.*, p. 509.

[45] M. Housden, *The League of Nations and the Organisation of Peace*. Harlow: Longman, 2012, chapter 3.

[46] *10 Years of World Co-operation*, p. 367.

[47] R.N. Kershaw, 'The League and the Protection of Linguistic, Racial and Religious Minorities' in *Problems of Peace. Third Series*. OUP, 1929, p. 157.

specific minority problems of countries which were affected by the peace settlement's application of self-determination.[48] Consequently minority protection did not grow up as a universal principle, but on the basis of bilateral agreements existing between first the Allied Powers, later the League of Nations, and the new and enlarged states of Central and Eastern Europe. So although the Assembly of the League of Nations passed a resolution in 1922 proposing that *all* states should treat national minorities in line with the minority agreements of the period, this had more the status of advice than binding legislation. A situation in which just 15 of the League's 55 member states were obliged to undertake minority protection formally was not favoured by Europe's minority leaders of the time,[49] but neither was it popular with statesmen of the countries concerned. They disliked having their sovereignty eroded, often disliked being treated differently to longer-established states and felt they were being patronised, since it appeared they needed to be taught 'the rules of civilized behaviour'.[50]

The very nature of the League of Nations was against it achieving the rights of national minorities in full measure. If it pushed an unpopular line too vigorously, member states could simply leave; and the more that would be motivated to leave, the more irrelevant the League would become. Correspondingly, Sir Eric Drummond, the first Secretary General of the League of Nations, maintained that declarations of minority rights could not be imposed on states and that it would always be vital for minorities to work co-operatively with their governments.[51] As a result, much work in the field of minority rights had to be achieved through informal means and attempted moral pressure rather than straightforward élite decision-making.

This also helps explain why politicians such as Guiseppe Motta and Austen Chamberlain stressed minorities should be loyal to the states in which they lived.[52] It wasn't just a matter of refraining from obviously treasonable acts. If milder acts by minorities provoked hostile responses from majority populations, being realistic there would be a limit to the extent to which the League could intervene to improve a situation. At the end of the day, in the inter-war world, minority rights would only be attained in line with the levels of desire existing among governments and the peoples they represented. Paul Schiemann's comment that the League was more interested in relations between states rather than within them perhaps was over-simplified, but in respect of nationality affairs, it held some truth.[53]

---

[48] I.L. Claude, *National Minorities. An International Problem*. New York: Greenwood, 1955, pp. 16–7 and Jackson Preece, p. 92.

[49] J. Hiden, *Defender of Minorities. Paul Schiemann, 1876–1944*. London: Hurst, p. 118–9.

[50] Z. Steiner, *Lights that Failed. European International History 1919–1933*. OUP, 2005, p. 362.

[51] 27.1.1922, Drummond to Rosting. R 1656. Minority Questions. Protection of Minorities in the Baltic States. 41 / 18723 / 10503.

[52] Robinson, Karbach, Laseron, Robinson and Vichniak., *Were the Minorities Treaties a Failure?* p. 99.

[53] Hiden, *Defender of Minorities*, p.119.

## 5. The growth of the League's minority protection system

The implementation of minority protection was always going to owe more to the work of the League of Nations than the minorities themselves.[54] The Council took up the duty in February 1920 as very much 'work in progress', and so it remained for the life of the organisation. It involved a steep learning curve and the formal systems employed were updated in 1921, 1923, 1925 and 1930. Nothing like it had been tried before on such a scale and the officials heading the relevant office were always allowed considerable scope to respond to the challenges at issue as they saw best.

A Minorities Section was established within the League's Secretariat which was managed initially by Norwegian diplomat Erik Colban (1876–1956). Its purpose was to gather information, discuss it with governments and minorities, and support the Council over minority affairs. A system of petition lay at the heart of the League's mechanism. A protected group could submit a petition of complaint to the Council which forwarded it to the Minorities Section to make sure it could be received (i.e. it was not couched in violent terms or was anonymous—and roughly half were found to be receivable). Thereafter the petition was returned to the Council and was forwarded to the government concerned for comment. If the document was found to contain substantive issues, an investigative 'Committee of Three' was convened, i.e. the President of the Council plus two other members. In keeping with the awareness that League member states were most sensitive to any interference in their sovereign affairs, the Committee of Three worked quietly. It sat in private, did not keep minutes and many of its findings were not publicised—generally not even being passed to the original petitioners. Committees of Three were kept busy throughout the 1920s especially, with over 350 petitions being lodged by protected minorities.[55] Although some minority spokesmen would have liked their complaints to have been dealt with as a matter of law, only very occasionally were cases referred to the Permanent Court of International Justice.

Negotiations between the League and the states accused of mistreating minorities often happened off-the-record and were carried out by Colban or his team. Over time, the Norwegian devised his own practical ways of dealing with frequently-cited states such as Poland and Romania, often visiting the regions affected to hold discussions, sometimes with local administrators accused of malpractice.[56] This way of working led to uneven outcomes, and while countries such as Greece and Romania were encouraged

---

[54] W. Hasselblatt, 'Neuzeitliche nationalpolitische Problem', *Baltische Monatsschrift* (1927).
[55] M. Scheuermann, *Minderheitenschutz contra Konfliktverhütung? Die Minderheitenpolitik des Völkerbundes in den zwanziger Jahren.* Marburg/Lahn: Verlag Herder Institut, 2000; *10 Years of World Co-operation*, p. 373.
[56] C. Fink, *Defending the Rights of Others. The Great Powers, the Jews, and International Minority Prrotection, 1878–1938.* CUP, 2004, p. 280.

to improve their record, others such as Poland and Czechoslovakia were not.[57] When states were unwilling to negotiate an issue, Colban had few sanctions he could recommend, not least because none of the original minority treaties and declarations specified what should happen if a state behaved poorly.[58]

## 6. The Baltic States, the League and the rights of minorities

Once, Aristide Briand declared the League of Nations could never be indifferent to 'the sacred cause' of minorities.[59] In line with this priority, on 15 December 1920 the first Assembly adopted a resolution stating that when Albania, the Caucasian States and the Baltic States applied for membership, they should agree minority protection provisions similar to those already in force for Poland.[60] Focussing on the Baltic States, on 12 May 1922 Lithuania was the first to make a declaration to the Council. It repeated the principles of the Polish treaty and recognised that such protection was a matter of 'international concern'.[61] The other two Baltic States moved much more slowly. Eventually, for Latvia, Mr Walters made a comparable declaration on 7 July 1923 and an Estonian one followed on 17 September. Given that Estonia originally had requested membership of the League in April 1920, obviously the process of undertaking an international commitment to protect minorities could turn out to be complicated.[62]

All the Baltic States had declared willingness to negotiate over minority protection in September 1921, when the Assembly admitted them to the League, but thereafter Latvia and especially Estonia dragged their feet.[63] Kaarel Pusta, a leading Estonian diplomat, maintained there was no need for any international guarantee for minorities and that the Council should simply note Estonia's relevant legislation. Anything else would infringe the state's sovereignty.[64] He argued strenuously that Estonia would have to hold a referendum before the government could enter into an internationally-binding guarantee such as this. He said there was no generally-recognised minority treaty which Estonia should adopt, nor any universal public or international

---

[57] Ibid, p. 281. Steiner, *The Lights that Failed*, p. 364.

[58] Fink, *Defending the Rights of Others*, p. 273.

[59] *10 Years of World Co-operation*, p. 378.

[60] Robinson, Karbach, Laseron, Robinson and Vichniak., *Were the Minorities Treaties a Failure?* pp.165–6.

[61] Hiden, *Defender of Minorities*, p. 118.

[62] Estonian Legation to Assembly of LON, 19.4.1920. S 342. Minorities. LoN Archive.

[63] Annex 289. Protection des Minorités en Esthonie, Lettonie et Lithuanie. Rapport présenté par M. Gastao da Cunha, 16th Session of the Council. *League of Nations. Official Journal*. 3rd Year. No. 2. February 1922. p. 123

[64] Report by M. da Cunha. Adopted by Council 14.1.1922. R 1664. Protection of Minorities in Estonia. 41 / 18460 / 15754. Eleventh Meeting (Private) held at Geneva, 20 Sept 1922, 5 pm. Twentieth Session of the Council. *League of Nations. Official Journal*. 3rd Year. No. 11 (Part II). November 1922, pp. 1197–99

law which could bind the state in this connection. Since Finland had never made a declaration on minority rights, Pusta held the Estonian state should not do so either—the fact that it had won its own independence militated against the need. The Estonian diplomat noted that the League's Assembly decision of 15 December 1920 had been a recommendation not an obligation and added that any possible minority declaration should only address problems that might arise if Estonia were to change its constitution. He also noted that Estonia had so few minority citizens that how it dealt with their rights bore little relationship to anything that was going on in other states.[65] Pusta also rejected the possibility of the League interference in Estonia's internal affairs and feared that enhanced rights for minorities might lead to German interference too, especially once Germany became a member of the League.[66]

The League's rapporteur, Brazilian diplomat Domicio da Gama, found Pusta's position unacceptable because, although Estonia's constitution was liberal at the time, that might change in the future.[67] He also recognised there might be a difference between what a constitution said and how it was implemented.[68] Helmer Rosting, a Danish official in the Minorities Section, believed also that, if Estonia looked likely to evade a declaration on minority rights, the possibility might encourage Lithuania and Latvia to try to do likewise.[69] Such a situation would present a serious challenge to minority protection as such. So the League had to confront Estonia and only after a protracted period of wrangling, Latvia's declaration and the personal intervention of Robert Cecil, was a declaration finally made offering Estonia's minorities international guarantees.[70] Estonia's reluctance to take this step undermined the good impression the liberal constitution had made on senior members of the League, including Eric Drummond.[71]

---

[65] Annex 404.a. Letter is dated Paris, 9.8.1922. Minorities in Estonia. Letter from M.Pusta to M. da Gama, submitted to the Council on September 1st, 1922, Annex 404a. Twentieth Session of the Council. *League of Nations. Official Journal.* 3 rd Year. No. 11 (Part II). November 1922, p. 1236. 23 rd Session of the Council. *League of Nations. Official Journal.* 4th Year. No. 3. March 1923. p. 233-4. 13th Meeting (private) of 21st Session of the Council. 20.9.1922. R 1664. Protection of Minorities in Estonia. 41 / 23587 / 15754. Memoranda, Colban 22.1.23 and EC 5.2.23. R 1664. Protection of Minorities in Estonia. 41 / 26094 / 15754. Detailed report of the position of the Est gvmt on the issue, 28.8.23. R 1664. Protection of Minorities in Estonia. 41 / 30475 / 15754

[66] EC 5.2.23. R 1664. Protection of Minorities in Estonia. 41 / 26094 / 15754.

[67] Annex 470. Protection of Minorities in Esthonia. Report by M. da Gama submitted to the Council on February 2nd, 1923. C. 127.1923. I, 23rd Session of the Council. *League of Nations. Official Journal.* 4th Year. No. 3. March 1923. pp. 379-82.

[68] Colban 22.1.23. R 1664. Protection of Minorities in Estonia. 41 / 26094 / 15754.

[69] Rosting memorandum, 7.2.23. R 1664. Protection of Minorities in Estonia. 41 / 26094 / 15754

[70] Section 1021. Minorities in Estonia. Second Meeting (Public). 31 August 1923, *League of Nations. Official Journal.* 4th Year. No. 11. November 1923. p. 1269. Section 1059. Minorities in Estonia. 17 September, League of Nations. Official Journal. 4th Year. No. 11. November 1923. pp. 1310–2.

[71] EC 5.2.23. R 1664. Protection of Minorities in Estonia. 41 / 26094 / 15754.

## 7. Ammende's interest in the League

Ewald Ammende's enterprise made it inevitable that he would interact extensively with the League. Sure enough, at the same time as he was promoting cultural autonomy within Estonia, and hand in hand with his interest in the Association of German Minorities in Europe, he tried to promote the rights of national minorities with the League. He came into contact with Helmer Rosting even before the League existed officially, since they met in Russia in 1919 while Ammende was making a trip concerning food shortages. Through Rosting, in 1922 Ammende met other League officials, apparently making a reasonable impression. At the same time, Ammende travelled around Europe cultivating contacts interested in minority affairs, including members of Germany's League of Nations Union.[72]

At a time when Secretary General Drummond was maintaining that minority rights could not be imposed on states but had to be negotiated and that minorities should feed their views into the process through contact with their state government, Ammende corresponded with League officials in order to influence the achievement of minority rights in the Baltic States more directly.[73] In January 1922 he wrote to Rosting asking for information about a recent decision of the Council concerning the protection of national minorities in the Baltic States.[74] Rosting replied that the states would provide appropriate declarations in due course.[75] Subsequently Ammende emphasised that very little information was leaking out about the processes under way and that the Baltic governments were trying to hush up negotiations with the League, indeed the whole matter of minority rights. He suggested the states were obscuring the issues by the use of old-fashioned secret diplomacy.[76] Ammende said Pusta would only make a declaration about the actual state of minority rights in Estonia and would not accept any international guarantee of the same. He added that minorities in Estonia believed an international guarantee was necessary to ensure they would not be affected by any adverse political changes in the future, also that it was necessary for minorities to be able to appeal to the international court at The Hague when there was no agreement between minority and majority populations.[77]

---

[72] Schot, *Deutschland und der Minderheitenschutz*, pp. 103–4. At this point Germany was not yet a member of the League, but nonetheless it had a League of Nations Union organisation.

[73] 27.1.22, Drummond to Rosting. R 1656. Minority Questions. Protection of Minorities in the Baltic States. 41 / 18723 / 10503.

[74] 20.1.22, Ammende to Rosting. R 1656. Minority Questions. Protection of Minorities in the Baltic States. 41 / 18723 / 10503.

[75] 26.1.22, Rosting to Ammende. R 1656. Minority Questions. Protection of Minorities in the Baltic States. 41 / 18723 / 10503.

[76] 1.2.22, letter from Ammende. R 1656. Minority Questions. Protection of Minorities in the Baltic States. 41 / 18723 / 10503. Commitment to openness in international relations was reflected in the first of Wilson's 14 points and point 18 of the Covenant.

[77] 25.2.22 Ammende to Rosting. R 1656. Minority Questions. Protection of Minorities in the

While Ammende was lobbying the League, he began using *Revaler Bote* to publicise minority rights. On 6 February 1922 the paper carried an interview in which Pusta stated international protection was unnecessary, that the League only needed a report about the domestic condition of minorities and that the existing constitution provided all the guarantees necessary. A copy of the article was conveyed to the League's offices, presumably by Ammende, as was a follow up piece.[78] On 16 February, Ammende highlighted that Estonia had to submit a report to the League about her minorities and recommended that these groups be part of the process, working with 'loyalty and stateliness'. He added that, in the case of a dispute, minorities should be able to appeal to the international court, and that small states should have a particular interest in guaranteeing the rights of minorities so that, in the event of a conflict with a larger neighbour, they would enjoy the sympathy of the world.[79]

At this time, Ammende was optimistic about the League and minority protection. In a memorandum from January 1922, he described the Brazilian diplomat then dealing with the Latvian and Estonian declarations (Gastoa da Cunha) as objective and decent, the latter quality said to be shared by Rosting. He concluded:

> The attitude of the League's Secretariat towards the question of minority protection must consequently be described as generally favourable to us.

Ammende understood that the League epitomised a new mood of international politics which enabled ethnic German leaders to meet without being regarded automatically as a threat. He wondered whether connections between Estonian, Latvian and Lithuanian Germans might become permanent so they could pursue their common interests as effectively as possible. True, such optimism was tempered. He recognised the League was imperfect, meeting too rarely and working too slowly. He also realised the Estonian government had been more active than the minorities in Geneva promoting its values. But still Ammende felt the very existence of the League brought the solution of global problems closer, including the protection of minorities. He welcomed that the League's system would necessitate the collection and dissemination of information about minorities from every corner of Europe. Consequently Ammende saw how world developments could assist the binding together of at least German minorities as a community of common interest and looked to the day that minorities would be represented

Baltic States. 41 / 18723 / 10503.
[78] 'Unser Gesandter in Paris. E.R. Pusta', *Revaler Bote* 6 February 1922. R 1656. Minority Questions. Protection of Minorities in the Baltic States. 41 / 18723 / 10503.
[79] E. Ammende, 'Zur Frage der Minderheitsrechte', *Revaler Bote* 16 February 1922. R 1656. Minority Questions. Protection of Minorities in the Baltic States. 41 / 18723 / 10503.

permanently at the League. He aspired to the start of a new cultural period: that of minority culture.[80]

Typically the Assembly of the League met in September and that month in 1922 Ammende published a lengthy article asking whether it could become 'a true association of nations' or would remain dominated by the Great Powers working through the Council.[81] At the same time, the paper reported on the Assembly's 6th Commission which dealt with minority affairs, including a speech by Gilbert Murray recognising the importance of loyalty on the part of minorities and justice on the part of the states in which they lived.[82]

Ammende's promotion of minority rights in particularly Estonia and Latvia continued into October 1922, when he published a discussion of resolutions concerning the protection of minorities during the meeting of the League's Assembly. Although he stressed that Walters (for Latvia) and Pusta (for Estonia) were trying to evade their responsibilities, Ammende's tone was positive. Gradually, he said, the League was moving towards recognition of universal minority rights, the demands of German minorities had been recognised and that minority protection was now one of the most important areas of the League's work. He quoted Swiss statesman Giueseppe Motta:

> ...Our effort to respect and love each other as colleagues
> and friends must be looked upon as a solemn goal worthy
> of respect, and Switzerland must be regarded as an example
> that is awe-inspiring and worthy of emulation everywhere
> different national groups coexist.[83]

Ammende's lobbying of the League could not be divorced from his involvement with the Association of German Minorities in Europe. Hence, in October 1922, he sent a copy of his founding memorandum for the Association to the League's Minorities Section.[84] The next month, he sent Rosting reports of the Association's recent meeting, emphasising that minorities wanted to pursue their principles in harmony with those of the

---

[80] Ewald Ammende, 30.1.22. Fond 1000, File 137. Riigiarhiiv, Madara branch. Tallinn. He followed this up with a further memorandum just a few days later: E. Ammende, 4 February 1922, 'Als Ergänzung zu meinem Memorandum von 30. Januar.' Fond 1000, File 137. Riigiarhiiv, Madara branch. Tallinn.

[81] E. Ammende, 'Kann die Genfer Völkerbundsversammlung zu einem Wahren Völkerbund werden', Revaler Bote 13 September 1922

[82] No author, 'Die Minoritätenfrage in der 6. Kommission des Völkerbundes', Revaler Bote 16 September 1922. Also 'Die Minoritätenfrage in der 6. Kommission des Völkerbundes', Revaler Bote 22 September 1922.

[83] E. Ammende, 'Beschlüsse über den Minoritätenschutz der dritten Völkerbundversammlung', Revaler Bote 7 October 1922. A mimeographed report of the Assembly written by Ammende is available as 'Die Ereignisse der dritten Völkerbundstagung', 1502–7–52. Moscow.

[84] Memo about desirability of a conference of representatives from all German minorities in Europe from Mr. Ammende, Riga. R 1684. Minority Questions. 41 / 24379 / 24379.

League, that they regarded the League as their protector, that they had no truck with irredentism, and that eventually national minorities should be recognised in their own right as subjects of international law.[85] Correspondingly he noted the meeting's feeling that, in order to remove minority issues from the field of Great Power politics, complaints should be dealt with by the Permanent Court at The Hague. More precisely, it was felt the Germans of South Tyrol should be guaranteed their rights and that disruption of the German minority education systems around Europe should stop immediately.

Ammende also proffered information about the state of German minorities in Europe (those in Romania were said to be in a favourable position, those in Hungary were said to live under conditions of terror, while in Estonia he assumed the situation facing minorities would change—presumably for the worse—once the minority declaration was made). He said that even though the German Foreign Ministry was unhappy about the initiative, he would hold a meeting of German minorities from around Europe (i.e. the Association) in spring of 1923. Berlin would not interfere with this and it would be based on the framework of the minority treaties.[86]

The Baltic German was presenting himself as someone committed to the League's principles and as a perfect collaborator. A meeting with Colban followed in which Ammende described the relationship between the Association of German Minorities in Europe and the German government as follows:

> It was in no way the intention of the Association to obtain
> favours from the German Government, or to act under any
> direction from that quarter. On the contrary, it was felt that
> the German Government could not possibly take the same
> long views with regard to the future position of the
> minorities as these populations had to take themselves, and
> it would be to the detriment of these minorities to cast in
> their lot with that of the German Reich.[87]

In other words, German minorities would not act as a cat's-paw for Berlin, would not be a tool for interference in the affairs of other states and would not be party to Pan-Germanism. Ammende's watchword was 'responsibility'.

---

[85] 12.11.22, Ammende to Rosting and 22.11.22, Ammende to Rosting. Conference of Representatives of German Minorities in Europe. R 1684. Minority Questions. R 41 / 24824 / 24379.

[86] Note by Rosting, 30.11.22. Conference of Representatives of German Minorities in Europe. (Ewald Ammende to Mr. Rosting). R 1684. Minority Questions. R 41 / 24824 / 24379.

[87] Note by Colban, 1.12.22. Conference of Representatives of German Minorities in Europe. (Ewald Ammende to Mr. Rosting). R 1684. Minority Questions. R 41 / 24824 / 24379.

It is unlikely that he impressed the League's officials a great deal. Colban's rather smug comments about the meeting suggest it was one-way traffic:

> I thanked Monsieur Ammende for his kindness in coming to see me, but I did not express any opinion as to the matter he put before me. He spoke for perhaps half-an-hour, and I don't think I said more than a very few words.

When Eric Drummond heard about the Association of German Minorities in Europe, he recognised some good in the initiative—up to a point anyway:

> Personally I doubt the formation of a central association is wise. It is certain to cause suspicion in the various states. However it is not our business to express an opinion on the subject, the association seems animated by excellent intentions.[88]

Drummond feared Ammende's good intentions would not yield fruit.

Nonetheless, it is possible that Ammende's lobbying had some impact. In January 1923 he contacted Rosting again expressing concern that Pusta and Walters did not want to place minority rights under international guarantee and saying this was causing unrest among minorities. Soon afterwards, Colban wrote to Secretary General Eric Drummond stating that unless Estonia made a declaration, nothing could be expected of Latvia or Lithuania, and perhaps there might even be consequences for Turkey's attitude to minority protection at the on-going Lausanne Conference.[89]

During this period, the minutes of the meetings of the Association of German Minorities in Europe show signs of hope in the League. When the group met in Vienna between 29 June and 2 July 1923 the tone, however, was relatively conservative given the effort Ammende had expended agitating with the organisation. So while the ethnic Germans present decided it was too soon either to open an office in Geneva or to enter into a union with non-German national minorities, it's quite possible that Ammende's mind already was on a different track. When the group recognised it would be helpful to have a contact inside the League and that all German minorities should set up groups belonging to the League of Nations Union, it was confirming what Ammende knew already.[90]

---

[88] Handwritten note by Eric Drummond, 5.1.23. Conference of Representatives of German Minorities in Europe. (Ewald Ammende to Mr. Rosting). R 1684. Minority Questions. R 41 / 24824 / 24379.

[89] 10.1.(23), Ammende to Rosting. 22.1.23, Colban (EC) to the Secretary General. S 342. Minorities.

[90] 'Tagung der Vertreter der Deutschen Minderheiten von 29 Juni - 2 Juli 1923 in Wien'. Fond 1000, File 142. Riigiarhiiv, Madara branch. Tallinn. This meeting was also covered in a

*Revaler Bote* kept up its focus on the affairs of German minorities across the summer of 1923. Ammende commented on the electoral successes of ethnic Germans in Yugoslavia and provoked a Hungarian minority commentator (Elmer Viranyi) whom he accused of under-estimating the extent of national consciousness among ethnic Germans in Hungary.[91] Yet the issue of Estonia's minority declaration was never far away. In April, Axel de Vries wrote about its enduring non-appearance. In July, reports followed about Latvia's declaration to the Council.[92] In September, finally articles appeared about Estonia's declaration, with information provided from Geneva by Ewald Ammende.[93] One article described the event as 'a happy solution', while another translated a section from the Estonian-language paper *Vaba Maa* noting that it was now clear that the fates of majority and minority populations had become intimately linked.[94]

In the early 1920s, Ewald Ammende had great hopes for the League of Nations. He was enthusiastic to work with it and believed benefits would follow. For him, to ignore the League was to swim against the tide and when the organisation showed imperfections, the point was to improve things.[95] Moreover, at an early point Ammende showed awareness of the benefits of approaching the League in multi-track fashion: he was aware of the value of lobbying officials within the organisation personally, but also of uniting German groups—and possibly other minorities too—in order to exert additional pressure. Perhaps already he had the idea of assembling a still more substantial weight of international minority opinion to influence the League. At this time, Ammende was prepared to be both an idealist (valuing the principles the League stood for), a *Realpolitiker* (attempting to wield practical power to influence that organisation) and a very active publicist harnessing the press in an attempt to achieve his ends.

---

newspaper article: 'Die Minoritätenrechte auf der Vollversammlung der Völkerbundligien in Wien in Juni 1923', *Revaler Bote* 13 July 1923

[91] E. Ammende, 'Der Deutsche Wahlsieg in Jugoslawien', *Revaler Bote* 24 April 1923. For Ammende's argument with Viranyi, see 'Die Minderheitenfrage in Ungarn. Eine Antwort an Herrn Viranyi Elemer', *Revaler Bote* 4 May 1923. E. Viranyi, 'Ungarn und das Minoritätenproblem', *Revaler Bote* 19 May 1923. E. Ammende, 'Ungarn und seine deutsche Minderheit', *Revaler Bote* 25 June 1923. E. Ammende, 'Was die deutschen und ungarischen Minderheiten voneinander trennt', *Revaler Bote* 30 June 1923.

[92] A. de Vries, 'Wie steht es um die Minderheiten-Deklaration?', *Revaler Bote* 12 April 1923. 'Die Minoritätenrechte auf der Vollversammlung der Völkerbundligien in Wien in Juni 1923', *Revaler Bote* 13 July 1923. 'Lettlands Minoritäten-Deklaration', *Revaler Bote* 21 July 1923. A.H. [Arnold Hasselblatt?], 'Von der Tagung des Völkerbundrat', *Revaler Bote* 3 August 1923.

[93] 'Der Schutz der Minderheitenrechte in Estland', *Revaler Bote* 3 September 1923. 'Der volle Text der estländischen Minderheitendeklaration', *Revaler Bote* 4 September 1923.

[94] 'Die estländische Minderheitenschutz-Deklaration vom Völkerbundrat angenommen!', *Revaler Bote* 18 September 1923. A. de Vries, 'Eine glückliche Lösung', *Revaler Bote* 18 September 1923. 'Presse-Rundschau', *Revaler Bote* 25 September 1923.

[95] E.Ammende, 'Genfer Völkerbundchronik', *Revaler Bote* 8 September 1924

## 8. Interest maintained

Estonia's declaration to the League was not the end of a story, in some ways it was only a start, since it gave rise to fresh sets of questions. In October 1924, Ammende compared the positive attitude of Gilbert Murray (Oxford academic and representative to the League of South Africa) favouring the League's status quo over minority protection, with the critical one of Count Apponyi (Hungarian representative to the Assembly).[96] Apponyi argued that Europe's stability depended on minorities feeling secure; in turn, this required complaints to the League being dealt with quickly and with the Permanent Court being a clear ultimate arbiter. Contrasting the views of the two, Ammende concluded that critics of the Council could do good work for minorities and that the Council could not silence well-founded criticisms of its procedures. He felt Germany's membership of the organisation was needed and that the defeated states had to represent themselves vigorously. He added that one day the Council should be put under the leadership of the Assembly and the solution of the minority question would be advantageous to minorities and states alike. The points were all insightful and mark him out as a thoughtful and constructive early critic of the League.

It bears emphasis that, at this point, Ammende was prepared to stand up for the League and its staff. When a Hungarian paper criticised Erik Colban for promoting the interests of states over minorities, Ammende defended him as impartial. His only culpability was listening too closely to information provided by states, adding that the Council was learning it had to do more to win the trust of minorities.[97] Articles about the League of Nations kept flowing from Ammende's pen. He wrote about the League's commission to Klaipėda (Memel) and autonomy there.[98] He wrote about disarmament and lessons from the First World War.[99] By degrees, he was becoming thoroughly knowledgeable not just about Baltic and ethnic German affairs, but about League of Nations affairs in general.

But he returned to national minority issues repeatedly. In October 1924, *Revaler Bote* carried an article from its 'Geneva Reporter' arguing there could never be peace and disarmament until the minority question was solved. This was especially the case while the Soviet Union was making play of unsatisfied minority demands:

> It is certainly not just a chance that at a time when in the near European East many millions of minority people are complaining bitterly about their masters, the Soviet Union is pursuing ostentatiously a very refined minority policy. It

---

[96] E. Ammende, 'Genf und die Minderheitenschutz', *Revaler Bote* 2 October 1924.
[97] E. Ammende, 'Das Völkerbundssekretariat', *Revaler Bote* 27 October 1924.
[98] E. Ammende, 'Die Völkerbundkommission in Memel', *Revaler Bote* 21 February 1924.
[99] E. Ammende, 'Das Genfer Werk', *Revaler Bote* 1 November 1924.

organises its non-Russian elements in little national republics, of which Communist obedience is demanded, but [there is] no sacrifice in linguistic or racial rights. The Ukrainian, White Russian, Volga German and Armenian Soviet Republics are precisely propaganda institutes for the members of the national groups concerned, but to whom otherwise the most decisive minority rights are denied.[100]

Suggesting that Russia would provoke instability using Europe's minority issue given the chance, the article concluded that addressing the minority problem was necessary in order to avoid future wars.

*Revaler Bote* kept up a stream of articles about national minorities from across Europe. They discussed ethnic German schooling systems, calling for them to be truly autonomous.[101] They related speeches by Romanian politicians rejecting intolerance and irredentism, but praising mother-tongue language in education and public life.[102] They discussed the impossibility of irredentism among Vojvodina's German minority (since it was located so far away from Berlin) and the poor treatment of ethnic Germans in Yugoslavia by local officials and Serbs determined to steal their land.[103] Articles recognised that that Lithuania's Germans were doing well, while Germans living in Czechoslovakia still were not enjoying all the rights due to them. Regarding Poland, the *Sejm*'s minority politics was said to be disjointed and Communist agitators were capitalising on inter-ethnic unrest in the country's eastern border areas.[104] In other words, everything to do with national minority politics was of interest to *Revaler Bote* and its team of commentators, including Ewald Ammende.[105] The paper wanted to be at the centre of minority debates. Its staff saw themselves as lobbyists for minorities and as opinion leaders for ethnic Germans in particular.

---

[100] 'Die Minderheitenfrage in Genf', *Revaler Bote* 1 October 1924.
[101] 'Zur Frage des Schulwesens der völkischen Minderheiten', *Revaler Bote* 1 September 1923. 'Die Schulen der Minoritäten in Rumänien', *Revaler Bote* 24 July 1924. 'Die Gründung des Ungarländischen Deutschen Volksbildungsvereins', *Revaler Bote* 29 August 1924
[102] 'Innenpolitik und Minderheiten-Frage in Rumänien', Revaler Bote 28 May 1924. 'Der Kampf um die deutsche Schule in Großrumänien', *Revaler Bote* 1 July 1924.
[103] 'Südslawiens Deutsche in Sorge und Unglück', *Revaler Bote* 4 July 1924.
[104] 'Die Minoritäten in der Tschecho-Slowakei', *Revaler Bote* 7 July 1924. 'Die Minderheitenfrage in Polen', *Revaler Bote* 10 July 1924. P. Meyer, 'Das Deutschtum in Litauen', *Revaler Bote* 18 July 1924. 'Die östliche Irredenta in Polen', *Revaler Bote* 3 September 1924. M. Lozyusky, 'Abschaffung ukrainischer Gymnasien in Ostgalizien.', *Revaler Bote* 24 September 1925
[105] See also L.v.B., 'Die neuen Sprachengesetze für die völkischen Minderheiten in Polen', *Revaler Bote* 14 August 1924. 'Neuer Kurs in der südslawischen Minderheitspolitik?' *Revaler Bote* 31 August 1924. 'Das Minoritätenproblem in Polen', *Revaler Bote* 30 August 1924.

## 9. Taking the Baltic Germans seriously

Ammende was not the only Baltic German to lobby the League. In 1921, Baron Stackelberg did the same, requesting that a commission of enquiry be sent to the Baltic to investigate minority rights there.[106] There was also Baron Alfons Heyking, a lawyer who hailed from Estonia. He was associated with a petition of complaint presented to the League in 1926 by two other Baltic Germans, Baron Schilling and E. von Bodisco.[107] Some of Heyking's arguments mirrored those of Ammende. He proposed that German groups should set up associations belonging to the League of Nations Union and criticised the League as an organisation of states that misunderstood minorities.[108] He, too, met with personalities working in the Minorities Section, had his views conveyed to Colban and corresponded with the Brazilian rapporteur da Gama.[109] Unsurprisingly, Heyking was disliked by at least some Estonian politicians, with Tõnisson once calling him 'a charlatan who lobbied in the anti-chamber'; he also had a rift with Ammende.[110] On one occasion, Heyking visited Rosting to lobby against the Association of German Minorities in Europe, since (he said) the project risked being usurped by Pan-Germanism. He doubted that, say, Volga Germans and Saxons from Transylvania had much in common anyway. He added that if the Association set up an office in Vienna to promote the rights of national minorities (as Ammende did), it would be in competition with a similar office he planned to create in Geneva.[111]

Certainly there were rivalries and jealousies among minority activists in the 1920s. Not that it mattered to the League's staff. They treated Heyking with as much suspicion as they did Ammende. So when Heyking finally organised a minority office in Geneva, Colban emphasised his staff should only provide him with information already released to the press.[112]

---

[106] Note by Rosting, 9.2.21. R 1656. Minority Questions. Protection of Minorities in the Baltic States. 41 / 10503 / 10503.

[107] See for example, Baron A. Heyking, 'Der notwendige Ausbau der Minderheitsrechte', Revaler Bote 11 July 1924. See his pamphlets on land reform in S 342. Minorities. For the petition, see R 1664. Protection of Minorities in Estonia. 41 / 51576 / 15754. Also see the letter from Schilling to the Secretary General of 8.6.27, R 1666. Minorities in Estonia. R 41 / 59912 / 15754. For Schilling lobbying Colban on 11.2.27, see S 342. Minorities.

[108] Baron A. Heyking, 'Die Union der Völkerbungsligen und die Minderheiten', Revaler Bote 2 January 1925.

[109] Note by Rosting, 7.2.23 on meeting with Baron Heyking. R 1664. Protection of Minorities in Estonia. 41 / 26094 / 15754. Letters of 5 and 7 March 1923. R 1664. Protection of Minorities in Estonia. 41 / 26971 / 15754. 21.5.26, R.M.Kershaw to Colban. A petition submitted to the Council by the exprpriated landowners. R 1664. Protection of Minorities in Estonia. 41 / 51576 / 15754

[110] Rosting, 20.3.23. 'Discussion in the Estonian Parliament about Cultural Autonomy for Estonia's Minorities.' R 1664. Protection of Minorities in Estonia. 41 / 27181 / 15754.

[111] 5.6.23 memorandum by Rosting. R 1684. Minority Questions. 41 / 28737 / 24379.

[112] 11.11.23, handwritten note by Colban. R 1684. Minority Questions. 41 / 25145 / 25145.

For all the reticence the League's staff displayed towards Ammende, Heyking and their associates, still they helped keep minority rights in the Baltic firmly on the League's agenda. Even Robert Cecil wrote to Eric Drummond stating his conviction that the ethnic German landowning class was being treated badly in Estonia.[113] Later, Eric Drummond met Paul Schiemann in the Latvian parliament to discuss agrarian reform and citizenship laws.[114]

## 10. Outside the League: the German state

But just as ethnic Germans had to manage life in 'foreign' states in the wake of the First World War, so the German state had to manage minorities living within its borders, and German minority policies displayed a tension. The *Reich* was sympathetic to German minorities abroad and, in so far as possible within the peace settlement's restrictions, supported their quest for autonomous existences. On the other hand, Germany's regional governments (*Länder*) did not favour the autonomy of national minorities living on their territories. Hence despite his efforts to the contrary, Stresemann could not persuade Prussia to adopt a truly progressive policy towards Polish and Danish schooling there.[115]

As early as autumn 1922, the League of Nations was gathering information about German schools in Poland and Polish schools in Germany. Inside Germany, no school had Polish as its official language, about 1,000 children were being taught Polish inadequately, the Prussian government did not help fund such teaching, and more than 100,000 Polish children attending German schools received no instruction in their mother tongue at all.[116] By contrast, in Posen and Pomerania (formerly part of the German Empire but now in Poland) there were 1,253 German schools with 81,470 pupils. Elsewhere, Erik Colban observed that the Polish government was living up to her 'moral obligations' towards minorities better than her German counterpart.[117]

This difficult reality restricted the support the German state could offer German ethnic minorities and highlighted the limits to the coincidence of their interests. Ammende's personal papers included a memorandum about the Polish minority in Masuria (Prussia) apparently written by Johannes Schmidt-Wodder.[118] It suggested the Polish community should not be

---

[113] 3.3.21 Cecil to Drummond. R 1656. Minority Questions. Protection of Minorities in the Baltic States. 41 / 11459 / 10503.

[114] ED, Riga, 27.2.25. S 342. Minorities.

[115] Schot, *Nation oder Staat?* p. 137 and p. 156.

[116] German schools in Poland and Polish schools in Germany. R 1684. Minority Questions in Estonia. 41 / 23875 / 23875.

[117] R 1648. Minority Questions. German schools in Poland and Polish Schools in Germany. 1.10.1922. 41 / 23875 / 23875.

[118] 'Denkschrift zur Frage der Behandlung der Nationalitäten in Deutschland mit besonderer

oppressed, but the area should be opened to free competition between Polish and German language and culture. Local populations ought to run their own schools, even if this meant the creation of autonomous Polish-language institutions. Admittedly Schmidt-Wodder felt certain that German schools would win the day and that, with them no longer having to take account of Polish-language students, it would be possible to promote more effectively a 'healthy, powerful German national consciousness'.

Schmidt-Wodder, then, was calling for Germany to establish a Central and Eastern European variant of self-determination by implementing a system analogous to the cultural autonomy Ammende wanted for Estonia. Once that happened, German minorities would be able to seize the moral high-ground in all subsequent negotiations over mother tongue schooling.[119] Unfortunately, no government in Weimar Germany could fashion domestic policy simply according to the needs of German minorities abroad, although this did not prevent sustained interest in what was happening to ethnic Germans. Certainly Gustav Stresemann took notice of cultural autonomy and in October 1924 a circular was sent around German diplomats inquiring about likely responses to the implementation of cultural autonomy inside Germany. The answers suggested foreign governments favoured Germany introducing the policy, but did not want to introduce cultural autonomy themselves.

In January 1925 Stresemann penned his famous memorandum anticipating Germany's joining of the League and the possibility of promoting minority protection in that forum. In order to do this effectively, he said, Germany would need to offer the same rights to the minorities within its own borders as it was demanding for ethnic Germans. Despite everything, therefore, by implication once again Stresemann was raising the possibility of a German state minority policy based on cultural autonomy.[120] Nonetheless, the Prussian *Land* remained resolutely opposed and so cultural autonomy was never introduced within the German state.

## 11. Conclusion

Minority issues were an international minefield and vitally important to the stability of Central and Eastern Europe. As such, they had to be of tremendous interest to the League of Nations. In a letter to da Gama dated 1922, Colban argued that small states such as Latvia and Estonia ought to support the rights of minorities for reasons of both principle and self-interest:

---

Rücksicht der Rückwirkung auf das bodenständige europäische Auslandsdeutschum' 28 October 1924. 1502–1–110. For the attribution, see S. Bamberger-Stemmann, p.163, fn. 96.
[119] 'Denkschrift zur Frage der Behandlung der Nationalitäten in Deutschland mit besonderer Rücksicht der Rückwirkung auf das bodenständige europäische Auslandsdeutschum' 28 October 1924. 1502–1–110. Schot, *Nation oder Staat?* p.120.
[120] Schot, *Nation oder Staat?* pp. 144–7.

> ... it should be remembered that it is to the great advantage
> of these small and newly created States that minorities
> protection should be the business of the League of Nations,
> as thereby the Governments of these countries will be able
> to repel any attempt on the part of any neighbouring
> country or any great power, to constitute itself protector of
> the minorities. It is obviously a better position for these
> countries to have minorities protection by the League of
> Nations than to risk constant quarrels with their neighbours
> on the subject of the conditions laid down for the minorities
> who may interest these neighbouring countries in
> particular.[121]

Protection of minorities implied protection of small states; but whether this
was recognised generally—even by small states themselves— was another
matter. In this respect, whenever the League received a set-back over the
cause of minority protection, the interests of small states were damaged
too.[122] It was indeed unfortunate, therefore, that a country such as Estonia
struggled so hard to avoid agreeing its international commitments.

And did the majority of statesmen in the 1920s know how to address
minority issues? Probably not. The lack of understanding was reflected even
in comments by figures in the League stating their expectation that minorities
eventually assimilate with majority populations. In December 1926, Brazilian
representative to the League, Afranio de Mello Franco told the Council that
minorities should 'enjoy a status of legal protection which might ensure
respect for the inviolability of the person under all its aspects and which
might gradually prepare the way for conditions necessary for the
establishment of a complete national unity.' In similar vein, British Foreign
Minister Austen Chamberlain said the aim of minority protection was 'to
secure for the minorities that measure of protection and justice which would
gradually prepare them to be merged in the national community to which
they belong.'[123] Other European statesmen, such as Greek Foreign Minister
Politis, concurred.[124] The comments were completely out of sympathy with
the aspirations of the minorities discussed in this chapter and shed additional
light on the inability of Ammende to receive a favourable hearing from the
staff of the Minorities Section.

Nevertheless, despite all setbacks, Ammende and like minds kept
publicising the cause of minorities. Certainly this involved bemoaning the

---

[121] 10.4.22, Colban to da Gama, S 342. Minorities.

[122] Robinson, Karbach, Laseron, Robinson and Vichniak., *Were the Minorities Treaties a Failure?* p. 260.

[123] Ibid, p. 150.

[124] His comments to a Council meeting of 5 June 1928 are cited in *Sitzungsbericht des Kongresses der organisierten nationalen Gruppen in den Staaten Europas. Genf 29.–31. August 1928*. Vienna: Wilhelm Braumüller, 1928, p.52.

loss of personal prestige and wealth, but still it had to involve important issues of principle. Ammende was highlighting how a whole category of people was being overlooked in the international affairs of the day. As he put it in an undated memorandum, minorities had to inform the League about their position on rights or else there would be no prospect of a non-partisan treatment of the subject.[125]

---

[125] E. Ammende, 4 February 1922, 'Als Ergänzung zu meinem Memorandum von 30. Januar.' Fond 1000, File 137. Riigiarhiiv, Madara branch. Tallinn.

## Chapter Six

## Establishing the European Congress of Nationalities

### 1. New challenge

Cultural autonomy had been achieved inside Estonia, the Association of German Minorities in Europe had been established for the benefit of ethnic Germans and Ammende was busy lobbying the League of Nations: now it was time for him to pull all of these initiatives together and create something major.

In 1925, Ewald Ammende played a formative role establishing the European Congress of Nationalities. The initiative was not without context. That same year moves were made to establish a World League of Minorities in Copenhagen. Previously, in 1916–17, Juosas Gabrys had organised minority congresses for the League of Russia's Foreign Peoples (*Liga der Fremdvölker Rußlands*), which had offices in Berlin.[1] But Ammende's undertaking took strength from Europe's atmosphere in 1925; it was the year of Locarno. At a time of optimism, the congress was supposed to help stabilise the continent further and routinise peace.[2]

Ammende's achievement should not be under-estimated. The minority movement was a camp riven with disputes and the more this is understood, the more significant the project appears. He was 'the organisational motor', to quote Max Hildebert Boehm, 'the essentially unifying and at the same time directive force' behind the congress. This is not to deny, of course that others played important parts. Paul Schiemann was Ammende's intellectual superior and was vitally important when it came to lobbying Berlin's Foreign Ministry;[3] but without Ammende, nothing would have happened—certainly not in 1925.

Ammende's activism was all the more impressive because already his health was failing. In March that year, a friend recommended he should give up alcohol completely.[4] Yet Ammende still engaged with one challenging initiative after another. With cultural autonomy achieved in Estonia, he set off on a trip through Lithuania, Latvia, Poland, Romania, Yugoslavia, Hungary and Czechoslovakia to contact personalities who might participate in the new venture.[5]

---

[1] S. Bamberger-Stemmann, *Der Europäische Nationalitätenkongreß 1925 bis 1938. Nationale Minderheiten zwischen Lobbyistentum und Grossmachtinteressen*. Marburg: Verlag Herder-Institut, 2000, pp. 76–7. J. Hiden, *Defender of Minorities. Paul Schiemann, 1876–1944*. London: Hurst, pp. 114–5.

[2] Bamberger-Stemmann, *Der Europäische Nationalitätenkongreß 1925 bis 1938*, p. 79.

[3] Hiden, *Defender of Minorities*, p. 115.

[4] 22.3.25, Popoff to Ammende. 1502–1–90, Moscow.

[5] 20.5.1925, Ammende to Lumby. 1502–7–19, Moscow.

## 2. Visionary memoranda

Ammende produced a series of memoranda designed to persuade influential individuals about the new project. 'How can peace and prosperity be secured for Europe through international co-operation?' was written with an eye particularly—although not solely—on the German Foreign Ministry. It argued that, with economic problems no longer critical, Europe should heal itself.[6] He argued that 'opinions, attitudes and psychological dispositions of the European nations' were the real problems facing the continent. He said nationalism was more of a challenge than economics, since it drew strength from the heritage of war. Equally, with millions of co-nationals left on the wrong side of existing borders, calls were being made for the freeing of oppressed peoples—calls which could only be answered by either territorial or non-territorial autonomy. Hence Ammende called for Great Power recognition of Estonia's cultural autonomy law and for Germany to provide something similar for its Danes and Poles. He proposed that the now disarmed country should take up the struggle for the rights of all oppressed peoples of the world. Such a role would facilitate Germany's entry into the League and strengthen her case for membership of the Council.

Ammende also recognised the enduring importance of border disputes. To deal with these, he recommended establishing a court of arbitration. This would offer benefit to German, Hungarian, Macedonian and Russian minorities, albeit at the cost of states giving up some elements of their sovereignty. For such a system to be effective, however, he felt the League of Nations should become more of a European venture than a global one. The peace settlement had resulted in the continent's political system becoming 'Balkanised'. To counter-act this, he recommended the League's Council comprise entirely European members—including both Russia and Germany, neither of which were members in 1925—and that there should be a solely European assembly too. In effect, he was proposing the League of Nations transform itself into a kind of European Union.

Ammende dashed across Europe's issues of the day. He wanted an international court to revise the provisions governing the Polish Corridor and Gdańsk (Danzig). He felt the League should assess whether Germany really was to blame for the start of the First World War and whether the Central Powers alone had committed war crimes. One-sided disarmament had to be re-visited. He outlined visionary steps to promote reconciliation in Europe. International high schools could help integrate different national groups. The press should experience more international organisation and there could be more international discussion of labour affairs. He wanted German minorities to become 'mediators and peace-promoters between the individual

---

[6] Letter to Herr Volkssekretär, 1502–7–19, Moscow.

nationalities'. He recommended that academics draw up a balance sheet of the damage done during the First World War.

Perhaps the memorandum displayed Ammende's greatest weakness—but arguably a strength too—his naivety. He was looking at international affairs as if they were a *tabula rasa* in which anything was possible. He wanted to re-build as much as possible afresh, with national minorities playing an integral role in the maintenance of peace. But his ideas would have called for a wholesale review of the post-war settlement.

A more important memorandum from the period following the achievement of cultural autonomy in Estonia was 'Principles, outlines and programme for a conference of the representatives of all national minorities in Europe'. This laid the foundations for the European Congress of Nationalities and was distributed to influential offices, such as the Minorities Section of the League.[7] It grew out of the talks Ammende held with the minority leaders from across Central and Eastern Europe in 1925.

The memorandum said that cultural autonomy in Estonia had provided a new set of goals for representatives of the national minorities of Europe. It added that, since the League's Secretariat was being pressured by majority nationality groups, the minorities required a special organisation to convey their particular views. Conditions for minorities were said to be deteriorating on a daily basis in states such as Italy and Spain, and since the League could not agree on the universal application of minority rights, a congress of European nationalities had to be convened quickly.

The memorandum outlined a possible congress programme. It repeated an extensive appreciation of Switzerland as a model for how multiple nationality groups could coexist peacefully. It proposed considering important aspects of the League's work, and perhaps holding a vote of confidence in the organisation. It would discuss the universalisation of minority rights, the possibility of group rights, a legal congress dealing with minority issues, the work of the League's Secretariat and the function of the minority treaties. The congress also would be interested in connections between different minority groups and the nationality question in the Soviet Union.

From the outset, Ammende conceptualised a European Congress of Nationalities as a pressure group acting on the League, he also understood that setting up such a body would be far from easy; hence the memorandum contained a section 'Difficulties'. He recognised that different minorities had different goals (e.g. border revision versus cultural autonomy) and felt a common platform would have to be created ahead of public meetings to

---

[7] For a copy of the document, see 'Gründe, Richtlinien und Program für eine Tagung der Vertreter aller nationaler Minderheiten in Europa' in R 1686. Minority Questions. Protection of Minorities. 41 / 44950 / 30181. The importance of the document is noted in the Introduction to the first published set of minutes to the first meeting of the European Congress of Nationalities. See *Sitzungsbericht des Kongresses der organisierten nationalen Gruppen in den Staaten Europas im Jahre 1925 zu Genf*. Vienna: Wilhelm Braumüller, 1926.

avoid damaging rifts making all the headlines. He recognised care would be necessary to ensure the proceedings did not contravene the terms of the peace settlement and that some resolution would be necessary to ensure *all* minorities were seen to be loyal to both the states in which they lived and the principles of the League.

Ammende knew that different minorities might be alienated from each other, but hoped the tendency would be overcome as they discovered common interests. He predicted that some would try to represent a congress as a gathering of those nations defeated in the First World War and recommended the counter argument that it was a gathering dedicated to free cultural development.

Care would be necessary to ensure that only true representatives of given nationality groups would attend the congress, individuals empowered genuinely to speak on their behalf. Thought would also have to be given to the languages employed in the congress, most likely German, French and Russian, although with the possibility of Hungarian too.

Ammende remained sufficiently positive to believe all these challenges could be addressed successfully. He wanted leading minority representatives to come together soon, so that the likely difficulties could be confronted in good time. Once an understanding had been reached, it might be possible for the project's initiator to approach the League's Secretariat and associated organisations looking for a connection. To maximise the congress's impact, Ammende identified Geneva as its venue and recommended its timing should coincide with the meetings of the Assembly so, for example, the latter's resolutions could be debated.

Ammende tried to define the groups he wanted to participate in the congress. He included ones from within the German state, for instance Danes, but noted that some Jewish groups could pose difficulties:

> Concerning the Jews, it has to be said that they are only organised as typical minorities in some individual states and only differentiate themselves from their environment there. In any case, participation in the congress would only come into question for the representatives of Jewish groups from these latter states.

Ammende was not expressing anti-Semitism, only recognising that some Jewish groups were unlikely to classify themselves as distinctive national groups. This was certainly the case for Germany's Jews, who, for the most part, saw themselves as Germans of Jewish faith. They would be unlikely participants at the congress. By contrast, however, Ammende assumed more nationally-minded Jewish groups would be represented from Romania, Hungary, Yugoslavia, Poland, Lithuania, Estonia and Latvia.

Ammende's memorandum emphasised the significance the congress would hold. Representatives would be reflecting the interests of some 50 million souls (his figure) who required equality with majority populations and freedom of cultural development. Accommodating them was in the interest of minority and majority alike. Ammende also proposed the congress would provide a new institution that would strengthen the League of Nations.

## 3. Responses and invitation

Not everyone accepted Ammende's case without question. On 11 September 1925, he visited Colban in Geneva, emphasising that the projected body was not 'revolutionary' and would not be 'hostile' towards governments. Ammende added that it would meet after the Assembly had dissolved so that no undue pressure would be exerted on its proceedings. A handwritten note by Eric Drummond followed a minute of the meeting. Unfortunately for Ammende it said that 'international meetings of minorities do not give evidence of great loyalty to the countries where they reside.'[8] In other words, the very convening of the congress was held suspect at senior levels of the League.

About a fortnight later, Ammende's fellow Baltic German Alfons Heyking (see chapter 5, section 9) also visited Colban:

> He himself [Heyking] was very upset about it [the congress], as it would certainly be to the detriment of the minorities because of the necessary implications that they were not loyal to their present governments.

When Colban said he could not take a position on what Ammende was attempting:

> Baron Heyking said that he entirely understood my attitude, which, he added, was ample proof that the contemplated Conference was a very great mistake.[9]

Ammende had travelled the length and breadth of Europe promoting the idea of the congress and holding conversations which informed his thinking.[10] Although some German groups and leaders remained as sceptical as Heyking, by late August Ammende was collaborating with colleagues to draw up invitations.[11] Each minority group would be able to send up to three

---

[8] Note by EC 12.9.25 followed by initialled note (ED) dated 14.9.25. R 1686. Minority Questions. Protection of Minorities. 41 / 44950 / 30181.
[9] Note by Erik Colban, 28.9.25. R 1686. Minority Questions. Protection of Minorities. 41 / 44950 / 30181.
[10] Introduction, *Sitzungsbericht 1925*.
[11] Copy of the invitation given to Colban by Ammende on 11.9.25, R 1686. Minority Questions.

representatives to Geneva, the congress would deal with principles rather than concrete cases and there would be a private organisational meeting before the public session took place. Tolerance would be recognised as a principle of international law and autonomy as a tool for peace. Resolutions would recognise that liberty of national conscience was a natural right; that minorities should be guaranteed cultural, economic and political development; that all minorities should be guaranteed autonomy if they desired it; and that the League of Nations should defend nationality rights (as should all international organisations interested in peace). Lacking from the final French-language invitation, however, was a clause included in an earlier, German-language, draft:

> ...The flouting of the natural rights of national groups by individual states is an essential reason why Soviet propaganda, which is already compromised in all other respects, still always provides a serious threat to Europe.[12]

The actual invitation was signed not by Ammende, but by Josip Wilfan (a Slovene from northern Italy), Paul Schiemann (a German from Latvia) and Count Szüllö (a Hungarian from Czechoslovakia).

### 4. Between Berlin and Budapest: official scepticism about Ammende

The invitations were backed up by another whirlwind of activity on Ammende's part. Having visited diverse minority representatives in Spanish Catalonia in July 1925 as they gathered for a meeting of the League of Nations Union, Ammende travelled on to the League of Nations' offices in Geneva to see Helmer Rosting and to discuss further his ideas for a European Congress of Nationalities.[13] He said the body would be based on principles already established by German minorities and would be open to all national minorities in Europe. He re-iterated that it would meet around the time of the Assembly, discuss only matters of principle and not promote irredentism. It would explore minority protection and the peace settlement, perhaps also the Soviet Union's system of autonomy. Ammende added that he was on his way from Barcelona to Warsaw and was in the process of holding a series of meetings with minority leaders.

Ammende did indeed meet with minority leaders in Warsaw on 8 July 1925.[14] With the agreement of representatives drawn from Spain's

---

Protection of Minorities. 41 / 44950 / 30181. For an earlier version of the invitation, which envisaged the congress occurring in early September, see R60462, Political Archive of the Foreign Ministry, Berlin.
[12] See R60462, Political Archive of the Foreign Ministry, Berlin.
[13] Congres General de Minorites. Entrevue avec M. Amende [sic.]. Date stamped 3 July 1925. R 1686. Minority Questions. Protection of Minorities. 41 / 44950 / 30181.
[14] Introduction, *Sitzungsbericht 1925.*

Catalans, Hungarians from Czechoslovakia, Ukrainians and White Russians from Poland, plus Germans from Poland and from South Tyrol, he called a further meeting in Dresden in August.[15] An additional meeting of German minority leaders, effectively of the Association of German Minorities in Europe, held in Vienna on 23 July also agreed on the need for the Dresden meeting. The meeting of the 23rd commissioned Paul Schiemann to contact the German Foreign Ministry about what was being planned.[16] This he did on 24 July. Noting that German officials wanted the event to be delayed, he said the congress was responding to on-going problems facing ethnic Germans in South Tyrol, Yugoslavia and Poland. He added that Hungarian and Slovene minorities favoured holding a congress, so if the Germans pulled out, it might go ahead without them anyway.

The German Foreign Ministry began taking an interest in Ammende's work, compiling a report about it.[17] Ammende believed, it was said, that since (according to the terms of the peace settlement) Germany could only assist ethnic Germans in cultural ways, these groups had to seek out additional allies, in effect other large minorities facing many similar problems. Hence, from now on, German minorities would have to frame their demands as principles with general European applicability. This would enhance their credibility and eradicate fears of Pan-Germanism. Looking forward, since the Great Powers conspicuously had not solved the minority issue, there was every chance that minorities as a whole could look increasingly towards German interests, even to Germany itself, for leadership. With this said, the memorandum also noted that the German state and German minorities increasingly were seen as separate from each other, even to the point where, on occasion, their interests could appear contradictory—which raised the possibility of a rift opening between the two. The report hoped that the congress could be postponed for a year and suggested the German minorities should consult with Berlin more closely before creating a *fait accompli*.

This position of the German Foreign Ministry had been informed, in part at least, by another memorandum penned by Ammende which outlined the rationale for a European Congress of Nationalities.[18] Ammende's document started provocatively: German minorities were 'cultural forward posts' for the German nation and so their development was absolutely vital. Following the war, Germany could only support them culturally, hence the need to form alliances with other nationalities and to appear genuinely

---

[15] Hiden, *Defender of Minorities*, pp.115–6.

[16] Memo for Reich Minister 23 July 1925, R60462, Political Archive of the Foreign Ministry, Berlin.

[17] Berlin, 15.8.25. Memo of Dept VI about the plans to convene an international conference of minorities. R60462, Political Archive of the Foreign Ministry, Berlin.

[18] Zur Frage der Organisation einer europäischen Nationalitätentagung. R60462, Political Archive of the Foreign Ministry, Berlin. Ammende is named as the author towards the end of the memorandum.

European. Such a strategy would yield all manner of benefits, for instance helping German minority parliamentarians build common fronts with other nationality groups around the continent. All of this, however, was premised on the successful creation of a European Congress of Nationalities.

Ammende rejected a series of objections to the congress. Recognising that the German state had not yet achieved reconciliation fully with its own minorities, this was taken not as grounds for the congress initiative to slow down, but for the German state to move more quickly to offer autonomy. To the idea that autonomy within Germany might lead to Danish and Polish groups uniting against the state, the memorandum said simply, 'This fear is unfounded.' It also rejected the idea that a congress involving the Catalans would lead to difficulties for the German state— although it was noted that in Vienna the German minority leaders had decided not to invite the Catalans to the congress yet, so that in the first place it retained more a 'Central European character' than a 'Pan-European' one.

Ammende stated clearly:

> In other words, if we succeed in bringing together in Geneva the large majority of all national minority groups, and establish them there on the foundation of our German demands and principles, then without doubt such a development will be a major and significant advantage for the entire German matter (and not even certain individual set-backs will alter that).

He added that the project should not be postponed because news of the preparatory work might leak out, making the event even more difficult to stage in the future.

The German Foreign Ministry had genuine misgivings about what was happening. When Ammende was received by Ministerial Director Dr. Köpke on 16 August 1925, he was told about Berlin's reservations concerning the planned timing and location of the congress.[19] In this light, it was clear the European Congress of Nationalities would never reflect simply the interests of the German state. Things were never going to be that easy.

Ammende needed a significant sponsor and straight after meeting Köpke, he went to Budapest for talks with Count Bethlen (Prime Minister of Hungary), telling him the initiative might founder on account of the German government's opposition. When German diplomats found out about this, they called in the Hungarian Ambassador to Berlin (Emich) to emphasise that a bad congress could cause trouble that would be hard to put right. They also worried about creating a block of minority interests, were concerned about

---

[19] Memo signed by Müller, 5.9.25. R60462, Political Archive of the Foreign Ministry, Berlin.

the impact of a congress on Germany's domestic politics and feared that internationally Germany would be considered the congress's prime mover.[20]

Yet not everyone in the German Foreign Ministry was quite so negative. Adolf Köster was German Ambassador to Riga. He explained in a letter:

> Although I appreciate them [i.e. the points against holding a congress], by reason of my years' long engagement specifically with these questions, and by reason of my professional experiences here in Latvia I would like to ask urgently, to check the points for and against one more time from the point of view that the minority question is not only a matter of German cultural expansion, but is an international political question of the highest dignity, the solution to which can be of immediate political significance for Germany and Europe. Despite everything, I am of the opinion that skilful leadership co-operation with the other European minorities can be an extraordinary important means to advancing the minority question. This co-operation would also, at least in part, help weaken one of the most serious accusations which today is made repeatedly against individual German minorities, namely that the whole German minority movement is nothing more than an official German action led from Berlin.[21]

Köster advised that Paul Schiemann meet with the Foreign Minister (i.e. Stresemann) and a State Secretary.

The German Foreign Ministry considered the congress in depth. On 20 August a meeting in Berlin was attended by German ambassadors from Prague, Belgrade, Copenhagen, Warsaw, Tallinn (Reval), Riga, Kaunas, Bucharest and Budapest, with Consuls from Karkov, Innsbruck and Geneva, plus a State Secretary representing the Minister. The tone of the meeting was conservative.[22] Although it recognised that co-operation between German minorities, indeed between all minorities, could be helpful in particular circumstances, it proposed the time was not yet ready to create an organisation like that being floated. The emergence of a 'questionable organisation' could de-rail the co-operation between states and German minorities that was starting to emerge in several locations. The diplomats

---

[20] Ibid.

[21] Letter from German Ambassador, Riga (Köster) dated 17.8.25. R60462, Political Archive of the Foreign Ministry, Berlin.

[22] Memo date stamped 20 August 1925. Record of meeting of Foreign Ministry staff. R60462, Political Archive of the Foreign Ministry, Berlin.

were sent away to take soundings among the leaders of the various German groups in their countries confidentially.

Ammende countered the evident lack of support with a barrage of propaganda before, also in August, inviting the German Foreign Ministry to send a representative to the congress's launch. He explained the event would be stage-managed so as to avoid the danger of controversy and disruption. The full public meeting would be a 'purely decorative event', with the key resolutions agreed beforehand.[23] But he maintained that the congress would have to meet quickly and that delay would threaten the whole procedure. Even with all of this said, disquiet about Ammende remained in official circles. One diplomatic letter from late August questioned who was the real driving force behind the project—Ammende or Schiemann?[24] The latter was to be preferred.

A German Foreign Ministry memorandum from early September 1925 amplified official disquiet about Ammende's activities.[25] It discussed his approach to the Hungarian government after being rebuffed by Berlin. It noted he had been holding discussions with Count Sierakowski, a parliamentary deputy and representative of Polish communities in Germany. There were notes about Paul Schiemann meeting with senior Foreign Ministry staff and Stresemann himself for an un-minuted conversation, but it was also said that differences were emerging between Schiemann and Ammende. In late August 1925, Schiemann voiced the desire to officials to postpone the congress until December, although he made clear that others (such as Josip Wilfan) felt this impracticable. Schiemann wondered if the 'congress' would amount to a confidential meeting between minority leaders held in private——although Ammende soon broadcasting that there absolutely had to be a public event.

The final form of Ammende's initiative, then, looked as if it would depend on which doors showed signs of opening or shutting. Under the circumstances, it was no surprise that even people relatively close to him ended up unclear about what was going to happen. Ammende was more intent on driving things forward than making sure everyone felt a participant in the process. But since his activity elicited a significant response from both nationality leaders and governmental institutions, even if the German Foreign Ministry didn't like what was happening, it could not be ignored.

As the German Foreign Ministry memorandum suggested, when minority leaders met in Dresden on 25 August, Wilfan rejected Schiemann's idea of postponing the congress. Schiemann also felt an agreement was reached for only a private meeting, a view he reported subsequently to

---

[23] Letter of 20 August 1920, Ammende, Zietenstr. 20, Berlin to Geheimrat. R60462, Political Archive of the Foreign Ministry, Berlin.
[24] Note stamped Ausw Amt VI, 31 August 1925. Signed by Söhrung. R60462, Political Archive of the Foreign Ministry, Berlin.
[25] Memo signed by Müller, 5.9.25. R60462, Political Archive of the Foreign Ministry, Berlin.

German diplomats but which Ammende soon contradicted. Unsurprisingly, in the days following Dresden tensions between Ammende and Schiemann peaked. In a letter dated 3 September to J.G. Bruns (legal adviser to the Association of German Minorities in Europe), which was copied to the German Foreign Ministry, Schiemann accused Ammende of going to Budapest and telling 'obvious untruths', which presumably revolved around the attitude of the Foreign Ministry to the congress and how the event would be organised.[26] Schiemann went on:

> I request that you tell him [Ammende] officially that if he is not obliged to stop completely every kind of independent action, I will have to inaugurate a vote of no confidence and demand that either he or I are relieved of our responsibilities.

A letter followed a few days later from Ammende to the German Foreign Ministry. Regretting that Schiemann's communication had caused upset in Berlin, he stressed that, when the congress met in Geneva in October, there would be a preparatory meeting ahead of a public one. The episode showed that Ammende was pushing the envelope of what the congress should be. He was more ambitious than at least some of his associates. There is also a hint that he was unscrupulous, since if he failed to find satisfaction in one place, at once he looked somewhere else.

The extent to which Ammende's strategies could alienate people was displayed clearly by Rudolf Brandsch, the leader of ethnic Germans in Romania.[27] Brandsch met a German Foreign Ministry official on 12 October.[28] He regretted not having done more to oppose Ammende's project determinedly in Vienna, believing that the 'unhappy conference' could have been prevented through skilled leadership. A report noted that Brandsch rejected Ammende's actions decisively and said that, since he no longer received money from his father, Ammende relied on foreign support for his project and tailored 'his adventurous politics accordingly'. Brandsch explained:

> ...Ammende's influence must be eradicated, he is irresponsible and only creates chaos. Mr. Brandsch is convinced personally that in this case Ammende is simply the tool of Count Bethlen.

---

[26] Letter from Paul Schiemann, Riga to Bruns, 3.9.25. R60462, Political Archive of the Foreign Ministry, Berlin.

[27] Although co-founder of the Association of German Minorities in Europe with Ammende, Brandsch once described him as a bankrupt adventurer looking for ways to boost his finances. Hiden, *Defender of Minorities*, p. 114.

[28] Report by Freytag written in Bucharest, 12 October 1925. R60462, Political Archive of the Foreign Ministry, Berlin.

He denounced Ammende for putting the interests of 'all the minorities of the world' ahead of German ones, a step 'just as fantastic and obscure' as it was 'dangerous'. Brandsch said German minorities would prefer to co-operate with each other and with the German state as a first priority, then with other minority groups only subsequently. He promised to get German groups to speak out against Ammende. Given the long-standing relationship that had existed between Ammende and Brandsch, this was strong criticism indeed.

Bransch's view was supplemented by a report of a German diplomat in the Baltic which amounted to rather a personal attack:

> The initiator of the Conference is the very active, but irresponsible and utopian Pärnu (Pernau) citizen Dr. Ewald Ammende. Without having taken soundings with the responsible local positions, Ammende, on his own initiative ... has stimulated the holding of such a conference. Unfortunately his efforts have fallen on fertile ground. The deeper reasons for his initiative are to be found in the fact that recently he has suffered serious financial losses as a result of deficient business transactions, and he hopes to create a secure material situation inside a minority organisation which he might well set up. Incidentally, his efforts are only supported here by a very small minority, to which belongs in any case the very active and equally utopian editor in chief of *Revaler Bote*, Axel de Vries.[29]

Here was someone else Ammende had alienated.

A memorandum circulated in the German Foreign Ministry around the time of the Brandsch interview noted that most Germans in Estonia had more practical concerns than those voiced by Ammende.[30] There was also a feeling that it was wrong to try to treat all minorities similarly, since 'in cultural terms they are not all on the same level and so cannot be valued the same'. This was a conservative critique of Ammende's agenda and took as read the superiority of German minorities.

### 5. Developments inside the League

League of Nations personalities remained sceptical about the congress in the period just before it met. Romania's permanent delegate, Mr. Commene, recommended that the Secretariat 'take a definite stand against this kind of

---

[29] K.H. Grundmann, *Deutschtumspolitik zur Zeit der Weimarer Republik*. Hanover: Hirschheydt, 1977, p. 287.
[30] Annex to Report of 5 October, No. 2542. R60462, Political Archive of the Foreign Ministry, Berlin.

activity'. Colban replied that the event was unimportant and the best thing was not to 'have any connection with it.'[31] He proposed that the differences between various minorities would prevent them co-operating in substantial ways anyhow. In a handwritten note, Eric Drummond commented: 'We can only leave the whole thing *severely* [?] alone for the present and watch developments.'[32]

But it would be wrong to suggest the League was uniformly against innovative responses to the question of national minorities. The Assembly regarded the issue as critical, in the process displaying how social problems increasingly were being prioritised as security issues. In September 1925, the Assembly accepted a Lithuanian resolution proposing a committee draft a universal convention on minority rights.[33] Lithuanian Minister President Galvanauskas (supported by Hungarian representative Count Apponyi) explained the aim was to enhance the prevailing uneven system of minority protection. He hoped a committee would be able to define 'minority', to examine the different needs of different minorities and to re-assess the petition system. The Lithuanian proposal added that a convention agreed by all would be particularly effective at preventing neighbouring states interfering in the affairs of others.

Unfortunately the Lithuanian proposal fell on too many deaf ears. When it was discussed by the Assembly's Sixth Committee, Eduard Beneš (Czechoslovakia) resisted viewing minorities as legal entities because to do so would change the terms of existing treaties; de Jouvenel proposed that his country, France, had no minorities and so the recommendation had nothing to do with him; while Robert Cecil, discussing Wales, felt global supervision of minorities 'would impose a crushing burden on the League', adding 'in a matter as delicate as that of minorities, prudence required that innovations should be avoided and that the prerogatives of the Council should be left intact.' Paul Hymans (Belgium) feared a new system might become 'a permanent cause of internal conflicts and disputes' leading to 'international conflicts'. Although some states spoke in favour of universalisation (in particular ones bound by minority agreements, such as Poland and Romania), eventually Galvanauskas withdrew the proposal and left the regulation of minority affairs to the discretion of the Council and the Committee of Three. He said 'the question was not yet ripe in the minds of the representatives of the various countries'.

The controversial nature of minority rights in 1925 helps explain the cautious line Colban recommended over the congress's first meeting, as he

---

[31] Erik Colban, 29.9.25. R 1686. Minority Questions. Protection of Minorities. 41 / 44950 / 30181.

[32] Ibid. In the text, 'severely' is difficult to read.

[33] Protection of Minorities. Resolution adopted by the Sixth Assembly. Geneva, October 10th, 1925. Extract from the Minutes of the Fourth Meeting of the Sixth Committee of the Sixth Assembly
16.9.25. R 1700, Minorities. Proposed Minorities Convention. 41 / 46391 / 46391.

explained in a memorandum for Secretary General Eric Drummond in early
October 1925:

> My personal opinion is that the Secretariat and its members
> should maintain an absolutely neutral attitude towards the
> meeting and have nothing to do, either officially or
> privately, with it. Of course we cannot prevent Minorities
> representatives meeting in Geneva from calling upon
> members of the Secretariat, but I am giving instructions to
> the staff of the Minorities Section to maintain an extremely
> careful attitude and not to enter into discussion with any
> members of the Congress. I wonder whether you might not
> consider it desirable to give directions to the Information
> Section and perhaps also to the Political Section in the same
> sense.

Drummond replied:

> I entirely agree.... As I said before, I feel that a meeting of
> this kind shows that the Minorities who come to it do not
> appreciate their obligations of loyalty towards their new
> countries.[34]

These concerns were at least understood by the congress participants. When
the congress met, notwithstanding 1925 being the year of Locarno, the
environment was difficult. At one point Josip Wilfan, the congress's
president, noted Europe was 'nervous' and emphasised the organisation
should prove itself through 'factual, practical political work.[35]

## 6. The European Congress of Nationalities meets

The creation of the congress has been interpreted as reflecting 'a spreading
disillusionment with League attitudes and procedures'.[36] Likewise, after the
Second World War, Pablo de Azcárate (who followed Erik Colban as leader
of the Minorities Section) said that 'discontent' on the part of minorities was
'very real' and led to the founding of the congress.[37] The view, however, was
true only up to a point (see also chapter 7, section 'Lobbying the League').
The congress aimed to influence the League based on values shared by some
League members at least. Admittedly some commentators have judged that

[34] E.C., 5.10.1925 and E.D., 5.10.1925. Note on the Conference of Minorities, 6 October 1925. S
338. General.
[35] *Sitzungsbericht 1925*, p. 72.
[36] Hiden, *Defender of Minorities*, p. 118.
[37] P. de Azcárate, *League of Nations and National Minorities. An Experiment*. Washington:
Carnegie Endowment. 1945, p. 131.

the congress never managed to achieve the influence it wanted, and instead settled 'for annual expressions of complaint directed as much against the League as against offending and host states'.[38] Yet this goes too far as well. Even if its effectiveness as a lobby group is open to debate, the congress still fulfilled useful functions. For example, the minutes of its meetings provide a record of the concerns of minorities—stated by themselves—at a time when international law and international organisations (governmental and non-governmental alike) were in their relative infancy.[39]

Had Ammende's view of the League of Nations been completely negative, the framework of the European Congress of Nationalities would not have been coined as it was. The preamble to the Covenant of the League of Nations spoke about the 'maintenance of justice and a scrupulous respect for all treaty obligations in the dealings of *organised peoples* with one another' (italics added). Several League of Nations commentators equated the 'organisation' of international affairs with the maintenance of peace, and disorganisation with war (see chapter 5, section 2).[40] So, the minutes of the first congress were published under the title 'Report of the First Conference of the *Organised* National Groups in the States of Europe in 1925 in Geneva' (emphasis added).[41] In due course, the congress's criteria for admission would take account of the level of organisation displayed by would-be members.[42] The implication was obvious: even though the congress was dealing with national minorities rather than states, by emphasising its 'organised' character, it was trying to make common cause with the League. Ammende and those around him were looking at the League in the hope of some manner of co-operation.

At this time Ewald Ammende was enthused by Switzerland. He was struck by life in an affluent state inhabited peacefully by multiple national groups. It seemed a model for Central and Eastern Europe. He was not alone in this optimism. An article published in *Revaler Bote* described Switzerland as an 'example of a harmonious solution, which satisfies both centralist as well as nationalistic, separatist strivings'.[43] The author of the piece was not only a professor at the University of Bordeaux, but also a general secretary in the League of Nations Union.

There was optimism, therefore, when Ammende—now designated General Secretary of the European Congress of Nationalities—delivered his

---

[38] R. Pearson, *National Minorities in Eastern Europe. 1848–1945*. London: Macmillan, 1983, pp. 123–4.

[39] Robinson, Karbach, Laseron, Robinson and Vichniak, *Were the Minorities Treaties a Failure?* p.247.

[40] A. Sweetser, 'The Non-Political Achievements of the League' in J.E. Johnsen (ed.), *Reconstituting the League of Nations*. New York: H.W. Wilson, 1943, p.149; W. Rappard, *The Geneva Experiment*. OUP, 1931, p. 69

[41] *Sitzungsbericht 1925*, 1926.

[42] Hiden, *Defender of Minorities*, p. 116.

[43] Dr. Theodor Ruyssen, 'Das Minderheitenproblem in der Zukunft', *Revaler Bote* 4 December 1924.

speech to the organisation on 15 October 1925. If the speech was critical of
the League, its tone suggested Ammende could help address the given
problems. Hence, he proposed there was a crisis in how the League of
Nations dealt with the nationality question because the rights of national
minorities had been imposed by force through the post-war settlement.
Consequently the rights lacked appropriate psychological underpinnings and
were not viewed as facets of justice. Ammende wanted the situation remedied
and recommended it should be done, in the first instance, on a European
rather than global scale. The problem of national minorities was said to be
too diverse globally for a sensible treatment to be possible, but once a model
solution was achieved in Europe, perhaps it could be applied to other parts of
the world.

Ammende could have pointed out that simply bringing together
representatives of Europe's different nationality groups was a major
achievement. Even people sharing the same nationality could look at their
position differently and could have very different ideas about how best to
respond to it. Hence, among Baltic Germans, Paul Schiemann's liberal
convictions contrasted the conservatism of Stackelberg and Hasselblatt.[44]
Where did this leave the likelihood for agreement in a congress full of
different national groups, at least some of which harboured traditional
animosities towards each other?

The congress's first full session was impressive. It included
Germans from Estonia, Latvia, Lithuania, Poland, Romania, Czechoslovakia,
Yugoslavia Denmark and Italy; Slovenes from Austria and Italy; Jews from
Latvia, Lithuania, Poland, Czechoslovakia and Romania; Danes from
Germany; Hungarians from Czechoslovakia, Romania and Yugoslavia; Sorbs
(*Wenden*) from Germany; Carpatho-Russians from Czechoslovakia;
Ukrainians from Poland; Poles from Germany, Latvia, Lithuania and
Czechoslovakia; White Russians from Poland; and Lithuanians from
Poland.[45] Observing were several additional groups from Poland, while
Russian and Swedish groups from the Baltic did not attend, but expressed
support for the event. The congress agreed four central resolutions:

> 1. National cultural freedom is as much a component of the
> civilised, cultured world as religious freedom, and this
> should be recognised legally; correspondingly, states should
> guarantee their minorities freedom of economic and cultural
> development as well as civic rights. It should be recognised

[44] See M. Garfleff, 'Nationalitätenpolitik zwischen liberalem und völkischem Anspruch.
Gleichklang und Spannung bei Paul Schiemann und Werner Hasselblatt' in J. von Hehn and C.J.
Kenez (eds.), *Reval und die Baltischen Länder*. Marburg: Herder Institute, 1980. Also X-M.
Núñez Seixas, *Entre Ginebra y Berlin. La Cuestion de las Minorias Nacionales y la Politica
Internacional en Europa 1914–1939*. Madrid: Akal. 2001, pp. 476–83.
[45] 'Die Teilnehmer und Resolutionen', *Revaler Bote* 12 December 1925.

that these principles are pre-requisites for understanding between nations and hence for peace in Europe.

2. All national groups should be supported to establish public legal organisations, based on either territory or persons depending on their characteristics, to assist in promoting the group. Self-administration represents a good way to promote understanding between minority and majority peoples. This system was seen as the best way to ensure "loyal co-operation" by minorities in the states in which they lived, enabling minorities and majorities to co-exist peacefully.

3. Peace in Europe requires a real commitment to mutual understanding and there should be a clear statement from the League of Nations about the rights of national minorities based on the first two sets of principles.

4. Finally, the congress applauds all international organisations which are attempting to address solutions to the minority question and asks for their support in working towards these goals.[46]

The main conference had been pre-empted by a pre-conference held on 14 October. This was opened by Dr. Josip Wilfan who recounted that 33 organised national groups would be represented in Geneva, being drawn from 12 nationalities located in 14 separate states.[47] An organising committee was chosen, which consisted of an appropriate array of national members: an Hungarian (Jakabffy), a Pole (Sierakowski), a Ukrainian (Wassitschuck), a White Russian (Jeremitsch), a Carpathian (Gerowski), a Lithuanian (Zajanskauskas) and a Dane (Christiansen). Unfortunately the Ukrainian and White Russian declared they could only participate under conditions the congress would not fulfil.

The full public meeting of the congress began the next morning. Now elected president of the congress, Josip Wilfan gave the opening speech arguing that understanding between peoples could not be based on formal treaties, but required heart-felt connections. In so far as solidarity between different national groups depended on mutual understanding, he maintained minorities could play important roles in generating it. He went on to emphasise that if Europe's minority question was important, then minorities themselves had to participate in finding a solution.[48]

Géza von Szüllő made a speech on behalf of Hungarians living in Czechoslovakia. Describing all those present as 'the disinherited of the

---

[46] *Sitzungsbericht 1925*, pp. 79–80.

[47] Ibid, pp. 12–3.

[48] Ibid, pp. 14–5. For a summary of the first day of the Congress, see 'Die erste europäische Nationalitätentagung', *Revaler Bote* 16 October 1925

world', he said the meeting was not convened to provoke problems but to recover the natural rights of minorities.[49] They only wanted justice and 'reciprocal loyalty' (i.e. their loyalty to the state in which they lived, and its loyalty towards them in return). Szüllö believed there were 50 million members of minorities across Europe. Disorganised, they were feeble; but organised, they would have power. He recognised that working with the groups was difficult, not least because it had to happen in a Europe in which Bolshevism would gladly use the minority issue for subversion.

The weightiest speech delivered on the first day of the congress came from Paul Schiemann.[50] He began discussing the 30 Years War, which proved conclusively that religious belief was so deeply felt that no state should try to intervene in the relationship between individual and God—a principle he thought applicable to nationality affairs. Schiemann suggested that an attempt by a state to interfere in an individual's claim to nationality was no different to a state intervening in religious devotion. Both religion and nationality were areas best left to conscience alone.

For Schiemann, once the genie of national consciousness had been released it could not be put back in the bottle, and attempts at assimilation would only damage the interests of peace. In fact, Schiemann argued that attempts to damage minorities harmed the majority too. So, a state which tried to weaken the culture of another person harmed its own culture; a state which damaged the economic position of some citizens damaged its general economy; and a state which differentiated between citizens of different nationalities destroyed the foundations of justice. Worse, discrimination fanned the flames of a 'will to annihilation' likely to threaten peace in Europe. It was a 'poison gas for many world wars'. By contrast, in the congress, hands were being extended between participants since, '[o]nly united, positive work creates peace.' He hoped that one day, historians would write about the liquidation of the nationality question with as little passion as the battle between the Churches was discussed in the 1920s.

Schiemann's speech epitomised the mood of Locarno Europe—and the Locarno conference was taking place while the congress met. Speakers at the European Congress of Nationalities lined up to express their support for peace. Dr. Kraft (a German from Yugoslavia) stressed that tolerance favoured minorities and majorities alike, since it promoted peace, as Schiemann re-iterated:[51]

> We believe that in all the lands where the principle of
> national tolerance is implemented in the cultural realm, the

---

[49] *Sitzungsbericht 1925*, pp. 15–6.
[50] Ibid, pp. 17–20.
[51] Ibid, pp. 36–8.

state is also strengthened, and hence the security of individual states.[52]

Deputy Nurok (a Jew from Latvia) argued that minorities split by a national border could only have their needs addressed through cultural autonomy.[53] Dr. Robinson (a Jew from Lithuania) emphasised they did not want the kind of autonomy that denied the existence of any state, only the kind that was actually anchored in the state.[54] And as the discussion progressed, people spoke up positively about the League of Nations. In the words of Dr. Margulies (a Jew from Czechoslovakia), the League was 'an idea and an institution which must lie on our path.'[55]

Of course, the congress did not please everyone. Ukrainian and White Russian groups from Poland were disappointed by its limited ambitions. Given the rhetoric of self-determination that accompanied the peace settlement they complained that Poland had been constituted as a state without them being consulted. As majority populations on roughly a third of Poland's territory, they demanded self-determination for themselves. In this light, the congress's primary focus on cultural autonomy and acceptance of existing borders was inadequate for them. Hence they only participated as observers. The Lithuanian group from Poland also withdrew from participation when it became clear the congress would not address specific political questions concerning them.[56] Dissatisfactions were also raised by minorities from within Germany. An ethnic Dane called Christiansen complained that cultural autonomy would not suit all national minorities. He felt it was too definite a model for societies where nationality did not follow clear lines of language or religion, or where important economic issues could be at stake depending on which nationality you chose.[57] In effect, he feared that many ethnic Danes in Germany would classify themselves as Germans for reasons of economic advantage if ever they had to make a firm choice of one nationality or another

So although critical voices were not very numerous at the congress in 1925, certainly they were present. Already they cautioned that Estonia's cultural autonomy law was not necessarily the universal solution to nationality issues that Ammende and those around him sometimes seemed to think. But the congress did not close on a negative note. President Wilfan delivered a rousing final speech. This had not been a gathering of 'mere minorities', rather 'the starting point of a free assembly of the peoples of Europe'. In Herderian fashion, he hoped the congress would prompt recognition of the 'natural units of nations' and would facilitate the 'free

---

[52] Ibid, p. 25.
[53] Ibid, pp. 44–7.
[54] Ibid, pp. 48–54.
[55] Ibid, p. 62.
[56] Ibid, pp. 21–2.
[57] Ibid, pp. 54–6.

associations between nations across all state boundaries'. He hoped that in this 'nervous Europe', a gathering could be repeated, not so much expressing the frustrations of 'oppressed national groups', but to achieve 'factual, practical political work'. He thanked Ammende for making the whole event possible.[58]

## 7. Reactions to the congress: participants, newspapers, officials

The European Congress of Nationalities was a highly unusual undertaking. Established at a point when state-thinking was the order of the day, it reflected the hopes of an unusual mixture of people looking to restrict state sovereignty and increase the scope for individual expression in public life. At a time when much thinking was dominated by ideas coming from Western Europe and the USA, it was an agenda originating in Central and Eastern Europe.[59] The emergence of this unconventional undertaking has, however, been received in very different ways, by contemporaries and historians alike. For Paul Schiemann, it was an institution promoting equality between national groups; for Rudolf Michaelsen it pursued a policy of peace. By contrast, the Foreign Office in London eventually came to see those involved as 'professional troublemakers', while Maria Rothbarth has said that 'in practice' the congress was 'an instrument of imperialist German revanche politics'.[60]

At the time, understandably the Baltic German press treated the European Congress of Nationalities favourably. Ammende wrote an article in which he outlined a process of consulting Swiss Federal politician Giuseppe Motta, who supported the idea, and journalist William Martin of *Journal de Genève*, who had more reservations. The latter was concerned that the congress would see accusations made against specific states, that arguments between co-national states might invade the undertaking, and that the whole event would become a gathering of those who had lost the First World War. Ammende said he tried to take account of all these points as he organised the proceedings.[61]

Ammende's journalism related the whole process he had undertaken in 1925 to bring about the congress. He listed the places he had visited, noted trips to a Zionist congress in Vienna and recorded his meeting with Wilfan in Venice.[62] It was as if he was writing for posterity. Without doubt, however, he had been completely overjoyed with the whole project. In a letter to de Vries after the congress, he hoped that they would see increased solidarity

---

[58] Ibid, pp. 73–7.

[59] Bamberger-Stemmann, *Der Europäische Nationalitätenkongreß 1925 bis 1938*, p. 2.

[60] Views cited in Ibid, pp.1–7.

[61] E. Ammende, 'Wie die Genfer Tagung zustande kam', *Revaler Bote* 12 December 1925.

[62] The places he visited included: Vilnius, Warsaw, Lviv (Lemberg), Czernowitz, Kischinew, Bucharest, Klausenburg, Temesvar, Belgrade, Agram, Trieste, Venice, Barcelona, Paris and Vienna.

between nationality groups leading to increased prospects for long-term peace in Europe.[63] Not only should Balts like himself strengthen their economic and cultural position in society, but work to shape relations across Eastern Europe to promote peace. Anything else, he said, amounted to 'sticking your head in the sand', not least because in the event of future war, the Baltic Germans would be destroyed. He said it was time to define a common platform for the East—a vision for all—and enthused that until recently, what they had achieved in Geneva have looked a fantasy.

In another letter, Ammende took satisfaction from good work the congress had accomplished over the Jewish Question.[64] He was delighted Jews had been so well represented. The proceedings had proved how important minority rights were for all Jews, not just for Zionists, since they all could be affected by anti-Semitism. Moreover, at the congress Jewish groups had been bound in with Hungarians, Slavs and Germans to pursue constructive, peaceful labour. He hoped the congress would be able to help solve the Jewish Question in places where voluntary assimilation was impossible, for example in East and South East Europe.

Ammende's positive spin on the congress was to be expected but, despite his earlier reservations, Paul Schiemann added praise too, this time in *Rigasche Rundschau*. As a gathering of nationality politicians not serving the interests of states, the congress had elevated the status of minority law as such.[65] A journalist from *Revaler Bote* who had not, apparently, represented a minority at Geneva was equally positive: the congress was a necessary supplement the League's Assembly and the Interparliamentary Union.[66]

*Revaler Bote* also published a digest of how Europe's press reported the congress. In Switzerland, it was praised by *Journal de Genève* and *Neue Zürcher Zeitung*—the former emphasising co-operation between minorities, the latter noting that security and minority issues had to go hand in hand.[67] Only *Gazette de Lausanne* worried that the congress might be a 'machination' by the German state. In France, *L'Oeuvre* noted that the congress raised interesting possibilities about the future drawing together of states in Europe, while in Italy (where assimilation was being practiced), the whole event was ignored.

Communist papers such as *Humanité* in France were more hostile, assuming most representatives to be agents of relevant governments. Such a response from the far Left, of course, was to be expected given Ammende's personal politics. In a widely circulated article, Axel de Vries also emphasised that the meeting of the congress would help proof Europe against Communist influence.[68] In a slightly later essay, de Vries repeated that if a

---

[63] 23.11.25, Ammende to de Vries, 1502–1–26. Moscow.
[64] 23.12.25, Ammende to Hirsch. 1502–1–26, Moscow.
[65] P. Schiemann, 'Die Genfer Minoritäten-Konferenz', *Rigasche Rundschau* 27 October 1925.
[66] Dr. N.v.G, 'Zur europäischen Nationalitätentagung', *Revaler Bote* 17 October 1925.
[67] 'Die Genfer Nationalitätentagung und die Presse der Welt', *Revaler Bote* 12 December 1925.
[68] A. de Vries, 'Europa und Moskau', *Baltische Blätter* (1925)

160 Martyn Housden

bourgeois alternative was not offered to the Soviet model of accommodating national minorities, then local Communists would have a useful basis for spreading propaganda helpful to Moscow.[69] Ammende also believed his congress was subverting the foundation of at least some pro-Communist propaganda circulating in Eastern Europe.[70]

In Yugoslavia, *Deutsche Volksblatt* applauded the congress for encouraging people to think about nationalities in new ways. In Germany, *Frankfurter Zeitung* said the event might mark the start of an era of free national conscience. The article finished with comments by German nationality leaders, including ones about specifically Ammende. Johannes Schmidt-Wodder called him 'a man of great selflessness and impulsivity' who lacked 'deviousness'.

Regarding more personal views of the congress, an ethnic German from Romania, Mr. Korodi, sent the German Foreign Ministry a confidential memorandum.[71] He applauded how Wilfan served as president 'skilfully and with tact'. He noted the event could not be accused of Pan-Germanism because of the extensive use of French language. He was also critical of Christiansen's complaint that Frisians and Lithuanians from within Germany were not present.

In a further memorandum, Korodi noted there had been some discussion 'behind the scenes' about Ammende's fitness to take the congress forwards. In particular there were doubts whether he had 'the diplomatic skill required to lead such proceedings.'[72] In particular, he was criticised for his negotiations with Hungarian Prime Minister Bethlen during the lead up to the congress, including the acceptance of Hungarian funding, all of which took place without consultation with ethnic German groups. Ammende was also accused of telling Bethlen confidential things about the pursuit of minority policies inside Germany. Korodi said that Ammende should not remain secretary when the congress met next.

The Romanian German noted that Poles, Danes and Sorbs from within German rejected cultural autonomy because they did not have the resources necessary to make it work. Apparently the Polish representative from Germany, Count Sierakowski, wanted an extensive declaration about the loyalty of minorities to the states in which they lived, something which separated him from the Ukrainians, Lithuanians and White Russians from Poland who assumed observer status at the congress. Korodi also recommended that it was the perfect time for the Prussian government to offer cultural autonomy to Poles and Danes. No doubt he was thinking that

---

[69] A.de Vries, 'Die Nationalitätenfrage und die kommunistische Partei', *Baltische Blätter* (1926).
[70] Ammende to Morokutti, 22.12.25, 1502–1–6. Moscow.
[71] Letter from Korodi about the essential outcomes of the congress, 13–16 Oct 1925. R60462, Political Archive of the Foreign Ministry, Berlin.
[72] Confidential memo written by Korodi, 'Von der Konferenz des deutschen Minderheiten-Ausschusses in Genf (16 u. 17 Okt. 1926)'. R60426, Political Archive of the Foreign Ministry, Berlin.

such a step would put pressure on the Polish government to accommodate its own, much more numerous, minorities with greater generosity.

Naturally, some interests still had reservations about the congress, not least the German Foreign Ministry. One of its reports explained that, as the congress met, some people still were concerned that Pan-Germanism was setting Ammende's agenda. Polish groups especially were nervous, suspecting Ammende was in the pay of the German government. These concerns, however, dissipated as the event unfolded and the observer noted that, eventually, the congress proceeded smoothly and without 'tension'.[73] A further report took the danger of Pan-Germanism a bit more seriously:

> ... it may not be forgotten that the initiators of this congress, Dr. Paul Schiemann, Dr. E. Amende [sic], the Hungarian Szulo [sic] and the Slav Dr. Wilfan, are not the kind of people to be suspected of sympathising with Pan-Germanism. However, it is also clear that these people must reckon with those leaders of German minorities who do support Pan-German endeavours.[74]

Pan-Germanism was said to motivate, to some extent, ethnic German leaders from Denmark and Czechoslovakia, and there was always a danger that the ideology would spread from these people to others. Nonetheless, the report added:

> The number of non-German delegates was sufficiently large to convince the Pan-Germans that their efforts to take over the congress were quite futile.[75]

The comments concluded that the congress was not Pan-German but was allowing minorities to participate in international affairs. Ammende personally was not participating enthusiastically in a Pan-German agenda and the addition of extra minorities at subsequent meetings was unlikely to allow the growth of German nationalism.[76]

---

[73] Report of 22 October 1925 by Junghann to General Konsul Aschmann, Geneva. R60463, Political Archive of the Foreign Ministry, Berlin.

[74] Memo of 27 October 1925. R60463. Foreign Ministry Archive, Berlin.

[75] 'Das Bestrebung der Deutschen auf dem Genfer Minoritätenkongress vereitelt.' Annex to a report of 29 October. R60463, Political Archive of the Foreign Ministry, Berlin.

[76] The tone of the report, therefore, was in harmony with the assessment of at least one subsequent commentator assessing the importance of minority rights for ethnic Germans between the wars:

> ... minority rights have become identified in the popular mind with German irredentism and Nazi pretensions to superiority and domination....
> [But the] majority of the great variety of national fragments were loyal and law-abiding persons who desired no more than to be assured of the full rights to citizenship and national freedom, including the right to employ

Nonetheless, there was surprise that the congress had been set up with such haste and that the minorities from especially Estonia and Latvia already were so well organised.[77] True, a report from *Rigasche Rundschau* argued the speed had been dictated by a desire to show that national minorities were not a threat to European harmony, but German diplomats probably did not find the argument persuasive.[78] Soon enough, the German Ambassador to Riga, Adolf Köster, was thinking that the longer the congress went on, the more considerable its demands would become.[79]

Köster highlighted that the congress was a challenge to the way the Great Powers and the League of Nations approached international relations:

> For this congress deprived France, Poland, Italy and other League of Nations Powers of the argument that ultimately the whole minority movement was a German revolt against the Treaty of Versailles deriving from the *Wilhelmstrasse* (German Foreign Ministry). And it showed the gentlemen of the Secretariat that a vital movement cannot be tamed with Mello Franco's soothing and theoretical formulae, which have forced Germans, Poles and Yugoslavs to a table.[80]

He said the congress had originated from the minorities themselves and had to be valued accordingly—in effect, it offered something which neither states nor the League of Nations could. It had to remain the minorities' own initiative, and had to be supported on this basis by Germany, even once that country had joined the League of Nations. The ambassador added that League politicians were indignant that minorities wanted to address openly issues which they preferred kept behind closed doors. He felt that just as Germany had to do all it could to prevent the League ossifying, so it had to promote the fight of European minorities for their rights, since the project had to be part of the pacification of Europe. Hence, when Germany supported

---

the mother tongue and maintain the identity of national cultural groupings. Nor did all Germans become irredentists or potential Nazis. A considerable element among the German minorities fought Nazism to the end, succumbing only to a violence and intransigence which had its birth in Hitler's Reich....
O.I. Jankowsky, *Nationalities and National Minorities*. New York: Macmillan, 1945, pp. 8–9.
[77] 'Das Bestrebung der Deutschen auf dem Genfer Minoritätenkongress vereitelt.' Annex to a report of 29 October. R60463, Political Archive of the Foreign Ministry, Berlin.
[78] 'Die Genfer Minoritäten-Konferenz', *Rigasche Rundschau*, 27.10.25, Nr. 242. R60463, Political Archive of the Foreign Ministry, Berlin.
[79] Bamberger-Stemmann, *Der Europäische Nationalitätenkongreß 1925 bis 1938*, pp. 85–6.
[80] Memo by Köster, 'Dissatisfaction of the small states with the minorities policy of the large states. Germany, the European Minorities and the Geneva Conference', German Embassy, Riga. 22 Feb 1926. R60463, Political Archive of the Foreign Ministry, Berlin. Afranio de Mello Franco was a Brazilian Council member to the League.

the rights of German minorities, it was also supporting the interests of Europe.

If the German Foreign Ministry gradually was becoming more favourably-inclined towards the congress, so perhaps was the League of Nations. Days after the congress met, Ammende visited Pablo de Azcárate in the Minorities Section of the Secretariat. While noting that the League's petition system caused 'very serious psychological difficulties' for national minorities, Ammende related that the congress would work constructively with majority populations and governments for the purpose of conciliation. Although Azcárate did not respond to the accusation that the League seemed not to like the congress, he did say that that the League could not respond unfavourably to any such efforts by minorities to develop strategies for conciliation with majority governments.[81] When, eventually, materials arrived at the League's offices detailing the congress's proceedings, even Eric Drummond admitted they seemed 'reasonable in substance and wording'.[82] When Azcárate suggested future communications might be unreasonable, Colban responded:

> I do not very much fear abuses. It is not so easy to hold
> international conferences. And their resolutions generally
> are well drafted and carefully worded. In case of abuse, we
> might consider the possibility of exceptional measures.[83]

Secretary General Drummond wrote to Wilfan,[84] and thereafter Ammende continued to send Colban materials.[85]

By January 1926, Ammende was suggesting little hostility existed in Geneva to the congress's work.[86] In May, he sent Colban a letter outlining preparations for the next meeting. He made sure to state the congress's peaceful purpose:

> As previously, our work will bear a strongly factual and
> loyal character.... it will be restricted to the question of how
> to facilitate the peaceful coexistence of nationalities within
> the framework of states.[87]

---

[81] Note by Azcárate, 22.10.25. R 1686. Minority Questions. Protection of Minorities. 41 / 44950 / 30181.

[82] 24.10.25, Note by Drummond. R 1686. Minority Questions. Protection of Minorities. 41 / 44950 / 30181.

[83] 3.11.25, note by EC. R 1686. Minority Questions. Protection of Minorities. 41 / 44950 / 30181.

[84] 4.11.25, Secretary General to Wilfan. R 1686. Minority Questions. Protection of Minorities. 41 / 44950 / 30181.

[85] E.g. 23.12.25, Ammende to Colban. R 1686. Minority Questions. Protection of Minorities. 41 / 44950 / 30181.

[86] 14.1.26, Ammende to de Vries. 1502–1–30, Moscow.

[87] 2.5.26, Ammende to Colban. R 1686. Minority Questions. Protection of Minorities. 41 / 44950

The same month, he visited Colban to discuss the congress. The latter heard Ammende heap praise on the League:

> M. Ammende further said that he had now come to the conclusion that the policy of the League of Nations in minorities matters had been very, very wise, as we had avoided unnecessary recourse to public action against individual Governments, and had tried to obtain satisfaction through private and friendly conversations with the Governments concerned. He felt that even should a minority, through official action by the Council, obtain certain advantages, such advantages were paid for three-fold by the set-back in the general relationship between the minority and its Government. The international organisation of minorities intended, he explained, to work on exactly the same lines as the League of Nations, carefully avoiding anything which might hurt the Governments concerned, and always endeavouring to be helpful.[88]

Ammende was trying to ingratiate himself.

Over the next few months, the League appeared to begin to accept the European Congress of Nationalities. Although Colban did not think members of the Minorities Section should attend any of its events, he agreed invitations to a reception could be sent to members of the Information Section. He also recognised that the congress's members were genuine representatives of their communities and 'very serious', capable individuals. Colban hoped personally to attend the congress's opening and perhaps one or two of the discussion sessions. Although Colban felt he could not receive an official delegation, he told Ammende individual congress delegates were welcome to visit him.[89] Eric Drummond, the Secretary General, agreed this position and said members of the Information Section could attend too, if they wanted.[90]

It is fair to say that the congress never completely overcame League suspicions, as Azcárate's later comments showed:

> It is hardly necessary to say that governments with minority obligations always regarded it [the congress] with disfavor,

---

/ 30181.

[88] EC, 19.5.26. R 1686. Minority Questions. Protection of Minorities. 41 / 51553 / 30181.

[89] Colban to Comert, 24.8.26. R 1686. Minority Questions. Protection of Minorities. 41 / 51553 / 30181.

[90] Handwritten note by Drummond, 24.8.26. R 1686. Minority Questions. Protection of Minorities. 41 / 51553 / 30181.

believing that its object was to prevent internal consolidation [of states] by provocative means, and that it was supported politically and financially by the German Government. My own impression is that this was not far from the truth; and the atmosphere of suspicion which always surrounded the Congress of Minorities did much to deprive it of authority and efficacy.

Still, it could not be ignored, as Azcarate went on to indicate:

...the organization achieved considerable importance and became on many occasions the authorized mouthpiece of the national minorities of Europe concerning questions of a common interest.[91]

In line with these comments, later Bastian Schot identified Ammende as 'the soul of the pan-European minorities movement.'[92]

And the League was well aware of the fearsome amount of work that still had to be done in respect of minority issues. Soon after the first congress met, for instance, ethnic German parliamentarians in Yugoslavia complained about the government seizing the German House in Cilli.[93] Documents from spring 1926 show the Minorities Section maintaining a watching brief on minority schooling in the Danish border area of Prussia.[94] Indeed, the Council faced a 'formidable' list of topics associated with specifically national minorities.[95] Under such circumstances, it was impossible for the organisation to ignore the sentiments and expertise found in the European Congress of Nationalities.

## 8. Conclusion

Although 1925 was the optimistic year of Locarno, organising the European Congress of Nationalities was far from straightforward. In the face of suspicions and detractors, Ammende had to persuade representatives to attend and had to seek out funding, all without official backing. The story is of him fighting to establish an unusual forum which could contribute towards the politics of Europe in a novel way. This does not mean the congress was a one-man show. Schiemann liaised with Berlin; Wilfan provided credibility with Slav groups; and Szüllö linked the undertaking to Budapest; but none of

---

[91] P. de Azcárate, *League of Nations and National Minorities. An Experiment.* Washington: Carnegie Endowment, 1945, p. 131.
[92] Schot, *Nation oder Staat?* p.105.
[93] R 1700, Minorities Questions. 41 / 47673 / 47673
[94] R 1700, Minorities Questions. German Minorities in South Denmark and Danish Minorities in North Germany. 41 / 49946 / 49946
[95] Handwritten note by Drummond, 2.3.26. R 1700, Minorities Questions. 41 / 50069 / 50069.

these actors showed the drive necessary to create a body like the congress at such an early point. In this respect, it is appropriate that Ammende has been called 'the motor' of the nationality movement.[96]

True, not everything about Ammende was praiseworthy. He was rather a 'chancer' prepared to root out funding opportunities ruthlessly. Perhaps there is also a suspicion that, quietly, he was prepared to work with German nationalism. After all, he was pressing an agenda which he knew would serve German ends because the logic of the number of German minorities dictated this.[97] Yet with this said, Ammende was setting up a forum which people could leave at any time. Members would only keep attending if they felt their interests genuinely were represented by it. For this reason, Ammende's undertaking could never have been simply a front for Pan-Germanism. So when, in a letter to de Vries from November 1925, Ammende said he was convinced that securing solidarity between different nationalities in Europe was one of the best ways to promote peace in Europe, there are no grounds, really, to disbelieve the honesty of his words.[98]

Regarding the League of Nations, certainly from the minorities' point of view it had multiple imperfections. It is easy to say it lacked ambition. The appointment of a low-key Secretary General like Eric Drummond has been read as symptomatic of the problem.[99] Perhaps the Council of the League was more an agent ready to prick a bad conscience than a knight in shining armour committed to rescuing the poor and oppressed of the world.[100] It was a role that proved too weak in the context of the inter-war period. As it was put later:

> Seen as a whole, the record of the minority states was discreditable. Newly liberated peoples, succumbing to the temptation to seek vengeance for past wrongs, seized upon the pretext of eliminating the special privileges which some minorities held as vestiges of their bygone hegemony in order to reduce those minorities to impotence.... The treaty-bound states not only failed, on the whole, to treat their minority groups in the prescribed manner, but they also seized every opportunity to nullify the international guarantee.[101]

---

[96] M. Garleff, 'Deutschbaltische Publizisten: Ewald Ammende—Werner Hasselblatt—Paul Schiemann', *Berichte und Forschungen* 2 (1994) 192.

[97] Although he was also happy to push an agenda such as cultural autonomy for Prussia which faced significant opposition within Germany.

[98] Ammende to de Vries, 23.11.25. 1502–1–26, Moscow.

[99] Z. Steiner, *The Lights that Failed. European International History 1919–1933*. OUP, 2005, p. 354.

[100] I.L. Claude, *National Minorities. An International Problem*. New York: Greenwood, 1955, p. 41.

[101] Ibid.

The statement is an over-simplification, not least in the light of Latvia's schooling law and cultural autonomy in Estonia. Nonetheless, when a state such as Italy (admittedly not comprising 'newly liberated peoples') had a permanent seat on the Council of the League, no international commitments to minority protection and a track record of persecuting minorities, precisely what message was being conveyed?

It is true as well that the rhetoric at the end of the war had been flawed. The emphasis on national self-determination soon enough met its limits:

> Self-determination is an anachronism. It asserts the sacred right of every nation to do as it pleases within its own frontiers, no matter how monstrous or how harmful to the rest of the world. It asserts that every aggregation of peoples has a sacred right to split itself into smaller and ever smaller units, each sovereign in its own corner. It assumes that the extension of economic or political influence through ever-larger units along centralised, interdependent lines is, in itself, unjust.... It was, let us hope, the last desperate expression of an ideal made obsolete by new conditions, the last catastrophic attempt to squeeze the world into a political pattern that had lost its relevance.[102]

Of course, it was impossible for national groups to organise themselves as self-contained, isolated territorial units. In this respect, national self-determination had to be balanced against other principles such as economic viability, geographical reality, history and demography.[103] In fact, trying to divide up the world into small, discrete political units flew in the face of international developments. With communications more extensive and efficient than ever, with possibilities for mobility growing all the time, the 1920s was not a time for isolation and introspection. As a later commentator put it, in the:

> ..highly integrated and industrialised world, we have to shift our standpoint and see all the nations and national matters in motion, in their interrelated functions, rotating according to the same laws without any fixed points created by our own imagination for our own convenience.[104]

---

[102] E. Reves, *The Anatomy of Peace*. London: Penguin, 1947. pp.168–9.

[103] For a similar argument, see W. Hasselblatt, *Über die Kulturautonomie. Buchmanuskript und Anlagen*. Riigiarhiiv, Tallinn. p.2.

[104] Reves, *The Anatomy of Peace*, p. 37.

At this time, to talk about self-determination excessively was to ignore reality.

The very promise of self-determination dictated dissatisfaction in the 1920s. Majorities were left irritated that minorities prevented its full achievement; for minorities, it was a sign of a promise made to others. Despite everything, perhaps the idea would have been less problematic had there been an adequate rhetoric of tolerance and countervailing state-building requirements; but generally an appropriate balance was missing. Consequently no one was satisfied and the League of Nations would be left in an impossible situation.

Nonetheless, the League was an advance on what had gone before:

> The League system undoubtedly helped to minimize international friction by providing a regularized, multilateral method of dealing with minority problems, and thus discouraging—and even making less necessary—the arbitrary, unilateral intervention of kin-states in the affairs of minority states.[105]

The League's approach to minorities clearly was imperfect and was not a finished piece of work; it was a tentative early effort at addressing a genuinely difficult problem likely to elicit all manner of resistance. This is the basis on which it should be judged, and this is the basis on which Ammende tried to become involved with the organisation.

And if the League's position over national minorities calls for careful assessment, so does that of German foreign policy during the Weimar period. Talk about readiness to use German minorities for revisionist purposes is too simple. Too much of the relationship between Berlin and the German minorities was undecided and open for negotiation: as yet, there was no common revanchist purpose. German officials disagreed whether to support Ammende, while he himself was prepared to look to Budapest rather than Berlin—again, this was a situation very much in the process of evolving.

---

[105] Claude, *National Minorities*, p. 29.

*Chapter Seven*

## The General Secretary: early optimism and its frustrations

### 1. A new Baltic German mission

In his more introspective essays, Ammende interpreted the congress as part
of a wider Baltic German mission. For centuries, he said, the lands between
Klaipėda (Memel) and Narva had been transit lands to Russia. Here, Baltic
Germans had pursued trade while also acting as pioneers of culture and
economic development. With this mission no longer possible in connection
with Soviet territory, Ammende argued ethnic Germans should engage more
fully in Central and Eastern Europe, an area plagued by nationality conflicts.
He said the Baltic Germans should draw on their centuries' long experience
of living in the midst of different national cultures to help address the
problem. Here, predictably he promoted the application of cultural
autonomy.[1]

     In line with his idea of mission, gradually Ammende began to turn
the congress into a prominent forum for national minority issues. As this
happened, naturally the organisation took it as read that national identity
provided the person, indeed Europe, with something fundamental. As Otto
Ulitz (a German from Polish Silesia) told congress participants in 1930:

> Our humanity grows out of our nationality. Our nationality
> is the foundation for everything we do and think.[2]

Ammende personally believed an individual's nationality could never be
extinguished.[3] Another commentator felt attempts to change a person's
nationality were unhealthy; they set up tensions within an individual.[4] These
terms of reference hearkened back to Herder and were associated with the
idea that the mixture of national groups offered something formative to
Europe. As another Baltic German put it, 'Europe cannot exist without
nationalities.'[5] It was assumed that, with a homogeneous population, Europe

---

[1] E. Ammende, 'Baltische Aufgaben. Die Arbeit auf internationalem Gebiet', *Revaler Bote*, 1
November 1929.
[2] O. Ulitz addressing the European Congress of Nationaliies, 1930. *Sitzungsbericht des
Kongresses der organisierten Nationalen Gruppen in den Staaten Europas. Genf, 3 bis 6
September 1930*. Vienna - Leipzig: Wilhelm Braumüller, 1931, pp. 31–4.
[3] E. Ammende, 'The Unsolved Minority Problem and the Peace of Europe.' S 338. 4 / 6638 /
6638. LoN Archive, Geneva.
[4] M.H. Boehm, Assimilation vom voelkerpsychologischen Geschichtspunkt, Nachlass Boehm
1077 / 16. Federal Archive, Koblenz.
[5] M.H. Boehm, 'Volksgedanke und Weltanschauung', 1932. Nachlass Boehm 1077 / 16. Federal
Archive, Koblenz.

would have been something different—something impoverished and inferior.[6]

The congress had arisen as a project pursued by members of minority nationality groups and provided a forum for the discussion of issues deemed important to them. To facilitate its work, the congress had an organising committee which became inhabited by a number of stalwart members. Ammende participated as General Secretary, likewise Josip Wilfan (a Slovene from Italy who was a member of the Italian parliament) as President. Also regular participants were Paul Schiemann (the famous ethnic German from Latvia who served in its parliament), Géza von Szüllö (an ethnic Hungarian who sat in the Czechoslovakian parliament) and Leo Motzkin (a senior figure among Jewish minorities).[7] The committee met several times a year, preparing the congress. It was also a focus around which subsidiary committees could be organised to address themes of particular interest, such as language, religion, culture or schooling. Behind everything, however, Ammende drove the congress along and from April 1927 he had an office in Vienna to facilitate his business, whether liaising with Basques from Spain, Lithuanians from Germany or Greeks from the Dodecanese.[8]

The congress met annually in early autumn. Arranged in advance by the organising committee, its proceedings were published and distributed to all interested parties, including the Minorities Section of the League of Nations and the Foreign Ministry in Berlin. Each year some new minorities joined the forum while others left, although throughout the 1920s a hard core of participants included at least the German, Hungarian and Jewish groups— their relative coherence and consistent membership helping underpin the congress's work.[9] What, then, were the main concerns of this unusual transnational body, particularly during the period when it enjoyed its greatest independence, namely from its inception to the remorseless rise of chauvinistic nationalism at the heart of Europe?

---

[6] See the comments of Director Paern to the congress in 1927. *Sitzungsbericht des Kongresses der organisierten nationalen Gruppen in den Staaten Europas. Genf 22.–24. August 1927.* Vienna: Wilhelm Braumüller, 1928, p. 111.

[7] Other members of the organising committee who served less length periods included Graf Stanisław Sierakowski (an ethnic Pole who sat in the Prussian *Landtag*), Michail Kurtschinsky and Francesc Maspons i Anglasell (a Catalan from Spain who belonged to the Academy of Law in Barcelona).

[8] *Sitzungsbericht 1927*, p.13

[9] For details of all the groups that belonged to the congress, see S. Bamberger-Stemmann, pp.397–405.

## 2. The language of peace: rhetoric and analysis in the European Congress of Nationalities, 1926–32.

*a. National minorities as pacifists*

For Ammende, minority problems were the main potential cause of war in Europe; [10] hence peace was a central theme for the congress and speakers emphasised repeatedly the importance of minority and nationality issues to it.[11] Paul Schiemann agreed. In the wake of the First World War, a spirit of conflict could be replaced by one of peace and the European Congress of Nationalities was work towards this end.[12] It was a project building 'a peaceful coexistence of nations',[13] while providing Europe with 'understanding' and 'satisfaction', also creating the prerequisites for 'a healthy and lasting peace.'[14] He believed peace had to be central to the concerns of minorities, peace both between states and within them.[15]

Catalan representatives from Spain first attended the congress in 1926 and soon declared, on behalf of all present, 'we are pacifists!'[16] Even in 1932, senior Jewish representative Leo Motzkin observed the congress was pursuing the pacification of Mankind.[17] Emil Margulies (a Jew from Czechoslovakia) agreed that leaving 15% of the continent's population embittered,[18] disappointed and hopeless was an enduring threat to peace.[19] Josip Wilfan maintained that peace in Europe required more than palliative measures for the minority question.[20]

---

[10] E. Ammende, 'Aktuelle Aufgaben im Kampfe um den nationalen Ausgleich', *Nation und Staat* Oct. 1929, p. 282.

[11] For instance, at the start of the 1926 congress, Michail Kurtschinsky (an ethnic Russian from Estonia) stated that the congress served 'the creation of peace between nations and states'. *Sitzungsbericht des Kongresses der organisierten nationalen Gruppen in den Staaten Europas. Genf 25.–27. August 1926.*Vienna: Wilhelm Braumüller, 1927, p. 23.

[12] *Sitzungsbericht des Kongresses der organisierten nationalen Gruppen in den Staaten Europas. Wien, 29. Juni bis 1. Juli 1932.* Wien-Leipzig: Wilhelm Braumüller, 1933, p. 16. Professor Bovet agreed when he spoke to the congress. He suggested that the mood of peace that had made the League of Nations possible after the First World War had also made the congress possible. *Sitzungsbericht 1932*, pp. 30–42.

[13] *Sitzungsbericht 1926*, p. 34. For a study emphasizing the contemporary relevance of Schiemann's thought, see I. Ijabs, 'Strange Baltic Liberalism: Paul Schiemann's Political Thought Re-visited', *Journal of Baltic Studies* 40 (2009) 496–515.

[14] *Sitzungsbericht 1927*, p. 23.

[15] *Sitzungsbericht des Kongresses der organisierten nationalen Gruppen in den Staaten Europas. Genf, 26 bis 28. August 1929.* Vienna and Leipzig: Wilhelm Braumüller, 1930, p. 94.

[16] *Sitzungsbericht 1927*, p. 65.

[17] *Sitzungsbericht 1932*, p. 21.

[18] *Sitzungsbericht 1926*, p. 31.

[19] *Sitzungsbericht des Kongresses der organisierten nationalen Gruppen in den Staaten Europas. Genf 29.–31. August 1928.* Vienna: Wilhelm Braumüller, 1928, p. 61.

[20] *Sitzungsbericht des Kongresses der organisierten nationalen Gruppen in den Staaten Europas. Genf, 26 bis 28. August 1929.* Vienna and Leipzig: Wilhelm Braumüller, 1930, p. 19.

Minorities had good reason to promote peace. As Joan Estelrich (a Catalan from Spain) said, in the event of war they were likely to suffer more seriously than most.[21] Wilfan agreed minorities were particularly prone to becoming victims of war and hence had a special interest in warning against it.[22] He might have added that national minorities often lived in sensitive border areas vulnerable to conflict and could find the state in which they lived fighting the state ruled by their co-nationals, a situation which could lead to them being stereotyped as potential enemies of the state in which they lived.[23]

Ammende shared these convictions. As he told the Royal Institute of International Affairs in London in May 1930, 'the problem of peace in Europe is indissolubly linked up with the problem of the minorities' question.'[24] In an article, he said he and his colleagues shared:

> ...the knowledge that the solution of this question forms the heart of the problem of coexistence among the European nations and therefore of the preservation of European peace.[25]

Summarising the proceedings from the congress in 1930, he maintained that unsolved nationality problems still threatened Europe's peace.[26] This was a message that everyone involved in the congress in the 1920s felt compelled to broadcast at every opportunity.

### b. Conditions for achieving peace

The congress outlined the conditions which could make peace possible. As Ammende put it, there was a need to satisfy the strivings that led to irredentism, but without re-drawing boundaries—a strategy which could only lead to new wars.[27] So how were satisfied national groups to be created? To quote Géza von Szüllő, if the congress was trying to identify the 'kernel of

---

[21] *Sitzungsbericht 1930*, p. 49.

[22] 'Bericht über die Teilsitzung des Kongressausschusses vom 11. Februar [1931] in Dresden.' R60528. Political Archive of the Foreign Ministry, Berlin.

[23] The point about the vulnerability of national minorities living in borderlands was, however, made by Josip Wilfan to the congress in 1932. See *Sitzungsbericht 1932*, p. 13.

[24] The Unsolved Minority Problem and the Peace of Europe. S 338. 4 / 6638 / 6638. LoN Archive.

[25] E. Ammende, 'Der Kampf um die Rechte der Nationalitäten und die neutralen Staaten', *Nation und Staat* May 1929, pp. 527–8.

[26] E. Ammende, 'Fünf Jahre europäische Nationalitätenbewegung', *Revalsche Zeitung* 30 August 1930.

[27] The Unsolved Minority Problem and the Peace of Europe. S 338. 4 / 6638 / 6638. LoN Archive.

poison' afflicting Europe (i.e. national intolerance), what would be the likely remedial medicine?[28]

Congress members knew nationalism in Europe had to be moderated. Elmér von Jakabffy (a Hungarian from Romania who served in parliament) agreed that all congress representatives should combat 'blind chauvinism' which denied any lasting value to the cultural achievements of nationalities other than one's own. This contributed nothing to the 'consolidation of Europe'.[29] Likewise, Schiemann felt Europe's minorities had to cool over-heated nationalism, changing it to a more restrained, healthy sense of national awareness which could offer something constructive to humanity. To this end, he felt minorities which were not compressed together in single nation states, had to criticise 'the national hatred of the world'.[30] Schiemann believed constructive national sentiment had an important role to play in Europe: positive nationalism (love of your own nationality) could assist in the pacification of the continent.[31] Leo Motzkin went further. To his mind, 'nationalism' became 'genuine' when you began to understand nations other than your own.[32] True nationalism had to be oriented to understanding others. It was not irredentist, since congress members were clear they wanted freedom to participate solely in the national culture of their co-nationals, not in the politics of their national group's state.[33]

Ewald Ammende agreed whole-heartedly. Just because national minorities valued their nationhood highly did not incline them towards chauvinism. Rather, their mission was 'strictly to be differentiated from national chauvinism, from domestic and international agitation'. Their interest in national identity had become something constructive and on this basis had to provide 'the foundation of the entire European nationality movement'.[34]

Congress members spoke up for national tolerance and against oppression, so it must have seemed like a voice from a different world entirely when, in 1929, Welshman Frederick Llewellyn-Jones (a member of the League of Nations Union and National Liberal MP for Bethesda, North Wales) attended the congress and emphasised the importance of good will rather than legislation in regulating minority affairs.[35] Good will was in too short supply in the societies inhabited by most of the congress participants. Hence, in 1926 the congress dealt with a theme Llewellyn-Jones could barely have imagined, as participants expressed outrage at steps taken in Italy to

---

[28] *Sitzungsbericht 1926*, p. 28.
[29] *Sitzungsbericht 1928*, p. 94.
[30] *Sitzungsbericht 1927*, p. 24–6.
[31] *Sitzungsbericht 1929*, p. 52.
[32] *Sitzungsbericht 1926*, p. 32.
[33] For example see the comments of Naumann, in *Sitzungsbericht 1927*, p. 84.
[34] E. Ammende, 'Baltische Aufgaben. Die Arbeit auf internationalem Gebiet', *Revaler Bote* 1 November 1929.
[35] *Sitzungsbericht 1929*, 1930, pp. 21–4.

change the names of minority individuals by force.[36] Schiemann argued such behaviour damaged Europe's peace. It was impossible for a state to achieve anything significant unless it was at peace internally and this required a solution to the minority problem.[37]

It was in keeping with Ammende's character and his position as General Secretary of the congress that he was deeply moved by the human costs of nationality-based persecution. It was logical for him to denounce the 'personal suffering' of innumerable people impoverished and rendered stateless by it. Such deplorable behaviour, he said, made subversion more rather than less likely, since it put people at odds with the state in which they lived.[38]   The sense that an oppressive treatment of minorities would only store up trouble for the future was voiced by Joan Casanovas (a Catalan from Spain):

> ...where there is tyranny, there are revolts, and from them
> spring war.... Every oppression of a nation means there is a
> danger of war.

Oppression of minorities increased the likelihood of other states attempting to intervene in the offender's domestic affairs. There was even the possibility of an enemy state using unrest on the part of minorities to destabilise the oppressive state.[39] In other words, in the world of the time, persecution of minorities posed a serious threat to peace because of the responses it could elicit from third-parties.

Repeatedly the congress made plain the desire to create a new kind of society in which it was possible to learn from national diversity. It was all part of a project to promote a better understanding of Europe, in the process creating the pre-conditions for lasting peace by consolidating the foundations of ethnically mixed states.[40]   In the process, participants were emphasising the value of Estonia's cultural autonomy model for multi-ethnic society. In 1928, Emil Margulies outlined his vision of a future in which society was not homogenised, perhaps through a slow process of assimilation, but in which majority and minority pursued independent lines of cultural development while constantly mixing on the basis of equality, giving and taking from each other in the process.[41] As another representative to the congress said, quoting Gottfried Keller, the goal was unity in diversity achieved on the basis of friendship rooted in freedom.[42] It followed, as another congress participant (Richard Csaki, a German from Romania) put it, they wanted to create a

---

[36] *Sitzungsbericht 1926*, pp. 126–7.
[37] *Sitzungsbericht 1928*, pp. 28–9.
[38] *Sitzungsbericht 1930*, pp. 21–2.
[39] *Sitzungsbericht 1927*, pp. 66–8.
[40] *Sitzungsbericht 1927*, p. 23.
[41] Ibid, p. 62.
[42] *Sitzungsbericht 1929*, p. 75.

situation where loyalty to the state in which you lived and loyalty to your national culture would not be in conflict. Everyone would be free to participate in their nation's great traditions and cultural events without fear of punishment, with the whole of society becoming richer as a result.[43]

The contention that diversity was intrinsically good was a million miles away from the demand that every nationality have its own exclusive state. For Ernst Flachbarth (a Hungarian from Czechoslovakia), minorities in Europe were like the colours of the spectrum, or a mixture of flowers in a great garden. If you lost even one element, the entirety would be damaged.[44]

It was unsurprising that congress participants saw national minorities as having the role of mediating between different national groups, of erecting bridges where previously there had been chasms. Obviously they had a burning desire to bridge any gap between themselves and the majority people in the state where they lived, but minorities realised that domestic rapprochement could lead to international rapprochement too. In 1928 Elmér Jakabffy proposed that minorities could mediate between the state in which they lived and the state inhabited by their co-nationals. So, for example, at least in cultural terms Baltic Germans could mediate between the Weimar Republic and Estonia and Latvia. This mediation was expected to produce greater understanding between national groups and states alike. Similarly, Emil Margulies argued that creating a united community out of different national groups in any given multi-ethnic state would only lead to the building of bridges between states. That is to say, the creation of domestic peace promoted the creation of international peace too.[45] In this connection, owing to their large numbers and geographical distribution, Ammende believed German groups had a unique role to play in generating 'understanding between nations'.[46]

### c. Law and morality

In the terms of its discussion, the European Congress of Nationalities was morally attuned. For Wilfan, they were pursuing 'policy for everyone, a policy of solidarity, a European policy, a policy for Mankind.' Motzkin hinted the congress was evidence of Europe's moral conscience awakening.[47] Unsurprisingly, law and justice were central concerns.

Géza von Szüllö believed peace grew out of specific conditions; in his words, 'no peace can exist without justice.'[48] For Joan Casanovas, order based on justice was the only conceivable way of ending international

---

[43] *Sitzungsbericht 1928*, pp. 67–80.

[44] Ibid, p. 99.

[45] Ibid, p. 62.

[46] E. Ammende, 'Völker-Verhetzung', *Revalsche Zeitung* 27 October 1931.

[47] *Sitzungsbericht 1927*, p. 15–21.

[48] *Sitzungsbericht 1928*, p. 25.

anarchy and war.[49] Michail Kurtschinsky (a Russian from Estonia) agreed that the key to peace was provided by just government, the kind allowing everyone the same rights and protection, so reflecting the existence of universal human rights as they had begun to be formulated in the late eighteenth century.[50]

For congress participants, the practice of one's own national culture had to be recognised as an inalienable right enshrined in definite minority legislation. Arthur von Balogh (a Hungarian from Romania) quoted a speech by Giuseppe Motta to the League of Nations Assembly made in 1921.[51] He demanded that the right to practice national cultural life become integral to the rule of law and that every state become a *Rechtsstaat* (a state based on the rule of law) enshrining this principle. Perhaps one of the most interesting critiques of Europe's prevailing legal systems was provided by Estonian German Werner Hasselblatt. For him, popular democracy had brought rule by national majorities leading the 'national state' to overshadow the idea of the *Rechtsstaat*.[52] So while state constitutions guaranteed all Europeans freedom and equality regardless of their national background, in practice these principles were overlooked repeatedly as administrators and officials applied their discretion against members of minorities. Consequently, no matter what it said in statute books, never before had there been such an outcry for freedom and equality. Hence Hasselblatt said:

> ...our solution should be this: back to law, to true law which
> is in harmony with moral ethos; back to law, to more law
> and a better moral order....[53]

He felt this was the most important idea abroad at the congress and believed eventually they would need to formulate a legal code to regulate relations between different nationalities.[54]

Minority thinkers emphasised more than just the fate of minorities was at stake if they were treated unjustly. Conflict ignited between neighbouring states by unjust treatment of minorities had to affect whole populations, not just sections of them. As Hasselblatt argued, however, there were consequences apart from war. Injustice practiced against a minority had a generally corrosive effect. It led to a general acceptance of injustice and corrupted society as a whole.[55]

---

[49] *Sitzungsbericht 1926*, p. 143 and *Sitzungsbericht 1927*, p. 65.
[50] *Sitzungsbericht 1926*, p. 25.
[51] *Sitzungsbericht 1927*, p. 44.
[52] *Sitzungsbericht 1928*, pp. 123–34.
[53] Ibid.
[54] Motzkin in *Sitzungsbericht 1926*, p. 33.
[55] *Sitzungsbericht 1926*, p. 93.

## d. Economics, security and disarmament

The congress's participants felt minority issues underlay all the major problems of the day. This was true of economics. Ewald Ammende was convinced that the economic unity of Europe would remain illusory until hatred between majorities and minorities was overcome.[56] Similarly, when the congress met during the Depression, Wilfan maintained Europe's economic problems could not be solved so long as the nationality question existed in the back of statesmen's minds when they met in conference. Their suspicions made it impossible for them to unite to solve even this most pressing problem.[57] It followed that, for congress members, Europe's organisation as a set of states was inadequate; it required organising as a system of nationality groups too. Only this two-fold organisation could secure genuine unity across the continent.[58]

By definition, the minority problem was tied to security and disarmament. On one occasion, the congress committee heard that so long as the matter remained unsolved, weapons would always proliferate. Unresolved minority questions led to demands that the peace settlement be revised, something which in turn caused politicians and states to feel threatened, consequently to demand greater security measures. In such an environment, significant disarmament was highly unlikely.[59] Hence Ewald Ammende maintained that national reconciliation had to be a pre-requisite of 'effective disarmament'.[60] The line gained support from other congress participants. British League of Nations Union activist Sir Willoughby Dickinson agreed that military security had to be supplemented by security based on satisfied nationhood, even if this meant living in a land where people spoke different languages, celebrated different festivals, where their children sang different songs and where people prayed in different ways.[61] Similarly, in 1931, Josip Wilfan argued there was no prospect of the World Disarmament Conference hosted by the League of Nations showing real success until it overcame the psychological barriers keeping different national groups apart.[62] At the same congress, Schiemann argued that efforts at piecemeal disarmament would not get far because the main problem of the age was defined by a destructive spirit. Although politicians spoke about the need to disarm, their states displayed 'over-heated nationalism'. Before substantial disarmament could happen, this mood had to change fundamentally; there had to be a break with

---

[56] *Sitzungsbericht 1930*, p. 96.

[57] *Sitzungsbericht 1931*, p.3.

[58] See Schiemann's comments in *Sitzungsbericht 1926*, p.43.

[59] 'Bericht über die Teilsitzung des Kongressausschusses vom 11. Februar [1931] in Dresden'. R60528. Political Archive of the Foreign Ministry, Berlin.

[60] E. Ammende, 'Die grundsätzlichen Ergebnisse der Genfer Auseinandersatzung', *Revalsche Zeitung* 29 January 1931.

[61] *Sitzungsbericht 1929*, p. 29.

[62] *Sitzungsbericht 1931*, p. 11.

aggressive nationalism.[63] In the same forum, Engelbert Besednjak (a Slovene from Italy), reiterated both that fear of irredenta drove the acquisition of armaments and also that no state would disarm so long as part of its national group was being persecuted abroad.[64]

Congress participants believed minorities should champion a more fundamental kind of disarmament than one involving only mutual reductions of men and materiel. Instead, the very root causes generating feelings of insecurity had to be tackled. Emil Margulies recommended 'spiritual disarmament' was necessary before anything else.[65] Similarly, Joan Estelrich advocated 'moral security', by which he meant that, before states could be secure, individuals had to feel secure in their personalities, in their ability to express fundamental cultural needs.[66]

But perhaps the most important phrase was 'moral disarmament'. It was used as a title for an article published by Ammende himself in 1932. Discussing how tensions still existed between national minorities and majorities, he made plain oppressive behaviour had to give way to something better in order to reduce tensions around Europe.[67] Wilfan agreed that material security had to be pre-empted by 'moral security' between Europe's nations.[68] Professor Ernest Bovet emphasised to the congress that Europe's moral disarmament and the creation of lasting peace required the universalising of minority protection.[69] In effect, moral disarmament involved removing all the ideological points which could cause tension in Europe and which might, therefore, one day contribute to war. Consequently it was logical that in 1931 the congress adopted the following resolution:

> Material disarmament cannot be implemented with good prospects and success without moral disarmament at the same time, which above all must involve the peaceful solution of the nationality question. Only this would result in a real securing of peace.[70]

### e. Solidarity between minorities

As it analysed peace, the European Congress of Nationalities attempted to be inclusive. To cite Leo Motzkin, the congress was supposed to draw together

---

[63] Ibid, pp. 97–8.

[64] Ibid, pp. 99–102.

[65] Ibid, p. 113.

[66] Ibid, pp.103–5.

[67] E. Ammende, 'Moralische Abrüstung', *Revalsche Zeitung* 17 November 1932.

[68] 'Von der bisherigen und künftigen Entwicklung der Europäische Nationalitätenkongresses.' R1687. Correspondence with Individuals. 41 / 56073 / 30181.

[69] *Sitzungsbericht 1932*, p. 31.

[70] *Sitzungsbericht des congresses der organisierten nationalen Gruppen in den Staaten Europas. Genf 29 bis 31 1931*. Vienna and Leipzig: Wilhelm Braumüller, 1932, p. 144.

lots of diverse groups and let them share their experiences.[71] To this end, the body aimed to create a sense of solidarity among participants. As Flachbarth said, 'Our motto is: one for all and all for one.' Only by pulling together would minorities, as non-state actors, create a critical weight likely to influence governments.[72] Hence Leon Reich (a Jew from Poland) advised minorities should never march against each other, even if at times neither could they march together. In a nutshell, and as Wilfan said in 1932, there had to be solidarity among minorities, no matter which group you belonged to.[73] Likewise Wilhelm von Medinger (a German from Czechoslovakia) stated people should work for the benefit of minorities as a whole rather than simply for the benefit of their own group.[74] Reich looked to the day when everyone would speak up for common interests.[75] More ambitiously, Wilfan hoped that the creation of solidarity among Europe's minorities would pave the way for more general solidarity among Europe's peoples 'as natural, especially cultural communities'.[76]

In the 1920s and early 1930s at least, congress participants were so committed to representing general interests that they advocated becoming active on behalf of even minorities living in the midst of their 'Mother Nation'.[77] As Eduard Pant (a German from Poland) put it:

> We must say clearly and openly, that every injustice, from whichever side it may come, remains an injustice. We may not approve injustice even if it comes from a side which we must give consideration to for certain reasons.[78]

He added that it would be inappropriate for people to call for reconciliation in the congress, but return home and promote measures oppressing other minorities. Minority representatives had to live up to their stated principles.

In this connection (and notwithstanding its critique of how mass democracies worked in practice), the congress was pro-democratic in principle. Géza von Szüllö held that true democracy protected minorities in their cultural demands.[79] Proposing that a society lacking every sense of

---

[71] *Sitzungsbericht 1927*, p. 18.

[72] *Sitzungsbericht 1926*, p.143.

[73] *Sitzungsbericht 1927*, pp. 99–100.

[74] *Sitzungsbericht 1926*, p.134. *Sitzungsbericht 1932*, p. 10. For a study of von Medinger, see S. Dyroff, 'Der Platz der Völkerbundbeschwerde in den politischen Strategien nationaler Minderheiten. Positionen aus dem Kreis "Europäischen Nationalitätenkongresses"' in M. Beer and S. Dyroff (eds.), *Politische Strategien nationaler Minderheiten in der Zwischenkriegszeit*. Munich: Oldenbourg, 2013.

[75] Reich in *Sitzungsbericht 1927*, p. 101 also see p. 14.

[76] *Sitzungsbericht 1926*, p. 19.

[77] See comments of Naumann in *Sitzungsbericht 1927*, p. 84.

[78] Ibid, pp. 97–8.

[79] *Sitzungsbericht 1927*, p. 22.

national consciousness would amount to Bolshevism, he advocated a kind of democracy based on the Bible and on the love of justice.[80]

Nor were the principles of congress participants without risk. In 1926, Josip Wilfan (despite being a senator in the Italian parliament) was arrested in Rome by Italian authorities.[81] Unsurprisingly, therefore, a few months later Paul Schiemann went out of his way to denounce Fascism as the greatest danger to the minority movement.[82] Given his long-standing interest in the Germans of the South Tyrol, naturally Ammende too spoke out frequently and passionately about the practices of the Italian government. On one occasion, he described the South Tyrol as a 'burning wound on the body of the German nation' and urged that Germany never sell out the South Tyrol.[83] Taking everything into account, there was at least some good reason for the congress's organising committee to term its organisation 'the strongest moral factor in the fight for national equality'.[84]

### 3. Eclectic interests

#### a. National intolerance

As General Secretary, Ammende was involved in much organisational hard work to make the congress function. Regularly he travelled the length and breadth of Europe networking and discussing minority issues. He was constantly guaranteeing the platform from which others could proclaim their messages of peace and tolerance. Occasionally, as in 1926, Ammende was so consumed with the job of actually running the congress that he had no energy left to address it personally. In his office in Vienna, he prepared congress minutes for publication, circulated newsletters about minority affairs and corresponded with all and sundry about congress business. In addition, he kept up a stream of articles for *Revaler Bote*. Through it all, naturally Ammende maintained an analytical commentary about minority affairs. In 1927 he addressed the congress about national intolerance as a cause of war, developing a thesis which he turned into a number of publications. To his mind, a mood of nationalism had been crucial in precipitating the First World War. Within states, it was associated with an atmosphere hostile to minorities. This mood also impacted on international relations such that, eventually, the unsolved minority question helped generate an explosion.[85] Of

---

[80] *Sitzungsbericht 1926*, p.29
[81] 'Dr.Wilfan—Slowenenführer in Italien verhaftet', *Revaler Bote* 13 November 1926.
[82] 'Dr Schiemann über die Tagung der deutschen Minoritäten', *Revaler Bote* 7 July 1927.
[83] E. Ammende, 'Das Schicksal der Deutschen Südtirols. "Eine brennende Wunde am Körper des deutschen Volkes"', *Revaler Bote* 10 January 1930.
[84] 'Protokoll der Sitzungen vom 5. Dezember 1931 in Wien.' Schiemann Papers. ENK Folder. Baltic Central Library, Riga.
[85] *Sitzungsbericht 1927*, pp. 57–64. See also E. Ammende, 'Der dritte Nationalitätenkongress', *Revaler Bote* 24 August 1927.

course the peace settlement, with its re-drawing of borders, did not remove the problem and millions of people still lived as minorities. Indeed, if anything the minority question had strengthened as a result of the war and peacemaking, since events had only increased popular national consciousnesses. Hence Ammende commented as follows in a memorandum written, apparently, for John Maynard Keynes:

> The Balts have become far more German now than they were under Russia. In Romania there are men with German names who before the war regarded themselves Hungarians. Now they have suddenly remembered that they are Germans; a typical instance of the revival of national consciousness.[86]

At the same time, the post-war possibility of greater international interaction allowed the more open recognition that national communities crossed borders. After the war, there was a greater feeling of cultural solidarity than ever and it had become impossible for a national community to ignore the fate of any of its splinters living on 'foreign' soil. Given that most nationality groups had a co-national state somewhere; it followed that unsolved minority questions within a state would impact on relations between states more than ever in the 1920s.

## b. Shortcomings of the League of Nations

Given that minorities were dedicated to developing their own narratives about minority protection and their place in any given state, it was hardly surprising that soon enough they found themselves at odds with those tasked by the post-war settlement to guarantee their well-being. From a relatively early point, as evidenced by a talk given in 1927, Ammende was prepared to be critical of how the League of Nations approached minority questions. For all its good intentions and despite the existence of a system of minority protection, to his mind the organisation did not take account adequately of the full importance of minority issues. He complained that already its minority protection system was inadequate; it appeared like a kind of charity rather than a system of law. He argued that appeals to the League when minorities had been treated poorly by the state in which they lived generally led to more difficulties than benefits, not least because the League attempted to negotiate with wrong-doers rather than enforce unassailable rights. As a result, sometimes treaties were being subverted in practice and some states were persecuting minorities with minimal repercussions. The consequence, to Ammende's mind, was that unhappiness with minority rights was increasing

---

[86] 'Germans outside Germany. A Movement for Consolidation. The Role of the Minorities.' 1502–1–61, Moscow.

and trust in the League was waning until a point just short of a crisis had been reached.

He accused the League of Nations of failing to clarify the minority problem. The management of petitions on a case by case basis by *ad hoc* Committees of Three had contributed to the 'artificial randomisation' of the issue. But since areas, such as border zones, often inhabited by minorities were the places most likely to suffer under the impact of war, Ammende felt it the duty of national minorities to warn the League and Europe's public of the danger of conflict growing greater every day; but would their warning be heard in time? Whether the League could underpin the principles of national tolerance would determine whether or not Europe went to war.[87] As he put it in 1927:

> ...we only need to remark that no other circumstance is endangering European peace in greater measure than precisely national intolerance.[88]

The European Congress of Nationalities condensed these concerns into a resolution stating that the position of national minorities in Europe was becoming worse. The principles of minority protection were being subverted and nothing was being done in response. The very principles of minority protection were being questioned and the foundations of the peace settlement likewise. Hence the congress called on the League to ensure that nationality rights were protected.'[89]

### c. Self-contradictory mentality and the opposite of reciprocity

To unmask the injustice of state policies towards national minorities, Ammende discussed the 'self-contradictory mentality'.[90] The trigger was a statement by the Italian government that it would Italianise German and Slovene minorities. To Ammende's mind, that government was replacing the principle of national tolerance with the demand for national uniformity. But there was a catch here because Italy demanded something different for Italian minorities abroad. Rome in no way expected Italians in Malta, Yugoslavia or France to lose their national character. It would tolerate neither the Anglicisation of Italians in Malta, nor their assimilation in France; it demanded their national cultural development.

---

[87] E. Ammende, 'Die Ergebnisse des dritten Genfer Nationalitätenkongresses', *Revaler Bote* 2 September 1927.

[88] *Sitzungsbericht 1927*, p. 64

[89] See E. Ammende, *Gefährdung des europäischen Friedens durch die nationale Unduldsamkeit*. Vienna: Friedrich Jasper. No date (presumably 1927), p. 11. Also *Sitzungsbericht 1927*, p. 131.

[90] E. Ammende, 'Zwiespältige Mentalität. Ein Beitrag zur Charakteristik der nationalen Krise' in *Nation und Staat*, March 1928. See also E. Ammende, 'Zwiespältige Mentalität', *Revaler Bote* 18 April 1928.

Ammende cited an article by Italian Senator Cirmeni which argued, quite illogically, that no one should be able to tell the Italian state how to act in its own house, but held that Italian minorities should maintain their own national identity. This was the 'self-contradictory mentality'. As Ammende summarised it: 'That which is allowed for me, is forbidden to someone else.'[91] While he admitted Italy was probably unique in expressing the mentality quite so clearly, he felt the basic sentiment was abroad in most European states. The congress had to play a major role in advancing beyond this way of thinking.

Naturally Ammende believed things could be better. In an interview with *The Times* of London given in October 1926, he said there were two ways to treat minorities: either to oppress them until some kind of catastrophe resulted or to allow them full cultural independence and economic equality. The latter avoided minorities complaining to the League of Nations and so subverting a state's prestige. Naturally this was the course Ammende favoured and he recommended it should be pursued on the basis of reciprocity. That's to say, given that a Polish minority lived in Lithuania, and a Lithuanian minority lived in Poland, wouldn't it make sense for both states to grant full rights to the minorities concerned?[92]

### d. Situation report and the importance of loyalty

Ammende's deep interest in European minority affairs led him to survey the situation of as many of their number as feasible. Unfortunately the project could not be definitive because, by the time he compiled his report, minorities from within Germany had left the congress and so did not participate in any of its initiatives. Still, Ammende, supported by the congress members, produced a massive study which publicised the situation facing minorities. Josip Wilfan greeted it as follows:

> In this book, the finger is laid on the wound. It shows where the European body is sick, what produces unbearable tensions within it, what tears asunder time and again this Europe that is striving for unity, and what must therefore be overcome.[93]

The report was supposed to show how poorly Europe's minorities were being treated towards the end of the 1920s, but it did more than this, providing a singular round up of information and insight regarding the

---

[91] Ammende, 'Zwiespältige Mentalität. Ein Beitrag zur Charakteristik der nationalen Krise' in *Nation und Staat*, March 1928, p.543.

[92] 'Fortschritt der Nationalitätenbewegung. "Times" Interview mit einem Estländer', 30.10.26 *Revaler Bote*. R60465. Political Archive of the Foreign Ministry, Berlin.

[93] *Sitzungsbericht des congresses der organisierten nationalen Gruppen in den Staaten Europas. Genf 29 bis 31 1931.* Vienna and Leipzig: Wilhelm Braumüller, 1932, p. 4.

character of many of Europe's national minorities at the time.[94] The report
was intended to cover 40 million members of nationality groups living in 14
different states.[95] It showed that while the minority question was particularly
pressing for Central and Eastern Europe, nonetheless minority questions
concerned Western Europe too, not least because 25% of Spain's population
could be counted as such. Furthermore, it was not just the size of minorities
that mattered: the fate of even numerically small minorities could be felt
deeply by co-nationals.

The survey proposed that most nationality groups in Europe had a
dual status. They lived as a majority population in a 'nation state', but also
some of their number lived as minorities in 'foreign' states. To Ammende's
mind, this showed Europe's minority problem did not concern solely
relations between minority and majority populations in any given state, it was
also a matter of relations between the 'mother nation' (*Stammvolk*) and co-
national minorities abroad. Ammende said:

> The truth is as follows: today the nations of Europe are
> communities whose international character can no longer be
> denied; they are unities which urge the creation of their
> national    organisations;    indeed    they    demand    most
> emphatically the recognition and respect of their national
> unity.[96]

This was why, Ammende reminded everyone, national groups could exercise
a self-contradictory mentality, because in different situations they were both
majority and minority.

Moreover, the survey displayed how many states were home to
numerous minorities. In Romania, Ammende said, there were minorities of
Hungarians, Germans, Ukrainians, Bulgarians, Jews and Russians; in Poland
there were Ukrainians, Germans, Jews, Russians, White Russians and
Lithuanians; and in Czechoslovakia there were Germans, Hungarians,
Russians, Poles and Jews. So he found simplistic ideas of the nation state
completely unacceptable; reality was far more complicated.

Ammende identified three different strategies applied by states to
oppress minorities. First there were open attempts to de-nation them. Second
there were cases where the theory and practice of minority rights were

---

[94] E. Ammende, 'Aktuelle Aufgaben im Kampfe um den nationalen Ausgleich', *Nation und Staat*
October 1929
[95] The summary here is taken from Ammende's speech to the congress given in 1930, when the
report was still being prepared. *Sitzungsbericht 1930*, pp. 17–24. In a further essay, Ammende
suggested that the congress represented 82% of Europe's minorities. 'Die Sprache der Zahlen',
*Nation und Staat* 4 (1930/31) pp. 650–56. The 14 states were Estonia, Lithuania, Latvia,. Poland,
Denmark, Germany, Czechoslovakia, Austria, Hungary, Yugoslavia, Romania, Bulgaria, Italy
and Spain.
[96] *Sitzungsbericht 1930*, p.18.

mismatched: on paper, a state was supposed to maintain a minority's rights, but in reality it was subverting them. This was the kind of persecution Ammende believed most common in Europe. And finally there were tactics designed to deny the very existence of a minority in the first place.[97] A state disputed there was any minority, maintaining it was only a part of the majority. Whatever the strategy for persecution, Ammende maintained they all caused considerable damage to the people in question. There were groups that had lost up to 75% of their national assets, and Ammende attested he personally had witnessed suffering on the part of innumerable people as a result.

To Ammende's mind, oppression of minorities stored up problems for the future. It made irredenta more likely. He recounted that if you travelled Europe's 'danger zones', as he did frequently, you'd see that despite the existence of the League of Nations and its mission to preserve the peace of the world, bad events were too close for comfort. To save Europe, he recommended a move away from 'negative' rights (emphasising how minorities should not be treated) to more positive rights (offering models for how to fulfil cultural freedoms—as happened through cultural autonomy).

Eventually the congress passed a resolution about the report. It said the document showed how all states (whether bound by national minority treaties or not) failed to understand minority issues. Both cultural rights and equality before the law were almost non-existent, assimilation was being applied with ever greater determination, while police and military power were being used against minorities.[98] Reviews of the book were suitably outraged at the picture it painted. *Revalsche Zeitung* said it made 'a shocking impression of immeasurable suffering and great injustice', and went on to quote from *Kölnische Zeitung*:

> A book of misery and indictment ... a black book, a horror-inspiring commentary to the pronouncements about the right to self-determination of nations and also, we hope, a reminder for the conscience of the League of Nations.[99]

---

[97] For a related article, see E. Ammende, 'Die augenblickliche Lage der deutschen Volksgruppen in den europäischen Staaten', *Revaler Bote* 9 July 1931.

[98] *Sitzungsbericht 1931*, pp. 142–3. For Ammende concluding text for the situation report, see 'Grundsätzliche Schlussfolgerungen, die sich aus den Lageberichten der Nationalitäten ergeben'. R60528. Political Archive of the Foreign Ministry, Berlin. For a summary of his arguments, see Avant-Propos. Geneva. R2161. Minorities. 4 / 31096 / 3817. Geneva. See also E. Ammende, 'Grundsätzliche Schlussfolgerungen, die sich aus den Lageberichten der Nationalitäten Europas ergeben.' Sonderausdruck aus der "Sammlung von Lageberichten über die Nationalitäten in den Staaten Europas". R2161. Minorities. 7th ENK. 29 to 31 August 1931. 4 / 31096 / 3817. Geneva. Also see E. Ammende (ed.), *Die Nationalitäten in den Staaten Europas. Sammlung von Lageberichten*. Vienna-Leipzig: Wilhelm Braumüller, 1931. Baltic Central Library, Riga.

[99] 'Die Nationalitäten in den Staaten Europas. Sammlung von Lageberichten des Europäischen Nationalitätenkongresses', *Revalsche Zeitung* 25 November 1931.

Ammende developed his ideas more fully when he spoke to the Royal Institute of International Affairs, London in May 1930.[100] He dismissed both the exchange of populations as practiced by Greece and Turkey after the First World War, as well as the 'direct annihilation' of cultural life Italy was pursuing in South Tyrol and the Dodecanese. He said it was inevitable that national minorities had to be included fully in the states they inhabited, hence it was necessary to find a mechanism permitting loyalty to both the state and their nationality. When Ammende identified potentially the most volatile parts of Europe owing to specific minority problems, interestingly he did not choose either areas ruled by Italy or populated, in the first instance, by Germans. Most dangerous were, in his opinion, parts of Europe populated by Ukrainians, White Russians and Lithuanians. As he put it:

> There is no doubt that if no improvement in the relations between the minorities and the majority is achieved here, we shall witness conflicts of far reaching consequences— events the incidence of which could easily spread to wider parts of Europe.[101]

Ammende feared tension between Poland and Lithuanian over especially Vilnius could lead to war while tension between the Polish state and Ukrainian communities could generate civil war—an event which might lead Soviet Russia to intervene. There could be no secure, peaceful development of Europe until these issues were addressed.

To Ammende's mind, the problem required a solution encouraging majority and minority to choose peaceful, loyal paths for themselves and vital here, of course, was the experience of cultural freedom:

> The growth of the loyal tendency and, at the same time, the decline of irredentism is in direct proportion to the opportunity for minorities to take an active part in the cultural life of the people to whom they belong by right of blood and descent. How utterly wrong is therefore the demand that loyalty must be the condition of granting nationality rights.

In other words, once appropriate rights were guaranteed, loyalty would follow. Trying to prove his point, Ammende claimed that cultural autonomy in Estonia had turned that country's German population into 'ardent supporters of the government'—a statement which was rather an exaggeration.

---

[100] The Unsolved Minority Problem and the Peace of Europe. S 338. 4 / 6638 / 6638. Geneva.
[101] Ibid.

Ammende advocated several steps to improve the position of minorities in Europe. He recommended a clear statement by the League of Nations emphasising that 'moral obligations' for dealing with minorities had 'general validity'. There should be a thorough investigation of the differences between Eastern and Western Europe over the treatment of minorities. Moves should be made to lessen the danger of irredenta, most importantly by encouraging states to deal with minorities on their territory in the same way they expected their co-nationals to be treated in other states. Lastly he argued the League should assume a more positive role in respect of minorities. It should not just deal with complaints of abuse, but investigate and broadcast good practices, for example by researching the implementation of cultural autonomy. (In a different essay, he suggested the League should help change the psychologies of all concerned regarding the minority question such that petitions would become things of the past.)[102]

### e. Germany's special role

Ammende was convinced that Germans had a special role in Europe, both in terms of championing the rights of national minorities and in binding together a continent fractured by war and the peace settlement. As he put it in the memorandum to John Maynard Keynes:

> The creation of national states has Balkanised Central Europe; the German minorities provide a sort of cement which may help consolidate it again. They consist in the main of steady, intelligent, middle-class people, shopkeepers, professional men, and farmers with a higher average of culture and understanding than the peoples among whom they live, and with no interest in anybody's quarrel. If Dr. Brandsch's idea is followed and each minority turns itself into a useful and indispensable ally of the government under which it finds itself, they may by working on parallel lines, contribute very greatly towards the peace and stabilisation of Europe.[103]

Ethnic Germans were well suited to becoming agents for reconciliation.

At the same time, and as Ammende recognised in another memorandum, German minorities had to be careful. In the post-war world, connections between Motherland and minorities could become more extensive than ever and so 'enemies' might argue that German minorities, if acting alone, were being directed from Berlin. Such scare stories could only

---

[102] E. Ammende, 'Die Sprache der Zahlen, *Nation und Staat* 4 (1930/31), p. 656.
[103] Memorandum by Ammende apparently to John Maynard Keynes, 'Germans outside Germany. A Movement for Consolidation. The Role of the Minorities.' 1502–1–61, Moscow.

be contradicted if German groups acted as just one element of a general European grouping of nationalities with an inclusive platform. In this framework, German minority projects would be European, rather than partisan.

It was imperative for German minorities to develop strong associations with the other major minorities in Europe, a development which might in turn permit the building of bridges between the German state and such groups. Eventually this would allow Germany to become an international leader in minority affairs—and naturally, for Ammende, the congress would help make all of this possible.[104] Yet, if German concerns were central to the business of the congress, interest in the work of the League of Nations—charged as it was with the protection of minority rights in many European states—was no less fundamental.

### 4. Lobbying the League

#### a. Optimism

At times, minorities displayed massive hopes for the League and that organisation gave them some grounds for optimism. In 1927, Catalan Professor Maspons i Anglassell took heart because the minorities had 'a League of Nations on their side'.[105] The next year, he added:

> We are the most convinced supporters of the League of Nations. We believe that it has opened up a new period in the political life of Mankind. We are perfectly convinced that without the League we would fall back into chaos and the most violent conflicts. We have and want to have trust in it. We expect from it the solution to our problems, which represent only one part of the problem of peace. We place all of our hopes in the League.[106]

In 1930, Joan Estelrich said of the League, 'We, the representatives of the minorities, still place all our hopes in it!'[107] Sudeten German Dr. Medinger agreed that, despite its shortcomings, the League of Nations remained 'the most important forum' for the 'petitions and wishes' of the national minorities.[108] He looked to a future in which the League might universalise minority rights. Prof. Balogh applauded the League as the greatest collective work achieved by civilised states. He recognised you should not blame the

---

[104] The Question of Organising a Congress of Nationalities. Moscow, 1502-1-112..
[105] *Sitzungsbericht 1927*, p. 17.
[106] *Sitzungsbericht 1928*, p. 29.
[107] *Sitzungsbericht 1930*, p. 54.
[108] *Sitzungsbericht 1926*, p. 131.

organisation for everything that went wrong and that it had been left important unsolved (maybe un-solvable) problems by the peace treaties.[109]

At least some resolutions passed by the congress were supportive of the League. Hence, the one relating to Ammende's speech on national intolerance included the following:

> It is our conviction that the League of Nations, as the only organisation competent for the treatment of all the questions which endanger peace in Europe, is obliged to be involved seriously in the treatment of the nationality problem and to take care that the holy rights of nationality are protected.[110]

Ammende kept on visiting the staff of the Minorities Section personally, always trying to persuade them to attend congress meetings. Erik Colban and Mr. Zilliacus (Information Section) attended the opening of the 1926 congress, and Ammende thanked the former when the two met at the League's offices a few days later.[111] Thereafter, Colban, or a representative, could be found frequently at the congress in Geneva. Routinely they received an invitation to the proceedings and were sent information about them.[112] Ammende did his best to employ a 'charm offensive' towards the League's staff. In a letter to Colban written in June 1927, he emphasised the congress would promote 'no aggression against states' and would work towards 'peaceful reconciliation'.[113] The next month, he wrote to Colban stressing that the congress was in harmony with everyone working towards 'European consolidation'.[114] Ammende maintained his strategy of personal contacts when Colban was replaced by Azcárate.[115]

Congress participants were also active in the League of Nations Union and Interparliamentary Union. In 1927, the congress's organising committee met in Brussels just ahead of the meeting of the League of Nations Union scheduled for the city and in which a number of the members would participate.[116] It is fair to say that during the 1920s, Ammende and those

---

[109] *Sitzungsbericht 1928*, pp.49–54.

[110] *Sitzungsbericht 1927*, p.131.

[111] Minute by Colban, 3.9.26. R 1686. Minority Questions. Protection of Minorities. 41 / 51553 / 30181. 'Der Nationalitätenkongreß', *Revaler Bote* 30 August 1926.

[112] 19.5.27, Colban to the Secretary General (Drummond). R1687. Correspondence with Individuals. 41 / 56073 / 30181. For an invitation, see 19.8.31 Ammende to Azcárate. R2161. Minorities. 4 / 31096 / 3817.

[113] 25.6.27, Ammende to Colban. R1687. Correspondence with Individuals. 41 / 56073 / 30181. Geneva. See also Ammende to Colban, 2.5.26. R 1686. Minority Questions. Protection of Minorities. 41 / 44950 / 30181.

[114] 15.7.26, Ammende to Colban. R 1686. Minority Questions. Protection of Minorities. 41 / 51553 / 30181.

[115] See The 7th Congress of European Nationalities. S 338. 4 / 6638 / 6638.

[116] Decisions. Committee sittings of 29 and 30 November 1927 in Berlin, Hotel Fürstenhof.

around him, were engaged in a multi-faceted strategy to influence the priorities of the League.

### b. Looming pessimism

Yet at the same time as Ammende and the congress were trying to create a working relationship with the League, there was also a sense that success would be fleeting. Minority spokesmen were alienated by comments made in the League to the effect that they were being prepared for assimilation (see chapter 5, conclusion). As Eugen Naumann put it in response:

> We want to keep ourselves as pure as possible and not be absorbed by the nation of the majority.[117]

In 1926 Géza von Szüllö—joined by other delegates such as the Leo von Déak (an Hungarian from Yugoslavia)—spoke out against Mello-Franco, complaining that attempts to make everyone the same were Bolshevist.[118] Ammende too rejected assimilation categorically. He thought even peaceful assimilation was 'immoral' and amounted to the 'removal of spirit' (*Entseelung*) from people.[119] Rudolf Brandsch put things as follows:

> It is demanded of us that we should assimilate. Even that shows again a lack of understanding of what a nation, a national minority, is. We are not adventurers and colonists who can go in one direction one minute and another direction the next. We do not belong to the modern nomads of the great cities who seek their fortune without having any inner connection to each other. Rather, we form living organisms which have become what they represent today through centuries of common development. Such an organism cannot be changed by external laws, ordinances or trickery so long as a grain of vital will is contained within it.[120]

For Brandsch, as for the other members of the congress, national minorities were living, breathing entities that deserved full respect. It was self-evident that statesmen failed to understand even the most basic truths about them. Even demands for loyalty were misplaced, as Brandsch explained:

Schiemann Papers. Baltic Central Library, Riga.
[117] Memo signed by P. Schiemann. 30.8.27, German Consulate. R60466. Political Archive of the Foreign Ministry, Berlin.
[118] *Sitzungsbericht 1926*, p. 29.
[119] *Sitzungsbericht 1930*, p. 23.
[120] *Sitzungsbericht 1928*, p. 55.

In addition to the decent fulfilment of our duty towards the state, an attitude—an external commitment to certain formulae—is demanded from us which we absolutely cannot have. Also it would be completely superfluous for statesmen to demand this from us, if they knew how deep and intrinsic the loyalty of the minority is. This is founded on us having an almost mystical connection with our homeland's (*Heimat's*) soil, with the earth on which we were born, and which our fathers transformed and worked. This fidelity, this connectedness, this intellectual harmony with the homeland's way of speaking, is the only foundation for our loyalty, but it is an absolutely secure one, this loyalty to the homeland.[121]

Admittedly members of the congress did try to re-interpret the unfortunate comments of Mello-Franco and Chamberlain. Hence Ammende made sure he reported on a speech given by Hungarian Count Apponyi to the League's Assembly in 1927:

I can only suppose that the Council meant this word 'absorb' exclusively as political absorption in the sense of the loyal fulfilment of all the rights of citizens towards the state.[122]

Ammende noted that Chamberlain was in the Assembly and had nodded his agreement. Talking to the congress in 1930, Josip Wilfan made a similar point. Although he too sometimes spoke out against crass assimilationism as propounded in some League circles,[123] nonetheless he suggested it would be advantageous to reach agreement with their opponents. He proposed the pursuit of 'assimilation in a civic sense' (in effect, integration), while leaving in place the most fundamental aspects of minority identities. Such an 'assimilation' would be acceptable so long as it relied on the methods of a 'civilised society'.[124]

---

[121] Ibid.

[122] E. Ammende, 'Gegen die Entnationalisierung. Die These Mello Francos widerlegt', *Revaler Bote* 15 September 1927. See also E. Ammende, 'Die VII Völkerbundversammlung und das Nationalitätenproblem', *Nation und Staat* 1927/28.

[123] *Sitzungsbericht 1928*, pp. 17–8.

[124] *Sitzungsbericht 1930*, pp. 9–10.

## 5. Proposing reforms to the League

### *a. General critique*

Given the divergence in mentalities between minority spokesmen and the statesmen inhabiting the League, it is no surprise that even in 1926 the former were displaying unhappiness with the latter. So, when Medinger made supportive comments about the League, he added constructive criticisms too. Medinger pointed out that the League was staffed by politicians who essentially represented majority populations and was a gathering of diplomats. ('Diplomats' was not supposed to sound like flattery. It identified people who did not act according to their consciences, but according an agenda set by others.) He recommended either that the League be extended by having some more representative forum added, or else it should include a more adequate diversity of deputies from multi-ethnic states (for example with the proportions of staff in Geneva reflecting the national proportions of the states from which they were drawn). He went on at length: all countries (rather than just treaty signatories) should protect minorities; the founders of minority protection had under-estimated the diplomatic games states could play in order to evade their responsibilities; the treatment of minority complaints by the Committee of Three was too secretive to be acceptable (it was reminiscent of a medieval system of justice); any member of the League (not just Council members) should be able to raise minority issues with the Council; more use should be made of the Permanent International Court; the League had to become more than a system for representing predominant interests and hence of perpetuating existing injustices; since the League depended on states, it always gave them the last word; and he recommended that perhaps in due course the Interparliamentary Union might develop into an alternative global parliament.[125]

It was axiomatic for congress members that the League did not understand their plight. In 1932, Deputy Rotenstreich (a Jew from Poland) was clear: the League needed to become a proper League of *Nations*, rather than just a League of *States*. He demanded that even minorities which lacked a home state should have some kind of representation in it.[126] Arthur von Balogh agreed, proposing the League found it convenient to overlook the interests of minorities. The League was dismissed as staffed by state servants, and its proceedings as more political than legal, leading 'law to sink and be buried in the swamp of politics.' The main thing for its minority protection system, he felt, was 'governments should not be damaged.'[127]

Ammende too began expressing concerns about the work of the League. During the congress of 1927, he discussed the inadequacies of its

---

[125] *Sitzungsbericht 1926*, pp. 131–4.

[126] *Sitzungsbericht 1932*, p. 133.

[127] *Sitzungsbericht 1928*, p. 60.

system of minority protection.[128] In particular he proposed that since minority rights were not universal, the majorities expected to respect them were reluctant to do so. It followed that sooner or later the rights of minorities were subverted and the prestige of the League was damaged in the process.

The next year, the congress passed a resolution on the topic. While recognising the League had a role to play in the establishment of trust between majority and minority populations, the resolution identified the complaint procedure as inadequate and proposed the League's statesmen had made unsatisfactory statements about it. It expressed concern that Europe's minorities had had their confidence in the organisation shaken, and went on:

> Thanks to the methods applied up to now by the League of Nations for the solution of the minority problem, nothing significant has been achieved.
>
> The guaranteeing of the rights of national minorities as a pre-requisite of the maintenance of peace is and remains an obligation of the League.
>
> We expect that in the future this obligation will be honoured.[129]

Increasingly the congress's participants voiced themes critical of the League of Nations. Many of the points outlined already were repeated several times over and others were added. The Committee of Three which deliberated over petitions was said to lack the expertise required to assess either the original complaints or the responses of named states to them—a situation not helped by the fact that committee members were statesmen and so, by nature, liable to greater understanding for other statesmen than minorities. The whole of the committee's system was described as overly secretive; in Michail Kurtschinsky's words it operated behind a veil.[130] Complaining minorities did not even hear if their petition was found 'receivable'; they did not find out what action was taken as a result of their petition and they did not participate in any deliberations associated with the complaint.[131] To Schiemann's mind, complaints became stranded in the Committee of Three.[132] Consequently minorities were left with an impression of organisational passivity.[133]

The institution of the Committee of Three also suffered from impermanence, since a different body was convened for each specific petition. Minorities felt the practice deprived it of authority. They wanted a

---

[128] *Sitzungsbericht 1927*, pp. 60–1.
[129] *Sitzungsbericht 1928*, p. 82.
[130] Ibid, p. 42.
[131] See comments of Margulies in *Sitzungsbericht 1926*, pp. 138–40.
[132] *Sitzungsbericht 1928*, p. 28.
[133] F. v. Üxküll-Guldenbrand, 'Nationalitätenkongress und Völkerbund', *Nation und Staat* October 1928.

permanent body capable of doing more than responding to complaints as they
arose.

### b. A permanent commission for minority affairs?

When the League of Nations Union met in Brussels in April 1928, the
committee members of the European Congress of Nationalities were present,
with Schiemann and Wilfan at least giving speeches.[134] At that meeting, the
delegation from Germany, led by Otto Junghann, called for the League to set
up a permanent minority commission, possibly comprising a mixture of
neutral and interested states. The proposal was taken up by the European
Congress of Nationalities that September, with Ammende promoting the idea
personally.[135] Ammende noted that as long ago as 1921, Gilbert Murray had
made a similar recommendation and the idea had been echoed by the
Interparliamentary Union in 1922.[136] He observed that a number of current
figures at the League, including Dutch Foreign Minister Jongheer van
Blokland and German Chancellor Herman Müller, supported exactly the
same proposal.[137] When a Czech representative addressed the League of
Nations Assembly that same month, arguing such a permanent commission
was impossible because there were no provisions for it in the peace treaties.
*Revaler Bote* reported his speech as an attack on the pacification of
Europe.[138]

The idea of a permanent minority commission was also discussed in
a League of Nations memorandum which accepted such a body might
improve the institution's management of minority affairs.[139] In a speech to
the congress, Wilfan agreed, pointing out that the Minorities Section did not
have enough autonomy to address minority issues on its own initiative, but
was supposed to act on commission of the Council or Assembly. Hence it
was not sufficiently independent to provide protection properly.[140] Similarly,
Leo Motzkin emphasised that a putative permanent minority commission
should not be a formal, bureaucratic office, but have decisive powers to
investigate situations comprehensively.[141]

---

[134] 'Wichtige Beratungen über das Minoritätenproblem. Die Brüsseler Tagung', *Revaler Bote* 20
April 1928.
[135] E. Ammende, 'Die Ergebnisse des vierten europäischen Nationalitätenkongresses', *Revaler
Bote* 10 September 1928.
[136] E. Ammende, 'Zur Gründung einer permanenten Minoritätenkommission beim Völkerbund',
*Revaler Bote* 20 September 1928.
[137] E. Ammende, 'Völkerbund und Minoritätenfrage. Die Versammlung kritisiert die
gegenwaertigen Methoden', *Revaler Bote* 17 September 1928.
[138] 'Eine Stimme gegen die Befriedung Europas. Die Tschechoslowakei und die
Minoritätenfrage', *Revaler Bote* 12 September 1928.
[139] Creation of a permanent Minorities Commission at the League of Nations. Geneva. R2161.
Minorities. 4 / 6738 / 3817.
[140] *Sitzungsbericht 1928*, p. 21.
[141] Ibid, p. 32.

The minorities' thinking became increasingly ambitious, so in 1929 Emil Margulies looked to the International Labour Office (I.L.O.) as a model for a permanent, comprehensive organisation to deal with minority affairs.[142] The I.L.O. brought together representatives from workforces, employers and the states to thrash out problems and to develop fresh initiatives to improve labour conditions. Hence Margulies had in mind creating a body to bring together, say, minorities, majorities and state representatives to improve the management of multi-ethnic societies. After explaining his thinking, Margulies tabled a resolution at the European Congress of Nationalities, stating that the organisation was ready to participate in any such initiative the League might inaugurate. It was adopted unanimously.[143] In due course, Ammende communicated this to the League as a proposal of the congress.[144]

### c. Not quite breaking with the past

There was a feeling that the League of Nations needed to break more thoroughly with old power-political ways of working and thinking. Motzkin felt that the notion of the nation state (i.e. the basic building block of the League) was premised on the ascendancy of strong majorities over weaker minorities. The only way to avoid this was to offer special support somehow to minorities.[145] Géza von Szüllö argued that the League tended to act with strength towards those who were weak, but displayed weakness in the face of those with strength. This, he said, was undemocratic. Speaking on behalf of a nationality without a 'home' state participating in the League at the time, Kurtschinsky proposed the League was indifferent about weak nationalities, implying it was easier to overlook their complaints than risk unsettling the states about which they complained.[146] Leo Motzkin agreed the League provided a platform for interests that were strong already. As early as 1928 he feared the organisation was overlooking 'bloody excesses' against minorities.[147] Wilfan was clear in alleging that the League preferred to ignore minority affairs. As he put it in 1929, 'For years the League of Nations has almost ignored our question.'[148] Likewise Szüllö maintained, 'The world of majorities cannot or does not want to understand our complaints.'[149]

The lack of readiness to offer understanding on the part of majority populations was explained artfully by Jacob Robinson (a Jew from

---

[142] *Sitzungsbericht 1929*, p. 126.
[143] Ibid, p.127.
[144] Memorandum of Ammende to Loesch. 18.10.29. R60493. Political Archive of the Foreign Ministry, Berlin. In this memorandum, he says the congress stands for an organisation like the ILO, while Stresemann stood for a permanent organisation along the lines of the Mandates Commission.
[145] *Sitzungsbericht 1928*, p. 38.
[146] Ibid, pp. 41–2.
[147] Ibid, pp. 34–6 and 40.
[148] *Sitzungsbericht 1929*, p. 17.
[149] *Sitzungsbericht 1930*, p. 56.

Lithuania). Majorities regarded national minorities as something that really should not be present—as blemishes on the beauty of the state which called for treatment through cosmetics or surgery. Statesmen would hardly heed a call, 'please nurture the blemishes'. Robinson also suggested you could not put a man in charge of a garden and expect him to tend flowers when he thinks he is actually dealing with weeds.[150] Robinson was convinced that statesmen, in the League and separate states, had to change their views of minorities fundamentally before anything constructive could be achieved.

### d. The League comes up short

Paul Schiemann found it critical that minorities did not have the status of legal subjects able to participate as full partners in the regulation of Europe's affairs. Instead, they were treated as 'objects' expected to experience passively machinations occurring between states and state communities. He went on:

> So long as the League of Nations is not an association of national communities, but rather is an association of states, of governments, then personally I consider that all efforts to create a positive minority law on the foundation of the League are illusory. Only when a positive law of nationality has been created among the European states could this state-legal relationship of an international European community be guaranteed by a national-legal relationship.[151]

As a contribution towards the necessary change, Schiemann developed the idea of the anational state. Here, the state would no longer promote any given national culture but would use its power to support the entire political population inhabiting its territory. With national culture no longer an affair of state, it could be recognised as an international matter, enabling Europeans to organise themselves in twofold fashion: as state communities and as national communities. In a Europe organised as a system of anational states, national communities would cut across political boundaries without difficulty, since their organisation would imply no threat to anyone at all.[152]

If this was the ultimate vision, then clearly the League was selling minorities short. In a memorandum for the German Foreign Ministry from 1927, Schiemann was critical of the League's secretive 'cabinet politics' and unclear responses to complaints by minorities. The characteristics were endangering its original purpose of being the 'bearer of the conscience of the

---

[150] *Sitzungsbericht 1926*, p. 59.
[151] Ibid, p. 37.
[152] Ibid, pp. 34–43.

world.'[153] Consequently minorities were left to wonder whether they should not try to assume the role of their own protector. In 1929, tired of the appearance of the interests of minorities not being pursued by the League, Leo von Déak (a Hungarian from Yugoslavia) recommended that the congress begin investigating and publicising abuses against minorities.[154] Although this would have been against the congress's original principle that it would not deal with specific cases, the proposal indicated the growing frustration experienced by minorities. Szüllö said this:

> We were promised that the minority question would be solved in the spirit of freedom; we were promised that the rights of minorities would be protected in the same generous spirit of freedom and good conscience. The belief which we attached to these promises has vanished and today we stand faced with a soulless and heartless bureaucratism, which pursues no other goal than to maintain that which the victors conquered, and to maintain that peace which is not a true, inner peace, to guarantee that apparent quiet which is not peace at all, but rather which only signifies the impotent silence of the vanquished.... Tyrants always justify their actions with the need to maintain peace....[155]

The congress was trying to apply all the pressure it could on the League. In summer 1928, Erik Colban was set to leave the Minorities Section and there were rumours that he was to be succeeded by, first, Polish Foreign Minister Zaleski, and then Colban's deputy from Spain, Pablo de Azcárate. The members of the congress's committee, however, were suspicious of any representative of a state with recognised minority problems taking over such an important post. Consequently the committee placed articles in the press outlining their concerns and wrote to the League's Secretary General, Eric Drummond.[156] As Wilfan and Ammende put it in their letter:

> In minority circles ... the view is held that the Section can only fulfil its weighty task if it has someone at its head who will not be influenced by any considerations of the nationality problems in his own country.[157]

---

[153] P. Schiemann, 'Der dritte Nationalitäten-Kongress', Un-named newspaper. Date stamped 22.8.27. R60466. Political Archive of the Foreign Ministry, Berlin.

[154] *Sitzungsbericht 1929*, p. 60.

[155] Ibid, p. 42.

[156] 'Zur Frage der Ernennung eines Nachfolgers fuer E. Colban als Leiter der Minoritätensektion im Voelkerbundsekretariat', *Revaler Bote* 9 July 1928. Also 'Die Nationalitäten protestieren', *Revaler Bote* 6 June 1928. See also 'Um Colbans Nachfolge', *Nation und Staat* March 1928.

[157] 25.5.28. Ammende and Wilfan to Drummond. R2161. Minorities. 4 / 3817 / 3817. For a

Without doubt, Ammende and those around him were desperate for a sign that the League took them seriously. Ammende visited Azcárate on 28 August 1928 to discuss Colban's successor, saying it would be a 'veritable offence' for an appointee to be drawn from a state with unresolved minority issues. Unsurprisingly, Azcárate minuted that he 'maintained an attitude of extreme reserve towards Mr. Ammende' and emphasised that it was wrong to think an appointee might be an instrument of the Spanish government.[158] In private, Ammende voiced support for a 'Scandinavian personality' who is 'competent and enjoys respect'. It was symptomatic of the deteriorating relationship that in the end Azcárate got the job.[159]

## 6. Conclusion

In its essentials, the story of the European Congress of Nationalities during its early years is simple. It is of hopes and best intentions gradually running aground as the organisation proved unable to capture the attention of statesmen and League of Nations officials in the way that had been anticipated. It is tempting to use Zara Steiner's phrase and say the congress was one of 'the lights that failed' in the 1920s.[160] To be fair to Ammende and those around him, such a judgement would be harsh. The very existence of the congress was an achievement that left a mark. That the mainstream political world was not ready to take these figures into account more adequately became particularly apparent in 1929.

---

report about the congress's debates about Colban successor, see Congress of European Nationalities. 4th Meeting, Geneva. R2161. Minorities. 4 / 6738 / 3817.
[158] 28.8.28. Memo by Azcárate. Geneva. R2161. Minorities. 4 / 6738 / 3817. Despite the clear confrontation between Ammende and Azcárate, the League still sent an observer to the congress's 1928 meeting, see 27.8.28. Memo for Drummond by Azcárate. Geneva. R2161. Minorities. 4 / 6738 / 3817.
[159] 17.1.28. Ammende to Schiemann. Schiemann Papers. Baltic Central Library, Riga.
[160] Z.Steiner, *The Lights that Failed. European International History 1919–1933.* OUP, 2005.

## Chapter Eight

## 1929: year of the minorities

### 1. Setting the scene: from spring 1928 to February 1929

#### a. Introduction

The year 1929 was critical, possibly even a turning point, in the history of Europe's national minorities. The developments which occurred during the year had been in the offing since at least Germany joined the League of Nations in 1926. The event was accompanied by high hopes on the part of especially German minorities that Berlin's place on the Council would pave the way for notable improvements in the way they were treated, since Germany was expected to prove a champion for minority issues across the continent. It was hardly surprising, therefore, that Germany's Foreign Minister, Gustav Stresemann, played a significant role in the drama of 1929.

That February Ammende wrote an article entitled 'Year of the Minorities' which noted a Swiss journalist had been the first to give the year that name.[1] Decisive developments were expected following a controversy which occurred in the Council between Stresemann and Polish Foreign Minister Zaleski, but also as a result of interventions in the Assembly by Dutch Foreign Minister Bleelarts van Blokland and Canadian representative Raoul Dandurand calling for reform of the League's minority system. Ammende argued that the European Congress of Nationalities had been instrumental in generating the hopeful situation, particularly through its activities in the League of Nations Union during 1928.

A number of characteristic lines of thinking about minority affairs had developed in subordinate League of Nations organisations during 1928. In Brussels that April, the League of Nations Union had heard calls for the creation of a permanent minority commission (see chapter 7, the section 'A permanent commission for minority affairs?') and when the League of Nations Union met at The Hague in August it produced a resolution amalgamating many familiar themes. Ammende commented that the resolution owed much to the British League of Nations Union activist Sir Willoughby Dickinson who had taken his ideas from the congress with which he had strong connections.[2] The resolution held that: legal obligations to minorities should be treated as constitutional elements of the League; all members of the League should accord minorities at least the same rights as outlined in the various protection treaties; the Council should play a higher

---

[1] E. Ammende, 'Das Jahr der Minoritäten', *Revaler Bote* 12 February 1929.
[2] E. Ammende, 'Die Union der Völkerbundligen auf neuen Wegen', *Revaler Bote* 29 August 1928.

profile role in supervising minority rights; and there should be a permanent
minority commission tasked to address minority questions across the year.
The resolution was presented by Professor Ernest Bovet of Lausanne
University and was agreed by all the national representatives present, except
the one from Italy. Bovet—who had contacts with the congress and addressed
it in 1932—also highlighted a number of points close to the heart of
Ammende. He bemoaned the lack of information which seeped out of the
organisation about the management of minority affairs, saying the League
was like a glass house with a dark chamber, and that only a fully independent
individual would be suitable as Colban's successor.

The scene was set for minority issues to come to the fore among the
League's leading statesmen. As Ammende reported subsequently, in the
Assembly in September 1928 Dutch Foreign Minister van Blokland
recommended that the League's minority system be changed.[3] The Minorities
Section, he said, was frequently over-burdened by the demands of the
Committee of Three. He recommended creating a permanent minority
commission, perhaps on the model of the Mandates Commission. The
proposal was supported by Germany's Chancellor, Herman Müller and, more
or less, by senior Swiss statesman Giueseppe Motta. It was, however,
contested by Polish Foreign Minister Zaleski who, unlike Blokland, Müller
and Motta represented a state actually bound by a minority agreement.
Zaleski opposed any move to increase the demands of minority protection
beyond what existed already.

Ammende was cock-a-hoop over van Blokland's intervention.
Optimistically he proposed that finally the congress's ideas were finding
resonance in the League.[4] He emphasised a permanent commission of
minority experts could help universalise nationality rights across Europe.[5]

There was no ignoring the fact that a division of opinion existed in
Europe over minority rights. Minorities themselves wanted them extended
and strengthened, and generally-speaking, were supported in this aim by
countries with co-nationals existing as minorities abroad but with relatively
few minorities living inside their own borders (e.g. Germany—which was not
a signatory to a general minority rights agreement, although it had a specific
agreement in place concerning German Upper Silesia—and Hungary, which
was a signatory state). On the other hand, a country such as Poland, which
had a substantial minority population and was a signatory to a minority
treaty, wanted to minimise its obligations. The basic divergence of attitudes

---

[3] E. Ammende, 'Völkerbund und Minoritätenfrage. Die Versammlung kritisiert die
gegenwärtigen Methoden', *Revaler Bote* 17 September 1928. See also F. v. Üxküll-Guldenbrand,
'Die Minoritätenfrage auf der Völkerbundtagung', *Nation und Staat* October 1928.
[4] E. Ammende, 'Völkerbund und Minoritätenfrage. Die Versammlung kritisiert die
gegenwärtigen Methoden.' *Revaler Bote* 17 September 1928.
[5] E. Ammende, 'Aktuelle Aufgaben der Nationalitätenbewegung', *Nation und Staat* October
1928 p. 84 ff

became particularly clear during a meeting of the League's Council in December 1928.

On 15 December 1928, both Stresemann and Zaleski were present when the League of Nations Council met in Lugano.[6] Representative of Japan, Mineitciro Adatci, reported a complaint by ethnic Germans from Polish Upper Silesia and this stimulated a passionate discussion of minority issues. Canadian representative Raoul Dandurand said that at the next meeting of the Council he would recommend significant changes to the League's system of protection, something which *Revaler Bote* interpreted as supportive of a permanent minority commission. Zaleski, however, intervened suggesting that minority protection was only supposed to prepare the way for the assimilation of minorities. He maintained that the ethnic German organisation in Silesia involved in the complaint (the *Volksbund*) was endangering peace and using minority protection as a shield behind which to hide whilst acting against the state. As he spoke, several times Stresemann showed his disagreement by thumping the table with his fist.

When Zaleski had finished, Stresemann spoke, criticising the Polish minister for talking in a 'spirit of hatred' and for promoting a campaign against German minorities in Upper Silesia. He emphasised that minority protection guaranteed independent schooling, language and religion to the Germans of Polish Upper Silesia and that, if they felt there was a problem, the minority was within its rights to appeal to the League for satisfaction. He demanded that minority issues be placed on the agenda when the Council met again.

In February, Dandurand's proposed changes to the system of minority protection were published by the Secretariat. He recommended that petitions of complaint should go, in the first instance, from the minority to the government concerned and should only be passed on to the League if the government did not respond to them. He also recommended that, once with the League, petitions should be considered not just by a Committee of Three, but by all 14 Council members.[7] Thereafter, the Council met on 6 March in Geneva and considered minority reform at length.[8]

### b. The Council meeting of 6–7 March

Dandurand spoke first, repeating his arguments from February; then Stresemann took the stage.[9] The German Foreign Minister emphasised that

---

[6] 'Für die Rechte der Nationalitäten. Schwerer Zusammenstoss zwischen Stresemann und Zaleski in Lugano', *Revaler Bote* 17 December 1928. Also A. de Vries, 'Entscheidende Wendung', *Revaler Bote* 22 December 1928.

[7] 'Verbesserung des Minderheiten-Rechts', *Vossische Zeitung* 22.2.29. R35801. Political Archive of the Foreign Ministry, Berlin.

[8] For the proceedings of the meeting see *League of Nations. Official Journal* (April 1929), pp. 516–41.

[9] For details of the speeches by Dandurand and Stresemann, see 'Die grosse Minderheitendebatte

minority protection was not a step on the way to assimilation, that
membership of a minority was not at odds with the fulfilment of civic duties
and that by speaking up for its rights, a minority was not attempting to
explode apart the state in which it resided since freedom and peace went
together well. Observing that a League report from 1920 held minority
protection was to be 'constantly applied' (i.e. by implication, by a system
more ambitious than an *ad hoc* Committees of Three), Stresemann added that
the enjoyment of cultural rights would not lead to irredenta, before observing
(in a phrase certain to annoy the Polish representative) that the political order
of the day would not stay the same forever. Stresemann went on to emphasise
that national minorities felt the petition system did not allow their voice to be
heard properly. He identified how little information about petitions was
circulated—certainly not to the minorities themselves. He suggested more
publicity should flow through the *League of Nations. Official Journal*. He
also maintained that the protection system would be more effective if all
interested governments were allowed to participate in complaint procedures,
if the minority at issue could represent itself in front of the League, if subject
specialists participated, and if the whole of the Council (rather than a
Committee of Three) considered complaints.

Thereafter he made four chief recommendations: that an
investigation be undertaken with a view to improving procedures for the
treatment of complaints by minorities; that in the future, concerned nations be
party to complaints tendered by minorities (which implied Germany should
participate in deliberations about complaints submitted by ethnic Germans);
that there should be an examination of how the League should fulfil its duty
to minorities in addition to its work regarding direct complaints; and that the
League's guarantees should be clarified. Given the extensive nature of these
issues, Stresemann also recommended that a special study commission be
inaugurated to consider all of the points in detail.[10] He concluded:

> The ideal towards which humanity is tending is the
> assurance of peace for all time, even though we may not
> share the belief that humanity will ever attain this ideal. We
> must do our utmost to create conditions favourable to such
> a peace. One of these conditions is peace between the
> various national civilisations. More effectively than by
> definite engagements and understandings, peace for all time
> may be assured by a regime of justice towards all those who

vor dem Völkerbundrat', *Nation und Staat* March 1929. For Stresemann's speech, see 'Der
Schutz der Minderheiten. Rede des Reichsministers des Auswärtigen Dr Gustav Stresemann in
der Sitzung des Völkerbundrats von 6 März 1929 über die Garantie des Völkerbundes für die
Bestimmungen zum Schutz der Minderheiten.' R35801. Political Archive of the Foreign
Ministry, Berlin.
[10] 'Lebensrechte der Minoritäten. Die grosse Reden Dandurands und Stresemanns', *Revaler Bote*
7 March 1929.

claim the vital and elementary right which is theirs to speak
their own language and to safeguard their faith and their
souls.[11]

Dandurand and Stresemann were bullish yet tightly reasoned in their
case for change to League procedures. Their basic arguments, in fact, could
have been made by the minorities themselves. Predictably, however, what
they said was contradicted by others also present at the meeting. Zaleski
spoke up in favour of the *status quo*—a system, which he said had been
agreed between the League's Council and the states concerned. These states,
he argued, would reject any attempt to impose additional commitments on
them. British Foreign Minister Austen Chamberlain added an air of
conservatism more endearing to the Pole than German and Canadian. He
emphasised that protecting minorities was a considerable job which was both
difficult and sensitive, since no state welcomed even 'friendly intervention'
in its domestic affairs. He feared the job was 'so great and invidious' that it
could never be done perfectly. In this light, he said that even if the existing
system had flaws, still it was working with 'scrupulous fairness' and
accomplishing the tasks for which it was designed. He argued that the
system's secrecy had advantages. Publicity could 'inflame passion' (exposing
the petitioners to additional dangers), while secrecy could provide a screen
behind which a government could make a concession to a complaining
minority without having to worry about looking weak to the rest of its
domestic population. In the light of his general tone, Chamberlain's re-
interpretation of Mello-Franco's ill-chosen words and argument, that he had
not meant to imply in the past that minorities should experience cultural
assimilation, sounded a little weak. He was floundering around in area which
he only half understood.

Aristide Briand too maintained the existing system was working in
its essentials, before suggesting that a committee investigating the whole
matter should probably be set up under Adatci. In the event, it was decided
that the representative for Japan, aided by those of Britain and Spain, would
draw up a report about the recommendations of Dandurand and Stresemann
in time for the next Council meeting in June. This was confirmed in a
Council resolution of 7 March 1929.

## 2. Lobbying Adatci

By early March 1929, therefore, there was substantial recognition that change
was due in how the League of Nations dealt with minority affairs. Adatci's
investigation was the response. From the outset, however, Ammende and
those around him were worried about how much Adatci would achieve. With
British and Spanish representatives set to participate alongside Adatci,

---

[11] *League of Nations. Official Journal* (April 1929), p. 522.

*Revaler Bote* pointed out that Chamberlain had already made anti-minority comments while Quinones de Leon was well known for his pro-French (and by implication anti-minority) views.[12] This did not, however, prevent the managers of the congress doing everything in their power to lobby the Adatci committee.

Almost immediately, a letter was sent under Wilfan's name to the Japanese diplomat emphasising that a solution to the minority question required the participation of all concerned—then an extensive memorandum followed.[13] It grew out of a meeting of the congress's committee held in Paris from 13 to 15 April which, unusually, was not attended by Ammende. The aim was to produce a document voicing the concerns of Europe's minorities and contributing to the reform process.[14] It rehearsed many familiar arguments, but in the end made six chief recommendations. The memorandum called for more publicity for how the League dealt with minority affairs. Receivable petitions should be published, as should responses by governments and reports of the Committee of Three—plus the Secretariat should publish an annual report on its work. Minorities should be able to provide more information to the League about complaints. That is to say, they should be able to respond to government replies to petitions and to participate in the proceedings that followed them. The Committee of Three should be improved. For example, it should work more quickly, should include all Council members and, indeed, the League should set up a permanent body to address minority issues. Recourse should be made to the Permanent Court more frequently to address minority complaints. A special committee of experts should be appointed inside the League to look at minority affairs and to explore possible solutions to them; and finally member states should live up to the Assembly's decision of 1922 which, of course, called on all states to act as if they were bound by minority treaties.[15]

Naturally the congress was far from alone in contributing ideas to Adatci. He received memoranda from 15 interested states and 11 independent organisations, many of which were published in *Nation and State* (the journal of the German minorities), alongside the memorandum from the congress's committee.[16] The German government, for instance stressed that the current system of minority protection was inadequate because it only responded to immediate complaints and did not provide long-term supervision of minority

---

[12] 'Adatschi findet einen Kompromiss. Der Ausschuss unter Kontrolle des Rates', *Revaler Bote* 7 March 1929.

[13] 'Denkschrift des Ausschusses der Europaeischen Nationalitätenkongresse', *Nation und Staat* May 1929.

[14] 'Nationalitätenkongress und Völkerbundrat', *Revaler Bote* 25 April 1929.

[15] 'Die Minoritätendenkschrift', *Revaler Bote* 16 May 1929. See also 'Denkschrift des Ausschusses der Europäischen Nationalitätenkongresse', *Nation und Staat* May 1929.

[16] *Nation und Staat* May 1929, p. 723. For texts of the memoranda from governments, see also *League of Nations. Official Journal* (July 1929), Appendix 1, 'Memoranda forwarded by the Governments'.

affairs. So, again, the German government recommended the establishment of a permanent commission for minority issues which would be able to act on its own initiative to address whatever matters it saw fit. It also re-stated problems with the Committee of Three: its findings typically were not sufficiently conclusive; its work did not have enough publicity; it needed more powers to investigate situations; and needed to be more inclusive.[17] The position of Germany, and that of Canada as it had been outlined by Dandurand to the Council, was supported by, amongst others, Bulgaria, Hungary, the Netherlands and Switzerland. The Committee for the Rights of Jewish Minorities also submitted a memorandum to the League, criticising it for inadequate, tardy responses to anti-Semitic excesses in Bessarabia in 1926 and 1927.[18]

Yet these critical arguments were balanced by contributions—often made by states bound by minority agreements—maintaining that the *status quo* was adequate. This was the position of the Estonian government, while Latvia said the existing system was 'both elastic and effective enough in practice to render considerable service'. Lithuania felt any changes to the existing system would have to be agreed by the current contracting parties.[19] Czechoslovakia, Greece, Poland, Romania and Yugoslavia were particularly outspoken over any move to update minority protection obligations and acted *in tandem* against such a possibility. Apparently in late February 1929 they had already published an open letter in the press arguing, amongst other things, that the existing practices of the Committee of Three were at odds with the spirit of the minority treaties; that it would be unacceptable to have to deal with complaints originating from co-national governments of minorities; that intervention in minority affairs based on Article 11 of the Covenant was unacceptable;[20] that minority states would need to be consulted over any changes to minority protection; that they should be allowed to participate in Council deliberations about minority affairs;[21] and that states bound by protection provisions would not stand for those being extended (including by the creation of a permanent commission) unless such provisions became general for all members of the League. Unsurprisingly, therefore, together, they made a case to Adaci that the imposition of minority rights on them was 'exceptional', 'should be construed in the most restricted sense' and certainly should not be extended. They maintained that, since they

---

[17] 'Bemerkungen der Deutschen Regierung zur Frage der Garantie des Völkerbundes für die Bestimmungen zum Schutze der Minderheiten', *Nation und Staat* May 1929.

[18] 'Das memorandum des "Rates für die Rechte der jüdischen Minderheiten (Komitees der Jüdischen Delegationen)" an das Adatci-Komitee', *Nation und Staat* May 1929.

[19] 'Schreiben der Estländischen Regierung', *Nation und Staat* August 1929. For the Latvian and Lithuanian positions, see *League of Nations. Official Journal* (July 1929), p. 1174–5.

[20] Article 11 permitted any League member to raise with the Council a situation likely to endanger peace.

[21] The Council set up a judicial committee to investigate this point, but rejected it on 6 March 1929. 'Die grosse Minderheitendebatte vor dem Völkerbundrat', *Nation und Staat* March 1929, p.493.

had either signed treaties or made declarations concerning minority rights, no
alteration to the minority system could be made without their explicit
agreement. To be clear, they said they could not accept the points made by
Stresemann and Dandurand. An expanded Committee of Three would only
become unwieldy; a permanent minority commission was unnecessary; lack
of publicity over investigations was 'a necessary state of affairs'; and
minorities could not expect to enjoy their rights fully until they 'have
genuinely given proof of loyalty and fidelity to their Governments.'[22] The
sceptical position was agreed by Jewish organisations based in Britain.[23]

As far as at least some minorities were concerned, there was a
pattern to the feedback. It seemed that the states with the biggest interest in
maintaining the provisions of the peace settlement (i.e. those who had gained
most and who tended to have signed minority treaties—i.e. the new and
extended states) were those most vocal in opposing alterations to minority
protection. They were the ones who, to some minds at least, had benefitted
from the losses of Germany and Hungary.[24]

## 3. The London Report

All these views informed the document Adatci completed on 18 May—the
London Report, so-called because the rapporteur, Chamberlain and de Leon
had met in London for discussions.[25] The recommendations did not make
happy reading for the minorities, since Adatci's first point disputed that the
peace treaties foresaw permanent supervision of minority issues. He argued
the Council should only become involved if a member state raised the
possibility of a breach of obligations. Hence, he turned his back on the
possibility of creating a permanent minority commission. The report also
rejected communications occurring directly between a minority and its
government. Adatci maintained minorities should only provide information
to the League, they should not participate in actual proceedings. Such
engagement, he said, would make friendly dealings within the Committee of
Three difficult to achieve. Although Adatci didn't mind if petitioners were
told whether their petitions were found justified or not, he refused to make a
practical recommendation on the point.

Regarding the Committee of Three itself, he refused to recommend
changes to its procedures. He refused to suggest that it be increased in size

---

[22] *League of Nations. Official Journal* (July 1929), pp. 1168–71.
[23] 'Die Denkschrift des Joint Foreign Committee of the Board of Deputies of British Jews und
der Anglo-Jewish Association an den Staatssekretär des Äusseren in London', *Nation und Staat*
August 1929.
[24] A. de Vries, 'Nach der Genfer Aussprache', *Revaler Bote* 11 March 1929.
[25] For the text of the London Report, see 'Der Bericht des durch die Entschliessung des
Völkerbundrats vom 7. März 1929 eingesetzten Komitees (Londoner Bericht)', *Nation und Staat*
August 1929.

and rejected the idea of a state which was co-national with a complaining minority participating in either the investigative or deliberative processes. Regarding the possibility of greater publicity for the League's treatment of minority issues, the report did not want the proceedings of the Committee of Three made public (although it accepted more information could be circulated to Council members), but it accepted that information about the outcome could be made public *if the state involved wished it* and that the Council should publish statistical information about the number of petitions handed in, accepted as receivable and disposed of each year.

The London Report was a very conservative document which sought only to tinker with existing minority procedures rather than to revise them fundamentally. No doubt its authors were intimidated by the opposition significant reform would elicit from the signatory states.

### 4. The final report and the Council's Madrid meeting

Predictably, Adatci's final report, presented to the Council's meeting in Madrid in early June 1929, sought only limited changes. It did not recommend the creation of a permanent commission, since the peace treaties made no provision for this and such a step would require the agreement of the signatory states. It noted that the Permanent Court could only become involved in a minority's case if governments could not negotiate a settlement. The final report also rejected Dandurand's idea that a petition should be sent to the government concerned before being forwarded to the League. The report stated that nothing should be done to turn the Committee of Three into some kind of tribunal and it refused to make any recommendations about the composition of the Committee of Three. There was, however, a suggestion to turn the body into a slightly larger Committee of Five. While it was accepted that petitioners should be told if their petition was not deemed receivable and that the investigating committee should send a letter to other members of the Council outlining the outcome of a case, nonetheless the final report held that detailed information about meetings should not be made public for the sake of the 'best interests of the persons belonging to the minorities'. To increase the flow of public information, the Council should just publish bare statistics about minority petitions annually, while outcomes could be published if the key state involved desired this.[26]

German representatives in Madrid expressed deep disappointment with Adatci's work. Although Stresemann, speaking on 11 June, understood there was no possibility of agreement being reached between himself and the

---

[26] Annex 1140. Protection of Minorities. Report of the Committee instituted by the Council Resolution of March 7th 1929. *League of Nations. Official Journal* (July 1929), pp. 1136–51. For a summary of the London Report, as received at the Madrid meeting of the Council in June, see 'Die Resolution des Völkerbundrates vom 13. Juni 1929 und die Vorentwürfe', *Nation und Staat* August 1929. For the key recommendations of the Adatci Committee as received at Madrid, see 'Bericht und Resolutionsantrag Adatci', *Nation und Staat* August 1929.

Little Entente over systems of minority protection, still he stuck to his guns and maintained he needed to reject Adatci's principles.[27] In an impassioned speech, Stresemann requested that a final decision about minority protection be postponed until the Assembly had a chance to debate the issue and until the Permanent Court make a decision about the extent of the League's responsibilities. He was, however, contradicted by Briand.[28] In fact, the Madrid meeting of the Council was a testy affair. At one point, Stresemann intervened in a speech by Briand. When the latter began to talk about assimilation, Stresemann stressed that minorities could be loyal without being assimilated.[29] So, by 13 June, although Stresemann was still expressing disappointment that, for example, co-national states could not participate in committee proceedings, ultimately he felt he had no option but to approve Adatci's report since it did mark an improvement on existing procedures— albeit a slim one.[30] In the end, the Council agreed the London Report in only slightly revised form (for example it was made explicit that the Committee of Three—or now Five—could meet between Council meetings as often as was required by its work).[31]

## 5. Reactions to Madrid

The responses of the minorities to the Madrid meeting were complicated. Perhaps echoing Stresemann's final, rather stoic assessment, Ammende penned an article arguing the changes were positive. He was pleased the investigating committee would have to send more information to the Council, also that there would be some enhanced publicity of the League's involvement in minority affairs. He qualified his enthusiasm, however, admitting the minorities certainly had not got everything they wanted and proposing the Madrid decisions were probably best seen as a stage in a discussion rather than an endpoint.[32] This interpretation can only have been strengthened by Stresemann's speech to the League in Geneva on 9 September 1929. Here he maintained that eventually the League would have to set up a special institution to deal with minorities, just as it had done for mandate and economic questions.[33] Clearly for him too, therefore, Madrid was best seen as just a step on the way to a much fuller engagement with the

---

[27] 'Die Protokolle der Sitzungen des durch den Beschluss des Rates vom 7. März eingesetzten Minderheitenkomitees', *Nation und Staat* August 1929, p. 823.

[28] 'Protest der Minoritäten gegen den Madrider Vorschlag', *Revaler Bote* 14 June 1929.

[29] 'Die Minoritätenverhandlungen beendet', *Revaler Bote* 14 June 1929.

[30] 'Das Protokoll der Sitzung des Rates am 13. Juni 1929 in Madrid', *Nation und Staat* August 1929, p. 836.

[31] 'Die Minoritätenverhandlungen beendet', *Revaler Bote* 14 June 1929.

[32] E. Ammende, 'Die kommende Völkerbundversammlung und die Nationalitätenfrage', *Revaler Bote* 23 July 1929.

[33] 'Stresemann spricht in Genf', *Revaler Bote* 10 September 1929.

rights of national minorities—and Ammende duly applauded all his work that year.[34]

Joan Estelrich also hoped the reform process would continue. He put it as follows to the European Congress of Nationalities:

> This is now the material result of this year of struggle; it is not very much; fortunately the intellectual results and the possibilities which they suggest are much greater....[35]

He felt Madrid left an unstable situation in its wake: now things had to keep moving. He looked to the eventual creation of a commission of neutral people within the League to supervise minority issues, also to the universalisation of minority rights. Beyond the congress, there was also a sense that additional movement was needed. In mid-1930 a sub-committee of the Interparliamentary Union recommended the now familiar idea that a permanent minority commission be created within the League.[36] There was, then, quite a widespread feeling (in some quarters at least) that a step forward had been taken in 1929 and that more steps should follow.

And there were a few reasons for a bit of satisfaction. The League's Council began publishing basic statistical information about the submission of petitions by minorities. So, by August 1930 the European Congress of Nationalities noted that 57 petitions had been submitted since the Madrid meeting, of which 31 were investigated.[37] The provision of such information allowed Ammende to observe with alarm the next year (1931) that the number of petitions had risen to 214 (with 73 deemed receivable)—an indication of both dissatisfaction on the part of minorities and their growing ill-treatment.[38] With such materials in the public domain, it was hard for anyone to argue against the mounting importance of minority issues.

## 6. Conclusion

Yet, if 1929 was supposed to be 'the year of minorities' there was no disguising the fact that it was a year of disappointments. Improvements were more than outweighed by lack of change which could only lead to, ultimately, disillusionment on the part of national minorities. Even before Adatci produced his final report, Paul Schiemann was expressing concern

---

[34] E. Ammende, 'Genf und die Minoritätenfrage', *Revaler Bote* 24 September 1929.

[35] *Sitzungsbericht des Kongresses der organisierten nationalen Gruppen in den Staaten Europas. Genf, 26 bis 28. August 1929.* Vienna and Leipzig: Wilhelm Braumüller, 1930, p. 36.

[36] 'Minderheiten und Interparlamentarische Union', *Revalsche Zeitung* 26 July 1930.

[37] 'Ausschuss der Europäischen Nationalitätenkongresse. Mitteilungen der Geschäftsführung'. August 1930'. R60528. Political Archive of the Foreign Ministry, Berlin. Also reported in 'Die Genfer Herbsttagung', *Revaler Bote* 18 August 1930.

[38] E. Ammende, 'Die Ergebnisse der diesjährigen Völkerbund-Diskussion über die Minoritätenfrage', *Revalsche Zeitung* 28 September 1931.

that he was offering too little progress.[39] It was symptomatic that, for all the benefit of publishing statistics about the petition system, in due course *Revaler Bote* was noting that very few actual decisions about petitions were made public—which meant, presumably, that the states concerned were opting to keep information about them secret.[40]

Almost as soon as the Madrid meeting had ended, sceptical voices were easy to find. The journal of the German minorities argued the congress had been unable to influence Adatci sufficiently and that his views remained framed by the Little Entente, Poland and Greece.[41] It was predictable, therefore, that the congress of 1929 heard a variety of complaints about the year as being an opportunity missed. Leo von Déak (an Hungarian from Yugoslavia) bemoaned the fact that the position of minorities had not improved over the last 5 years, that the League's work was poorly informed, that protection was little more than the prerogative of the majority and that, if the League would not investigate abuses properly, then the Congress should do so, perhaps in association with the League of Nations Union.[42]

Disappointment was also evident in an article Ammende wrote following the 1929 congress meeting. Really, he said, the solution to the nationality problem did not lie with improving complaint procedures, much more it lay with actual work for reconciliation between the different national groups. To promote this, he called on the League of Nations to create a forum for minorities equivalent to the International Labour Organisation, where all interested parties could be called together to thrash out the key issues of the day—a call also heard from Emil Margulies (a Jew from Czechoslovakia) and Joan Estelrich (a Catalan from Spain) at the congress meeting of 1929 when a resolution was passed proposing that the League set up such an organisation.[43]

Time only made the sense of disillusionment deeper and encouraged bitterness. By 1932, Ammende was voicing views which were as critical of the League as ever. It was, he said, an organisation dominated by the interests of states in which minority issues were thoroughly politicised and in which states were preventing the publication of critical materials. He felt it axiomatic that minorities should be bound in to the League's system and be able to refute materials deployed by complained-about states. Perhaps this could happen in a revised forum more akin to the Mandates Commission. If the League would not take such necessary steps, then maybe private people, possessing moral respect, should set up an independent, neutral institution to

---

[39] P. Schiemann, 'Von Genf nach Madrid', *Nation und Staat* May 1929.
[40] 'Öffentlichkeit der Minoritätenverfahren verlangt Curtius in Genf', *Revalsche Zeitung* 16 September 1931.
[41] 'Madrid', *Nation und Staat* July 1929.
[42] *Sitzungsbericht des Kongresses der organisierten nationalen Gruppen in den Staaten Europas. Genf, 26 bis 28. August 1929*. Vienna and Leipzig: Wilhelm Braumüller, 1930, pp. 55–61.
[43] E. Ammende, 'Die Ergebnisse des 5. Nationalitätenkongresses', *Revaler Bote* 5 September 1929. For the comments of Margulies and Estelrich, see *Sitzungsbericht 1929*, pp. 125

judge minority petitions. At this meeting of the congress, resolutions were agreed demanding the creation of a permanent minority commission inside the League and that all European states sign a convention on minority protection.[44] There was no escaping the feeling that, after 1929, Ammende and those around him were more convinced than ever that the League exhibited fundamental flaws. As Emil Margulies argued, current League procedures were deficient and despite all of the ideas conveyed to the organisation, its decisions for change (or lack thereof) were thoroughly unsatisfactory.[45]

---

[44] 'Abschluss des Nationalitätenkongresses', *Revalsche Zeitung* 6 July 1932.
[45] *Sitzungsbericht 1929*, p. 124.

*Chapter Nine*

# International national community thinking and a different kind of Pan-Europe

## 1. Non-universalisation

The burgeoning disillusionment within the European Congress of Nationalities about the League took many forms and encompassed several different issues. Antipathy to Colban's successor, Azcárate, surfaced quickly enough. Kurt Graebe (a senior ethnic German from Poland) wrote to Ammende concerned he was proving more a representative of state interests—and particularly Polish ones—than those of the minorities. He proposed that minorities needed to deal with Azcárate personally to convince him that his current conduct would never gain their trust.[1] Relations between the Minorities Section and the national minorities were indeed cooler than had been the case in Colban's time. Under Azcárate—and perhaps predictably given the unfortunate conversation he had held with Ammende before being appointed to lead the Minorities Section (chapter 7, sub-section 'The League comes up short')—, the League's offices seemed to become increasingly critical of the congress. In September 1931, for example, a League report of the recent congress meeting observed cohesion within the organisation was weak. It questioned whether there was a single thing to be identified as the 'minorities problem', or lots of separate ones. Hence the report suggested the congress consisted of various groups all following their separate goals with only an external impression of an overarching organisation.[2]

When Ukrainian minorities presented a petition to the League complaining about Polish repression in eastern Galicia, Ammende was outraged by its handling. The rapporteur, Mr. Sato of Japan (who recently had been spending much time dealing with the Manchuria crisis), was criticised for producing a report so shoddy that it was—Ammende implied—rejected by representatives from Norway, the UK and Germany. The report's

---

[1] 5.6.31. Graebe to Ammende. Schiemann Papers. ENK Folder. Baltic Central Library, Riga. For a study of Graebe, see S. Dyroff, 'Der Platz der Völkerbundbeschwerde in den politischen Strategien nationaler Minderheiten. Positionen aus dem Kreis "Europäischen Nationalitätenkongresses"' in M. Beer and S. Dyroff (eds.), *Politische Strategien nationaler Minderheiten in der Zwischenkriegszeit*. Munich: Oldenbourg, 2013.
[2] 5.9.31, memorandum for Azcárate. R2161. Minorities. 7th ENK. 29 to 31 August 1931. 4 / 31096 / 3817. To be fair to the League's observer, members of the minorities recognised something similar about the congress. For example, Axel de Vries once said it represented a full 'kaleidascope' of 'goals, passions, desires and anxieties' on the part of different minorities. He also thought, however, that the organisation was a political necessity and had done many things to improve relations between nations in Europe. A. de Vries, 'Genf', *Revalsche Zeitung* 9 September 1931.

conclusions were shaped by pro-Polish ways of thinking, for instance suggesting that the current problems were only temporary and that 'pacification' measures by the Polish state were justified responses to Ukrainian terrorism. The proceedings left Ammende with the impression that some members of the Council were too ready to sell out the needs of minorities in favour of those of states and reinforced his belief there was a structural problem in the League. He proposed that only minorities with co-national states present in the Council had any hope of getting a fair hearing, so the position of Ukrainians was hopeless.

Ammende felt that even after Madrid, political interests could still overpower legal ones, especially in the Council. He kept arguing that improvement could only occur if minority protection was removed from that thoroughly politicised body and was given to a permanent minority commission. There remained, in his opinion, a case for publishing petitions, the observations of governments about them, plus comments from minorities on the latter. Only then would European public opinion learn what was really happening to Europe's minorities—and this offered a way forward:

> The judgement of this public ... today is more significant
> than even a favourable example of a lazy compromise by
> the statesmen sitting in the Council.

It was only because of public opinion that Polish pacification of Ukrainians was condemned at all.[3]

Writing in *Revalsche Zeitung* (the renamed *Revaler Bote*), in 1931 Eric Drummond, General Secretary of the League of Nations, termed his organisation a 'peace machine'.[4] Notwithstanding the changes of 1929, members of the minorities increasingly were convinced that this 'machine' had fundamental deficiencies which were being overlooked. They became increasingly outspoken on the point too. Talking to the congress in 1932, Ammende complained that things had actually become worse since the Adatci reforms.[5] He bemoaned the fact that the League no longer possessed so many great and neutral statesmen, figures like Branting and Nansen who could put general interests at the heart of the League's agenda. If the League would not take the minority problem seriously, Ammende looked to the congress to set up its own body to publicise minority affairs and to support the drafting of future petitions.

---

[3] E. Ammende, 'Die "geheiligten Rechte" der Nationalitäten. Zum Genfer Ratsfiasko', *Revalsche Zeitung* 9 February 1932. For a report from Tallinn on what had been happening in Ukarinian territories, see 'Die Bedrückung der Ukraine. Wie Polen die Ukrainer befriedete!' *Revalsche Zeitung* 28 October 1930.
[4] E. Drummond, 'Elf Jahre Völkerbund', *Revalsche Zeitung* 9 January 1931.
[5] For his speech, see *Sitzungsbericht des Kongresses der organisierten nationalen Gruppen in den Staaten Europas. Wien, 29. Juni bis 1. Juli 1932*. Wien-Leipzig: Wilhelm Braumüller, 1933, pp. 102 ff.

Professor Ernest Bovet also spoke to the congress in 1932 and highlighted fundamental problems with the League's protection system. At the inception of minority protection, the Great Powers prevented the system becoming universal because they believed they treated their citizens well enough and did not want any intrusion to their domestic affairs. Unfortunately a situation had been reached where protection could not progress until provisions were universalised because, Bovet felt, bad conscience on the part of the non-signatory Great Powers subverted any possible efforts to underpin existing protection measures.[6]

At the same meeting of the congress, Emil Margulies also addressed the problem of non-universal minority rights. To his mind, Europe was divided between non-signatory states which regarded themselves as free of obligations, and signatories which felt they were under some kind of moral servitude. Margulies suggested the only way forward was for minority rights to be universalised and, to this end, he proposed a common convention should be established for states to adopt voluntarily. He looked to individual states which recognised the moral significance of the step to take the idea forwards.[7] The congress duly approved a resolution demanding universal minority rights in Europe.

When Kurt Graebe addressed a meeting of German minority representatives in Austria in June 1932, he underlined the feeling that since 1929 the protection of minorities had become worse not better. Time and again, interested states were preventing the publication of reports about the treatment of petitions, while those that were published seemed inadequate anyway.[8]

For members of the minorities, the League of Nations was missing its opportunities. There was even a sense that members of the organisation were overlooking the most important issues quite deliberately. As an article in *Revaler Bote* put it in 1932:

> As usual in Geneva, the 13th League Assembly has also understood with unusual skill how to avoid mentioning the great questions of international politics.[9]

Fundamentally important issues such as disarmament and the protection of minorities were glossed over, suggesting that the organisation did not understand basic responsibilities. It was hardly surprising under the circumstances that, in 1931, the congress had found that:

---

[6] *Sitzungsbericht 1932*, p. 34.

[7] *Sitzungsbericht 1932*, p.162.

[8] 'Jahrestagung des Verbandes der deutschen Volksgruppen in Europa.' *Revalsche Zeitung*, 4 July 1932.

[9] 'Der Niedergang des Völkerbundes', *Revalsche Zeitung* 25 October 1932.

...even petitions to the League of Nations concerning the gravest attacks upon life and property were treated in a manner calculated to shatter the faith of those affected.[10]

## 2. Disillusionment

In 1929, some voices already had been heard trying to caution about the consequences of disillusionment on the part of minorities. Talking to the congress that year, Sir Willoughby Dickinson warned the minorities not to expect too much. He feared that many states in Europe actually favoured the assimilation of minorities and felt minority protection had been a mistake. This, he said, was true even of some members of the League's Council. Nonetheless, he also warned that when trying to deal with problems, minorities should still—and despite all the difficulties—'turn to the League of Nations and only to it'.[11] He emphasised, 'it is not desirable that they are compelled to turn to Germany'. He was clear that minority issues could be dealt with in the most peaceful way only through a fully international organisation since appealing to a sponsoring state might lead Germany to attempt to intervene in the domestic affairs of a European neighbour. Such a situation would heighten political tensions and, in an extreme case, might even provoke war.

Dickinson's words were honest, but he was proclaiming them in an environment where people were not always prepared to listen. In mid-October 1929, Ammende was already contacting an official in the Foreign Ministry in Berlin suggesting the creation of a committee to bring together all German minorities:

> Only through the coming together of the international German national community—the meeting of the German national council and the election of a permanently convened executive / national committee—will the largest nation in Central Europe be given the sure foundation for the national cultural co-operation of all the parts of its German community of blood, language and culture. Moreover, since this example would lead to a corresponding development among very many other European nations, sooner or later the possibility would be reached of giving Europe's nations a new foundation for cultural exchange and national co-operation.[12]

---

[10] J. Robinson, O. Karbach, M.M. Laserson, N. Robinson and M. Vichniak, *Were the Minorities Treaties a Failure?* New York: Antin Press. 1943, p. 253.

[11] *Sitzungsbericht des Kongresses der organisierten nationalen Gruppen in den Staaten Europas. Genf, 26 bis 28 August 1929.* Vienna-Leipzig: Wilhelm Braumüller. 1930, p. 28–9.

[12] In S. Bamberger-Stemmann, *Der Europäische Nationalitätenkongreß 1925 bis 1938. Nationale Minderheiten zwischen Lobbyistentum und Grossmachtinteressen.* Marburg: Verlag

The readiness to take such a project forward in co-ordination with the German Foreign Ministry marked rather a step away from the practices of both the Association of German Minorities and of the congress, which very much were initiatives from the minorities themselves and in which the German state played a secondary role.

Pessimism subverted Dickinson's words too. In the past, when Ammende had looked at Europe, he saw a series of areas threatened by nationality-based conflict, including Vilnius, Polish Ukrainian territory and Bessarabia.[13] Others however, soon were becoming even more concerned about the prospects for the future. Werner Hasselblatt thought the experiences of the minorities symptomatic of an increasing malaise throughout Europe. Addressing the congress in the wake of the League's Madrid meeting, he expressed the worry that 'Europe, as a continent, as a cultural unity is in absolute decline', since it was characterised by 'contradictions, and not least by national contradictions'.[14] In particular, he warned of the deeply corrupting impact of a situation in which legal guarantees existed, but were not enforced. It would, he said, be better if such laws had never been created in the first place. Two years later he returned to the theme, warning the congress of a possible collapse of the continent if conditions continued to worsen.[15] Europe, he said, did not contain particular 'danger zones', rather he thought the continent as a whole was 'completely wild' in its toleration of legal and moral outrages.[16] By contrast, he noted that the USSR had taken at least some steps towards addressing the minority question. Axel de Vries shared this pessimism. In 1931 he argued that a Spenglerian decline of the West was at hand, that Europe was breaking down.[17] The same year, he spoke about 'Europe's serious illness' and gave little reason to think the patient would ever get better.[18]

## 3. The death of Stresmann and its consequences

1929 and the failure of the League of Nations to do more to meet the concerns of the minorities led them to ask the question 'if not the League as our saviour, then whom?' Despite Willoughby Dickinson's warnings about the dangers of looking to Germany, that country was in many ways an

---

Herder-Institut, 2000, p. 185.

[13] E. Ammende, 'Zwischen Rußland und dem Westen', *Revaler Bote* 16 August 1926 and E. Ammende, 'Zwischen Rußland und dem Westen', *Revaler Bote* 17 August 1926

[14] *Sitzungsbericht 1929*, p. 79.

[15] *Sitzungsbericht des congresses der organisierten nationalen Gruppen in den Staaten Europas. Genf 29 bis 31 1931.* Vienna and Leipzig: Wilhelm Braumüller, 1932, pp. 31–3.

[16] Discussing the state of minorities issues in Europe in 1931, Josip Wilfan felt the right phrase was 'Europe's open wounds'. See 'Vom Genfer Nationalitätenkongress', *Revalsche Zeitung* 4 September 1931.

[17] A. de Vries, 'Europäische Götterdämmerung', *Revalsche Zeitung* 18 July 1931.

[18] A. de Vries, 'Genf', *Revalsche Zeitung* 9 September 1931.

obvious guarantor. Since 1926 it had been not just a member of the League, but held a seat in the Council. It was a nation state which could not ignore ties to some 8 million members of ethnic German minorities and, as the words of Stresemann plus diplomats such as Köster showed, it was home to both statesman and officials sympathetic to their plight.[19]

In early October 1929, however, everything changed for German foreign policy: Gustav Stresemann died. With his steady hand absent, radical possibilities would soon begin to intrude. Ammende was quick to recognise the significance of the event. Given the support Stresemann had given the minority movement, his loss would leave a big hole. Ammende felt he would need to be followed by another person who could serve as a unifying figure in the interests of 'all-German' initiatives. He also feared that, with such a towering figure absent, the enemies of the minority movement, and possibly of Germany too, would seize the day.[20] In this connection he noted that the Czech statesman Eduard Beneš was becoming active. Ammende believed Beneš had played a part in the League's apparently worsening attitude towards minorities, as it had been experienced from about 1923 on. Beneš viewed minority leaders as 'complainers and propagandists', and unfortunately had found too many allies in the Minorities Section. The new circumstances, Ammende feared, would increase the room for manoeuvre available to him.[21] Ethnic Germans needed to unite to plan a response.

### 4. Changes in the ethnic German camp: the rise of Hasselblatt and ties to Berlin

1929 also saw a subtle but significant change in how German minorities presented themselves. The same year as the disappointment with the League and Stresemann's death, the Association of German Minorities in Europe changed its name to the Association of German National Groups (*Volksgruppen*) in Europe.[22] The move, arguably, suggested a new mood of assertiveness among at least the German 'minorities' who came to reject that

---

[19] Most obviously this sympathy was because before the First World War, Germans living in the Polish Corridor and Polish Upper Silesia, for example, had been Reich citizens. Equally, it was hard to ignore the existence of a millions-strong ethnic German community in the Sudetenland. In addition, Baltic Germans, such as Ammende and Schiemann, not to say Rudolf Brandsch in Romania, were pursuing a great deal of work to establish connections between German communities in their home regions and Berlin.

[20] Memorandum, Ammende to Loesch. 18.10.29. R60493. Political Archive of the Foreign Ministry, Berlin.

[21] Memorandum by Ammende. 'Eduard Benesch's wahres Gesicht'. R60493. Political Archive of the Foreign Ministry, Berlin.

[22] M. Garleff, 'Baltische Minderheitenvertreter auf den Europäischen Nationalitätenkongressen 1925–1938', *Jahrbuch des baltischen Deutschtums* 33 (1986) 117–31. Baltic Central Library, Riga, p. 118. See also 'Nationalitätenpolitik zwischen liberalem und völkischem Anspruch. Gleichklang und Spannung bei Paul Schiemann und Werner Hasselblatt' in J. von Hehn and C.J. Kenez (eds.), *Reval und die Baltischen Länder*. Marburg: Herder Institute, 1980, p. 118.

word as indicative of some kind of second class status. By calling themselves 'national groups' they were claiming full equality with majority national groups in any given state and emphasising their belonging to a larger, overarching entity—the German nation as a whole.

Nor did the changes stop there. Carl Georg Bruns had led the Berlin office of the Association of German Minorities / National groups since the organisation was established. In 1931, however, he died. A disability had prevented Bruns fighting in the First World War and consequently he had served in the military administration in Brussels. Here, apparently, he was introduced to nationality issues for the first time.[23] After the war, he worked for the German fraction in the national council in Posen and West Prussia, and subsequently never lost an interest in Poland's German minorities.[24] From 1923 on, however, he led the Association's secretariat, a role he fulfilled with tact and skill.[25] Over the years, Bruns developed a reputation as an honest-broker promoting the interests of German groups honourably. As a result, he received a favourable obituary in the *Manchester Guardian*, which described this legal adviser to German minorities as:

> ...one of those truly great men who, although unknown to the wider public, have done at least as much for the world's peace as those who will figure in the history books of the future as the peacemakers of our age.... Had Dr Bruns been a propagandist he would have achieved nothing. But he met falsehood with fact, prejudice with an open mind, and casuistry with precise legal knowledge.[26]

Paul Schiemann also wrote an appreciative recollection of Bruns, stressing the productive way he had tackled minority rights as a legal issue. He regretted the fact that, in all probability, whoever took over his position in the Association would lead it with more of an eye on organisational and political issues than legal ones.[27]

Ammende recognised the pity of the death of Bruns. This, he told Schiemann, had left a large gap in their movement.[28] Where Schiemann and Ammende disagreed, however, was over the appointment of a successor. Ammende wanted the post filled by his fellow Estonian German Werner

---

[23] E. Kaufmann, 'Carl Georg Bruns als Persönlichkeit und Vorkämpfer der deutschen Minderheit', *Nation und Staat* March 1931.

[24] For a further obituary, see FuG, 'Dr Carl Georg Bruns', *Nation und Staat* March 1931.

[25] 'Carl Georg Bruns', *Revalsche Zeitung* 28 February 1931. For his cremation, see 'Der Trauerfeier in Anlass des Hinscheidens von Dr C.G. Bruns', *Revalsche Zeitung* 9 March 1931.

[26] 'A Champion of Minorities. Death of Dr Bruns. Intricate Work of Legal Adviser', *Manchester Guardian* 2 March 1931. R60493. Political Archive of the Foreign Ministry, Berlin.

[27] P. Schiemann, 'Carl Georg Bruns. Der Rechtsberater der deutschen Minderheiten', *Frankfurter Zeitung* 6 March 1931. R60493. Political Archive of the Foreign Ministry, Berlin.

[28] 27.2.31, Ammende to Schiemann. Schiemann Papers. ENK Folder. Baltic Central Library, Riga.

Hasselblatt. In early March he told Schiemann as much in a letter which admitted that Hasselblatt had 'many failings', but still would be a 'first class' choice—although he recognised that Schiemann might think otherwise.[29] Quickly, Ammende was promoting Hasselblatt's case. In a letter to the German Foreign Ministry he indicated that, before long, most people would support Hasselblatt's candidacy.[30] Accordingly, later in March he contacted Schiemann again.[31] Now Ammende stressed that already Hasselblatt had extensive support among German minority leaders in Poland, Romania and Denmark. He emphasised that Hasselblatt was a well-regarded lawyer with considerable experience dealing with legal questions concerning the League of Nations. By contrast, a certain Professor Kaufmann (who presumably was Schiemann's preferred replacement), was more of a theorist. Ammende felt the Association did not need a choice that would be either a temporary stop-gap or a pure academic. He went on:

> What we need is a jurist with a proven constructive intellect, who stands in the middle of our struggle for our rights, who in addition has a reputation and who, on account of his whole authority, would be in the position to have an impact on the gentlemen in Geneva ... just as Bruns did with the greatest success. There is not the least doubt that, since the struggle over the autonomy law in Estonia and more, Hasselblatt has the reputation of an eminent, skilful and constructive jurist, yes, if you wish, even the capacity of one—even if you think otherwise.[32]

Ammende emphasised that someone like Hasselblatt would be far more likely to impress, say Azcárate than would an unknown legal theorist.

Hasselblatt was once described as a 'diplomat' who could use a 'moderate voice' and careful arguments. He was also sufficiently realistic to know that 'the time of privileged minorities' was over. If all of this sounded progressive, the same source recognised that he interpreted the nation as a 'national estate' (*Nationalstand*), a phrase which hearkened back to conservative, organic inclinations.[33] Nonetheless, Ammende supported Hasselblatt staunchly. In early April he wrote to Schiemann again. He wanted a unanimous vote for Hasselblatt among the representatives to the Association of German National Groups since anything else would look

---

[29] 5.3.31, Ammende to Schiemann. Schiemann Papers. ENK Folder. Baltic Central Library, Riga.
[30] 17.3.31, Ammende to Geheimrat, AA. R60493. Political Archive of the Foreign Ministry, Berlin.
[31] 17.3.31, Ammende to Schiemann. R60493. Political Archive of the Foreign Ministry, Berlin.
[32] Ibid.
[33] 'Kämpfer für deutsches Volkstum. Auslandsdeutsche Führerköpfe. 2. Werner Hasselblatt', *Vossische Zeitung*, 29.12.32. R 60494. Political Archive of the Foreign Ministry, Berlin.

strange to Berlin's officials.[34] Unfortunately, to Schiemann's mind Hasselblatt stood too close to the German Foreign Ministry for comfort. While Bruns consistently had steered an independent course, Schiemann feared Hasselblatt would try to align German minorities too closely with the *Reich*, making them a tool for the pursuit of Berlin's foreign policy. For Schiemann, Hasselblatt was too ready to conform to Berlin's demands to be a credible advocate of the minorities' needs. This is why at least one commentator has observed that 1931, with Hasselblatt's eventual appointment to replace Bruns, marked the Association's loss of independence.[35] By this point, however, and in the light of his recommendation to Berlin of October 1929 that a co-ordinating committee be set up for German national groups around Europe, clearly Ammende also was looking to the German state to become involved increasingly in minority affairs.

Now, as Schiemann gave way to Ammende and Hasselblatt, a kind of generational change was under way in the German minority leadership— and it would not prove to be for the better. For all his work on cultural autonomy, Hasselblatt seemed more comfortable with basically conservative, corporatist and even *völkisch* thinking than progressive alternatives. He interpreted democracy as dictatorship by the voting majority and parliamentary decisions as decided by arithmetical politics coupled with horse-trading, materialistic thinking and departure from traditional values. His vision of Europe essentially was Nordic-Protestant, with a sense that Germans in the eastern parts of Europe were facing an increasing tide of Slavs, against whom they provided a bulwark for western culture. So he saw himself as part of a German mission to strengthen the truly significant cultural core of the continent.[36] Accordingly, Hasselblatt seems to have helped bring about the change in name of the Association of German Minorities to National Groups.[37] Once he was installed as Bruns's successor, he gave up his home in Estonia and moved to Berlin.[38]

The closeness of relationship between Hasselblatt and Berlin's policy circles soon showed an effect. As soon as he knew he was to take over from Bruns, Hasselblatt wrote to the Foreign Ministry to discuss funding. He expressed the hope that there would be enough resources to maintain himself and his family in the capital, not to say to provide removal costs and money

---

[34] 7.4.1931, Ammende to Schiemann. Schiemann Papers. ENK Folder. Baltic Central Library, Riga.
[35] Bamberger-Stemmann, *Der Europäische Nationalitätenkongreß 1925 bis 1938,* pp. 191–7.
[36] 'Nationalitätenpolitik zwischen liberalem und völkischem Anspruch. Gleichklang und Spannung bei Paul Schiemann und Werner Hasselblatt' in J. von Hehn and C.J. Kenez (eds.), *Reval und die Baltischen Länder.* Marburg: Herder Institute. 1980, pp.123–6.
[37] X-M. Núñez Seixas, *Entre Ginebra y Berlin. La Cuestion de las Minorias Nacionales y la Politica Internacional en Europa 1914–1939.* Madrid: Akal, 2001, pp.480–2.
[38] 'Abschiedsehrung für Abg. Werner Hasselblatt', *Revalsche Zeitung* 20 May 1932.

for travel.[39] In return for official support, Hasselblatt did his best to impress the Foreign Ministry. A diplomatic report of the Association's meeting of August 1931, the first organised by Hasselblatt, said the event stood out from previous events by virtue of the level of presentations and discussion.[40] Soon thereafter a memorandum of the Foreign Ministry noted:

> The activity of the Association of German National Groups in Europe is of special significance for the promotion of German interests abroad, particularly in the minority sphere. It is therefore urgently necessary that the Association is given the necessary financial transfers abroad regularly for the exercise of this activity, without delay and implemented without reserve.[41]

Thereafter, in December, the Reich Chancellor, together with State Secretary von Bülow and *Oberregireungsrat* Planck received a delegation from the Association, at which the leaders of the group (including presumably Hasselblatt) gave a speech and handed over a list of things they would like done. The Chancellor declared his readiness to assist the group, even to consider setting up a crisis fund for their use.[42] In other words, if Ammende had looked to Hasselblatt as someone to tighten relations between the German minority movement and the German Foreign Ministry, he had backed the right horse. Unfortunately, the link would come with a hefty price tag attached.

### 5. Minority or national group? *Volksgruppen* (national group) thinking and Pan-Europe

In November 1925, Theodor Oberländer wrote to Ewald Ammende arguing that the tension between the Anglo-Saxon Powers and the Russian-Asiatic bloc necessitated the creation of a strong new Europe. This, he said, should not be accomplished under the leadership of France, but under Germany and Central Europe. German minorities had to make a contribution here, including through the promotion of cultural autonomy as a mechanism likely to reduce national tensions in Europe.[43] Yet, as the 1920s ended, and as the renaming of the Association of German National Groups in Europe showed,

[39] 8.4.31, Hasselblatt to the AA. R60494. Political Archive of the Foreign Ministry, Berlin.
[40] 'Bericht über die Jahrestagung des Verbandes der deutschen Volksgruppen in Europa in Bad Schandau vom 23.–26.8.1931'. R60493. Political Archive of the Foreign Ministry, Berlin.
[41] 14 October 1931. AA (VI A) to Verband. R60494. Political Archive of the Foreign Ministry, Berlin.
[42] Aktennotiz. R60494. Political Archive of the Foreign Ministry, Berlin. Between March 1931 and March 1932, RM 46,600 fromwed from the Foreign Ministry to the Association. 9.6.32. Graebe (Verband) to AA. R60494. Political Archive of the Foreign Ministry, Berlin.
[43] 15.11.25, Oberländer to Ammende. 1502–1–26. Moscow.

increasingly there was a feeling that being labelled a 'minority' was not helpful. It left a feeling of inadequacy. From the perspective of minorities, the main reason to adopt the label was to lay claim to minority rights. Yet if they were being administered badly regardless of what the post-war settlement said, then why even bother with this—especially if you aspired to being seen as part of an over-arching national whole? Furthermore, to be truthful, some of the members of the German minorities had never liked being termed a 'minority' anyway. Hasselblatt thought minority protection smacked of something donated to those inferior to most other people, like the needy, the sick and the poor.[44] Schiemann too rejected the idea of minority rights as a kind of charity; he wanted legal rights.[45] The rights had to be your due, not an act of generosity on the part of majority populations.

As an alternative to a nation state incorporating minority rights, some—such as Schiemann—looked to the Swiss state. Here (according to his interpretation), different groups were not so much thought of as 'minorities' but as different nationality groups, all of whom co-operated equally in the state.[46] Professor Max Laserson (a Jew from Latvia), speaking to the congress in 1927, pointed out that there was a tendency for the national group predominating in a state to feel it could tailor that state towards its own national self-realisation alone, but the minority struggle was directed against such over-simplified ways of thinking.[47] Correspondingly, in 1929 Wilhelm von Medinger argued strongly that Germans in Czechoslovakia were more than 'just' a minority. They were in the majority in some areas and were participants in government. They wanted political equality and to be considered 'one of the nations of the state'—i.e. on a par with a recognised state-bearing nation such as Czechs and Slovaks.[48] Talking to the same congress, Franz Jesser (a Sudeten German) was even more blunt:

> We want constitutional recognition as a second state-forming and state-bearing nationality.[49]

He insisted that one day Czechoslovakia should organise itself along the same lines as Switzerland, where diversity did not preclude a significant sense of unity.[50] A few years later, Hans Otto Roth, a German from Romania,

---

[44] *Sitzungsbericht des Kongresses der organisierten nationalen Gruppen in den Staaten Europas. Genf 25.–27. August 1926.*Vienna: Wilhelm Braumüller, 1927, p. 47.
[45] *Sitzungsbericht des Kongresses der organisierten nationalen Gruppen in den Staaten Europas. Genf 22.– 4. August 1927.* Vienna: Wilhelm Braumüller, 1928, p. 24.
[46] Ibid, p. 25.
[47] Ibid, p. 35.
[48] *Sitzungsbericht 1929*, 1930, p. 63.
[49] Ibid, p. 74.
[50] Ammende was so taken with the strength of the Sudeten Germans, he wondered if they should try to pursue some kind of territorial autonomy. Memorandum, Ammende to Loesch. 18.10.29. R60493. Political Archive of the Foreign Ministry, Berlin.

declared that minorities were not just 'minorities', but 'co-deciding, state-leading nations'.[51]

This way of thinking became centrally important as a result of the disappointments of 1929 coupled with Richard Coudenhove-Kalergi's ideas as explained in his book *Pan-Europe* (1923) which later were given popular political character by Aristide Briand.[52] As Otto Ulitz (a German from Polish Silesia) told the European Congress of Nationalities, Briand had addressed the League of Nations on 9 September 1929, raising the question of creating a specifically European association of states. The following May he presented the League with a memorandum discussing the establishment of a European Union based on his model.[53] Ulitz, however, argued there were important flaws in the conception of Pan-Europe. Briand seemed to be suggesting that an association of equal sovereign states could secure peace in Europe; but Ulitz felt there were problems. On the one hand, groups of European states were aligning against each other; on the other hand, there was a resurgence of national identity that was impacting badly on Europe's minorities. Hence in Briand's vision there was no space for minorities to participate in the shaping of European life and that, consequently, the plan was omitting something fundamental. As Ulitz put it:

> Our humanity awakens from our nationality. Our nationality is the foundation for all our action and all our thought.[54]

Accordingly, he proposed a Pan-Europe should be established not just on the foundation of sovereign states, but of nationality too. He wanted ideas of Europe to reflect national communities (*Volksgemeinschaften*), not just state borders. The more that happened, with national communities establishing ever stronger international connections, the more political borders would become irrelevant or maybe even start to vanish. He looked to the day when Europe's nations could relate to each other directly, from the North Cape to the Mediterranean, from the Atlantic to the Urals. Then, he said, it would be possible to have a pan-European community.[55]

---

[51] *Sitzungsbericht 1932*, p. 45.

[52] See 'Briands Paneuropa', *Revaler Bote* 6 September 1929 and 'Frankreichs Paneuropaplan gescheitert', *Revalsche Zeitung* 9 September 1930.

[53] Subsequently, in 1930, Briand called a meeting of 20 Foreign Ministers from across Europe to promote the idea. See 'Frankreichs Paneuropaplan gescheitert', *Revalsche Zeitung* 9 September 1930.

[54] *Sitzungsbericht des Kongresses der organisierten Nationalen Gruppen in den Staaten Europas. Genf, 3 bis 6 September 1930*. Vienna - Leipzig: Wilhelm Braumüller, 1931, p. 33. For a summary by the German Foreign Ministry of this meeting of the congress, see 'Die Minoritätenkongress und das Paneuropaproblem', R60528. Political Archive of the Foreign Ministry, Berlin.

[55] *Sitzungsbericht 1930*, pp. 29–35.

At the same meeting of the congress—1930—, Joan Estelrich (a Catalan from Spain) maintained that, despite all the political planning for an association of European states, the national minorities actually were most committed to the idea of a European Union. As he put it:

> No one can deny our attachment to the European idea, even the fact of our congress is one of the most effective adverts for the European Union; we fight against unity to be achieved through force, but at the same time we are the strongest example of a European union....[56]

Estelrich had doubts about Briand's plan. His European Union would subvert the authority of the League of Nations, lacked psychological and moral foundations, and overlooked completely the minority question. Hence Estelrich called for a union of Europe based on national groups rather than states:

> In order to realise the union, one must direct a call to the nations, not just to the states and their ministers. We want a European Union, but a true one, one of nations and not governments. (Very good!)[57]

Other speakers lined up to add their views on a united Europe. Michail Kurtschinsky (a Russian from Estonia) felt Briand's idea ignored the minority question completely. Jacob Robinson (a Jew from Lithuania) agreed, saying the minority question was 'all too European', and adding that minorities by their very nature (inhabiting one country, but being tied culturally to another, as well as being connected to other minorities) were particularly Pan-European.[58] Engelbert Besednjak (a Slovene from Italy) agreed with Estelrich that a united Europe had to be based on a union of nationalities rather than states (which were not rooted so profoundly in the human condition). He believed national communities, including their minorities:

> ... are the foundation on which European intellectual life rests and through which ultimately the political fate of states is shaped.[59]

By implication, a European Union could only be achieved once the minority problem was solved and peace existed between all national groups.

---

[56] Ibid, p. 49.
[57] Ibid, p. 54.
[58] Ibid, pp. 39 and 74.
[59] Ibid, p. 71.

Ukrainian congress participants were particularly hostile to Briand's idea of Pan-Europe. Vasyl Mudry (a Ukrainian from Poland) dismissed the scheme as fossilising existing borders—something Ukrainians could not accept. Since talk of changing borders was at odds with the principles of the European Congress of Nationalities, President Wilfan had to intervene to halt his talk. Nonetheless Mudry added that, to his mind, a European federation should be based on a right to self-determination, not on the status quo.[60] Mudry was followed by another Ukrainain (from Romania), Volodymyr Zaloziecki, who argued that according to current plans, only western Ukraine (with 8 million inhabitants) would be included in Pan-Europe, while eastern Ukraine (home to 35 million) would be excluded. He thought this was unacceptable.[61]

More moderate was the intervention of Ambassador von Ugron (a Hungarian from Romania). He interpreted Coudenhove-Kalergi's orginal plan as a response to Europe being in danger of decline after the First World War. Briand's vision, he felt, was less ambitious, involving essentially a pulling together of existing sovereign states for political consultation and economic benefit. Von Ugron thought it possible that Europe did need some kind of union, but felt that before it could happen the continent's inhabitants had to feel they belonged together; there had to be a kind of European patriotism. Although Coudenhove–Kalergi had recognised the need for language and cultural rights, he felt Briand's plan offered minorities nothing. Before Pan-European plans could work, all groups needed to be involved and all nations had to be united behind the plan.[62]

It was decided that the congress would send a memorandum to Briand. The document expressed doubts that his proposals would lead to peace, being overly concerned with states as the units of European organisation. Unfortunately there were millions of people for whom the striving after national unity could not be achieved in terms of state membership, and as a result a European Union would have to be build not just on a foundation of states, but on one of nations too. Equally, a European Union could not just be a mechanism for building bridges between states; it had to facilitate understanding between nations. For this to be achieved, every European had to be able to live in closest harmony with his co-nationals. The memorandum, which was signed by President Wilfan, ended by calling on Briand to use his power to promote 'a vital pan-European community' based not just on the economy and states, but on justice and co-operation between nations.[63]

---

[60] Ibid, p. 89.
[61] Ibid, pp. 91–2.
[62] Ibid, pp. 62–5.
[63] Ibid, p. 119.

The minorities could not have had great hopes of Briand. Take his comments to the Council of the League of Nations of March 1929 in which he tried to define the purpose of minority protection:

> ...it is a question of protecting minorities in the preservation of their language, their culture, their religion and their traditions in order to maintain this kind of little family in the lap or the large one, not in order to weaken the larger one, but rather to secure the harmony of all the constituent parts. It is not a question of the minorities vanishing, but of a kind of assimilation, which lets the nations become greater, without diminishing the small family. Gentlemen, I understand the problem of minorities in this way.[64]

Briand's comments showed that statesmen were still struggling to find an appropriate way to think about minorities. His talk certainly made it harder for him to win over minorities to his wider agenda.

## 6. Discussing Pan-Europe and international national communities

The congress had so much to say about Pan-Europe at the 1930 congress that it was clear the topic would run and run; but even before Briand made his comments, the minorities had shown an interest in Pan-European ideas. For instance, in 1926 *Revaler Bote* reported about the first Pan-European congress in Vienna.[65]

Ammende had some concerns about Pan-Europeanism. Although he was sure minorities supported a united Europe, he was concerned that if a separate organisation, called perhaps the European Union, began to function, then it might usurp the work of the League of Nations in Europe (and the congress had been attempting to influence this organisation for the last five years). Given that the League worked with authority on a variety of European issues directly relevant to minorities, he felt such a change could be dangerous—particularly since Briand's planning paid scant attention to minorities. This was why he emphasised that European unification should happen within the framework of the League; it was the option he preferred even if he was often critical of the League's work. It was also why he warned that the establishment of a committee of Foreign Ministry officials drawn from European states, even if organised within the League (as Briand had suggested), eventually would lead to a separate, independent association of

---

[64] 'Die grosse Minderheitendebatte vor dem Völkerbundrat', *Nation und Staat* March 1929, p. 511.
[65] 'Paneuropa. Einige kritische Bemerkungen anläßlich des paneuropäischen Kongresses in Wien', *Revaler Bote* 8 October 1926 and H.Hütter, 'Nach dem paneuropäischen Kongreß in Wien', *Revaler Bote* 13 October 1926.

those same states. He preferred the idea of creating a European Section in the League's Secretariat to pursue Europe's unification. He felt that Europe didn't really need a committee of Foreign Ministers all to sit around wringing their hands (especially since many of them already attended the League annually anyway). Instead he wanted effective work towards a clear understanding of the problems which prevented good relations between nationalities. Paper promises were unnecessary; practical national reconciliation was what was needed.[66]

Talking to the congress in 1930, Ammende explained that the leaders of the Pan-European movement were not interested in people like them. Minority spokesmen were not representatives of states and had no state apparatus behind them; hence they could be overlooked.[67] But so far as Ammende was concerned, until the nationality question was solved, there could be no united Europe. Hence, in his eyes, removing tensions between nationalities was work towards European unity, and congress President Josip Wilfan wondered if Europe's minorities might promote European union by establishing solidarity among themselves.[68] Likewise for Schiemann, Europe as a unity of states could not be at peace unless supplemented by an international structure of national communities.[69] The trouble was, to Ammende's mind, there could never be a united Europe so long as national oppression, hatred and conflict between different national groups continued. There could be no European unity until the minority problem was solved.[70]

For Ammende and those around him, nationality issues took precedence over relations between states and a German consular note about the 1930 congress emphasised that, for that organisation, Pan-Europe was unachievable until the minority question was solved.[71] As Wilfan pointed out the same year, it was the nationalities not the states that were the real sources of 'friendship and animosity, of love and hate'. They and their sentiments provided the driving force behind international relations. So, Wilfan continued, it was hopeless for statesmen to talk of friendship between countries if the masses wanted nothing to do with it 'in their heart and soul'.[72]

---

[66] *Sitzungsbericht 1930*, p. 95. E. Ammende, 'Die Aufgaben des VI. Nationalitätenkongresses', *Revalsche Zeitung* 4 September 1930. E. Ammende, 'Das "geeinte" Europa Briands und die nationalen Minderheiten', *Neue Zürcher Zeitung* 8.7.30. R60528. Political Archive of the Foreign Ministry, Berlin. Ewald Ammende, 'Das "geeinte Europa" Briands und die Stellungnahme der Nationalitäten', *Revalsche Zeitung* 17 July 1930.
[67] *Sitzungsbericht 1930*, p. 94.
[68] *Sitzungsbericht 1929*, p. 117. *Sitzungsbericht 1926*, p. 19.
[69] *Sitzungsbericht des Kongresses der organisierten nationalen Gruppen in den Staaten Europas im Jahre 1925 zu Genf*. Vienna: Wilhelm Braumüller, 1926, p. 43.
[70] E. Ammende, 'Aktuelle Aufgaben im Kampfe um den nationalen Ausgleich', *Nation und Staat* October 1929.
[71] Letter from the German Consulate, Geneva. 10.9.1930. R60528. Political Archive of the Foreign Ministry, Berlin.
[72] *Sitzungsbericht 1930*, pp. 8–9.

It was impossible to have harmonious relations between neighbouring states so long as tensions remained between the nationalities inhabiting them.

Paul Schiemann was clear that a harmonious, united Europe called for both competition between states and tension between nations to be superseded.[73] As he put it in August 1930:

> Without resolving the nationality problem, a European Union—even the beginning of such—is hopeless.[74]

This did not mean Schiemann failed to understand peace and economic success were part and parcel of the European project, rather he believed no such goals were attainable so long as the nationality question remained unresolved. For additional support he quoted Prinz Rohan's ideas about the unification of Central and Eastern Europe. Although Rohan felt this should happen for economic reasons, he understood that it would be impossible until the cultural lives of different national groups were secured adequately.[75]

In the light of concerns such as these, Ammende and those around him began developing an alternative idea of Pan-Europe with nationalities at the core. With Europe 'Balkanised' by the Treaty of Versailles, Ammende believed the creation of international connections was imperative, otherwise the continent would suffer catastrophe. While he accepted that a union of states might be a first step towards creating a Pan-Europe, alone it would not be enough. Pan-Europe would need to take account of minorities fully.[76]

Ammende sent a memorandum to the German Foreign Ministry outlining how a European Union might develop.[77] The plan, he said, should be based on universal minority rights and would be in the interests of both Germany and Europe. He envisaged a growing together of the continent's nationalities in harmony with increasing European unification. Part of the process would involve the German nation drawing together—in fact, Germany might pioneer the whole project—but, he spelled out, 'not on the foundation of connections to the German state organism and its political interests'; the growing together was to be a cultural affair. Gradually a national organism (*Volkstumsorganismus*) would emerge with links between the main population within the German state (*Stammvolk*) and the national groups around the continent (*Volksgruppen*). Since this would be an entirely cultural development, there would be no concern at all about political liaison

---

[73] *Sitzungsbericht 1926*, p. 43.

[74] 'Ausschuss der Europäischen Nationalitätenkongresse. Mitteilungen der Geschäftsführung'. August 1930'. R60528. Political Archive of the Foreign Ministry, Berlin.

[75] P. Schiemann, 'Coudenhove und Rohan', *Nation und Staat* July-August 1930.

[76] 'Überstaatliche Kulturgemeinschaft. DAZ 1 Februar 1930'. R60528. Political Archive of the Foreign Ministry, Berlin.

[77] 'Gesichtspunkte zur deutschen Nationalitäten-Politik.' R60528. Political Archive of the Foreign Ministry, Berlin.

with the German state.[78] To ensure that the whole process took place successfully, Ammende felt there needed to be a number of organisational innovations:

> Only through a realisation of the international German national community—the convening of the German national council [a body representing different ethnic German populations] and election of an executive and national community committee meeting in permanent session—will the largest nation in Central Europe receive the secure foundation for the national cultural co-operation of all parts of the community of German blood, language and culture. Moreover, since this example would trigger the corresponding development of very many other European nations, sooner or later it would be possible to give European peoples a new foundation for cultural exchange and national co-operation.[79]

It should be underlined that Ammende still maintained the German minorities could belong to an international national community (*Volksgemeinschaft*) for cultural purposes while fulfilling their duties to the state communities (*Staatsgemeinschaft*) in which they lived.[80] The formation of these national cultural bodies was understood as a way to recognise the centrality of nations to Europe and, at the same time, to ensure their coherence so they could play the part of historic actors.[81] Without these developments, Pan-Europe was misconceived.

In 1932, Josip Wilfan published an article stressing the fundamental link between nations, culture and Europe.[82] He argued that European culture resides in its nations, and that the constant interplay of different national cultures gave Europe its cultural and intellectual richness. Hence, when every European nation promoted its cultural character, it contributed to European culture as a whole. It followed that every nationality should be in a position to organise its national community regardless of state borders and he called

---

[78] For another discussion by Ammende of the creation of an organic national community, see E. Ammende, 'Die Aufgaben des VI. Nationalitätenkongresses', *Revalsche Zeitung* 4 September 1930.

[79] 'Gesichtspunkte zur deutschen Nationalitäten-Politik.' R60528. Political Archive of the Foreign Ministry, Berlin.

[80] For arguments see, for instance, R. Brandsch, 'Fünf Jahre Minderheitenarbeit', *Nation und Staat* 1927/28 and of course the seminal P. Schiemann, 'Volksgemeinschaft und Staatsgemeinschaft', *Nation und Staat* v. 1. September 1927.

[81] F. v. Üxküll-Güldenbrand, 'Der VI Nationalitätenkongress. Genf 3 bis 5 September 1930'. *Nation und Staat* October 1930. Also 'Briands Paneuropaplan auf dem Minoritätenkongress', *Revalsche Zeitung* 4 September 1930.

[82] J.Wilfan, 'Die Organisierung der Volksgemeinschaft. Referat auf dem VI. Nationalitätenkongreß', *Nation und Staat* April 1932.

for a Pan-Europe in which nations organised themselves across the continent for cultural co-operation in the belief that the action of each would promote the achievement of all. Such a social model was deemed a pre-condition for reconciliation between nations and solidarity among them; it was a psychological pre-requisite for the successful union of European states too. He emphasised that no national community should ever misuse its organisation as a 'means of battle' against any other. In harmony with his argument, in 1930 Wilfan had already presented the congress with eight resolutions entitled 'The Development of National Communities among the Individual European Nations'. The points included the clear statement that Europe's culture is an expression of the intellectual life of its nations; also that to promote the culture of Europe, every nationality must be able to nurture its own culture. Correspondingly, Wilfan proposed that all European nations be permitted to create 'pan-national' organisations for cultural purposes.

In 1932, Ammende too made a strong statement about the fundamental connectedness of all the members of a given national group:

> The congress establishes that without reciprocal cultural connections of the same nationality groups among themselves, that is to say with the *Stammvolk* [i.e. the population of the 'home' national state], a prosperous cultural development is impossible. Left on their own, and without mental stimulation, individual national groups must waste away, [something] which cannot lie in the interests of states. The cultural isolation of individual nationalities makes their freedom of development illusory. As a result, the cultivation of these reciprocal connections is an absolute necessity for a fruitful cultural life. The congress considers it part of the foundation of the nationality system that the individual parts of the nation [*Volk*] maintain and nurture cultural connections among themselves and with the entire nation, that is, with the *Stammvolk*. The state may, by no measures of any kind, prevent these reciprocal cultural connections and their practical activity.[83]

He reiterated a point already made to the German Foreign Ministry: that there should be some kind of central organisation to manage relations between the co-national state (e.g. Germany) and the minorities beyond it. He also outlined rules for how the international national community should be developed, which included: it should only deal with cultural issues; it should be above party political and religious divisions; it should only consist of

---

[83] E. Ammende, 'Richtlinien zur Begründung der Volksgemeinschaft', *Nation und Staat* April 1932, pp. 464–5.

nationally-conscious individuals; it should be completely independent of state control; and there should be mutual tolerance between all such structures.

For Ammende and his friends, national communities had to lie at the heart of what Europe is: they had to be crucial building blocks for any Pan-European or European Union structure. It was also understood that in achieving such a union, minorities had to beware political involvement. Wilfan had emphasised that national communities should be used exclusively for cultural purposes, and in so doing was echoing points made by other minority thinkers.[84] Paul Schiemann had already observed that the more minorities rejected participation in the politics of the 'mother' state, the better they were situated to create an international national community.[85] At the same time, he recognised that politically and economically they had to be rooted in their *Heimat* (i.e. the state in which they lived); anything else invited accusations of irredenta and disloyalty.

Clearly the idea of Pan-Europe had a big impact on the European Congress of Nationalities, but the participants developed it in their own way. In the process, however, the congress began to see itself as able to become an addition to the League of Nations. Mayer Ebner (a Jew from Romania) made exactly this point in 1931.[86] If, despite its title, the League was in fact really a League of 'States', then the congress might one day be recognised as a true League of 'Nations' or 'Nationalities'. It could be a cultural supplement to the work of the political organisation.

## 7. The German angle and Ammende's 'new order'

This growth of interest in the international national community was accompanied by increased interest in the fortune and future of specifically the German national community (*Volksgemeinschaft*). In December 1929, the Association of German National Groups in Europe met in Prague. Present, among others, were Ammende and Hasselblatt. A report of the meeting noted there was a danger that if German minorities too frequently expressed sympathy for foreign nations, they could create the impression they were prepared to give up the right to create their own national group. It could strengthen the will of those who would oppose them and damage German solidarity.[87] Such a development hinted that, in the wake of disappointments over Adatci, German minorities were starting to prioritise in significant fashion their own welfare ahead of that of others, and this corresponded well with an interest in creating a Pan-German cultural community. Two months

---

[84]   J.Wilfan, 'Die Organisierung der Volksgemeinschaft. Referat auf dem VI. Nationalitätenkongreß', *Nation und Staat* April 1932.

[85] *Sitzungsbericht 1927*, p. 26.

[86] *Sitzungsbericht 1931*, p. 16.

[87] Extracts from 'Der Auslanddeutsche', 2nd Volume 1930. R60493. Political Archive of the Foreign Ministry, Berlin. See also 17.12.1929. German Embassy to AA. R60493. Political Archive of the Foreign Ministry, Berlin.

prior to the Association's meeting, Ammende had written to the German Foreign Ministry as follows:

> I must time and again stress anew that precisely we Germans need a more stable platform than the Nationality Congress for the further development of our mission in the nationality question and thereby for the organisation of our own nationality (likewise its connections to the other groups). More precisely expressed, our work may not be limited only to the congress meetings and their preparation.[88]

He spelled out that, in response to ideas of Pan-Europe coming from Western Europe, there was a need to set up a Pan-German committee as the 'kernel of our forthcoming German cultural community.' Clearly he had something in mind more weighty than the Association of German National Groups in Europe—something based in and somehow backed by the German state.

By this point, Ammende's frustrations were becoming manifest and he was threatening to cross the boundary between cultural and politico-economic action. For example, in discussions of the on-going persecution of Germans in the South Tyrol he recommended that Germans begin a tourism boycott of Italy. There was also talk that a unified German national community based around a committee in Germany could become quite an aggressive tool for the pursuit of minority rights. An anonymous article in the journal of the German minorities, *Nation und Staat*, argued that a cultural organisation based in Germany should be recognised under international law and be allowed to act as a plaintiff against states failing in their commitments to protect national minorities.[89] Thus the cultural organisation would also play the role of proactive legal advocate, possibly also a co-ordinator of appeals to the League of Nations.

In 1932, Ammende began appealing for something more radical still: a 'new order' for Europe's states.[90] He wanted the free cultural development of every national group in every state to be facilitated by minority rights, territorial or personal self-administration (depending on the demographic and settlement patterns of the minorities concerned) and, if necessary, the federal organisation of relevant states.[91] Hence Ammende felt minority rights were no longer good enough to satisfy the demands of all minorities in Europe. It really was time to break with the ideology of the

---

[88] Memo, Ammende to Loesch. 18.10.29. R60493. Political Archive of the Foreign Ministry, Berlin.

[89] 'Zur Verwirklichung der überstaatlichen Volksgemeinschaft', 'Aus Zeitschriften und Zeitungen', *Nation und Staat* November 1932 v. 6.

[90] In 1932, the phrase 'new order' did not yet have a Nazified meaning.

[91] E. Ammende, 'Neuordnung im europäischen Staat. Föderalismus, Selbstverwaltung und Nationalitätenrechte', *Nation und Staat* October 1932.

nation state, and for states to adapt their structures to take account of the patterns of national minorities inhabiting them. Only such a readiness to accommodate the needs of national minorities with very different characteristics would suffice to incorporate them properly into the state.

Seizing on examples, Ammende highlighted the dangerous situation in the Ukrainian part of Poland. He also proposed the Soviet Union's attempts to take account of national minorities had been so successful that émigré groups felt a post-Bolshevik state might do the same. Meanwhile, in Spain the introduction of self-administration for Catalonia in 1932 had been associated with some moves towards reconciliation between the region and the Spanish state. Having deployed all of these arguments and more, he said there was no going back for Europe; the continent required:

> ...union of the nations and national groups in the states through the recognition and consideration of independent national life....[92]

Ammende also suggested that such an arrangement of states in multi-national ways need not lead to the creation of purely 'anational' structures. He felt that, as the example of Spain and Catalonia showed, in practice the state might maintain the character of the majority population—hence Catalans understood they inhabited a self-administering unit of a Spanish Republic. The most important thing remained simply that national minorities felt they were given full and appropriate rein to develop their national culture within the state in which they lived.

## 8. Other nationalities

Writing about the results of the 6th meeting of the European Congress of Nationalities in 1930, Ammende had already argued that international national communities were being formed across Europe and that the congress was the pioneer in the re-configuration of Europe's nations.[93] The contention sat rather uncomfortably with the observation that Poles were particularly busy developing an international structure for themselves, because by this point Polish minority groups had left the congress. Nonetheless, the previous year Ammende had written about the meeting in Warsaw of an organisation of Poles Abroad which elected a council with 18 members and 4 representatives which was to work out the details of forming an All-Polish World Cultural Association. Even this development, however, in Ammende's mind had only been made possible after the congress brought together Europe's minorities and, in fact, two key members of the Polish organisation

---

[92] Ibid, p. 341.
[93] E. 'Die Ergebnisse des VI. Genfer Nationalitätenkongresses', *Revalsche Zeitung* 17 September 1930.

(Jan Kaczmarek and Stanisław Sierakowski, both from Germany) had been representatives to the congress.[94] Ammende expected Hungarian national groups to experience similar developments and felt certain that other nations would follow suit.[95] He was sure a point of 'no return' had been passed and that Europe was on the way to re-shaping itself as a continent built on nationalities as much as states. In Autumn 1929, reports began to emerge of Russian minorities beginning to meet in Riga.[96] Later, in summer 1932, their efforts to create an international national community seemed more concerted still, with congress member Michail Kurtschinsky playing a leading role.[97]

Ammende was not completely uncritical of the movement to create international national communities. In one essay, written in 1932, he criticised the Polish organisation especially. Apparently it took exception to comments by US senator Borah about Polish access to the Baltic. It also complained about US interference in Polish domestic affairs and called for Poles abroad to protest too. Ammende objected that such a call drew Polish minorities into the purely political (rather than cultural) affairs of the Motherland and raised the prospect of, say, Poles in Germany pressuring the German government to consider its position over the Polish Corridor. This, of course, would threaten a conflict between the obligations of these people as members of the German state and of the Polish nation, so creating mistrust between the Polish minority and German majority. Also it would raise the possibility of other minorities starting to protest over other issues, such as Lithuanians over Vilnius. Ammende feared such developments would come to threaten the very existence of the minority movement.[98]

With all of this said, Ammende still felt the move towards supra-state national communities could not be halted. He stressed his belief that these international national communities would grow and promote harmony between peoples and states. It was a duty of the European Congress of Nationalities to strengthen such an outcome.

---

[94] E. Ammende, 'Zum V. europäischen Nationalitätenkongress. Die Frage der organisierten Nationen', *Revaler Bote* 29 August 1929. For more details on the Polish meeting, see F. Üxküll-Güldenband, 'Ansätze zur Verwirklichung des Volksgemeinschaftsgedankens. Die nationale Organisation des Polentums', *Nation und Staat* April 1932. Apparently there were 98 delegates from 18 different European states present and it took place in the *Sejm* building. Also see 'Der Kongress der Auslandspolen in Warschau', *Nation und Staat* October 1929 and 'Die Organisation des Auslandpolentums', *Revaler Bote* 14 August 1929.
[95] The following article mentions a meeting of Hungarians Abroad: 'Der V. Minoritätenkongress', *Revaler Bote* 27 August 1929.
[96] 'Die erstmalige Tagung der russischen Minderheiten', *Nation und Staat* October 1929.
[97] 'Die erstmalige Tagung der russischen Minderheiten', *Nation und Staat* v. 3 October 1932
[98] E. Ammende, 'Auf falschem Wege. Eine Gefährdung der Volksgemeinschaftbewegung', *Nation und Staat* April 1932. pp. 594–98.

## 9. Conclusion

In 1929 the minorities experienced the disappointment of the Adatci report, Briand gave momentum to talk of Pan-Europe and Stresemann left the international scene. The minorities responded with greater self-assertiveness, perhaps even impatience, demanding they be considered as more than 'just' minorities, namely as representatives of their specific national group as a whole. The unfortunate aspect of this thinking, of course, was that it tempted people to consider themselves *German* (or Polish, or Russian etc. etc.) first, and a minority sharing something in common with similarly positioned other national minorities only subsequently. As a result, ultimately it risked overshadowing common European interests shared by all minorities with awareness of nationally-specific interests. As such, it threatened to make the European Congress of Nationalities more than ever a convocation of groups experiencing too little in common—something which was not part of its vision.

To construct a Europe of diverse culturally sophisticated international communities was not an impossibility, but certainly would have required substantial tact, principle and skilful moral leadership. So, from this point on, ever more the question would be posed about national communities, what should their purpose be? Should they promote common interests? Should the stronger stand up for the weaker? Or should they divide according to the politics of the day? These issues came to the fore increasingly as the minority agenda shifted away from the purer, more inclusive idealism of 1925 to something more partial and divisive. A politician such a Stresemann or Schiemann might have been able to avoid the pitfalls of the age; Ammende and Hasselblatt proved unequal to the challenge.

# Chapter Ten

# Critical challenges

## 1. Dissenting voices: the Frisian Question

From 1929, the congress was facing ever greater challenges to constructive engagement with European affairs, but dissenting voices had been taking issue with the organisation well before that point. Dissent emerged most clearly and most quickly from minorities located inside the German state. In 1926 Jan Skala (a leading figure from Germany's Polish minority) admitted the organisation offered a good opportunity for 'creating a working community of Slavic minorities',[1] but already there were signs of problems to come. In early July 1926, Wilfan and Schiemann had held talks with Jan Kaczmarek, an ethnic Pole and senior member of the Association of National Minorities in Germany. The grouping included representatives drawn from Poles, Danes, Lithuanians and Sorbs, all of whom at some point were represented in the congress. It also, however, represented Frisians and Kaczmarek wanted this group to join the congress as a national minority too. Schiemann was doubtful, feeling the step would make the congress a laughing-stock. He foresaw trouble on the horizon.[2]

Schiemann read the situation correctly. When the congress met in 1927, Kaczmarek intervened to state that the congress had done nothing to accommodate the Frisian minority even though, against their better judgement, the minorities from within Germany had supported cultural autonomy within the congress. Hence he declared that the groups represented by him (in effect the Poles, Lithuanians, Danes and Sorbs from within German) had decided to leave.[3] Ernst Christiansen, a Dane from Germany who had been critical of cultural autonomy at the 1925 congress (see chapter 6, section 6), stated his solidarity with Kaczmarek. Wilfan spoke against what was happening, with Motzkin, Casanovas (a Catalan from Spain), Hasselblatt (a German from Estonia), Jakabffy (a Hungarian from Romania) and Krakalia (a Ukrainian from Romania) adding their support, but still the minorities from within Germany left the congress and did not return. In fact, from the next year no Polish minority group at all attended the congress. Without question, the upheaval of 1927 marked a serious crisis; it even raised questions about whether the congress could present itself as an advocate for all of Europe's national minorities. Sensitive about the consequences of the upheaval, soon Ammende was contacting Colban about the Frisian question.

---

[1] J. Skala, 'Der Kongress der nationalen Minderheiten in Genf 1926', *Serbske Nowiny* 8.9.26. R60464. Political Archive of the Foreign Ministry, Berlin.

[2] Report 20.7.26. Fond 1000, File 139. Riigiarhiiv, Madara branch. Tallinn.

[3] *Sitzungsbericht des Kongresses der organisierten nationalen Gruppen in den Staaten Europas. Genf 22.–24. August 1927.* Vienna: Wilhelm Braumüller, 1928, pp. 123–4.

He emphasised that no group would be admitted to the congress unless a majority of its number considered it a national group.[4]

From the outset and in a resolution of 1926, the congress had taken as read that cultural autonomy as practiced in Estonia could promote the welfare of national minorities. (The congress never suggested it was the *only* way to achieve this end, only that it was a particularly promising strategy appropriate to some circumstances.) Rudolf Brandsch (a German from Romania) argued, for instance, that his national group had, in effect and to great benefit, enjoyed various systems of cultural autonomy in Transylvania since the twelfth century. He proposed there was no better way to promote national consciousness than this.[5] But now cultural autonomy became a key issue for debate between those inside and outside the congress as the members of the Association of National Minorities in Germany made a case that the congress's failure to accept the Frisians and its continued promotion of cultural autonomy along the Estonian model were seriously alienating for many national minorities.

Immediately after the congress of 1927, Jan Skala published an article differentiating 'strong' and 'weak' minorities.[6] He had used the categories in an essay published that January and he might have been responding to comments by Rudolf Brandsch after the 1926 congress when Brandsch suggested some groups were 'linguistically and culturally so weak' they faced serious problems defending their rights.[7] Skala observed that 'strong' minorities (such as Germans, Hungarians and Jews) tended to be better off financially and outnumbered weaker groups at the congress by 20 to 13. The failure of the congress to admit the Frisians, Skala maintained, highlighted a fundamental split in the organisation between the 'power political aspirations of the well-to-do minorities' and the more modest expectations of the 'proletarian minorities' for legal protection. Skala suggested that talk about the solidarity of minorities at the start of the congress project had just been a ploy on the part of 'imperialistic groups' to promote their own 'ideology and real-political purposes', for example building up a convenient power-base in advance of Germany joining the League. The congress and its principles no longer met the requirements of the 'weaker, pacific minorities' and Skala wondered whether attempts to apply cultural autonomy to some minorities might not leave them fractured, weakened and even more susceptible to pressures for assimilation. As a result, he said, the minorities from within Germany had left the congress.[8]

---

[4] 9.12.26. Ammende to Colban. R1687. Correspondence with Individuals. 41 / 56073 / 30181.

[5] Ibid, p.73.

[6] Jan Skala, 'Der III Genfer Minderheitenkongress', *Prager Presse*, 1.9.27. R60466. Political Archive of the Foreign Ministry, Berlin.

[7] 'Strong and weak minorities. On the genesis of a Schuldlage'. Schiemann Papers. Baltic Central Library, Riga.

[8] For Skala's views, see S. Bamberger-Stemmann, *Der Europäische Nationalitätenkongreß 1925 bis 1938. Nationale Minderheiten zwischen Lobbyistentum und Grossmachtinteressen*. Marburg:

In a memorandum written during the 1927 congress committee meeting, Wilfan accepted that some minorities were indeed stronger than others but denied that the distinction necessarily was damaging to the weaker groups. Rather, the congress gave potentially weaker groups access to the international stage. Noting that some weaker minorities (such as the Slovenes of Carinthia) were interested in enacting some model of cultural autonomy, he argued that strong minorities could only retain their strength by representing the interests of all. Equally, however, he accepted that the congress needed better rules for deciding which groups could and could not join.[9]

Schiemann also wrote a memorandum about the withdrawal of the Association of National Minorities in Germany. He said Kaczmarek proposed the congress gave more space to 'irredentist groups' than 'small loyal' ones such as the Frisians; the accusation, Schiemann felt, should not be taken at face value. He argued that Polish minorities were not really interested in the Frisians, but wanted to express dissatisfaction with the minority policy implemented by the German state and to support the Polish government in its long-standing dislike of the European Congress of Nationalities.[10] Schiemann noted that representatives of the Polish ministries were present at the congress when the difficulties broke out and the fact spoke of events as some kind of political manoeuvre. An article from *Revaler Bote* agreed there was a hidden agenda. The walk out, it said, reflected how Poles within Germany did not like the cultural autonomy model as they had proved unable to establish their own effective cultural organisation. They preferred to leave responsibility for Polish cultural life to the German state, which accordingly had to finance it in full. Hence they were demanding rights without recognising their responsibilities. The walk out was said to be a pretext.[11]

Polish criticisms of the congress continued. In August 1927, the same month as the congress took place, Skala denounced moves towards cultural autonomy in Carinthia supposed to benefit ethnic Slovenes. Apparently two Slovene deputies in the Austrian parliament did not support the initiative. Skala said that establishing a cataster was 'enimical to minorities' and could lead to their future persecution. Skala argued that trying to force a system of cultural autonomy on Slovenes was unacceptable; that

---

Verlag Herder-Institut, 2000, pp. 175–7.

[9] 'Von der bisherigen und künftigen Entwicklung der Europäische Nationalitätenkongresses.' R1687. Correspondence with Individuals. 41 / 56073 / 30181.

[10] Arguably Poland was suspicious of the organisation because it had a large German involvement and because it gave voice to at least German, Jewish, Ukrainian and Lithuanian minorities based in Poland, all of which were unhappy about their treatment by the Polish state. It was also plausible that Poland saw the congress as a site for playing out general Polish-German tensions.

[11] 'Die Polen verlassen den Nationalitäten-Kongress', *Revaler Bote* 26 August 1927.

the group should be allowed to come up with its own solution to its situation.[12]

Naturally Schiemann kept pressing his position in the face of Skala and those who had left the congress. He argued it was highly unlikely for any national minority to be so 'weak' it could not take advantage of what cultural autonomy offered.[13] Likewise he felt it silly to maintain German minorities were 'strong' but Slavic ones intrinsically 'weak'. Schiemann felt there was a biased agenda at work and in another article Ferdinand von Üxküll accused the journal of the Association of National Minorities in Germany, *Kulturwehr*, of pro-Polish and anti-German bias.[14] Naturally Ammende had little time for Skala. A few years later, he accused him of being 'a master of poisoning streams', of pursuing 'a systematic incitement between nations' and being consumed by a 'pathological hatred against Germandom'.[15] Nonetheless, after the events of 1927, Ammende became a bit more careful about how he promoted cultural autonomy. So, speaking to the congress in 1930, whilst maintaining that cultural autonomy in Estonia was working well, he went out of his way to highlight that the system did not 'hold the monopoly' on ways to solve nationality issues and recognised there had been important initiatives carried out elsewhere.[16]

## 2. A minority?

Without doubt, the Frisian question—the idea that Germany's Frisians were a genuine national minority and should be represented in the European Congress of Nationalities—caused the congress tremendous problems; appropriately, it took the issue very seriously. In 1926, at the request of the Association of National Minorities in Germany, the congress had begun looking at whether the group was suitable for membership or not.

Ammende began collecting information. A memo from July 1926 suggested there were perhaps 4,200 Frisians living along Germany's North Sea coast leading towards Denmark, yet the group was divided. The nationally-aware Schleswig Frisian Society had established a political party around Johannes Oldsen, yet 9 Frisian homeland associations, with roughly 2,000 members, were at odds with the party. They regarded themselves as Frisian but German. Hence the memorandum concluded that half of Frisians

---

[12] J. Skala-Luzican, 'Die Kärntner Kulturautonomie', *Kulturwehr* August 1927. S 342. Minorities. Geneva. At this time, Skala's writings led to a sharp exchange with Baltic German author, adn supporter of cultural autonomy, Ferdinand Üxküll. See for example F. v. Üxkuell-Guldenbrand, 'Nochmals die Kulturwehr', *Nation und Staat* March 1928.

[13] P. Schiemann, 'Die Spaltung im Nationalitätenkongreß', *Nation und Staat* 1 (1927).

[14] F. v. Üxküll-Guldenbrand, 'Unzulässige Methoden', *Nation und Staat* 1927/28.

[15] E. Ammende, 'Völkerverhetzung', 18.11.31 *Kölnische Zeitung*. R60529. Political Archive of the Foreign Ministry, Berlin. See also E. Ammende, 'Völker-Verhetzung', *Revalsche Zeitung* 27 October 1931.

[16] *Sitzungsbericht des Kongresses der organisierten Nationalen Gruppen in den Staaten Europas. Genf, 3 bis 6 September 1930*. Vienna - Leipzig: Wilhelm Braumüller, 1931, p.24.

did not have national autonomy as a goal and suggested the matter needed closer investigation.[17] Given the tenor of the memorandum, it was unsurprising that the Frisians were not invited to the 1926 congress. As Motzkin told the German Foreign Ministry, the Frisians were neither properly organised nor actually wanted to be recognised as a separate national group in sufficient numbers. To invite them would risk the congress looking silly.[18] At about the same time, Brandsch also wrote an essay warning against spurious minorities joining the congress.[19]

The Frisian population at the time was complicated and was discussed in a memorandum which detailed the views of Rudolf Muss, a senior figure among North Frisians. Although some Frisians lived beyond Germany's borders, those within the Weimar Republic were split into at least two groups. Those living south of the River Elbe (the West Frisians) looked towards the Netherlands in cultural terms, while those to the north of the river (the Northern Frisians) looked towards Denmark. It was the latter group which were at the heart of the difficulties encountered by the congress. The West Frisians were led by a man called Kalma who had written to the northern counter-parts asking that they stop looking for recognition by the congress. Apparently not all Northern Frisians favoured the move anyway, and it was said to be rejected by the radical 'young Frisian' wing of the Dutch Frisians too. The memo noted:

> Both parts of the clan want to promote their literature, traditional dress and special affairs of the *Heimat* in co-operation with their home state, not in opposition to it.[20]

A memorandum kept by the German Foreign Ministry showed a slightly different picture. It said the investigation by the members of the congress over the Frisian question had yielded the following main points: North Frisians were German-minded; they felt linked to Schleswig-Holstein and German culture; they want to stay true to this heritage; they want to promote their culture and language in Frisian schools and churches; and they rejected being called a national minority. They considered their position different to that of, say, ethnic Danes living in Central Schleswig or Poles and Sorbs in Germany. These views were approved by a meeting of the North Frisian Association on 12 September 1926 and, apparently, attracted 13,100 signatures.[21] Under the circumstances, the memorandum suggested,

---

[17] Report of 20.7.1926. Fond 1000, File 139. Riigiarhiiv, Madara branch. Tallinn.

[18] Memo. Berlin, 7.9.26. R60464, Political Archive of the Foreign Ministry, Berlin.

[19] R. Brandsch, 'Die Nationalitätenkonferenz in Genf', *Deutsche Politische Hefte*, vol 4, Oct 1926. R60465. Political Archive of the Foreign Ministry, Berlin.

[20] Anschrift. Vertraulich. Nicht für die Presse! betr. nordfriesische Frage. By Rudolf Muuss— Tating. Erster Vorsitzender des Nordfriesischen Vereins für Heimatkunde und Heimatliebe. Schiemann Papers. Baltic Central Library, Riga.

[21] 'Friesen-Frage auf dem Internationalen Minderheiten-Kongress in Genf'. R60466. Political

Kaczmarek's insistence on a Frisian group joining the congress was most likely a ruse to help build an anti-German block within the organisation.

Clearly the situation was complicated and the congress formed a committee comprising Wilfan, Kaczmarek and Brandsch—although Ammende participated too when Wilfan proved unable to travel to a meeting in Berlin—to assess the Frisian affair carefully. According to the prevailing rules of the congress, any member group had to be organised, had to agree the congress's principles and had to consider itself a national minority. A meeting of the sub-committee held in October 1926 again voiced some doubts about whether significant numbers of Frisians wanted to be considered a separate nationality to make adoption by the congress reasonable and a study trip to Frisia was foreseen.[22]

At a further meeting held in November 1926, attended by Kaczmarek, Brandsch and Ammende, differences of opinion between the Pole and others seemed entrenched. Brandsch highlighted that 7,800 Frisians had signed a statement saying they felt German, bound to Schleswig-Holstein and did not want to be considered a national minority. He added that at the last election, only 300 to 600 people had voted in favour of specifically Frisian deputies. Kaczmarek countered saying that many of the 7,800 had been pressured economically to sign and he questioned how much significance should be given to the document given that only about 5,800 people actually spoke Frisian.[23]

In June 1927, *Wieser Zeitung* reported that ethnic Danes were promoting the idea that Frisians on the west coast of Schleswig and the islands were a separate national minority. Traditionally, it was said, churches and schools had never used Frisian language, but the report noted that currently there were some moves to promote Frisian language and culture. In some schools, therefore, Frisian language was being taught and some Frisian songs were being sung; occasionally prayers were said in Frisian in some churches; and Frisian societies were promoting Frisian language and culture. Nonetheless, the report suggested that the German state was happy to facilitate these developments because the Frisians were not a separate national group; they were German in the same way that Schwabs and Bavarians were. That is to say, Frisians were part of the German nation.[24] A couple of months later an article appeared in *Revaler Bote* describing the position of the Frisians as 'unequivocal and clear', with Polish agitation to

---

Archive of the Foreign Ministry, Berlin.

[22] Bericht über den bisherigen Stand der Friesenfrage. R60465. Political Archive of the Foreign Ministry, Berlin.

[23] Protokoll über die Zusammenkunft am Dienstag, den 16. November 1926 in Sachen Friesenangelegenheit. R60465. Political Archive of the Foreign Ministry, Berlin. See also 'Die Nordfriesen an den Minderheitenkongress', *Tägliche Rundschau*, 17 December 1926. R60465. Political Archive of the Foreign Ministry, Berlin.

[24] 24.6.27, 'Die friesische Minderheit', *Weser Zeitung*. R60465. Political Archive of the Foreign Ministry, Berlin.

recognise them as a separate national group described as 'a comedy'. The article suggested that Danish interests might also have been behind the initiative, the hope being eventually to remove North Schleswig from German territory.[25] It was no wonder that about this time a committee meeting of Wilfan, Motzkin, Schiemann, Sierakowski and Ammende heard the former express doubt over whether the Frisians actually wanted to participate in the congress or whether there was any documentation to establish such a desire.[26]

The Frisian question certainly was interesting. In terms of principle, it highlighted the difficulty of deciding what was and what was not a national group, but there were practical issues too. The absence from the congress of minorities from within Germany plus of Polish minorities in general meant the congress was more prone to appearing German-dominated, possibly even as shaped by the interests of the German state. Schiemann, for example, understood such impressions had to be avoided since the organisation's strength resided in its non-partisan character.[27] With this said, in a further memorandum from the German Embassy in Riga, Schiemann was quoted as believing several national minority spokesmen were glad the Polish minorities had left the congress. In the past, for instance, some German minorities had regarded the Poles as potential 'trouble-makers'. Schiemann proposed that Polish minorities had engineered the crisis of 1927 in a deliberate attempt to discredit international minority affairs as a possible weapon in the hands of *Reich* policy. He said the following:

> The situation is very earnest. If we cannot prove the integrity of our policy to the public, and put the Poles in the wrong, such that they have to return to us, then in a foreseeable time the minority movement will stop being a factor in international politics.[28]

In an attempt to force the Poles back to the congress on their terms, Schiemann recommended Germans and German minorities should become more active in promoting minority rights. He suggested to Riga's German diplomats that steps should be taken to improve the situation of minorities in Germany, followed by a concerted effort to improve minority protection as offered by the League. Only such steps would shore up the prestige of the congress and so of the German groups operating within it. A reply from the Foreign Ministry in Berlin, however, was lukewarm, and while it recognised

---

[25] 'Die Polen verlassen den Nationalitäten-Kongress', *Revalter Bote* 26 August 1927
[26] 7/8 June 1927. Protocol of the organising committee of the 3rd European Congress of Nationalities. 299 / Nachlass Wilfan 1250, 1.
[27] Memo signed by P. Schiemann. 30.8.27, German Consulate. R60466. Political Archive of the Foreign Ministry, Berlin.
[28] 5 January 1928. German Embassy, Riga. R60466. Political Archive of the Foreign Ministry, Berlin.

the need for an active minority policy within the German state, it found Schiemann's recommendations not particularly 'friendly towards Germany' (*'deutschfreundlich'*). The reply held that the Polish minorities now had isolated themselves.[29] In essence, exiting the congress was a Polish problem not a German one.

Given the gravity of the issues, meetings between congress representatives and supporters of Frisian attendance continued. In November 1927, the congress's committee considered the conditions under which a national group could be accepted for membership of the organisation. These were: it must be a specific nation; it must be European; it must be organised; it must have an independent cultural will; the majority of its number should wish to participate; it should have a manifest national culture; and delegates should be sent from the relevant areas in question.[30] Of course, a number of these points were less than straightforward. How, for example, could you identify the extent of a possible national group in order to decide whether a majority wanted to be identified as a distinct entity? If such people did not want to be so identified, were they actually members of the group in the first place? Despite such conceptual difficulties, the points informed a meeting which took place in Flensburg in 1928.[31] This was prefaced by an article in *Revaler Bote* entitled 'The North Frisians are German' suggesting that the move to recognise Frisians as a separate nationality might have been stimulated by Danish activists and noting that pro-Danish Frisian separatist groups had only received 241 votes in the *Reichstag* elections of 1924.[32] Schiemann and Wilfan met with members of the Association of National Minorities in Germany. The outcome was to underline that most Frisians did not want recognition as a national minority, although a definitive decision on the matter of membership was deferred until a further meeting of the congress's managing committee.[33]

Meanwhile, Berlin's diplomats continued to mull over the consequences of the Poles leaving the congress. Whilst there was recognition that the congress was valuable to German minorities and deserved official financial support, some felt a decision on further funding should wait until a final decision was taken on whether or not the congress would admit the Frisians—the implication being that admission would result in lower funding being passed from the Foreign Ministry.[34]

---

[29] Letter of 14.1.28. 60466. Political Archive of the Foreign Ministry, Berlin.

[30] Decisions. Committee sittings of 29 and 30 November 1927 in Berlin, Hotel Fürstenhof. Schiemann Papers. Baltic Central Library, Riga.

[31] *Sitzungsbericht des Kongresses der organisierten nationalen Gruppen in den Staaten Europas. Genf 29.–31. August 1928.* Vienna: Wilhelm Braumüller, 1928, p.9.

[32] 'Die Nordfriesen sind deutsch', *Revaler Bote* 12 November 1926

[33] 'Die Flensburger Minderheitenbesprechung. Die künstliche Friesenfrage. Eine Unterredung mit Dr. Schiemann', *Hamburger Fremdenblatt* 8.4.28. R60467. Political Archive of the Foreign Ministry, Berlin.

[34] Memo of 10.5.1928. R60467. Political Archive of the Foreign Ministry, Berlin.

Debate about the Frisian issue dragged on among the members of the congress's organising committee, but there was no decision to admit the Frisians.[35] Despite the tensions between the congress and the Association of National Minorities in Germany, Ammende tried to keep communications open. In 1930 he was exchanging letters with Pastor Cyz, a representative of the Sorbs.[36] Ammende said he knew the Frisian issue raised questions of solidarity for the association, but emphasised that in the light of the Flensburg meeting, the majority of Frisians were against identifying themselves as a national group and hence there was no 'collective, cultural statement of life'. Ammende stressed the failure to adopt the Frisians was not a 'German machination', a 'political machination' or any other act of ill will. Furthermore, he expressed the hope that soon minorities within Germany would start working with German minorities again, since the support of German minorities had helped Poles in Germany make advances over Polish language schooling. He suggested more help from German minorities might assist in the establishment of Lithuanian and Lausitz-Serb schools in Germany too. Ammende even suggested the congress might look again at Frisian membership at some point in the future.

In his reply, Cyz was pleased by the talk of the groups all returning to the congress one day—although this only happened to a limited degree a few years later when Ammende persuaded a break-away group of Lithuanians from within Germany to attend.[37] Skala tried to prevent even this happening.[38]

Those leading the congress tried to take the Frisian affair in their stride. Talking to the gathering in 1927, Wilfan highlighted that their difficulties reflected the need to define properly their key concepts such as *nationality* and *minority*. [39] In due course, the congress publicised clearly the criteria which groups had to fulfil if they were to join. In 1929 Ammende told the congress the following:

> Every group that is to be accepted as a new member must be organised in the state, further it must display its own national will. The latter is assumed without further ado if the majority of the group is in favour of participating in the congress, or at least is not against it, but also must be

---

[35] For on-going discussion, see 'Der nächste europaeische Nationalitätenkongress', *Nation und Staat* March 1928.

[36] 9.8.30. Ammende to Pfarrer Cyz. Schiemann Papers. ENK Folder. Baltic Central Library, Riga. 19.8.30, Cyz to Ammende. Schiemann Papers. ENK Folder. Baltic Central Library, Riga.

[37] 3.6.30, Ammende to Geheimrat, R60528. Political Archive of the Foreign Ministry, Berlin. Also 22.8.30. Ammende to Schiemann. Schiemann Papers. ENK Folder. Baltic German Library, Riga.

[38] Letter from the German Consulate, Geneva. 10.9.1930. R60528. Political Archive of the Foreign Ministry, Berlin.

[39] *Sitzungsbericht 1927*, p. 141.

proven by collective cultural expressions of a lasting kind
on the part of the group registering itself.[40]

### 3. More criticisms of the congress and cultural autonomy

Nor did criticism of the congress end with the Frisian question; in the early
1930s it might even have become more barbed. In September 1931, the
*Review of Nationalities and National Minorities*, edited by P.J. Gabrys and J.
Pelissier, published an article—signed by the editors—criticising the
European Congress of Nationalities.[41] Its democratic credentials were
questioned as the author described the representatives of 'this strange
congress' as only 'more or less authorised by the national minorities in
Europe'. The organisation was held to exhibit a democratic deficit in so far as
resolutions were said to be prepared 'in advance behind the scenes' and
voting was always unanimous. The key posts of President and General
Secretary always fell to Wilfan and Ammende (the latter described as
'shrewd', with the suggestion he had tricked a group of Lithuanians from
Prussia to join the congress with 'fallacious promises') without any obvious
elections to confirm them in post. The article asserted German dominance of
the proceedings and proposed that Germans were the only people present
who actually complained—something said to be hardly justified given their
relative material prosperity. The article highlighted that German Foreign
Minister Curtius was a senior protector of German minorities—another
reason why they had little about which to complain. Predictably, the article
suggested:

> The congress occupies itself especially with general
> problems of political order which serve directly or
> indirectly the goals of German policy.[42]

Hence Ammende was said to have presented a resolution which amounted to
the German state's view on disarmament. The real purpose of the congress
was to prepare 'world opinion for revisionist German policy.' By contrast, it
was said, minorities which genuinely lacked elementary rights did not have
their voices heard, and this was why the minorities from Germany had left.
The article concluded that the congress would only be able to achieve good
work if it could 'emancipate itself from the inopportune tutelage in which it
is held by its secretary general' (i.e. Ammende).

---

[40] *Sitzungsbericht des Kongresses der organisierten nationalen Gruppen in den Staaten Europas.
Genf, 26 bis 28. August 1929.* Vienna and Leipzig: Wilhelm Braumüller, 1930, p. 3.
[41] 'Le Congrés des minorités nationales a Genève', *Révue des Nationalités et des Minorités
Nationales*, September 1931. R2161. Minorities. 7th ENK. 29 to 31 August 1931. 4 / 31096 /
3817.
[42] Ibid.

Not everything included in the article was incorrect. Key figures in the congress did seem to have jobs for life and the organisation's important discussions and resolutions certainly were well prepared beforehand; but to suggest that the body was simply a tool of German foreign policy just repeated an old accusation which might have been expected of, say, Polish interests at odds with most things German. At this time, the congress provided a platform for at least German, Jewish and Ukrainian minorities, all of which had complaints about their treatment by Warsaw. Nonetheless, it was not just Gabrys and Pelissier who were critical of the congress, League staff voiced misgivings too.

In 1931, the Minorities Section of the League of Nations began to take a closer look at the European Congress of Nationalities. A memorandum written that September by Elmer Radisics of the Information Section for the head the Minorities Section, Pablo de Azcárate, discussed that year's congress proceedings. What he found was not described in particularly flattering terms, since he believed unity between the different participants was superficial. Cohesion was weak and the congress was described as a movement of different groups all following their separate goals under the mantle of a general organisation. This did not provide a promising foundation for the League to take the congress seriously, but Radisics added that the congress had recommended the League examine cultural autonomy as implemented in Estonia with a view to recommending it to other states.[43] Over the next few weeks, Ludvig Krabbe (who was Danish), deputy director of the Minorities Section, produced an assessment.

Krabbe's memorandum discussed whether cultural autonomy was 'as ideal as M. Ammende seems to find it.'[44] He soon doubted this, stating 'it is not absolutely certain' that all the groups in the congress actually shared the General Secretary's point of view that cultural autonomy was a 'panacea'. Krabbe highlighted that the Association of Minorities in Germany had left the congress three years previously and had not returned, feeling that cultural autonomy was against their best interests. The League's official also criticised how the congress had discussed cultural autonomy during its proceedings in 1931. There was no proper debate about it, just pre-prepared lectures by, for instance, Axel de Vries (a German from Estonia) and Michail Kurtschinsky (a Russian from Estonia who explained why Estonia's Russians had not adopted the model). Krabbe maintained Estonia's Germans were well positioned to take advantage of a system such as cultural autonomy, being relatively small in number (less than 8,000), mostly urban (84% or so), and exhibiting substantial economic and intellectual prowess. Estonia's Jews shared some characteristics, numbering only 4,000 souls, being 75%

---

[43] 5.9.31, memo by Elmer Radisics for Azcárate. R2161. Minorities. 7th ENK. 29 to 31 August 1931. 4 / 31096 / 3817.

[44] 'Cultural Autonmy as a solution to the problem of minorities. Note by M. Krabbe dated 18 November 1931.' R2161. Minorities. 7th ENK. 29 to 31 August 1931. 4 / 31096 / 3817.

urbanised and living in groups deemed easy to organise. By contrast, Russians constituted Estonia's largest minority (21,000 people) and Kurtschinsky gave 'a veritable apology for his compatriots having not introduced cultural autonomy'. The Russians controlled their affairs through the local government administration. Kurtschinsky added they were susceptible to possible economic burdens that might accompany cultural autonomy, that—as a largely rural population—they were difficult to organise and, as a separate point, that they lacked initiative. Krabbe's report noted that Estonia's Swedes had not adopted cultural autonomy because local government administration offered them an adequate basis for self-government too and the group could not bear the economic burden of the system.

Krabbe's scepticism about cultural autonomy showed through as he observed Latvia's Germans did not enjoy full cultural independence, yet extensive autonomous rights in education permitted them to organise their cultural life effectively. He criticised Schiemann for not saying more about this when he spoke to the congress. Krabbe maintained that, 'the expression "cultural autonomy" says nothing in itself'. He analysed the rules and regulations applied in Estonia to maintain minority schools and discovered that, if applied to Denmark, the prescriptions would lead to minority schools being closed. From this perspective, he wondered whether the idea of cultural autonomy was not, perhaps, misconceived. Was it sensible to set up 'an administrative machinery' dedicated to a group's whole cultural life, or should there not be a clearer focus simply on running good public schools?

Krabbe also highlighted that not all minorities favoured the idea of a cataster. Some feared persecution if they identified themselves as members of a minority, while others were concerned they would be identified as a different caste if they did so. Krabbe noted that Germans in Danish Schleswig had not wanted to identify themselves in this way for fear of stimulating suspicion. There was a similar feeling among Germans in Hungary. So Krabbe wondered if the introduction of cultural autonomy could lead to only some members of a possible national group signing up to a cataster, while the rest would be de-nationed. Furthermore, Krabbe noted that cultural autonomy was not adequate as an indicator of national tolerance. He noted that, although Estonia permitted cultural autonomy, its agrarian reforms had hit the German minority more severely than any other minority in Europe. He wondered, therefore, if unenlightened attitudes also informed other areas of Estonia's policies.

The memorandum's conclusions were, at best, lukewarm over cultural autonomy. It was an interesting experiment in lessening friction between majority and minority populations, but did little to prevent confrontations in areas not regulated by it (e.g. the economy). As such, it was not a 'solution' to the minority problem even in the countries which had introduced it. As a system, it could not be recommended to everyone, since minorities often found themselves in different circumstances (e.g. geographical, economic, social, and intellectual); and some minorities did not want it anyway. Finally, Krabbe felt that the real solution to the nationality problem lay not with the introduction of a given system, but in the cultivation in mixed populations of a spirit of 'national tolerance and liberalism'.[45]

## 4. Discussion

By the period 1930–31, therefore, there was an established body of criticism concerning the European Congress of Nationalities. Some came with a distinctly anti-German, pro-Polish—perhaps even pro-Danish—hue. Certainly a number of figures denied the congress was led by German interests and in 1931, for instance, Catalan deputy to the congress Francesc Masferrer denied it promoted German-inspired policy, only liberal and humane action.[46] Nonetheless, there was no denying that the congress provided a good stage for the interests of German minorities.[47]

The congress came from an initiative originating among German minorities and ethnic Germans played formative roles in it. Schiemann, Ammende and Hasselblatt all had ties to German diplomats and lobbied the German Foreign Ministry regularly. Also German groups from around Europe were, by and large, sufficiently well-organised to be in a good position to take advantage of the stage afforded by it. Likewise the congress promoted cultural autonomy—a social form favoured by ethnic Germans in Estonia. Of course, that ethnic Germans had such a high profile in the congress was not in itself insidious. It reflected the substantial numerical presence of ethnic Germans across Europe plus their genuine involvement in political and cultural affairs where they lived. Equally it did not prevent the demands of the German groups offering benefit to other minority groups; but it did raise the possibility that German interests, whether consciously or unconsciously, could over-power those of other groups. It also raised issues of public relations: it meant that initiatives really did need to be presented in ways that underlined their general, rather than specifically German, nature. Other groups consistently had to be encouraged to 'buy in' to what the German groups wanted. It meant that German groups always needed to take account of accusations that they were hi-jacking Europe's minority movement. The extent to which this was the case is underlined by the fact that some Polish interests even argued that by attacking the League of Nations, the congress was hoping to subvert its position as protector of minorities in Europe and replace it with the German state.[48]

[45] Ibid.
[46] *Sitzungsbericht des congresses der organisierten nationalen Gruppen in den Staaten Europas. Genf 29 bis 31 1931*. Vienna and Leipzig: Wilhelm Braumüller, 1932, p. 46.
[47] It is worth observing that although the interests of German minorities and the German state could intersect, they could also differ.
[48] Memorandum, 22.9.26. Fond 1000, File 139. Riigiarhiiv, Madara branch. Tallinn.

Perhaps the congress's structure also played to the interests of German minorities. The fact that Josip Wilfan was president was not just chance. Although not a German, there was a case for saying his was a political appointment. With a Slav as president, it created the impression that the congress was about more than just German groups; and yet, as a Slovene from Italy he was inextricably linked to at least some key ethnic (although not necessarily *state*) German agendas. Ammende experienced long-standing personal outrage at the treatment of Germans in South Tyrol and, as a Slovene from Italy, Wilfan too had a major interest in that country's minority policy. So something about Wilfan marked him out as placeman whose interests could be trusted to mirror those of at least some ethnic Germans.[49]

Perhaps the understanding extended to Ukrainian affairs by the congress reflected German interests too. On a number of occasions, the congress heard fiery speeches (some of which had to be stopped for their strong language) by Ukrainian representatives. Providing a platform for such talk suited German interests because they highlighted alleged abuses of minorities inside Poland, a topic directly of interest to German minorities from the Polish Corridor and Upper Silesia who also felt badly treated by the same government.

The European Congress of Nationalities frequently criticised the League of Nations for working according to the interests of states, yet there remains an impression that the congress was invaded by nationality-based state interests, not least German ones. Taking everything into account, perhaps this was inevitable—after all, every representative at the congress had to be sensitive to the interests of the groups with which he was linked by culture—but sometimes particular interests came to the fore. Occasionally the process was so notable it divided the congress into factions. This happened in 1926 over the Frisian issue, but also in 1932 when Hungarian, Ukrainian and German minorities seemed to ally to criticise states in which they had minorities, such as Poland and Czechoslovakia. The same year Germans, Ukrainians and Russians came together to criticise the Soviet Union too.[50] The experiences showed how difficult it was to insulate congress proceedings from specific interests and factionalism; they displayed what a sensitive structure it was.

Relatedly, Géza von Szüllö (a Hungarian from Czechoslovakia) commented as follows to the congress in 1930:

> Let's not forget that peace is the result of the satisfaction of
> nations, but is not the foundation of it. So long as 'peace'

[49] The suggestion here is that Wilfan would have supported Ammende's horror at Italy's policy of assimilation. Not all German groups wanted to fight this point, however. In his 'second book', for example, Hitler played down the importance of the Germans of the Tyrol. See *Hitler's Secret Book*. New York: Grove Press, 1961, p. 167.
[50] More than most, however, Jewish groups tended to float free from this possible building of factions.

divides the world in two—victors and vanquished—, armed and disarmed—, majorities and minorities—, advantaged and oppressed—, you do not have the above mentioned foundation for satisfaction.[51]

There was an impression that at least some of those involved most vigorously in the congress could be counted members of groups defeated in the war and losers under the terms of the peace treaties. Hence, through the congress they were trying to pursue their particular restorationist agendas by whatever means were available. This did not help the congress's credibility either—but there were even worse problems waiting in the wings.

## 5. An Achilles heel: finances

Between 1929 and 1931, several things were happening at once which had a cumulative impact on the congress. The members felt that they were let down by the League of Nations' failure to update its systems of minority protection adequately. Briand's talk of Pan-Europe encouraged the delegates to start conceptualising a continent organised not just according to states, but increasingly according to international national groups. Also manpower changes occurred with, first, the death of Stresemann, then the death of Carl Georg Bruns. In addition to these developments, however, there were changes in how the congress was funded.

Without doubt, by establishing the congress Ammende had achieved something remarkable for a private individual—albeit one with good connections. He personally was tireless in his travels around Europe, networking and promoting minority issues. The fact was, however, that all of this work had to be financed and money was always an issue for Ammende— one which became increasingly important after his family's reduced circumstances led to their possessions being sold to Pärnu town in February 1928.[52]

Ammende's correspondence gives an impression that, financially, the congress and his work on its behalf was always balanced on a knife's edge. The congress, and specifically Ammende as General Secretary, was supposed to receive funds (subscriptions) from the groups belonging to it on an annual basis in order to support its work. German state funds were particularly important to the continuation of business and were supplied to Ammende by the German Foreign Ministry via the Association of German National Groups in Europe. Yet even these subscriptions—which turned out to be perhaps the most reliable single source of income—were not always made available, certainly not in good time.

---

[51] *Sitzungsbericht 1930*, p. 55.
[52] 6.2.28, Ammende to Schiemann. Schiemann Papers. Baltic Central Library, Riga.

In September 1927, Ammende wrote to Rudolf Brandsch (a senior figure in the Association and long-standing ethnic German colleague from Romania), saying 'There are thousands of bills to pay here. People are arriving from all sides and I don't know what to do'—adding that the German minorities should not let everything fall apart for purely financial reasons.[53] Nor was this just a passing problem. In January 1928, Ammende wrote to Schiemann saying the financial situation was 'more muddled than ever' and he felt he was being left in the lurch by German groups not doing enough to offer financial support.[54] He asked if Schiemann could request Reichsmarks (RM) 1,500 from Graebe (a German from Poland who was another senior figure in the Association with links to the German Foreign Ministry), plus maybe something from Brandsch and even from a friend of Schiemann from Hamburg. A few days later he sent another letter to Schiemann in which he expressed satisfaction that 'our work is developing well', while bemoaning 'unbearable financial difficulties'.[55]

And the difficulties just kept coming. In September 1929 Ammende informed Graebe that the congress's finances had been in a dire situation for the last 6 months. He was left to complain that time and again he had to deal with the consequences of groups not paying their subscriptions. The Ukrainians had not paid this year and he wanted the money made good; he also wanted RM 3,000 promised by German sources made available.[56]

In February 1930, Ammende wrote to Graebe again emphasising the extent of the difficulties he was facing. He was waiting for German and Jewish contributions to the work of the congress,[57] and since they were late, he had not been able to pay his rent or telephone bill, nor was he able to send support to his family. He stated the situation bluntly:

> I have decided to tell you that, in the case of further difficulties with the German contributions, I can no longer be responsible for our work. Up to today, I have only received a portion of the payment which is due.... At the start of next week, payments are once more due, for which I absolutely need the rest of the contribution.[58]

Money earmarked for congress funds had been used for unexpected initiatives by the German group and so Ammende went short. Ammende's obvious distress met was recognised since, in just a little over a week, Graebe made the money available.[59]

---

[53] 4.9.27, Ammende to Brandsch. R60466. Political Archive of the Foreign Ministry, Berlin.
[54] 13.1.28, Ammende to Schiemann. Schiemann Papers. Baltic Central Library, Riga.
[55] 17.1.28, Ammende to Schiemann. Schiemann Papers. Baltic Central Library, Riga.
[56] 13.9.29, Ammende to Graebe. R60493. Political Archive of the Foreign Ministry, Berlin.
[57] Those attending the congress were supposed to pay an annual contribution to fund its work.
[58] 8.2.30, Ammende to Graebe. R60528. Political Archive of the Foreign Ministry, Berlin.
[59] 17.2.30, Ammende to Graebe. R60528. Political Archive of the Foreign Ministry, Berlin.

In 1932, with finances tighter than ever owing to the Depresssion, to save money it was decided to hold the congress in Vienna rather than Geneva.[60] Yet for all the money-saving measures Ammende devised, it was German funding that kept the organisation going. Money was channelled from the German Foreign Ministry to the Association of German National Groups in Europe and on to the congress. This movement was less than flawless, with issues arising consistently concerning how much money the Foreign Ministry should release, when exactly it should be made available and also the speed with which the Association passed it on.

Getting money out of the Foreign Ministry required regular appeals by leading members of the Association. German Foreign Ministry archives hold an undated memorandum from Carl Georg Bruns detailing an Association committee meeting which certainly tried to push as many right buttons as possible as it encouraged financial support. German communities abroad were said to require money to champion German culture and to advertise for the German nation. A drop in funding would threaten a flood of refugees to Germany, weakening the outlying communities whilst causing problems inside the German state. Withdrawal of finances would threaten the existence of ethnic German cultural institutions precisely at a time when East European states were putting pressure on those communities. Damage to the minorities would lessen Germany's trade opportunities, harm economic life inside that country and lessen the 'economic and cultural influence' of the 'Motherland'.[61]

Economic support to the German minority movement was vital. Roughly a third of the Association of German National Groups in Europe's income was provided by the Foreign Ministry, and Bruns received relatively generous support for his work as legal adviser to the group (e.g. RM 8,000 in May 1928).[62] In this light, some financial support for Ammende and the congress was obvious.

In summer 1927, Brandsch and Schiemann requested Swiss Francs (SF) 20,000 to cover German subscriptions to the congress for 1928. A Foreign Ministry memorandum noted that RM 4,300 and RM 5,000 had been paid for this purpose in 1925 and 1926, but now the amount requested had risen considerably. The author, Freytag, suggested that German funding should not be relied upon for the future and proposed that, since SF 10,000 was required urgently, maybe that amount alone ought to be paid.[63] Freytag's argument underlined that Foreign Ministry support for the congress was no

---

[60] 'Protokoll der Sitzungen vom 5. Dezember 1931 in Wien.' Schiemann Papers. ENK Folder. Baltic Central Library, Riga. 'Der VIII. Nationalitäten-Kongress', *Revalsche Zeitung* 12 May 1932.

[61] 'Der Auschuss der deutschen Volksgruppen in Europa zur Kürzung der Fondsmittel.' R60493. Political Archive of the Foreign Ministry, Berlin.

[62] 8.5.29, Graebe (?) to Consul Reinebeck. R60493. Political Archive of the Foreign Ministry, Berlin. 25.5.28. AA to Bruns. R60493. Political Archive of the Foreign Ministry, Berlin.

[63] Memorandum by Freytag, 10.9.27. R60466. Political Archive of the Foreign Ministry, Berlin.

foregone conclusion at this point. Despite its reticence, the Foreign Ministry did release RM 6,000 which in due course was passed on to Ammende. It was supposed to last him until August 1928.[64] By December 1927, however, Brandsch was once again contacting the Foreign Ministry requesting SF 6,000 to cover the cost of congress business. Putting the request in perspective, he noted that the Slovene group in the congress contributed SF 5,000 while the Hungarians added SF 8,000. He said they were not asking a lot to keep such an important forum functioning.[65] By January, Ammende was complaining about lack of money again, while that same month another reluctant Foreign Ministry memorandum discussed Brandsch's latest request in a tone which was less than completely helpful.[66] It noted that Brandsch had received SF 6,000 (or RM 4,000) to cover the costs of German groups attending the congress and observed that German groups should get used to the idea of financing the organisation themselves.[67] So even though Brandsch eventually received RM 3,000 to help finance Ammende's office in Vienna, once again it was clear that at this point the German Foreign Ministry supported the European Congress of Nationalities to only a limited extent.[68]

Paul Schiemann contacted the German Foreign Ministry at this time too. He emphasised that German membership subscriptions for the congress had to be paid punctually and that increased funding was necessary. He maintained that since the General Secretary was an ethnic German and since ethnic Germans had established the congress, it was appropriate for Berlin to provide more generous funding.[69] Clearly getting the money required to run the congress was a major challenge, a reality which threatened to be at odds with the ambitions of the organisation, as Ferdinand von Üxküll noted:

> A movement which serves all Europe's humanity really must have substantial means at its disposal.[70]

Part of the problem was that the German Foreign Ministry had reservations about Ammende personally. He was only a private individual who lacked any elected governmental post in his home country of Estonia. From the Foreign Ministry's point of view, his only significance was as General Secretary, but this post could have been filled by anyone—maybe by someone of greater political importance in their homeland. Hence, from Berlin's point of view, there was no need to secure Ammende personally, and by August 1932 the

---

[64] 13.9.27, Brandsch to Ammende. R60466. Political Archive of the Foreign Ministry, Berlin. 20.9.27. AA to Brandsch. R60466. Political Archive of the Foreign Ministry, Berlin.
[65] 6.12.27, Brandsch to the AA. R60466. Political Archive of the Foreign Ministry, Berlin.
[66] 2.1.28, Ammende to Graebe. Schiemann Papers. Baltic Central Library, Riga.
[67] Memorandum of 10.1.28. R60466. Political Archive of the Foreign Ministry, Berlin.
[68] 13.3.28, Brandsch to AA. R60466. Political Archive of the Foreign Ministry, Berlin.
[69] Memorandum, 26.3.28. R60467. Political Archive of the Foreign Ministry, Berlin.
[70] F. v. Üxküll, 'Der III. Kongress der Organisierten Nationalen Gruppen Europas', *Nation und Staat* 1927/28, p. 52.

Foreign Ministry was wondering if he should not stand down from his congress post. Certainly Berlin funded others more generously than Ammende.[71] This Foreign Ministry perception hardly helped the congress function effectively.

The problem of funding the congress did not just lie with Germany. Ammende had long realised that the congress was important to Jewish groups. They were well represented, not just by Zionists, and the forum provided a good stage from which they could speak out against anti-Semitism.[72] Yet consistently there were problems when it came to them paying their contributions. In October 1929, Ammende wrote to the German Foreign Ministry regretting the death of Stresemann, but also stating that Jewish groups were short of funds and so could not pay their full subscription.[73] In February 1930 he was complaining that Motzkin and the Jewish groups owed SF 4,800.[74] By May 1930 payment had not been made and Ammende began to think that he would need to visit the German Foreign Ministry to try to access more funding.[75] The situation did not improve quickly since, in June 1931, Ammende was contacting Schiemann for assistance in getting money out of the Jewish groups.[76] But things only got worse and by November 1931 there were fears that the Jews might leave the congress over SF 7,000 debts—a possibility which would have led to (incorrect) suspicions that they had been forced out by 'German machinations'.[77] The situation was so serious that Ammende wrote to the German Foreign Ministry again about the Jewish groups.[78] This lack of money compounded the difficulty caused by Ukrainian groups failing to pay their subscription either.[79] Under these circumstances, Ammende was all the more reliant on the money that did make its tortuous way to his account from Belin.[80] As Ammende put it in April 1932, given the problems with funding from other minorities (at this point, specifically Jews and Catalans), German involvement was vital to make sure the congress did not collapse.[81] That

---

[71] Bamberger-Stemmann, *Der Europäische Nationalitätenkongreß 1925 bis 1938,* pp. 155–6.

[72] Ammende to Prof Julius Hirsch, Berlin, 23.12.25. 1502-1-26, Moscow.

[73] 23.10.29, Ammende to Geheimrat Reinebeck. R60493. Political Archive of the Foreign Ministry, Berlin.

[74] 22.2.30, Ammende to Schiemann. Schiemann Papers. ENK Folder. Baltic Central Library, Riga.

[75] Beschlüsse der Ausschussitzung Linz, den 3. Mai 1930. Schiemann Papers. ENK Folder. Baltic Central Library, Riga. 6.5.1930. Ammende to Schiemann. Schiemann Papers. ENK Folder. Baltic Central Library, Riga.

[76] 2.6.31, Ammende to Schiemann. Schiemann Papers. ENK Folder. Baltic Central Library, Riga.

[77] 27.11.31, Graebe to Hirsch. R60529. Political Archive of the Foreign Ministry, Berlin.

[78] 4.12.31, Ammende to Geheimrat (Roediger?). R60529. Political Archive of the Foreign Ministry, Berlin.

[79] 13.9.29, Ammende to Graebe. R60493. Political Archive of the Foreign Ministry, Berlin.

[80] Memo by Ammende. 'Auszug aus dem Brief an Oberstleutnant Graebe.' R60493. Political Archive of the Foreign Ministry, Berlin.

[81] 2.4.32, Ammende to Roediger. R60530. Political Archive of the Foreign Ministry, Berlin.

year, the Foreign Ministry did step into the breach, covering the congress's losses of RM 8,000.[82]

Precisely because money from other sources was so unreliable, time and again Ammende had to depend on Berlin's modest assistance. And Berlin did have a record of providing at least some funding for minority-related activities. Funds were passed to the Association of German Minorities in Europe to help set up a journal called *Nation und Staat*. When approached by Carl Georg Bruns about the journal, the Foreign Ministry responded enthusiastically that such a venture would be good for both the German minorities and German foreign policy. Initially the Foreign Ministry foresaw generous support since a confidential memorandum spoke of first year costs running as RM 50,000—although a further memorandum proposed covering costs of only RM 30,000 over three years.[83] Since *Nation und Staat* was understood by Berlin to provide a counter-balance to *Kulturwehr* (the journal of the Association of National Minorities in Germany), the Prussian Interior Ministry offered to contribute between RM 20,000 and 25,000, while the Reich Interior Ministry agreed to contribute RM 10,000.[84] A further memorandum noted that RM 57,000 was paid to support the journal in 1927 and RM 52,000 was budgeted for 1928—figures which again, by way of comparison, emphasise the limited nature of the funding which found its way from Berlin to the congress.[85]

Perhaps all along Ammende looked on Foreign Ministry funding as a kind of 'gravy train' which he wanted to jump aboard. He was probably aware, for instance, that in 1932 the German Foreign Ministry supported Hasselblatt's activities in Berlin to the tune of RM 46,600. Maybe he wanted comparable resources for himself. There is no question that German Foreign Ministry archives show consistent agitation on his part. When he wasn't asking for money, he was sending copies of his publications, newsletters and situation reports to diplomatic offices, as if trying to remind them constantly of the good work he was trying to achieve. On one occasion he asked a *Geheimrat* if a press digest he was distributing was useful. He mentioned that others found it so—but then said that his work on it required funding.[86] In addition, at times Ammende seemed anxious to prove to the German Foreign Ministry that he could pass on detailed information (perhaps even

[82] Bamberger-Stemmann, *Der Europäische Nationalitätenkongreß 1925 bis 1938.* pp. 157–8.

[83] Confidential memo signed by Freytag, dated 16.11.26. R60426, Political Archive of the Foreign Ministry, Berlin. Also 'Aufzeichnung über den Plan einer Zeitschrift der deutschen Minderheiten'.'R60426. Political Archive of the Foreign Ministry, Berlin.

[84] Memo 12.1.27, R60426. Political Archive of the Foreign Ministry, Berlin.

[85] Account for 1927 for funding to *Nation und Staat*. R60427. Political Archive of the Foreign Ministry, Berlin.

[86] 18.2.30, Ammende to Geheimrat Reinebeck. R60528. Political Archive of the Foreign Ministry, Berlin.

intelligence) about people and negotiations relating to minority affairs that could have been of interest to diplomats.[87]

Little by little Ammende's efforts to acquire consistent funding from the Foreign Ministry began to pay off; to a limited extent anyway. Memoranda from late spring 1928 show that the Foreign Ministry was slowly becoming prepared to support the organisation. A document from this period noted that the congress lacked 'tight organisation and purposeful leadership' but still felt it was worth supporting since the organisation more or less coincided with German foreign policy's aims for German minorities. The memo implied the organisation would be able to exert pressure on the League of Nations, but added that there would have to be a way of checking how the money was used.[88] Another memorandum from the period observed the congress deserved additional support because its demise would be a severe loss for German minorities, although it also commented that a number of issues needed to be sorted out, such as precisely which minorities should be eligible to join it.[89] During that summer, when Graebe approached the Foreign Ministry for a further RM 6,000, a memo noted: 'Even the leaders of the minorities will have to learn that the readiness of the Foreign Ministry to help (which is proven to them constantly) has its limits.'[90] Hence in 1928 the German Foreign Ministry's perception of the congress was that it should be supported, but under specific conditions and within limits. As a result it offered a restricted kind of patronage to Ammende during the late 1920s.

### 6. Strings attached

Admittedly there are signs that from 1929 on, the Foreign Ministry began viewing Ammende and the congress a bit more favourably. True, in August that year a memorandum still specified that for money to be granted it would be necessary to show 'an urgent interest in heightened activity of the congress of nationalities'.[91] Also a memorandum from April 1929 gave a clear impression that money from Berlin would have strings attached. While it favoured money going to the congress, it specified this should happen in such a way that influence could be exerted over its leadership.[92] This impression was re-iterated in August 1930 in a memorandum prepared for the State Secretary and the Foreign Minister which noted that the congress had developed into a significant factor in the international minority movement,

---

[87] See for example 22.1.32, Ammende to Therdenge. R60529. Political Archive of the Foreign Ministry, Berlin.

[88] Memo of 7.4.28 for v. Weizsäcker. Illegible (Treusgen?) signature. R60467. Political Archive of the Foreign Ministry, Berlin.

[89] Memorandum of 10.5.1928. R60467. Political Archive of the Foreign Ministry, Berlin.

[90] Aufzeichnung, Geheim! 8.8.29. R60527. Political Archive of the Foreign Ministry, Berlin.

[91] Bülow, 13.8.29, R60527. Political Archive of the Foreign Ministry, Berlin.

[92] Memo of 26.4.29 (Bülow). R60527. Political Archive of the Foreign Ministry, Berlin.

offering ethnic Germans a good international platform from which to represent their interests. It continued:

> The Foreign Ministry has supported the congress through the Association of German National Groups in Europe. This support proceeds on condition that, in exerting influence on the leadership of the congress the German national groups do not ignore necessary consideration of the official policy of the *Reich*, in particular they take soundings with the Foreign Ministry before embarking on important initiatives.[93]

In other words, any increased funding from Berlin was likely to come with an agenda. True, at issue was consultation rather than control, but still it made plain that Berlin's money would only flow so long as the congress was aligned with German foreign policy goals.

These circumstances add to an understanding of why the Frisians were never likely to be accepted by the congress and why it was all the more ready to adopt positions which could be construed as anti-Polish. Anyone could understand that (in a narrow sense at least) it was not in Germany's interests to encourage the activity of a fresh national minority within the state—although recognition of a Frisian national group might also have complicated relations between Germany and the Netherlands—, and competition between Berlin and Warsaw was well entrenched. So even if it goes too far to say that the congress operated along lines that were straightforwardly in favour of the German government (e.g. regarding attitudes to South Tyrol), it goes too far to say that the congress leaders (especially ethnic German ones through whom German Foreign Ministry funds were channelled) could have remained unaware of background expectations in Berlin. The German state's money was necessary to keep the congress going and was delivered on the understanding that German interests were taken into account.

The situation, of course, highlighted the difficulties involved in running the congress. It needed German state money and had to take account of German state interests yet, these were not always and necessarily the same as even the interests of German minorities, never mind the interests of other national groups. The observation highlights the complexity of any possible attempt to draw together German foreign policy interests and those of the interests of Europe's national minorities. It also suggests that, notwithstanding German state funding, at least some non-German interests had to be incorporated into the congress or else it would be discredited as a just a façade which no one would respect.

---

[93] Memo for State Sec and Finance Minister, 28.8.30. R60528. Political Archive of the Foreign Ministry, Berlin.

These were the tortuous circumstances under which Ammende kept requesting money and by 1931 there were a few more signs that the Foreign Ministry was prepared to be helpful—to some extent at least. That January, a memorandum noted Ammende had been in touch several times for financial support for a press digest about minority affairs which he compiled and circulated. This was described as 'a generally valuable organ for everyone concerned with minority affairs' and it was recommended that the Foreign Ministry pay Ammende RM 2,000 to support publication for 6 months.[94] Thereafter Ammende received 'dribs and drabs' of money in support of this venture, for example RM 1,000 in June 1932.[95]

Further limited assistance followed. In 1931 Ammende published *Die Nationalitäten in den Staaten Europas* based on information collected through the nationality groups making up the congress. The German Foreign Ministry was so impressed they decided to buy 50 copies—a number which went a long way towards covering the title's costs.[96] From this point on, Ammende had a bit more joy when it came to getting small sums of money from the Foreign Ministry. In February 1932, he was given RM 5,000 towards the cost of the title he had just published.[97] The next month Ammende was contacting the Foreign Ministry again discussing the transfer of money to help support his work on the press digest—and in due course he received RM 1,000 through the Association's accounts.[98] In May 1932 he was in touch again raising the possibility of the Foreign Ministry giving him RM 6,000 to translate his book into English.[99] Eventually RM 5,000 was authorised, with the first contribution paid in June.[100]

At one point Ammende was so short of money he considered applying to the Carnegie Foundation for a grant.[101] His desperation, however, can only have emphasised how much he valued the money from the German Foreign Ministry; and the flow of money supporting his publishing ventures during 1931–32 certainly was not loosening the complicated ties between Ammende and Berlin—ties which would gain in importance as German nationalism became ever more strident there.

---

[94] 12.1.31, Confidential memo (Roediger). R60528. Political Archive of the Foreign Ministry, Berlin.
[95] 23.6.32, AA to Verband der deutschen Volksgruppen. R60530. Political Archive of the Foreign Ministry, Berlin.
[96] Memo (e.o. VI A 1699), Oct 1931. R60529. Political Archive of the Foreign Ministry, Berlin.
[97] 25.2.32, Terdenge to Ammende. R60529. Political Archive of the Foreign Ministry, Berlin. Note of February 1932. R60529. Political Archive of the Foreign Ministry, Berlin.
[98] 5.3.32, Ammende to Therdenge. R60530. Political Archive of the Foreign Ministry, Berlin. 8 April 1932, AA (Freytag) to the Verband. R60530. Political Archive of the Foreign Ministry, Berlin.
[99] Extracts from 17.5.32, Ammende to Terdenge. R60530. Political Archive of the Foreign Ministry, Berlin.
[100] 19.5.32, Terdenge to Ammende. R60530. Political Archive of the Foreign Ministry, Berlin. 22.6.32 Memo from AA to Ammende. R60530. Political Archive of the Foreign Ministry, Berlin.
[101] 7.6.32, Ammende to Terdenge. R60530. Political Archive of the Foreign Ministry, Berlin.

## 7. Conclusion

Having been established, did the European Congress of Nationalities achieve its potential; or did it too quickly begin to stagnate, particularly from 1928 on?[102] Although some high hopes (for example of influence with the League of Nations) ran aground, stagnation was not really the word. For all the difficulties and challenges the congress faced, notwithstanding that it could not please everybody all of the time and accepting that cultural autonomy was not regarded as ideal by all minorities, still it remained a much-noticed platform for principled discussion of nationality issues. It remained open to a wide range of contributors and constantly was on the lookout for relevant issues of the day which it could re-interpret according to the perspective of minorities.

It offered comment on the inability of statesmen to understand the situation of national minorities. It offered criticism of the League's in-built political biases, while equally rejecting Soviet efforts at state-building.[103] The congress supported the alternative of democratic, essentially free-market multi-ethnic societies built on national autonomy—especially on Estonia's model of cultural autonomy, but also (and rather differently) the model introduced in Spain to accommodate the Catalans. (Ammende made sure he was on hand to promote the Spanish project as a further contribution to Europe's minority problem—see chapter 9, section 7.)[104] The vision was to create a Europe of harmonious societies marked by lots of vibrant, achievement-oriented national cultures which would take strength from each other.

Through his work in the congress, Ammende managed to turn himself into an expert on Europe's minority issues. Max Hildebert Boehm described him as a real European committed to establishing a united front of European nationalities.[105] He was a dynamo working tirelessly for a deeply felt cause. True, he was not without his critics. Ulitz once wrote to Schiemann complaining that Ammende was more of a propagandist and organiser than a politician able to assess different possibilities.[106] There was also a tendency for Ammende to tailor his language to the expectations of his audience so, for example, he might talk more about peace to League of Nations staff and German interests to officials in Berlin; but that reflected the different natures of the institutions he was dealing with as well as

[102] Bamberger-Stemmann, *Der Europäische Nationalitätenkongreß 1925 bis 1938,* p. 180.
[103] *Sitzungsbericht des Kongresses der organisierten nationalen Gruppen in den Staaten Europas. Genf 25.–27. August 1926.* Vienna: Wilhelm Braumüller, 1927, p. 29.
[104] E. Ammende, 'Die Mission des Spanischen Staates', *Revalsche Zeitung,* 28 December 1931. E. Ammende, 'Historische Umwälzungen', *Revalsche Zeitung,* 22 September 1932.
[105] M.H. Boehm, 'Portätskizzen baltische Deutschtumsführer.. Nachlass Boehm 1077 / 14. Koblenz.
[106] 28.1.31, Ulitz to Schiemann. Schiemann Papers. ENK Folder. Baltic Central Library, Riga.

Ammende's desperation to acquire support for himself, the congress and its agenda.

Criticism of Ammende should also take account of his health. In July 1930 he wrote to Schiemann saying he had been diagnosed with diabetes and would need to enter a sanatorium after the forthcoming congress.[107] Later the same year he contacted Schiemann complaining that he had had to return to Vienna on account of raised sugar levels and so had been unable to visit him. In the New Year he was complaining something would have to be done about his health.[108] A few months later he was taking a '*Kur*' in Bad Pistyan. Given this background of health problems, it is all the more remarkable that Ammende contributed as much as he did to the congress and minority issues alike.

None of this is to ignore that by the start of the 1930s there were warning signs about the possible future of the congress. A financial tie to the German Foreign Ministry had not been a problem so long a politician such as Stresemann was in place, but it did raise question marks about how the relationship would develop as more cynical figures took over. Equally, with Hasselblatt installed as a critical figure in Berlin, a great deal would depend on how he chose to mediate between the nationality congress and the Foreign Ministry. Susceptibility to future influences from Berlin was only heightened, of course, by the disillusionment experienced in respect of the League of Nations as a protector of minorities. If the League could not or would not help, for Ammende the only possible alternative was liaison with Berlin.

In this respect, the judgement of Robert Cecil is relevant. Writing in his memoirs, he felt the work of the League of Nations did assist minorities, but accepted the minority system was not as effective as it should have been.[109] Commentators generally agree that the organisation's procedures had flaws. They lacked rules and systems for the enforcement of decisions taken in response to complaints by minorities, perhaps minorities could have been granted some kind of standing in the League's procedures, and maybe officials should have investigated complaints more rigorously than they did.[110] Hence just as money was a force pulling Ammende and the congress into Berlin's orbit, so the deficiencies of the League were pushing in the same direction.

---

[107] 29.7.30, Ammende to Schiemann. Schiemann Papers. ENK Folder. Baltic Central Library, Riga.

[108] 7.10.30, Ammende to Schiemann. Schiemann Papers. ENK Folder. Baltic Central Library, Riga. 12.1.31. Ammende to Schiemann. Schiemann Papers. ENK Folder. Baltic Central Library, Riga.

[109] R. Cecil, *A Great Experiment*. London: Jonathan Cape, 1941, p.120.

[110] J. Robinson, O. Karbach, M.M. Laseron, N. Robinson and M. Vichniak, *Were the Minorities Treaties a Failure?* New York: Antin Press. 1943, pp. 107–8. I.L. Claude, *National Minorities. An International Problem*. New York: Greenwood. 1955, p.27. O.I. Jankowsky, *Nationalities and National Minorities*. New York: Macmillan. 1945, p. 125.

*Chapter Eleven*

# The new nationalist wave

## 1. Introduction

Europe had been experiencing new kinds of authoritarian government from the points at which Lenin took over Russia and Mussolini assumed power in Italy. Nonetheless with, first, National Socialism's electoral success in Germany in 1930 and, second, Hitler becoming Chancellor on 30 January 1933, the continent's political situation deteriorated notably. Given that personnel changes within the German national minority organisation had signalled a new atmosphere there since at least the death of Bruns, it was unlikely that the Association of German National Groups in Europe would be able to put up serious resistance to increasing nationalism emanating from Berlin.

Hitler was an ethnic German and was acquainted with others, not least Alfred Rosenberg (born in Tallinn). Life in the Habsburg lands had sensitised Hitler to the inter-play of nationalities. Although in his *Second Book* he showed himself ready to sell out the Germans of South Tyrol, still a Germany with Hitler at the helm could never overlook the position of German minorities.[1] Most obviously, he would never be able to ignore the Sudeten Germans. It was also inevitable that difficulties would emerge over the relations between Berlin and Europe's ethnic German groups because, regardless of cultural autonomy's principles, for Nazism it was impossible to draw a line between cultural and political life. With Hitler in power, ethnic German communities could not have a cultural tie to Germany without there being a political one too. The game had changed.

The naked jingoism of Nazism could only threaten the national minorities within Germany, inevitably provoking their co-nationals abroad. Hitler's clear disdain for the Treaty of Versailles had to unsettle newly created border states such as Poland and Czechoslovakia. Yet, Nazism's fundamental antipathy to the very existence of a Polish state (which a treaty of friendship barely masked), together with the demonization of Soviet Communism, were attractive qualities to some. Many Ukrainians, for instance, were unhappy about the lack of their own nation state and the division of their homeland between the Soviet Union and Poland. In fact, Ukrainian passions were heightened by a massive event during the early 1930s: famine. During the years of the Russian Empire, Ammende had enjoyed business contacts with Ukraine. In due course the famine would take on considerable importance for both him and the organisations in which he

---

[1] A. Hitler. *Hitler's Secret Book*. Introduction by Telford Taylor. New York: Grove Press, 1961, p. 167.

participated. He was especially attuned to the position of national minorities in the Soviet Ukraine, especially ethnic Germans in the Volga and the North Caucasus. He could never accept that a famine threatening their lives could be left as an affair of domestic politics to be addressed—or not—according to Moscow's priorities. He was committed to the necessity of an international response.

In the final phase of his life, therefore, Ammende was faced with Hitler in Berlin and Stalin in Moscow. The ultimate impossibility of being able to influence the dire politics of either locus gave a defining character to the final phases of his life.

## 2. Baltic German interpretations of the rise of National Socialism

Throughout the years of international turmoil which followed the crash of the New York Stock Market, the Baltic German press maintained a detailed commentary on events and their implications.[2] *Revalsche Zeitung* (formerly *Revaler Bote*) editor Axel de Vries proposed that the catastrophic Depression was shaking popular confidence in historical progress and the 'decline of the West' was threatening to be made real.[3] But what did the Baltic German press have to say about specifically the rise of National Socialism in Germany?

From an early point, there had been some signs of sympathy. In spring 1923 *Revaler Bote* reported Germans were being enthused not just by Hitler's personality and oratory, but by his ideas.[4] It reported he was exciting people with talk of national belonging, adding he was also attacking exponents of 'international Jewish high finance'. Supporters were said to number uncritical youths of all classes, workers disillusioned with Socialism and déclassé, dispossessed members of the middle classes. Even if the paper felt Nazism was unlikely to bring about Germany's resurgence on its own, it could contribute to just such an end. More sceptical was a piece written in the wake of the Munich Putsch in which Hitler was described as a building site labourer who had been unable to articulate his plans to an audience.[5] His party was said to lack a constructive programme.

In the early 1920s, of course, there was little appreciation that Hitler's rather small following would ever hold substantial significance for Estonia's Germans, but interest began to pick up with the 1930 *Reichstag* elections, although reporting was prepared to highlight the possible dangers associated with Hitler's politics. Quoting *Kölnische Zeitung*, *Revalsche Zeitung* commented of the NSDAP's 107 seats that:

[2] 'Katastrophe an der Neuyorker Börse. Kursverluste biz 20 Prozent', *Revaler Bote* 25 October 1929; Der 13. Juli', *Revalsche Zeitung* 17 July 1931.
[3] A. de Vries, 'Europäische Götterdämmerung', *Revalsche Zeitung* 18 July 1931.
[4] 'Der Nationalsozialismus', *Revaler Bote* 17 March 1923.
[5] 'Niederwerfung des Münchener Putsches', *Revaler Bote* 10 November 1923.

> Now economic need and unscrupulous rabble-rousing by
> the radicals has created a parliamentary situation such that
> no one knows how things will work out.[6]

As the new *Reichstag* met, there were reports of Nazis and Communists clashing in the surrounding streets, Nazis chanting 'Germany awakens!' and of shop windows being smashed.[7]

    *Revalsche Zeitung* always reported clearly that Germany's National Socialist Party was surrounded by violence. It reported the Boxheim documents, hinting at revolutionary planning within the party.[8] It explained how the Prussian police took action against the party and how Hindenburg banned the SA.[9] There were reports about the Potempa trial which made plain how senior Nazis, such as Alfred Rosenberg, rejected the prosecution of party comrades for the political murder of a Polish Socialist.[10] Over the critical period 1930–32, *Revalsche Zeitung* provided its readership with adequate reporting of the nature of Hitler's politics. Nonetheless it was possible to identify strands justifying a feeling that even if Hitler was bad, the possible alternative to him was worse. In late 1930, the paper reported that 226 Nazi Party members had been murdered by Communist and Socialist paramilitaries—it did not mention how many Communists had been killed by Nazis.[11]

    Responding to the recognition that even in 1931 the NSDAP was exerting a substantial power of attraction on German minorities abroad, Axel de Vries began developing an astute critique. He was dismissive of the quality of its political programme, which he thought little more than a 'lure'. In terms of economic policy, he thought the party comparable to Marxism. Regarding Nazism's racism, however, de Vries was particularly dismissive notwithstanding his own penchant for anti-Semitism (see chapter 2, sections 2 and 4). He insisted that the German 'race' was not something 'united', but was a mixture of four different races. He emphasised that Nazism completely overlooked how membership of a national group did not depend on biology, but on the decision to belong to a given cultural group. In other words, he was clear that Nazism's programme was built on illusion. In the end, when evaluating the party, personalities, passion and irrationality were more important than doctrine.[12] By 1932, however, de Vries was recognising that

---

[6] 'Wahlsieg der Nationalsozialisten', *Revalsche Zeitung* 15 September 1930.

[7] 'Schwere Ausschreitungen in Berlin', *Revalsche Zeitung* 14 October 1930.

[8] 'Deutschlands innerer Kampf', *Revalsche Zeitung* 26 November 1931.

[9] The SA (*Sturm Abteilungen*) were Hitler's paramilitaries. 'Preussische Polizei gegen NSDAP', *Revalsche Zeitung* 17 March 1932; 'Verbot der SA und SS', *Revalsche Zeitung* 14 April 1932.

[10] 'Rosenberg kommentiert Beuthen. Die nationalsozialistische Auffassung von Recht', *Revalsche Zeitung* 25 Augst 1932.

[11] 'Mord Terror gegen Nationalsozialisten', *Revalsche Zeitung* 19 November 1930.

[12] A. de Vries, 'Die nationalsozialistische Bewegung', *Revalsche Zeitung* 25 April 1931 and 'Die

people in 'the East' were going to have to take a position on Nazism because its foreign policy brought with it an orientation away from the West. Rather contradicting his previous arguments, de Vries observed that for German communities abroad, National Socialism was not important as a party, but as an 'ideological orientation and as a movement'. While National Socialism had re-awakened German self-confidence, he recognised it could bring problems, not least because its imperialism and emphasis on nation state thinking could meet resistance both from eastern nations and given that the nation state was not appropriate to the territories stretching from the Baltic to the Black Sea where peoples were interspersed. Referring specifically to the party programme which defined a German as someone of German blood, he also noted that Nazism's concepts about nation, race and citizenship were inadequate. He maintained that if the eastern peoples took up Hitler's programme for themselves, all ethnic German communities would be extinguished.[13]

Across 1932, *Revalsche Zeitung* provided stimulating commentary about events in Germany. De Vries interpreted the transition from Brüning to Papen as part of a process likely to bring about the re-building of Germany's post-war state. The only question was whether national conservative elements, especially Nazism, would be incorporated into the state with or without a revolution. He hoped that Hindenburg and the army would help Hitler's movement become a pillar of the state by an organic, rather than a dramatic, process of change.[14]

By November, the paper was reporting that Germany's democracy was hitting the buffers.[15] There were stories of Hitler telling Hindenburg that purely parliamentary measures could not solve Germany's problems and of a 'dark prognosis' facing a country in which the powers of Nazism and Communism were becoming balanced. With 'very dangerous' developments increasingly likely, the paper warned it had 'never covered up or glossed over the shortcomings and dangers of the NSDAP.'[16] Having reported in detail on the politicking which occurred inside Germany following the *Landtag* elections in Lippe, by late January 1933 *Revalsche Zeitung* was wondering if the country would have to declare a state of emergency.[17]

Reporting became extensive as the NSDAP began the process of seizing power. All of the main events were covered, whether torch-lit parades, the burning of the *Reichstag*, the March elections, the imposition of

nationalsozialistische Bewegung II', *Revalsche Zeitung* 26 April 1931.
[13] A. de Vries, 'Deutsche Ostpolitik I', *Revalsche Zeitung* 29 April 1932. See also A. de Vries, 'Deutsche Ostpolitik II', *Revalsche Zeitung* 30 April 1932.
[14] A. de Vries, 'Deutsche Wende I', *Revalsche Zeitung* 11 June 1932.
[15] Dr. S., 'Grabgesang des Parlamentarismus', *Revalsche Zeitung* 7 November 1932.
[16] 'Wer wird Reichskanzler? Hitlers Antwort an Hindenburg', *Revalsche Zeitung* 24 November 1932; 'Schlechte Prognose für Deutschland!' *Revalsche Zeitung* 26 November 1932.
[17] 'Das Wahlergebnis in Lippe', *Revalsche Zeitung* 16 January 1933; 'Staatsnotstand in Deutschland?' *Revalsche Zeitung* 24 January 1933.

*Reich* Governors or the occupation of trades union offices (interpreted as a step towards corporatism), not to say the banning of the Socialist party.[18] Hitler was quoted as saying Marxism would be eradicated in Germany over the next ten years and applauded for opening people's eyes to the true nature of Communism.[19] Certainly the anti-Communist agenda helps explain why the tenor of reporting about Hitler's coming to power often was positive. Likewise, noting that Hitler was the first ethnic German to become Chancellor, de Vries observed:

> The fact of the creation of a German government under Adolf Hitler as *Reich* Chancellor justifiably has been greeted with joy by every nationalistically-inclined German.[20]

Finally, the piece went on, Hitler had been built into government on the basis of compromise. Even if people did not know exactly where the whole process would lead, there were grounds simply for being pleased that 'national Germany' had found itself.

### 3. Hitler in power: minorities and the German nation

As Hitler settled into the Reich Chancellery, a more positive picture of the man and his politics began to emerge through the press, one which struck a number of chords likely to appeal to even responsible Baltic Germans. Nazism was said to have psychological roots, whether in an ecstasy of youth, a reaction to wretchedness and despair, or the need for weak people to band together for 'warmth and power'. In a world where individuals felt let down by 'modern humanism', democracy and capitalism, they were left with a choice between Communism and Fascism. Nor were Germans to blame for what Europe had become. Responsibility lay with decision-makers in Paris, London, Warsaw and Prague. This left National Socialism looking rather like a millenarian movement of marginalised people—'a doctrine of healing through belief'—but clearly the argument did not view Germans as to blame for electing the new Chancellor.[21]

---

[18] 'Fackeln in der Wilhelmstrasse', *Revalsche Zeitung* 31 January 1933; 'Kommunisten stecken den Reichstag an', *Revalsche Zeitung* 28 February 1933; 'Die nationale Revolution', *Revalsche Zeitung* 10 March 1933; 'Die Gleichschaltung in Deutschland', *Revalsche Zeitung* 20 March 1933; 'Auf dem Weg zum korporativen Staat', *Revalsche Zeitung* 8 May 1933; 'Die Entwicklung in Deutschland. Das Ende der SPD', *Revalsche Zeitung* 23 June 1933.
[19] 'Deutschlands Kampf gegen den Marxismus', *Revalsche Zeitung* 9 February 1933; 'Die nationale Revolution', *Revalsche Zeitung* 10 March 1933.
[20] A. de Vries, 'Hindenburg und Hitler. I' *Revalsche Zeitung* 11 February 1933.
[21] 'Der nationalsozialistische Glaube I', *Revalsche Zeitung* 3 July 1934; 'Der nationalsozialistische Glaube II', *Revalsche Zeitung* 4 July 1934.

On another occasion, Hitler was praised for beginning to create a
national community transcending class—an achievement which resonated
with traditional Baltic German interests in creating a social model which
rooted the individual in the community.[22] Hitler's grand domestic project was
held to dictate the kind of foreign policy open to Germany. *Revalsche
Zeitung* quoted Hitler directly:

> We National Socialists have a massive domestic project. It
> obliges us to seek peace and friendship with the outside
> world.[23]

He was praised for standing for reductions in tension and for peace.[24]
Germany had disarmed, so Hitler called on other states to do the same.[25]
When it was recognised that the maintenance of peace required the revision
of the post-war settlement, *Revalsche Zeitung* highlighted that this process
could only happen by peaceful means and that just such aims were, indeed, at
the heart of Berlin's initiatives. To quote directly: '...Germany's foreign
policy is a policy of peace.'[26]

The Baltic German press recognised that events in Germany would
have consequences for their community owing to their ties of 'blood and
culture'.[27] Clearly not all would be good as, for instance, was reflected in
reporting about anti-Semitic disorders committed by Latvian Nazis in
February 1933.[28] Although some Baltic German commentators were quick to
question whether Nazism was suitable for their community,[29] for whatever
reason—whether through ideological affiliation or acceptance of Berlin's
propaganda—the movement found a foothold. An unsigned letter to Paul
Schiemann, written by someone who had participated in the European
Congress of Nationalities' committee meeting proposed that National
Socialism was 'in its roots, a healthy and strong movement' which German
minorities should not oppose. It went on:

> No one can foresee what will become of the National
> Socialists. The primitive quality of their thinking is
> disarming, but I really do esteem (presumably more
> strongly than you) the élan of the national idea.[30]

---

[22] A. de Vries, 'Zwischen Ost und West', *Revalsche Zeitung* 11 March 1933; H.N.,
'Volksgemeinschaft', *Revalsche Zeitung* 10 October 1933.
[23] 'Hitlers neue Friedensrede', *Revalsche Zeitung* 19 June 1934.
[24] A. de Vries, 'Klare Aussenpolitik', *Revalsche Zeitung* 27 May 1933.
[25] 'Für Recht und Frieden', *Revalsche Zeitung* 18 May 1933.
[26] 'Wege zur Revision', *Revalsche Zeitung* 28 August 1933.
[27] v. Wr, 'Deutschland und wir', *Revalsche Zeitung* 16 February 1933.
[28] 'Lettische Nationalsozialisten', *Revalsche Zeitung* 6 February 1933.
[29] W. Baron Maydell, 'Die politischen Strömungen im Lager der Deutsch-Balten', *Revalsche
Zeitung* 25 March 1933.
[30] 10.12.30, Anonymous, Berlin to Schiemann. Schiemann Papers. ENK Folder. Baltic Central

With Hitler in power, such a senior figure in the *Revalsche Zeitung* as Axel de Vries increasingly left his initial scepticism about the party to one side.[31] In so doing, no doubt he hoped that the new regime would back the cause of German minorities abroad. As early as 23 March 1933, Hitler told the *Reichstag* he would promote the rights of ethnic Germans with all means.[32] On 17 May 1933, he gave a speech to the German parliament rejecting categorically assimilation as a policy for dealing with national minorities inside Germany. He represented the view that all national groups had their own cultural traditions, just as German communities had.[33]

> ... while we are connected in boundless love and fidelity to our own nation, from this same conviction we respect the national rights of other nations and from the very depths of our hearts would like to live with them in peace and friendship. (Lively applause.)
> Consequently we do not recognise the idea of Germanisation. This intellectual mentality of the last century, according to which you believe it is possible to turn maybe a Pole or Frenchman into a German, is so very foreign to us that we reject passionately attempts to do the reverse. (Stormy and sustained applause.) We regard the European nations around us as established facts. The French, Poles etc. are our neighbouring nations and we know that no historically conceivable event can alter this reality....[34]

A week later he emphasised Germans would never try to Germanise others and would defend members of their own nation threatened with removal from it.[35] On 25 May former Chancellor Franz von Papen told a gathering of borderland ethnic Germans held at Iburg that the peace settlement had

---

Library, Riga.
[31] E.g. compare A. de Vries, 'Die nationalsozialistische Bewegung', *Revalsche Zeitung* 25 April 1931 and 'Die nationalsozialistische Bewegung II', *Revalsche Zeitung* 26 April 1931 with A. de Vries, 'Klare Aussenpolitik', *Revalsche Zeitung* 27 May 1933. In the latter article, de Vries applauds Hitler particularly for his stance against assimilation—a message that was popular among German minorities in its own right.
[32] 'Kundgebungen Hitlers und v.Papens zur Volkstumspolitik', *Nation und Staat* June 1933
[33] S. Bamberger-Stemmann, *Der Europäische Nationalitätenkongreß 1925 bis 1938. Nationale Minderheiten zwischen Lobbyistentum und Grossmachtinteressen*. Marburg: Verlag Herder-Institut, 2000, p.249.
[34] 'Auszugsweise Abschrift der Rede des Herrn Reichskanzlers aus der DAZ vom 18 Mai 1933, Nr. 230', R 60594. Political Archive of the Foreign Ministry, Berlin. The speech was widely reported in the Baltic German press, see F. von Üxküll, 'Deutschlands volkspolitisches Programm', *Nation und Staat* June 1933.
[35] 'Kundgebungen Hitlers und v.Papens zur Volkstumspolitik', *Nation und Staat* June 1933.

fragmented Europe, leaving a third of the German nation outside the German state. The situation was compounded by the deterioration of minority rights. Hitler's revolutionary response, he said, was to recognise the independence of nations (*'die Eigenständigkeit der Völker'*). Papen wanted Germany to lead a project to secure and unite nationalities in Europe.[36] Repeatedly in the period after the seizure of power, Nazi leaders emphasised that this attitude towards nationality was devoid of imperialistic intent since there was no point invading a state if conquered peoples could never become 'yours'.[37]

De Vries, Hasselblatt and Üxküll all welcomed National Socialism's rejection of assimilation.[38] The latter maintained that in this attitude, National Socialism differentiated itself from Italian Fascism, since the latter took the extent of a state's territory as defining 'the nation' and was committed to assimilating everyone who lived there. By contrast, for Germany, the nation was defined as the community of Germans, regardless of where they resided and there was no desire to absorb non-Germans interspersed with them.[39] Although some non-German commentators, such as Kazimierz Smogorewski, maintained that Hitler's concept of the national community eventually would yield an initiative for a Greater Germany,[40] ethnic Germans were not so pessimistic. So while Üxküll noted that Germany's neighbouring nations opposed Hitler's national revolution, he still applauded how ethnic Germans were being transformed increasingly into parts of a greater whole.[41]

Nor were ethnic Germans necessarily alone in failing to apply their critical faculties properly. While Josip Wilfan recognised that Nazism wanted to create a Greater Germany in terms of people, he did not sound a warning about the project. Instead, he contrasted it with Italy's assimilationism.[42] In some respects and for some people at least, there was a distinct unwillingness to dwell critically on Hitler's project. Believing that the German government would oppose assimilation and thinking that it focused on people rather than borders, also noting that it appeared to forego attempts to revise the peace settlement, too many observers spent too little time considering the wider meaning of Nazism's racism and aggression.[43] Hence Hasselblatt wrote to Schiemann stating that Nazism was 'strong and young', and hoping that it

---

[36] 'Papen: Sicherung der Volkstuemer ist nötig', *Berliner Lokalanzeiger*, 26.5.33. R 60594. Political Archive of the Foreign Ministry, Berlin.
[37] See for example Culture Minister Rust's speech in 1935 to a gathering of ethnic Germans held at Königsberg, 'Friede zwischen Völkern', *Revalsche Zeitung* 14 June 1935.
[38] A. de Vries, 'Klare Aussenpolitik', *Revalsche Zeitung* 27 May 1933. W. Hasselblatt, 'Volkstumspolitik in der völkerrechtlichen Entwicklung', *Nation und Staat* March 1935. F. von Üxküll, 'Deutschlands volkspolitisches Programm', *Nation und Staat* June 1933.
[39] F. von Üxküll, 'Das neue Deutschland', *Nation und Staat* April 1933.
[40] Bamberger-Stemmann, *Der Europäische Nationalitätenkongreß 1925 bis 1938*, pp. 249–50.
[41] F. von Üxküll, 'Volk im Umbruch', *Nation und Staat* October 1933.
[42] 'Volkstums- und Territorialprinzip', *Nation und Staat* April 1933
[43] Bamberger-Stemmann, *Der Europäische Nationalitätenkongreß 1925 bis 1938,* pp. 249–50.

would stand alongside Europe's national minorities which had been persecuted for 13 years.[44]

It bears emphasis that these miscalculations were made against a significant background. On 1 April 1933, the boycott of Jewish shops had begun in Germany.

## 4. Nazism, the association and the congress: 'the new nationalist wave'

Whatever the official rhetoric, by degrees Hitler's regime set about co-ordinating ethnic German organisations. The task was made all the easier by the prior personnel changes and the ideological shift that had already begun among the membership (reflected in the renaming of the Association of German Minorities in Europe as the Association of German National Groups [*Volksgruppen*] in Europe). In other words, Hitler's regime encountered ethnic German institutions which, if not already Nazified, were experiencing a change which predisposed them to co-operate with the new Berlin.[45] One of the more worrying indicators about the alterations was the publication in *Nation und Staat* in October 1932 of an anti-Semitic article written by a member of the NSDAP.[46] The motives behind the decision to carry the piece need not have included ideological agreement, but clearly at least some of the editors of the journal (who included Üxküll, Brandsch and Schiemann—although Schiemann surely could not have agreed to the article) were prepared to accommodate Nazi perspectives into the mainstream of German minorities' discourse. In the process, they helped legitimate the ideas.

Not all members of the German minorities were content as the Nazis approached political power. Just a few months before *Nation und Staat* carried the anti-Semitic essay, the association assembled for its annual meeting at Baden, near Vienna. Here, Paul Schiemann made an epic speech entitled 'The New Nationalist Wave' which assaulted Hitler's politics.[47] He said it was a time of crisis when the spirits of war and peace were locked in battle. A growing force, he said, which regarded peace as the continuation of war by other means, was heightening tensions in society and diminishing the prospects for the future. The development had been marked by the flight of individuals into a 'community', such that the 'mass' had become the decisive factor in politics and the importance of personal conviction had been replaced by irrationality and loyalty to symbols. There had been a rise of a 'will to annihilation' and the conflation of the national community with state community. Under these conditions, true national sentiment had been transformed. In its ideal form, this should represent a 'piety of spirit', but it

[44] Undated, Hasselblatt to Schiemann. Schiemann Papers. Baltic Central Library, Riga.
[45] Bamberger-Stemmann, *Der Europäische Nationalitätenkongreß 1925 bis 1938*, p. 255.
[46] N. Gürke, 'Der Nationalsozialismus, das Grenz- und Auslanddeutschtum und das Nationalitätenrecht', *Nation und Staat* October 1932, v.6 pp. 7–30
[47] The speech was given on 26 June 1932 and was published subsequently. P. Schiemann, 'Die neue nationalistische Welle', *Nation und Staat* September 1932.

had been amplified by its association with the state. As a result of its application in struggles for political power, it had been coarsened and had become associated with hatred. Whoever denounced foreigners the loudest, seemed the best patriot. Things had gone too far such that the very foundations of the state community were being destroyed. With characteristic skill, Schiemann turned phrase after phrase laying bare the dreadful nature of what was happening:

> Service to the nation cannot be placed above moral law, if
> we do not want to destroy completely the meaning of moral
> law.

Slowly but surely 'a new nationalist wave' was washing over their multi-ethnic region, bringing with it new, and entirely inappropriate, ideas of power based on the nation state. Increasingly, 'sermons' were coming from the west, damaging their young people and their fight for nationality rights. How could they demand equality when their own co-nationals were committed to racism? So he concluded:

> We must not only lead a [sense of justice] against the
> nationalism found in foreign camps among our majority
> peoples, rather we must determinedly and righteously lead
> it against the nationalism in our own camp, even against the
> nationalism of our own national comrades.

This speech marked the end of Schiemann's ties with the Association of German National Groups in Europe.

Schiemann's speech was not matched by comments from, not least, Ewald Ammende. In fact, Ammende had even tried to get Schiemann to moderate the content of his 'new nationalist wave' speech. He asked Schiemann not to discuss the 'spirit of war', rather the 'spirit of hatred' and suggested that the talk not be phrased as a treatment solely of what was happening within German communities. Ammende added that in offering this advice he was only thinking about Schiemann's 'success' and 'interests'.[48] In fact Ammende was not the only one attempting to influence Schiemann, Hasselblatt had done so a few months earlier.[49] Naturally Schiemann took no notice. In a robust reply, he told Ammende he could 'in no way approve' the recommendations. He had no intention of putting his name to a list of 'trivialities' If the committee didn't like what he was going to say, then he would withdraw from the proceedings and recognise that there was no longer a place for him in the association.[50]

---

[48] 11.6.32, Ammende to Schiemann. Schiemann Papers. Baltic Central Library, Riga.
[49] 29.2.32, Hasselblatt to Schiemann. Schiemann Papers. Baltic Central Library, Riga.
[50] 19.6.32, Schiemann to Ammende. Schiemann Papers. Baltic Central Library, Riga.

The difference between the men would have been more readily comprehensible had Ammende become a member of the NSDAP, but this was not the case. Key figures from the German minority movement, such as Ammende, Graebe and Hasselblatt have been termed 'traditionalists' rather than Nazis.[51] That minority rights activists stood for something fundamentally different to the Nazis was reflected in an extract from Alfred Rosenberg's writing:

> Today, those supporters of 'national rights' who yet preach the ideal of a 'united mankind' and laud a single, organized, visible, ecumenical church which is to determine and embrace all public life, all science, all art, all ethics, on the basis of a single dogma, display the end result of those ideas, born of racial chaos, which have poisoned our true nature through the centuries. This is exemplified by the kind of commentator who says: 'What Austria is striving for, the whole world must attain on a vaster scale.' This is racial pollution and spiritual murder elevated to a world political program.[52]

For die-hard National Socialists, the liberalism and tolerance of minority rights activists pointed to the corruption and collapse of the race. Something more determined and élitist was required.

Members of the German minority movement apart from Schiemann recognised that Nazism was not necessarily in harmony with its aims. An article in *Nation und Staat* noted that Nazism had alliances abroad with nationalist groups inimical to German minorities living in their country (e.g. as was the case in Romania). The article observed that the creation of Nazi groups in ethnic German settlements sometimes produced negative effects; that the movement's anti-Semitism was a problem; that Nazism was committed to nation-state thinking and that it saw the problem of German minorities as separate from that of European minorities.[53] As observed already, differences between Nazism and the minority movement were also visible in attitudes towards the South Tyrol. According to Hermann Rauschning, Hitler said he would put a stop to 'the absurdly sentimental views about the South Tyrol. He would not let this 'deflect' him from the aim of 'an alliance with Italy'.[54] In his *Second Book*, while discussing *Reich* foreign policy, Hitler criticised those who became emotional over the South Tyrol:

---

[51] See Bamberger-Stemmann, *Der Europäische Nationalitätenkongreß 1925 bis 1938*, p. 391.
[52] A. Rosenberg, *The Myth of the Twentieth Century*. Torrance, CA: Noontide Press, 1982, p. 42.
[53] 'Aus Zeitschriften und Zeitungen', *Nation und Staat* November 1932 v. 6, p. 133.
[54] H. Rauschning, *Hitler Speaks*. London: Thornton Butterworth, 1939, pp.40–7.

... the foreign policy task of the German *Reich* as such cannot be determined by the interests of the parts split off from the *Reich*. For in reality these interests will not be served thereby since practical help indeed presupposes the regained power of the motherland. Hence the sole viewpoint that warrants consideration in regard to the foreign policy position can be only that of the fastest and earliest restoration of the independence and freedom of the remaining part of the nation united under a government.[55]

In other words, Hitler had more pressing priorities than standing up for all and just any ethnic German community. In particular, he didn't want to risk a confrontation with Mussolini over a few hundred thousand people who probably could not be extirpated in even 20 or 30 years anyway.[56] Quoted in the Baltic German press, Alfred Rosenberg agreed that the question of the South Tyrol would not prevent Fascist Italy and a Nazi Germany coming together.[57] Given that Ammende felt as strongly about the region in the early 1930s as in the early 1920s (criticising German authors who refused to back the Tyroleans' cause), this marked a serious cleft between himself and Hitler's movement.[58]

Less significant but still existent was a difference over state-building in Spain. An article apparently written by Ammende in late 1933 recommended increased decentralisation based on enhanced rights to self-administration for Catalans, Galicians and Basques.[59] This was not an argument likely to be shared by senior figures in the NSDAP; but the fact remained that Ammende and those around him were under pressure. They were facing the stark choice of either recognising their differences with Berlin's new government, leading to open criticism and even opposition to it, or else leaving the differences to one side in order to take funding. For Schiemann, no such compromise was possible, but for Ammende—a generation younger, with more of a history of anti-Soviet activism and perhaps, in the end, with less moral clear-sightedness—a dedicated anti-Nazi mission was too difficult a choice. It would have risked throwing away a life's work (not least the congress) and consigning himself to insignificance. Although co-operation with Hitler's regime necessitated compromises, it kept him 'in the game' and even held open the promise of enhanced work against a common enemy—Moscow.

---

[55] A. Hitler. *Hitler's Secret Book*. Introduction by Telford Taylor. New York: Grove Press. 1961, pp. 180–1
[56] Ibid, p. 193.
[57] 'Rosenberg über Legalität und Südtirol', *Revalsche Zeitung* 26 November 1932.
[58] E. Ammende, 'Das Schicksal der Deutschen Südtirols. Eine brennende Wunde am Körper des deutschen Volkes', *Revaler Bote* 10 January 1930.
[59] 'Spanien am Scheidewege', *Europäische Nationalitäten-Korrespondenz*. Sondernummer 4 (1933) pp. 1–10. R 60531. Political Archive of the Foreign Ministry, Berlin.

Personnel changes, and especially Hasselblatt's relocation to Berlin,[60] enabled the Association of German National Groups in Europe to adapt quickly to the new mood in Germany.[61] Meanwhile Ammende kept up requests for money from the new paymaster. By early 1934, for instance, he was asking that the German Foreign Ministry pay an outstanding debt of RM 10,000 relating to the cost of running the congress (owing particularly to unpaid subscriptions from the Jews and Catalans), plus provide a subsidy of RM 10,000 during the forthcoming financial year.[62] Within weeks, RM 8,000 was made available and was channelled, as usual, via the Association of German National Groups in Europe.[63]

In 1933–4, ethnic German groups followed a path amounting to self-inflicted 'co-ordination'. Faced with a choice of being by-passed or else participation based on compromise, as a group they displayed few scruples about choosing the latter. By the time the Association of German National Groups met in Bad Saarow in September 1933, regardless of precise motivations (and whether or not those present bought into Nazism's racism with commitment), most had decided to align themselves with the new power-holders.[64] The situation had to have serious consequences for the congress, not least because Ammende was a little too quick to liaise with them. It has been suggested his trip to Spain in 1933 took on the characteristics of an official mission, while a memorandum he wrote about the South Tyrol facilitated the Nazificiation of ethnic German organisations there.[65]

Even Paul Schiemann could not escape the consequences of Hitler coming to power in Berlin. He stood down from the committee of the Baltic German National Community in Latvia and as leader of the parliamentary party of Latvian Germans. He was also replaced as chief editor with *Rigasche Rundschau* by Ferdinand von Üxküll.[66] And so far we have hardly raised the most significant problem of the period: the rise of anti-Semitism.

---

[60] 'Abschiedsehrung für Abg. Werner Hasselblatt', *Revalsche Zeitung* 20 May 1932.

[61] Bamberger-Stemmann, *Der Europäische Nationalitätenkongreß 1925 bis 1938*, p. 274.

[62] 'Zur Frage der Teilnahme und des Beitrages am Europäischen Nationalitäten—Kongress. Regelung des Dezizites.' R 60531. Political Archive of the Foreign Ministry, Berlin; 22.2.34. Ammende to Herr Doktor. R 60531. Political Archive of the Foreign Ministry, Berlin.

[63] 14.3.34. Reich Foreign Minister. R 60531. Political Archive of the Foreign Ministry, Berlin.

[64] Bamberger-Stemmann, *Der Europäische Nationalitätenkongreß 1925 bis 1938*, p. 257.

[65] Ibid p. 330. See memorandum written by Ammende, 'Spanien als Faktor der Europäischen Nationalitäten-Politik. Barcelona—Madrid—Bilbao. Reisebericht, October 1931.' R60529. Political Archive of the Foreign Ministry, Berlin.

[66] Bamberger-Stemmann, *Der Europäische Nationalitätenkongreß 1925 bis 1938*, pp. 60–1. 'Wechsel in der Leitung der Rigaschen Rundschau', *Revalsche Zeitung* 4 July 1933.

## 5. 1932-33: failure of principle

Jewish minorities were outraged by *Nation und Staat*'s publication of Norbert Gürke's anti-Semitic essay. He was the leader of the NSADP's Law Department in *Ostland*-Vienna District[67] and the piece was entitled 'National Socialism, Border and Ethnic Germans and Nationality Rights'.[68] The essay's racism was surprisingly crude, its political agenda unmistakable:

> The nation is a unit of blood and culture. The individual national citizen is incorporated into a nation according to his racial pattern, that's to say the inheritance from his ancestors and his own mentality and achievement— language, state and cultural education, profession. Nor is the present day legal view decisive when it comes to deciding membership of a nation. The nation cannot, therefore, be compelled to absorb every person who leaves another nation. This is demanded by the present day view of the intrusive Jews and immigrants who lose their own sense of life and who, mostly for economic reasons, play at being German.[69]

Replete with Greater German and revisionist thinking, the essay looked to the spread of Nazi ideas beyond Weimar's borders.[70] It envisioned the eventual unification of all Germans into a Greater Germany that would be at least the equal of all other nations. Suffering of ethnic Germans beyond Germany's borders, as it had happened since 1918, was blamed firmly on the peace settlement, French interference in Central and Eastern Europe, and the corrupt manipulation of 'superficially democratic constitutions' in new states as a result of the numerical superiority of national majorities over minorities. Under these circumstances, the creation of a strong German nation state was seen as a necessary step on the way to protecting ethnic German communities.

Gürke put an exclusionary spin on the notion of cultural autonomy. He insisted that in Germany, foreigners should carry out their cultural lives 'in a special self-administration'—in effect, in a kind of cultural ghetto.[71] He recommended that 'Mongols' and 'blacks' be kept away from public life; and Gürke's view of Jews was no different. Characterised as bearers of a spirit at

---

[67] 'Aus Zeitschriften und Zeitungen', *Nation und Staat* November 1932 v. 6, p. 133.

[68] Gürke, 'Der Nationalsozialismus, das Grenz- und Auslanddeutschtum und das Nationalitätenrecht', pp. 7–30

[69] Ibid, p. 26.

[70] Although the essay said the NSDAP would not look for members beyond Germany's frontiers, it said the ideological movement could not be stopped by artificial borders.

[71] Gürke, 'Der Nationalsozialismus, das Grenz- und Auslanddeutschtum und das Nationalitätenrecht', p. 26.

odds with the German character, they were said to favour democracy as a means to securing equality, exploitation and domination. They would not and could not become participants in a Third *Reich*. Believing them to be a race in the first instance and a religious minority in the second, he maintained that Jewish half-breeds (*Mischlinge*) were damaging to the national body and that their birth should be prevented by appropriate marriage laws and criminal legislation. Gürke noted that Nazi doctrine regarded the Jews as a completely different order of problem than that posed by any other national group in Europe.[72]

Such a discussion was new to the pages of *Nation und Staat*. It was poles apart from arguments deployed by Paul Schiemann (not least in the speech 'New Nationalist Wave') who took it as axiomatic that nationality was a matter of personal conviction, certainly not any kind of objective characteristic such as biological inheritance.[73] Consistently Schiemann had sought to incorporate Jews into the nationality movement and he recognised that at key times, such as when the minorities from within Germany left the congress, German groups had been supported by the Jews.[74] He personally found the ideas of Jewish thinkers on nationality issues useful, but equally he recognised that it was difficult to categorise all Jewish groups as national.[75] He felt that in Western Europe, for the most part Jews were assimilated into the cultures where they lived, while the Jews of Eastern Europe more typically maintained their own exclusive national identity.[76] He also recognised that there was an on-going process led by Zionists to create a Jewish nation in a European sense, based on a clear territory and with a common language (Hebrew or Yiddish). For Schiemann, then, Jews actually were quite complicated in nationality terms, far more so than Gürke's blanket prejudice suggested.

Perhaps Ammende was always more attuned to ideas of German mission in the East than Schiemann. Equally he did not show as much interest in Jewish intellectual tendencies as did his elder colleague. He was, however, aware from a relatively early point that the position of Jews in Germany was particularly important. In late 1931, he wrote to a member of the German Foreign Ministry:

> German Jews must now prove whether they are in a
> position to act nationally. Their noses really do need to be
> rubbed in that point. Incidentally, the affair is so serious

---

[72] Ibid, pp. 22–3.
[73] The point about Schiemann being at odds with Gürke was noted in 'Aus Zeitschriften und Zeitungen', *Nation und Staat* November 1932 v. 6. This press review rather took odds with Schiemann's thoroughly negative attitude to Nazism.
[74] Vertraulich. 9.1.30. R60528. Political Archive of the Foreign Ministry, Berlin.
[75] See his reference to Sadinsky's work in P. Schiemann, 'Volksgemeinschaft und Staatsgemeinschaft', *Nation und Staat* v. 1. September 1927
[76] Ibid, p. 31.

that an exit of the Jews [from the congress] at the present moment would be extremely disadvantageous for us politically. They owe us around Swiss Francs 5,000 for the past year and we have to take this into consideration first and foremost.[77]

Ammende's language (*'Das sollte man ihnen gründlich unter die Nase reiben.'*) emphasised he had little fellow feeling for Germany's largely assimilated Jewish population—in fact, like most other members of the congress, Ammende always found it difficult to know how to deal with people who favoured assimilation. Nonetheless, he did not deploy the same sort of anti-Semitic stereotyping as did Gürke and he recognised that the congress needed Jewish support, both politically and economically.

Ammende's desire that German Jews take up the mantle of declaring themselves a national minority was expressed by other minority figures too. Max Hildebert Boehm's views perhaps came with a more clearly pro-Nazi nuance than those of Ammende. So, an article written by him in spring 1933 minimised the importance of the Jewish Question as it was emerging during Germany's National Socialist revolution and criticised how it was being used in the international media as anti-German propaganda.[78] In this context, Boehm challenged Germany's Jews to declare themselves a national minority, a step he must have known to be very unlikely.

Undeniably the views of Ammende and Boehm flagged up difficulties on the part of German minority figures regarding the Jewish Question as it was unfolding in Germany. In 1932–3, in fact, there was a mood that too many people among German national minorities were prepared to accommodate anti-Semitism. That at least some were content to work with Nazism was underlined in a letter sent by Üxküll to Schiemann in January 1932 saying that an article sent by the latter, which attacked the NSDAP directly, was giving him a headache. He didn't know if he could publish something like that and noted that, in time, the NSDAP could exert influence on Germany's nationality policy.[79]

The views of Ferdinand von Üxküll were worrying because he not only replaced Schiemann as editor of *Rigasche Rundschau*, but also became increasingly influential in *Nation und Staat*. Writing in the latter in April and June 1933, he expressed approval of Hitler's coming to power and hoped that in the 'new Germany', state and nation would soon be brought into harmony.[80] A couple of months later, Üxküll published a piece quoting Hitler's recent speeches and the talk given by von Papen at Iburg on 25 May.

[77] 4.12.31, Ammende to Geheimrat (Roediger?). R60529. Political Archive of the Foreign Ministry, Berlin.
[78] M.H. Boehm, 'Minderheiten, Judenfrage und das neue Deutschland.' Special edition of *Der Ring*, 28.4.33. R 60595. Political Archive of the Foreign Ministry, Berlin.
[79] 23.1.32, Üxküll to Schiemann. Schiemann Papers. Baltic Central Library, Riga.
[80] Üxküll, 'Das neue Deutschland'.

On this foundation, he denounced attempts by Germany's Jews to assimilate with the German nation. According to Üxküll, assimilation had been deleterious for his own group:

> It was painful for Germandom, that in many cases it could
> no longer represent itself internally or externally.[81]

This was held a particular problem because Jews in Germany were, in Üxküll's eyes, representatives of many of the qualities against which the German revolution of 1918–19 had been directed. So he also posed a rhetorical question:

> Does a great nation have the right to reflect on its own
> character, and to remove elements which have remained
> foreign from its spirit, from its soul? In principle, we can
> only say 'yes' to this question.[82]

In the pages of *Nation und Staat*, therefore, Üxküll was accepting that assimilation could be reversed by compulsion and that Jews might be ejected from the German nation—a process which came to be known as *dissimilation*. In this light, what sense could be made of Üxküll's proposal that what was happening in Germany at the time was temporary and that a lasting regulation of relations would have to happen in accordance with international law? Also, what should be made of his argument that the nationality principles represented by the congress should be applied to Jews in Germany?[83] Certainly the comments indicated convoluted thinking characteristic of how the congress had difficulties understanding the best way to deal with groups desiring assimilation, or which wanted an ambiguous status. The congress always saw its purpose as to stand up for national minorities that had a clearly defined sense of self; apart from when it was forced to (e.g. over the Frisian question), it spent little time dealing with 'grey areas' of national identity. In this respect, the issue of Germany's Jews was highlighting the limits of those participating in the congress. It was a forum for people who were consistently one thing or another, not both and not sometimes one, sometimes the other.

But Üxküll's words were an obvious problem. Their tone and arguments were at odds with the messages a minority journal should have been conveying. Assuming that recognition of basic human dignity is an integral part of nationality or minority rights, quoting extensively from politicians purveying anti-Semitism was at odds with the true mission of a minority movement. Given that the minority movement had long accepted

---

[81] Üxküll, 'Deutschlands volkspolitisches Programm', p. 541.
[82] Ibid, p. 541.
[83] Ibid, pp. 541–2.

that people classify their nationality according to inner conviction, how could dissimilation by a third party make sense? Political power, finances, perhaps dislike of the very idea of national ambiguity, and the rejection of assimilation *tout court* were the issues winning the day—perhaps even anti-Semitism for Üxküll. Fellow feeling for those experiencing discrimination and respect for individual choices were both losing ground.

In the wake of the NSDAP coming to power, *Nation und Staat* failed to report adequately on key issues which had to be of major interest to Europe's nationality movement. There was little comment on the boycott of Jewish shops in Germany which occurred in April 1933, little discussion of the Bernheim petition submitted to the League of Nations concerning the treatment of Jews in German Upper Silesia in May 1933 and, two years later, little analysis of the Nuremberg Laws on citizenship. This lack of discussion was deafening and told its own story.

## 6. Boehm on dissimilation

The idea of dissimilation owed much to Max Hildebert Boehm and his book *The Independent Nation*.[84] Boehm maintained that when different nations lived in close proximity, they tended to seek to maintain their individuality. This, he implied, was good, because without individuality, there would be paleness of character. Boehm felt the individuation of national groups had become more difficult in the past 200 years owing to the rise of cosmopolitanism (promoting similarities rather than differences) and the possibility of nations being penetrated by foreigners.[85] Boehm clearly was against assimilation. He maintained that attempts to change nationality could create unhealthy tensions within an individual.[86] He was equally sure that one of Europe's great strengths was that it consisted of a complex of different, vibrant national groups rather than of a homogeneous population. As he put it, 'Europe cannot exist without nations.'[87] In fact, for a long time Boehm had found it difficult to fit Jews into his scheme, regarding their thinking as anti-European and 'un-German'.[88] In his later writing, he supported their removal, or 'dissimilation', from the German nation, arguing it was the exact opposite of an oppressive act.[89]

---

[84] M.H. Boehm, *Das eigenständige Volk*. Göttingen: Vandenhoeck and Ruprecht, 1932.

[85] Ibid, pp. 305–8.

[86] M.H.Boehm, 'Assimilation vom völkerpsychologischen Geschichtspunkt.' Nachlass Boehm 1077 / 16. Koblenz.

[87] M.H. Boehm, 'Volkegedanke und Weltanschauung', 1932. Nachlass Boehm 1077 / 16. Koblenz.

[88] M.H. Boehm, 'Vom jüdisch-deutschen Geist', *Preussischen Jahrbuch* 1915. Nachlass Boehm 1077 / 17. Koblenz.

[89] M.H. Boehm, *Volkstumwechsel und Assimilationspolitik*. Jena: Verlag der Frommannschen Buchhandlung. 1938. Nachlass Boehm 1077 / 18. Koblenz.

This was the intellectual background for a minor review article in *Nation und Staat*, published in 1933, which argued that, in a difficult time, Germany's Jews should look to their Jewish heritage and culture as a means to protect themselves and to secure an existence worthy of a human being.[90] Lines of argument such as these were based on the premise that Germany's Jews should give the Nazis what they wanted: denial of any claim to German belonging in favour of a claim to solely Jewish identity. The arguments were deployed without any reference what was actually happening 'on the ground' in Germany or to the hatred which accompanied the persecution under way.

### 7. Conclusion: Jews, Germany and the 1932 Congress

Jewish groups were horrified at the treatment of Jews in Germany and the response of ethnic German groups to it. Leo Motzkin had been involved in the European Congress of Nationalities from its commencement, working alongside German groups and supporting them when other minorities left the congress. He could not believe his eyes when *Nation und Staat* became a vehicle for 'hatred between nations' pedalling 'the very blackest anti-Semitism'. Writing to Josip Wilfan (and copying the letter to Ammende), he deplored 'such language of hatred and narrow-mindedness' which compromised so obviously the congress's ideal of 'fraternity between nations'. In the light of what had happened, he was left to wonder 'Where is Dr Wilfan? Where are the other colleagues in the committee of the congress of nationalities?' He could not believe that anti-Semitism had been deployed in such a 'cold-blooded fashion', yet with such 'passionate hatred'.[91]

On the same day, Motzkin sent a letter to Ammende personally. He complained that Gürke's piece had singled out Jews and that once you failed to treat minorities equally, then the minority movement was reduced to nothing. He mentioned that the kind of denunciations applied against the Jews could be applied against anyone and questioned whether Jewish groups could have anything to do with an international movement that took anti-Semitism seriously, since 'a minority movement is absolutely incompatible with anti-Semitism.' He wanted a declaration by the German minorities on the matter.[92]

In June 1932 Motzkin already had been warning of the rise of anti-Semitism in Central and Eastern Europe, particularly as personified by Hitler. A letter sent to Ammende stated the situation unambiguously:

> As you know perhaps better than I, an outrageous and brutal anti-Semitism is raging in a series of countries in

---

[90] 'Zur Frage der Juden in Deutschland' in 'Aus Zeitungen und Zeitschriften', *Nation und Staat* September 1933.
[91] 16.11.32, Motzkin to Wilfan. Nachlass Wilfan 1250, FC4407. Koblenz.
[92] 16.11.32, Motzkin to Ammende. Nachlass Wilfan 1250, FC4407. Koblenz.

Eastern and Central Europe; ever since Hitler has collected
such large crowds around himself, it cannot be denied that
the sedition has assumed the very worst of pogrom forms
even in Central Europe; therefore not only in Eastern
Europe, but also in Central Europe the Jewish population is
facing the greatest danger. In my opinion the European
Congress of Nationalities cannot let such a phenomenon
pass by in silence, if it wants to stay true to its basic
principles. It would be more correct if the President in his ...
[illegible] human way would raise his authoritative voice
against the all-poisoning propaganda of hatred against a
part of humanity and against the brutal actions bound up
with it. Now I really do believe that President Wilfan and
you also have thought that it is time to undertake some kind
of worthy action connected to this in the framework of the
congress. Specifically it will be a matter of a precise
statement, defined not by form but by principle, which the
president can elucidate during his general round up—
something which I regard as an urgent necessity.[93]

Time did not make the situation better. As the *Reichstag* elections
were taking place in March 1933, Leo Motzkin visited Berlin. He found an
atmosphere so volatile that Jews could barely walk the streets. He had a
conversation with Hasselblatt in which he emphasised that anti-Semitism and
the minority movement were incompatible.[94] A few weeks later, it became
clear that the patience of the congress's Jewish members was wearing thin
with the prevailing attitude of their German 'colleagues'. In early April,
Jacob Robinson (a Jew from Lithuania) wrote to Motzkin complaining about
the lack of criticism of Hitler's government in the German minority press.
They just denied the plight of Germany's assimilated Jewry.[95] That same
month, Ammende was approached by a Jew called Feinberg based in Geneva
who had been pained by a recent edition of *Nationalitäten-Korrespondenz*
and its lack of treatment of the Jewish Question in Germany.[96] In reply,
Ammende said he had been in Berlin attempting to influence people,
including the chief editor of *Deutsche Allgemeine Zeitung*, over the Jewish
Question. He had been in touch with Jews in the city, including ones whom
Motzkin knew, but had been unable to influence them since they did not want
their fate to be internationalised. In particular, 'whether rightly or wrongly'
they believed it would be 'precisely catastrophic' if any steps were taken to

---

[93] 24.6.32, Motzkin to Ammende. Nachlass Wilfan 1250, FC4407. Koblenz.
[94] 10.3.33, Motzkin to Robinson and Margulies. A 126 / 635. Central Zionist Archives,
Jerusalem.
[95] 2.4.33, Robinson to Motzkin. A 126 / 635. Central Zionist Archives, Jerusalem.
[96] 11.4.33, Ammende to Feinberg. A 306 / 113. Central Zionist Archives, Jerusalem. Feinberg's
original letter was dated 3.4.33.

support the idea that they were not part of the German nation, but a national minority. Ammende said that under the circumstances, it was hard for the congress to take a position.

Jewish members of the congress began to lose faith in General Secretary Ammende. On 17 April 1933 Emil Margulies (a Jew from Czechoslovakia) wrote to Motzkin suggesting that Ammende was 'on a slippery slope' (*'im Rütschen'*) and stating that Schiemann and Wilfan agreed. Ammende was criticised for being prepared to differentiate between the rights of German nationalities and those of others, also for considering that it might be possible to maintain the rights of national minorities under a fascist regime. Increasingly he was said to be concerned with events in the Soviet Union, not Germany.[97]

The shock the Jewish members of the congress undoubtedly felt at the position of ethnic Germans such as Hasselblatt and Ammende was not alleviated by the genuine complexities of Jewish history and identity which, of course, they understood very well. Among Europe's Jewish communities there were multiple differences, whether between those who were more assimilation-minded (groups which tended to be in Western Europe), and those which were more self-contained (which tended to be drawn from Eastern Europe), Zionists (who looked ultimately to Palestine for a homeland) and Bundists (who perhaps were more content with a Jewish future in Europe).[98] At the end of the day, anti-Semitism could affect any Jew at all, so all had to reject it decisively.

By mid-1932, therefore, Wilfan and Ammende were perfectly clear that anti-Semitism was a major issue. Although Ammende tried to pursue 'business as usual', for example wondering if the European Congress of Nationalities might soon be in the running to receive a Nobel Prize,[99] at a deeper level he must have understood the gravity of the situation. It is possible that he was experiencing the effects of stress. Just two months after that year's congress meeting, Ammende was in a sanatorium undergoing a cure for his long-standing high blood pressure. Apparently he soon lost 7 kgs, but found the necessary dietary restrictions (no sugar, fat or alcohol) a challenge.[100]

The 1932 Vienna congress had been difficult to organise. Although there were plans to address religious persecution, roughly two months before the event was scheduled, Ammende wrote to Schiemann noting that German groups were reluctant to deal with the topic, while adding that he saw no

---

[97] 17.4.1933, Margulies to Motzkin. A 126 / 635. Central Zionist Archives, Jerusalem.
[98] For a study of Bundist thought, see R. Gechtman, 'Conceptualizing National Cultural Autonomy—From the Austro-Marxists to the Jewish Labor Bund' in the *Simon Dubnow Institute Yearbook* (2005) pp. 17–50.
[99] 30.8.32, Ammende to Schiemann. Schiemann Papers. Baltic Central Library, Riga.
[100] 2.8.32, Ammende to Schiemann. Schiemann Papers. Baltic Central Library, Riga. 8.8.32. Ammende to Schiemann. Schiemann Papers. Baltic Central Library, Riga.

reason to omit it from the agenda.[101] Already, however, it seems German interests were lining up against those of Jews. A few days later, Wilfan wrote to Ammende observing that suggestions were being made for the congress only to deal with persecution and the churches, not with religion as a whole. He noted this would prevent Jewish representatives participating in the proceedings.[102] Ammende's response was interesting. He said it would indeed be hard for Jews to participate in such a discussion, but proposed that Leo Motzkin be asked to give a keynote speech during the event, perhaps addressing 'the solidarity of the minorities'.[103]

So, Ammende wanted a discussion that would not provoke discussions of anti-Semitism, but equally wanted to bind Jewish groups into the proceedings. The strategy was pragmatic but cynical; it also reflected the looming impossibility of keeping German and Jewish representatives within the same organisation.

---

[101] 2.5.32, Ammende to Schiemann. Schiemann Papers. Baltic Central Library, Riga.
[102] 8.5.32, Wilfan to Ammende. Nachlass Wilfan 1250, FC4397. Koblenz.
[103] 11.5.32, Ammende to Wilfan. Nachlass Wilfan 1250, FC4397. Koblenz.

## Chapter Twelve

## When friends won't help

### 1. The 1932 Congress

Josip Wilfan opened the congress in 1932 with a strong speech highlighting the rise of national intolerance and warning of the repetition of massacres of minorities resembling the Sicilian Vespers and Bartholomew's Night. He said minorities should respond to the threat with solidarity. As planned, Leo Motzkin made a keynote speech in which he thanked Wilfan for showing 'understanding for the serious suffering which has afflicted the Jewish nation especially in recent years.' He emphasised that while Jews had become particular objects of hatred, their problem was not to be isolated: their treatment subverted the very system of minority protection. Motzkin went on to identify the difficulties they were facing:

> We live in a time when hatred celebrates with orgies, in a time when hatred is good business and nourishes the very worst instincts. In this sense, our congress is a contradictory phenomenon which can contribute to the pacification of Mankind.[1]

The 1932 congress was marked by a number of strong speeches. Schiemann reprised his 'new nationalist wave' speech delivered to the Association of German National Groups in Europe, warning that hatred was threatening to become a core ingredient of the state.[2] Géza von Szüllö added that the spirit of universalism was at war with that of the separate nation.[3] Professor Bovet argued that bad consciences on the part of the Great Powers, which sat in the League's Council but which were not bound by minority agreements themselves, prevented the proper enactment of the necessary rights.[4] Even more pessimistically, and echoing a sentiment familiar to readers of Oswald Spengler, Hans Otto Roth warned that Europe stood before the threat of collapse. In words that would prove sadly prophetic, he noted that national minorities could indeed be 'annihilated physically', but so long as they remained alive, so would the minority problem. He called for a new spirit in Europe.[5]

---

[1] *Sitzungsbericht des Kongresses der organisierten nationalen Gruppen in den Staaten Europas. Wien, 29. Juni bis 1. Juli 1932.* Wien - Leipzig: Wilhelm Braumüller, 1933, pp. 20–2.
[2] Ibid, pp. 14–8.
[3] Ibid, p. 19.
[4] Ibid, pp.30–42.
[5] Ibid, pp. 45–52.

Given such a weighty context, Wilfan's introduction (on the afternoon of the second day) of nationality rights and the churches was distinctly pedestrian, as were the subsequent talks. Father Drexel discussed the importance of religion to ethnic German groups in Soviet Russia, while Ukrainian churchman Mr. Hornykewytsch plus former cultural minister in the Russian Empire Prof. Karataschoff discussed the importance of the Ukrainian United and Greek Orthodox Churches. Clearly, however, there was an elephant in the room. It was flagged up late in the day when Jewish representative Mordechai Nurok (Latvia) interjected that the Jews could not participate in discussion since matters of religion and nationality raised a different set of issues for them.[6] Correspondingly, when congress resolutions were agreed, they covered the need for the League to do more for minorities and the importance of churches to national identity but said nothing directly about the Jewish Question. It was almost ironic, therefore, that Jewish representative Emil Margulies (Czechoslovakia) read the resolution calling for the incorporation of minority rights into the legislation of all European states.[7]

As early as 1932, congress participants who should have known better were failing to confront anti-Semitism adequately. So, if the League of Nations was rendered less effective on account of bad consciences, perhaps the same was true for the congress and its leaders as well. This was particularly the case since Jewish deputies were on hand to keep breaking through the patina of respectability. In addition to Motzkin's words, Nurok maintained that Europe's Jews were suffering a medieval kind of persecution.[8] Margulies made a well-judged speech, emphasising that Jewish communities were particularly vulnerable since they only existed as minorities and had no homeland.[9] Rotenstreich (from Poland) added (no doubt with one eye on the German groups) that minority rights should never be used as tools for power politics. He warned that minorities should not 'overlook what evil effects the hatred of Jews must bring with it in all lands.'[10] He advocated that stateless minorities must, somehow, be allowed to sit in the League of Nations.

Two months later, some of the congress's Jewish deputies attended the Jewish World Conference held in Geneva where they repeated their condemnation of the rise of anti-Semitism.[11] This was the background against which *Nation und Staat* published Gürke's anti-Semitic essay. On occasion, the piece provoked self-reflection among Jewish activists. Motzkin wrote to Robinson saying it was no good for them to complain about what was being

---

[6] Ibid, p. 91.
[7] Ibid, pp. 161–2.
[8] Ibid, p.145.
[9] Ibid, pp.116–7.
[10] Ibid, p.133.
[11] The event was reported by the ethnic German press, see 'Jüdische Weltkonferenz', *Nation und Staat* November 1932, p. 138.

published, it was the Jews' own fault for failing to secure themselves more firmly in the minority movement. Doing that would have made such publications impossible.[12] This, however, did not prevent him recognising:

> You get the impression spontaneously that some of the German minority leaders are riding in the wake of National Socialism.....[13]

He felt that some others might join them and in a letter to Wilfan, Motzkin protested against the 'shadows of anti-Semitic thinking' which he sensed in the congress.[14] Actually, Gürke's article was discussed by a committee meeting of the congress held in December 1932. It was the subject of correspondence in the weeks beforehand, with Ammende trying to justify publication by saying it provided 'an authentic standpoint' about Nazism's view of the minority question and permitted others to respond to it. He added that it was not appropriate to doubt the upright nature of any of the minority leaders.[15] In time, Margulies requested that the issue be removed from the committee's agenda on the grounds that Jewish groups were undecided how to respond. Schiemann maintained there should be no differentiation of civic rights by ethnic group and expressed astonishment that anyone could ever think Gürke's piece could be produced without a reply.[16]

An odd thing about the events of 1932 was that they had been prefaced, in late 1931, by concern among ethnic German minorities leaders that Jewish groups might be pressured to stay away from the congress, so damaging its standing. In December 1931, Graebe had complained there was a danger of the Jews leaving the congress and that such an outcome would please Polish interests but damage German ones.[17] He suggested to Ammende that the Polish government was pressuring Jews for a boycott.[18] Yet, for all his lack of understanding when it came to dealing with anti-Semitism, Ammende consistently was clear that keeping the Jews within the congress was most important. He stuck to this line even when they were not paying their subscriptions.[19] He re-iterated his position in spring 1932, stating that if the Jewish groups departed the congress without doubt Wilfan would be forced to stand down as president.[20] Ahead of the congress's committee meeting which took place in Berlin in May 1932, he made sure that Motzkin

---

[12] 11.11.32 Motzkin to Robinson. A 126 / 633. Central Zionist Archives, Jerusalem.

[13] 16.11.32, Motzkin to Margulies. A 126 / 633. Central Zionist Archives, Jerusalem.

[14] 16.11.32, Motzkin to Wilfan. A 126 / 633. Central Zionist Archives, Jerusalem.

[15] 21.11.32, Ammende to Robinson. A 126 / 633. Central Zionist Archives, Jerusalem.

[16] 1.12.32, Margulies to the Committee. A 126 / 633. Central Zionist Archives, Jerusalem.

[17] 4.12.31, Graebe to Prof. Hirsch. R60529. Political Archive of the Foreign Ministry, Berlin.

[18] 30.11.31, Graebe to Ammende. R60529. Political Archive of the Foreign Ministry, Berlin.

[19] Undated (presumably late 1931) memorandum by Ammende. 'Auszug aus dem Brief an Oberstleutnant Graebe.' R60493. Political Archive of the Foreign Ministry, Berlin.

[20] 15.3 and 13.3.32, Letter from Ammende. A 126 / 633. Central Zionist Archives, Jerusalem.

could attend and that Schiemann would be able to meet with Rosmarin (a Jew from Poland).[21]

For all of this, Ammende just could not put himself into the position of Germany's Jews. Hence he was also clear with Motzkin that he felt there was a limit to what the European Congress of Nationalities could do to assist them. For instance he told Motzkin:

> The assimilated gentlemen in Germany and elsewhere do not consider claiming the position of a national minority for themselves.[22]

Since the congress was supposed to promote the rights of national minorities, if someone did not want to identify him- or herself as a national minority, how could the congress offer assistance? In a narrow sense, of course, Ammende had a point, but his position left far too much unsaid—and would condition the crisis faced by the congress in 1933.

Despite Ammende's desire to maintain contact with Europe's Jewish groups, he showed a major failing of both imagination and principle in trying to gloss over what National Socialism meant for them; and he was not alone. Under the headline 'No Pogroms in Germany', *Revalsche Zeitung* carried a story in March 1933 about the Association of Jewish Front Soldiers writing to the US Ambassador in Germany to point out there had been only a few outrages against Jews and that the state authorities had intervened to stop them.[23] When anti-Jewish boycotts were about to start in Germany, *Revalsche Zeitung* reported them as a response to foreign threats for an economic boycott of Germany.[24] And while the paper reported on senior Nazis organising the boycott (as about other anti-Jewish measures),[25] it also reported on responses to Nazi Germany. Hence a conference of Latvian Jews was reported which agreed a resolution to break 'all connections with Germany'.[26] The paper was creating a spurious impression of 'tit-for tat-ism', perhaps even that things were not really so bad for Jews inside the Third *Reich*.

---

[21] 29.4.32, Letter from Ammende. A 126 / 633. Central Zionist Archives, Jerusalem.

[22] 7.11.12 Ammende to Motzkin. A 126 / 633. Central Zionist Archives, Jerusalem.

[23] 'Keine Pogrome in Deutschland', *Revalsche Zeitung* 25 March 1933.

[24] 'Die deutsche Gegenaktion', *Revalsche Zeitung* 29 March 1933.

[25] 'Abwehrkampf und Boycott', *Revalsche Zeitung* 31 March 1933. 'Boycottpause in Deutschland. Der Boykott der NSDAP wird von Montag bis Mittwoch unterbrochen', *Revalsche Zeitung* 1 April 1933. 'Numerus clausus an deutschen Schulen und Hochschulen', *Revalsche Zeitung* 26 April 1933.

[26] 'Die Deutschenhetze in Lettland', *Revalsche Zeitung* 10 June 1933.

## 2. 1933

Probably the difficulty of the situation at the start of 1933 had an impact on Ammende because that March, he was in a clinic again on account of high blood pressure.[27] Without question, things were going on behind the scenes. On 7 April 1933 Ammende wrote to Wilfan about a forthcoming edition of *Nation und Staat*. The letter made plain the problem the Jewish Question in Germany posed for the journal and said that it simply could not deal with the boycott of Jewish shops.[28] External circumstances were restricting what German minorities could and could not do. The next day Wilfan wrote to Ammende about Üxküll's essay on the new Germany that was about to be published in *Nation und Staat*. Wilfan observed that the author seemed to favour Hitler's movement and pointed out that perhaps it had not thought through its minority policy properly yet (implying that Üxküll should discuss this point). He mentioned that Üxküll's piece was strangely silent on the Jewish Question.[29] When Ammende wrote back, he left all these points to one side. Instead he noted that the congress's financial situation was worse than ever and that there was a danger of 8 years of work culminating in a financial mess. Furthermore, 15 years of stress had left his constitution weakened—so how could they get out of their current plight, given that German and Hungarian groups could only help to a limited extent? He asked Wilfan if it would be possible for Yugoslavia's groups to supply a subsidy of SF 5,000.[30] Ammende was making a point. If the congress was to continue, it needed funding; this, in turn, required reliance on Germany unless someone new filled the gap.

But the Jewish Question would not go away. In May 1933 Wilfan wrote to Ammende saying that Grünbaum, a Jewish leader from Poland, had visited him in Vienna saying the Jews still definitely wanted to co-operate with the minority movement, but stating that German groups simply had to take a position on all that had been happening recently. Wilfan commented that he knew how difficult this would be for the Germans, but maintained that the Jewish Question had to be addressed urgently, perhaps through discussion of issues that were 'general and common', maybe concerning the position of all national minorities in Germany. He wondered if Ammende should meet with Motzkin and Margulies to take matters forward.[31]

Within days, Ammende was telling Wilfan he was in touch with Motzkin and Feinberg trying to prevent a complaint against Germany being lodged with the League of Nations. He was wondering if some kind of appeal over Jewish issues could be sent to the German government, but felt this just

---

[27] 10.3.33, Ammende to Wilfan. Nachlass Wilfan 1250, FC4397. Koblenz.
[28] 7.4.33, Ammende to Wilfan. Nachlass Wilfan 1250, FC4397. Koblenz.
[29] 8.4.33, Wilfan to Ammende. Nachlass Wilfan 1250, FC4397. Koblenz.
[30] 12.4.33, Ammende to Wilfan. Nachlass Wilfan 1250, FC4397. Koblenz.
[31] 23.5.1933, Wilfan to Ammende. Nachlass Wilfan 1250, FC4397. Koblenz.

couldn't come from ethnic German groups.[32] Nor was the situation likely to
improve with time. A fortnight later, following discussions with other ethnic
German leaders (Graebe from Poland and Roth from Romania), Ammende
told Wilfan that German groups might well have to play the role of martyrs.[33]
He did not spell out exactly what he meant by this, but if they did nothing,
they risked being reviled by the other minority groups in Europe, although if
they protested about the Jewish Question to Berlin, they risked provoking
major internal divisions and having their subsidies cut to boot.

By the end of June 1933, the situation was getting so fraught that
Ammende felt potentially high risk action was required. On the 21st, he wrote
to Wilfan:

> I feel obliged to tell you in confidence that the sacrifice of
> this journey to Berlin is justified above all by the
> facilitation of a conversation with *Reich* Propaganda
> Minister Dr. Goebbels which will take place tomorrow at
> 1.30. I have decided to tell him openly how much the
> present situation regarding the Jewish Question is
> heightening the critical situation of German national groups
> and naturally also the *Reich*. I am telling you this so that
> you are in the picture and so that, if there are renewed
> attacks from the Jewish side, there is clarity over the way
> responsible German representatives (among whom I must
> count myself in this case) have in reality taken a position on
> the Jewish Question despite all the cheap suspicions which
> are stacked up against them. Or does Herr Motzkin believe
> that I or some other personality from German circles in
> general still would have the possibility of intervening
> directly with the leading personalities in Berlin if we had
> been tempted by the public statements on the Jewish
> Question laid before us?[34]

Ammende may well have used his visit to Goebbels to justify his failure to
say much about the Jewish Question in public (and it is interesting that he
even received any consideration from Goebbels at all), but (although no
minute of the meeting survives) there is little reason to believe Ammende had
much of an impact on the *Reich* Minister. In fact, it is very hard indeed to
think what Ammende could possibly have said in an attempt to change
Berlin's trajectory. Probably he suggested that persecutions within the *Reich*
were likely to inspire persecutions of ethnic Germans abroad, but even such
an argument would hardly have led to a fundamental re-think of a policy as

[32] 28.5.33, Ammende to Wilfan. Nachlass Wilfan 1250, FC4397. Koblenz.
[33] 9.6.33, Ammende to Wilfan. Nachlass Wilfan 1250, FC4397. Koblenz.
[34] 21.6.33, Ammende to Wilfan. Nachlass Wilfan 1250, FC4397. Koblenz.

important to National Socialism as anti-Semitism—particularly given Hitler's view on South Tyrol and the ethnic Germans living there. Ammende was a small 'tail' trying to 'wag' a 'dog' that was both large and determined.

Ammende was not alone in trying to influence Nazi policy. Towards the end of March, Hasselblatt and Graebe had approached *Reich* Minister without Portfolio Göring requesting that German minorities be consulted in advance over *Reich* policy.[35] The next month, Hasselblatt contacted *Geheimrat* Rödinger in the German Foreign Ministry about the Law for the Re-professionalisation of the Civil Service, which allowed for the removal of Jewish civil servants.[36] He told Rödinger that the introduction of comparable laws directed against ethnic Germans, would be disastrous. He requested that it be made clear that the legislation was directed against only assimilated Jews rather than Jews as a national minority. Hasselblatt's concerns were forwarded to the *Reich* Interior Ministry.[37] Rödiger also penned a note stating that Nazism's opponents abroad were trying to use the country's treatment of Jews as grounds to deny Germany the role of guardian of minorities. It was possible that these events could be used as evidence for a complaint to the League of Nations, also that they could be taken as a pretext for the ill-treatment of German minorities abroad. He requested that debates within the *Reich* take account of the position of German minorities abroad and also that German embassies report to Berlin about any discrimination against ethnic German communities as a result of the Jewish policy.[38]

In this instance, Hasselblatt's protest was very limited in scope (ignoring assimilated Jews) and limited in impact—particularly since, in due course, *Reich* Interior Minister Frick sent a letter to Foreign Minister von Neurath stating there were no grounds for changing the Law for the Re-professionalisation of the Civil Service.[39] Still, Hasselblatt kept on trying. In early May he visited State Secretary Stieve in the Foreign Ministry, again highlighting that persecution of the Jews in Germany could lead to a corresponding persecution of Germans abroad. The State Secretary noted that the Foreign Ministry would try to take account of the interests of ethnic Germans.[40] As a result, Stieve sent a circular around Germany's embassies requesting frequent reports on the treatment of German minorities.[41] Apart from a basic sensitisation of people to the potential vulnerability of German minorities and a flow of memoranda, however, there was always a limit to

---

[35] 20.3.33, Hasselblatt and Graebe to Goering. R 60494. Political Archive of the Foreign Ministry, Berlin.
[36] 3.4.33, Hasselblatt to Geheimrat Roediger. R60595. Foreign Ministry Archive, Berlin.
[37] Foreign Ministry note of 7 April 1933. R60595. Foreign Ministry Archive, Berlin.
[38] Note by Roediger, 12 May 1933. R60595. Foreign Ministry Archive, Berlin.
[39] 22.5.1933, RMI Frick to von Neurath. R 60596. Political Archive of the Foreign Ministry, Berlin.
[40] 4.5.33, Memorandum by Stieve. R 60595. Political Archive of the Foreign Ministry, Berlin.
[41] 19.5.33, Circular from Stieve to German Embassies. R 60595. Political Archive of the Foreign Ministry, Berlin.

what Hasselblatt was going to achieve. There was never any sign of him being likely either to cause the Third *Reich* to re-visit its Jewish policy or to make a personal sacrifice on behalf of Europe's Jewish communities.

### 3. Preparing for the European Congress of Nationalities in 1933

Against this difficult background, Ammende and the committee started preparing for the meeting of the congress. As the event approached, apparently Ammende maintained contact with Jewish delegates, in particular Motzkin and some of his friends in Geneva.[42]

The Jewish Question was always going to be crucial to the 1933 congress. As early as 2 April, when the preparatory committee met, Margulies was asking how it would be dealt with. Wilfan recommended it happen in the context of a discussion of the nationality question in the authoritarian state, a topic which would allow contrasts to be made between the situations in Germany and Italy. Even though Germany's Jews strictly were not a national minority but an element of the majority population, he felt their situation could be addressed. Rather inscrutably, Ammende added that the aim should be to encourage every regime to recognise nationality rights, although he did not explain how this would apply to Germany's Jews.[43] By June, Ammende was in Barcelona with Roth and Graebe but still wondering how best to deal with the Jewish Question at the forthcoming congress. Maybe the German minorities would have to keep quiet on a number of issues.[44]

When the congress's committee met in July, it consisted of Wilfan, Margulies, Schiemann, Roth, Besednjak (a Slovene from Italy) and Ammende.[45] Wilfan said he had participated in the World Association of the League of Nations Union meeting at Montreux, where a special interest had been taken in the Jewish Question. The commission reporting on it recognised that a nation had a right to delimit itself as it wanted (in effect to eject or 'dissimilate' those it no longer regarded as its own), but added that Germany's methods of doing this, and of depriving people of their rights in the process, were wrong. Ammende discussed directly developments inside Germany, which he said had serious consequences for German minorities. The discussion which he stimulated came to the conclusion that, since German minorities were currently being criticised for failing to take a stand on the Jewish Question, it was absolutely essential that the congress meet in 1933. Bern was chosen as a venue on account of a poor atmosphere said to be abroad in Geneva. It was foreseen that the congress would open with an

---

[42] 26.5.33, Ammende to Schiemann. Schiemann papers. Baltic Central Library, Riga.

[43] 2.4.33, Protocol of meeting of board of the ENK 2 April 1933 in Vienna. Nachlass Wilfan 1250, FC4397. Koblenz.

[44] 9.6.33, Ammende to Wilfan. Nachlass Wilfan 1250, FC4397. Koblenz.

[45] 'Report about the proceedings and decisions of the committee and council sitting of 2–3 July in Vienne VI, Schadekgasse, No. 8.' Nachlass Wilfan 1250, FC4397. Koblenz.

appropriate declaration by the German groups (i.e. about the Jewish Question).

The meeting also discussed 'dissimilation'. It was proposed that the views of German and Jewish representatives to the congress pretty much coincided. Reportedly Margulies made a statement saying nations could delimit themselves however they wanted, but the methods applied in Germany were against nationality rights and motivated by hatred. It was agreed that in about a month there would need to be a meeting between Motzkin, Margulies, Schiemann, Hasselblatt and Roth in order to finalise a statement for the congress.

Later in its proceedings Schiemann asked Wilfan what he would say about the Jewish Question during the congress. He said he'd repeat his line from Montreux: that a nation had the right to define its conditions of membership. Given all that had been said about everyone having the right to choose their own nationality, and that a statement of national identity was akin to a religious conviction, Schiemann at least must have wondered what was going on. With little else to be said on the subject, in due course Ammende began to talk about the famine in southern Russia which could lead to the deaths of 10 million people.

A whole series of letters followed between Wilfan and Ammende about dissimilation. Ammende even said he was becoming optimistic about how the topic would be dealt with.[46] Wilfan accepted that dissimilation would have to be addressed, including the Nazi view of it. He wondered, though, if a title 'national exclusivity and national tolerance' would be better than 'dissimilation and nationality rights' for a topic of debate.[47] The correspondence suggested that Ammende had a significant problem conceptualising how to deal with a group of people who, essentially, were assimilated. He just couldn't conceive how to address the Jewish Question in Germany apart from if the German Jews declared themselves a separate national group.[48]

Setting up the 1933 congress involved an inordinate amount of effort. Ammende tried to re-incorporate national minorities from within Germany, a project which led to a whirlwind tour of the country for conversations with community leaders. At one point he had to spend 6 out of 8 nights on trains.[49] The purpose behind these efforts was obvious: to provide a wider context for discussion of the Jewish Question because the presence of the other groups would enable nationality rights in Germany to be addressed from different perspectives.

None of this prevented scepticism about what was going on in the congress. In late July 1933, Natan Szwalbe attacked the organisation in an

---

[46] For example, 4.7.33, Ammende to Wilfan. Nachlass Wilfan 1250, FC4397. Koblenz.

[47] 10.7.33, Wilfan to Ammende. Nachlass Wilfan 1250, FC4397. Koblenz.

[48] 20.7.33, Ammende to Wilfan. Nachlass Wilfan 1250, FC4397. Koblenz.

[49] 21.8.33, Ammende to Wilfan. Nachlass Wilfan 1250, FC4397. Koblenz.

article published in *Nasz Przegląd*.[50] Noting that National Socialism exerted substantial influence over all German publications, he alleged that Üxküll was representing the interests of Alfred Rosenberg and specified that he had taken over *Rigasche Rundschau* after Schiemann had withdrawn. Under the circumstances, he proposed Ammende had to be in an utterly impossible situation:

> The Congress office is still in the hands of Dr. Ammende, who is enveloped in a sad glory, since open conflict broke out between World Jewry and Hitlerian barbarity. During this period, the gentleman has stood deaf and dumb and was cheeky enough to show himself in Geneva during the May session.[51]

Quite rightly, Motzkin's position was said to be hopeless too. It was clear either the congress would explode or individual delegations would leave.

Aware of such criticisms, Ammende kept pushing things along, especially through negotiations with the German groups. By mid-August he felt the ethnic Germans would make all the statements required of them about nationality rights. Not even Jewish delegates would dispute the statements (he believed), even though German delegates were concerned some Jewish speakers might cause trouble. So long as Motzkin and Margulies stayed on top of things, Ammende thought discussions would reach an amicable solution. He proposed that the debate about the relationship between Jews and Germans within the German state was of fundamental importance because it could determine how relations between Jews and majority populations would develop in other European states. Ammende suggested that if Germans claimed nationality rights, Jews should be allowed to do the same:

> Expressed differently, apart from the clear conclusion that Germany's Jews have in every case a claim to the full extent of nationality rights, clearly there would also need to be an independent law for the Jewish collectivity in Germany.

Ammende advised that German and Jewish leaders, such as Hasselblatt and Margulies, should meet to organise what would happen next.

Ammende was at odds with the persecution of Jews in Germany, but his fixation on national identity backed up by the money flowing from Berlin restricted how he could respond to what was happening. An article he wrote

---

[50] *Nasz Przegląd*, Warsaw, 28 July 1933 by Natan Szwalbe. Nachlass Wilfan 1250, FC4397. Koblenz.
[51] Ibid.

in summer 1933 epitomised his difficulties.[52] He said it was wrong to criticise the European Congress of Nationalities for failing to take a position on events inside Germany since its rule of eight years standing precluded discussion of individual cases; he added that the forthcoming congress would discuss 'dissimilation and nationality rights'. Ammende went on to quote Baron von Üxküll that current problems had to be solved according to international law and moral principles, as well as to talk about both the boycott of Jewish shops in Germany *and* the boycott of ethnic German businesses outside Germany organised by Jewish leaders.

So how did Ammende think the Jewish Question should be addressed? With approval, he quoted German *Reichstag* Deputy, Baron Freytag-Loringhoven arguing that current legislation about the Jews was wrong:

> People are being discriminated against who only have one Jewish grandparent. In an individual case where the given person has dissolved [his or her] internal ties to the Jewish community, that can represent a real tragedy and even an injustice.

He went on to recommend that Jews in Germany declare themselves a separate nationality in order to claim the relevant minority rights. Then, under supervision, they would be able to administer their own cultural and religious affairs as well as receive state subsidies. By the same token, however, they would have to keep their distance from German life.

The idea that Jews in Germany should declare themselves a national minority and opt for cultural autonomy certainly was in line with the principles of the European Congress of Nationalities, but emphatically was not what German Jews wanted. As a community leader from the Central Association of German Citizens of Jewish Faith explained:

> ... The great majority of German Jews remains firmly rooted in the soil of its German homeland, despite everything.... But according to the ruling of the laws and regulations directed against us only the 'Aryans' now belong to the German people. What are we, then? Before the Law we are non-Germans without equal rights; to ourselves we are Germans with full rights. We reject it, to be a folk or national minority, perhaps like the Germans in Poland or the Poles in Germany, because we cannot deceive our own innermost [feelings]. We wish to be subject as Germans with equal rights to the new Government and not

---

[52] 'Zur Frage der Juden in Deutschland', *Europäische Nationalitäten-Korrespondenz*. Sondernummer 4 (1933) pp. 1–10. R 60531. Political Archive of the Foreign Ministry, Berlin.

to some other creation, whether it is called the League of
Nations or anything else. As far as we are concerned that
also closes the question of Geneva which at present
occupies Jewish people everywhere. Thus we are
suspended between heaven and earth....[53]

The Jews saw themselves as German, not as an independent nation, so opting
for a separate status was not an option, even if it might confer practical
advantages. In accordance with Schiemann's idea that nationality should
reflect inner convictions, these sentiments determined that Germany's Jews
could not divorce themselves from their German roots.

### 4. A strategic diversion

Given the fundamental problems likely to occur during the 1933 congress,
Ammende developed a diversionary strategy. It hearkened back to one of his
earlier concerns: conditions inside the Soviet Union. Increasingly he showed
an interest in the treatment of European national minorities there as well as
the spectre of starvation. At the start of September, Ammende wrote to
Wilfan suggesting he'd address the famine in Ukraine because it affected
many minorities with co-nationals in the congress. (In the same letter,
Ammende also said that Margulies should not be allowed to address
specifically the situation inside Germany. So, quite illogically given the
congress's rule that no specific cases be discussed, Ammende was advocating
a direct treatment of one case but not of the other. These were double
standards.)[54] The strategy was supposed to forge a common interest to bind
people into the congress regardless of reactions to what was happening inside
Germany, also to underline that the Soviet empire was no Eldorado for
minorities. Ammende knew that while, say, Ukrainian groups had a clear
interest in discussing what was happening in Soviet Ukraine, so did ethnic
Germans (since large German groups lived in the Volga), but hopefully Jews
too (since Ukraine contained a Jewish community). Ammende even asked
Leo Motzkin if he'd like to talk about famine in Ukraine since he was from
the region.[55] Furthermore, Emil Margulies had a history of involvement in
projects oriented towards Ukraine, co-operating with Ammende on this score
in 1922, so hopefully he would be attracted by the topic as well.[56]

---

[53] A. Wiener of the Leadership of the Centralverein, *C.V.-Zeitung*, No.22, 1 June 1933 in Y.
Arad, I. Gutman and A. Margaliot (eds.), *Documents on the Holocaust*. Jerusalem: Yad Vashem,
1999, pp. 50–1.
[54] 9.9.1933, Ammende to Wilfan. Nachlass Wilfan 1250, FC4395. Koblenz.
[55] See Frank's article on Motzkin.
[56] S. Bamberger-Stemmann, *Der Europäische Nationalitätenkongreß 1925 bis 1938. Nationale
Minderheiten zwischen Lobbyistentum und Grossmachtinteressen*. Marburg: Verlag Herder-
Institut, 2000, p. 337.

Ammende planned that a string of reports be presented by the minorities straddling 'Europe' and the western Soviet Union. His initiative found influential friends, not least William Martin, editor of the *Journal de Genève* who, in 1924, had been chairman of the International Committee for Georgia.[57] Yet fears over the 1933 congress would not completely go away. In a letter to Ammende, Hasselblatt spelled out his worry that, despite everything, Jewish groups would try to disrupt the event and it would fall to Wilfan to deal with the situation.[58] Ammende passed on the expectation to Wilfan that the Jews should not be allowed to discuss specifically the situation inside Germany.[59]

### 5. Jewish responses in advance of the congress

Jewish groups refused to be bought off so easily. They were determined to push the issue of persecution in Germany at the international level. In May 1933, Franz Bernheim, a Jewish resident of Upper Silesia, lodged a complaint with the League of Nations. Since a convention agreed between Germany and Poland in 1922 extended minority rights to Upper Silesia, the League was entitled to address the issue, and in time the petition led to the suspension of discrimination there.[60] Ammende discussed this case in *Europäische Nationalitäten-Korrespondenz*, regretting that whereas in the past Germany had been fêted as a champion of nationality rights, now it was being put in the dock. He feared the Bernheim petition would be used to stimulate an anti-German campaign.[61]

Naturally officials in Berlin were exorcised by the issues around Bernheim's initiative. In early April 1933, Count Adelmann, the German Consulate in Katowice (Kattowitz), met with the president of the League's Mixed Commission, Mr. Calonder, to hear that the treatment of Jews in Upper Silesia was unacceptable under the terms of the Upper Silesian treaty.[62] Pressure on the German government was heightened when two additional petitions were submitted to the League, one by the Jewish Club in the Polish *Sejm*, the other by a number of signatories including Motzkin and Margulies.[63] The Secretary General of the League considered the topic to be urgent, while some members of the German Foreign Ministry hoped the issue

---

[57] Bamberger-Stemmann, *Der Europäische Nationalitätenkongreß 1925 bis 1938,* pp. 333–5.

[58] 7.9.33, Hasselblatt to Wilfan. Nachlass Wilfan 1250, FC4395. Koblenz.

[59] 9.9.1933, Ammende to Wilfan. Nachlass Wilfan 1250, FC4395. Koblenz.

[60] See M. Housden, *The League of Nations and the Organisation of Peace.* London: Longman, 2012, pp. 108 and 153–5.

[61] 'Die internationalen Auseinandersetzungen. Zwei bedeutsame Erfolge' in *Europäische Nationalitäten-Korrespondenz.* Sondernummer 4 (1933) pp. 1–10. R 60531. Political Archive of the Foreign Ministry, Berlin.

[62] 7.4.33. Graf Adelmann, German Consulate, Kattowitz. R 60595. Political Archive of the Foreign Ministry, Berlin.

[63] 24.5.33. Telegram from Geneva to AA. R 60595. Political Archive of the Foreign Ministry, Berlin.

might just vanish without anything needing to be done. One official suggested that maybe the Jews of Upper Silesia were not really a minority, another that Bernheim was not affected personally by the issues he outlined.[64]

Events in Germany were discussed at the World Jewish Congress. It took place in Geneva from 5 to 8 September, that's to say, very shortly before the staging of the European Congress of Nationalities in Bern. This fact probably helps explain why Ammende re-located his congress. Under the circumstance, it would have been difficult to follow so closely behind an international Jewish event held in the same city. Some familiar names gave notable addresses to the World Jewish Congress. Emil Margulies delivered a tough speech warning that members of the Jewish nation were involved in a mortal conflict. They were used to pogroms between the Dnieper and the Volga, not between the Danube and the Elbe. If Jewry's human rights could be removed in Germany, the same could happen anywhere. He connected this fight for survival with the battle Jews also had to create a homeland where they might no longer be threatened.[65] Leo Motzkin gave a speech accusing the Nazis of anti-nationalism. True nationalism, he said, begins when you stand up for another national group: if you are only acting on your own behalf, it was a misuse of the idea. He admitted to being more shocked by what was happening in Germany than by the massacres of Jews in Ukraine which followed the First World War.[66] He said, 'It is the Middle Ages with the refined instruments of modern times.'

Interestingly, Motzkin also emphasised the separate nature of Jews and debated how assimilation-minded Jews were responding to events inside Germany. He criticised the Central Association of German Citizens of Jewish Faith for protesting persecution based on their assimilated credentials. The position encouraged Jews to forget millennia of their culture. He also seemed to accept the possibility of dissimilation when he said:

> ... it is an elementary fact that an element of a population
> can no longer claim membership of a nation if the main part
> of the nation, the uncontested one, does not recognise it as
> such.

Hence he thought slogans such as 'Do not let yourself be de-germanised' were misplaced. Clearly Motzkin, not unlike Ammende, found it difficult in at least some ways to understand the position of assimilated Jews.

A string of notable Jewish community leaders, such as Stephen Wise and Nathan Goldmann, added to the weight of words. The latter insisted

---

[64] 1.6.33. Bülow, AA to German delegation Geneva. R 60595. Political Archive of the Foreign Ministry, Berlin.

[65] *Protocol of the 2nd World Jewish Conference, 5–8 September 1933, Geneva.* Hebrew Union College, Cincinnati. In another speech he warned that they should expect no help from the League because 'the wastepaper bin is big.'

[66] Ibid, pp. 84–5.

equality had to be achieved for the Jews in the lands of the diaspora before a solution to Palestine would become possible. Then it fell to Motzkin to read out the resolution calling on Jews to defend themselves against Nazism's agenda.

For all the differences that existed between Jewish groups over how to respond to the problems of specifically assimilated Jews, basically everyone present at the World Jewish Congress in Geneva was fundamentally opposed to what was happening in Germany. In this light, there could have been no doubt that a confrontation was going to happen between the Jewish members of the European Congress of Nationalities and both the German groups and management committee. The impression was underlined in correspondence between Jacob Robinson (a Jew from Lithuania) and Motzkin. In early August 1933, Robinson complained that the European Congress of Nationalities had lost its purpose for the Jews. It had been a valuable forum when Germany had been an advocate for national minorities with a permanent seat on the League's Council. More recently, however, the congress had become a vehicle for Hungaro-German revisionism. Now, at a key time, its leadership had failed. German minority leaders had failed as well, allowing their journal to be used to promote anti-Semitism. Sooner or later Jews would have to leave the congress and so they ought to pursue a policy of 'participation in order to leave.' He specified they should demand a resolution condemning Germany's Jewish policy outright, and when the ethnic Germans refused to accept it, they could leave the congress in a blaze of publicity.[67]

A month later, Robinson stepped up the pressure over participation in the congress. He proposed to Motzkin that Jews could only participate if the ethnic Germans distanced themselves from the *Reich* government. There had to be a resolution 'which calls the things in Germany by name'. It would have to identify the dangers of racial theory and anti-Semitism.[68] A few days after this letter (and with the congress scheduled to start meeting on 16 September), Motzkin sent an ultimatum to Wilfan laying out the conditions for Jewish involvement. First there would have to be a clear statement that events in Germany were a crime against the laws of Mankind; second, there would have to be an open discussion of what was happening, by implication allowing direct reference to events inside Germany. If there was no satisfactory reply by 13 September, Motzkin said the Jewish groups would not attend the congress. Motzkin complained it was still unclear where the congress's committee stood over events in Germany. He added that if his position seemed tough, it was actually a compromise since half of the Jewish delegates already wanted to distance themselves from congress. If the conditions were unacceptable, or if there was no reply by 13 September, Motzkin said the Jews would stay away.

---

[67] 7.8.33, Robinson to Motzkin. A 126 / 635. Central Zionist Archives, Jerusalem.
[68] 3.9.33, Robinson to Motzkin. A 126 / 636. Central Zionist Archives, Jerusalem.

Wilfan wrote back the very next day complaining that he had only been able to discuss Motzkin's position with Ammende by telephone and said that it was impossible to carry out the sort of discussions required by the demands with all of the German representatives affected by them in the timeframe allowed—they were scattered all over Europe before coming to Switzerland for the meeting.[69] Hence, the congress's committee would not meet until 15 September—an event to which Motzkin was invited. In reply, Motzkin demanded that Wifan's personal position be clarified by the quickest means of communication available: a telegram.[70]

When Wilfan replied, he seemed to stand with the German groups. Noting that Graebe and Hasselblatt had tried without success to find Motzkin and Margulies during the Zionist Congress in Prague, he denied Ammende had done anything that called for the congress's committee to justify its actions.[71] He also denied the congress could draft a resolution addressing specifically the German situation since it would have to adhere to the usual rules of procedure.

### 6. Bad Saarow and Montreux

There was no doubting that a collision would happen, particularly since Jakob Robinson was looking to make capital out of a confrontation. To make any kind of agreement more remote still, in early September 1933 the Association of German National Groups in Europe took steps to align itself with National Socialism at its meeting in Bad Saarow. Those present declared their loyalty to the Nazi regime while at the same time (and unrealistically) stating a desire to maintain a level of independence from Berlin.[72] As was recorded:

> The representatives of the German national groups declared unanimously their full trust in the new German state leadership, but remarked correspondingly that the relationships in the *Reich* could not be exported directly to the German national groups living in the midst of foreign nations; the national groups are ready, under guarantee of their independence, to co-operate in the great cultural and economic tasks of the German nation.[73]

---

[69] 8.9.33, Motzkin to Wilfan and 9.9.33, Wilfan to Motzkin. Nachlass Wilfan 1250, FC4407, Koblenz.

[70] 9.9.33, telegram Wilfan to Motzkin. 9.9.33 letter of Wilfan to Motzkin. 11.9.33, Motzkin to Wllfan. A 126 / 636. Central Zionist Archives, Jerusalem.

[71] 11.9.33, Wilfan to Motzkin. A 126 / 636. Central Zionist Archives, Jerusalem.

[72] Bamberger-Stemmann, *Der Europäische Nationalitätenkongreß 1925 bis 1938*, p. 257.

[73] Wochenbericht der Abteilung VI, 10–16 September 1933. 16 September 1933. R60494. Foreign Ministry Archive, Berlin.

German interests proved very sensitive to international responses to the Jewish Question. When the League of Nations Union met at Montreux in June 1933, the topic could not be avoided and although, according to later judgements, German representatives were not put under the spotlight adequately, still, they were on the defensive.[74] According to a German Foreign Ministry report, the meeting had as an agenda item 'Persecutions in Germany', but discussions were limited, dealing for instance with the legislative detail of persecution rather than the inhumanity abroad on Germany's streets. German delegates were shocked by the strength of feeling shown over the Jewish Question, even by League of Nations Union delegates who previously had been sympathetic towards Germany. They found Robert Cecil's attitude to display 'hatred and contempt'.[75] With their backs to the wall, the members of the German contingent maintained the Jews were not a national minority and stressed Germany had signed no minority protection agreement. By implication they were characterising events inside Germany as purely domestic matters. The German delegation was left feeling the world was sympathetic towards the new Germany, but it did not understand the Jewish Question.

A report in the Polish press provided a bit more colour about Montreux. Apparently German delegation leader Dr. Schnee tried to head off discussion of the Jewish Question at every opportunity, while Professor Bovet—anxious to avoid the Germans leaving the forum—attempted to play the peacemaker between them and others at every turn. When Schnee attempted to deny there was a problem over the Jewish Question in Germany, Leo Motzkin simply called him a liar.[76]

In the face of all the difficulties, from an early point some, such as Elmer Jakabffy (a Hungarian who sat in the Romanian parliament) wondered if 1933's congress shouldn't be postponed. Ammende, however, insisted it go ahead and looked to Hasselblatt to smooth the way with the German Foreign Ministry.[77] Bit by bit, word leaked into the press that the congress would discuss 'national dissimilation and the rights of nationalities'.[78] Ammende recognised Jewish groups probably would try to address the German situation directly and, if that happened, he wanted Wilfan to use his authority as congress president to intervene and stop them.[79] And where did Ammende think the congress would end up in its treatment of the Jewish Question? In a

---

[74] Bamberger-Stemmann, *Der Europäische Nationalitätenkongreß 1925 bis 1938*, p. 284.

[75] 'Bericht über die Behandlung der Frage der gegen jüdische Bevoelkerungskreise in Deutschland getroffenen Regierungsmassnahmen. Jahreskongress des Weltverbandes der Völkerbundligen in Montreux. (30 Mai bis 10 Juni 1933).' R 60596. Political Archive of the Foreign Ministry, Berlin.

[76] 8.6.33, *Nasz Przeglad*. Nachlass Wilfan 1250, FC4407, Koblenz.

[77] Krabbe, 'Neuvieme Congress des Nationalites Européennes tenu a Bern du 16 au 19 Septembre 1933', 4/6638/6638. S338. League of Nations Archive, Geneva.

[78] 'Der XI Europäische Nationalitätenkongress', *Revalsche Zeitung* 2 August 1933.

[79] 9.9.33, Ammende to Wilfan. Nachlass Wilfan 1250, FC4407, Koblenz.

letter to Wilfan written in early September 1933 he said the congress
probably would be able to agree unanimously that Germany's Jews should
enjoy full nationality rights as defined by the forum's principles.[80] Two
months earlier he had expressed comparable views, again to Wilfan: he
thought the only way for Germany's Jews to save themselves was to re-join
'the community of their own old nationality.'[81]

There certainly was a dreadful consistency in Ammende's position.
He was seeking to impose the principles underlying the congress on the
German situation, while resolutely failing to take seriously that it was not an
option for Germany's Jews themselves. What was his motivation? Was he
being naive or wilful? Perhaps he was experiencing the desperation born of
facing an impossible situation, but it was hard to see how events could result
in anything other than an explosion.

### 7. Sad spectacle: the start of the Bern congress

When the congress finally convened on 16 September, it was without
Schiemann (on account of ill health) and without the Jewish groups.
Regarding the latter, the published minutes recorded the whole sorry saga
that had led to the situation.[82] The congress committee had met several times
across the year discussing how best to deal with dissimilation and had taken
note of Motzkin's letter to Wilfan of the 8th. A Jewish group consisting of
Motzkin, Margulies and Farchy had met with the congress committee on 16
September to discuss a resolution on dissimilation and nationality rights.
There was no agreement since Jewish demands would have breached the
congress's established rules (they would have led to Germany being
discussed directly). Consequently the Jewish groups refused to participate.

Wilfan opened the congress in the federal parliament building of the
Bern canton. He greeted the delegates (now including Galicians from Spain)
with the words that the world was more tense and dangerous than ever. Using
tortuous arguments, he addressed 'dissimilation' or 'making dissimilar again'
(*Wieder-unähnlich-Machen*). Wilfan struggled as he explained they needed to
think about solidarity and recognise how much everyone present had come to
like the representatives of the German groups over the years. The key thing,
he said, was that one of the oldest, most culturally elevated nations in Europe
was experiencing a transformation in which it was developing a new idea of
the nation that excluded some people with certain characteristics. The
consequences, he said, should not be discussed in concrete terms, but as
principles. He observed that no one should be declared of lesser value than
others, and no one should be deprived of their rights.

---

[80] 9.9.33, Ammende to Wilfan. Nachlass Wilfan 1250, FC4407, Koblenz.

[81] 20.7.33, Ammende to Wilfan. Nachlass Wilfan 1250, FC4407, Koblenz.

[82] *Sitzungsbericht des Kongresses der organisierten nationalen Gruppen in den Staaten Europas.
Bern, 16. bis 19. September 1933*. Vienna-Leipzig: Wilhelm Braumüller, 1934.

The congress was a disjointed affair. No sooner had Wilfan staggered to the end of his speech than Michail Kurtschinsky (a Russian from Estonia) began talking about the famine in Ukraine.[83] He said the crisis was affecting 100,000s of Russians, Germans, Ukrainians, Jews, Poles, White Russians, Estonians, Latvians, Bulgarians and many others. He painted a terrible picture of human suffering, of people being sacrificed so that the Soviet economy could grow. Milena Rudnycka (a Ukrainian deputy in the *Sejm*) intervened, complaining that a disaster was taking place in a land rich in natural resources—in the breadbasket of Europe. Its population was being sacrificed so that corn could be distributed to Soviet industrial centres, the military and the secret police. All over the world, people were failing to recognise what was going on; they were closing their eyes to starvation, corpses in the streets and cannibalism. Recently Ukrainian communists had been shot when they complained about the situation; others committed suicide. As she began denouncing 'the crimes of the Red Russian dictatorship in the Ukraine' Wilfan interrupted to say she was moving into political territory.[84]

According to the congress's rules, Wilfan's intervention was long overdue. As soon as Ukraine was mentioned, rules had been breached. Yet Wilfan let things run. Certainly it was a very welcome distraction from the Jewish Question. At this point Ammende finally broke his silence, admitting that he had written a memorandum about the Ukrainian famine several weeks earlier and saying that although it raised political issues, his main concern was humanitarian. He suggested that Rudnycka was only moved by humanitarianism too. Ammende insisted the congress should take a position on the famine because so many of its groups had co-nationals suffering grievously in the Soviet Union. In some areas, he said, already 50% of the ethnic German population had died. He proposed that no one attending the congress wanted to look on, as the rest of the world was doing, while these people died.[85]

The peculiar nature of the congress was underlined as its focus swung back to dissimilation. Hans Otto Roth (a German from Romania) made a statement on behalf of the German groups. He said, with no apparent hint of shame:

> We regard the exclusion of a different kind of people
> (especially of a different race—as one has seen recently)
> from a national culture basically to be permissible. In this
> connection, efforts should also be made to maintain the
> integrity of the rights for which our congress has stood for
> the groups of people turned into minorities through

---

[83] Ibid, p. 17.
[84] Ibid, pp. 22–3.
[85] Ibid, pp. 24–5.

> dissimilation. At the same time, we declare that we stand, as before—without reduction or limitation—on the principles of the congress which have been expressed in its resolutions and its 9 years of work.[86]

After the declaration, Wilfan once more warned the congress it could not discuss specific cases.

The congress broke up and reconvened the next day to discuss territorial autonomy for closely settled groups (introduced by a Sudeten German, Dr. Medinger who talked about developments in his home region),[87] the lack of rights being delivered for Lithuanians in Vilnius and East Prussia, and the state-building ambitions of Catalans (with the talk delivered by Professor Maspons i Anglasell). The presentations were so specific they created the impression there was only one topic that could not be addressed by name: the Jewish Question in Germany. Ammende himself delivered a lack-lustre talk about territorial autonomy, which perhaps showed how much things were changing in the minority movement. Territorial autonomy was coming to the fore as cultural autonomy, rooted in the person, receded. Ammende recognised territory was important in Barcelona, San Sebastian, Galicia and Sudetenland. He declared:

> We must enable compactly settled groups to be able to administer themselves.... [In a resolution agreed by the congress in 1926] ...we said we would not only promote personal autonomy and minority rights, but we would have to recognise that in certain areas of Europe self-administration is necessary and achievable without being the first step towards separation.[88]

He recommended that local populations in especially Vilnius and Carpatho-Russia be afforded self-administration.

A mood of dissatisfaction pervaded the proceedings. Géza von Szüllö complained that, although the congress was meeting for the ninth time, the forum had barely achieved any of its goals. He said it had been too well-behaved since, typically, good children received no rewards, but those who screamed and shouted did. Along with Dr. Zalozieckyj (a Ukrainian from Romania), he suggested that real progress required the congress to start dealing with specific cases. To quote Zalozieckyj: 'The congress would lose nothing if it would allow us to call facts by their name.'[89]

---

[86] Ibid, p. 26.
[87] Sudeten Germans had been participating in the congress since 1929.
[88] Ibid, pp. 40–2.
[89] Ibid, p. 52 and p. 54.

This, then, was a period of crisis for the congress. Old ways of doing things were being re-evaluated, established priorities were being re-balanced, and it was happening in the context of the Nazified co-ordination of German minorities through whom key funding flowed. It was no surprise that Ammende often sat through proceedings quietly. He must have been experiencing considerable turmoil as his life's work underwent a pretty thorough examination. And this examination was about to become more probing still.

## 8. A fresh Jewish input

On 18 September, the congress returned to national dissimilation. This was occasioned by the managing committee receiving a letter dated 17 September sent by a Jewish delegation of Rosmarin, Margulies, Farchy and Motzkin. It asserted that the declaration by Hans Otto Roth made in the name of the German groups during the opening session had destroyed the foundations for common work between nationalities. As he interpreted the contents for those present, Wilfan suggested that the letter was in error, since it had failed to appreciate fully the positive side of what the German had said. The letter asserted that events inside Germany were 'without example in the civilised world'.[90] In impassioned fashion, it noted that no one in the congress had ever approved assimilation, but nonetheless assimilation was best left to be negotiated between nations directly. When congress participants were rejecting assimilation, in fact they were rejecting intervention by state power in that process. Hence, if the congress condemned state intervention to promote assimilation, it should also reject state intervention to prevent assimilation (as was the case in Germany).

　　In any event, the letter from Margulies, Motzkin, Rosmarin and Farchy, proposed that a narrow focus on assimilation and dissimilation risked missing the point. The actions of the German government were not just about rejecting assimilation, but about removing rights from the Jews, denying their equality and defaming them on account of their ancestry. Minority rights were being denied, but so were the basic human rights of Jewish people. If events were not challenged passionately, the whole system of minority protection in Europe would be replaced with simply the power of the stronger. Wilfan went on to quote directly from the letter:

> The declaration of the German national groups uses, approvingly, only the word 'removal' [*Ausgliederung*] of one nation by the other to stand for German Jews being deprived of their rights, robbed, raped and defamed. It

---

[90] Ibid, p. 64. For a copy of the original letter from Motzkin, Margulies, Rosmarin and Farchy, see 17.9.33, Letter from Motzkin, Rosmarin, Margulies and Farchy to President of ENK. R 60531. Political Archive of the Foreign Ministry, Berlin.

> approves explicitly this removal, as it has happened in
> Germany: the expulsion of Jewish civil servants, the
> ousting of Jews from the free professions, the removal of
> their means of existence built up over long years of work,
> blocking their entry to places of education, public
> incitement and defamation (even in schools and among
> young people), as well as systematic boycott constructed on
> hatred and envy, and aiming at complete annihilation.[91]

Motzkin, Margulies, Rosmarin and Farchy said the German declaration had approved all of this.

The summary of the letter completed, Wilfan then embarked on a lengthy justification of what had been happening in Germany:

> If a nation ... gains a sharper, a more detailed idea of itself,
> about its own essence, according to which it is impossible
> to include everyone who previously regarded themselves as
> belonging to it...., then nothing can be done.

It was tragic, when the majority of a population told a group it no longer belonged to them, but for eight years the congress had stood for principles which permitted such a decision. Wilfan felt the ejection of people from the national group rested on the rejection of past processes which had extended the nation in question; it amounted to the rejection of assimilation. Members of the congress had always rejected assimilation and protested against the application of state power to bring it about; hence dissimilation was in harmony with their position.[92] The congress's president made some particularly mealy-mouthed comments about maintaining the rights and dignity of those being dissimilated before proposing a resolution which included the following:

> In the case of the introduction and implementation of
> national dissimilation, the freedoms and rights which the
> European Congress of Nationalities has incorporated in its
> speeches and decisions from the outset remain unaffected.[93]

This was the sort of thing that could only be said because it stood in a vacuum, deprived of any grounding in the reality of what was actually happening inside Germany.

Hans Otto Roth then intervened again to make another statement on behalf of German groups:

---

[91] Ibid, p. 65.
[92] Ibid, pp. 67–8.
[93] Ibid, p. 69.

German groups have always fought national assimilation most keenly. This fundamental standpoint excludes the denial of the right of a nation to national dissimilation. We do not underestimate that the implementation of dissimilation in itself is an unusual and in many ways a painful process and that its character will be so always and everywhere, but we do not consider it compatible with the principles of the congress to take a position on the matter of specific events relating to the methods applied in the process of dissimilation.[94]

Roth was not going to criticise Berlin.

When it came to a vote on Wilfan's resolution, Szüllő abstained on behalf of Hungarian groups, as did Maspons i Anglasell for the Catalans of Spain. Zaloziecky initially abstained but then changed his mind. Kurtschinsky made a speech on behalf of Russian groups from Estonia and Poland, Lithuanians from Poland, the Catalans and all Hungarian groups. He stated plainly that the wave of out-spoken anti-Semitism obvious in several lands was against human rights and contradicted the ideals of the congress. Nonetheless, after a great deal of politicking, Wilfan declared that, apart from the abstention of the Hungarian groups, the resolution was passed and that, consequently, unanimity had been achieved. On this basis he hoped that soon enough their Jewish colleagues would return to participate in their work.[95]

Now a dreadfully wounded beast, the congress staggered on discussing nationality, religion and language, also the character of the national community. Nonetheless, the shock waves of what had happened radiated out. With Ammende sitting dumb for most of the time (although thanked fulsomely by Graebe for organising the congress), Roth appeared again, displaying a particular gift for casuistry. The congress, he said, stood firmly on the principle of rejecting assimilation, but he added that all present rejected the idea that—in the process of its construction—a nation state could bring about the destruction of any national group within its borders. As the congress drew to a close, Wilfan made a final statement which included words of regret that Schiemann and Motzkin were not present. Then he presented a series of resolutions, which included a statement specifically on the famine in Ukraine. He left the congress saying that, although the participants had been facing a crisis, if they remained true to their principles they would survive. He looked forward to the next meeting, because it would mark the congress's tenth gathering.[96]

---

[94] Ibid, p. 69.
[95] Ibid, p.71.
[96] Ibid, p. 97.

## 9. Conclusion: what would Schiemann have said?

Wilfan might have regretted the absence of Schiemann and Motzkin, but they were not the kind of people to participate in an event like this. It seems, however, that at about this time Schiemann did prepare a text on dissimilation, although apparently it was never presented or published. His argument shows just how difficult a topic it was for minority activists at this time.

Schiemann agreed that the congress had always stood against assimilation, but said this was because it supported the freedom of the individual to define his or her own nationality.[97] Yet even with that said, Schiemann struggled to identify dissimilation as purely unacceptable:

> Let's consider this dissimilation process in the first place as a purely intellectual event, as a drawing of a boundary conducted by one nation between itself and a group of people who number themselves among them. No one will be able to mistake the tragic situation forced on those who are rejected in such a way, those who suddenly have the emotional and rational foundations of their mental existence pulled from under their feet. On the other hand, it is hardly possible to deny a nation the right to stipulate the boundaries of its own community. That is also the standpoint of the German groups which the president of our congress has represented in his speech in Montreux.

He realised he was struggling with two potentially conflicting principles:

> 1. A national community is not an association which has the right to exclude its members. A nation has responsibility for the mentally, morally or physically sick members of its community too. And the reverse.
> 2. No one can compel a national community to accept foreign elements damaging to it, even if these confess themselves part of it.

Nonetheless, Schiemann was clear that 'objective characteristics of descent' (racial characteristics) could not be used to determine whether or not an individual belonged to a given national group. Membership was entirely a

---

[97] Text dated 4 September 1933. Presumably it is the speech Schiemann would have given had he attended the 1933 Congress. Nachlass Wilfan 1250, FC4407. Koblenz. In a letter sent a few months later, Wilfan offered Schiemann advice on how best to tackle the topic of dissimilation. Obviously, then, it was a topic about which Schiemann was thinking over this period. 30.3.34, Wilfan to Schiemann. Nachlass Wilfan 1250, FC4400. Koblenz.

matter of 'psychological reality'. So, if a national group ever had grounds to eject individuals, this could only happen if there was reason to doubt 'the truthfulness of the confession' which they made about their sense of national belonging; but they could not be ejected on account of biological inheritance. For Schiemann, dissimilation had to reflect the lack of a common bond of national identity:

> What is membership of a nation? It is an independent self-identification with a single nation. Just as the consciousness of being 'me' is the prerequisite for the individual person, so the personality's consciousness of 'us' in respect of a specific nation is the prerequisite of national membership— the consciousness of 'us' in respect of the culture of a nation, its fate and not least its deficiencies and its blame. Such a consciousness cannot be proved through a family tree, through declarations and songs, not even through individual acts of impulse. It is a content of life [*Lebensinhalt*]. The right to dissimilation therefore rests on the presupposition that this consciousness does not exist completely in those being rejected. There is no institution which could be in a position to prove or disprove the existence of such a consciousness in individual cases. And so in practice we must allow the exercise of such a right to the national community.

This is not to say Schiemann was pleased by his conclusion. What if there were moves to dissimilate 'Germans' who had assimilated with different national groups 500 years previously? How could they be accepted once more into the German national body? It followed that the process of dissimilation might create groups of nationless individuals. Under the circumstances, he sounded a warning about how dissimilation should be implemented:

> Our congress, which has fought against assimilation throughout its existence, cannot dismiss the right to dissimilation. But we should not forget that our fight against the assimilation policy of governments in the first place has been directed against the attempt to compel these goals using state power.

When it had opposed assimilation, the congress had done so on the grounds that it was something enforced by state power arbitrarily, but there was no opposition to assimilation as chosen by individuals and as reflecting genuine changes in their identity. No matter what happened, however, Schiemann emphasised that no person should be deprived of civil rights even if he or she was to be dissimilated.

Although Schiemann's text (with its rejection of inheritance as the defining characteristic of the individual) clearly was directed against Nazi racism, still he might have discussed at a bit more length whether, for instance, the concept of 'us' existed between Germans and the Jews living among them. Also he did not really discuss multi-dimensional identities—the possibility that someone could identify with both German and Jewish categories—perhaps even with an individual's identity changing according to circumstances. So, at a family gathering an individual might be aware of a Jewish identity, but in day-to-day life maybe German identity predominated. Perhaps it would have been asking a great deal for Schiemann to have taken up issues such as these, but there seems to have been something just stopping his rejection of dissimilation completely. Perhaps he might even have wondered why someone with a name like 'Hasselblatt' should be considered German. Nonsense needed to be called by its name. Really, from the perspective of a committed liberal, dissimilation cried out for a more forthright rejection.

But Schiemann was not at the congress and his text—apparently— was never made public. Meanwhile, people who should have known better continued to get away with nastiness. On the closing day of the congress, from the German groups, Graebe, Roth and Hasselblatt wrote a letter to Wilfan which they hoped would be passed on to Motzkin, Margulies, Rosmarin and Farchy. Responding to the communication from the Jews dated 17 September, they pointed out that the German groups had not supported what was happening in Germany; they had not taken sides and refused to take a position.[98] This observation was delivered in a way that suggested it was worthy of applause. That's how far ethics had declined in the circles of German minorities by autumn 1933.

---

[98] 19.9.33, Graebe, Roth and Hasselblatt to Wilfan. Nachlass Wilfan 1250, FC4407. Koblenz.

# Chapter Thirteen

## Aftermath

### 1. Damned

The European Congress of Nationalities was damned by its inactivity over the Jewish Question. The organisation had always experienced tensions between different power blocs but the dismal events of 1933 exacerbated them more than ever. Although some kind of unity emerged between German and Ukrainian groups as both prioritised work on the famine in the Soviet Union, more important by far was the chasm that opened up between those prepared to tolerate the treatment of Jewish groups and those, like the Hungarians, who were not. 1933, therefore, signalled more than ever that the congress was a house divided.

As various, especially German, congress members reflected on what had happened that September, it was not obvious that they understood properly the position of the organisation. When Graebe wrote to Schiemann on 21 September, he was almost triumphant. Having noted that Roth and Hasselblatt effectively were the leaders of the Association of German National Groups in Europe, he criticised Jewish leaders for becoming increasingly intransigent as the date of the congress had approached. He blamed especially the Polish Jews—and maybe the Polish state behind them. Yet, Graebe said, Wilfan's skill and the composure of the German groups, had enabled them to navigate the troubled waters. The Jews had not exactly left the congress, they had just stayed away from its public sessions. They had not managed to 'put Germany in the dock' because no other group wanted such a precedent. The only disappointing feature of the congress had been Ammende's poor form. He had lost his composure occasionally for fear that the organisation would explode apart. Consequently, he lost respect in the eyes of some the German groups. Graebe proposed that maybe Ammende had experienced ill-health and would soon take a cure to restore him.[1]

*Revalsche Zeitung* also tried to interpret things as positively as possible. The paper implied the congress had suffered due to tensions between Zionist and non-Zionist Jewish groups. This had caused difficulties at the Zionist Congress in Prague (held just before the European Congress of Nationalities) and motivated subsequent Jewish actions.[2] The article maintained that Germany's Jews had never seen themselves as a national minority and had never attended the congress. The question of whether they were a minority had only arisen since Nazism came to power. The congress's committee had decided not to take a position on events inside Germany

---

[1] 21.9.33, Graebe to Schiemann. Schiemann papers. Baltic Central Library, Riga
[2] 'Recht des Volkstums', *Revalsche Zeitung* 21 September 1933.

because they did not really concern a national minority; since they disagreed with the position, the Jewish groups decided to stay away. The newspaper denied the congress had been 'co-ordinated' under Nazi leadership and described as slander the accusation it was promoting German and Hungarian revisionism, not least because Catalans and various Slavic groups belonged to it. More unexpectedly, the article also suggested it was time to move beyond ideas of individual rights based in the ideals of the French Revolution and towards notions of rights and duties based on communities:

> The corporatist idea, which has already gained pioneering significance in many states, should also point the way for the organic incorporation of national groups into the modern state.

According to the article, corporatism would suit Baltic Germans very well, since they were used to realising their nationality not as individuals, but as communities, estates and corporations. The article showed clearly which way the wind was blowing: towards conservative ideals.

Wilfan was not so pleased with developments in the wake of the congress. Within weeks he was complaining the Jews were not briefing honestly and proposed that Ammende should become active to set the record straight.[3] The Jewish Press Centre had issued a statement saying the civil rights of Jews were being broken in Germany and that Jewish groups would only return to the congress once it spoke out on this point. The centre quoted Roth's statement and commented:

> ... this statement approved current German legislation based on racial principles, which naturally was completely unacceptable to the Jews.[4]

On 23 September, Natan Szwalbe published 'The Nationality Congress: Hitlerism exposed' in the Warsaw publication *Nasz Przegląd*.[5] He complained that once the Poles had left the congress in 1927, Ammende had fallen increasingly under the influence of the German Foreign Ministry. With a base in Vienna, Ammende was susceptible to German influence and so avoided dealing with minority issues inside Germany. Hence the Jewish Question could only be addressed in a limited way. Wilfan was criticised for his performance at Montreux, where he delivered a speech defining him as a sociologist of dissimilation. In effect he justified Hitler's politics.

---

[3] 18.10.33, Wilfan to ?. Nachlass Wilfan 1250, FC4397. Koblenz.
[4] '9. Europäischer Minoritätenkongress in Bern.' *Jüdische Presszentrale*. R 60531. Political Archive of the Foreign Ministry, Berlin.
[5] N. Szwalbe, 'Der Nationalitätenkongress. Der Hitlerismus entlarvt' in *Nasz Przegląd*, 23.9.33. Nachlass Wilfan 1250, FC4407. Koblenz.

Furthermore, Wilfan's exact status was put in question when Szwalbe suggested he had the same sort of relationship to Belgrade as Ammende had to Berlin. Russian groups were also accused of cynicism over their engagement with the congress. They just wanted a springboard for anti-Soviet propaganda even though the issues had nothing to do with minority rights. Swalbe guessed at what was really happening. He thought the congress was responding to orders from Alfred Rosenberg (Hitler's champion of anti-Communism). Hence Ammende was pressing an anti-Soviet cause which in fact was stimulated by a cynical Nazi agenda in the background.

Szwalbe went on: although Catalan and Hungarian representatives to the congress had made efforts to oppose the spectre of Hitlerism, without the presence of Polish and Jewish delegations they were too weak. So if the 1933 congress witnessed one good thing, it was that 'finally the Hitlerite directors of the congress have pulled down their masks'. Now it was clear the German minority movement had fallen under the influence of Nazi ideology. Terming the congress 'this corrupt institution', Szwalbe criticised Wilfan and Ammende for 'monkey fun' when they elected Motzkin to their executive committee again. (Naturally Motzkin turned down the post.[6])

## 2. Ammende

Ammende's post-congress publicity was more muted than usual. His piece for *Revalsche Zeitung* held few surprises.[7] He seemed too worn out to argue with real conviction; perhaps he realised the death-knell was sounding for the congress's reputation. Certainly his line lacked the conviction radiating from Szwalbe's journalism. Predictably, Ammende cited Roth's statement that ethnic Germans supported minority rights, both in the states where they lived and in Germany itself. Of the session on dissimilation he said:

> ... the fundamental decision was agreed unanimously, that
> when national dissimilation is introduced and implemented,
> the freedoms and rights for which the congress has stood
> since the beginning .... should remain unimpaired.

Again it was a clear statement of support for nationally-conscious groups and of indifference towards assimilated individuals.

Ammende was under a lot of pressure and his health was cracking. In October he asked Schiemann to approach Jewish groups with a view to building bridges. Meanwhile he prepared to go to a sanatorium near Lakatos. Once in the clinic, he planned to write to the *Neue Zürcher Zeitung* which

---

[6] 26.9.33, Motzkin to Wilfan. Nachlass Wilfan 1250, FC4407. Koblenz.
[7] E. Ammende, 'Zum Abschluss des 9. Europäischen Nationalitätenkongresses', *Revalsche Zeitung* 25 September 1933.

was accusing him of taking a *Reich* German line.[8] His health problems were not dealt with easily, however. In late December 1933 and in late January 1934, he was in a sanatorium in Baden taking a cure. When his secretary visited him, she recorded he was not feeling himself.[9] In November 1934, he was back in the sanatorium at Baden.[10] The crisis in the health of the congress, therefore, was echoed in a crisis in the health of its General Secretary.

### 3. Wider impacts

Events from 1933 rippled out from the congress. Ludvig Krabbe had attended the proceedings as an observer for the League of Nations.[11] He was clear that the forum had been hamstrung by the Jewish Question. Given that Hasselblatt had been working closely with the German Foreign Ministry, there had been no doubt that the congress would end up in an impossible position: either Germans or Jews would be forced to leave. Krabbe recognised the importance of the German groups for the organisation, but believed the Hungarians had no desire to be left as a cat's-paw for German interests.

Krabbe sensed the German government standing behind the German groups and the Polish government behind the Jews. Rosmarin, he said, was a Polish Jew and a member of the *Sejm*. Krabbe believed he had been tasked to create a resolution condemning Germany even if it meant the German groups would walk out. Meanwhile, Roth's statement was taken as supportive of the German state. No wonder Ammende approached Krabbe at one point saying, 'The work to which I have dedicated my life is broken.' He asked Krabbe to speak to Hasselblatt and Graebe, to ask them to be more conciliatory for fear of isolating Germany. Krabbe emphasised the extent of the bond between the German groups and the German state by observing it was only after a telephone conversation with Berlin that the German groups approved the general resolution on dissimilation and Kurtschinsky's resolution on anti-Semitism.

Apparently Hungarian representatives spoke with Krabbe too, maintaining that dissimilation by a state was unacceptable. Szüllö was particularly dissatisfied with the congress's principle that specific cases should not be discussed. The Jews had long played such an important role in congress affairs that their absence would leave German groups in such a predominant position that it might alienate those who remained. As Jakabffy

---

[8] 20.10.33, Ammende to Schiemann. Schiemann papers. Baltic Central Library, Riga.
[9] 27.12.33, Ammende to Wilfan, 29.12.33 Schwartz to Wilfan and 27.1.34 Ammende to Wilfan. Nachlass Wilfan 1250. FC4397. Koblenz.
[10] Correspondence between Ammende and Wilfan from late 1934, located in Nachlass Wilfan 1250. FC4397. Koblenz.
[11] Krabbe was a member of the Minorities Section. 22.9.33, Memorandum by Krabbe. 'Neuvieme Congrès des Nationalites Européennes Tenu a Berne du 16 au 19 Septembre 1933.' S338. Minorities Coniference. 4 / 6638 / 6638. LoN Archive, Geneva.

told Krabbe, 'We [Hungarians] don't want to prop up a German facade after the Jews depart.' At the end of the day, Krabbe concluded, the congress had only been saved by the extreme efforts of President Wilfan, and even then at the expense of serious ambiguity, 'sybilline' resolutions, votes taken against the better judgement of most of the delegates, and by leaving open the question of whether the Jews would ever return to the organisation. The unflattering report was sent to both the head of the League's Minorities Section, Azcárate, and its Secretary General. The only rider to be added here concerning Krabbe's criticism of the congress is that in another report he expressed the belief that the Jews would still return to participate in the 1934 congress.[12]

This was not the sort of publicity the congress needed in influential circles and Ammende tried to counter-act the bad press. Writing to Krabbe, he maintained that before the congress took place, even the Jews agreed dissimilation was valid.[13] The participants had not expressed an opinion about whether dissimilation was desirable, only that if it happened, it should do so in accordance with the congress's freedoms and principles. It was wrong, he said, to suggest that the organisation was in cahoots with the *Reich*. The *Journal des Nations*, for instance, had declared that he, Wilfan and Kurtschinsky were 'an instrument of German propaganda' and that 'in the future, independent public opinion will no longer be interested in the machinations of these gentlemen.' Ammende suggested that the congress's debacle had been caused because Margulies changed his mind over dissimilation just a few days before the event took place, leading the Jews to issue an ultimatum which contravened the basic tenets of the organisation by demanding the naming of a specific state and specific events. (Ammende made a similar point about Margulies in a letter to Professor Ruyssen. Margulies was said to have agreed dissimilation at the congress's July committee meeting, but subsequently changed his mind.)[14] Wilfan, Ammende said, had complete integrity and the German groups did not approve what was happening in Germany. In due course, Ammende represented this line in an article in *Revalsche Zeitung*, maintaining that *Journal des Nations* was backed by Polish-French interests which were attempting to use the Jewish issue as a lever to disrupt the solidarity of the congress.[15] By this point, however, Ammende's chances of influencing anyone at all in the League of Nations, never mind the Minorities Section, had become next to zero.[16]

---

[12] Reprt signed by Krabbe on 23.9.33. 'Neuvième Congres des Nationalites Européennes Tenu a Berne du 16 au 19 Septembre 1933.' R3932. Minorities. Congress of Organised National Groups in the States of Europe. Berne. September 1933. 4 / 6638 / 6638. LoN Archive, Geneva.

[13] 21.10.33, Ammende to Krabbe. Nachlass Wilfan 1250, FC4398. Koblenz.

[14] 11.11.33, Ammende to Ruyssen. Nachlass Wilfan 1250, FC4397. Koblenz.

[15] E. Ammende, 'Genf—Paris—Warschau. Wie es gemacht wird', *Revalsche Zeitung*, 23 October 1933.

[16] Many of these points were repeated in Ammende's letter to Ruyssen. 11.11.33, Ammende to Ruyssen. Nachlass Wilfan 1250, FC4397. Koblenz.

The seriousness of the situation was underlined two days later when Ammende wrote direct to Azcárate, head of the Minorities Section of the League.[17] He said it was 'grotesque' that people were complaining that the congress should address specific issues because in the past the very same people had said the exact opposite—a situation which they had termed 'objectivity'. Ammende requested that Azcárate publicise the truth about the congress in Geneva, such that it would be clear that criticisms of it were incorrect.

## 4. Caught out glossing the truth: Margulies's attack

Ammende knew the congress was in trouble after the 1933 meeting. He wrote to all its deputies, trying to explain what had happened.[18] Personally, he hadn't expected Otto Roth to make his declaration on Saturday morning. The statement had only been prepared in general terms by the German groups, and it was made all of a sudden and in such a way that its meaning was misunderstood. The main thing, Ammende maintained, was that dissimilation should only happen in such a way that the freedoms and rights of those affected were maintained (although he did not explain how the rights of those Jews who felt thoroughly German could ever be maintained through dissimilation). Equally he apologised that Kurtschinsky's declaration (condemning anti-Semitism) had not been prepared beforehand. In thoroughly unconvincing fashion, Ammende tried to maintain there were still grounds for solidarity between Germans and Jews. In fact, this concern to keep up the impression that the congress was determinedly attempting to do the right things in the face of difficult circumstances never left Ammende. Writing to Schiemann even in April 1934 he said that it was important the congress fight the 'false impression of capitulation before the totalitarian claims of states.'[19]

Despite everything, Ammende remained desperate at least to keep lines of communication open with Jewish groups. In early November 1933 he wrote to Schiemann noting that, following the death of Leo Motzkin, Wilfan was in touch with Zionist Jews in Belgrade. He believed Grünbaum (a Jew from Poland who had attended the congress) and Jakobsen (both Zionists) understood the situation well.[20] He asked Schiemann to contact Margulies too in order to build bridges. Meanwhile he, Ammende, was off to Berlin to talk to Graebe and Roth because Germany had just left the League of Nations and so a whole new situation had been created.

---

[17] 23.10.33. Ammende to Azcárate. R3932. Minorities. Congress of Organised National Groups in the States of Europe. Berne. September 1933. 4 / 6638 / 6638. LoN Archive, Geneva.
[18] 9.10.33, Ammende to the ENK representtaives. Schiemann Papers. Baltic Central Library, Riga.
[19] 4.4.34, Ammende to Schiemann. Schiemann Papers. Baltic Central Library, Riga.
[20] 9.11.33, Ammende to Schiemann. Schiemann Papers. Baltic Central Library, Riga.

Ammende was trying to sanitise things in his mind. In January 1934, in a letter written just before he went for his cure, Ammende contacted Wilfan complaining that the Jews were trying to represent Roth's statement as anti-Semitic when it was no such thing. He said the congress could not accept a refusal by Jewish representatives to sit down for discussions with their German counter-parts. He wanted Graebe to develop a dossier of documents outlining a boycott of German businesses in Poland—i.e. implying that it wasn't just Jews who were the subject of prejudice at the time. Nonetheless, he feared the Jews were planning a spectacular way to leave the Congress once and for all.

Ammende contacted directly some of the Jewish representatives with whom he had the greatest differences. He asked Margulies for understanding over what had happened. Nothing had been planned out in advance, he said. He hoped things could still be saved if the German groups made another declaration about rights and freedoms. He had drafted one himself and had sent it to Graebe for Roth and Hasselblatt to see. Ammende proposed Roth's first declaration had been a mistake. Only after everyone read his wording had it become clear it could be misinterpreted. There had been no intention to defend the *Reich*'s policy over the Jews and Roth's subsequent statement tried to put this right. Ammende wished the Jews had attended the congress because then they might have been able to table additional resolutions.[21] Also he wrote to Motzkin, stressing that the misunderstanding of Roth's words on the part of the Jews was damaging the congress and giving its opponents ammunition against it. He requested that nationally-minded Jews take the initiative and throw their weight behind the organisation. He recommended that a group of Jews be found at once in Germany to organise themselves as a national minority.[22]

Likewise, Wilfan contacted Motzkin with a view to setting up a meeting to defend himself against the bad publicity in the Jewish press.[23] Motzkin's reply, however, was lukewarm to say the least. Until there was a significant change in the situation, Jews could not co-operate with the congress, even if this caused them heavy hearts. Wilfan had been weak and they would only discuss matters with him when he had a concrete proposal.[24]

At the start of the New Year, Ammende was still trying to set up meetings with members of the Jewish groups, despite a lack of encouragement from the Jewish side.[25] In a particularly telling letter, just a few weeks beforehand, Margulies had already contacted Wilfan telling him the time was not ripe for a meeting between the two of them plus Schiemann and Ammende.[26] He made it plain the Jews considered themselves outside

---

[21] 6.10.33, Ammende to Margulies. A 126 / 636. Central Zionist Archives, Jerusalem.
[22] 9.10.33, Ammende to Motzkin. A 126 / 636. Central Zionist Archives, Jerusalem.
[23] 19.10.33, Wilfan to Motzkin. A 126 / 636. Central Zionist Archives, Jerusalem.
[24] 30.10.33, Motzkin to Wilfan. A 126 / 636. Central Zionist Archives, Jerusalem.
[25] 29.1.34, Ammende to Wilfan. Nachlass Wilfan 1250, FC4397. Koblenz.
[26] 1.1.34, Margulies to Wilfan. Nachlass Wilfan 1250, FC4406. Koblenz.

the congress and had no desire to participate in planning a new event. Margulies thought Ammende got his money from German sources and so he could not be his own man. Ammende had railroaded through his personal anti-Soviet agenda in the last meeting by virtue of his position of General Secretary. Margulies admitted that he too was anti-Soviet, but Ammende was acting as a 'paid tool of the Hitler-Rosenberg policy', which had nothing to do with the purpose of the congress. Margulies went on:

> He is a tool of NS world politics which, in the face of the rest of the world, wants to play the part of saviour of European culture in the face of Bolshevism; and, by this manoeuvre, he wants to divert attention from what is happening in Germany, what is happening to the Jews.

Of the need to solve the issues that came out of Bern by negotiation, Margulies said:

> ...I can only do that with people with whom I feel solidarity in terms of world view, in my attitude to human problems, to concrete political problems, and in whom I have trust.
> I do not have trust in Dr. Ammende.

Perhaps Margulies was on less firm ground when he complained about the Jews being defamed and ejected from 'the ranks of nations' to 'that place where the gypsies stand.' More worthy was the sentiment, 'It's not about nationality rights. It's about being human.' Margulies argued strongly that the minority movement had been held together by the principle of equality, but since German groups had singled out the Jews as a special problem, they could no longer sit alongside them. But was it just the Germans who were culpable? As Margulies put it:

> And now Herr Doctor, check your own declarations again to see if you have done it! In your own declarations!

Margulies closed by recognising that if the Jews left the nationality movement once and for all, it would be 'untenably compromised'.

## 5. Acrimony intensifies

This was a stinging attack on Ammende's character and, even though directed to Wilfan, drew a rather fatigued response from the man himself. Ammende told Margulies he was not using the famine in Ukraine to deflect attention from the Jewish Question in Germany, rather as a citizen of the former Russian Empire he had an interest in the matter, had lots of personal connections in the area affected, and had been promoting interest in famine as long ago as the 1920s. Perhaps trying to be dismissive, although also showing how hard it was for him to remain completely committed to the work of the congress, Ammende said he would be away from his office as General Secretary for three months on account of ill health. During this period he would be pursuing work associated with aid to Russia.[27]

Margulies, however, was not yet ready to let things go. In mid-February 1934 he launched a savage assault on Ammende personally. It was fine for Ammende to pursue the Russian agenda as a private individual, but as the General Secretary of the congress, he thought it outrageous:

> This is not a matter to do with your honour, it concerns your activity as General Secretary; it concerns the view that the role confers on you a number of obligations and rights, and militates against your political actions, against your political expediency, against your political tact.
>
> For instance, if you really were a Nazi, if you really were a propagator of Hitlerite ideas, from a human standpoint I'd have no right to prevent you doing that. You are a German, I am a Jew. What is right for a German, seen from the German standpoint, is his affair. As a Jew, since this party's programme is also directed against Jews, I would only have the right to draw your attention to the consequences for me, relating to your politics and my behaviour.
>
> In addition to this, however, I have the right and the duty [to intervene] if I believe, for instance, that the General Secretary of the Congress of Nationalities, to which I have belonged for many years, not only possesses this political view, but rather also represents [it], and indeed represents it in his activity as General Secretary.
>
> The accusation raised against you is that you, as General Secretary, have undertaken actions which must create the public impression that in this position you (1) are under the influence of Nazi ideology and (2) are pursuing Nazi world politics.

---

[27] 6.2.34, Ammende to Margulies. Nachlass Wilfan 1250, FC4406. Koblenz.

I say explicitly: this is the impression. In politics carried out in public, not only realities are important but appearances too. A responsible politician must also consider the appearances which result from his actions and which are associated with him. For public opinion does not have the possibility of grappling with all different kinds of proof. It seizes on rumour on appearance, and if it cannot be contradicted decisively, then appearance becomes reality in public opinion.[28]

Margulies had been hurt by what happened in September 1933. He told Ammende that for some time now people, such as Motzkin and Szwalbe had distrusted him, but he (Margulies) had always been loyal. Now, however, he was convinced Ammende did not understand the Jewish Question. He accused him of, 'Insincerity which must not be malicious, but which can no longer be unconscious.' Margulies could only think Ammende was in a hole he could not get out of.

Clearly exasperated, Margulies went on: could Ammende really not understand why the Jews did not trust him? He was supposed to be a General Secretary protecting the rights and principles of minorities, yet he was treating Jews as if human rights did not apply to them; he was denying their status. If Ammende could not understand such an obvious point, Margulies said they did not share any convictions. And Margulies's attack continued:

National Socialism is my opponent, because it is a sworn mortal enemy of the Jewish nation. But I have neither desire nor time to fight every individual war. Before I will consider the question of returning to the congress, I must know that I will not be dealing with people who deny me, who deny my nation equality among nations, treatment on the same legal foundation and human dignity.

For Margulies, at the end of the day, dissimilation had raised a matter of human rights not just nationality rights, and the consequences were inescapable.[29]

Ammende was slow to reply to this apposite, wounding communication. He explained it had taken so long because he had been in a sanatorium and had needed time before he could respond calmly.[30] He said all the accusations against him were based on false premises. His assistance

---

[28] 16.2.34, Margulies to Ammende. Nachlass Wilfan 1250, FC4397. Koblenz.
[29] At first sight at least, the UN's Universal Declaration of Human Rights seems to agree with Margulies's analysis. According to Article 15, 'No one shall be arbitrarily deprived of his nationality nor denied the right to change his nationality.' Whether 'nationality' meant the same to Margulies as it does to the UN is, however, another question.
[30] 3.4.34, Ammende to Margulies. Nachlass Wilfan 1250, FC4397. Koblenz.

for ethnic Germans in Soviet Russia suffering the effects of famine were in opposition to the foreign policy of Hitler's Germany which resisted all connections (even humanitarian ones) with that place. Was he dependent financially on Germany? Well, Ammende expressed pride at funding the congress from all manner of different sources. To the suggestion that he, as a private person, should fulfil the congress's business even if poorly paid, he became particularly irate: he worked for the congress night and day.

If there was a problem with Ammende's response, it was that he was 'protesting too much', that he was failing to recognise any grounds at all for the accusations levelled against him. In reply to any accusation of wrong-doing over the Jewish Question, he said simply, 'I must reject this accusation most decisively.' He said that time and again he personally had rejected Nazism's policy on the Jews. He maintained ethnic Germans were ready to support German Jews, but it was not at all clear whether the latter wanted to fight discrimination on the basis of nationality rights. He said it was unfortunate that they had not decided to wage a war based on this foundation, but it left him unable to intervene. Hence the situation involved a group of Germans being deprived of their rights, not of a national minority being deprived of its rights. Ammende said he was telling this to Margulies without bitterness.

### 6. Pointless communications

There were no grounds for rapprochement between Ammende and Margulies, so even though lines of communication between congress managers and Jewish groups remained open, there was precious little chance of the two coming together. Still, as early as 20 October 1933, Ammende wrote to Schiemann encouraging him to communicate with the Jews with a view to building bridges.[31] A few days later, Ammende added he wanted Schiemann to explain that Roth's first declaration at Bern was a mistake and the second was supposed to be a clarification. He requested Schiemann to persuade the Jews that the German minorities were not Hitler's tools.[32] Ammende also recommended Schiemann that he do more than talk to Margulies, whom he felt was something of an outsider. He recommended that Schiemann contact Motzkin.[33] Unfortunately, the congress's long-time collaborator Leo Motzkin had suffered a heart attack in early November.[34] The next December and January, Ammende was largely reduced to the position of a spectator as he spent time in a sanatorium trying to deal with his own health problems. By his own admission, these had been made worse by the recent stresses.[35]

---

[31] 20.10.33, Ammende to Schiemann. Schiemann papers. Baltic Central Library, Riga.
[32] 23.10.33, Ammende to Schiemann. Schiemann papers. Baltic Central Library, Riga.
[33] 23.10.33, Ammende to Schiemann. Schiemann Papers. Baltic Central Library, Riga.
[34] 9.11.33, Ammende to Schiemann. Schiemann papers. Baltic Central Library, Riga.
[35] 21.12.33, Ammende to Schiemann. Schiemann papers. Baltic Central Library, Riga.

In the background, things began to happen. Following a meeting of mid-November 1933, Margulies contacted Wilfan suggesting Jewish groups might consider returning to the congress if a declaration addressed the following: the Jews should be treated equally with all other national minorities and should have their civic and political equality guaranteed; the congress's committee should reject any attempt to defame or remove the rights of a minority on the grounds of race; and congress membership required certain standards of behaviour.[36] By December, Wilfan was drafting letters to the Jews, telling them it was in their interests to return to the congress. He wondered if he and Schiemann should meet Nurock (a Jewish representative from Latvia) and Margulies in January, perhaps in Vienna.[37]

Things did not progress quickly. In January 1934, Wilfan wrote to Margulies expressing condolences over the death of Motzkin and stating that the congress's managing committee had authorised discussions with leading Jews to explore how to move things forward.[38] Already Ammende had been in touch with Nathan Goldmann (who was stepping into Motzkin's shoes).[39] In February 1934, Wilfan told Schiemann he had been talking to influential Jews in Prague, including Goldmann and congress representatives Nurock, Rosmarin, Rotenstreich, Margulies and Farchy. Subsequently Goldmann said they were supportive of working out a new congress declaration and he suggested that, amongst others, Margulies get in touch with Wilfan and Schiemann to organise something.[40] Quickly Ammende jumped on reports from the Jewish press, specifically *Eastern Jewish News* (*Ostjüdische Zeitung*), saying the mission to Prague had been a success.[41] As the month progressed, Wilfan reported to Schiemann that the Jews in Prague were prepared to discuss re-joining the congress. Over at least the next month or so Wilfan and Schiemann discussed a possible new resolution addressing dissimilation.[42]

Already, at the end of January 1934, Ammende had written to Schiemann saying he had been talking to Jewish representatives in Geneva and they were calmer than in autumn. In particular, he had been communicating with Goldmann, a former resident of Berlin. Apparently Goldmann liked the idea of driving forward a discussion with Schiemann and Wilfan.[43] Ammende kept working away at the Jewish issue. He wrote to Wilfan making a series of suggestions about how best to engage with the

[36] Undated, Margulies to Wilfan. Schiemann Papers. Baltic Central Library, Riga.
[37] 21.12.33, Wilfan to Schiemann. Schiemann Papers. Baltic Central Library, Riga.
[38] 21.1.34, Wilfan to Margulies. Schiemann Papers. Baltic Central Library, Riga.
[39] 22.1.34, Wilfan to Schiemann. Schiemann Papers. Baltic Central Library, Riga.
[40] 20.2.34, Wilfan to Schiemann. Nachlass Wilfan 1250, FC4400. Koblenz.
[41] 20.2.34, Ammende to Schiemann. Schiemann Papers. Baltic Central Library, Riga.
[42] 20.2.34, Wilfan to Schiemann and 30.3.34, Wilfan to Schiemann. Nachlass Wilfan 1250, FC4400. Koblenz.
[43] 25.1.34, Ammende to Schiemann. Schiemann Papers. Baltic Central Library, Riga.

Jews.[44] Since they imputed anti-Semitism to some Germans, he recommended they identify which German representatives the Jews would sit down and talk to. If the Jews refused to sit down with some people and created a serious situation, then maybe the German groups would make counter-accusations over boycotts of ethnic German shops in Poland. He recommended that talks should be channelled through agents of the committee rather than through arbitrary members of any particular group. They had to refute Jewish accusations that events had been stage managed and he foresaw that perhaps the congress should clarify a number of resolutions. The Jews needed to understand their approach to the congress had been mistaken, but Ammende recommended that no excuse be given to make it easy for the Jews to stay away again—which he felt Jews from Poland were anxious to do, given the opportunity.

Ammende and those close to him (excepting probably Schiemann) never developed understanding for Jews who favoured assimilation. Hence in March 1934 Wilfan complained to Schiemann that in any declaration they could not use the word 'excluded' (*ausgegliedert*) to describe dissimilation because it annoyed Jews and neutrals, while adding they had not viewed dissimilation as 'not permitted' but it could be seen as something positive.[45] By this point, someone in Wilfan's position should have had a bit more insight than that. Although he recognised the thrust of the policy should be for the German Jews to be seen as a national minority rather than a sub-section of the majority population, the terms of his letter suggested he was fooling around with forms and phrases rather addressing matters of substance.

Discussion with Jewish groups plodded on. In May 1934, another letter from Wilfan to Schiemann suggested Jewish representatives were about to meet in Prague with a view to leaving the congress, and yet the exit never happened.[46] In a letter to Dr. Feinberg (based in Tel-Aviv) written in late 1934, Ammende still hoped that a group of German Jews would come forward demanding nationality rights. Only then would new possibilities be created for protecting the community.[47] Ammende was at least being consistent. Writing to Nathan Goldmann in October 1934, he had said a group coming forward like this within Germany was critically important since it could decide which would be the stronger in the future: assimilated or nationally-minded Jews.[48] Ammende tried to spell out his position clearly:

---

[44] 29.1.34, Ammende to Wilfan (Herr Doktor). Schiemann Papers. Baltic Central Library, Riga.

[45] 30.3.34, Wilfan to Schiemann. Schiemann Papers. Baltic Central Library, Riga.

[46] 11.5.34, Wilfan to Schiemann. Schiemann Papers. Baltic Central Library, Riga.

[47] 10.12.34, Ammende to Dr. N. Feinberg. A 306 / 113. Central Zionist Archives, Jerusalem.

[48] 8.10.34, Ammende to Dr. N. Goldmann. A 306 / 113. Central Zionist Archives, Jerusalem. Discussions between Schiemann and Goldmann were reported briefly in the Congress proceedings of 1935, see *Sitzungsbericht des Kongresses der organisierten nationalen Gruppen in den Staaten Europas. Genf, 2 bis 4 September 1935*. Vienna-Leipzig: Wilhelm Braumueller, 1936, p. 14.

> ... I would like the emphasise explicitly that I certainly take
> the position that genuinely assimilated elements among the
> Jews cannot be marginalised or separated further from the
> community of the majority nation.

He added that eventually, in order to solve the prevailing difficulties, the
whole of German Jewry should declare itself a nation.

Ammende confirmed this view repeatedly, although he did it with
particular clarity in a letter written in London and sent to his long-term
associate Werner Hasselblatt. To quote him:

> Things are much more difficult with the Jews: the longer
> things go on, the more they turn out to be assimilationists.
> Today it is clearer than last year that, from the Jewish side,
> it is not a fight for the rights of the Jewish nation in
> Germany, but concerns a category of Germans and so is a
> matter of the rights of part of the majority nation—in the
> eyes of the Jews anyway. That means, ultimately, that
> increasingly one turns away from the platform of the
> nationality congress—which has to act for the rights of the
> nationalities and not for elements of majority peoples.
> Incidentally, it is very interesting that the 'members of the
> German nation of Jewish religion' who arrive here [i.e.
> London] only possess one wish: to assimilate in England as
> quickly as possible. The majority do not think about
> protecting or fighting for the rights of their own
> nationality.[49]

He went on:

> ... the Jews take the view that their fight in Germany should
> not be about the rights of a national group, but as always
> about the equality of a part of the majority population—
> therefore about the rights of assimilated Jews and not about
> the members of minorities. We would do a favour to the
> Jews who really do experience a national sentiment if this
> factual situation was clarified. Personally, I am of the view
> that this fight conducted exclusively henceforth on the basis
> of the rights of assimilated Jews, as also about assimilation
> law, will end with an extraordinary debacle for the ideology
> of national Jewry if things don't change.

---

[49] 16.6.34, extract from a letter from Ammende to Hasselblatt. Schiemann Papers. Baltic Central
Library, Riga.

## 7. Conceptual naivety

It was easy to criticise Ammende for this view, as Margulies did. Equally it is possible to provide apologies for him: it was an early period in conceptualising minority rights; it was the pre-Holocaust era; if the Bernheim petition had led to a pause in persecution in Upper Silesia, maybe other German Jews should have tried to claim something similar; and perhaps a demand on the part of the whole of German Jewry for similar nationality rights would have led to the internationalisation of the Jewish Question in Germany. Yet the strategy of defining themselves as a national minority did not sit well with Germany's Jews, hence the strategy was impossible. Furthermore, the position adopted by Ammende and those around him, while offering potential benefits to Germany's Jews, also risked slipping into conformity with National Socialism's aims because it demanded that Germany's Jews define themselves as non-Germans. Hence both Ammende and Hasselblatt agreed with a speech given to the congress by Besednjak in 1935 which said the Jewish Question was not a minority issue, but concerned Jews laying claim to a dual identity—which was against the desire of the German nation. But by accepting the position of 'the German nation', in effect Ammende and Hasselblatt were accepting dissimilation.[50] On this basis, Ammende and Hasselblatt were due more criticism than understanding.

Nonetheless, certainly members of the congress experienced genuine problems integrating Europe's Jews into their understanding of the world. When Paul Schiemann discussed whether or not Europe's Jews constituted a nation, he found the conclusion less than clear cut. Traditionally, he thought, they had not been a nation in the European sense (since they did not share a single common language and were not attached to a single territory), but perhaps they were becoming one as a result of Zionism. Still, he implied, this was a work in progress.[51] Schiemann's position, incidentally, found some kind of echo in M.H. Boehm's work. As early as 1917, Boehm had observed a change within Jewry. In previous centuries, he said, Jews had lived as a nation within other nations, but now they were becoming a nation among other nations.[52] This was due to Zionism.

The congress had fundamental difficulties conceptualising how to deal with assimilated groups. So much of its work had been carried out

---

[50] S. Bamberger-Stemmann, *Der Europäische Nationalitätenkongreß 1925 bis 1938. Nationale Minderheiten zwischen Lobbyistentum und Grossmachtinteressen.* Marburg: Verlag Herder-Institut, 2000, pp. 286–7.
[51] P. Schiemann, 'Volksgemeinschaft und Staatsgemeinschaft', *Nation und Staat* v. 1, September 1927, pp. 29–30.
[52] M.H. Boehm, 'Emanzipation und Machtwille im modernen Judentum', *Der Jude.* 1917. Nachlass Boehm 1077 / 17. Federal Archive, Koblenz.

resisting attempts by states to assimilate national minorities, as happened in Italy over the Germans of South Tyrol, that its members struggled to understand the needs of people who chose to assimilate. Congress members shared a caste of mind exhibited by M.H. Boehm when he argued that assimilation involved denying one's essential character.[53]

To put this in context, we have to remember that at least some important Jewish members of the congress certainly shared difficulties in understanding how to deal with people who chose assimilation. This was shown by Leo Motkin's talk to the World Jewish Congress given in 1932 (see chapter 12). Comments like this shed a slightly different light on Ammende's contention that Germany's Jews should dissimilate and claim the rights due a national group.[54] Based on Motzkin's position declared at the World Jewish Congress, Ammende had some grounds for thinking his position was accepted by at least some of the Jews attending the European Congress of Nationalities. As, however, a former member of the Russian Empire, a place which had seen no small number of severe anti-Semitic outrages, really Ammende should have been more sensitive (although Motzkin had belonged to that Empire as well).

In the light of the charges laid out in Margulies's letter of February 1934 to Ammende, this was a crisis unlikely ever to be resolved. Hence, although at the end of November 1934 Ammende was telling Schiemann that thanks to his efforts and those of Wilfan relations with the Jews had improved over the last year,[55] nonetheless this was said in the context of Jewish representatives attending neither the 1934 congress nor managing committee meetings. Relations might have improved, but there were still fundamental differences between the two sides and no sign of them being bridged.

And yet the congress retained contact with the Jewish groups. At the opening of the congress in 1935 Wilfan even reported that contacts with Goldmann were being pursued (especially by Schiemann), but Goldmann felt the Jews would only return if Germany's Jews declared themselves a national minority. Wilfan went out of his way to emphasise that nothing on the side of the congress prevented a return.[56]

The situation was as tragic as its consequences were serious. If the minorities' own movement could not agree how best to deal with Germany's Jewish Question, if it could not provide a clear steer for governments, then what was its point? Whether Ammende and those around him suffered a genuine failure of understanding over this question, or whether he was being wilful, the outcome could only be damaging for the cause of minority rights.

---

[53] M.H. Boehm, 'Assimilation vom völkerpsychologischen Geschichtspunkt.' Nachlass Boehm 1077 / 16. Federal Archive, Koblenz.
[54] See, for instance, 13.7.33, Ammende to Wilfan. Nachlass Wilfan, Section 5, FC4397. Federal Archive, Koblenz.
[55] 28.11.34, Ammende to Schiemann. Schiemann papers. Baltic Central Library, Riga
[56] *Sitzungsbericht 1935*, p. 14.

The situation certainly did not enhance the moral authority of Ammende's organisation.

## 8. Conclusion: favourable German responses

Some German responses to the Jews removing themselves from the European Congress of Nationalities, while leaving the organisation still running, were particularly cynical. Just a few days after the 1933 congress ended, a report from the German consulate in Bern expressed quiet satisfaction at how events had proceeded. Motta, who made the meeting room available for the event, had worried there would be trouble even before the proceedings began, but that did not really happen because the Jews just stayed away.[57] In the event, the Jews did not wreck the congress and neither did Kurtschinsky's declaration about anti-Semitism turn everyone against Germany. The report quoted from *Neue Zürcher Zeitung* of 24 September 1933, saying Jewish demands had gone too far. Otto Junghann was similarly positive about the effect of the Jews staying away from the congress, since their absence left the German groups victors. That the Jews failed to return in 1934, made him similarly optimistic because they would not pose fresh difficulties.[58]

When the German representative to the League of Nations, Ambassador Keller, spoke to the League's Sixth Committee in October 1933, he emphasised a number of points that fitted well with the congress's position. He argued that Germany had always supported national minorities and would continue to do so.[59] Underlining the importance of international connections between different elements of the same nation, he rejected both Germanisation and assimilation. Apparently he felt no shame in proposing there were no grounds for internationalising the Jewish Question:

> In the first place, the Jews in Germany are neither a linguistic nor a national minority. In the first instance, it is a question about a demographic-political and social problem which has taken on a particular seriousness in the post-war period as a result of significant migration of Jews from Eastern Europe to the West.

He was presenting the Jewish Question as a domestic German affair.

Perhaps the conduct of the congress had been appreciated in Berlin. A few months after it was held, Graebe requested an extra RM 10,000 from the German Foreign Ministry. He argued that the congress had been

---

[57] 25.9.33, Deutsche Gesandtschaft, Bern. 'Tagung des IX Europäischen Nationalitäten Kongresses in Bern vom 16–19 September 1933.' R 60531. Political Archive of the Foreign Ministry, Berlin.

[58] Bamberger-Stemmann, *Der Europäische Nationalitätenkongreß 1925 bis 1938*, pp. 281–5.

[59] 'Das neue Deutschland und der Minoritätenschutz', *Revalsche Zeitung* 5 October 1933.

particularly successful in dealing with criticism aimed at the German state.[60] At about the same time, Ammende also wrote to the Foreign Ministry requesting the same amount of money on the grounds of some minorities (e.g. Catalans and Jews) failing to pay their subscriptions. He pointed out specifically that the congress had survived the Jewish crisis.[61] Soon thereafter RM 8,000 was transferred from the German Foreign Ministry for use by Ammende.[62]

It is indeed possible that something fundamental was changing in 1933 concerning the relationship between the congress and Berlin. It is quite possible that something had been sold out for a 'mess of pottage'. Money kept flowing from the Foreign Ministry, and even if there had been no formal agreement between Berlin and Ammende over particular ties that were supposed to accompany it, there didn't need to be.[63] There only needed to be a tacit understanding that, so long as the congress and its members kept saying and doing the 'right' things, then the organisation would be bankrolled—to some extent anyway.

True, some responses were more critical. In early 1934 there was talk of Hungarian minorities leaving the congress. A Hungarian ambassador, for instance, said congress proceedings were too theoretical and the organisation had proved ineffective, for instance failing to influence the League of Nations at all. The Hungarian source wondered if Ammende actually enjoyed as much support from the German Foreign Ministry as he claimed and questioned whether the organisation would keep going if a large group withdrew from it.[64]

In an even more depressing piece of writing, Max Hildebert Boehm used phrases such as 'pessimistic scepticism' in connection with the 1933 congress.[65] He said that increasingly it was becoming a victim of stronger political forces. Liberalism in Europe was falling prey to stronger political powers promoting authoritarianism about which it could do nothing. In effect, Boehm was articulating that the days of the European Congress of Nationalities were now strictly numbered. With Hitler in Berlin, effective minority rights in Europe were less of a possibility than ever.

---

[60] 21.2.34. Graebe to Foreign Ministry, Berlin. R 60531. Political Archive of the Foreign Ministry, Berlin.

[61] 19.2.34. Ammende to ?. R 60531. Political Archive of the Foreign Ministry, Berlin and 'Zur Frage der Teilnahme und des Beitrages am Europäischen Nationalitäten-Kongress. Regelung des Dezizites.' R 60531. Political Archive of the Foreign Ministry, Berlin.

[62] 14.3.34. Reich Foreign Minister. R 60531. Political Archive of the Foreign Ministry, Berlin.

[63] For example, 4.12.35, Gravenhorst to AA. R 60532. Political Archive of the Foreign Ministry, Berlin and 4.12.35 Ammende to AA. R 60532. Political Archive of the Foreign Ministry, Berlin.

[64] 17.4.34. Memorandum. R 60531. Political Archive of the Foreign Ministry, Berlin.

[65] M.H. Boehm, 'Der 10. Europäische Nationalitätenkongress.' R 60531. Political Archive of the Foreign Ministry, Berlin.

# Chapter Fourteen

## Fateful context

### 1. The mood of the 1930s

The congress's dire response to the Jewish Question in Germany occurred within a deteriorating wider context. Just like other newspapers across Europe, in October 1929 the Baltic German press carried extensive coverage of the collapse of the New York Stock Market.[1] Subsequently, European history took place against a background of profound economic uncertainty and memories of the same. Further stories followed about the failure of the League of Nations to deliver successful disarmament negotiations in Geneva, also of the Manchuria crisis.[2] Although the 1920s had not exactly been crisis-free for Europe—not least there had been the Vilnius, Corfu and Greco-Bulgarian crises—, nonetheless as the world headed into the 1930s, international affairs seemed in a worse state than ever. Post-war optimism was wearing thin as popular presses questioned whether the League had anything left to offer.[3]

The bleakness affected Ammende. By the start of 1932 he was writing about the poor treatment of national minorities in various situations, not least the persecution of Ukrainians in Galicia. He (like the Ukrainian representative to the congress Milena Rudnycka) was particularly depressed that petitions submitted by that group to the League had no impact on apparent Polish persecutions.[4] Reports were also circulating about breaches of Klaipèda's (Memel's) autonomous status, difficulties facing autonomous schooling in Latvia, problems over minority schooling in Poland and the closure of the Ministry for Minorities in Romania.[5] When, in October 1932, Germany's ambassador to Geneva, von Rosenberg, called for the improved treatment of minority issues by the League in terms of greater inclusion of minorities and more thorough investigation of complaints, Ammende was soon on hand to explain why the proposals were duly rejected by an 'anti-

---

[1] 'Katastrophe an der Neuyorker Börse. Kursverluste biz 20 Prozent', *Revaler Bote* 25 October 1929.

[2] For example,'Schluss der Abrüstungsverhandlungen', *Revalsche Zeitung* 10 December 1930 and 'Der mandschurische Konflikt vor dem Völkerbund', *Revalsche Zeitung* 7 October 1931.

[3] 'Der Niedergang des Völkerbundes', *Revalsche Zeitung* 25 October 1932.

[4] 16.2.32, Ammende to Therdenge. Schiemann Papers. Baltic Central Library, Riga, also *Sitzungsbericht des Kongresses der organisierten nationalen Gruppen in den Staaten Europas. Wien, 29. Juni bis 1. Juli 1932.* Wien-Leipzig: Wilhelm Braumüller, 1933, pp. 118–22.

[5] For example, see E. Ammende, 'Die "geheiligten Rechte" der Nationalitäten. Zum Genfer Ratsfiasko', *Revalsche Zeitung* 9 February 1932. Other articles in *Revalsche Zeitung* from this time include 'Der Staatsstreich in Memel', *Revalsche Zeitung* 8 February 1932, 'Ein Schlag gegen die Minoritätenschulen in Polen', *Revalsche Zeitung* 27 February 1932, 'Aufhebung des Minoritätenministeriums in Rumänien', *Revalsche Zeitung* 28 December 1932 and 'Neue Massenverhaftung von Ukrainern', *Revalsche Zeitung* 30 December 1932.

minority front' of Yugoslavia, Romania, Czechoslovakia, Poland and Greece.[6]

Ammende believed there needed to be 'moral disarmament' over the minority question, but he was not so clear about how the change could be enacted.[7] At this time he was aware of only one positive development: the Catalans were winning more autonomy within the Spanish state.[8] This was an event of such importance, he felt, that soon the Basques would follow and the idea of the unitary Spanish state would have to be reconceptualised in favour of something involving greater decentralisation.[9] Then, where the Catalans had led, he expected the Sudeten Germans and Ukrainians of Poland to follow. But articles and arguments like this were not the rule of the day. More typical was the tone set by an article written by Axel de Vries in which he argued that belief in the inevitable progress of Europe had been shaken deeply in recent times.[10]

Against this background of hopelessness, once Hitler was in power the Baltic German press kept reporting about changes being driven forward inside Nazi Germany, for example the 'co-ordination' of the *Länder* to create a more unified state.[11] When the Röhm Putsch was reported, drastic measures were said to have been necessary to deal with subversive elements which had suspicious foreign connections.[12] When an interview with Hitler was reported (originally carried out by Ward Price of the British *The Daily Mail*), the piece emphasised his peaceful intent.[13] This was notwithstanding Germany leaving the League of Nations' disarmament process (14 October) and the League itself (21 October 1933).[14] Already, however, *Revaler Bote* was arguing that a peaceful process of revising the post-war settlement would be necessary for the preservation of peace in Europe and, one way or another, would have to happen in Central and Eastern Europe especially.[15]

When the Baltic German community met to discuss its relationship to the new Germany, it had to be careful. A speech given by the chairman of the Baltic German Party in Estonia, *Rittmeister* von zur Mühlen, in late 1933 stressed the need to be loyal to Estonia, that there should be no political links

---

[6] 'Deutschland und der Minoritätenschutz. Eine Erklärung des Gesandten v. Rosenberg in Genf', *Revalsceh Zeitung* 6 October 1932 and E. Ammende, 'Der Kampf geht weiter.... Gegen die Anti-Minoritätenfront', *Revalsche Zeitung* 20 October 1932.
[7] E. Ammende, 'Moralische Abrüstung', *Revalsche Zeitung* 17 November 1932.
[8] E. Ammende, 'Die Mission des Spanischen Staates', *Revalsche Zeitung* 28 December 1931 and E. Ammende, 'Historische Umwälzungen', *Revalsche Zeitung* 22 September 1932.
[9] 'Spanien am Scheidewege', *Europäische Nationalitaeten-Korrespondenz*. Sondernummer 4 (1933) pp. 1–10. R 60531. Political Archive of the Foreign Ministry, Berlin.
[10] A. de Vries, 'Europäische Götterdämmerung', *Revalsche Zeitung* 18 July 1931.
[11] Dr. S., 'Ein Jahr nationalsozialistisches Deuschland. Die innerpolitische Entwicklung', *Revalsche Zeitung* 1 February 1934.
[12] 'Adolf Hitlers Säuberungsaktion', *Revalsche Zeitung* 2 July 1934.
[13] 'Ein Friedensinterview Hitlers', *Revalsche Zeitung* 6 August 1934.
[14] 'Das Lebensrecht der deutschen Nation', *Revalsche Zeitung* 23 October 1933.
[15] 'Wege zur Revision', *Revalsche Zeitung* 28 August 1933.

with Germany's National Socialist Party, and that these connections offered economic advantages. The Jewish Question was marginalised as a German domestic affair which did not affect Estonia's Germans directly, even though they recognised they might have to address their own 'blood-based purity and renewal' in due course.[16] But in the difficult, more threatening situation of the 1930s, precisely what kind of strategy should German minorities try to pursue on the international stage?

## 2. Germany out of the League

Von zur Mühlen had clear sympathies with the new Germany; but not all ethnic Germans were in his mould. As the consequences of Germany leaving the League of Nations began to sink in, with ethnic Germans once more lacking the voice of a sympathetic state in the Council of the League, at least some German minority presses began to discuss the situation. There were some calls for minorities to keep their faith in the League of Nations.[17] While an alternative might involve the Third *Reich* trying to assist minorities through bi-lateral treaties, these were recognised as imperfect because they would reflect the quality of relationship existing between Germany and any partner state.

Even with Germany outside the League, Ammende maintained some kind of effort to engage with and influence the organisation. Within weeks of Germany's departure, he wrote an unusually positive article which, amongst other things, noted that petitions could lead to helpful interactions between the different parties involved.[18] He had in mind a complaint about the ethnic German Cilli House in Yugoslavia; but Ammende was promoting a fresh agenda too. With Germany having departed the League, he proposed that the obligation fell to England and the neutral states to protect the rights of national minorities. He spelled out the enduring importance of national minorities:

> Without a solution to the European nationality problem, the implementation of border corrections based on consensus ... is unthinkable. The denial of the protection of national minorities means irredenta without end, increasing confrontations, indeed a development which ultimately must lead to war-like disputes between states and nations.

---

[16] 'Rede des Vorsitzenden der D-B Partei Rittmeister B. v.z. Mühlen-Eigstser', *Revalsche Zeitung* 27 November 1933.
[17] 27.8.35, 'Auslandsdeutsche Politik mit oder ohne Völkerbund', *Deutsche Presse* (Prague) R 60496. Political Archive of the Foreign Ministry, Berlin.
[18] E. Ammende, 'Die Lage in Genf zum Beginn des Jahres', *Revalsche Zeitung* 4 January 1934.

In another article written after Germany had left the League, Ammende continued to speak up for the petition system which previously he had criticised so roundly. Chauvinism, he said, would be much greater without such a system in place. He added that even if the League had its deficiencies, the world was better off for its existence.[19]

When the congress met in 1934, Ammende spoke positively of both the changes in minority procedures introduced at Madrid and the League's staff.[20] During a discussion about a Polish proposal for the universalisation of minority rights, he recognised openly the moral purpose of the organisation.[21] Following that congress, Ammende still wrote to Azcárate in the minority office of the League, telling him that Maspons and Wilfan were on the way to Geneva to hand over a record of the congress's proceedings to the President of the Council.[22] Yet the interface between congress and League remained unlikely to be productive. The following year, in 1935, Ammende, Hasselblatt, von Szüllö and Karl Frank (a German from Czechoslovakia) all visited Rosting in the Minorities Section. A minute of the meeting reported that the discussion was general and that the visitors did not have anything new to say.[23] A report by the League's observer at the congress that year was similarly dismissive.[24]

### 3. History of criticism

It was hardly surprising the League's officials did not really take these contacts seriously. There was too much of a history of contrary attitudes on the part of the congress. In 1932, Ammende had made it clear the League had failed to engage properly with minority issues (see chapter 9). Amongst other things, he argued that the Council was staffed by people who only followed the interests of their states not ethical principles. Milena Rudnycka (a Ukrainian from Poland) added to the list of dissatisfactions. She highlighted the extreme difficulty of a minority that lacked a co-national state in the League, since no one would fight for it.[25] Rotenstreich (a Jewish member of the *Sejm*) made a similar point when he said stateless minorities should be represented in the League somehow.[26]

---

[19] E. Ammende, 'Genf und die Nationalitäten', *Nation und Staat* 7 (1933–4) p. 81.
[20] *Sitzungsbericht des Kongresses der organisierten nationalen Gruppen in den Staaten Europas. Bern, 4 bis 6 September 1934.* Vienna-Leipzig: Wilhelm Braumüller, 1935, p. 23.
[21] Ibid, p. 58, although Ammende did also suggest the League was undergoing a moral crisis at the time.
[22] 6.9.34, Ammende to Rosting. R3932. Minorities. Congress of European Nationalities. 10th Congress, Berne, 4–6 Sept 1934. 4 / 13142 / 6638.
[23] 9.9.35. Minute by Rosting. R3932. Minorities. 11th Congress of European Nationalities, 2–4 Sept.1935, Geneva. 4 / 19664 / 6638.
[24] 7.9.35. Memo by Kremer for Rosting. R3932. Minorities. 11th Congress of European Nationalities, 2–4 Sept.1935, Geneva. 4 / 19664 / 6638.
[25] Ibid, pp. 119–21.
[26] Ibid, pp. 131–5.

League of Nations observer Ludwig Krabbe was on hand to witness the congress's 1932 proceedings. He noted how Ammende spoke out against the League in a violent tone. When Krabbe encountered Ammende afterwards, the latter greeted him with good humour, shouting 'Have I said something incorrect?' The League's man suggested that Ammende lacked 'tact' and 'understanding'. He recommended that the congress should meet in a way that was more open and frank. A report like this did the organisation little benefit because it was passed right up the League's organisation such that even Drummond commented that it was an 'excellent report' which he had read 'with greatest interest'.[27]

Even though the 1933 congress was dominated by dissimilation, delegates still found time to criticise the League. Professor Arthur von Balogh (a Hungarian from Romania) provided a ten point critique. He recommended, amongst other things, that the League's rapporteur on minority affairs should not come from outside Europe, that the committee investigating any petition should cross-check what it was told by a government with the petitioning minority, that solutions to petitions should be based on legal principles, that the Council should be less accommodating to governments, that the Council should ensure its decisions were implemented, and that all Council members (rather than just *ad hoc* committees) should address minority affairs.[28] It was a hard hitting critique which underlined the depth of division between League and minorities. Graebe added to the list of criticisms. He said the League could never achieve much so long as politics took precedence over justice, or 'power is given priority over what's right.'[29] He criticised the committees which investigated petitions for lacking the courage to put complaints on the order of the day for the whole Council, he proposed that only co-national states would ever stand up for a persecuted minority, and he recommended that the Council should forward more complaints to the Permanent Court at The Hague.[30]

True, the 1930s saw especially Poland start to press for the universalisation of the rights of national minorities. The initiative was launched in a speech given by Poland's Foreign Minister Beck to the League's Assembly on 13 September 1934, followed by a speech to the 6th Commission by Count Raczinski on 20 September.[31] Beck observed that the prevailing and unequal minority protection regime was entirely the product of chance political circumstances which followed the war and which had no principled justification. Raczinski proposed that, initially, 'universalisation' should be confined to Europe, but he was supported by at least

[27] 4.8.32. Azcarate to Secretary General. R2161. Minorities. 8th European Congress of Nationalities. Vienna, 29 June–1 July 1932. 4 / 37541 / 3817. League of Nations Library.
[28] *Sitzungsbericht des Kongresses der organisierten nationalen Gruppen in den Staaten Europas. Bern, 16. bis 19. September 1933.* Vienna-Leipzig: Wilhelm Braumüller. 1934, pp. 43–6.
[29] Ibid, p. 28.
[30] Ibid, pp. 52–3.
[31] 'Die Genfer Aussprache', *Nation und Staat* October 1934.

representatives from Yugoslavia and Iraq.[32] Unfortunately, Poland's recommendation most likely was not made for pure motives.

As Hans Otto Roth (a German from Romania) suggested to the European Congress of Nationalities in 1934, Poland wanted to use minority rights as a weapon against the Soviet Union which was set to join the League that September.[33] Engelbert Besednjak (a Slovene from Italy) agreed.[34] Poland was concerned that, once the USSR was a member of the League, the latter might try to unsettle Ukrainian and White Russian minorities in the east of Poland. By pressing for the universalisation of minority rights, Besednjak argued Poland was playing a cynical game. Its policy-makers knew that other states, not currently bound by minority agreements, would never agree to universalisation, so in the end Poland would declare itself no longer bound by minority provisions. Hence the League stood before a choice: the universalisation or collapse of minority protection.

It was ironic that this talk of universalisation was happening at a time when the minority protection system was being used less frequently than ever by minorities themselves. In 1931, 204 petitions were submitted to the League by minorities and 101 in 1932. In 1933 and 1934, however, the numbers fell to 57 and 68.[35] Talk, therefore, of making the system more robust risked missing the point. Apparently minorities themselves were looking for other ways to vent their grievances.

## 4. Hitler and the minority question

As commitment to the League's protection system faded, so Baltic Germans looked increasingly to Berlin. That the interests of a numerically small minority far from Germany's borders and those of an increasingly self-confident *Reich* government were not so easy to reconcile had to be obvious to any thinking person who read the Baltic German press. Hitler was quoted from a speech delivered at Nuremberg during the same party congress at which the Nuremberg Laws were promulgated:

> National Socialism is forced to be intolerant. It is not a question of whether intolerance is foreign to the German nation, it is a matter of whether it is useful to the German nation.[36]

---

[32] 'Minoritätenprobleme in Genf. Die Erklärungen in der Vollversammlung des Völkerbundes', *Nation und Staat* October 1934.

[33] *Sitzungsbericht 1934*, pp. 46–54.

[34] Ibid, pp. 39–44.

[35] J. Robinson, O. Karbach, M.M. Laserson, N. Robinson and M. Vichniak, *Were the Minorities Treaties a Failure?* New York: Antin Press, 1943, p. 128.

[36] 'Der Abschluss in Nürnberg', *Revalsche Zeitung* 17 September 1935.

The statement clearly contradicted points made by Ammende previously. Likewise, at least some ethnic Germans might have wondered what the majority peoples among whom they lived would make of such a world view.

In an article published a couple of days later, the *Revalsche Zeitung*'s editorial staff approved Hitler's statements on the Jewish Question and the fact that he had given it legislative form (i.e. the Nuremberg Laws). From now on, therefore, there would be less scope for the disorganised persecution of Germany's Jews. The paper even proposed a situation had been created where German Jews could develop their own system of cultural autonomy.[37] This was, of course, a cynical mis-stament of the situation 'on the ground' in Germany where, for instance, Jews were banned from using some swimming baths at the same time as 'Aryans' or even sitting on the same park benches.

### 5. The position of national minorities around Europe

How was the treatment of minorities across Europe developing at this time? Werner Hasselblatt suggested there was a bloodless civil war taking place across the continent, with a rise in the persecution of minorities by states.[38] Certainly during the 1930s, too many progressive steps achieved in the 1920s were reversed. In Latvia in 1932, for instance, moves were made to start rolling back language rights and minority schooling.[39] Within a year, reports were circulating, first, that Latvia's Education Minister Kehninsch was aiming to close minority middle schools and, later, that measures were to be introduced compelling Latvia's middle schools to teach in Latvian language.[40] In June 1934, following the Ulmanis coup, several Baltic German publications were banned, including *Baltische Monatshefte*.[41] A month later, the German school administration was dissolved and a number of key Baltic Germans lost their positions in the Education Ministry.[42] At the start of 1936, steps were taken by the Latvian Finance Minister to dissolve

---

[37] 'Reichstag in Nürnberg', *Revalsche Zeitung* 19 September 1935.

[38] W. Hasselblatt, 'Volkstumspolitik in der völkerrechtlichen Entwicklung', *Nation und Staat* March 1935. To Hasselblatt's mind, however, this persecution took the form of assimilation, so he applauded Hitler for being a statesman who rejected this strategy.

[39] 'Dr Schiemann fordert Recht. Das Sprachengesetz vom Parlament nicht angelehnt', *Revalsche Zeitung* 25 February 1932 and 'Russifizierung—Lettifizierung', *Revalsche Zeitung* 29 February 1932.

[40] 'Kehninsch will alle Minoritäten-Mittelschulen schliessen', *Revalsche Zeitung* 20 January 1933 and 'Zur Frage der Minoritätenschulen in Lettland', *Revalsche Zeitung* 31 January 1933.

[41] 'Die "Baltische Monatshefte" verboten', *Revalsche Zeitung* 13 June 1934. Other titles banned were *Deutsche Tageszeitung*, *Der Deutsche Bote* and *Unser Werk*.

[42] 'Der Verwaltung des deutschen Bildungswesen in Lettland zum Abschiede', *Revalsche Zeitung* 20 July 1934, also see 'Das deutsche Schulwesen Lettlands', *Revalsche Zeitung* 12 November 1935.

Riga's guilds, a step described by the Baltic German press as tantamount to the liquidation of 'German social and cultural' organisation.[43]

Measures were also taken against minority schools in Poland.[44] In addition, *Revalsche Zeitung* was soon reporting that the Lithuanian government was trying to increase its control over Klaipėda (Memel), a former area of the German Empire which had been guaranteed extensive autonomy under international agreements.[45] Kaunas's actions led the German government to protest.[46] In due course, the situation became so serious that Klaipėda was even identified as a risk to Europe's peace.[47] When Klaipėda's elected body was re-opened in November 1935 after a hiatus, its German fraction alleged persecution by Lithuanian authorities.[48] With the area situated adjacent to the borders of East Prussia, it was a difficult situation indeed.

Nor was this the end of it. In 1935 *Revalsche Zeitung* reported the arrest of four ethnic Germans in Eupen-Malmedy, Belgium. They were to have their Belgian citizenship removed for writing letters to German statesmen and trying to maintain a 'cultural bridge' to Germany.[49] The proceedings elicited a letter of complaint from Belgium's *heimattreue* Germans (i.e. they were loyal to Belgium) who expressed confusion over what was going on.[50]

The years following the Great Depression saw a rising tide of intolerance directed against national minorities in many locations across Central and Eastern Europe. The advent of a stridently nationalist government in Berlin did not help the situation of specifically German minorities. Hence, as early as April 1933 Axel de Vries was warning about a perceptible rise in Estonian nationalism and the possibility of attacks against the local German minority.[51] He specified that this hostility was at least partly in response to Nazism's rise in Germany and that the best course for Estonia's Germans was to act with complete loyalty to their homeland. De Vries's call re-iterated Carl Schirren's demand that Baltic Germans hold out (*Ausharren*). Cut-backs in the education budget had, for example, begun to threaten German educational provision in at least the small towns.[52] Over the summer of 1933, a number of German schools were struck off the list of

---

[43] 'Zur Auflösung der Rigaer Gilden', *Revalsche Zeitung* 8 January 1936
[44] 'Ein Schlag gegen die Minoritätenschulen in Polen', *Revalsche Zeitung* 27 February 1932.
[45] 'Deutschtum in Memel', *Revalsche Zeitung* 17 February 1934.
[46] 'Eine litauische Note an Deutschland zur Lage im Memelgebiet', *Revalsche Zeitung* 26 March 1934 and 'Zuspitzung der Memelfrage', *Revalsche Zeitung* 3 April 1935.
[47] 'Das Memelland als Gefahrenherd', *Revalsche Zeitung* 2 October 1935.
[48] 'Erste Sitzung des Memellandtags', *Revalsche Zeitung* 7 November 1935.
[49] 'Land und Leute gehoeren zusammen! Eindrücke vom Prozess gegen die vier Heimattreuen aus Eupen und Malmedy', *Revalsche Zeitung* 25 October 1935.
[50] 'Das Lütticher Fehlurteil', *Revalsche Zeitung* 29 October 1935.
[51] A. de Vries, 'Notwendige Klärung', *Revalsche Zeitung* 22 October 1933.
[52] 'Aus der Arbeit unserer Kulturverwaltung. Bericht des Vizpräsidenten Baron Wrangell vor dem Kulturrat', *Revalsche Zeitung* 28 March 1933.

public institutions, leading to all manner of fears being expressed by some Baltic Germans.[53] More moves to reform education, with an eye on economies, would follow in 1934.[54]

## 6. Nazi sympathies in Tallinn

Of course, how persuasive Estonia's Germans might find a call such as this was an open question. In a discussion of minority rights which followed the European Congress of Nationalities in 1933, an anonymous article carried by *Revalsche Zeitung* advocated rights for national minorities based on collective principles rather than individual ones.[55] Having noted that Germany's Jews had never regarded themselves as a national minority, the article specified that Estonia's existing cultural autonomy legislation was based on individual rights (attached to separate persons) rather than collective rights, since the Estonian constitution did not recognise the rights of whole national groups as such. The author proposed that Baltic Germans were more used to thinking in terms of collectivities and suggested that corporatist thinking (as existed in other European rightist regimes at the time) if applied to nationality might offer a suitable way forward in the achievement of nationality rights. This was a very conservative response to the challenges facing Estonia's Germans in 1933.

Too frequently, from January 1933 on, reporting in *Revalsche Zeitung* became cheer-leading for Hitler. For instance:

> All the clans and classes of the German nation are pulling
> together. It is the historical mission of National Socialism
> to bring to a good conclusion this work of unification based
> on the will of the nation.[56]

How could ethnic Germans remain unaffected by such a powerful mission? Soon enough the head of the German cultural council, Harry Koch, was echoing Nazi concerns which highlighted the need for Estonia's Germans to create their own national community (*Volksgemeinschaft*).[57] True, Baltic Germans (including Ammende) had used that word before it became associated with National Socialism, but once it was taken up by Hitler, it was hard to avoid some kind of association.

It was predictable, then, that the Nazi-sympathising Viktor von zur Mühlen took over the leadership of the Baltic German Party in November

---

[53] 'Abbau deutscher Schulen. Bedauerlicher Regierungsbeschluss in Sachen des deutschen Schulnetzes', *Revalsche Zeitung* 16 June 1933 and S.K., 'Ein schwerer Schlag', *Revalsche Zeitung* 22 June 1933.

[54] 'Zur Schulreform', *Revalsche Zeitung* 26 May 1934.

[55] 'Recht des Volkstums', *Revalsche Zeitung* 21 September 1933.

[56] H.N., 'Volksgemeinschaft', *Revalsche Zeitung* 10 October 1933.

[57] 'Die Tagung des Deutschen Kulturrats', *Revalsche Zeitung* 21 November 1933.

1933. The step was applauded as a natural development. Writing about the
event, Axel de Vries denied it was a result of deliberate co-ordination
orchestrated from Berlin, rather it was a manifestation of Estonia's Germans
looking at the state of Europe and drawing their own conclusions.[58] De Vries
commended the development:

> Estonia's German community is the first of German
> national groups in Europe to give itself a national political
> leadership.

De Vries argued that Estonia's Germans had been deeply influenced by the
renewal movement occurring in Germany and said this was now the only
possible ideological foundation for the community. On this basis he judged,
'We are standing at the beginning of a new epoch in the development of our
nation.' He believed there was 'a fresh and keen wind blowing through
Central Europe'.

Von zur Mühlen had been a member of the Baltic Regiment that
fought for independence against Bolshevik forces. In 1928–29 he had been
received by Hitler and was favourably impressed. By 1931–32 a Nazi impact
was becoming discernible among Estonia's Baltic Germans and in 1933 an
overtly pro-Nazi paper, *Der Aufstieg* (*The Ascent*) began appearing. The
paper carried articles such as 'Principles of the Baltic National Socialist
Movement in Estonia', 'The Jews' War', 'Adolf Hitler's Call to the German
Nation' and Adolf Hitler on 'Nation and Race'.[59]

When von zur Mühlen addressed the German cultural council as
chairman of the Baltic German Party in late November 1933 he side-stepped
the Jewish Question entirely while still managing to hint at a racial mission
for Baltic Germans:

> We regard the Jewish Question as a domestic affair of the
> German *Reich* which does not concern out nation directly.
> The question of keeping our blood pure and of renewing
> our nation must be given our earnest consideration.[60]

In this light, his declaration that there were only intellectual ties between
Estonia's Germans and Berlin was not very persuasive. No one should have
been too surprised, therefore when, in December 1933, the Estonian
parliament witnessed accusations directed against Nazi sympathies in the

[58] A. de Vries, 'Der Weg der Zukunft', *Revalsche Zeitung* 28 November 1933.
[59] 'Grundsätze der baltischen nationalsozialistischen Bewegung in Estland', *Der Aufstieg* 25 June
1933; 'Der Juden Krieg', *Der Aufstieg* 2 April 1933; Adolf Hitler, 'Volk und Rasse', *Der
Aufstieg* 16 April 1933 and 'Adolf Hitlers Aufruf an das deutsche Volk!' *Der Aufsteig* 22
October 1933. Estonian National Library, Tallinn.
[60] 'Rede des Vorsitzenden der D-B Partei Rittmeister B v.z. Mühlen-Eigstser.' *Revalsche Zeitung*
27 November 1933.

Baltic German Party and the cultural autonomy administration. The *Riigikogu* passed a series of resolutions declaring Nazism an anti-state movement, demanding revision of cultural autonomy, calling for the banning of Nazi publications, the expulsion of Nazi agents, and the cleansing of cultural autonomy organisations of Nazi sympathisers.[61] The Estonian government closed the German Club, where von zur Mühlen's group met, and banned *Der Aufstieg*. The German cultural council was suspended on the proviso that fresh elections would be held three months later.[62]

Baltic Germans were slow to understand the situation. In early January 1934, *Revalsche Zeitung* was complaining not only that ethnic Germans were being persecuted across Europe, but also that the Nazi movement was being caricatured. The article maintained it was quite possible to be loyal to both the German nation and the Estonian state.[63] A few days later it was reported that 30 Baltic Germans, including von zur Mühlen, were being investigated by the Estonian police.[64] Meanwhile, the Estonian state was suffering a crisis of its own. In November 1932, the Baltic German press was already reporting that Konstantin Päts—leader of the government—was demanding the right to issue emergency decrees for the sake of stability.[65] To maintain public order, on 11 August 1933 a state of emergency was declared which was scheduled to last until 1 January 1934. It authorised the closure of a number of organisations, including Estonia's Association of Young Socialists and the Legion for the Protection of the North.[66] Later, action would be taken against Estonia's organisation of Freedom Fighters too.[67]

Elements within Estonia's Baltic German community tried to put a brave face on things. Axel de Vries interpreted Estonia's 15 year period of democracy as over, yet he retained some optimism. The purpose of the state of emergency, he said, was to maintain a 'democratic dictatorship' in the face of a plausible fascist threat. He looked to the emergence of a new kind of authoritarian state which would take into account the territory's social and national diversity.[68] In effect, he was expecting the creation of a corporatist state able to accommodate the Baltic Germans in an updated system of

---

[61] 'Grosse Aussprache im Parlament über den Nationalsozialismus', *Revalsche Zeitung* 6.12.33
[62] J. v.Hehn, 'Zur Geschichte der deutschbaltischen nationalsozialistischen Bewegung in Estland', *Zeitschrift für Ostforschung* 26 (1977) 597–650, also 'Der Deutsche Kulturrar aufgelöst. Die Kulturverwaltung und die Kulturkuratorien arbeiten weiter. Neuwahlen des Kulturrats binnen 3 Monaten', *Revalsche Zeitung* 7 Dezember 1933.
[63] 'Das Ergebnis der von der politischen Polizei eingeleiteten Untersuchung in Sachen der nationalsozialistischen Gruppe in Estland', *Revalsche Zeitung* 4 January 1934.
[64] 'Das Ergebnis der von der politischen Polizei eingeleiteten Untersuchung in Sachen der nationalsozialistischen Gruppe in Estland', *Revalsche Zeitung* 4 January 1934.
[65] 'Die Regierung Päts. Die neue Regierung verlangt Dekterecht', *Revalsche Zeitung* 1 November 1932 and 'Das Ermächtigungsgesetz', *Revalsche Zeitung* 8 November 1932.
[66] 'Verhängung des Ausnahmezustandes ueber ganz Estland', *Revalsche Zeitung* 12 August 1933.
[67] 'Regierungsmassnahmen gegen die Freiheitskämpfer', revalsche zeitung, 13 March 1934 and 'Bisher 500 Personen verhaftet', Revalsche Zeitung 14 March 1934.
[68] A. de Vries, 'An der Schwelle einer neuen Zeit', *Revalsche Zeitung* 19 August 1933.

cultural autonomy. De Vries discussed this on a number of occasions.[69] Most
notable, however, was an article written in March 1933 in which he identified
Bolshevism as a deadly enemy of Baltic peoples and a mortal threat to Baltic
Germandom. In this context, he emphasised the influence of men from the
Baltic, such as Alfred Rosenberg and Otto von Kursell, on Nazism's anti-
Bolshevik direction. He maintained that Balts traditionally amalgamated the
values of 'community' (*Gemeinschaft*) and corporation, to conceptualise the
person as intimately rooted in his or her society. Hence he demanded that
Baltic Germans uphold the idea of corporatism.[70] In due course, de Vries also
spoke warmly of Päts's new government, expressing the hope that he could
adapt it to the new form of state without difficulty.[71]

In the midst of the difficulties, Estonia received a new constitution
which came into force on 24 January 1934. *Revalsche Zeitung* interpreted its
main difference in terms of a separation of powers, with the president being
elected by the people directly and so independent of parliament.[72] Yet the
Baltic German community did not remain unscathed. In addition to the
suspension of the cultural council and the banning of Nazi publications, for a
period, publication of *Revalsche Zeitung* was suspended in 1934 because of
the use of the word 'Reval' (i.e. the old German name for Tallinn) in its title.
For a while it changed its name to *Estländische Zeitung* before resuming its
former name on 1 April 1935.[73] There was a tendency for the Estonian press,
however, to be a little too zealous in its readiness to interpret German get-
togethers as proto-Nazi events. For instance a celebration of President von
Hindenburg's birthday in 1933 was viewed in this way.[74] The next year, the
electoral propaganda issued by the Estonian Association for Renewal and the
Centre Party were criticised for containing anti-German slogans.[75]

With the state of emergency over, new elections to the German
cultural council were held late in January 1934. The results were predictable,
with Harry Koch, Axel de Vries and Viktor von zur Mühlen all re-elected.[76]
Eventually Baron Wrangell was elected president.[77] Some of the council's
issues remained the same too, with commentators recommending that the
social order of the Baltic Germans be re-structured to create a more inclusive
national community. There were complaints that the cultural organisation
remained overly dominated by traditional élites, such as the *Literaten*

---

[69] A. de Vries, 'Schlussfolgerungen', *Revalsche Zeitung* 14 July 1934 and A. de Vries,
'Schwankender Boden', *Revalsche Zeitung* 31 July 1934.
[70] A. de Vries, 'Zwischen Ost und West', *Revalsche Zeitung* 11 March 1933.
[71] A. de Vries, 'Die neue Regierung', *Revalsche Zeitung* 23 October 1933.
[72] 'Der Geist den neuen estlaendischen Verfassung', *Revalsche Zeitung* 22 January 1934, also A.
de Vries, 'Um die Zukunft', *Revalsche Zeitung* 24 January 1934.
[73] 'Revalsche Zeitung', *Revalsche Zeitung* 1 April 1935.
[74] 'Deutschefeindlichkeit um jeden Preis', *Revalsche Zeitung* 7 Oct 1933.
[75] 'Übel Deuschenhetze', *Revalsche Zeitung* 13 January 1934.
[76] 'Ordentlicher Delegiertentag der D-B Partei', *Revalsche Zeitung* 29 January 1934; 'Das
Ergebnis der Kulturratswahlen', Revalsche Zeitung 7 March 1934.
[77] 'Erste Tagung des IV Deutschen Kulturrats', *Revalsche Zeitung* 7 April 1934.

(intellectuals) and people with white collar jobs, while those in trades and manual occupations were marginalised.[78] The position both reflected fears that the birth rate was declining among Baltic Germans such that they faced eventual extinction and also the desire to create a national community along the lines of that under construction—in theory—in Hitler's Germany.[79]

The re-formed cultural council did seem to have a future in Estonia. Later in 1934, for instance, *Nation und Staat* reported on the rise of authoritarianism in the country in the context of comments made by Interior Minister Einbund.[80] The tenor of the reporting was that, in the new authoritarian mood of the time (and in line with the broadly corporatist ideas held by Baltic Germans already), cultural autonomy organisations would have to be bound firmly into the structure of the state and contribute to the common good. By implication, the article was arguing that minorities still had a role to play in Estonia—although a further article in the same publication recognised austerity measures had forced the re-organisation of German middle schools, that some ethnic Germans had been fired by Tallinn council, that some Germans had been put on trial for belonging to subversive organisations and that steps were being taken against the use of ethnic German place names and the use of German language in business. Nonetheless, the reporting implied Estonia's German community would survive such setbacks and understood that the situation facing Latvia's ethnic Germans was more serious.[81]

The public statements by the head of the cultural council, Baron Wrangell, were stoic. When the Estonian state was given a new legislative basis in January 1935, he interpreted the changes as in line with a corporatist project likely to include minorities in the state in a new way. He observed that the new Education Minister understood the importance of tuition in the mother tongue.[82] He maintained that while increased authoritarianism could impinge on cultural self-administration, nonetheless many people in the government—including the state president—were speaking up for cultural autonomy. Hence Wrangell made a clear declaration that Estonia's Germans were rooted firmly in their homeland (*Heimat*).[83] In an article celebrating ten years of cultural autonomy, Axel de Vries was even more positive. He maintained that a system of cultural self-administration could fit well with an authoritarian state and hoped, in line with statements made by the state president, that one day the German minority would be represented in the

---

[78] S. Klau, 'Nationale Lebensfrage', *Revalsche Zeitung* 11 May 1934.

[79] 'Zum Kampf gegen den Geburtenrückgang', *Revalsche Zeitung* 8 May 1934. Among Germans, the birth rate in Estonia was 19.3 per thousand as against 25.7 in Germany and 40.3 in Romania.

[80] 'Estland', *Nation und Staat*, November 1934, pp. 105 ff.

[81] 'Ein Jahr des Gegenangriffs', *Nation und Staat*, January 1935.

[82] 'Das Deutschtum und der Neuaufbau des Staats', *Revalsche Zeitung* 1 April 1935.

[83] W. Baron Wrangell, President of the German Culture Administration, 'Vom Wesen der Kulturautonomie', *Revalsche Zeitung* 12 October 1935.

national parliament through the system of cultural self-administration.[84] By
the start of 1936, de Vries assumed this would be the main way the German
minority would be able to wield influence in the Estonian state.[85]

### 7. Rise of the Sudeten Germans

Estonia's Germans were determined to weather a difficult period. Yet, as they
were working hard to survive, other minorities were becoming more
ambitious. Some, in fact, were increasingly determined no longer to represent
themselves as minorities, but as nationalities sharing their home state with
other nationalities.[86] Ammende spoke about this at the congress's meeting in
1934.[87] One significant group that epitomised this attitude most clearly, the
aspiration to be a partner in the state rather than a minority, was the Sudeten
German community. In 1933–34 the Baltic German press was describing
Sudeten Germans as persecuted, impoverished and occupying a place in
society radically different to the equal one outlined to them by
Czechoslovakia's founding fathers.[88] During the same period, *Nation und
Staat* published an article describing a war of nerves occurring between the
German National Socialist Workers' Party and the Czech state.[89] In 1935,
however, there was a sea change as Konrad Henlein's Sudeten German Party
captured the bulk of the ethnic German vote in May's elections and secured
44 seats in the Czech parliament. Henlein was quoted as believing the age of
nation states was past, that henceforth nationalities had to live side by side in
full equality.[90] Soon he was making demands such as German language
education for all ethnic German children.[91]

These developments could not pass without discussion. According
to Ammende, the electoral result disproved Beneš's claim there was no
Sudeten German issue and underlined that a large national group with a
coherent settlement pattern had to be allowed its cultural and administrative

---

[84] A. de Vries, 'Zehn Jahre Deutsche Kulturselbstverwaltung', *Revalsche Zeitung* 16 November
1935.
[85] A. de Vries, 'Klare Sicht,' *Revalsche Zeitung* 2 January 1936.
[86] A similar idea of claiming equality with other national groups inhabiting the same state
certainly helped inspire the change of name for the ethnic Germans Association of German
Minorities in Europe to the Association of German National Groups in Europe which happened
in 1929 (see chapter 9, section 4).
[87] *Sitzungsbericht 1934*, 1935,
[88] Bohemicus, 'Die sudetendeutsche Tragödie', *Revalsche Zeitung* 6 November 1933,
'Furchtbares Kinderelend in Sudetenland', *Revalsche Zeitung* 9 February 1934 and Dr W.W.,
'15 Jahre Verdrängungspolitik. Eine Verlustbilanz des Sudetendeutschtums', *Nation und Staat*
March 1934.
[89] 'Eine Kundgebung der sudetendeutschen Nationalsozialisten', *Nation und Staat*, July-August
1933
[90] 'Gewaltiger Erfolg der Sudetendeutschen Partei', *Revalsche Zeitung* 20 May 1935 and 'Die
Mission Konrad Henleins', *Revalsche Zeitung* 28 June 1935.
[91] 'Kulturgemeinschaft aller Deutschen. Henlein: Das Sudetendeutschtum verurteilt den
unwürdigen Seelensang der Entnationalisierung', *Revalsche Zeitung* 2 March 1936.

rights.[92] It was a startling rejection of the Czech state's policy of trying to break up the cohesion of the German minority through the settlement of Czech railway workers and other officials in ethnic German areas, also of the marginalisation of minorities from key areas of public life (such as the Justice Ministry). Elsewhere he commented that if 3.5 million Sudeten Germans could not press for equality within their state, what hope could there be for smaller groups that were culturally and nationally weaker?[93]

The growing organisation and assertiveness of the Sudeten German community had international consequences. For example, in 1933 the ethnic Germans elected to the key posts in the Association of German National Groups in Europe were Graebe (Poland), Roth (Romania) and Hasselblatt (Estonia), but this staffing changed after the Czech elections of 1935.[94] That September, 100 ethnic German representatives (including ones from the Soviet Union) turned up for a meeting of the Association held in the Sudeten German town then known as Gablonz but now Jablonec nad Nisou. Apparently Werner Hasselblatt had recommended to the German Foreign Ministry that such a location was now desirable.[95] The meeting was opened by the chairman of the Sudeten German Party, Karl-Heinz Frank, and a new chair of the Association was elected—Max Richter who was also from Czechoslovakia. In fact, the Association's managing committee became packed with Sudeten Germans, including Rutha, Frank-Eger and Kundt. The German diplomatic report of the meeting noted that the leadership of the Association had been placed in the hands of Sudeten Germans, and the Sudeten German Party was particularly well-represented by them.[96] Naturally the meeting was accompanied by the customary declarations that minorities were completely loyal to the states in which they lived and an appropriate telegram was sent to Masaryk, the President of Czechoslovakia.[97] Ammende attended this meeting too, but his contribution was not really appreciated.[98] He was criticised for failing to understand the history of loyal work the Sudeten Germans had achieved in the Czechoslovak state.[99]

---

[92] E. Ammende, 'Der Kampf um die Nationalitätenrechte und der tschechoslowakische Staat', *Revalsche Zeitung* 8 July 1935.

[93] E. Ammende, 'Der Kampf um die Nationalitätenrechte und der tschechoslowakische Staat', *Nation und Staat*, June 1935, p. 560.

[94] 'Eine Kundgebung der sudetendeutschen Nationalsozialisten', *Nation und Staat*, July-August 1933

[95] 'Der Europäische Nationalitätenkongress', R 60495. Political Archive of the Foreign Ministry, Berlin.

[96] 3.9.35. Deutsche Gesandtschaft, Prague. R 60496. Political Archive of the Foreign Ministry, Berlin.

[97] 'Volkstreue und Staatstreue', Deutsche diplomatisch-politische Korrespondenz, 30.8.35. R 60496. Political Archive of the Foreign Ministry, Berlin.

[98] 'Jahrestagung des Verbandes der deutschen Volksgruppen in Europa', *Nation und Staat*, October 1935.

[99] 'Zur Tagung der deutschen Volksgruppen in Gablonz', *Deutsche Landpost* 4.9.35. R 60496. Political Archive of the Foreign Ministry, Berlin.

The changes had consequences for the European Congress of Nationalities. By 1934 Schiemann was ill and marginalised, while older and (relatively speaking) more moderate ethnic German figures such as Steinheil and (from the Sudetenland) Medinger were dead. There had, therefore, been a further changing of the guard in the ranks of the ethnic German minority movement.[100] Against this background, Sudeten German representatives turned up at the 1935 congress in significant numbers, bringing with them the hopes of a large, coherent community settled right on the borders of the Third *Reich*. Their perspectives were not the same as those of smaller, more far flung minorities. Their heightened engagement with the congress has been interpreted as a turning point after which the organisation became a tool for Nazi agitation and foreign policy.[101] Whether or not this is exactly correct (because, and despite statements from Berlin to the contrary, Germany's influence among ethnic Germans, including within the congress, had been rising since before 1933), the group did impart a new confidence to proceedings.[102] Subsequently commentators suggested the Sudeten Germans at least saw themselves as a future ruling élite.[103]

In 1935, therefore, the Sudeten Germans and their politics became increasingly influential in the Association and congress alike. The influence in the latter, of course, was magnified all the more given that funding to the congress was still funnelled through the Association; but this did not mean everything would run harmoniously in the ethnic German camp. Reporting in the Christian democratic press in Prague following the Jablonec meeting was critical of the attitude of the NSDAP's leadership in Berlin, which it blamed for putting in jeopardy the claims to independent lives of ethnic German communities. The reports suggested ethnic Germans should take responsibility for their own existences and do their best to maintain connections with the League of Nations. Some ethnic Germans at least still felt they needed to remain independent from the politics of Berlin.[104] There was still a contest within the group for hearts and minds.

---

[100] *Sitzungsbericht des Kongresses der organisierten nationalen Gruppen in den Staaten Europas. Genf, 2 bis 4 September 1935.* Vienna-Leipzig: Wilhelm Braumüller, 1936, p.16.

[101] S. Bamberger-Stemmann, *Der Europäische Nationalitätenkongreß 1925 bis 1938. Nationale Minderheiten zwischen Lobbyistentum und Grossmachtinteressen.* Marburg: Verlag Herder-Institut, 2000, p. 272.

[102] For statements that there was no intention to 'co-ordinate' ethnic German organisations, see, for example A. de Vries, 'Grundsatzliche Klärung', *Revalsche Zeitung* 26 May 1934. Later, for a statement that the movement of ethnic Germans does not work for the Reich also see Friedrich Carl Badendieck, 'Ergebnis der VDA Tagung. Frieden im Geiste der Volkstumstreue', *Revalsche Zeitung* 18 June 1935. For a statement by Gauleiter Burckel that Nazism oculd not be transplanted beyond Germany's borders, see 'Aufgaben des Auslanddeutschtums', *Revalsche Zeitung* 10 October 1935.

[103] Ibid.

[104] 28.8.35. Deutsche Gesandtschaft, Prague. R 60496. Political Archive of the Foreign Ministry, Berlin.

## 8. International context

By late 1935, the atmosphere surrounding nationality issues was deteriorating even compared to what it had been in 1933. The situation was not helped by growing international disillusionment over the League of Nations. As one early commentator put it, the 'failure' of the organisation became associated with 'the disintegration of the moral foundations of international order.'[105]

The League had not been able to check Japanese aggression in Manchuria and censure had only led the country to leave the organisation. Initially the Baltic German press had been optimistic about the League's disarmament project, but by March 1935 Germany was re-introducing conscription.[106] The Abyssinia crisis made things worse. Events in Africa were broadcast across the pages of *Revalsche Zeitung*. It was noted, for instance, that Latvia and Estonia both agreed to participate in sanctions against Italy.[107] Reports pulled no punches, noting that if the Hoare-Laval initiative was accepted, Mussolini would become the most powerful man in Europe and the League would have become a vehicle for imperialism.[108]

By the end of December 1935, *Revalsche Zeitung* was reporting the impending collapse of collective security.[109] At the same time, worries were beginning to circulate in the Baltic arena about the formation of power blocs. De Vries began to worry that the trend could pull the Baltic States into a conflict. So, for example, he hypothesised that a Franco-Russian axis could lead to a demand for Russian troops to pass through Baltic territories, perhaps as part of an operation carried out under the League's auspices.[110] Correspondingly, de Vries stated openly that it was impossible for the Baltic States to put all their trust in the League of Nations, particularly if they aimed to stay neutral in the event of a conflict. Speculatively, he suggested neutrality might require a treaty between the Soviet Union, Germany and Poland under the guarantee of Britain, plus perhaps France and Italy. De Vries also recognised that Estonia and Latvia faced the security challenge posed by Lithuanian-Polish relations. It was not impossible that one day Lithuania and Poland might go to war. Such an event could easily drag in Latvia and Estonia.[111] Articles like this exemplified a new phase of pessimism, even fatalism, in international relations.

---

[105] I.L. Claude, *National Minorities. An International Problem.* New York: Greenwood, 1955, p. 46.
[106] 'Neugestaltung Europas?' *Revalsche Zeitung* 27 April 1932.
[107] 'Baltische Neutralitätspolitik', *Revalsche Zeitung* 19 November 1935.
[108] 'Die heikle Lage des Völkerbundes. Mussolini wird der mächtigste Mann Europas', *Revalsche Zeitung* 12 December 1935.
[109] 'Der Bruch im Kollektivsystem', *Revalsche Zeitung* 28 December 1935.
[110] A. de Vries, 'Aussenpolitischen Gefahren', *Revalsche Zeitung* 27 April 1935.
[111] A. de Vries, 'Baltische Assenpolitik', *Revalsche Zeitung* 4 May 1935.

In this context, de Vries even cited Adolf Hitler in an essay about European security.[112] The *Reich* Chancellor's speech to the *Reichstag* of early March 1936 sounded the death knell of the Versailles order once and for all. De Vries's suggestion that this would be the start of a period of stabilisation for Europe was, of course, unrealistic: within days the Rhineland was re-militarised. In this context, what could the League of Nations do to help anyone, never mind national minorities?[113] This was recognised by Josip Wilfan at the congress in 1936. By this point, statesmen and average citizens alike felt they had more important things to worry about other than the rights of national minorities.[114]

## 9. Arrival of the Soviet Union

The politics of the League of Nations was transformed not only by the departure of Germany from its structures, but also by the arrival of the Soviet Union in September 1934. This development was widely regarded by the national minority movement, certainly as represented in the European Congress of Nationalities, as a disaster. At the congress held in September 1934, Ukrainian representative Milena Rudnycka made an intervention described by the German Foreign Ministry observer as 'particularly emotional'.[115] It was not untypical for Ukrainian speeches to have much in common with German interests, typically being oriented against either Poland or the USSR, and this was no exception. She argued that the entry of the Soviet Union into the League of Nations compromised the other members of the organisation and was insulting to them since the Soviet Union's politics very simply amounted to a 'crass denial and violation of the League's principles'.[116] Perhaps Ammende was even more outspoken, emphasising the Soviet Union's nationality policies contradicted the principles recognised by the League. In fact, the Soviet Union represented a 'fundamental negation' of 'all the rights of minorities as we represent them'.[117] So now the precedent was set that states could sit in the League while openly oppressing their minorities.[118] To quote one of Ammende's interventions:

> If one ... accepts a new member, of whom it is known that
> for a year and a half it has been pursuing a policy of

[112] A. de Vries, 'Europäische Sicherheit I', *Revalsche Zeitung* 9 March 1936.
[113] 'Ein permanentes Minderheitenkomitee der Weltverbände?' *Nation und Staat*, April 1936, p. 525.
[114] *Sitzungsbericht des Kongresses der organisierten nationalen Gruppen in den Staaten Europas. Genf, 16 bis 17 September 1936.* Vienna-Leipzig: Wilhelm Braumüller, 1937, p. 47.
[115] 'Der X Europäische Nationalitätenkongress. Die Ergebnisse.' R 60531. Political Archive of the Foreign Ministry, Berlin.
[116] *Sitzungsbericht 1934*, pp. 77–9.
[117] Ibid, p. 80.
[118] Ibid, pp. 81–2.

exterminating national minorities, without an undertaking being agreed that this policy be changed, and if such a member will be sitting in the Committee of Three the very next day in order to guarantee the rights of minorities, then the general validity of minority rights is being undermined and weakened.[119]

Ammende and many of his fellow congress participants were outraged by the entry of the Soviet Union into the League. He had undertaken several trips, for example to the USA, Canada and Ireland, agitating against the development. Now, however, the congress was left to rage impotently. In the context of the times, the organisation was beginning to look more than a little futile.

## 10. Life after the Jews

The 10th anniversary meeting of the European Congress of Nationalities, held in 1934, was a time for stock-taking. In a reflection sent to the German Foreign Ministry, Ammende observed the organisation had been established during the Locarno period—a time of optimism.[120] Things, however, had changed:

Today we have to establish that healthy national spirit has given way only to boundless chauvinism. Lack of tolerance towards nationalities has reached a new high point. Even in states that previously were held nationally tolerant, no longer is the least understanding on display for the rights and individuality of the nationalities.

Increasingly voices were heard stating that if minority rights were not universalised, then no individual state should be bound by them. In other words, the rising new mood of the age was threatening to destroy all of the work to create a legal foundation for minority rights which had been achieved since the end of the war. Yet Ammende declared that national minorities would fight on for their rights because, in an ethnographically mixed continent, their ultimate concern was for the peace of Europe. The observer from the German Foreign Ministry picked up on this point especially.[121]

Ammende still relied on money from Germany to keep his initiative on the road. Following the 1934 congress, he wrote to the Foreign Ministry

---

[119] Ibid, p. 60.
[120] E. Ammende, '10 Jahre europäische Nationalitätenbewegung. Kampf in entscheidender Stund.' R 60531. Political Archive of the Foreign Ministry, Berlin.
[121] 'Der X Europäische Nationalitätenkongress. Die Ergebnisse.' R 60531. Political Archive of the Foreign Ministry, Berlin.

suggesting, rather wishfully, that the Jewish press was moving towards the congress again and stating that *Nationalitäten-Korrespondenz* (*Nationality Correspondence*) was influencing public opinion over minority affairs.[122] In due course a subsidy of RM 4,000 was paid to support it, while a similar sum followed to support the congress.[123] The funding tie between Ammende and Berlin was just too fundamental to be severed—by Ammende anyway—and he rarely missed an opportunity to request money. On one occasion, he cited anti-Soviet activity in Geneva, Vienna and London as grounds for support.[124] In 1935, the year the Sudeten Germans arrived at the congress in force, more money flowed for Ammende's publication (RM 4,000) and to support the congress (RM 8,000 and RM 6,000).[125] By early 1936, Hasselblatt was estimating that Berlin was subsidising the congress (directly and through the Association of German National Groups in Europe) to the tune of about RM 20,000 per year. Even so, it was still said to be in deficit by RM 8,000 for 1935.[126] In other words, without assistance from Berlin probably there would have been no European Congress of Nationalities.

After 1933 especially, Berlin's money can only have come with significant strings attached, but nonetheless we have to be careful about how to interpret this. For example, Ammende was such a dedicated anti-Communist that he would have criticised the Soviet Union even without this financial support. Also, despite Hitler's shadow in the background, speakers at the congress still managed to make valid points. At the 1935 congress, for instance, Szüllö denounced their age as one of hypocrisy. No matter what laws were agreed for the protection of minorities, their application was subverted by national administrations.[127] Lorenz Karall (a Croat from Austria), reminded everyone it was only the democratic world that had enabled national minorities to come together. He added that the position of minorities in authoritarian states was particularly precarious, with the exercise of their rights entirely dependent on the discretion of the power-holder.[128]

With an eye on bigger pictures in politics, L. Makaruschka (a Ukrainian from Poland) and Karall blamed Bolshevism for damaging

---

[122] 9.10.34, Ammende to Geheimrat. R 60531. Political Archive of the Foreign Ministry, Berlin.
[123] 7 November 1934. Memorandum by Roediger of the Foreign Ministry, Berlin. (Sent to Hasselblatt, of the Verband.) R 60531. Political Archive of the Foreign Ministry, Berlin; 21.5.35. Ammende to AA, Dept IV. R 60531. Political Archive of the Foreign Ministry, Berlin.
[124] 15.2.35. Ammende to Geheimrat. R 60531. Political Archive of the Foreign Ministry, Berlin.
[125] 22.3.35. Ammende to AA Sec IV. R 60531. Political Archive of the Foreign Ministry, Berlin; 22 March 1935. Ammende to AA, Section IV. R 60531. Political Archive of the Foreign Ministry, Berlin; 23.8.35. Hofrat Pollow and Roediger to Verband. R 60531. Political Archive of the Foreign Ministry, Berlin; 4.12.35, Gravenhorst to AA. R 60532. Political Archive of the Foreign Ministry, Berlin; 4.12.35 Ammende to AA. R 60532. Political Archive of the Foreign Ministry, Berlin.
[126] 20.2.36. Hasselblatt to AA. R 60496. Political Archive of the Foreign Ministry, Berlin.
[127] *Sitzungsbericht 1935*, p. 26.
[128] Ibid, pp. 46–8.

Europe's political system. Makaruschka maintained that Bolshevik propaganda methods had infected European democratic practises, while the very existence of the Soviet Union was stimulating non-Communist states to re-think how to protect themselves—leading to authoritarianism. Karall proposed that the Soviet Communist state provided a model on which fascist dictatorships drew.[129] (How that comment could have played out in Berlin was anybody's guess.)

And if officials in Berlin were perplexed by Karall's words in 1935, they would have been even more challenged by those of Josip Wilfan a year later. He criticised thinking of national cultures in terms of hierarchies, with some cultures being superior, with a richer history and holding greater significance. He advocated equality among nations.[130]

Although by 1934–36, the European Congress of Nationalities clearly was 'damaged goods', still it retained a final few vestiges of significance. When it met in Bern in September 1934, Jean Kremer was observer for the League. With proceedings finished, Wilfan and Ammende went to visit *Bundesrat* Motta and members of the League's committee were received by Eduard Beneš in Geneva.[131] The congress had also been attended by a Jewish observed (Motzkin's press secretary), who (to Ammende's mind) was 'extraordinarily happy' with the proceedings.[132] Generally the members of the congress present showed a united front.[133] Hence there was still something plausible in Ammende's contention that, for all its weaknesses, the congress retained some kind of significance as a tool for influencing public opinion.[134]

Interesting debates continued to occur in the congress. With Germany out of the League and that organisation declining in status, Hasselblatt and Ammende discussed whether bilateral treaties could provide an adequate foundation for effective minority protection. Hasselblatt felt that such a system would not deal with complaints properly, since a state could only take action against a neighbour if the prevailing constellation of political powers in the international arena was favourable. While Ammende recognised that common interests between neighbours would provide an incentive to make bilateral minority agreements work, he also recognised that all bilaterals might not include the same terms and so some groups might be more favoured than others.[135] In 1935 Ammende also addressed the congress on the use of mother tongue place names. This was notable because it was the same year that *Revalsche Zeitung* had had to change its name temporarily

---

[129] Ibid.
[130] *Sitzungsbericht 1936.*
[131] *Sitzungsbericht 1934*, introduction.
[132] 6.9.34, Ammende to Schiemann. Schiemann Papers. Baltic Central Library, Riga.
[133] 'Nationalitäten-Kongress 1934.' Geneva, 15 Sept. 1934. R 60531. Political Archive of the Foreign Ministry, Berlin.
[134] 9.10.34, Ammende to Geheimrat. R 60531. Political Archive of the Foreign Ministry, Berlin.
[135] *Sitzungsbericht 1934*, pp. 62–71 and 75–6.

because the use of the old German name for Tallinn (i.e. 'Reval') was no longer acceptable to the Estonian government. Ammende almost expressed surprise that the issue of native language place names was more important than they had previously thought. It was wrapped up with the very feeling of being rooted in the soil on which you lived (*Bodenständigkeit*).[136]

## 11. Minority rights in authoritarian states?

One of the more unusual strands of discussion held by the congress was whether minority rights—as products of a democratic age—could flourish under authoritarian systems. Some, such as Max Hildebert Boehm, had begun to question whether, as a product of a democratic age, the congress itself could survive if democracy did not.[137] When the topic was tackled, the points made by speakers, of course, could be applied to both Soviet and fascist states. Besednjak questioned directly whether the fate of minorities was concomitant with that of democracy.[138] He maintained (rather hopefully) that although the minority movement had grown up in a democratic context, it was not simply a component of democracy: it had an independent existence. He went so far as to suggest that in some cases (for example, the Slovenes of Carinthia and Croats of Burgenland), the advent of authoritarianism had led to improvements for minorities. All authoritarian states, he said, were not like Italy. They did not necessarily want to impose a single national culture throughout their territory. Some, he said (citing Nazi Germany) rejected assimilation. Deliberately identifying the Jewish Question as a topic outside the realm of congress interests, Besednjak argued that minorities could indeed demand their rights in authoritarian systems and presented a declaration stating the congress was aligned with no specific political regime but would work with any given system.

An interesting discussion followed in which representatives showed genuine disagreement. Of course there had long been elements of the minority movement more firmly attached to ideas of nationhood than democracy. Likewise, speakers at the congress had shown themselves capable of regarding democracy critically. In 1932, Prof. Kartaschoff argued that 'chauvinism' rooted in democracy was particularly difficult to combat.[139] In 1935, there was criticism of what minorities could achieve in democracies. Karall argued that the rights of minorities had been virtually cancelled out in Poland. By contrast, high hopes were expressed for authoritarianism. Johann Starc (a Slovene from Austria) proposed the position of minorities could be improved more easily under such systems—at least if government was

---

[136] *Sitzungsbericht 1935*, pp. 55–8.
[137] M.H. Boehm, 'Der 10. Europäische Nationalitätenkongress.' R 60531. Political Archive of the Foreign Ministry, Berlin.
[138] *Sitzungsbericht 1935*, pp. 33–8.
[139] *Sitzungsbericht des Kongresses der organisierten nationalen Gruppen in den Staaten Europas. Wien, 29. Juni bis 1. Juli 1932.* Wien-Leipzig: Wilhelm Braumüller. 1933, p. 86.

underpinned by ethical foundations and Christian values. He proposed that an authoritarian system had the potential to be more thoroughly moral than a democracy and looked to such a state constructing corporatist institutions permitting the representation of minority interests. Dionisios Strelitzky (a Hungarian from Yugoslavia), made a similar recommendation, but was perhaps more realistic. He expressed more fully the threats that authoritarianism could present for national minorities. He recognised that the spaces available in public life for them could be reduced drastically and that they might not be able to challenge such developments.

In the context of this discussion, Makaruschka displayed the limits of correspondence between his national group and the German state. Certainly he made a variety of points a die-hard Nazi would have applauded. For instance, he felt Europe was experiencing a mood of immorality generated by the Treaty of Versailles and coupled with the existence of the Bolshevik state. Nonetheless he added that Bolshevism's methods could only be fought effectively in states in which democracy was anchored deeply. Makaruschka stated clearly that his group opposed the authoritarian state as a phenomenon that was regressive rather than progressive.[140] His scepticism was echoed by Leo von Déak (a Hungarian from Yugoslavia) who pointed out that while, in theory, you could have minority rights in an authoritarian state, in practise censorship made them meaningless.[141]

## 12. Conclusion

Although discussion of authoritarianism was interesting, there was no disguising its defensiveness. Delegates seemed to be choosing between the lesser of two evils—which system marginalised their interests less severely: democracy or authoritarianism? So if the congress had been construed at least in part as a lobby group, by 1934–5 there was no disguising how close to a dead end it was. Its members recognised that the League of Nations could barely respond to their needs and felt they faced irrelevance in either mass democracy (which could be subject to popular nationalism) or authoritarianism (which would not necessarily permit their representation and could promote assimilation).

Moreover, no matter how ethnic Germans tried to interpret the implications of National Socialism, they could not disguise from themselves the fundamental conflict between the Nazi state and many of their own ambitions, particularly for cultural autonomy. Worse, their position in their home state was only made worse by the suspicions generated as a result of Nazism's growth, influence and impending threat.

In this respect, the story of those driving the congress was a sad one. Bamberger-Stemmann assesses them not as Nazis, but as the kind of

---

[140] Ibid, pp. 38–50.
[141] Ibid, p. 27.

bourgeois people to whom Nazism held out promises. She suggests that, without Nazism in the world, the organisation could have become a stable organ representing Europe's nationalities. Unfortunately, the vulnerabilities of the congress and its leaders ensured it missed the opportunity to become a genuine 'instrument of peace and international understanding'.[142]

Bamberger-Stemmann is also correct that the Allied Powers played a part in pushing the national minorities towards Hitler. They failed to incorporate adequately national minorities into the structure and functioning of post-war Europe.[143] Hence the groups were given inadequate mechanisms for representation in the League of Nations, deficient international protection and, in fact, were viewed more as a hindrance to the smooth running of international affairs than a necessary component of a successful continent. As it stood after the First World War, therefore, the international system facing national minorities was not modern, democratic, principled and open. At best it was more pragmatic, although with time it came to appear to the minorities themselves exclusionary and increasingly threatening. With the international system failing to respond to the minorities' concerns decisively, increasingly they were pushed into liaison with a co-national state (or in the case of stateless minorities, such as Ukrainians, any state that offered support). This position, however, made it all but impossible for them to play the role of purely independent forces at the international level.

Yet even with all of this said, it would be naive to maintain that all of Europe's national minorities were simply the victims of a derelict international system. Some of their number were too ready to capitalise on the nationalistic possibilities which that same deficient system made available.

---

[142] Bamberger-Stemmann, *Der Europäische Nationalitätenkongreß 1925 bis 1938,* p. 395.
[143] Ibid, p. 396.

*Chapter Fifteen*

## At Stalin's throat

### 1. Re-direction

From the moment the Jewish groups absented themselves from the congress, Ammende must have known the organisation had lost its credibility. As the Sudeten Germans engaged increasingly with the Association of German National Groups in Europe and then the European Congress of Nationalities, it must also have been plain that the intellectual ground associated with the minority movement was shifting. The demands of national groups a few thousand strong, sometimes thinly dispersed among host populations and located a long distance from Germany's borders were never likely to match those of a group numbered in millions, settled relatively cohesively and living in close proximity to the borders of the *Reich*. As the years progressed from 1933, it was clear the game had changed.

But Ammende was not a person to sit on the sidelines watching things happen without him. His energy required a purchase somewhere, and so increasingly he switched focus from Europe's national minorities to the possibilities associated with the Soviet Union. Some opponents were scathing about this. Hence in early 1934 Margulies alleged Ammende's interest in the Ukrainian famine of the 1930s was a ploy to distract attention from the Jewish Question in Germany.[1] But even if Ammende recognised an instrumental value in the famine, there is no denying that his interest in Ukraine and the Soviet Union was long-standing. It is also true that Ammende was content to accept support from the Third *Reich*. In 1934 the German Foreign Ministry backed his visit the USA where he publicised the need for humanitarian intervention in Ukraine.[2] Ammende's connections with individuals based in Berlin, such as Karl Loesch of the German Association for the Protection of Germandom in Border Areas and Abroad, raised suspicions in the Austrian Chancellor's office that perhaps Ammende was some kind of agent for Hitler.[3] Ammende, then, even if he was not a card-carrying Nazi, was dabbling in the Third *Reich*.

### 2. Reporting on the Soviet Union

The Baltic German presses were fascinated consistently by the Soviet Union. Narrating crisis after crisis, short-coming after short-coming, there was a sub-

[1] 6.2.34, Ammende to Margulies. Nachlass Wilfan 1250, FC4406. Federal Archive, Koblenz.
[2] S. Bamberger-Stemmann, *Der Europäische Nationalitätenkongreß 1925 bis 1938. Nationale Minderheiten zwischen Lobbyistentum und Grossmachtinteressen*. Marburg: Verlag Herder-Institut, 2000, pp. 321 and 330.
[3] Ibid, p. 263.

text of expectation that the Communist empire would soon collapse. Yet there was more to the reporting than *Schadenfreude*; there was awareness that people with whom there had once been a shared citizenship were suffering. This sensation became particularly apparent when those in misery were fellow ethnic Germans—likewise, although to a lesser extent, members of another nationality with links to western Europe—and seems to have involved a genuine humanitarian quality. Since famine had been a particular problem in the early 1920s, so it remained of special interest into the 1930s and was reflected in the pages of *Revaler Bote*, later *Revalsche Zeitung*.

In 1929 that newspaper was reporting a hunger crisis in Siberia affecting perhaps 10,000 German farmers. Calls for charitable assistance were issued by the German Red Cross and *Brüder in Not* (Brothers in Crisis).[4] Reports followed about the persecution of ethnic German refugees by Soviet authorities, successful attempts by President Hindenburg and the German government to assist them and, ultimately, their transportation to German ports.[5] Articles published in 1930 continued to give a shocking image of conditions in rural Russia. There was a sad letter from a Mennonite family.[6] There was a story of an Estonian farmer fleeing westwards because life in the East was unbearable, also of general refugee movements of farmers across the borders into Latvia and Poland.[7] In time, reports emerged of hunger revolts in the Caucasus.[8] And supplementing all these stories, there were reports of Stalin's collectivisation of agriculture, including early talk of annihilation of the kulaks.[9]

Ammende's interest in German communities in Russia went right back to his time as a student. There is also a suggestion that in 1917 he participated in a congress of the Empire's national minorities.[10] It was natural, therefore, that as fresh stories of crisis seeped out of the region, Ammende began interpreting them. Mistreatment of ethnic Germans during the First World War, he said, had caused many to wonder whether to remain

---

[4] 'Brüder in Not!' *Revaler Bote* 13 November 1929.

[5] 'Die deutsche Rgierung schreitet ein', *Revaler Bote* 15 November 1929. 'Der Leidensweg der Kolonisten', *Revaler Bote* 19 November 1929. 'Helft den deutschen Kolonisten!' *Revaler Bote* 20 November 1929. 'Das deutsche Leid', *Revaler Bote* 20 November 1929. 'Keine Pässe! Das Elend der deutschen Kolonisten', *Revaler Bote* 21 November 1929. 'Hilfsaktion der deutschen Regierung', *Revaler Bote* 23 November 1929. 'Weitere Zwangsverschickung deutscher Bauern', Revaler Bote 25 November 1929. 'Endlich doch Auswanderungserlaubnis?', *Revaler Bote* 26 November 1929. 'Was die Kolonisten erzählen. Der erste Seetransport in Swinemünde', *Revaler Bote* 3 December 1929.

[6] 'Trostloser Brief aus Russland. Entsetzliche Lage der deutschen Kolonisten', *Revaler Bote* 15 January 1930.

[7] 'Die Not in Russland', *Revaler Bote* 10 February 1930. 'Bauerntragödie. Massenflucht aus Sowjetrussland', *Revaler Bote* 11 March 1930.

[8] 'Die Unruhen in Südrussland. Hungerrevolten—Russische Flüchtlinge in Persien', *Revaler Bote* 17 June 1930.

[9] 'Stalin entwickelt seine Agrartheorie. Ohne Struvel auf zur völligen Kollektivierung!' *Revalter Bote* 3 January 1930. 'Die Vernichtung der Kulaken geht weiter', *Revaler Bote* 28 March 1930.

[10] A. de Vries, 'Dr Ewald Ammende', *Revalsche Zeitung* 15 April 1936.

in Russia.[11] Most believed they were a 'community of fate' and were prepared to stay. Unfortunately their situation worsened as a result of most Germans sympathising with anti-Bolshevik groups during the Russian civil war and persecution followed. Things worsened further due to the famine of 1923. The advent of Stalinism, however, had made a dire situation worse again. Although some ethnic Germans (also called 'colonists' in much of the contemporary documentation) had been permitted to leave the Soviet Union, Ammende maintained this would not be repeated. Hence about a million ethnic Germans were facing a dangerous future.

Even at this point, citing reports from German 'colonists' in Russia about food shortages, Ammende warned about the possible repeat of the famine of 1922–3 (see chapters 1 and 2). He argued that international intervention for humanitarian ends was becoming unavoidable:

> The problem of Russia has once again reached a point where it is no longer a question of experiments carried out by the Communist powerbrokers and their effects, but rather concerns the existence and life of numerous people. Becoming involved is not only a matter of rights but, more important still, belongs to the duties of civilised humanity.

Ammende returned to the theme seven months later, this time criticising the German government.[12] Since 1929, he said, it had been clear Germans in Russia needed protection but Berlin refused to address the issue. The German government was reacting to Russia's crisis as if it were a purely domestic affair. This, he said, was too simple. Given that the German nation constituted a coherent cultural community, it was impossible for the main body to look on while co-nationals died or were brutalised. Again, Ammende had particularly harsh words for Stalinism and collectivisation. For people who had moved historically from the West to colonise Russian lands, collectivisation implied they should be 'psychologically and spiritually broken'. They were to be deprived of 'family life, religion and customs'. The policy amounted to an attack on a whole way of life. The German nation could not remain passive while ethnic brothers were enslaved by the Soviet system. He proposed that these people ought to be offered transportation elsewhere and called for a *Reichstag* investigation into the whole affair.

In 1932, however, news began to break that something really major was happening that affected the Soviet Union's ethnic Germans. At the start of June, it was reported that farmers were streaming into Odessa in search of bread. They were from newly collectivised areas and the paper judged: 'Ukraine, Russia's richest and most well-fed land, is suffering a severe

---

[11] E. Ammende, 'Soll das Russlanddeutschtum untergehen?' *Revaler Bote* 2 January 1930.
[12] E. Ammende, 'Zum Untergang des Russland-Deutschtums', *Revalsche Zeitung* 7 August 1930.

famine.'[13] Things remained quiet until, at the start of September, de Vries reported that the Soviet government was adopting emergency measures in the face of a famine that could affect as many as 20 million people. The author commented that it was all the same to Moscow if several million starved on account of their impending policies.[14]

By January 1933, the prediction was coming true as *Pravda* warned about the dangers of famine owing to passive resistance on the part of farmers refusing to bring in the harvest.[15] In response, Molotov and Stalin authorised special measures to ensure as much grain as possible was collected.[16] By April, *Revalsche Zeitung* was reporting that only 33% of the expected harvest had been supplied in Ukraine, with just 8.5% collected around Odessa and 2.4% in Moldova. A letter allegedly from an official in Ukraine said the original farming class had been 'robbed, deported and shot', only to be replaced by an artificial agricultural proletariat that knew nothing about what it was doing. Hence, food shortages had started in February and dead horses could be seen in the streets.[17]

Stories often were based on letters originating within the Soviet Union warning of famine.[18] Reports flowed describing a degenerating situation. One detailed the death of a Protestant churchman from the Volga German community.[19] At the start of July, the Baltic German press highlighted high food prices in Russia and forecast agricultural collapse across the key grain areas of Ukraine, the Volga, the North Caucasus and Siberia. Stories leaked out via especially Protestant press services telling of villages losing a third of their population and up to a million ethnic Germans living in the area threatened by the consequences of idiotic Soviet agricultural policies. By way of response to the crisis, *Brüder in Not* was planning a major assistance project.[20] According to Ammende, it was responding to letters from Germans in the areas affected by hunger and comprised an alliance of Red Cross and church organisations.[21]

Days later, stories became significantly more alarming. 10 million people already were starving and 100,000 Germans had died. Plague was abroad in Siberia and cannibalism was frequent. It was alleged that ethnic Germans had been affected most severely by the rise of Bolshevism with its desire to root out national difference and to dispossess small farmers. 70,000

[13] 'Hunger in der Ukraine', *Revalsche Zeitung* 1 June 1932.

[14] A. de Vries, 'Das Hungergespenst', *Revalsche Zeitung* 10 September 1932.

[15] 'Hungersnot in Russland', *Revalsche Zeitung* 10 January 1933.

[16] 'Zwei neue Dekrete Stalins', *Revalsche Zeitung* 24 January 1933.

[17] C. von Kügelgen, 'Hungernde Ssowjet-Ukraine', *Revalsche Zeitung* 19 April 1933.

[18] 'Notschreie aus Russland. Die Hungersnot in der SSSR', *Revalsche Zeitung* 13 June 1933.

[19] J. Schlenning, 'Ein Märtrer für Volkstum und Glauben. Dem Gedächnis Nathanael Heptner, des Propstes der Wolgadeutschen', *Revalsche Zeitung* 9 June 1933.

[20] C. von Kügelgen, 'Brüder in Not. Hilferufe aus dem Lande des Hungertodes', *Revalsche Zeitung* 1 July 1933.

[21] E. Ammende, 'Die russische Hungerkatastrophe', *Europäische Nationalitäten-Korrespondenz* 4 (1933) pp.1-10. R 60531. Political Archive of the Foreign Ministry, Berlin.

German kulaks were languishing in concentration camps. This was 'a robber economy' (*Raubwirtschaft*) which had lasted 15 years and which could cause the death of up to 20 million people in the near future.[22] At the same time, Soviet authorities were requisitioning increasing amounts of grain from farming communities.[23] By mid-August, *Revalsche Zeitung* was discussing traumatising images from Ukraine reproduced in Nazi mouthpiece *Völkischer Beobachter*. Hunger had seized a land that once fed half of Europe.[24]

Travel to Soviet Ukraine was not easy in summer 1933, not least on account of bans preventing journalists journeying outside of Moscow, but still information appeared to be flowing from various sources.[25] Occasional foreign press correspondents penetrated the famine area to relay harrowing tales. For example, Gareth Jones published in *The Daily Standard* and *The Daily Express* early that year.[26] Gradually diplomatic reporting reflected concern over what was happening behind Stalin's frontiers. Hence a specialist report circulated by the German Foreign Ministry said clearly that crisis was not caused by natural causes, but by the brutal enactment of the harvest and its collection. The state was said to go about its business without any interest in the human consequences. The report continued:

> It is quite conceivable that a solution to the Russian agrarian crisis will happen in such a way that the balancing of production and consumption will be created not through an increase in production, but though the dying out of those millions who can no longer be nourished by a shattered agricultural economy.[27]

News was passed from ethnic Germans within Russia to organisations and relatives abroad. The German Foreign Ministry came into possession of correspondence from an anonymous German churchman with a parish in the North Caucasus outlining not just starvation, but the constant fear of being under suspicion of Soviet authorities and of the possibility of deportation to Siberia.[28]

---

[22] '20 Mill. Menschen müssen verhungern. Totalhungersnot in Russland', *Revalsche Zeitung* 4 July 1933.

[23] 'Hungersnot', *Revalsche Zeitung* 14 July 1933.

[24] 'Das Massensterben in Ssowjetrussland', *Revalsche Zeitung* 19 August 1933.

[25] 'Reisen in Russland verboten', *Revalsche Zeitung* 10 August 1933.

[26] For example *The Daily Standard*, 31 March 1933 and The *Daily Express*, 4 April 1933, 'Bread We are Dying'. For details of Gareth Jones's life and for more information on his reporting on the famine see http://www.garethjones.org/ (accessed 18 June 2013).

[27] 'Bericht eines hervoragenden Sachkenners über die Lage in einem Teile des südlichen Sowjet-Russland im Frühjahr 1933.' R 127510. Political Archive of the Foreign Ministry, Berlin.

[28] 11.8.33, Anonymous to Dr Schröder. R 62162. Political Archive of the Foreign Ministry, Berlin. Information leaked out through both Potestant and Greek Orthodox Churches. 'Der Todeskampf der Sowjet-Ukraine', *Revalsche Zeitung* 4 August 1933.

Now Ewald Ammende began to consider possible relief projects. By early July 1933 (i.e. during the lead up to the fateful 1933 congress) he was talking about the need to launch a massive aid initiative for Russia. He believed the winter of 1933 would see starvation so serious that not even Soviet authorities would be able to deny it. Then the world would have to decide whether it would stand by while millions died in the heart of Europe. He recommended that steps be taken to influence public opinion in grain-rich areas such as the USA, in order to help pave the way for the delivery of major amounts of assistance.[29]

### 3. Ammende and anti-Communist agitation

There were many reasons for Ammende to push an initiative regarding famine in Soviet Ukraine. Certainly it reflected his personal long-standing interest in Germans in Russia; it reflected his family's former business interests in Ukraine; and it built on personal links he had with ethnic Ukrainians through the congress. It was a channel for him to express his established anti-Bolshevism. It played to his hopes that one day the Soviet Union would collapse and Russia could return to Europe, leading to the improvement of the continent's economy. Concern over the famine was related to Ammende's belief that the Soviet Union's nationality policy was oriented, ultimately, towards eradicating true diversity on Soviet territory. Here, he'd have agreed with the thrust of a slightly later essay written by Ferdinand von Üxküll maintaining that any Bolshevist support for national minorities was tactical and temporary. The long term aim was, much more, to create a nationless Mankind of undifferentiated proletarians.[30] To quote Üxküll from 1934:

> This is the situation facing us today. There is a fundamental
> negation by Moscow of all the rights of national minorities
> as we represent them.[31]

True, the famine did offer an alternative focus for outrage at a time when the congress was struggling over Germany's Jewish Question. It offered the possibility of some minorities trying to promote the well-being of co-nationals inside Russia so long as they were prepared to leave the Jewish Question to one side. It also offered a clear means for Ammende to prove the congress was a useful tool for Hitler's Germany in a propaganda war against the Soviet Union.

---

[29] 6.7.33, Ammende to Prof. Sallet (Berlin, Verein des Deutschtums für das Ausland). R 127510. Political Archive of the Foreign Ministry, Berlin.

[30] F. von Üxküll, 'Die bolschewistische Lösung des Nationalitätenproblems', *Nation und Staat* July - August 1935.

[31] *Sitzungsbericht des Kongresses der organisierten nationalen Gruppen in den Staaten Europas. Bern, 4 bis 6 September 1934.* Vienna-Leipzig: Wilhelm Braumüller, 1935, p. 80.

Under the circumstances, according to Sabine Bamberger-Stemmann, it was inevitable that Ammende be drawn into the orbit of the Third *Reich*'s anti-Comintern politics, particularly as championed by Hitler's Baltic German ideologue Alfred Rosenberg.[32] Certainly archive holdings about the Third *Reich*'s anti-Comintern policies do contain documents carrying Ammende's name but, relatively speaking, there are not that many of them. His name is not stitched into the system as neatly as, say, that of Karl Loesch (linked to the Association for the Protection of Border Germans and Germans Abroad) or a number of others (e.g. Drs. Leibbrandt and Ehrt).[33] So although Ammende was helpful to the anti-Comintern project in so far as he, for instance, visited Canada and met Prime Minister Bennett, then visited Ireland and met de Valera, agitating against the Soviet Union's position in the League of Nations, nonetheless his position was more of a bit-part player than a policy-driver.[34] He was less of a load-bearing element in Nazism's anti-Communist system, more of a figure who would work reliably on its behalf and who could be used by it.[35]

Ammende's writings were nothing like those of Rosenberg. The Nazi ideologue maintained crudely that race and culture went hand in hand, also expressing himself more mystically with phrases such as 'Race is the image of soul.'[36] Rosenberg absolutely abhorred the multicultural model of society which Ammende, Hasselblatt and Schiemann had championed across the 1920s. Likewise there was clear difference between the views of someone like Ammende and a convinced Nazi such as Helmut Nicolai who wrote legal ideology for the Party.[37] When Nicolai, a bureaucrat in the Prussian civil service, was posted to Upper Silesia in 1928, he wrote a treatise arguing that the different population groups in the area had been locked in a bitter racial struggle for supremacy for centuries.[38] There was no counterpart to such work among Ammende's writings. So Ammende and members of the Nazi Party were not really kindred spirits; rather they shared certain things in common (such as national pride and dedicated anti-Soviet convictions) and could co-operate on this basis. Also the *Reich* had something Ammende still needed desperately: resources.

## 4. Innitzer Committee

Determined to take steps to engage with the famine in Russia, Ammende made contact with the well-established aid organisation *Brüder in Not*. He

---

[32] Bamberger-Stemmann, *Der Europäische Nationalitätenkongreß 1925 bis 1938,* p. 333.

[33] See documents located at MA 128/3, Institute for Contemporary History, Munich.

[34] 2.10.34, 'Aktennotiz for Rosenberg about Antikomintern'. MA 128/3, Institute for Contemporary History, Munich.

[35] Bamberger-Stemmann, *Der Europäische Nationalitätenkongreß 1925 bis 1938*, pp. 338–9.

[36] A. Rosenberg, *The Myth of the Twentieth Century*. Torrance, CA: Noontide Press. 1982, p. 4.

[37] Most famous was H. Nicolai, *Die rassengesetzliche Rechtslehre*. Munich: Eher and Son, 1932.

[38] H. Nicolai, *Oberschlesien im Ringen der Völker*. Breslau: Grass, Barth and Co., 1930.

attended one of the organisation's meetings in August 1933 which heard that already over half a million *Reichsmarks* had been collected by the organisation. During the proceedings, Ammende argued that Vienna—the base of his own office—would be a good hub from which to arrange the organisation's humanitarian initiatives.[39]

A few weeks before this meeting, and as reported in the press, Ammende had written a memorandum calling for a major international aid effort on behalf of Germans in Russia.[40] He was quoted directly:

> Hundreds of thousands and millions of people are starving while overseas agricultural areas are choked with grain, while in Kansas industrial ovens are heated with maize, while there are fresh negotiations between Canada, the USA, Argentina, and Australia (the richest corn baskets in the world) about a 15 to 20% reduction of land for sowing. The agricultural economy of these territories faces ruin on account of over-production, as do shipping firms, since ocean-going boats are laid up owing to a lack of freight.... Hundreds of thousands and millions of people are being destroyed while in the London Conference, statesmen from all countries are concerning themselves with the economic reconstruction of the world, and especially our part of it. For months and weeks there are debates about how individual economic factors, money, merchandise, transport and so on, can be put at the service of all humanity once more. But the most important topic is passed over in silence, namely the question of how many millions of people—really the most valuable asset—can be saved for the world and its economy.

Ammende went on to discuss the key characteristics of any aid effort to be extended to the Soviet Union: it should be a purely humanitarian action; it should have no political motivation; it should be led by humanitarian organisations, not least the Red Cross; it should be international; inside the Soviet Union, aid agency staff should supervise closely how aid would be distributed; it should be implemented regardless of religious difference; and it should be responsive to public opinion.

Further instances of publicity generated by Ammende soon appeared. A few weeks later, *Revalsche Zeitung* discussed the famine memorandum. It said assistance to Russia was a moral obligation and its

---

[39] 4.8.33. Deutsches Rotes Kreuz. Niedrschrift über die Sitzung des Arbeitsausschusses "Bruder in Not" am 1 August 1933. R 127510. Political Archive of the Foreign Ministry, Berlin.

[40] 'Die russische Hungerkatastrophe. Sollen Millionen von Menschen in Russland verhunger?', *Revalsche Zeitung* 19 July 1933.

rejection would have an incalculably dreadful result. The article observed that Catholic Archbishop of Vienna Theodor Innitzer was also demanding an aid action.[41] According to Ammende, he personally had been instrumental in persuading Innitzer to engage decisively with the project.[42] So in summer 1933, just as the Jewish Question in Germany was becoming critical for the nationality movement, Ammende was throwing himself into the issue of the famine.

In late August 1933, another article analysed what was happening in Soviet Ukraine, and later its substance would be published as the start of Ammende's book *Muss Russland hungern?*, later translated as *Human Life in Russia*. A further article published in January 1934 also carried Ammende's fingerprints. Making use of material deployed in his book, the piece maintained that when foreign statesmen visited the famine areas and found few signs of starvation, they had been given a false impression, one manipulated deliberately by Soviet authorities. Ammende maintained that true conditions were absolutely dire, with grain being wrenched from Ukraine for supply to industrial areas and political troops.[43] At about the same time, *Revalsche Zeitung* also reported that Moscow was checking carefully all news communications about famine before they were sent abroad and was preparing to organise a trip for diplomats through the affected areas.[44] The implication was obvious: Moscow was doing all it could to control the flow of information about what was happening and trying to make sure only acceptable impressions of the situation could circulate.

Information from German sources flatly contradicted Moscow's version of events. German-language press broadcast that hundreds of thousands of letters had been sent by 'colonists' in the Soviet Union describing mass death in Ukraine, the North Caucasus and the Volga. In response, *Brüder in Not* had forged links with the Protestant and Catholic Churches, creating a national movement. Reports said that gifts of money and food already had saved 12,000 families of between 6 and 15 people from starvation, but the effort had to be continued, even extended.[45]

In late October, Cardinal Innitzer called a meeting of leaders from the Catholic, Greek Orthodox and Protestant Churches, plus Jewish leaders. They met in Vienna to create an aid committee for the famine areas of the Soviet Union. Innitzer demanded the crisis be publicised as much as possible. Other churchmen added their voices in support, including Monsignor Dr.

---

[41] 'Die russische Hungerkatastrophe. Solen Millionen von Menschen in Russland verhungern?' *Revalsche Zeitung* 23 August 1933.
[42] A.D. McVay and L.Y. Luciuk (ed.), *The Holy See and the Holodomor. Documents from the Vatican Secret Archives on the Great Famine of 1932–1933 in Soviet Ukraine*. University of Toronto, 2011, p. 44.
[43] 'Die Hungerkatastrophe in Russland', *Revalsche Zeitung* 11 January 1934.
[44] 'Meldungen über die russische Hungersnot sind verboten', *Revalsche Zeitung* 24 August 1933.
[45] C. von Kügelgen, 'Augenzeugen aus der russischen Hungershölle', *Revalsche Zeitung* 31 August 1933.

Hornykewitsch. Ammende was present too, contributing a talk 'The Fight about the Truth'.[46]

The calling of this committee came at the end of a process. As long ago as 1925, Pius XI had established the Pro Russia commission to deal with all religious affairs inside the USSR.[47] Interest in Russia was maintained when, in 1933, the Vatican received an agricultural expert called Otto Schiller (an agricultural attaché of the German Embassy in Moscow) who had travelled through the Volga and North Caucasus and who, as a result, was familiar with the famine area. Bishop d'Herbigny of the Pro Russia Commission tried to get Pius XI to sanction a papal relief mission, and his proposal was placed before the Pope on 24 March 1933. The Pope, however, felt it an impossible task because the action would have to stretch beyond solely Catholic faith groups. There were also fears that attempts by the Vatican to engage in Russia might stimulate a wave of anti-Catholic persecution in the Soviet Union, also that the aid would never reach those most in need. By late summer 1933, clearly the Vatican as such was not going to act on the famine in the Ukraine but still, on 29 September, d'Herbigny recommended that the Pope contact Cardinal Innitzer to undertake some manner of relief action. The Pope agreed on the strict understanding that the Pro Russia Commission would not be involved directly in the project.[48]

At this point, the linkage between Ammende and Innitzer became significant. From early August Ammende was pressing Innitzer to act over the famine, although he was also in touch with Quaker organisations. At the time Ammende was set to circulate his memorandum about the famine— supplemented with photographs—to the wider public.[49] In due course, he described himself as assuming the post of Honorary Secretary of the Interconfessional and International Vienna Relief Committee for the Russian Famine Areas.[50] Apparently Ammende's colleague from the congress and ethnic Ukrainian Milena Rudnycka was also associated with Innitzer's committee, as were Mennonite groups.[51]

At the time Ammende hoped the Pope endorsed his efforts. Once he even wrote that the Vatican supported its work 'in every way'.[52] Unfortunately he was mistaken. Correspondence among Catholic churchmen shows reservations about working with Ammende because he was not

---

[46] 'Das Weltgewissen erwacht. Bildung eines interkonfessionellen und übernationalen "Hilfskomitees für die Hungergebiete der Ssowjet Union" in Wien', *Revalsche Zeitung* 21 October 1933.

[47] For an article on early Papal engagement with the Soviet Union, see 'Katholische Aktion in Russland. Commissione Pontifica per la Russia', *Revalsche Zeitung* 7 October 1933.

[48] McVay and Luciuk (ed.), *The Holy See and the Holodomor*, pp. 10–5.

[49] Ibid, pp. 42–4.

[50] E. Ammende, *Human Life in Russia*. Cleveland: Zubal, 1984 (first published 1936), p. 10.

[51] F. von Üxküll, 'Brüder in Not', *Nation und Staat* January 1934, p. 207.

[52] Letter of 9.8.33, Giobbe to Orsenigo in McVay and Luciuk (ed.), *The Holy See and the Holodomor.*, footnote 53.

himself a Catholic and could never guarantee assistance would be given 'proportionally' to Catholics.[53]

Just as he had travelled internationally promoting minority rights, Ammende did the same promoting awareness of the famine and proposing a 'moral initiative against the Soviet Union'.[54] In London in 1934, Ammende liaised with Willoughby Dickinson, a long-standing acquaintance through the European Congress of Nationalities, and contacted groups of Ukrainian and Russian exiles. He was invited to a reception of about 100 dignitaries, including the Archbishop of Canterbury. But just as Ammende was only accepted by the German Foreign Ministry up to a point, likewise he was only accepted by the famine organisations up to a point. The Chancellor's office in Vienna had advised Innitzer not to provide Ammende with an official letter of introduction for use in London on the grounds that his involvement in any aid action might make it appear too much of an anti-Soviet project and hence subvert its humanitarian aims. Even so, apparently Ammende mobilised British groups over the famine leading to the creation of a petition directed against the Soviet Union's prevailing church policy.[55]

As far as Berlin was concerned, the project launched by Ammende and Innitzer was marginal. It was not understood to promise effective, long-lasting assistance to Russia and so interest in it soon waned.[56] Nor did Ammende stimulate a major effort on the part of the already reluctant Holy See. Hence by December 1933 voices within the Catholic Church were complaining the Pope should have done more to help relieve distress in Russia.[57] This does not mean, however, that Ammende had no impact at all in respect of the Soviet famine.

## 5. Anti-Sovietism

The press kept up a steady stream of reports about dire conditions in Russia, particularly stories alleging that Soviet authorities were responsible for either the actual famine or how its consequences developed. One report alleged that people were only being fed if they were deemed useful to the Soviet state. Hence 2 or 3 million party members and industrial workers in Russia were living relatively privileged lives while farmers were being allowed to starve.[58] Another proposed that resources were being deployed to make sure the Soviet Union looked good when foreign dignitaries visited, and foodstuffs were still being exported in exchange for gold while people in

---

[53] Letter of 9.8.33, Giobbe to Orsenigo in McVay and Luciuk (ed.), *The Holy See and the Holodomor.* p. 49.
[54] Bamberger-Stemmann, *Der Europäische Nationalitätenkongreß 1925 bis 1938,* p. 344.
[55] Ibid, pp. 340–2.
[56] McVay and Luciuk (ed.), *The Holy See and the Holodomor*, pp. 68–9.
[57] Ibid, p. 77.
[58] Dr S., 'Klassensstaat Ssowjetrussland', *Revalsche Zeitung* 25 September 1933.

Ukraine, the Volga, the Caucasus and Siberia were suffering.[59] In January
1934 there were discussions about whether 5 or 15 million people had died
already.[60] By March 1934, Ammende was reporting problems with the most
recent harvest which suggested the crisis of 1933 (which had seen 140,000
ethnic Germans die) would be repeated. Soviet authorities and newspapers
such as *Pravda* blamed 'local factors' for existing difficulties, but Ammende
dismissed the idea.[61] In late May, reports appeared about refugees crossing
the border into Poland near Lviv (Lemberg). About 10 million people were
said to be starving and the story was supplemented once again with tales of
cannibalism.[62] By summer 1934, stories had also started to circulate about
steps to stamp out independence movements in Ukraine, including the
shooting of intellectuals and the deportation of 100,000 farmers to Siberia.[63]
At the same time, reports emerged of heightened government demands for
grain from the kulak class.[64] A year later there were, if anything, even more
depressing reports of the persecution through shooting or sentences of forced
labour for ethnic German community leaders, such as pastors, who had
requested assistance from abroad on account of enduring famine.[65]

   Ammende was always a publicist and his response to the Ukrainian
famine reflected a determination to show the Soviet Union was not the
paradise for minorities it was supposed to be.[66] The more Ammende and his
colleagues observed the Soviet management of nationality affairs, the more
critical they were of them. They argued, for instance, that Moscow's policy
of promoting regional languages was just a means more efficiently to purvey
Communist ideas to the population.[67] Üxküll wrote an article publicising
inhuman deportation and settlement policies which involved the removal of
whole villages from west and south west Russia, while filling spaces in the
area (caused by famine and deportations) with groups from Kirgizia, Baschka
and Russia.[68] In a further piece, he argued that although Bolsheviks
recognised the national question was a source of propaganda to motivate the
population, nonetheless the ultimate goal remained to create a humanity no

---

[59] J. Schmied-Kowarzik, 'Russland hungert', *Revalsche Zeitung* 14 October 1933.
[60] 'Die russische Hungerkatastrophe. Die Russen selbst geben 10 bis 15 Millionen Opfer an', *Revalsche Zeitung* 24 January 1934.
[61] E. Ammende, 'Die neue Phase der Hungersnot in der Ssowjetunion', *Revalsche Zeitung* 5 March 1934.
[62] 'Der Hunger in der Ssowjet-Ukraine', *Revalsche Zeitung* 23 May 1934.
[63] 'Ssowjetunion, Völkerbund und Nationalitätenproblem', *Revalsche Zeitung* 9 August 1934.
[64] 'Schlechte Ernteaussichten in Russland', *Revalsche Zeitung* 13 August 1934.
[65] Friedrich Carl Badendieck, Bundesleitung des BDA, 'Vernichtungskampf gegen das Deutschtum in Russland', *Revalsche Zeitung* 3 June 1935.
[66] Bamberger-Stemmann, *Der Europäische Nationalitätenkongreß 1925 bis 1938*, p. 333.
[67] C. von Stamati, 'Zur Nationalitätenpolitik der Sowjetunion', *Nation und Staat* January 1935, p.227.
[68] F. von Üxküll, 'Der Todesweg der Deutsche in der Sowjetunion', *Nation und Staat* July - August 1935.

longer divided by nationality. It would be a unity based on labour and a proletariat.[69]

Ultimately for Ammende and those around him, Soviet nationality policy was a vehicle for oppression, not for liberation and independent development. He became convinced that Soviet nationality policy, especially as implemented in the west of the Soviet Union, was having such damaging repercussions that those lands had become centrifugal forces threatening to break the state apart. This was why, he felt, repressive measures were being applied against the local populations.

Ammende's anti-Soviet convictions often informed his interventions in congress proceedings. In 1934, he expressed outrage that Soviet nationality policy contradicted openly the League's policy on minorities. He questioned whether the League should adopt a member who so clearly rejected its principles.[70] There followed a resolution, read by Josip Wilfan, which called for states to have their protection of national minorities checked before joining the League and, if they were found wanting, they should be refused membership.[71]

## 6. Ammende's interpretation of famine in Ukraine

Ammende understood the Ukrainian famine to be a national phenomenon, a conviction he expressed in an essay published in *Nation und Staat* in early 1934.[72] The piece supplemented an anti-Soviet diatribe written by Üxküll, which said 6 million people had died in Ukraine (15% of the rural population) as a result of a tragedy caused largely by collectivisation and the over-zealous collection of the harvest. He called for global intervention (e.g. involving the importing of grain through Odessa and Rostov) to save lives.[73] Two months later Ammende continued to paint a vivid picture of crisis facing 1.2 million Germans in Ukraine, Volga and Siberia. Their situation was made all the worse, according to Ammende's analysis, because the administration in the Volga region was staffed by Communists from Bela-Kun's former regime in Hungary, people said to be deeply hostile to ethnic German colonists and their way of life. Consequently many ethnic Germans had become refugees, with 60 even fleeing through Turkestan to British India. Under the circumstances, Ammende called on the whole German nation to

---

[69] F. von Üxküll, 'Die bolschewistische Lösung des Nationalitätenproblems', *Nation und Staat* July - August 1935.

[70] *Sitzungsbericht des Kongresses der organisierten nationalen Gruppen in den Staaten Europas. Bern, 4 bis 6 September 1934.* Vienna-Leipzig: Wilhelm Braumüller, 1935, pp. 80–2.

[71] Ibid, p. 86.

[72] E. Ammende, 'Eine Pflicht der Nation. Zur Tragödie des Russlanddeutschtums.' *Nation und Staat* March 1934. A few months later, an article was published offering a population round up of ethnic Germans in Russia, S. Klau, 'Die deutsche Minderheit in der UdSSR.' *Nation und Staat* November 1934, pp. 79–88.

[73] F. von Üxküll, 'Brüder in Not.' *Nation und Staat* January 1934.

demand that ethnic Germans be allowed to leave the Soviet Union, until which point they should receive foreign aid. Ammende kept up a fearsome propaganda drive over the famine supported by the *Journal de Genève* and its editor, William Martin who had been an enthusiastic supporter of Georgian independence in 1924.[74]

Ammende's extended intellectual engagement with the famine had begun with the memorandum written for the Innitzer Committee: 'The Russian Hunger Catastrophe. Do Millions of People in Russia have to Starve?'[75] As General Secretary of the European Congress of Nationalities, he said, he was interested in the famine because many European national groups had co-nationals being affected. Citing sources including Gareth Jones, Ammende proposed Russia was gripped by a crisis reminiscent of 1922–4 which could affect as many as 10 million people and which would not climax until the next winter. He proposed the basic disaster was manmade, caused by the complete ignoring of psychological responses to Soviet economic policy. The harvest of 1932 had broken down due to the hasty collectivisation of agricultural systems, ripping farmers from the soil and producing a de-motivated and de-skilled rural workforce. Dissent led the rural population not to bring in the harvest efficiently, while farmers also slaughtered their animals before their assets were 'collectivised'. Hence between 1928 and 1932 the number of cattle in Russia fell from 70.5 million to 29.2 million. Meanwhile, farm machinery was allowed to fall into disrepair. Consequently Russia's key food surplus areas were now producing only a fraction of what they had done previously. Yet supplies from these areas traditionally had fed the large urban areas constituting the heartland of Russian industry. If these industrial areas were absolutely vital to the continued survival of the Soviet Union, then grain had to be ripped out of the traditional agricultural surplus areas at all costs.

Ammende believed the harvest of 1933–4 would be even worse than that of 1932–3 because disruption to agriculture had prevented all but superficial planting and sowing. With this in mind, in June 1933 Soviet Commissar to Ukraine Postyschew gave a speech to the Plenum of the Communist Central Committee of Ukraine which outlined Moscow's determination to deliver grain from agricultural to urban areas come what may. As Ammende observed, provisioning the industrial and government populations would necessitate pushing rural populations into starvation. Ammende found it a 'disgrace of the twentieth century' that more was not already being done to save innocent Soviet citizens:

---

[74] S. Bamberger-Stemmann, *Der Europäische Nationalitätenkongreß 1925 bis 1938. Nationale Minderheiten zwischen Lobbyistentum und Grossmachtinteressen*. Marburg: Verlag Herder-Institut, 2000, pp. 334–5.

[75] E. Ammende, 'Die Russische Hungerkatastrophe. Sollen Millionen von Menschen in Russland verhungern?' R 127510. Political Archive of the Foreign Ministry, Berlin. It was published as E.Ammende, 'Die russische Hungerkatastrophe', *Europäische Nationalitäten-Korrespondenz* 4 (1933) 19 August 1933. R60531. Foreign Ministry Archive, Berlin.

The famine in the Soviet Union can no longer be concealed. The civilised world will be confronted by the question: do they want to be onlookers while in the forthcoming winter, just as in the last half year, millions of innocent people starve in the Soviet Union—in the Volga, the North Caucasus and Siberia, even though an aid action can be carried out without facing difficulties. Now this question must be answered clearly. If the decision is in favour of aid, then no more time must be wasted. Otherwise it could be too late.[76]

Over the next couple of years, Ammende turned his memorandum into a book which subsequently was translated into English and published by Allen and Unwin in 1936 (*Muss Russland hungern?* which became *Human Life in Russia*). A re-printed version was published in 1984 in Cleveland with the support of The Foundation to Commemorate the 1933 Ukrainian Famine. At an early point in the text, Ammende stated his long-standing interest in publicising the horrors accompanying the collectivisation of agriculture. As early as December 1929 he had written a letter to *Neue Zürcher Zeitung* predicting acute famine in Stalin's lands:

In view of the poor harvest and the results of Stalin's experiment [i.e. collectivisation], a severe food crisis can be foretold with certainty, in which case the coming spring may bring another catastrophe... It is the duty of the European public to take the initiative in order that timely preparations may be made on behalf of the victims in Russia.[77]

Yet while Ammende was clear that Stalin's policies were the immediate cause of millions of deaths, he also blamed the western powers—and possibly by implication the League of Nations—for failing to engage with the problem in timely fashion, for example by launching an international enquiry.[78] Ammende did not, however, stop to consider whether an external investigatory body would ever be allowed into the Soviet Union.[79]

On the topic of the controversial photographs contained in his book, at least some seem to have been drawn from the famine of the 1920s rather than the 1930s (being identified as belonging to Nansen's Commission), but

[76] Ibid, p. 8.
[77] E. Ammende, *Human Life in Russia*. Cleveland: Zubal, 1984. (first published 1936), p. 18.
[78] Ibid, p. 19.
[79] During the period of the famine from the early 1920s, the Soviet government had refused to have anything to do with a possible League of Nations commission of inquiry.

Ammende's preface proposed that some were taken in Kharkov in 1933 by an 'Austrian specialist' using a Leica camera not available in 1922, while the English edition also contained images 'supplied' by Dr. F. Dittloff who had been Director of the German Government Agricultural Concession in the North Caucasus.[80] Notwithstanding that political purpose had always be written through Ammende's interest in the Soviet Union, he contended:

> My book differs from most of those written about Russia in that it was written with a purely humanitarian object. Its kernel is simply the fate of the inhabitants of the Soviet State, and all other questions, such as the success or the failure of the five-year plans, collectivisation, the construction of the industrial monster works and the rest are of subsidiary importance. The only question is, 'Is it desirable and is it possible to render help to the people who are starving in Russia?'[81]

This declaration conflicted with the fact that the book was financed by the *Reich* Ministry for National Education and Propaganda and the German Foreign Ministry, hence Bamberger-Stemmann interprets it as constituting just one of many initiatives carried out by Ammende on behalf of Rosenberg's anti-Comintern project.[82]

The crux of Ammende's argument was that the famine of 1933–4 differed from that of 1921–2 because it was largely man-made. Essentially it grew out of the 'fiasco' of collectivisation coupled with the deliberate choice to supply grain to the industrial towns of the Soviet Union while leaving the rural, producing areas with a profound shortage.[83]

Ammende maintained that the 'experiment' of collectivisation had failed.'[84] Quoting Otto Schiller, of the German Embassy in Moscow, he said this was the result of ignoring 'the human factor' in the economy.[85] For instance, Russian peasants had proved too backward to use the mechanical aids offered them, with the result that large 'tractor cemeteries' were strewn across the countryside. To quote Ammende:

---

[80] Ibid, pp. 22–3. For an argument that at least some of the photographs are from the 1920s, see D. Tottle, *Fraud, Famine and Fascism: The Ukrainian Genocide Myth from Hitler to Harvard*. Toronto: Progress Books, 1987, pp. 84–5. For an argument that at least some are genuine, see the web site dedicated to investigative journalist Gareth Jones. It is contended that some of the shops shown in Kharkov were not in existence in 1921–2. http://www.garethjones.org/soviet_articles/thomas_walker/muss_russland_hungern.htm (accessed 26 June 2013). For comments about the photographs as drawn from Nansen's Commission, see Bamberger-Stemmann, Ibid, p. 336.
[81] Ammende, *Human Life in Russia*, p. 24.
[82] Bamberger-Stemmann, *Der Europäische Nationalitätenkongreß 1925 bis 1938*, p. 336.
[83] Ammende, *Human Life in Russia*, p. 29.
[84] Ibid.
[85] Ibid.

> The whole fault lies in the illusion that, in a country with a
> largely illiterate population, a grandiose State Socialist
> apparatus could be swiftly improvised and a system created
> which would render the country independent of all foreign
> imports.[86]

The situation was made worse because the over-pressured Soviet economic system was producing shoddy goods that were not really up to the demands made of them. Furthermore, deprived of any 'inducement' to participate in the project, farmers were exhibiting passive resistance; they were refusing to work.[87] On top of all this, the kulak class was persecuted relentlessly, depriving the rural population of its traditional leaders. Hence Ammende commented:

> The lack of farm managers, combined with all the results of
> Stalin's agricultural policy, is one of the chief reasons of
> the famines of 1933 and 1934.[88]

For all these 'human' reasons, the Soviet rural economy gradually ground to a halt, leaving the central authorities to rip whatever grain was remaining out of it for the industrial and military populations, also to export it for the benefit of the non-agricultural economy and to boost foreign reserves regardless of the human cost.

Ammende divided the famine into three phases. The first stretched across 1933 until autumn and marked the beginnings of tragedy. According to *Le Temps* journalist Pierre Berland, it was a period of struggle between 'a Government of fanatical ideologues' and 'a peasant mass hostile to collectivisation'.[89] 25,000 dedicated Communists were sent into the countryside to drive forward collectivisation and Commissar Postyschew was deployed to Ukraine to procure the harvest regardless of local opposition. Across the summer, people began starving in, for instance, Kiev, Kharkov and Rostov. From autumn 1933 until autumn 1934, Ammende believed the famine exhibited a second phase during which hardship again was the result of ruthless grain collection.[90] Now Postyschew enforced the principle 'away with compassion' and treated as an enemy of the state anyone who tried to resist Moscow's demands. Consequently the situation facing average people was even worse than it had been the previous year. During this period the state embarked on a 'cleaning up process' so that starving people were

---

[86] Ibid, p. 52.
[87] Ibid, p. 32.
[88] Ibid, pp. 48–9.
[89] Ibid, p. 58.
[90] Ibid, p. 74.

removed from towns and cities to 'invisible' areas.[91] A third, and perhaps the worst phase, started in autumn 1934 during which at least some large ethnic German villages in the Volga saw their populations fall to 40 or 50% of their prior levels.[92] Discussing estimates of numbers of people who had died by this time, Ammende noted that they ranged up to fully 10% of the population of Ukraine and North Caucasus.[93]

### 7. Starvation and nationality

In Ammende's mind, intersecting with famine in Ukraine was Bolshevism's attitude to the rights and 'cultural individuality' of the territory's nationalities.[94] The areas from which grain was being ripped so mercilessly were not, for the most part, inhabited by ethnic Russians but other nationality groups. Moscow's policy on grain amounted to an assault on these local populations. The situation was creating serious tensions within the Soviet system because it highlighted a fundamental difference between the politics of Lenin (for whom the national question was simply a source of propaganda) and regional leaders (for whom national differences had to be taken seriously). Now, when regional intellectuals complained about what was happening to their nationality, they were being denounced for anti-Soviet behaviour.[95] This tension between the needs of the centre and of the peripheries also meant that as local Communists resisted collecting grain from starving areas, they provoked a confrontation that became a 'fight against local nationalist tendencies', a situation that was most severe in the Ukrainian Soviet Socialist Republic.[96]

Nikolai Skrypnik had been an associate of Lenin, but was a Communist leader from Ukraine who took local national difference seriously. During 1933, however, Pavel Postyschew became a senior commissar. For him, the demands of the central Soviet system took priority completely over all local needs. The ruthless exploitation of Ukrainian agriculture which followed, led Skrypnik to protest.

In the background was a decision by the Central Committee of the Communist Party and the Council of People's Commissaries dated 14 December 1932 that called for the elimination of all 'bourgeois nationalist' elements in Party and Soviet organisations. Perhaps with this in mind, when Postyschew arrived in Ukraine prepared to do Moscow's bidding, he considered the place awash with foreign agents and counter-revolutionaries. He became convinced that Skrypnik's work had shown proletarian internationalism could not be aligned with national difference and that

---

[91] Ibid, pp. 75–7.
[92] Ibid, p. 89.
[93] Ibid, pp. 97–9.
[94] Ibid, p. 104.
[95] Ibid, p. 104–6.
[96] Ibid, p. 108.

attempts to do so only led to nationalist counter-revolution.[97] Consequently—according to Ammende—a major confrontation developed between Skrypnik and Postyschew when the Central Committee of the Communist Party of the Ukraine met at Kharkov on 10 June 1933. While Skrypnik protested that Ukraine's culture and land were being ruined, Postyschew denounced him as an enemy of the state and alleged his offices contained 'harmful counter-revolutionary and nationalistic elements', 'poisoners' and 'spies'.[98] Within days of the altercation, Skrypnik's suicide was announced. Thereafter Postyschew set about removing grain from a starving land and purged thousands of offices around the Ukraine. The situation turned into a *de facto* national struggle, as Moscow's famine-producing policies targeted non-Russian groups with particular severity. Ammende made plain that non-Russian nationalities, including German settlements scattered across Ukraine and the Caucasus, fared badly:

> ... Moscow now has a direct interest in the destruction of a large part of the generation currently living in the Ukraine and in other autonomous districts.... The nationalities of these districts, especially the Ukrainians, are thus engaged in a struggle for their existence and for the salvation of a part of their national being. But they are wholly at the mercy of Moscow and can do nothing to defend themselves.... So it is that in the middle of the twentieth century, at a time when influential Soviet statesmen are praising the Soviet Union as a factor making for peace, a systematic war of destruction is proceeding in the interior of Russia—a war carried on not with artillery and machine-guns, but by banishments, executions and famine. I think I have shown that this war is directed in particular against the members of the various nationalities, millions of whom have already been sacrificed to it.[99]

For Ammende, Moscow lacked any moral compass at all:

> What has the Soviet Government done in the face of the catastrophe within its borders? It has kept silence; it has simply denied the existence of the famine; it has not even attempted to ameliorate it by rapid distribution of the grain available for export among the starving population. More than that, by exporting part of the grain wrung from the peasantry, Moscow has contributed to increase the number

---

[97] Ibid, p. 118.
[98] Ibid, p. 123.
[99] Ibid, p. 146–49.

> of victims of the catastrophe.... So long as an economic
> order destined to last forever is achieved, the death of
> millions becomes insignificant. It follows from this general
> assumption that human life in Bolshevist eyes has little, if
> any, value: man is an economic factor, like labour in the
> abstract, and nothing more.[100]

The Soviet Union possessed massive reserves of manpower, so it was too
easy for policy-makers to become indifferent to the suffering of average
people. Hence Ammende cited an official called Sklar who said the death of
6 million people would be an acceptable loss for the benefit of
Communism.[101] He also characterised Stalin as 'insensitive to every human
emotion' likely to interfere with the achievement of his 'grand conception'.[102]
Stalin was a 'sinister man' who presided over a system in which
'[t]yranny and fear dominate everything.'[103] Ammende proposed Moscow
was using 'destruction by indirect means' to get rid of potential opponents.[104]
Hence, for instance, some Ukrainians had been banished to work in
horrendous conditions on the canal being constructed from the Baltic to the
White Sea. To Ammende's way of thinking, under Stalin the Soviet Union
was experiencing a deliberate policy of extermination as a means to
achieving a political vision:

> Moscow's aim is clear: the present generation, in so far as it
> remains loyal to the principles of nationhood, religion and
> family, is to be exterminated, to clear the way for the
> conquest of the rising generation. The young are to be
> uprooted and set free from old-world influences, that they
> may be won over to the ideals of a world proletariat—
> unencumbered by God, nation or family.... To achieve this
> object it is essential first to destroy the old generation
> which still believes in God and nation. This explains the
> fanatical hatred with which Moscow—despite the denials of
> its friends and agitators abroad—is obliterating the
> remnants of religious life and exterminating the clergy of
> all denominations in the country.[105]

---

[100] Ibid, p.150.
[101] Ibid, p. 152.
[102] Ibid, p. 155.
[103] Ibid, pp. 165–6.
[104] Ibid, p. 169.
[105] Ibid, p. 185.

To Ammende's mind, the general aim of Moscow's policies was, at the very least, to turn younger people against ideas of religion, family and nationhood—'the very foundations of Western civilization'.[106]

Ammende was critical of western institutions for failing to do more to assist Moscow's victims. Through political pressure and propaganda, the Soviet Union was denying what was really happening within its borders. When Édouard Herriot visited the country and was taken to famine areas, Ammende said his experiences were completely stage-managed, such that his subsequent statements that there was no famine subverted humanitarian efforts.[107] States were afraid to address the reality of the Russian famine owing to 'political and economic considerations', namely they did not want to confront the Soviet Union over events for fear of damaging their national interests.[108] Hence he said the Vatican and churches should take moral leadership. This was especially important because 'the daring experiment of agricultural communization' was causing 'the death of an appallingly large number of people who were innocent even in the eyes of Moscow'.[109] He advocated that, now the USSR had joined the League of Nations, a commission of inquiry should be sent to investigate the true situation of distress there.[110]

## 8. Conclusion

It follows that as the European Congress of Nationalities was foundering as a result of the Jewish Question in Germany, so Ammende had found a cause for his substantial energies. His denunciation of the famine in Ukraine— including the central argument that it was a man-made tragedy—was both resolute and impassioned. From today's vantage point, however, the credentials of his study as an objective piece of work were undermined in a major way by Ammende's acceptance of funding from the Third *Reich*.

---

[106] Ibid.
[107] Ibid, p. 257.
[108] Ibid, p. 280.
[109] Ibid, p. 283.
[110] Ibid, pages 306 and 319.

*Chapter Sixteen*

## Admitting defeat

### 1. Moving on

Even in the 1930s, not everyone who read Ammende's analysis of famine in Ukraine was impressed. Take the following review:

> Dr.Ammende's work cannot be recommended as an impartial study of the grain question in Soviet Russia. The author has obvious emotional predilections which make it difficult for him to give an objective presentation of his arguments. His facts may be true, but by selecting only those which support his arguments and suppressing all others, he gives a distorted and exaggerated view of the situation. He relies too much on assaulting the reader's emotions by harrowing descriptions of starving children, corpse-strewn streets, and other grisly accompaniments of famine, all lavishly illustrated by photographs. But these facts do not in themselves prove the futility of the economic policy pursued by the Soviet Government: pre-War Russia also had her famines although she had no Five-Year Plans.[1]

There was never a concerted international campaign to bring humanitarian standards to bear in Stalin's Russia. Inevitably, however, the crisis that had moved Ammende began to pass and by the end of 1935 *Revalsche Zeitung* was reporting that after five years of disruption owing to collectivisation, finally Russia had experienced a normal harvest.[2] Stalin was accepted as a fact of life by the international community.

Meanwhile, Ammende was still facing disappointments within the European Congress of Nationalities. Jewish groups were no closer to returning and the Sudeten agenda was coming ever more to the fore while Estonia's model of cultural autonomy was left increasingly in the shadows. Under the circumstances, many congress participants were demoralised and the meetings of 1934 and 1935 were shadows of former events. Ammende too showed signs of de-motivation. Previously a workaholic, by 1935 his named contributions to *Revalsche Zeitung* had all but ended. By this time, it Ammende was looking for something new.

---

[1] Margaret Miller, review of E. Ammende, 'Human Life in Russia', *International Affairs* 15 (1936) pp. 956–7.
[2] A.W. Just, 'Getreide-Ernten in der Räteunion', *Revalsche Zeitung* 14 December 1935.

By 1935 it was also clear that Ammende's health was suffering more than ever. In June of that year he noted his condition was 'fully reduced' following the League of Nations Union meeting which had taken place in Brussels. He ended up with congested lungs on account of high blood pressure.[3] By October 1935 once again he was writing letters from a sanatorium near Baden.[4] In December he told Wilfan that for the sake of his health he needed to spend several months without stress and recommended that Nazi-sympathising Üxküll should be treated as his deputy.[5] Nonetheless there was more than a shadow of a new initiative in the offing, one that tied up with Ammende's trips to the USA, Canada and Ireland during which he campaigned against the Soviet Union's entry to the League.

Ammende was planning to undertake a world cruise with a purpose in mind, as reflected by the Berlin Propaganda Ministry's backing for the trip.[6] He set out from Germany abroad the steamer *Reliance* on 28 December 1935.[7] At the start of January it became clear he wanted German consulates all around the world to be told about his trip so they could be prepared for visits. His activity was discussed at least in vague terms when Hasselblatt met with German Foreign Ministry staff that month.[8] A circular was indeed sent around German consulates telling them that Ammende was undertaking 'scientific research' about Communism and the work of the Comintern abroad.[9] He was to be offered assistance should he need it.

## 2. World cruise

Ammende's world cruise probably reflected more than one purpose. Firstly, he seems genuinely to have wanted to contact different ethnic German groups around the globe, perhaps with a view to establishing not just a European association of German national groups, but a global one. Such an aim would have built on his prior work and would have mirrored moves already undertaken by Polish groups.[10] Secondly, in a letter to an official in the

---

[3] 26.6.35, Ammende to Bahr. Schiemann Papers. Baltic Central Library, Riga.

[4] Various etters from Ammende dated October 1935. Nachlass Wilfan 1250, FC4398. Federal Archive, Koblenz.

[5] 2.12.35, Ammende to Wilfan. Nachlass Wilfan 1250, FC4398. Federal Archive, Koblenz.

[6] 28.1.26, Vermerk zu dem Briefe des Herrn Dr. Ewald Ammende an Herrn Geheimrat Roediger vom 6.XII.1935. R 31832. Political Archive of the Foreign Ministry, Berlin.

[7] Amongst other places, Reliance was to dock in New York, San Fransisco, Honolulu, Manila, Kobe, Shanghai, Penang, Java, Bombay, Durban, Cape Town, Bilbao and Havana. See Hapag-Weltreise 1936 des Dreischrauben-Luxusdampfers "*Reliance*". R 31832. Political Archive of the Foreign Ministry, Berlin.

[8] 2 January 1936, Gravenhorst (Verband) to Roediger. R 31832. Political Archive of the Foreign Ministry, Berlin. Also 25.1.36, Hasselblatt to Geheimrat v. Twardowski. R 60496. Political Archive of the Foreign Ministry, Berlin.

[9] 14.1.36, Roediger circular to German diplomatic representations in Asia and the Far East. R 31832. Political Archive of the Foreign Ministry, Berlin.

[10] 'Weltverband der Polen', *Revalsche Zeitung* 14 August 1934 and 'Nach der Tagung der Ausland-Polen', *Revalsche Zeitung* 18 August 1934.

Foreign Ministry, Ammende indicated plans to launch a campaign in the USA in summer 1936 to raise money for victims of famine in the USSR. Thirdly and probably most importantly, in line with German Foreign Ministry demands, he suggested he would have an opportunity to study Moscow's engagement in the places his cruise put to shore. To this end, he indicated he was already in touch with the German representative in Brazil and that one of his brothers had been based in Mukden for some years, so he was planning to draw together information which would provide some insights about Georgi Dimitroff's leadership of the Comintern. In a note, Ammende emphasised his conviction that Moscow should be placed in the dock before world opinion, and not other states which had been accused in a 'grotesque' way.[11] (In other words, he was suggesting that an anti-Soviet campaign might alleviate international pressure on Germany over the Jewish Question, for instance.) In a further note sent to a German representative in Brazil, Ammende's purpose was said to be the study of 'the activity of the Comintern and its methods', also research into revolutionary propaganda (*Umsturzpropaganda*) deployed by Moscow abroad.[12]

It's interesting to observe that Ammende's world cruise moved in tandem with a number of concerns reported in *Revalsche Zeitung*. In August 1935, the paper carried articles about 'world revolution' by Axel de Vries and Baron Ungern-Sternberg which discussed Moscow's strategy and tactics for fomenting global unrest.[13] They proposed Bolshevik ideals could be pursued best in 'chaos' and 'collapse', also that the Comintern was planning a new global offensive. There were stories about Washington protesting over the activities of the Third International and accusations that Moscow was provoking unrest in French ports, not to say 'infecting' French school teachers with Communism.[14] At times the stories about Moscow were delivered with a real sense of threat, for instance there were reports of Soviet troops massing on Finnish, Latvian and Estonian borders.[15] They also hinted at the massive potential that Communist successes could yield. So, for instance, there were reports of the proliferation of Communist troops across China, of Moscow drawing Mongolia into its orbit and of the Soviet Union starting to exert pressure on Chinese Turkestan. There was no question, then, that Moscow was seeking to turn itself into an Asiatic power of even greater magnitude than was already the case.[16] What would be the implications for the rest of the world?

---

[11] 6.12.35, Ammende to Roediger. R 31832. Political Archive of the Foreign Ministry, Berlin.
[12] 3.1.36, Letter to Legationsrat Hencke (AA). R 31832. Political Archive of the Foreign Ministry, Berlin.
[13] A. de Vries, 'Weltrevolution und Räte-Union', Revalsche Zeitung 10 August 1935. Baron E. v. Ungern-Sternberg, 'Weltrevolution', *Revalsche Zeitung* 21 August 1935.
[14] 'Die 3. Internationale im Angriff', *Revalsche Zeitung* 31 August 1935.
[15] 'Räterussland droht. Truppenkonzentration an der finnländischen und lettländischen Grenze', *Revalsche Zeitung* 7 September 1935.
[16] 'Moskau greift nach China', *Revalsche Zeitung* 29 October 1935.

In the context of growing international disillusionment over collective security,[17] the fact that Communism had been defeated in Germany was not taken as grounds for complacency because as Adolf Ehrt, leader of the anti-Comintern, explained to *Revalsche Zeitung*, this had only increased its danger for other parts of the world.[18] Latin America, India and China were all on the itinerary of Ammende's world cruise and the Baltic German paper cast its eye across all three. From Brazil, there were reports of Communist uprisings in Pernambuco and Rio Grande de Norte, as well as stories of widespread strikes. A revolutionary Communist had been arrested in Buenos Aires.[19] From Uruguay came stories of the breaking of diplomatic relations with the Soviet Union on account of subversive activity there.[20] From India, there were reports about Britain taking steps to deal with terrorism motivated by Communism and religious hatred.[21] From China, there were stories about a 20,000-strong Communist army and of autonomist strivings in the northern provinces of Schantung, Hopeh, Schanft, Suiyuan and Tschanchar, also of fresh possibilities of war between China and Japan.[22] Ammende's ship docked in Hong Kong at the end of March 1936 and proceeding on to other Chinese ports, including Shanghai, in early April. At about this time *Revalsche Zeitung* was carrying reports about heavy Soviet fortifications along their border with Manchuria.[23] Further reporting wondered whether increasing Soviet influence in Mongolia might lead to tensions with Japan.[24] The previous summer there had already been stories about Manchuria—a key site of international tension following the prior Japanese campaign—having become effectively an autonomous state.[25]

In other words, there was a rough correspondence between the reporting in *Revalsche Zeitung* and Ammende's movements while on the world cruise. His on-going interests were reflected in a letter written following his stay in Rio. There, he had met the leader of the Russian Department in the Brazilian Foreign Ministry, Odette de Carvalho. They agreed that, even though Brazil was no longer a member of the League of Nations, the government should be encouraged to present a formal complaint about the recent conduct and words of Soviet diplomat Maxim Litvinov.

---

[17] 'Der Bruch im Kollektivsystem', *Revalsche Zeitung* 28 December 1935.

[18] 'Aus der Arbeit der Anti-Komintern. Ein Interview mit ihrem Leiter Dr. Adolf Ehrt', *Revalsche Zeitung* 25 November 1935.

[19] 'Die Hand der III. Internationale' and 'Ein Agent der Komintern verhaftet', *Revalsche Zeitung* 8 January 1936.

[20] 'Kommunistenaufstand in Brasilien', *Revalsche Zeitung* 26 November 1935. 'Moskaus Haende in Süd-Amerika. Abbruch der diplomatischen Beziehungen zwischen Raeterussland und Uruguay', Revalsche Zeitung 28 December 1935.

[21] 'Aktivität der kommunistischen Streitkraefte in China', *Revalsche Zeitung* 8 January 1936. 'Der Kommunismus in Indien', *Revalsche Zeitung* 28 November 1935.

[22] 'Chinas Reichsarmee marschiert', *Revalsche Zeitung* 6 December 1935.

[23] 'Russland Kriegsvorbereitungen in Sibirien', *Revalsche Zeitung* 1 April 1936.

[24] 'Die Aussere Mongolei', *Revalsche Zeitung* 3 April 1936.

[25] 'Nordchinas Monroe-Doktrin', *Revalsche Zeitung* 9 August 1935.

They also agreed that Latin American countries still inside the League should raise questions in Geneva about the work of the Comintern. Ammende observed that a former German Communist Parliamentary Deputy called Ewert (also known as Harry Berger) had been in Brazil by order of Moscow in order to manage Brazilian Communists. Secret documents shown to Ammende suggested that Ewert had been involved in Communist plots in China in 1932. There was also discussion of how money originating in Russia and intended to finance Comintern work had been moved back and forth between firms in Brazil and Uruguay. Hence Ammende was both ascertaining how Soviet sympathisers were becoming active around the world and agitating among government officials against Soviet interests.

Ammende added that the heat plus the hustle and bustle in Rio had affected his health adversely and that he would have to recuperate on the ship as it travelled to Cape Town.[26] Nonetheless his letters to his family suggest he was enthused by the cruise. He wrote to his mother telling her about his plans to visit Singapore and Beijing (Peking), about the Panama Canal and about his anticipation at seeing Los Angeles.[27] By the time Ammende reached Mumbai (Bombay), he was saying his health had improved thanks to an opportunity to relax onboard the ship.[28] From India, he wrote to Wilfan saying that the trip was really interesting, but it was possible to trace the 'tremors' of the time everywhere, likewise 'Moscow's persistent work'. For this reason, he felt it was vital that the minority movement held firm to its principles and thought it would be all the more important to undertake a project about national minorities in association with England.[29] He added that he would travel to Agra, Delhi and the Taj Mahal before steaming to Thailand, Java and the Far East.

When *Reliance* reached China, Ammende appears to have called in at the German Embassy in Nanking and then decided to travel around the country. The precise reason for the trip is unknown, but reasonably it can be assumed to have involved a general desire to see China, an interest to assess the development of Communism in that country, a desire to visit his brother in Mukden, and also, possibly, a desire to witness the security situation in Manchuria (a critically important area at the time). Ammende was, however, on a train just outside Beijing when his ill-health finally took its toll and he suffered a stroke. He was taken to the German hospital in Peking where he died on 15 April 1936.[30] His brother Edgar arrived with an unsigned last will which he wanted to pass to the other brother, Erich, in Vienna.[31] According to the Nanking Embassy, Ammende left behind lots of political notes which,

---

[26] 11.2.36, Gravenhorst to Roediger. R 31832. Political Archive of the Foreign Ministry, Berlin.
[27] 5.2.36, Ammende to his mother, 1502-1-88, Moscow.
[28] 22.2.1936, Ammende to Geheimrat. R 31832. Political Archive of the Foreign Ministry, Berlin.
[29] 1.3.36, Ammende to Wilfan. Nachlass Wilfan 1250, FC4398. Federal Archive, Koblenz.
[30] 16.4.36, German Embassy, Peping. R 31832. Political Archive of the Foreign Ministry, Berlin.
[31] 20.4.36, German Embassy, Peping. R 31832. Political Archive of the Foreign Ministry, Berlin.

in the first instance, were to go to Erich Ammende and which, it seems, would later be passed on to Werner Hasselblatt.[32]

## 3. Obituary

Several decades after Ammende's death, Max Hildebert Boehm wrote a short appreciation of his life.[33] He had been well-liked, vital and energetic—one of the strongest personalities existing in the European nationality movement prior to 1933. Neither a member of the *Literaten* nor an aristocrat, he had been less of a theorist and more of a practitioner in search of minority rights. Never a dogmatist, he had been a publicist, agitator and organiser. In his own way, Ammende had also been a kind of a diplomat, seeking out connections, driving things forward and embodying an irrepressible dynamism. He had always been prepared to build bridges. Although Boehm's piece was perhaps a bit damning by virtue of its silence regarding Ammende's intellect, and a bit irreverent in its noting that Ammende had been called 'the fat doctor', nonetheless it was quite an affectionate piece.

Naturally, Ammende's death was marked by an outpouring of recognition at the time as well. Government offices noted his passing, so the Cultural Department of the Foreign Ministry sent a telegram to Ammende's mother in Pärnu expressing sympathy and stating that he would be remembered as a 'champion for the legal position of minorities'.[34] A comparable telegram was sent to Max Richter, President of the Association of German National Groups in Europe. In due course, a memorial event in Berlin was organised by Richter and Hasselblatt.[35]

Ammende's death was reported widely in the press, including in National Socialist mouthpiece *Völkischer Beobachter*.[36] There was a piece in *Rigasche Rundschau* which recalled his engagement with that newspaper particularly between 1919 and 1922. It praised him for his considerable 'judiciousness' and 'energy', also for his organisational prowess.[37] A further piece praised his 'boundless will' and his 'unfailing civil courage'. Without being either a statesman or diplomat, but based entirely on the strength of his personality, Ammende had attempted to participate in the shaping of post-war Europe.[38]

---

[32] 'Nachlass Dr Ewald Ammende', Deutsche Botschaft, Nanking, 13.5.36. R 60532. Political Archive of the Foreign Ministry, Berlin.

[33] M.H. Boehm, 'Ewald Ammende als Mittler der europäischen Volksgruppen', *Jahrbuch des Baltischens Deutschtums*, 10 (1963) pp. 55–60.

[34] 15.4.36, Telegram from Stieve. R 60532. Political Archive of the Foreign Ministry, Berlin.

[35] Invitation to memorial for Ammende. R 60532. Political Archive of the Foreign Ministry, Berlin. The event took place in Kaiserallee 189, Berlin-Wilmersdorf. It was reported by the press, see 'Gedenkfeier für Dr Ammende', *Rigasche Rundschau* 23.4.36.

[36] 'Dr. Ewald Ammende', *Völkischer Beobachter*, 16 April 1936. R 60532. Political Archive of the Foreign Ministry, Berlin.

[37] 'Dr. Ewald Ammende', *Rigasche Rundschau*, 16 April 1936.

[38] C. von Kügelgen, 'Dr Ewald Ammende zum Gedächnis', *Rigasche Rundschau*, 16 April 1936.

Naturally *Revalsche Zeitung* published extensively about Ammende. The newspaper left no doubt that someone of immense significance had been lost. It carried death notices placed by Ammende's family, the paper's editorial office, the German cultural administration and the Association of German National Groups in Europe.[39] The judgements passed on him were even more generous than those in Riga's press. Axel de Vries suggested that, from a European perspective, Ammende had been among the most significant and able members of the post-war generation active in the Baltic—a true 'nationality politician (*Volkstumpolitiker*), colleague and friend'.[40] In a further piece, de Vries said Ammende had been a restless spirit who had left a gap no one else could fill.[41] He had been a true 'diplomat' skilled at negotiating with people, regardless of their nationality or personal background. He had been a force for life who knew just how to deal with people. Given the number of journeys Ammende had made during his lifetime, he was likened to a 'meteor'—a person who stayed in his *Heimat* for periods that were always too brief. De Vries's evaluation of Ammende's life recognised he had been a determined opponent of revolutionary Communism whose book *Muss Russland hungern?* was yet to be published at the time of his death. Tantalisingly, the piece recognised that the book paved the way for a fresh project with which Ammende was engaged at the time of his death, but it did not spell out exactly what this project had been. The piece stated Ammende had not been a Nazi and the new situation in Germany had caused him great (but unspecified) difficulties in his work.

Naturally Werner Hasselblatt described Ammende's temperament as having been irrepressible, but noted that his health had not been similarly robust. He observed that the mixture of Ammende's high blood pressure and a heart condition always threatened that this 'unique personality' would be removed too soon. His 'passionate' nature, 'civic courage' and 'drastically open way of speaking' marked him out as someone who was 'irreplaceable'.[42]

Perhaps one of the most flattering and personal obituaries of Ammende was written by Üxküll von Guldenbrand. Describing Ammende as 'a subtle knower-of-men' he was said to have engaged with the Association of German National Groups in Europe with passion and spirit ('*leidenschaftlicher und temperamentvoller Weise*').[43] He was said to have worked in the mould of Immanuel Kant, namely by looking for connections between people and constantly seeking to create unity. Equally he recognised that politics was the art of the possible. Üxküll believed that Ammende lived

---

[39] *Revalsche Zeitung*, 15 April 1936.
[40] A. de Vries, 'Dr Ewald Ammende', *Revalsche Zeitung*, 15 April 1936.
[41] Ibid.
[42] W. Hasselblatt, 'Dr. Ewald Ammende.' R 60532. Political Archive of the Foreign Ministry, Berlin. See the text also as Werner Hasselblatt, 'Dr Ewald Ammende', *Rigasche Post* 19 April 1936. Latvian State Library, Riga.
[43] F. Üxküll von Guldenbrand, 'Ewald Ammende', *Nation und Staat* April 1936, pp. 533–4.

by his own principles and was certain Europe's future depended on the solution of the nationality question. He showed it was possible to be a good European at the same time as being faithful to your *Heimat* and nation. Getting to grips with Ammende's personality, Üxküll went on:

> Considered superficially, he seemed a primitive type. Basically his thoughts and actions were very simple, but they were of that kind of simplicity which is the result of clarity of thought and unity of personality.[44]

Ammende had a strong personality, one possessed entirely by the task he was pursuing, and would never harm anyone deliberately. Although sometimes lacking in diplomacy, nonetheless he was said to be a great diplomat. Prepared to make substantial demands on people, he never asked for more commitment than he would supply himself. When he encountered a problem, he addressed it with 'full force'. He was 'a true friend and good comrade', a genuine European—but always a Balt with a deep sense of duty to his community. Üxküll went on:

> Ammende was the purest kind of idealist, but an idealist who stood with both feet firmly in reality. He had the courage to see things as they are and to believe in the final victory of ethical principle, in the power of truth.[45]

Üxküll's words were supplemented by a statement from the European Congress of Nationalities:

> As an unsurpassed knower of the relationships and needs of individual nationalities, as a convinced and courageous champion of the ideal of free and just reconciliation of national conflicts, as a prudent and far-sighted organiser of our common work, he was purposeful and vigorous, the soul and driving force of our congress.[46]

Naturally the congress provided its own tribute to Ammende at its 1936 meeting. The congress leaders sent a special invitation to the League of Nations asking if a representative might attend.[47] When the congress convened in Geneva in September, Wilfan praised Ammende's 'will and spirit'. He had been a 'lively, exuberant, agile-minded' person equipped with

---

[44] Ibid, p. 536.
[45] Ibid, p. 537.
[46] *Nation und Staat*, April 1936, pp. 536–7.
[47] 15.9.36. Wilfan to Pelt (LoN Information Dept). R3932. Minorities. Congress of Organised National Groups in the States of Europe. Berne. September 1933. 4 / 6731 / 6638.

'an open heart and an open mind'; he had been 'German through and through'. In Wilfan's opinion, the congress owed its life to Ammende. It would not have been established and would not have been able to continue without his engagement. Working like a dynamo, producing a constant stream of letters, essays and memoranda, Ammende had overcome terrific difficulties to ensure people from very different backgrounds could participate. According to Wilfan, Ammende represented his convictions openly and courageously; he was never unfaithful to his 'ideal goals'.[48]

Géza von Szüllő gave an appreciative speech emphasising Ammende's work had not been motivated by racism. Just as all individuals have a right to life regardless of their height, hair colour or sportiness, the same was true of nations: 'whether they are large or small, Semitic or Aryan, it is all the same! It is a nation and has a right to life!'[49] (Admittedly the obituary in *Deutsche Allgemeine Zeitung* did jar with this evaluation. It identified Ammende's motivation as '[l]ove of his own nationality and at the same time a shining feeling of justice'.)[50] Hasselblatt contributed to the congress's discussion. He believed Ammende's commitment to creating a successful multi-ethnic society was rooted in his early experiences in Pärnu, where nationalities lived together without difficulty and without cosmopolitanism detracting from their identities. Again commenting on Ammende's personality, Hasselblatt quoted a friend who described him as an 'elephant in a porcelain shop'—but one which never broke any porcelain due to his sensitivity, wit and jovial nature. He proposed that Ammende's death had caused a crisis for the nationality movement.[51]

### 4. The congress's demise

Ammende's death was symbolic of the fact that his main life's work, the European Congress of Nationalities, had run its course. Too often discussion at the 1936 event showed there was little constructive the organisation could do. Wilfan recognised that, at the time, thinking about national communities was going backwards in Europe, probably because people felt they were facing more important issues. He warned that so long as there was a tendency in Europe to place different national groups in some kind of hierarchy, there was a danger of them breaking the very principles they were trying to uphold. All nations had to be seen as equal.[52] Engelbert Besednjak (a Slovene from

---

[48] *Sitzungsbericht des Kongresses der organisierten nationalen Gruppen in den Staaten Europas. Genf, 16 bis 17 September 1936.* Vienna-Leipzig: Wilhelm Braumüller, 1937, pp.3–4.
[49] Ibid, p. 7.
[50] 'Zum Tode Ewald Ammendes', *Deutsche Allgemeine Zeitung*, R 60532. Political Archive of the Foreign Ministry, Berlin.
[51] *Sitzungsbericht 1936*, pp. 8–12.
[52] Ibid, p. 50.

Italy) observed that as the League of Nations faltered, so belief in Europe as a community built on law began to fail too.[53]

Even more difficult was the congress meeting of 1937 which took place in London. Depending on your point of view, the venue either reflected the hope that Britain was a relatively neutral state in respect of national minority affairs which could be relied on to promote justice in Europe (not least through its influential position in the League); or it was taken as a machination by especially German minority groups to promote pro-German propaganda there. The quest to set up a meeting in London had a long history. Even before the 1936 congress had been convened (and within weeks of Ammende's death), Hasselblatt had been in touch with Berlin's Foreign Ministry in search of funding to support a meeting in London.[54] Very soon he visited that city, holding discussions with Willoughby Dickinson (who had long been interested in the organisation), C.A Macartney (a Foreign Office expert on Central and Eastern Europe) and former Foreign Secretary Sir Samuel Hoare.[55] In fact, Hasselblatt headed a multi-national delegation from the congress which included Germans, Hungarians, Catalans and Ukrainians. They met with MPs, members of the League of Nations Union, the diplomatic corps and the international press. Lord Noel-Buxton, well-known for his extensive engagement in League of Nations affairs, was present and must have enjoyed von Szüllö's speech which likened the League to a doctor who was a bit sick himself.[56]

When the congress convened in London in 1937, its propaganda purpose was barely concealed. The London proceedings dwelt at length on the congress's work during its halcyon days. There was talk of it representing three quarters of Europe's national minorities (or 30 million people), its Christian values and rights of self-administration.[57] Furthermore, a number of the speeches were tailored directly to drawing Britain into support for the cause of minorities. This was very clear in, for instance, Graebe's presentation:

> At the previous meeting it was decided to hold this meeting
> in London, in the expectation that England would show
> more appreciation than other countries for the position of
> European Minorities in mind at the impending reform of the
> League of Nations and to ensure that their rights, laid down

---

[53] Ibid, pp. 62–8.
[54] 28.4.36. Hasselblatt to v. Twardowski. R 60496. Political Archive of the Foreign Ministry, Berlin.
[55] 'Notiz betr. Londoner Aktion des Nationalitäten-Kongresses.' R 60532. Political Archive of the Foreign Ministry, Berlin.
[56] 'Besuch einer Delegation des Nationalitätenkongresses in London', *Nation und Staat* July - August 1936, p. 735.
[57] *The Congress of the European National Minorities. London Meeting 14–15 July 1937.* Vienna and Leipzig: Wilhelm Braumüller, 1938, pp. 20, 53 and 56–9.

in obsolete Minorities Treaties, be incorporated in the League of Nations Covenant as general International Law applicable to all Minorities, whether mandated or not.[58]

He went on:

> In the concert of the Powers, Great Britain's word is so effective and carries so much weight that it will be quite sufficient to secure recognition for the wishes of the Minorities, viz.: incorporation of their National rights in the League of Nations Covenant, Creation of a Committee of Investigation and of a permanent Minorities Committee in the League of Nations.[59]

He was stating directly an expectation that Britain assume a special responsibility to assist Europe's national minorities.

More erudite and subtle was Hasselblatt's presentation. Discussing 'British Endeavours and Proposals for the Improvement of the Rights of Minorities in Europe', he played on the victimhood of minorities, maintaining they had been 'absolutely left in the lurch' by the League of Nations.[60] He made it plain who could be their saviour: 'In no other country [apart from Britain] is there such an unselfish public interest in minority questions.'[61] Throughout his talk, Hasselblatt emphasised the extensive interest Britain had always shown in the affairs of national minorities, particularly in the League (for example, the speeches of Gilbert Murray, H.A.L. Fisher's role in securing appropriate declarations from the Baltic States and a memorandum drawn up by the British League of Nations Union in 1931). Having also discussed the interest of Britons such as Seton-Watson, Dickinson and Llewellyn-Jones in the affairs of minorities in Central and Eastern Europe, he concluded:

> If the rights of the minorities are disregarded, psychologically and politically, European peace will be seriously imperilled.[62]

His talk had amounted to a plea for London to take up the cause of national minorities as its own.

Yet there were clear omissions in the congress proceedings which cannot have gone unnoticed. Most notably, the Jewish Question was never

---

[58] Ibid, p. 75.
[59] Ibid, p. 78.
[60] Ibid, p. 38.
[61] Ibid, p. 40.
[62] Ibid, p. 50.

mentioned despite the fact that the Nuremberg Laws had been in place for two years. By the same token, London did not necessarily understand the congress properly. Those in the British capital were not always aware of the connections that existed between the different elements that comprised it. They did not necessarily appreciate its links to, say, the Association of German National Groups in Europe. Furthermore, British attitudes towards the members of the minorities could be dismissive. A London Foreign Office memorandum referred to them as 'professional trouble makers' and soon expressed the view that little could be done to assist them anyway.[63] The mood surrounding the proceedings was not helped by one of the congress's supporters, George Popoff, being expelled from the country thanks to MI5's intervention.[64] With time, London's suspicion that the congress was being run for the sake of German interests increased and British officials came to see Konrad Henlein as a voice for national minorities more worthy of support than that organisation.[65] The balance of opinion, however, was that London had no intention of engaging with the lives of Europe's national minorities when the state of international relations was so precarious. In any event, the 1937 congress had hardly any impact on British opinion, whether official or public.

### 5. Conclusion: giving Ammende context

This study has made quite clear that Ammende was far from a perfect character and, correspondingly, the minority politics in which he participated has been evaluated negatively by a number of authors. Sabine Bamberger-Stemmann, for example, maintains the European Congress of Nationalities became a propaganda tool for a sophisticated, multi-level revisionist foreign policy pursued by Weimar governments. Coming to power, the Nazis took over this policy and began re-forging it in their image. Specifically in terms of the congress, they took over an instrument already functioning in the interests of the *Reich* and proceeded to manipulate its purpose away from revisionism and towards expansionism. In this context, the exit of the Jews from the congress marked the end of opposition to essentially German initiatives and hence the organisation became ever more a vehicle for Nazi power politics. As Weimar ended, therefore, so did the hope of a viable and effective democratic minority lobby likely to have purchase on policy-making in Berlin and, indeed, Europe. So even though Bamberger-Stemmann believes Ammende, Hasselblatt and Graebe personally were traditionalists rather than Nazis, nonetheless from 1933 onwards they became facilitators

---

[63] S. Bamberger-Stemmann, *Der Europäische Nationalitätenkongreß 1925 bis 1938. Nationale Minderheiten zwischen Lobbyistentum und Grossmachtinteressen*. Marburg: Verlag Herder-Institut, 2000, pp. 361–3.

[64] Ibid, p. 365.

[65] Ibid, pp. 370–2.

for Hitler's foreign policy. They have been described as a 'front' masking the activity of a more fundamental policy drive coming not from roughly democratic activists, but from 'agitating functionaries'.[66]

Although Bamberger-Stemmann recognises that the congress *could* have become a 'strong, enduring and successful representation and movement of European minorities' the chance was lost owing to its intrinsic weaknesses and the context in which it operated. In the end, she says, the 'history of the European Congress of Nationalities is one of breakdown.' Ammende's quest for funding drove the organisation into the arms of Hungarian and German nationalism. In this light, the departure of the Jews was not the result of anti-Semitism among the minorities *per se*, but reflected the dependence of particularly German ethnic groups on Berlin.[67]

Bamberger-Stemman assesses the achievements of the congress as mediocre:

> The effect of the ECN ultimately was weak. None of the goals Ammende had when he founded the ECN were achieved, neither the solidarity of minorities, nor the reform of the petition system, nor the recognition of minorities as subjects of international law.[68]

The author also makes plain, however, there was always a limit to how much Ammende and those around him were ever likely to achieve, particularly since the Allies had not accepted national minorities as independent actors on the world stage when they formed the post-war order. Given the strictures of the time, neither were they likely to develop and function like modern lobbying bodies in present-day democracies.[69] Equally, once Hitler was in place in Berlin and Germany had left the League of Nations, the chance of the congress existing as an independent force became slimmer than ever because it needed desperately some kind of active sponsor which could only be an interested big state. So despite all of their efforts, the national minorities just were not in a position to drive forward an independent policy; in the context of the times, they always needed a connection with either a co-national state or some other one.[70]

Bamberger-Stemmann's judgements can be bleak. In connection with Ammende, for instance, she says that, in the end, minority politics became 'purely a vehicle for national egoism'.[71] Although Ammende was always acutely aware of the priorities attached to the German nation, for a long time he was quite right that the interests of ethnic Germans were closely

---

[66] Bamberger-Stemmann, *Der Europäische Nationalitätenkongreß 1925 bis 1938*, pp. 389–91.
[67] Ibid, pp. 391–3.
[68] Ibid, p. 395.
[69] Ibid, p. 396.
[70] Ibid, pp. 396–7.
[71] Ibid, p. 348.

related to those of other national minorities. Hence, at its inception, the congress did represent a forum with the potential to pursue general interests. These would have offered benefits to the 8 million or so members of the German nation beyond the borders of the Weimar Republic, but they would have offered benefits to other minorities too. The fact that Ammende's agenda slimmed down over the years until it was left very much reflecting German interests was not caused just by his own mentality, it also reflected how the international world increasingly fragmented along the lines of national interests narrowly construed. Given that the sense of unity epitomised by the creation of the League of Nations broke up into something more fractured and antagonistic, it is hard to see how a non-state actor perpetually in need of resources could have remained insulated from the wider trends and master of his own destiny. Nonetheless, the trouble with Ammende was that even though he was affected by general developments, still at key points (such as over the Jewish Question) he did not do enough to take a stand based on principle. So this is why we should recognise Ammende's better motives and the beneficial possibilities his work made available (in the 1920s at least), but at the same time recognise fully his feet of clay (as well as those of the people around him).

Yet for all their ultimate complicity with Hitler's politics, it is interesting to notice that, in different ways, the Baltic Germans named here all remained outsiders from the Nazi regime. The most obvious case was Paul Schiemann, who lived under house arrest in Riga during the period of Nazi occupation. Also, however, Ammende's world cruise and death in China can be seen as a sign of him having reached a dead end. His agenda for Europe's minorities had gone as far as it could go, so what exactly was left? From his perspective, why not take some more money and conjure up a reason for a world cruise? Even Hasselblatt must have come to realise his superfluity in the Third *Reich*. As war started in 1939, he found himself writing essays about Baltic German history and compiling a timeline of key dates. The chronology ended with the note:

> 18 October 1939: the first steamer with Baltic German settlers leaves Estonia[72]

In other words, from helping draft the cultural autonomy law of 1925 which was supposed to underpin the future of Baltic Germans in Estonia, Hasselblatt found himself co-operating with a *Reich* government which negotiated their emigration (or *Umsiedlung*) ahead of the absorption of their homeland into a Soviet sphere of interest.[73] So even though Hasselblatt became attached to Rosenberg's office, writing racially-attuned memoranda

---

[72] W. Hasselblatt, 'Einsatz der Baltendeutschen', *Nation und Staat* (1939) November, p. 59.
[73] For a study of the '*Umsiedlung*', see D. Loeber, *Diktierte Option. Die Umsiedlung der Deutsch-Balten aus Estland und Lettland*. Neumünster: Karl Wachholtz, 1972.

for it, he must have been under no illusion of the hopeless quality that his life had taken on.[74] More dramatically, now living in Vienna, on 8 December 1939 Üxküll von Guldenbrand committed suicide. The act was comment enough.

At the end of the day, all of the ethnic Germans identified in this study, including even Paul Schiemann, were believers in some kind of German mission in the East. They were part of a long tradition of demographic and cultural transfer from Germany eastwards, first introducing then underpinning 'Germanic' or 'European' values to lands where there was perceived to be an interface with oriental, Asiatic or even barbarian values. Building on centuries of hegemony in the Baltic region, including long-established service to the Tsar, Baltic Germans felt a special calling and affinity for this mission. Hence, even though Baltic Germans could only be numbered in thousands, still they felt a sense of purpose and importance that far-outstripped their population size. They felt their role and the culture which supported it to be vital to the preservation of European values in the face of a constant threat from the East.

The sense of importance that went with being a Baltic German could have been one of the problems intrinsic to this period's nationality movement. By way of comparison, it is often said (at least partly as a joke) that the problem with policemen and -women starts with the kind of people who want to join the police force. The role attracts people who like the idea of wielding authority, or being law and order personified. By way of comparison, it is possible that in the 1920s and 1930s, they very people who became most active in respect of minority rights had something about them which subverted their role. That is to say: why would someone become so very actively engaged with minority rights in the first place? Certainly there was a role for those standing up for justice and wanting to fight persecution based on prejudice, but these 'positive' motives were not the sole ones. At least some of those who were motivated to engage forcefully with national minority affairs at this time felt the superiority of their national identity most keenly. Baltic Germans, by virtue of their material and cultural inheritances, both had plenty to lose (i.e. their privilege in the Baltic arena), and believed they had a duty to champion particular values in Central and Eastern Europe. Hence it is easy to appreciate that, for people like Ammende, engagement with national minority affairs, if not motivated by nationalism pure and simple, could still have spoken of a kind of intrinsic superiority or sense of mission that, eventually, became less than helpful to his cause.

---

[74] See M. Housden, 'Ambiguous Activists. Estonia's Model of Cultural Autonomy as Interpreted by Two of its Founders: Werner Hasselblatt and Ewald Ammende', *Journal of Baltic Studies* 35 (2004) pp. 231–53.

## Conclusion

## The need for more histories of national minorities

### 1. Alternative Europe

Ammende's life and particularly his work in the European Congress of Nationalities provides a glimpse into a different Europe—one with a far higher proportion of self-conscious, indigenous national minorities (particularly Germans, Jews and Ukrainians) and in which there was the possibility of states being less 'national' and more multi-ethnic. In this light, the study hints at a different way Europe could have evolved: as less of a continent built on nation states and more of a continent built on states of nations—or 'anational states', to use Paul Schiemann's word. But for this to have happened, there would have had to have been a much greater readiness for statesmen, both in national governments as well as in the League of Nations, to have heeded the challenging arguments posed by minority spokesmen. Not least was the idea that by foregoing the status of a simple nation state (i.e. by devolving some sovereignty to national cultural organisations), state structures would have become more flexible and resilient in the face of ethnically and politically complicated domestic and international environments. By offering national minorities less cause for dissatisfaction, the adaptation promised to forestall irredenta and the receptiveness of minority communities to targeted political propaganda.

Based on such a model, in the 1920s Europe could have set itself on a different kind of trajectory to that which emerged. Of course, to have succeeded ultimately it would have required a different historical context. Not least, it would have needed a still more determined German state fighting for the rights of national minorities over a longer period inside the League of Nations—something which called for Stresemann to have lived and worked for at least five years longer. Also it would have required either Carl Georg Bruns to have lived longer or else for his replacement as legal advisor within the Association of German National Groups in Europe to have had less of a *völkisch* caste of mind than Werner Hasselblatt. The latter observation underlines that, for Europe to have had a good chance of capitalising on these alternative options concerning the management of national minorities, certainly states (led by Germany) would have had to have adopted different sets of attitudes and practices, but equally key national minorities really would have had to have chosen different options themselves.

Nonetheless, before Stresemann died and before Hasselblatt was in Berlin, the European national minority movement, led by German groups and with ties to a basically democratic German Foreign Ministry, held out the possibility of different options for the continent. In this context, a connection between Berlin and the congress leadership need not be interpreted as

indicative of a drive to revise the terms of the Treaty of Versailles.[1] Support
by Berlin for German national minorities—with the latter located firmly in
the context of a pan-European minority movement—also had the possibility
of promoting a peaceful multi-cultural continent. Furthermore, the longer
Europe's post-war borders remained unchanged and the more populations
became used to the status quo, the more the multi-cultural option would have
become routinised for the long-term.

## 2. Peace, national identity and missed opportunities

As history actually unfolded, however, constructive possibilities were
swamped by destructive realities. So how are we left to evaluate the idea of
using the language of national identity to talk peace?

In the 1920s there was not necessarily a conflict between
recognising national difference and providing security in Europe. There is
scope to maintain that the main difficulty was as much that of ineffective
international management regimes (on the part of the League of Nations and
individual states alike) as of the prior existence of tensions between different
national groups 'on the ground'. By the mid-1920s at least, lots of
possibilities were still open. There was still dynamism associated with new
state-building projects. Democracy was still accepted across most of Europe;
there was the optimism associated with Locarno; yet the positive spirit did
not make the transition to the 1930s. There is little doubt, for instance, that
the League of Nations missed an opportunity over the 'Year of Minorities' in
1929. Despite a strong case for reform being made by a series of senior,
thoughtful politicians, Adatci's final proposals were feeble. In the light of
them, what status should anyone with a serious interest in national minorities
have accorded that organisation and its key players? In other words, even if
we question whether the League of Nations had sufficient strength to become
a truly effective champion of national minorities in inter-war Europe, in the
light of lukewarm documents such as the Adatci report it appears as though
the statesmen staffing Geneva's corridors were hardly dedicated to fighting
for them. Thereafter, the drift within the German minority movement, the
readiness to accept anti-Semitism and the rise of the Sudeten German agenda
encountered far too few countervailing forces.

During the inter-war period, it is fair to say that the language of
nationality always had different strands, being used differently by given
individuals, contested by some and misunderstood by others. On balance,
however, in the 1920s it was mostly about preserving valued identities and
seeking accommodation within the *status quo*: to cite Carl Schirren from the
previous century, at this point the concern of most nationality spokesmen

---

[1] For example, S. Bamberger-Stemmann, *Der Europäische Nationalitätenkongreß 1925 bis
1938. Nationale Minderheiten zwischen Lobbyistentum und Grossmachtinteressen*. Marburg:
Verlag Herder-Institut, 2000, p. 390.

identified in this study was to survive and to become accepted as part of the prevailing reality rather than to change that reality as such. As time progressed, however, concerns with national identity became increasingly wrapped up with self-interest, exclusivity and asserting superiority. Roughly speaking, it was a story of liberal nationalism losing its 'liberalism' and becoming something more exclusionary and, ultimately, threatening. In other words, while clearly it is possible to talk peace using the language of national identity (as the 1920s showed), the dangers are obvious. It is an undertaking that can only be pursued carefully and when subjected to constant critical evaluation for fear of the agenda being subverted over time by less honestly motivated factions.

## 3. Institutionalising national differences

And what of the institutionalisation of national differences? Was the establishment of a system such as cultural autonomy really suitable as a foundation for the self-confident co-operation of diverse elements in a multi-ethnic society, or was it solidifying social divisions where they did not need to be solidified—retarding social mobility and becoming wrapped up with 'othering' in the process? We might also wonder whether the creation of a system such as cultural autonomy can be viewed as a transitional step appropriate to, say, a post-colonial society where a segmented population was being prepared eventually for less conservative, less hide-bound ways of life. Was it a step on the way to longer term social modernisation and liberation leading to a still more free-wheeling kind of diversity? Hence, it could be seen as the mid-point of a progression: imperial society—transition (including cultural autonomy or a similar system)—modernity / postmodernity. Expressed differently, the same progression might represent a transformation as follows: imperial society incorporating traditional divisions and antagonisms—a phase of confidence-building (incorporating a system such as cultural autonomy) during which formerly alienated groups experience processes of reconciliation and adjustment to each other—the emergence of a more united society in which inhabitants can construct their identities as they see fit without requiring the support of elaborate state-backed institutions.

Looking at social developments from the perspective of the Baltic German community, it is easy to see cultural autonomy as a half-way house between empire and full-blown democratic pluralism. The Baltic Germans were a former élite who felt their national identity strongly. They experienced a difficult war, a major socio-economic upheaval, the existence of a tremendous external threat (Bolshevism), democracy smashing the old traditional corporatist mechanisms of social organisation, the subsequent rise of fascist possibilities and an international society which could not offer them unequivocal protection. They were members of a community with a strong sense of self which for centuries had managed to exist autonomously in a system coined by foreign powers. They had even survived in the face of Russification. In this light, for them, a system of social organisation that retained some characteristics of corporatism, but updated them to a new social situation, and which permitted a geographically dispersed population to pull together, surely met the needs of the time. It reflected what the Baltic Germans had been, recognised the realities of the situation in which they found themselves, and at least allowed the group to bind together and experience some kind of common roots in the *Heimat* into the future. As such, it was likely to be a much less fraught option than, say, emigration or cultural assimilation. But was cultural autonomy likely ever to become a long-standing means of organising multi-ethnic society?

Perhaps an individual's response to the question reflects the way he or she reacts to the idea of national identity: can it be reflected in just one choice or is it something more malleable and vacillating? It is conceivable that under some circumstances national belonging involves a single, unequivocal, unchanging commitment and is an utmost priority in an individual's life. Under such circumstances, commitment to a single established institution defining the extent of a person's educational and cultural life would not be difficult to make. What happens, however, when the possibilities facing individuals are more complicated? What happens if families have parents from different national groups, if children use more than one language in everyday life, if people appreciate authors and folk tales in more than one language, if they come from a land inhabited by several different nationalities? What if, in other words, some degree of ambiguity and shifting of national identity, possibly even by any given situation, is par for the course for a given region? What if some people at least would choose to be both, say, German *and* Estonian in various ways or at various times? Would a system like cultural autonomy make sense in a circumstance such as that; or would it rely on an artificial, unhelpful fixity?

In reply, it is important to be realistic about what cultural autonomy both was and could ever be. It was and is no universal panacea for the organisational and policy-resourcing challenges posed by multi-lingual, multi-cultural, multi (and unequally)-resource-based society. It could never hope to make society's fracture lines and suspicions disappear miraculously. No matter how multi-ethnic society is organised, sooner or later decisions have to be taken about how to divide resources—for example over expenditure on culture and education—and in Central and Eastern Europe in the 1920s, cultural autonomy was one method that came to the fore as a means to achieving this distribution relatively fairly. As such, it was never supposed to be a magic wand, it was always more like one tool in the box; something available to be applied if the situation was appropriate. But whether or not it was applied, the problem of the fair apportionment of resources, indeed the underlying just treatment of all members of society, was an issue that remained to be addressed by all interested citizens.

Cultural autonomy was important in its context. It was applied at a time and in a place where many people felt their nationality keenly and where it represented a significant characteristic of life. It is an entirely contingent point as to whether national identity still takes on such significance today. Is national identity still likely to be felt to such a deep extent that it could justify splitting children into different schools for their education? Does this one variable still take on such significance that it is more important than bringing different children together in the same school and managing in that one institution difficulties surrounding multi-lingualism and multiple cultures? Organisation and management as it actually happens has to be the subject of a conversation between minority, majority and government institutions—a conversation which, by its very nature, needs to take account of the requirements of all sides and which, no doubt, needs to be returned to frequently as different organisational possibilities are implemented and as society (along with those comprising it) changes. And for those engaged with actual or possible projects for separate cultural lives and perhaps separate schooling by national culture, the experiences from inter-war European history, not to say the strengths and weaknesses of the proponents of cultural autonomy both nationally and internationally, provide food for thought and stand as an example of one particular attempt to manage diversity.

The promotion of cultural autonomy was accompanied by hopes for survival, a quest for personal fulfilment and the desire for security and harmony, but also by weasel words, beliefs in national superiority and some kind of a desire to insulate aspects of community life from wider historical trends. Even accepting its mixed reality, however, it was certainly better than some of the other nationally-based possibilities occurring at the time, whether—on the side of the majority—persecution and forced assimilation, or—on the side of the minority—revanche and irredentism. In comparative perspective at least, therefore, it was more than just a negative historical phenomenon.

Of course there will always be different ways to try to manage ethnically and linguistically complicated environments. In Wales, for instance, today the aim is to manage a multi-lingual environment on a school by school basis, as the following extract from an official paper explains:

> The term 'bilingual provision' is used to refer to a wide range of teaching and learning settings which include varying amounts of Welsh language in the delivery. Bilingual schools can include those where a large proportion of the curriculum is delivered through the medium of Welsh, those where there are two streams— Welsh-medium and English-medium—taught separately

(sometimes called 'dual stream' schools), and those where
only a few elements of the curriculum or only a small
number are taught through the medium of Welsh. In further
education colleges in particular, bilingual provision can
refer to situations where classes are taught simultaneously
in the two languages, or where courses contain Welsh-
medium modules.[2]

Decisions about how individual schools organise their language requirements
are taken locally, under the auspices of the local authorities rather than
central government.[3] Actually, during the inter-war period the German
minority movement had shown an interest in what was happening in Wales,
with Carl Georg Bruns visiting the country to examine education there in
1925, but that approach did not fit with the requirements of German
minorities.[4] Naturally the regulation of schooling in Wales had not simply
grown up over night; it is a topic with a history all of its own (and it is worth
noting that what Bruns observed cannot have been exactly the same as what
happens today).[5] In any event, the situation being addressed by Ammende
and his colleagues in the 1920s had a different historical context, a different
cultural heritage, a different immediate political framework and a different
geo-political position. The system they chose, therefore, played best to their
situation and character. It was only to be expected that a former colonial élite
had the self-confidence to promote it at the international level too. As such,
however, Ammende and those around him became unique: essentially private
individuals, members of Central and Eastern European minorities rather than
governments, engaging in not just national but continental debates about the
terms of the world they were inhabiting. It was quite appropriate for them to
act in this way. At the time in question, if they had not done so, how many
established, responsible statesmen would have come forward to speak up
with determination on their behalf?

---

[2] *Welsh-medium Education Strategy.* Information document 083/2010. Welsh Assembly
Government, April 2010, pp.8–9.
[3] Ibid, p.13.
[4] Bamberger-Stemmann, *Der Europäische Nationalitätenkongreß 1925 bis 1938,* p. 350.
[5] The information document already mentioned gives the following recent details: the first
Welsh-medium state primary school opened in 1947 and by 2009 438 (29%) primary schools in
Wales were classified as Welsh medium; the first Welsh-medium secondary school opened in
1956 and by 2009 55 (25%) secondary schools in Wales were classified as Welsh-medium.
*Welsh-medium Education Strategy,* p. 4.

# Bibliography

## Archives

**Baltic Central Library, Riga**
Schiemann papers.

**Latvian State Library, Riga**
*Rigasche Post.*
*Rigasche Rundschau.*

**National Library of Estonia, Tallinn**
Fond 85, Nimistu 1, Sāilik 60, Leht 166: Hasselblatt's manuscript, *Über die Kulturautonomie.*
Fond 1000: Baltic German affairs in the 1920s.

**Estonian State Library, Tallinn**
*Revaler Bote.*
*Revalsche Zeitung.*

**Federal Archive, Koblenz**
1250. Wilfan papers.
1077. Boehm papers.

**Johann-Gottfried Herder Institute, Marburg**
Manuscript 53. W.Hasselblatt, Von der Kulturautonomie zum Nationalitätenkongress.
Published *Sitzungsberichte* of the European Congress of Nationalities (see published primary sources for details).
*Nation und Staat.*

**Political Archive of the German Foreign Ministry, Berlin**
R31832, R35801, R60426, R60427, R60462, R 60463, R60464, R60465, R60466, R60467, R60493, R60494, R60495, R60496, R60527, R60528, R60529, R60530, R60531, R60532, R60533, R60594, R60595, R60596, R62162, R127510.

**Institute for Contemporary History, Munich**
ED224/21. Balling papers.
MA128/3. Documents dealing with Nazi authorities and German national minorities.
NG3908. Details of a memorandum written by Hasselblatt on the character of Nazi occupation policies.

**League of Nations Archive, United Nations Library, Geneva**
*League of Nations. Official Journal.*
R 656. Famine in Russia.
R 657. Famine in Russia.
R 1648. Minority Questions.
R 1656. Minority Questions.
R 1664. Protection of Minorities in Estonia.
R 1684. Minorities Questions in Estonia.
R 1686. Minority Questions.
R 1687. Correspondence with Individuals.
R 1700. Minorities.
R 1754. Famine in Russia.
R 2161. Minorities.
R 3932. Minorities.
S 338. General.
S 340. Minorities.
S 342. Minorities.
S 364. Minorities

**Hebrew Union College, Cincinnati**
Protokoll der jüdischen Welt-Konferenz. Genf, 14–17 Auguat 1932.
Protocol of the 2nd World Jewish Conference, 5–8 September 1933, Geneva.

**Central Zionist Archive, Jerusalem**
A126 and A 306. Covering correspondence with and about Ammende involving Goldman, Margulies, Motzkin and Robinson.

**Russian State Military Archive, Moscow**
Fond 1502. Ammende papers.

**Published primary sources**

*Texts from before 1945 and written by key participants in the book's main events. Historical journals and newspapers are identified by their titles alone. For the specific articles used in this study, please see the footnotes provided in each chapter.*

Amende [sic], E., *Europe and Soviet Russia*. Riga: R. Ruetz and Co, 1921.

Ammende E. (ed.), *Die Nationalitäten in den Staaten Europas. Sammlung von Lageberichten*. Vienna-Leipzig: Wilhelm Braumüller, 1931.

Ammende, E., *Gefährdung des europäischen Friedens durch die nationale Unduldsamkeit*. Vienna: Friedrich Jasper, undated.

Ammende, E., *Human Life in Russia*. Cleveland: Zubal, 1984. Originally published as *Muss Russland hungern? Menschen und Völkerschicksale in der Sowjetunion*. Vienna: Wilhelm Braumüller, 1936.

Azcárate, P. de, *League of Nations and National Minorities. An Experiment*. Washington: Carnegie Endowment, 1945.

*Baltische Blätter.*

*Baltische Monatsschrift.*

Barnard F.M. (ed.), *J.G. Herder on Social and Political Culture*. CUP, 1969.

Boehm, M.H., *Die Krise des deutschbaltischen Menschen. Eine Studie zum Kulturproblem der Ostseeprovinzen Russlands*. Berlin: Verlag der Grenzboten, 1915.

Boehm, M.H., 'Ewald Ammende als Mittler der Europäischen Volksgruppen', *Jahrbuch des Baltischen Deutschtums* 10 (1963) 55–60.

Carr, E.H., *Nationalism and After*. London: Macmillan, 1945.

Cecil, R., *A Great Experiment*. London: Jonathan Cape, 1941.

*Der Aufsteig.*

*Deutsche Politische Hefte.*

Donath, H. (ed.), *Paul Schiemann. Leitartikel, Reden und Aufsaetze. Band II 1919-19.33. Heft 1: Juli 1919 bis April 1920*. Frankfurt a.M., 1986.

*Europäische Nationalitäten-Korrespondenz.*

*Estland*. Reval: Nord- und Ostdeutsche Forschungsgemeinschaft, 1924.

*Estländischdeutscher Kalender.*

*Europäische Nationalitäten-Korrespondenz.*

*Europäische Revue.*

*Frankfurter Zeitung.*

Greaves, H.R.G., *The League Committees and World Order. A Study of the Permanent Expert Committees of the League of Nations as an Instrument of International Government*. OUP, 1931.

Hitler, A., *Hitler's Secret Book*. Introduction by Telford Taylor. New York: Grove Press, 1961

Johnsen, J.E. (ed.), *Reconstituting the League of Nations*. New York: H.W. Wilson, 1943.

Kellor, F., *Security against War. Volume 1*. New York: Macmillan, 1924.

Kershaw, R.N., 'The League and the Protection of Linguistic, Racial and Religious Minorities' in *Problems of Peace*.

*Kölnische Zeitung*.

*League of Nations. Official Journal*—proceedings and documents as indicated in the footnotes.

Macartney, C.A., *National States and National Minorities*. OUP, 1934.

Maddison, E., *Die nationalen Minderheiten Estlands und ihre Rechte,.* Tallinn: 1926.

*Manchester Guardian*.

Miller, M., review of E. Ammende, *Human Life in Russia, International Affairs* 15 (1936) pp. 956–7.

*Nation und Staat*.

*Nasz Przegląd*.

*Neue Zürcher Zeitung*.

Nicolai, H., *Die rassengesetzliche Rechtslehre*. Munich: Eher and Son, 1932.

Nicolai, H., *Oberschlesien im Ringen der Völker*. Breslau: Grass, Barth and Co., 1930.

*Prager Presse*.

*Problems of Peace*. Third Series. OUP, 1929.

Rappard, W.E., *The Geneva Experiment*. OUP, 1931.

Rauschning, H., *Hitler Speaks*. London: Thornton Butterworth, 1939.

*Revaler Bote / Revalsche Zeitung / Estländische Zeitung*.

*Rigasche Rundschau*.

Robinson, J., O. Karbach, M.M. Laserson, N. Robinson and M. Vichniak, *Were the Minorities Treaties a Failure?* New York: Antin Press, 1943.

Rosenberg, A., *The Myth of the Twentieth Century*. Torrance, CA: Noontide Press, 1982.

Schiemann, P., *Zwischen zwei Zeitaltern. Erinnerungen 1903–1919*. Lüneburg: Verlag Nordland-Druck, 1979.

*Sitzungsbericht des Kongresses der organisierten nationalen Gruppen in den Staaten Europas im Jahre 1925 zu Genf*. Vienna: Wilhelm Braumüller, 1926.

*Sitzungsbericht des Kongresses der organisierten nationalen Gruppen in den Staaten Europas. Genf 25.–27. August 1926*.Vienna: Wilhelm Braumüller, 1927.

*Sitzungsbericht des Kongresses der organisierten nationalen Gruppen in den Staaten Europas. Genf 22.–24. August 1927*. Vienna: Wilhelm Braumüller, 1928.

*Sitzungsbericht des Kongresses der organisierten nationalen Gruppen in den Staaten Europas. Genf 29.–31. August 1928.* Vienna: Wilhelm Braumüller, 1928.

*Sitzungsbericht des Kongresses der organisierten nationalen Gruppen in den Staaten Europas. Genf, 26 bis 28. August 1929.* Vienna and Leipzig: Wilhelm Braumüller, 1930.

*Sitzungsbericht des Kongresses der organisierten Nationalen Gruppen in den Staaten Europas. Genf, 3 bis 6 September 1930.* Vienna - Leipzig: Wilhelm Braumüller, 1931.

*Sitzungsbericht des congresses der organisierten nationalen Gruppen in den Staaten Europas. Genf 29 bis 31 1931.* Vienna and Leipzig: Wilhelm Braumüller, 1932.

*Sitzungsbericht des Kongresses der organisierten nationalen Gruppen in den Staaten Europas. Wien, 29. Juni bis 1. Juli 1932.* Wien-Leipzig: Wilhelm Braumüller, 1933.

*Sitzungsbericht des Kongresses der organisierten nationalen Gruppen in den Staaten Europas. Bern, 16. bis 19. September 1933.* Vienna-Leipzig: Wilhelm Braumüller, 1934.

*Sitzungsbericht des Kongresses der organisierten nationalen Gruppen in den Staaten Europas. Genf, 2 bis 4 September 1935.* Vienna-Leipzig: Wilhelm Braumueller, 1936.

*Sitzungsbericht des Kongresses der organisierten nationalen Gruppen in den Staaten Europas. Genf, 16 bis 17 September 1936.* Vienna-Leipzig: Wilhelm Braumüller, 1937.

*The Congress of the European National Minorities. London Meeting 14–15 July 1937.* Vienna and Leipzig: Wilhelm Braumüller, 1938.

Smuts, J., *The League of Nations: a Practical Suggestion.* London: Hodder and Stoughton.

Sweetser, A., 'The Non-Political Achievements of the League' in Johnsen (ed.), *Reconstituting the League of Nations.*

*Tägliche Rundschau.*

*Ten Years of World Co-operation.* Geneva: Secretariat of the League of Nations, 1930.

*The Daily Express.*

*The Daily Standard.*

*Vossische Zeitung.*

Vries, A. de, *Das Deutschtum in Estland.* Brandenburg: Sidow and Co., undated.

*Zehn Jahre Deutschpolitisches Arbeitsamt.* Reichenberg: Sudetendeutschen Verlag, 1929.

## Secondary sources

Agamben, G., 'We Refugees',
   http://jft-newspaper.aub.edu.lb/reserve/data/soan201-sk-mod7-
   agamben/Module7-G_Agamben-WeRefugees.pdf (accessed 12.13).
Alderman, G. (ed.), *Governments, Ethnic Groups and Political
   Representation*. Aldershot: Dartmouth Publishing, 1993.
Alenius, K., 'The Birth of Cultural Autonomy in Estonia: How, Why and for
   Whom?' *Journal of Baltic Studies* 38 (2007).
Arendt, H., 'We Refugees',
   www.stanford.edu/dept/DLCL/files/pdf/hannah_arendt
   _we_refugees.pdf (accessed 12.13).
Auer, S., *Liberal Nationalism in Central Europe*. New York:
   RoutledgeCurzon, 2004.
Auestad, L. (ed.), *Psychoanalysis and the Nation*. London: Karnac, 2014.
Auestad, L. (ed.), *Psychoanalysis and Politics. Exclusion and the Politics of
   Representation*. London: Karnac, 2012.
Aun, K., *Der völkerrechtliche Schutz nationaler Minderheiten in Estland von
   1917 bis 1940*. Hamburg: Joachim Heitmann, 1951.
Bamberger-Stemmann, S., *Der Europäische Nationalitätenkongreß 1925 bis
   1938. Nationale Minderheiten zwischen Lobbyistentum und
   Grossmachtinteressen*. Marburg: Verlag Herder-Institut, 2000.
Barbieri, S., *National Minorities in Post-Revolutionary and Soviet Russia
   (1917–1932). Theoretical Framework and Institutional Arrangements*.
   Doctoral thesis: University of San Marino, 2007/2010.
Beer, M. and S. Dyroff (eds.), *Politische Strategien nationaler Minderheiten
   in der Zwischenkriegszeit*. Munich: Oldenbourg, 2013.
Biagini, E.F. (ed.), *Citizenship and Community. Liberals, Radicals and
   Collective Identities in the British Isles 1865–1931*. CUP, 1996.
Claude, I.L., *National Minorities. An International Problem*. New York:
   Greenwood, 1955.
Cobban, A., *The Nation State and National Self-Determination*. London:
   Collins, 1969.
Dyroff, S., 'Der Platz der Völkerbundbeschwerde in den politischen
   Strategien nationaler Minderheiten. Positionen aus dem Kreis
   "Europäischen Nationalitätenkongresses"' in Beer and Dyroff (eds.),
   *Politische Strategien nationaler Minderheiten in der
   Zwischenkriegszeit*.
Figues, O., *A People's Tragedy*. London: Jonathan Cape, 1996.
Fink, C., *Defending the Rights of Others. The Great Powers, the Jews, and
   International Minority Prrotection, 1878–1938*. CUP, 2004.
Fromm, E., *Fear of Freedom*. London: Routledge and Kegan Paul, 1960.
Friedman, L., *The Lives of Erich Fromm: Love's Prophet*. New York:
   Columbia University Press, 2013.

Fromm, E., *The Sane Society*. London: Routledge and Kegan Paul, 1963.

Fromm, E., *To Have or to Be?* London: Continuum, 2009.

Garleff, M., *Deutschbaltische Politik zwischen den Weltkriegen*. Bonn-Bad Godesburg: Verlag Wiisenschaftliches Archiv, 1976.

Garleff, M., 'Deutschbaltische Publizisten: Ewald Ammende—Werner Hasselblatt—Paul Schiemann', *Berichte und Forschungen* 2 (1994) 189–229.

Garleff, M., 'Nationalitätenpolitik zwischen liberalem und völkischem Anspruch. Gleichklang und Spannung bei Paul Schiemann und Werner Hasselblatt' in Hehn and Kenez (eds.), *Reval und die Baltischen Länder*.

Garleff, M., 'Relations between the Political Representation of the Baltic Provinces and the Russian Government, 1850–1917' in Alderman (ed.), *Governments, Ethnic Groups and Political Representation*.

Gechtman, R., 'Conceptualizing National Cultural Autonomy—From the Austro-Marxists to the Jewish Labor Bund' in *The Simon Dubnow Institute Yearbook* (2005).

Gilbert, P., *The Philosophy of Nationalism*. Boulder, Colorado: Westview Press, 1998.

'Gorky—The Humanitarian', Russian Review, 27 (1968) 351–3.

Grundmann, K.H., *Deutschtumspolitik zur Zeit der Weimarer Republik*. Hanover: Hirschheydt, 1977

Hehn, J v. and C.J. Kenez (eds.), *Reval und die Baltischen Länder*. Marburg: Herder Institute, 1980.

Hehn, J. von, 'Zur Geschichte der deutschbaltischen nationalsozialistischen Bewegung in Estland', *Zeitschrift für Ostforschung* 26 (1977) 597–650.

Hiden, J., *Defender of Minorities. Paul Schiemann, 1876–1944*. London: Hurst, 2004.

Housden, M., 'Ambiguous Activists. Estonia's Model of Cultural Autonomy as Interpreted by Two of its Founders: Werner Hasselblatt and Ewald Ammende', *Journal of Baltic Studies* 35 (2004) 231–53.

Housden, M., 'Ewald Ammende and the Organisation of National Minorities in Inter-war Europe', *German History* 18 (2000) 439–60.

Housden, M. and D. Smith (eds), *Forgotten Pages in Baltic History. Diversity and Inclusion*. Amsterdam: Rodopi, 2011.

Housden, M., 'Psychoanalysis and Peace: Erich Fromm on History, Politics and the Nation' in Auestad (ed.), *Nationalism and the Body Politic*.

Housden, 'Securing the Lives of Ordinary People. Baltic Perspectives on the Work of the League of Nations' in Housden and Smith (eds.), *Forgotten Pages in Baltic History*.

Housden, M., *The League of Nations and the Organisation of Peace*. Harlow: Pearson, 2012.

Housden, M., 'When the Baltic Sea was a "bridge" for humanitarian action: the League of Nations, the Red Cross and the repatriation of prisoners of war between Russia and Central Europe 1920–22', *Journal of Baltic Studies* 38 (2007) 61–83.

Ijabs, I., 'Strange Baltic Liberalism: Paul Schiemann's Political Thought Revisited', *Journal of Baltic Studies* 40 (2009) 495–515.

Jackson Preece, J., *National Minorities and the European Nation-States System*. Oxford: Clarendon, 1998

Jankowsky, O.I., *Nationalities and National Minorities*. New York: Macmillan, 1945.

Killy, W. (ed.), *Deutsche Biographische Enzyklopädie*. Munich: K.G.Sauer, 1995.

Koch, F.C., The *Volga Germans. In Russia and the Americas, from 1763 to the Present*. Pennsylvania State University Press, 1977.

Lenz, W. (ed.), *Deutschbaltisches Biographisches Lexikon. 1710–1960*. Cologne: Böhlau Verlag, 1970.

Loeber, D., *Diktierte Option. Die Umsiedlung der Deutsch-Balten aus Estland und Lettland*. Neumünster: Karl Wachholtz, 1972.

Macedo, S., *Liberal Virtues. Citizenship, Virtue, and Community in Liberal Constitutional-ism*. Oxford: Clarendon Press, 1990.

March, U., *Die deutsche Ostsiedlung*. Bonn: Bund der Vertriebenen, 1998.

Margaliot, A. (eds.), *Documents on the Holocaust*. Jerusalem: Yad Vashem, 1999.

McVay, A.D. and L.Y. Luciuk (ed.), *The Holy See and the Holodomor. Documents from the Vatican Secret Archives on the Great Famine of 1932–1933 in Soviet Ukraine*. University of Toronto, 2011.

Miller, D., *On Nationality*. Oxford: Clarendon Press, 1995.

Mühlen, H. von zur. z., *Die baltischen Lande. Von der Aufsegelung bis zum Umsiedlung*. Bonn: Bund der Vertriebenen,1997.

Musgrave, T.D., *Self-Determination and National Minorities*. Oxford: Clarendon, 1997.

Myers, K., *Watching the Door*. Brooklyn: Soft Skull Press, 2009.

Newsome, W.B., '"Dead Lands" or "New Europe"? Reconstructing Europe, Reconfiguring Eastern Europe: "Westerners" and the Aftermath of the World War', *East European Quarterly* 36 (2002).

Nimni, E., 'National-Cultural Autonomy as an Alternative to Minority Territorial Nationalism' in Smith and Cordell (eds.), *Cultural Autonomy in Contemporary Europe*.

North, M., *Geschichte der Ostsee. Handel und Kulturen*. Munich: Beck, 2011.

Núñez Seixas, X-M., *Entre Ginebra y Berlin. La Cuestion de las Minorias Nacionales y la Politica Internacional en Europa 1914–1939*. Madrid: Akal, 2001.

Page, S., *The Formation of the Baltic States. A Study of the Effects of Great Power Politics upon the Emergence of Lithuania, Latvia and Estonia*. Cambridge: Harvard University Press, 1959.

Pearson, R., *National Minorities in Eastern Europe. 1848–1945*. London: Macmillan, 1983,

Plakans, A., *A Concise History of the Baltic States*. CUP, 2011.

Plasseraud, Y., *Les États Baltiques des Sociétés Gigognes*. Brest: Armeline, 2006

Rauch, G. von, *The Baltic States. The Years of Independence. Estonia, Latvia, Lithuania 1917–1940*. London: Hurst, 1974.

Reves, E., *The Anatomy of Peace*. London: Penguin, 1947.

Scheuermann, M., *Minderheitenschutz contra Konfliktverhütung? Die Minderheitenpolitik des Völkerbundes in den zwanziger Jahren*. Marburg/Lahn: Verlag Herder Institut, 2000.

Schlau, W. *et al, Die Deutsch-Balten*. Munich: Langen Müller, 1995.

Schot, B., *Nation oder Staat? Deutschland und der Minderheitenschutz. Zur Völkerbunds-politik der Stresemann Ära*. Marburg-Lahn: Herder Institute, 1988.

Sharp, A., *The Versailles Settlement: Peacemaking in Paris, 1919*. Basingstoke: Palgrave, 1991.

Smith, D.J. and K. Cordell (eds.), *Cultural Autonomy in Contemporary Europe*. London: Routledge, 2008.

Smith, D.J. and J. Hiden, *Ethnic Diversity and the Nation State*. London: Routledge, 2012.

Steiner, Z., *Lights that Failed. European International History 1919–1933*. OUP, 2005.

Tamir, Y., *Liberal Nationalism*. New Jersey: Princeton University Press. 1993.

Tottle, D., *Fraud, Famine and Fascism: The Ukrainian Genocide Myth from Hitler to Harvard*. Toronto: Progress Books, 1987.

Uibopuu, H.J., 'The Estonian Republic in its Constitutional Development 1918–40', *Internationales Recht und Diplomatie* (1972).

Walters, F.P., *A History of the League of Nations*. OUP, 1952.

*Welsh-medium Education Strategy*. Information document 083/2010. Welsh Assembly Government, April 2010.

Zetterberg, S., *Der Liga der Fremdvölker Russlands 1916–1918*. Helsinki: Finnish Historical Studies, 1978.

# Index

Acton, Lord, 73, 109
Adatci, Mineitciro, 2, 201, 203, 204, 206, 207, 208, 210, 214, 232, 236, 392
Alenius, Kari, 65, 89
Ammende family, 13
Anational state, 62, 391
Anti-Comintern activity, 358–9, 376
Anti-Soviet sentiment, 363–5
Apponyi, Count, 132, 151, 167, 191
Arendt, Hannah, 8
Association of German Minorities / German National Groups in Europe, 50, 53, 126, 128, 129, 130, 139, 145, 148, 218, 221, 222, 223, 232, 238, 240, 252, 253, 256, 258, 263, 271, 272, 275, 300–2, 343, 348, 386, 391
Auer, Stefan, 108
Aun, Karl, 58, 116
Authoritarianism, 350–1
Autonomous schooling law, Latvia, 64, 329, 335
Azácarte, Pablo de, 64, 116, 152, 163, 164, 165, 189, 197, 198, 213, 220, 247, 315, 316

Balkanisation of Europe, 140, 229
Baltic German population, 66
Baltic Regiment, 21
Bamberger-Stemmann, Sabine, 351–2, 358, 368, 386–90
Bauer, Otto, 74
Beermann, Johannes, 78, 105
Beneš, Eduard, 151, 218, 342
Berg, Hermann von, 75, 77
Bern, 292, 302–5, 318
Bernheim petition, 280–1, 297, 325
Bethlen, Count, 146, 160
Biography, 2
Blokland, Jongheer van, 194, 199, 200
Bock, Max, 22
Boehm, Max Hildebert, 23, 26, 139, 260, 278–80, 325, 326, 328, 350, 380
Bolshevism, 40, 41, 47–8, 99–102, chapter 15
Bovet, Ernest, 178, 200, 215, 285
Brandsch, Rudolf, 52, 149, 150, 190, 238, 241, 242, 252, 253, 254, 271
Brest-Litovsk, Treaty of, 115
Briande, Aristide, 123, 203, 208, 224, 227, 236, 251
*Brüder in Not*, 354, 356, 359, 361
Bruns, Carl Georg, 148, 218, 251, 253, 256, 263, 396

Casanovas, Joan, 174, 175, 237
Catalonia, 234, 260, 304
Cecil, Robert, 114, 125, 135, 151, 261
Chamberlain, Austen, 122, 137, 191, 203, 206
*Cheka*, 36
Chicherin, 33, 34
Christiansen, Ernst, 157, 237
Churchill, Winston, 116
Cobban, Alfred, 73, 115, 116–7, 189
Colban, Erik, 123, 124, 130, 135, 143, 150, 151, 152, 163, 164, 197, 198, 200, 213, 237
Collective security, 114
Committee of Three, 123
Committee on New States and the Protection of Minorities, 118–9
Congress of Berlin (1878), 119
Congress of Nationalities, 72, 119
Corporatism, 312
Coudenhove-Kalergi, Richard, 224
Cultural autonomy law, Estonia, chapter 3, chapter 4, 338, 394–5

Dandurand, Raoul, 199, 201, 203, 205, 206, 207
Dickinson, Willoughby, 177, 199, 216, 363, 384
Disarmament, 177, 330
Dissimilation, 280–1, 302, 309, 323
Drummond, Eric, 122, 125, 126, 130, 135, 143, 151, 152, 163, 164, 166, 198, 214
Dubnow, Simon, 74

Ebner, Mayer, 232
Einbund, Karl, Interior Minister, 48, 92, 94, 95, 97, 100, 102, 105, 106, 341
Estelrich, Joan, 172, 178, 188, 209, 210, 225
Estonian constitution, 65, 74, 77, 82, 83

Famine, 37–8, 42–6, chapter 15, 375
Flachbarth, Ernst, 175, 179
Freytag-Loringhoven, Baron, 295
Frick, Wilhelm, 291
Frisia, 237–46
Fromm, Eric, 6, 7, 8

Gabrys, Juosas, 139, 246, 247
Galvanauskas, Ernestas, 151, 167
Gama, Domicio da, 125, 134, 136
Geneva, 142, 146, 189, 292, 348

Genoa conference, 32–5
George, Lloyd, 115
German House, Cilli, 165, 331
Goebbels, Josef, 290
Goldmann, Nathan, 322, 323, 326
Göring, Hermann, 291
Gorky, Maxim, 41, 46
Graebe, Kurt, 213, 215, 252, 257, 273, 287, 290, 292, 300, 307, 310, 311, 317, 327, 333, 343, 384, 387
Gürke, Norbert, 276–80, 281, 286, 287

Hasselblatt, Werner, 1, 2, 4, 61, 62, 63, 68, 70, 75, 79, 80, 83, 88, 90 , 93, 94, 95, 97, 102, 103, 105, 106, 107, 109, 154, 176, 217, 219, 220, 221, 222, 223, 232, 236, 237, 249, 256, 270, 273, 275, 282, 283, 291, 292, 293, 294, 297, 300, 301, 310, 311, 314, 317, 324, 325, 332, 343, 348, 349, 359, 376, 380, 381, 383, 384, 387, 388, 389, 391
Headlam-Morley, J.W., 116, 121
Henlein, Konrad, 342, 386
Herder, J.G., 18, 169
Herriot, Édouard, 373
Heyking, Alfons, 134, 135, 143
Hitler, Adolf, 69, 263–71, 273–4, 275, 330, 334–5, 337, 346, 352, 387
Holocaust, 9
Hymans, Paul, 151

Innitzer, Cardinal Theodor, 359–63
Intolerance, 180, 334, 336, 347

Jaakson, Jüri, 90, 91, 92, 93, 96, 100, 102, 105
Jesser, Franz, 223
Jewish issues, 142, 159, chapter 11, chapter 12, chapter 13, 331, 338, 388
Jones, Gareth, 357, 366
Junghann, Otto, 194, 327

Kaczmarek, Jan, 235, 237, 239, 242
Kant, Immanuel, 18
Karall, Lorenz, 347–8, 350
Kartaschoff, Prof., 351
Kershaw, R.N., 121
Keynes, John Maynard, 181, 187
Koch, Harry, 22, 68, 70, 87, 105, 106, 337, 340
Köster, Adolf, 147, 162, 218
Krabbe, Ludvig, 247, 248, 314, 315, 333
*Kulturrat*, 105–8

Kurtschinsky, Michail, 175, 193, 195, 225, 247, 248, 303, 314, 315, 316, 327

Laserson, Max, 223
Laun, Karl, 74
Lausanne Conference, 119, 130
League of Nations, 37, 46, 49, 51, 63, 64, 73, 86, 95, 102, chapter 5, 141, 142, 143, 150–2, 153, 162, 164, 166, 168, 181–2, 188–98, 327–8, 329, 331, 333, 345–7, 351, 367, 385, 387–90
League of Russia's Foreign Peoples, 139
Liberalism, 58–9
Llewellyn-Jones, Frederick, 173, 385
Locarno, 165
Loesch, Karl, 353, 359
London meeting of the European Congress of Nationalities, 383–6
London Report, 206–7

*Maapäev*, 21
Maddison, Eugen, 81, 96
Madrid, 207–9, 214, 217, 332
Macartney, C.A., 64, 384
Makaruschka, L., 348, 349, 351
Margulies, Emil, 157, 171, 174, 178, 194, 210, 211, 215, 286, 287, 289, 292, 293, 294, 296, 298, 302, 305, 306, 310, 315, 316–8, 319, 321, 326, 353
Martin, William, 158, 296, 366
Masferrer, Francesc, 249
Maspons i Anglassell, Prof., 188, 304, 332
Medem, Vladimir, 74–5
Medinger, Wilhelm von, 179, 188, 192, 223, 304, 344
Mello-Franco, Afranio de, 136, 190, 191
Mickwitz, Christoph, 19
Mill, John Stuart, 61
Miller, David, 109, 110
Minorities Section of the League of Nations, 123
Minority protection and Baltic States, 124–5
Mission, 23–5, 41, 67, 68, 169–70, 187–8, 389
Montreux, 292, 293, 300–2, 308, 312
Moral disarmament, 178, 330
Morality, 175–6
Moscow's new offensive, 48–50
Motta, Giuseppe, 51, 122, 128, 158, 176, 200, 327
Motzkin, Leo, 169, 171, 173, 175, 178, 194, 195, 237, 241, 243, 255, 281, 282, 284, 285, 287, 288, 289, 290, 292, 293, 294, 296, 297, 298, 299, 300, 301, 302, 305, 306, 307, 308, 310, 313, 316, 317, 320, 321, 326
Mühlen, Vikton von zur, 22, 330, 331, 337, 338, 339, 340

Murray, Gilbert, 132, 194, 385
*Muss Russland hungern?*, 365–73
Myers, Kevin, 6

Nansen, Fridtjof, 45, 119, 214, 367
National identity, 5, 39, 63, 79–82, 392–6
National community, 69, 70, 71
Neuilly, Treaty of, 119
Nicolai, Helmut, 359
Nuremberg Laws, 334–5
Nurok, Mordechai, 157, 286, 322

Oberländer, Theodor, 222
Obituary, 380–3

Pan-Europe, 222–32
Pantenius, Heinrich, 68, 71, 77, 78, 79, 104, 105, 107
Papen, Franz von, 270
Pärnu, 13, 14, 15, 76, 93, 251, 380, 383
Päts, Konstantin, 22, 89, 90, 92, 94, 339, 340
Peace, 5, 9, 10, 171–5, 392–3
Polish Minority Treaty, 52, 64, 119
Polish schooling in Germany, 135–6
Population exchanges, 119
Postyschew, Pavel, 365–73
Pusta, Kaarel, 124, 125, 126, 128

Quakers, 41, 44, 45, 362

Rada, Ukraine, 83
Railways, 15, 16, 27, 32
Rappard, William, 114
Rathenau, Walter, 32
Rauschning, Hermann, 273
Renner, Karl, 74, 75, 85
*Revaler Bote / Revalsche Zeitung*, 15, 24, 29, 30, 50, 51, 57, 67, 72, 79, 80, 83, 84, 86, 91, 92, 95, 97, 101, 127, 131, 132 ,133, 150, 153, 159, 180, 185, 194, 201, 209, 214, 215, 227, 239, 242, 244, 264–7, 288, 311, 313, 315, 335, 336, 337, 339, 340, 345, 349, 354, 356, 357, 360, 361, 375, 377, 378, 381
Rights of national minorities, chapter 5
Robinson, Jacob, 157, 196, 225, 282, 299
Rohan, Prinz, 229
Rosenberg, Alfred, 263, 265, 273, 274, 313, 318, 340, 359, 388
Rosting, Helmer, 125, 126, 128, 144, 332

Rotenstreich, Mr., 192, 286, 322, 332
Roth, Hans Otto, 223–4, 285, 290, 292, 293, 303, 305, 307, 310, 313, 317, 334, 343
Rudnycka, Milena, 303, 329, 332, 346, 362
Russia, 31–7, 40–2
Russification, 19, 24

Schiemann, Paul, 1, 19, 25, 62, 86, 101, 115, 122, 135, 139, 144, 145, 147, 148, 149, 154, 156, 158, 159, 161,165, 169, 171, 173, 174, 177, 180, 193, 194, 196, 197, 209, 219, 221, 223, 228, 229, 232, 236, 237, 239, 240, 243, 244, 249, 252, 253, 261, 268, 271, 272, 275, 277, 278, 283, 285, 292, 293, 294, 296, 307, 308, 309, 311, 313, 316, 321, 322, 323, 325, 326, 343, 359, 388, 389, 391
Schirren, Carl, 19, 24, 98, 336, 392
Schmnidt-Wodder, Johannes, 135, 136
Schooling, 73–9
Security, 72–4
Self-contradictory mentality, 183–4
Self-determination, 10, 50, 73, 115
Sierakowski, Stanisław, 148, 154, 235, 243
Skala, Jan, 237, 238, 239, 245
Skrypnik, Nikolai, 365–73
Smuts, Jan, 114
Sources, 3
South Tyrol, 55–7, 180, 232, 250, 263, 273–4, 275, 326
Soviet Union, 234, 260, 296, 346–7, chapter 15
Spindler, August, 68, 77, 79, 81, 84, 89, 92, 93, 95, 104, 105, 106
Stackelberg, Baron Eduard von, 22, 47, 80, 106, 109, 154
Steiner, Zara, 198
Stresemann, Gustav, 109, 136, 199, 201, 202, 206, 207, 208, 218, 255, 261, 391
Sudeten Germans, rise of, 342–4
Switzerland, 51, 62, 141, 153, 223
Szüllö, Géza von, 144, 155, 156, 165, 169, 172, 179, 190, 195, 196, 197, 250, 285, 304, 307, 314, 332, 348, 383, 384
Szwalbe, Natan, 293, 312–3, 320

Tamir, Yael, 108
Tallinn putsch, 99–102
Tõnisson, Jan, 21, 87, 88, 89, 90, 91, 92, 93, 102, 103, 134
Tourism, 14, 15
Trade, 16, 17, 27, 28–31
Trieste, 28

Ukraine, 296, 303, chapter 15
Ulitz, Otto, 169, 224, 260
Universalisation of minority rights, 141, 209, 332, 333, 334
Üxküll-Guldenbrand, Ferdinand von, 1, 240, 270, 271, 275, 278, 289, 294, 358, 376, 381–2, 388

*Vaba Maa*, 91, 131
Volga Germans, 44
Vries, Axel de, 1, 24, 41, 47, 64, 68, 75, 87, 90, 91, 95, 97, 98, 99, 101, 102, 103, 131, 150, 159, 166, 217, 247, 264, 265, 266, 267, 269, 270, 336, 337, 338, 339, 340, 341, 345, 346, 356, 381

Wales, 151, 395
Wilfan Josip, 144, 152, 154, 157, 160, 161, 163, 165, 169, 171, 172, 177, 178, 180, 183, 191, 194, 196, 204, 226, 228, 230, 237, 239, 242, 243, 244, 245, 246, 250, 270, 281, 283, 284, 285, 286, 287, 289, 292, 297, 299, 300, 301, 302, 303, 304, 305, 306, 310, 311, 312, 313, 315, 319, 322, 323, 326, 332, 349, 376, 383
Wilson, Woodrow, 115
World cruise, 376–80
World League of Minorities, 139
Wrangell, Baron von, 71, 106, 340, 341

Zaleski, August, 197, 199, 200, 201, 203

Lightning Source UK Ltd.
Milton Keynes UK
UKOW03n0634130814

236821UK00001B/30/P